ASSESSMENT

IN SPECIAL AND REMEDIAL EDUCATION

ASSESSMENT

IN SPECIAL AND REMEDIAL EDUCATION

THIRD EDITION

JOHN SALVIA
The Pennsylvania State University

JAMES E. YSSELDYKE
University of Minnesota

Houghton Mifflin Company   Boston

Dallas   Geneva, Illinois   Hopewell, New Jersey   Palo Alto

CONTENTS

PREFACE

Audience for This Book

Assessment in Special and Remedial Education, Third Edition, is intended for a first course in assessment for those whose careers require understanding and informed use of assessment data. The primary audience is those who are or will be teachers in special and remedial education at the elementary or secondary level. The secondary audience is the large support system for special and remedial educators: child development specialists, counselors, educational administrators, nurses, preschool educators, reading specialists, school psychologists, social workers, speech and language specialists, and specialists in therapeutic recreation. In writing for those who are taking their first course in assessment, we have assumed no prior knowledge of measurement and statistical concepts.

Purpose

Students have the right to an appropriate education in the least restrictive educational environment. Decisions regarding the most appropriate environment and the most appropriate program for an individual should be data-based decisions. Assessment is one part of the process of collecting the data necessary for educational decision making, and the administration of tests is one part of assessment. To date, tests have sometimes been used to restrict educational opportunities; many assessment practices have not been in the best interests of students. Those who assess have a tremendous responsibility; assessment results are used to make decisions that directly and significantly affect students' lives. Those who assess are responsible for knowing the devices they use and for understanding the limitations of those devices and the procedures they require.

Teachers are confronted with the results of tests, checklists, scales, and batteries on an almost daily basis. This information is intended to be useful to them in understanding and making educational plans for their students. But the intended use and actual use of assessment information have often differed. However good the intentions of test designers, misuse and misunderstanding of tests may well occur unless teachers are informed consumers and users of tests. To be an informed consumer and user of tests, a teacher must bring to the task certain domains of knowledge, including knowledge of the basic uses of tests, the important attributes of good tests, and the kinds of behaviors sampled by particular tests. This text aims at helping education professionals acquire that knowledge.

The New Edition

The third edition does not represent a radical departure from the style, content, and organization of the first and second editions. However, we have made a significant effort to produce a text that is even more applied than its predecessors. We have clarified and simplified difficult portions, updated information on tests that have been revised since publication of the last edition, added reviews of tests that were not included in previous editions, and provided a new part on the use of assessment information in educational decision making.

The new text, in five parts, is an introduction to psychoeducational assessment in special and remedial education. Parts 1 and 2 provide a general overview of and orientation to assessment. In Part 1, testing is placed in the broader context of assessment, assessment is described as a multifaceted process, the kinds of decisions made using assessment data are delineated, and basic terminology and concepts are introduced. Chapter 3, "Legal and Ethical Considerations in Assessment," is new to this edition; it covers issues in current practice that are dictated in the courtroom and mandated by legislation and includes guidelines on collection, maintenance, and dissemination of pupil records that were discussed in a separate chapter in previous editions of the text. In Part 2, we introduce the student to the basic concepts of measurement. We have reordered chapters and increased the number of examples used to illustrate statistical concepts. Part 2 gives readers a basic understanding of the measurement principles needed not only to comprehend the content in Parts 3 and 4 but also to apply and use information obtained from tests they may administer.

In previous editions, we have had one part devoted exclusively to reviews of the most commonly used formal assessment devices in each domain. In order to distinguish more clearly between tests that measure processes (such as intelligence, sensory acuity, and personality) and those that assess skills (for example, reading, mathematics, and adaptive behavior) we have divided the chapters that evaluate tests in the third edition into two parts—Assessment of Processes and Assessment of Skills. As a result of this reorganization, we have written separate chapters on domains that were combined in the first and second editions. Two chapters on language assessment appear in this edition —one covers oral language (process) and the other deals with written language (skill). Assessment of personality and adaptive behavior has also been divided into two separate chapters so that processes and skills are clearly differentiated.

In addition to the reorganization and updating reflected in Parts 3 and 4, we have prepared new opening and closing sections for chapters in those parts in response to student reactions to previous editions of the text. Each chapter that contains reviews of tests now opens with a discussion of the reasons for assessing students in particular domains and closes with consideration of ways to cope with the dilemmas created when tests fail to meet specific standards of excellence.

Each chapter that includes test evaluations follows a similar format. Initially, we describe the kinds of behaviors typically sampled by tests in the domain under discussion. Representative tests are then reviewed. For each test, we describe its general format, the kinds of behaviors it samples, the kinds of scores it provides, the nature of the sample on whom it was standardized, and evidence for its reliability and validity. The technical adequacy of the tests is evaluated in light of the standards set forth by three professional associations (American Psychological Association, American Educational Research Association, and National Council on Measurement in Education) in their document entitled *Standards for Educational and Psychological Tests.*

Part 5 is entirely new to this edition and emphasizes the text's strengthened focus on application and practice. We examine the ways in which assessment data are used in educational settings to make decisions about students. We do this not only by considering the various procedures that are involved in educational decision making but also by including case studies that apply the procedures to students at various grade levels with a range of learning difficulties. Part 5 is organized according to three different kinds of decisions: referral, classification, and instructional planning. In Chapter 23, we describe the ways in which assessment information is used to make referral decisions and we include specific coverage of the very important process of prereferral intervention. We also discuss the ways in which teachers and related services personnel can gather information on instructional effectiveness and how such information can be used to make referral decisions. In Chapter 24, we describe the use of assessment information in making classification decisions about students who have been referred for special services. Chapter 25 examines the process of using assessment information to plan instructional programs for students who have been classified. The case studies in the chapters follow this same decision-making process, continuing throughout Part 5 to illustrate the activities that correspond to each stage.

A summary of chapter content, additional readings, and study questions appear at the end of each chapter in the text to help readers expand their knowledge and apply the fundamental concepts developed. Chapters in Part 2 also include problems related to the measurement concepts discussed in the text; answers are provided to give students immediate feedback. Appendixes at the end of the text include three tables of statistical data, a list of equations used in the text, a directory of test publishers, and suggestions for how to review a test. Complete bibliographical references for in-text citations follow the appendixes. For this edition we have added an index of tests discussed in the text and continue to present separate indexes for subject matter and authors cited in text.

Assessment is a controversial topic; we have attempted to be objective and even-handed in our review and portrayal of current assessment practices.

Acknowledgments

Many people have been of assistance in our efforts. We wish to express our sincere appreciation to the following individuals who have provided constructive criticism and helpful suggestions during the development of this text:

A. Edward Ahr, Chicago State University

Bob Algozzine, University of Florida

Ellen Brooks, Manhattanville College

James Clark, Central Missouri State College

Leonard Curtis, Georgia State University

David Grigsby, Stephen F. Austin State University

Philip Hansen, California State University at Northridge

J. Melvin Lane, University of Northern Colorado

Gerald Mahoney, University of Michigan

Dale Scherba, California State University at Carson

Clyde Shepherd, Keene State College

Linda Siegelman, Pacific Lutheran University

Steven Spaner, University of Missouri

Robert Suppa, Lehigh University

John Wasson, Moorehead State University

Danielle Zinna, Bowling Green State University

We especially appreciate the contributions of Tom Frank who wrote the section describing the assessment of auditory acuity in Chapter 12 and Ed Klein who helped prepare Chapter 13 on the assessment of oral language. We thank Audrey Thurlow for her cheerful, rapid, and accurate assistance in typing the revised manuscript.

This text represents a collaborative effort and we believe we have produced an integrated text that speaks for both of us.

John Salvia   James Ysseldyke

ASSESSMENT

IN SPECIAL AND REMEDIAL EDUCATION

PART 1

ASSESSMENT: AN OVERVIEW

School personnel regularly use assessment information to make important decisions about students. Part 1 of this text is a description of basic considerations in psychological and educational assessment of students.

Chapter 1 is a description of assessment and includes a delineation of the factors that must be considered in assessment, the various kinds of assessment information school personnel collect, and a description of the steps in the assessment process. In Chapter 2, assessment is more specifically defined, the purposes of assessing students are described, and fundamental assumptions underlying assessment are discussed. Chapter 3 is a description of fundamental legal and ethical considerations in assessment.

The concepts and principles introduced in Part 1 constitute a foundation for informed and critical use of tests and the information they provide.

CHAPTER 1

THE ASSESSMENT OF STUDENTS

All of us have taken tests during our lives. In elementary and secondary school, tests were given to measure our scholastic aptitude or intelligence or to evaluate the extent to which we had profited from instruction. We may have taken personality tests, interest tests, or tests that would assist us in vocational selection and career planning. As part of applying for a job, we may have taken civil service examinations or tests of specific skills like typing or manual dexterity. Enlisting in the armed forces meant taking a number of tests. Enrolling in college meant undergoing entrance examinations. Those of us who decided to go on to graduate school usually had to take an aptitude test: many of those who became teachers had to take a national teacher examination. Physicians, lawyers, psychologists, real estate agents, and many others were required to take tests to demonstrate their competence before being licensed to practice their profession or trade. It is estimated that students attending America's public schools take more than 250 million standardized tests each year.

Throughout their professional careers, teachers, guidance counselors, school social workers, school psychologists, and school administrators will be required to give, score, and interpret a wide variety of tests. Because professional school personnel routinely receive test information from their colleagues within the schools and from community agencies outside the schools, they need a working knowledge of important aspects of testing.

According to the joint committee of the American Psychological Association (APA), the American Educational Research Association (AERA), and the National Council on Measurement in Education (NCME), a test "may be thought of as a set of tasks or questions intended to elicit particular types of behaviors when presented under standardized conditions and to yield scores that have desirable psychometric properties . . ." (1974, p. 2). *Testing,* then, means exposing a person to a particular set of questions in order to obtain a score. That score is the end product of testing.

Testing may be part of a larger process known as *assessment;* however, testing and assessment are not synonymous. Assessment in educational settings is a multifaceted process that involves far more than the administration of a test. When we assess students, we consider the way they perform a variety of tasks in a variety of settings or contexts, the meaning of their performances in terms of the total functioning of the individual, and the likely explanations for those performances. Good assessment procedures take into consideration the fact that anyone's performance on any task is influenced by the demands of the task itself, by the history and characteristics the individual brings to the task, and by the factors inherent in the setting in which the assessment is carried out.

Assessment is the process of collecting information. Some of the information that is collected may be test data; much of it will likely be other forms of information. However, assessment is more than just the collection of information; it is collection with a purpose. *Assessment is the process of collecting data for the purpose of (1) specifying and verifying problems and (2) making decisions about students.* As shown in Figure 1.1, five[1] general types of decisions are made: referral, screening, classification, instructional planning, and pupil progress evaluation. Also, as shown in Figure 1.1, in the schools we specify and verify problems in three areas: academic, behavior, and physical.

Problem Area	Type of Decision				
	Referral	Screening	Classification	Intructional Planning	Evaluating Pupil Progress
Academic					
Behavior					
Physical					

FIGURE 1.1 Assessment is the collection of data to specify and verify problems and to aid in decision making

1. Actually, there are at least three more reasons for assessment. Individuals may be assessed because they are curious about themselves, because they are participants in research studies, or because a school district is evaluating educational programs.

TYPES OF DECISIONS

Referral Decisions

Referral decisions are decisions about the need to seek additional assistance from other school personnel. Although anyone can refer students (for example, parents, the students themselves, or other individuals), teachers are generally the ones who make referrals. Teachers regularly refer students to other professionals in the school and sometimes to professionals or agencies outside the school. Recent surveys show that 3 to 5 percent of the students in public schools are referred each year for psychological and educational assessment. About 92 percent of those students who are referred are tested, and about 73 percent of those who are tested are placed in special education (Algozzine, Christenson, & Ysseldyke, 1982).

Who do teachers refer for evaluation? That question can be answered simply: they refer students who bother them. Although the question can be answered simply, it is not easy to predict whether a student will be referred. Different teachers are bothered by different behaviors, although some behaviors and characteristics would probably bother most, if not all, teachers.

Screening Decisions

Since there is some variability in teachers' tolerances for and awareness of various problems, there may be students in classrooms who are exceptional and who are not having their needs met. School districts want to find these students and provide special services to them so screening programs are started. Thus, screening decisions are essentially administrative in nature. All students in particular schools or school districts are given cursory examinations to ascertain whether any of the students who are evaluated need further, more intensive assessment. Tests may be administered to identify students who differ significantly from their agemates (in either a positive or a negative sense) and who therefore require special education services. Just as vision and hearing tests are routinely given to identify pupils with vision or hearing problems, intelligence tests are administered to identify students who may need special attention, either because of limited intellectual capacity or because of highly superior intellectual ability. Achievement tests, measures of what has been taught to and learned by students, are routinely given to identify students who are experiencing academic difficulty and for whom further assessment may be appropriate.

Screening is an initial stage during which those who may evidence a particular problem, disorder, disability, or disease are sorted out from among the general population. Screening has its origins in medicine and uses terminology from medical screening practices. We speak of individuals who perform poorly on screening measures as being "at risk"; we describe individuals as "false positives" when they perform poorly on screening measures but later do well on follow-up assessments. Sometimes students show no problems at the time of screening and are screened "normal." Later, these same students may evidence the very problems for which screening was conducted; these students are said to be "false negatives." Finally, when we talk about the accuracy of screening decisions, we often speak of the "hit rate" (proportion of accurate positive decisions) for screening.

Classification Decisions

Classification decisions take several forms. In the schools, classification decisions concern a pupil's eligibility for special services: special education services, remedial education services, speech services, and so forth. In this book, we are primarily concerned with eligibility for special education services. Thus, we are interested in whether a pupil is exceptional. Usually, special services are much more costly than the services provided to students in general education. Moreover, these extra costs (sometimes called excess costs) are paid in part by federal and state governments. Governments want to insure that tax money goes to programs for individuals who have been specially targeted for services, those who are *eligible* for services at government expense.

In addition to the classification system employed by the federal government, every state has an education code that specifies the kinds of students considered handicapped. States have different names for the same handicap. For example, in California some students are called educationally handicapped; in other states, such as Texas, the same kinds of students are called learning disabled. Different states have different standards for classification of the same handicap. In Pennsylvania, the maximum IQ for mentally retarded individuals is 80; in Minnesota, the maximum IQ is 70; in California, a black student cannot be tested with an individual intelligence test for classification as mentally retarded. Some states consider gifted students as exceptional and entitled to special education services; other states do not. In some states, brain-damaged students are considered exceptional; in others, there are no provisions for a category of students termed brain injured. Each state has its own criteria for each type of handicap for which special education is provided. In most states, students must be evaluated by certified diagnostic specialists before they are eligible for special education services. Public Law 94-142, the Education for All Handicapped Children Act of 1975, specifies that eligibility, classification, and/or placement decisions are to be made by teams of professionals with the concurrence of the pupil's parents.

In assessment for classification, those persons responsible for determining a pupil's eligibility develop a plan to clarify and verify that the student is handicapped. Data are then gathered (that is, tests are administered, systematic observations made, interviews conducted, and so forth) to clarify and specify the extent to which students meet the eligibility requirements for services for handicapped persons. Although there are many problems apparent in the use of tests to make classification decisions, most federal and state regulations require that decisions be test based. This requirement is designed to protect students. If teachers, diagnosticians, and administrators were allowed to make classification and eligibility decisions on the basis of subjective impressions, classification could be haphazard and capricious.

Instructional Planning Decisions

Assessment data are often used to clarify and specify how and where a pupil is to be taught. Thus, tests are administered in an effort to assist teachers and administrators in planning education programs for individuals or groups of students. Test information might be used to decide placement in reading groups or assignment of students to specific compensatory or remedial programs. Observations and interviews may be used to decide whether special services will be delivered in the regular classroom or in a special education environment. Test results are also used in deciding what goals to stress, what objectives to teach, and how to teach, for individuals as well as for groups.

With the increase in the attention given to learning disabilities and with federal and state requirements for individualized education programs for exceptional students, we have seen an expansion in the use of diagnostic profiles in planning instructional efforts. The merits and limitations in the use of tests in planning specific education programs are discussed in several chapters in Parts 3 and 4 of this text. Chapter 25 is in large part devoted to a discussion and illustration of this purpose of testing.

Pupil Progress Decisions

Finally, assessment data are used to verify that a pupil has made progress and to specify the particular objectives that have (and have not) been attained in the prescribed educational curriculum. Various kinds of assessment data are used to monitor a pupil's day-to-day progress so that teachers can fine-tune education programs. Other kinds of assessment data are used to tell teachers, parents, and the students themselves the extent to which progress has been made during longer periods of time (for example, over the semester). Grades on teacher-constructed tests and scores on standardized achievement tests are the usual indicators of academic progress. Some newer tests tell teachers and parents what specific educational objectives have or have not been achieved. Evaluation of pupil progress is intimately related to the particular program in which a student is enrolled. It is absolutely essential that the content of the assessment parallel the curriculum exactly. Should this not be the case, the decisions about progress will quite likely be incorrect. Thus, we must distinguish between attainment and achievement. *Attainment* is what an individual has learned, regardless of where it has been learned. *Achievement* is what has been learned as a result of instruction in the schools. Any test of factual information measures attainment; however, a test of factual information is an achievement test only if it measures what has been directly taught. Only achievement tests can be used to monitor pupil progress. It would be pointless to use a test that did not assess what a teacher had covered.

PROBLEM AREAS FOR SPECIFICATION AND VERIFICATION

Assessment is a process of collecting data for the purposes of (1) specifying and verifying problems and (2) making decisions about students. We just described the kinds of decisions that are made in educational settings. We now describe three kinds of problems with which assessment is usually concerned: academic problems, behavior problems, and physical problems. In doing so, we describe the specification and verification of problems for the purpose of making different kinds of decisions.

Academic Problems

The most common reason students are referred for psychological or educational assessment is that a teacher or parent believes they are not performing as well as could be expected academically. Teachers usually make that decision on the basis of their observations of pupil performance in academic content areas: reading, mathematics, spelling, science, social studies, and so forth. When students are referred for assessment, it is necessary that teachers specify their concerns. Teachers who refer students for assessment because of "reading problems" provide diagnostic personnel with limited information. To the extent that teachers describe and specify the nature of a student's problems (for example, "Richy is the poorest reader in the class and consistently has difficulty associating letters with sounds"), they help diagnostic personnel. Some very effective teachers regularly gather information on pupil progress in academic content areas and use those data to make referral decisions.

Academic performance is nearly always assessed in making classification decisions. For example, a student referred for reading problems may be given a reading test to provide a comparison of the development of reading skills relative to other students in the school or even the nation. The results of the test would be used to verify the existence of a problem.

Academic performance is nearly always assessed in making instructional decisions. In deciding what to teach a student it is necessary to specify those skills that the student does and does not already have.

Behavior Problems

Students are often referred for psychological or educational assessment because they demonstrate behavior problems. Students for whom severe behavior problems can be specified and verified are often declared eligible for special education services.

Behavior problems include failure to get along with peers, delinquent activities, and excessive withdrawal, as well as disruptive and noncompliant behavior. For example, Ms. Swanson may be troubled because Larry is so quiet and withdrawn. She might begin to verify that this is actually the problem by counting the frequency of Larry's interactions with his peers. A low count would not, by itself, indicate a problem. Therefore, Ms. Swanson might select another boy whose behavior she judged to be appropriate and count the frequency of his interactions with his peers. She could then verify that Larry interacted much less frequently than a boy who had no problems interacting.

Ms. Swanson might plan a behavior-modification program for Larry to increase the number of positive interactions that he had with his classmates. She could systematically collect data on the effectiveness of this new program and reach some decisions about Larry's progress.

Physical Problems

Physical problems include sensory handicaps (vision and hearing), problems of physical structure (for example, spina bifida or cerebral palsy), and chronic health problems (diabetes or asthma).

Severe physical problems are often first brought to the attention of parents by physicians before a child enters school. When a child with a severe physical problem enters school, the parents might supply specific information from physicians that confirm and specify the physical nature of the child's problem. Milder, but nonetheless important, problems that have not been noticed by the parents are often discovered during routine screening. For example, White Haven Area Schools might require that the school nurse (Ms. Slique) regularly conduct hearing tests (for example, a puretone audiometric test for hearing within the speech range). When the first-grade students are screened, Ms. Slique notes that Jane has a 65 decibel loss in her better ear. A hearing loss of such magnitude, if confirmed, would have serious educational implications and would necessitate substantial educational modifications so that Jane could profit from her education. However, the screening assessment was conducted in the nurse's room, which had not been soundproofed, and with equipment that had not been checked recently for accuracy. Therefore, Ms. Slique decides that it would be best to have an audiologist see Jane and diagnose her hearing problem.

SUMMARY

Testing is part of a larger concept—assessment. In assessment information is gathered for two reasons. First, assessment data are used to clarify and verify the existence of educational problems in the areas of academic functioning, behavioral and social adaptation, and physical development. Second, assessment provides data to facilitate decision making. Five types of decisions are especially pertinent in special education assessment: referral, screening, classification, instructional planning, and evaluation of pupil progress.

STUDY QUESTIONS

1. Differentiate between testing and assessment.
2. Read the Eaves and McLaughlin paper listed in Additional Reading and identify the three levels of assessment that the authors describe.
3. Differentiate between specification and verification.

ADDITIONAL READING

Cronbach, L. J. (1970). *Essentials of psychological testing.* New York: Harper & Row. (Chapter 2: Purposes and types of tests, pp. 22–43.)

Eaves, R. C., & McLaughlin, P. (1977). A systems approach to the assessment of the child and his environment: Getting back to basics. *Journal of Special Education, 11,* 99–111.

Green, B. F. (1981). A primer of testing. *American Psychologist, 36,* 1001–1011.

McCutcheon, G. (1981). On the interpretation of classroom observations. *Educational Researcher,* 5–10.

Poland, S. F., Thurlow, M. L., Ysseldyke, J. E., & Mirkin, P. K. (1982). Current psychoeducational assessment and decision-making practices as reported by directors of special education. *Journal of School Psychology, 20,* 171–179.

Ysseldyke, J. E. (1983). Current practices in making psychoeducation decisions about learning disabled students. *Journal of Learning Disabilities, 16,* 226–233.

Ysseldyke, J. E. (in press). The use of assessment information to make decisions about students. In B. Blatt & J. Morris (Eds.), *Perspectives in special education: The state of the art.* Chicago: Scott, Foresman.

CHAPTER 2

BASIC CONSIDERATIONS IN ASSESSMENT

Assessment is a process of collecting data for two purposes: (1) specification and verification of problems and (2) making decisions for or about students. Assessment data are used in making many different kinds of decisions about students as described in the first chapter.

Those who assess students must be aware of several assumptions inherent in assessment and of how failure to meet those assumptions directly affects the validity of obtained results. They must consider many factors in assessment, going beyond the student to gather additional kinds of information. In this chapter we describe factors to be considered and the various kinds of information collected in the process of assessment, and we differentiate between formal and informal assessment.

Those who assess students need to identify a starting point for assessment and decide the specific kinds of data that will be collected. We address several questions commonly asked in deciding how students will be assessed. We end the chapter with a set of guidelines for teacher administration of standardized tests.

ASSUMPTIONS UNDERLYING ASSESSMENT

A number of assumptions underlie the valid assessment of students. To the extent that these assumptions are not met, test results and interpretations lack validity. Newland (1971) has identified and discussed the following five assumptions underlying assessment.

The Person Giving the Test Is Skilled

When pupils are tested, we assume that the person doing the testing has adequate training for the purpose of testing. We also assume that the tester knows how to—and indeed does—establish rapport with pupils; students generally perform best in an atmosphere of trust and security. We further assume that the tester knows how to administer the test correctly. Testing consists of a standardized presentation of stimuli. To the extent that the person giving the test does not correctly present the questions or materials, the obtained scores lose validity.

We also assume that the person who administers a test knows how to score the test. Correct scoring is a prerequisite to the attainment of a meaningful picture of a student. Finally, we assume that accurate interpretation can and will be made.

Test administration, scoring, and interpretation require different degrees of training and expertise depending on the kind of test being administered and the degree of interpretation required to draw meaning from the test taker's performance. Although most teachers can readily administer or learn to administer group intelligence and achievement tests, a person must have considerable training to score and interpret most individual intelligence and personality tests. Most states now require that a person be certified or licensed as a psychologist in order to administer these types of tests. Licensing or certification, in turn, is often contingent on the demonstration of competence.

Obviously, a terribly important point is implicit in this first assumption. Professionals should administer only the tests they are qualified to administer. Too often, unfortunately, we hear of people with no training in individual intelligence testing who nonetheless administer individual intelligence tests; or we see people with no formal training in personality test administration or interpretation giving personality tests. Such tests may *look* easy enough to give; however, the correct administration, scoring, and interpretation are complex. Because tests are so often used to make decisions that will affect a child's future, this assumption of a skilled observer or tester is especially important.

Error Will Be Present

No psychological or educational measurement is free from error. A certain amount of error is always present when we test. Although measurement error is dealt with extensively in Chapter 7, a few points are appropriate here. Nunnally (1978) differentiates between two kinds of error in any measurement effort: *systematic error,* or bias, and *random error.* He illustrates systematic error by the example of a chemist who uses an inaccurate thermometer, one that always reads 2 degrees higher than the actual temperature of a liquid. All of the readings the chemist takes will be biased, but they will be biased systematically; that is, all readings will be in error by 2 degrees.

In the measurement process, random error occurs in two ways. First, the measurer may be inconsistent. Nunnally's illustration of this is a near-sighted chemist who reads an accurate thermometer inaccurately. The readings will be in error, but the amount and direction of error will be random. In some cases, the chemist may read the thermometer 5 degrees high, in others 4 degrees low. An indeterminate amount of error, then, affects obtained measurements. Second, measurement devices may produce inconsistent results. For example, an elastic rubber ruler produces inconsistent measures of length.

Reliability concerns the extent to which a measurement device is free from random error. A test with very little random error, an accurate test, is said to be reliable, while one with considerable random error, an inaccurate test, is said to be unreliable. Tests differ considerably in degree of reliability. To the extent that unreliable devices (devices with considerable random error) are used to make decisions about students, those decisions may, in fact, be erroneous. Factors that contribute to lack of reliability in testing are discussed in Chapter 7.

Acculturation Is Comparable

Every schoolchild has a particular set of background experiences in educational, social, and cultural environments. When we test students using a standardized device and compare them to a set of norms to gain an index of their relative standing, we assume that the students we test are similar to those on whom the test was standardized; that is, we assume their acculturation is comparable, but not necessarily identical, to that of the students who made up the normative sample for the test.

When a child's general background experiences differ from those of the children on whom a test was standardized, then the use of the norms of that test as an index for evaluating that child's current performance or for predicting future performances may be inappropriate. Incorrect educational decisions may well be made. It must be pointed out that acculturation is a matter of experiential background rather than of skin color, race, or ethnic background. When we say that a child's acculturation differs from that of the group used as a norm, we are saying that the *experiential background* differs, not simply that the child is of different ethnic origin, for example, than the children on whom the test was standardized.

Unfortunately, many psychologists, counselors, remedial specialists, and others who select tests to be administered to students often do so with little regard to the characteristics of the students who constitute the normative samples. Many school administrators routinely purchase tests with more concern for price than for the technical adequacy and appropriateness of those tests.

The Quick Test, for example, was standardized on white children in Missoula, Montana; yet it is used daily to measure the "intelligence" of black ghetto children, children whose educational, social, and cultural background *may* differ extensively from that of the children on whom the test was standardized.

The performance section of the Wechsler Intelligence Scale for Children–Revised (WISC–R) consists of a variety of tests (mostly manipulative, like putting puzzle pieces together to form objects) that require no verbal response by the child. The fact that the child does not have to speak has encouraged psychologists to use the test in an effort to test deaf children. Levine (1974), in a survey of testing practices used by psychologists who work with the deaf, reported that the test most frequently used to measure the intelligence of deaf children is the WISC performance section: norms based entirely on the performance of youngsters who can hear are used to interpret the performances of deaf children! Appropriate application of the norms presumes that the child evaluated can *hear* the directions and has had acculturation comparable to that of the children on whom the test was standardized. Several nonverbal subtests of the Wechsler scales (for example, Picture Completion and Picture Arrangement) require verbal competence.

Behavior Sampling Is Adequate

A fourth assumption underlying psychoeducational assessment is that the behavior sampling is adequate in amount and representative in area. Any test is a sample of behavior. If we want information about a student's math skills, we give the student a sample of math problems to solve. Similarly, if we want to know about spelling skills, we ask the student to spell a representative number of words. When we administer a math or spelling test, we assume that we have a large enough sample of items to enable us to make statements regarding a student's overall skill development in that area. Few teachers would ask a student to solve only two arithmetic problems and presume that the results would tell much at all about that student's skill development in arithmetic. Testing requires an adequate sampling of behavior to assist in decision-making processes.

Not only do we assume that the behavior sampling is adequate in amount, but we assume that the test measures what its authors claim it measures. We assume that an intelligence test measures intelligence and that a spelling test measures spelling skills. A test of addition would be a poor measure of overall skill in math, because math entails much more than addition. Similarly, a measure of a student's skill in addition of single-digit numbers provides only one part of a test of that student's skill in addition. We cannot rely on a test's name as we attempt to define the behaviors sampled by the test. Many tests, for example, are called "reading" tests. Yet reading has several subcomponents, such as recognition, comprehension, and phonetic analysis. As we shall show in Chapter 17, no reading test samples reading per se. Each test samples one or more reading behaviors. The user of reading tests —or any tests, for that matter—must go beyond test names in an effort to ascertain the behaviors that the tests measure.

To the extent that tests used to measure students' performances are incomplete or fail to measure what they claim to measure, decisions based on students' scores on those tests may well be wrong.

Present Behavior Is Observed; Future Behavior Is Inferred

When we give a test, we observe only the test taker's performance on one sampling of behavior, at a particular time, under particular testing conditions, and in a particular situation. We observe what a person *does;* we may or may not observe what that person is capable of doing. We sample a limited number of behaviors and generalize the individual's performance to other, similar behaviors. For example, because Heathcote correctly works ten of ten problems in single-digit addition, we infer that he could add any two single digits correctly. Moreover, judgments or predictions about an individual's behavior at some future time may be made. These predictions are inferences in which we may place varying degrees of confidence. We may better trust the inferences we make about future performance if we have seen to it that the other assumptions about assessment have been satisfied. If we have administered a test that is adequate in its behavior sampling and representative in area, that is relatively free from error, and that was accurately administered, scored, and interpreted, using as norms students of background comparable to the background of those we tested, then we may put a reasonable amount of faith in the adequacy of observed data. Data obtained from such an administration may be used with greater assurance in making predictions than data obtained under conditions in which any of the assumptions were not met. Human behavior is extremely complex, and we must remember that any prediction about future behavior is an inference.

FACTORS CONSIDERED IN ASSESSMENT

Current Life Circumstances

An individual's performance on any task must be understood in light of that individual's current circumstances. We must understand current circumstances to be aware of what a person brings to a task.

In educational assessment, health is a significant current life circumstance. Health and nutritional status can play an important role in children's performances on a wide variety of tasks. Sick or malnourished children are apt to be lethargic, inattentive, perhaps irritable.

Children's attitudes and values also should contribute to our evaluation of their performance. Willingness to cooperate with a relatively unfamiliar adult, willingness to give substantial effort to tasks, and belief in the worth of the task or of schooling have their influence on performance.

Finally, the level of acculturation children bring to a task is of utmost importance. A child's knowledge and acceptance of societally sanctioned mores and values, use of standard English, and fund of general and specific cultural information all influence performance on school-related tasks.

Developmental History

A person's current life circumstances are shaped by the events that make up his or her history of development. Deleterious events in particular may have profound effects on physical and psychological development. Physical and sensory limitations may restrict a student's opportunity to acquire various skills and abilities. A history of poor health or poor nutrition may result in missed opportunities to acquire various skills and abilities. An individual's history of reward and punishment shapes what that person will achieve and how that person will react to others. In short, it is not enough to assess a student's current level of performance; those who assess must also understand what has shaped that current performance.

Extrapersonal Factors

In addition to the skills, characteristics, and abilities a pupil brings to any task, other factors affect the assessment process. How another person interprets or reacts to various behaviors or characteristics can even determine whether an individual will be assessed. For example, some teachers do not understand that a certain amount of physical aggression is typical of young children or that verbal aggression is typical of older students. Such teachers may refer "normally" aggressive children for assessment because they have interpreted aggression as a symptom of some underlying problem.

The theoretical orientation of the diagnostician (the person responsible for performing the assessment) also plays an important part in the assessment process. Diagnosticians' backgrounds and training may predispose them to look for certain types of pathologies. Just as Freudians may look for unresolved conflicts while behaviorists may look for antecedents and consequences of particular behaviors, diagnosticians may let their theoretical orientation influence their interpretation of particular information.

Finally, the conditions under which a student is observed or the conditions under which particular behaviors are elicited can influence that student's performance. For example, the level of language used in a question or the presence of competing stimuli in the immediate environment can affect a pupil's responses.

Interpretation of Performance

After an individual's behavior and characteristics have been considered in light of current life circumstances, developmental history, and extrapersonal factors that may influence performance, the information is summarized. This often results in classification and labeling of the individual being assessed. The assessor arrives at the judgment that when all things are considered, the child "fits" a particular category. For example, a child may be judged mentally retarded, emotionally disturbed, learning disabled, educationally handicapped, culturally or socially disadvantaged, backward, normal, gifted, or a member of the Red Birds reading group.

Assessors, especially when they have assigned negative labels, often attempt to impute a cause for an individual's status. Classification according to cause *(etiology)* is common in medicine but less common in education and psychology. In some cases the cause of the condition is highly probable. For example, Kevin may be developing quite normally until he sustains a severe head injury, after which his performance and development are measurably retarded. However, in most instances, the causes are elusive and speculative.

Prognosis

All assessments and classifications of students contain an explicit or implicit *prognosis,* a prediction of future performance. A prognosis may be offered for students both in their current environment and life circumstances and in some therapeutic or remedial environment. For example: "If Rachel is left in her current educational placement, she can be expected to fall further and further behind the other children and to develop problem behaviors. If she is placed in an environment where she will receive more individual attention, she should make more progress academically and socially." Such prognoses are made, it is hoped, on the basis of sound data rather than speculation.

KINDS OF ASSESSMENT INFORMATION

Although this book is concerned primarily with tests and testing, it is well to remember that a test is only one of several assessment techniques or procedures available for gathering information. Figure 2.1 shows that there are six general

TIME AT WHICH INFORMATION IS GATHERED

	Current	Historical
Observations	Frequency counts of occurrence of a particular behavior Antecedents of behavior Critical incidents	Birth weight Anecdotal records Observations by last year's teacher
Tests	Results of an intelligence test administered during the assessment Results of this week's spelling test given by the teacher	Results of a standardized achievement-test battery given at the end of last year
Judgments	Parents' evaluations of how well the child gets along in family, neighborhood, etc. Rating scales completed by teachers, social workers, etc. Teacher's reason for referral	Previous medical, psychological, or educational diagnoses Previous report cards Parents' recall of developmental history, of undiagnosed childhood illnesses, etc.

TYPE OF INFORMATION

FIGURE 2.1   Sources of diagnostic information classified according to type of information and time at which the information is collected

classes of diagnostic-information sources; the classification shown in the figure depends on the time at which the information is collected (current or historical) and on how the information is collected (from observation, tests, or judgments).

Current vs. Historical Information

Diagnostic information can be categorized according to the currentness of the information: information that describes how a person is functioning now and information that describes how that person has functioned in the past. Obviously, the distinction between current and historical information blurs, and the point at which current information becomes historical information depends in part on the particular fact or bit of information. For example, if Johnny had his appendix removed *three years ago,* we know he currently has no appendix.

On the other hand, if 9-year-old Jane weighed 56 pounds *three years ago,* we could not conclude that she weighs the same today.

There are several advantages in having and using current information. The first is the most obvious. Current information describes a person's current behavior and characteristics. It offers two more subtle advantages as well: (1) the diagnostician can select the information to be collected, and (2) the information can be verified. However, current information alone cannot provide a complete picture of a person's present level of functioning, because the antecedents of this functioning are not considered. This is the advantage of historical information. School diagnosticians cannot go back in time to observe previous characteristics, behaviors, and situations. A diagnostician who wishes to incorporate a student's history into the assessment procedure must rely on previously collected information or the memory of individuals who knew the student.

Historical information has four limitations of which diagnosticians must be aware. First, a diagnostician cannot control what information was collected in the past; crucial bits of information may never have been collected. Second, past information is difficult and sometimes impossible to verify. Third, the conditions under which the information was collected are often difficult to evaluate. Fourth, remembered observations may not be as reliable as current observations.

Types of Information

Diagnostic information can also be categorized according to the type of information: observations, tests, and judgments. Each of the three types of information has advantages as well as disadvantages. Each type can be collected by a diagnostician (in which case the data become *direct information*) or by another person *(indirect information).* Diagnosticians do not have the time, competence, or opportunity to collect all possible types of information. In cases where specialized information is needed, they must rely on the observations, tests, and judgments of others. If a behavior occurs infrequently or is demonstrated only outside school, the diagnostician may have to rely on the observations and judgments of others who have more opportunity to collect the information—parents, perhaps, or ward attendants in institutional settings. For example, bed wetting does not occur at school, but few diagnosticians would question the accuracy of parents' reports of bed wetting. Moreover, if a child is an intermittent bed wetter, a diagnostician might have to spend several nights at the child's home in order to observe the behavior directly. In such cases indirect information is usually adequate.

Observations can provide highly accurate, detailed, verifiable information not only about the person being assessed but also about the contexts in which the observations are being made. There are two types of observation: nonsystematic and systematic. In *nonsystematic observation,* the observer simply watches an individual in his or her environment and takes note of the behaviors, characteristics, and personal interactions that seem of significance. Nonsystematic observation tends to be anecdotal and subjective. In *systematic observation,* the observer sets out to observe one or more behaviors. The observer specifies or defines the behaviors to be observed and then typically counts or otherwise measures the frequency, duration, magnitude, or latency of the behaviors. The major disadvantage of systematic observation is that it may allow other important behaviors and characteristics to be ignored.

There are two major difficulties in collecting systematic and nonsystematic observational data. The first is that observation is very time consuming; a diagnostician pays for the highly accurate, specific information that observation provides by not being able to collect other information. The second problem is that the very presence of an observer may distort or otherwise alter the situation to such a degree that the behavior of the individual being observed also is altered.

Tests are a predetermined set of questions or tasks to which predetermined types of behavioral responses are sought. Tests are particularly useful because they permit tasks and questions to be presented in exactly the same way to each person tested. Because a tester elicits and scores behavior in a predetermined and consistent manner, the performances of several different test takers can be compared no matter who does the testing. Hence, tests tend to make many extrapersonal factors in assessment consistent for all those tested. Basically, two types of information, quantitative and qualitative, result from the administration of a test. *Quantitative* data refer to the actual scores achieved on the test. Examples of quantitative data include such statements as "Lee earned a score of 80 on her math test," or "Henry scored at the 83rd percentile on a measure of scholastic aptitude." *Qualitative* information consists of nonsystematic observations made while a child is tested and tells us how the child achieved the score. For example, in earning a score of 80 on her math test, Lee may have solved all of the addition and subtraction problems with the exception of those that required regrouping. Henry may have performed best on measures of his ability to define words, while demonstrating a weakness in comprehending verbal statements. When tests are used in assessment, it is not enough simply to know the scores a student earned on a given test; it is important to know how the student earned those scores.

The *judgments* and assessments made by others can play an important role in assessment. In instances where a diagnostician lacks competence to render a judgment, the judgments of those who possess the necessary competence are essential. Diagnosticians seek out other professionals to complement their own skills and background. Thus, referring a student to various specialists (hearing specialists, vision specialists, reading teachers, and so on) is a common and desirable practice in assessment. Judgments by teachers, counselors, psychologists, and practically any other school employees may be useful in particular circumstances. Expertise in making judgments is often a function of familiarity with the student being assessed. Teachers regularly express professional judgments; for example, report-card grades represent the teacher's judgment of a student's academic progress during the marking period; referrals for psychological evaluation represent a different type of judgment based on experience with many students and observations of the particular student. Judgments represent both the best and the worst of assessment data. Judgments made by conscientious, capable, and objective individuals can be an invaluable aid in the assessment process. Inaccurate, biased, subjective judgments can be misleading at best and harmful at worst. Finally, all assessment ultimately requires judgment.

Integration of Assessment Information

To see how the various types of information can come into play in an assessment, consider the following example. Mary, who is 6 years old, is falling behind in reading, her teacher reports (a current judgment). The teacher also reports that Mary does not listen or pay attention and does not associate sounds with letters (current observations). An inspection of Mary's kindergarten records indicates that she was absent thirty-one days in January and February (past observation). Mary's scores on the reading-readiness test administered in June of her kindergarten year were sufficiently high that her teacher recommended her promotion to the first grade (past judgment). An interview with Mary's parents revealed that Mary has a history of treated middle-ear infections (past observations and judgments) during the winters. According to her parents, she currently has an ear infection that is being treated by the family doctor (current observation). Pulling together all this information, the school authorities hypothesize that Mary is having hearing difficulties. They obtain a hearing examination (current test), which indicates that Mary is currently suffering from a moderate hearing loss of sufficient magnitude to affect her progress in phonics adversely (current judgment). With background and current information, it is now possible to assess (understand and interpret) Mary's classroom behavior. With medical treatment for her ear problem and some classroom intervention by the teacher, Mary can be expected to do better in school.

Formal vs. Informal Assessment

Increasingly, educators are advocating informal over formal assessment, especially in instructional decision making and in evaluating pupil progress. When such a distinction is made, any assessment that involves collection of data by anything other than a norm-referenced (standardized) test is generally considered informal assessment. Collection of information by means of observation is often thought of as informal assessment, as is information gathering by interviewing and by means of teacher-constructed tests.

Over the last decade there has been a significant increase in curriculum-based assessment. Curriculum-based assessment includes (1) direct observation and analysis of the learning environment, (2) analysis of the processes used by students in approaching tasks, (3) examination of pupil products, and (4) control and arrangement of tasks for students. Focus is on assessment of a student's ongoing performance in the existing curriculum.

Observation of the learning environment involves looking at the kinds of instructional materials being used with students as well as at the basis for selection of the materials. Specific observation techniques include systematic analysis of the way in which instruction is organized and sequenced, with specific attention to potential pitfalls in instructional organization; looking at and examining the adequacy of the ways in which instruction is being presented (lecture, workbook, programmed instruction, and so on); and examination of the extent to which sufficient time is allocated to instruction and the extent to which the student is actively engaged in responding to academic content.

Evaluation of the ways in which students approach tasks, student demeanor, student attention to tasks, and the extent to which students read and follow instructions are also part of curriculum-based assessment. Teachers who follow curriculum-based assessment attend carefully to the products students produce in an effort to analyze the specific kinds of errors students make. For example, teachers may examine errors on math worksheets in order to spot patterns of difficulties. Curriculum-based assessment is often called diagnostic teaching because teachers or diagnostic specialists have an opportunity to modify several aspects of instruction and to study the impact of such adaptations on pupil performance.

Increasingly, school personnel are using the kinds of informal assessment strategies noted above. In this text, we choose to concentrate on formal assessment. In our opinion, the topic of informal assessment requires adequate treatment in a separate book.

APPROACHES TO ASSESSMENT

There are three different approaches to assessing students that differ primarily in what is assessed and where the assessor begins assessment. Each approach is described below.

Assessing the Learner

Most often, when students are referred for evaluation because they are experiencing academic or behavior problems, school personnel use an approach in which they assess the learner. This type of assessment addresses the question

"What is wrong with the student?" Tests are administered in an effort to identify within-student deficits or disabilities, or efforts are made to find strengths and weaknesses in the development of specific skills.

As noted, assessment of the learner is the most frequently used approach, and it is the approach most often taught in college and university courses. This approach is based on several assumptions. Students who experience academic difficulties are assumed to suffer from internal conditions (called *deficits, disorders, disabilities,* or *dysfunctions*) that cause their academic difficulties. It is assumed that tests can and should be used to identify the students' deficits, that the deficits can be reliably and validly identified, and that instructional approaches can be selected based on pupil performance on tests. Thus, we see school personnel engaged in assessment of perceptual, perceptual-motor, psycholinguistic, and other kinds of abilities and in attempts to remediate those abilities.

The approach that begins assessment by diagnosing the learner has been criticized repeatedly and strongly. It has been shown that the assumptions underlying the approach are not met (Ysseldyke & Salvia, 1974), that the approach is technically inadequate (Ysseldyke & Marston, 1982), and that the approach seldom leads to effective instruction (Arter & Jenkins, 1979; Engelmann, Granzin, & Severson, 1979).

Diagnosing Instruction

Engelmann, Granzin, and Severson (1979) recommend that assessment begin with instructional diagnosis, the purpose of which is "to determine aspects of instruction that are inadequate, to find out precisely how they are inadequate, and to imply what must be done to correct their inadequacy" (p. 361). In such an approach, emphasis is on initiating assessment by asking, "To what extent are the student's problems caused by poor instruction?"

Instructional diagnosis consists of systematic analysis of the instruction and of the appropriateness of instruction to the learner. It includes engaging in activities described earlier in the discussion on curriculum-based assessment: observation of the learning environment, evaluation of the ways in which students approach tasks, evaluation of the products of instruction, and diagnostic teaching.

Assessing Opportunity to Learn

Ysseldyke and Algozzine (1982) describe an approach to assessment that begins with asking the questions "To what extent does instruction actually occur?" and "To what extent is the learner actively engaged in instruction?"

Ysseldyke and Algozzine recommend assessing the extent to which pupils are actively engaged in responding to instruction for a sufficient amount of time that they can be expected to learn what they are being taught. They argue that the nature of instruction should be assessed only after it has been shown that instruction is actually occurring. They advocate assessing the learner only after it can be demonstrated that the student is actively engaged in responding to academic content for sufficient amounts of time and that the instruction is appropriate to the developmental level of the learner.

CONSIDERATIONS IN TEST SELECTION AND ADMINISTRATION

Who Is to Be Tested?

In answering the question "Who is to be tested?" we must address two issues. First, we must decide whether we want to test a single student or a group of students. Second, we must determine to what extent the single student (or any student in the group) demonstrates special limitations that must be taken into account in testing.

Group vs. Individual Tests

The distinction between a group test and an individual test is both obvious and subtle. Group tests can be given to one person or to several people simultaneously; individual tests must be administered to only one person at a time. Any group test can be administered to an individual; no individual test should be administered to more than one person at the same time. This is the obvious distinction. There are several subtle distinctions, however.

In an individual test, the questions and demands usually are given orally by a tester who also observes the individual's responses directly and in many cases records these responses. The tester is able to control the tempo and pace of the testing and often can rephrase or clarify questions as well as probe responses to elicit the best performance. If a student undergoing testing becomes fatigued, the tester can interrupt or terminate the test. If a student loses his or her place on the test, the tester can help; if the student dawdles, the tester can urge; if the student lacks confidence, the tester can reinforce effort. Individual tests usually allow the tester to encourage a test taker's best efforts and to gather a considerable amount of qualitative information. Thus, the examiner can infer strengths and weaknesses in terms of both quantitative *and* qualitative information.

With a group test, the examiner may provide oral directions for younger children, but for children beyond the fourth grade, the directions usually are written. The pupils write or mark their own responses, and the examiner must monitor the progress of several test takers simultaneously. The examiner typically cannot rephrase, probe, or prompt responses. Even when a group test is given to a single student, qualitative information is very difficult, if not impossible, to obtain.

The choice between an individual or a group test is determined in part by the decision to be made and the efficiency with which that purpose can be achieved. Basically, when we test for program evaluation, screening, and some types of program planning (for example, tracking students into ability groups), group tests can be appropriately used. Individual tests *could* be used, but the time and expense would not be justified in terms of the information desired. When we plan individual programs, individual tests are more appropriate. Typically, when a student is to be placed in a special education program, an individually administered test is required by law.

Special Limitations and Considerations

A particular student may have special limitations that make a group test inappropriate. As previously discussed, most group-administered tests are limited in their applicability because of the way the questions are presented (that is, they require that test takers be able to read) and the way responses are to be made (generally, by writing or marking). Common sense tells us that if a student cannot read the directions or write the responses, a test requiring these abilities is inappropriate. In such cases, the test measures inability in reading directions or writing answers rather than skill or ability in the content of the test. A child without arms may know the content of the test but may not answer any questions correctly because she cannot write. Similarly, children without speech or with severe speech impediments may know the answers to the questions a test asks but be unable (or unwilling) to respond to *even* the most sensitively administered individual test that requires oral answers. Children with physical or sensory handicaps may perform more slowly than nonhandicapped children simply because of their handicaps. A test that awards "points" for the speed as well as the accuracy of response would not be a valid test of such children's mastery of content.

A related concern is the relationship between a person's functional level and social maturity. Often, older individuals with relatively low levels of skill development are assessed. In such cases, the tester must be careful to select test materials that reflect the test taker's social maturity. An adolescent who is just learning to read may well resent test materials geared to 6-year-old children. The use of test materials that are inappropriate in terms of the older individual's social maturity may reduce or eliminate rapport and thereby jeopardize the accuracy of the test results.

What Behaviors Are to Be Tested?

Any test is a sample of behavior. In deciding what behaviors to test, an examiner must take into account three subquestions: What stimulus and response demands will be made? What domain (content) will be measured? How many domains will be tested?

Stimulus and Response Demands

A test or an individual test item measures an individual's ability to receive a stimulus and then express a response. These demands are present in *all* tests. Skill in the content of a test cannot be measured accurately if the stimulus and response demands of a question are beyond the capabilities of the test taker. As noted earlier, tests can be administered orally or visually: an examiner can show written materials to a student while simultaneously reading them. There is little reason why a test could not be tactilely administered, too, so that specially limited students could understand its basic stimulus demands.

Response demands can also vary. Test instructions may call for an oral *yes* or *no* response or for oral definition or elaboration. Tests may also require written responses that can range from a simple yes-no, true-false, or multiple-choice response to an elaborate, written essay.

A tester should be sensitive to any limitations a student may have. Such limitations are especially important in relation to the stimulus and response demands of testing. The tester should also have quite specific intentions to measure a particular skill or trait. How to measure should be considered as well as what to measure. For example, all spelling tests are not the same. Writing words from dictation is a different kind of spelling test than recognizing a correctly or incorrectly spelled word in a multiple-choice format.

The Domain

The content domain that is tested is generally what we think of as the "kind" of test. There are many kinds of tests, many traits or characteristics that can be measured: intelligence, personality, aptitude, interest, perceptual-motor development, linguistic ability, and so on. Most general traits or characteristics can be further subdivided. For example, intelligence can be divided into performance abilities and verbal abilities or fractionated into as many as 120 separate abilities (Guilford, 1967). There are also many skills and knowledge areas that can be measured: reading, mathematics, social studies, and anatomy are only a few. Some tests are designed to measure skill development in one specific content area (for example, reading) whereas other tests measure skill development in several different areas. The former are known as *single-skill tests* while the latter are *multiple-skill batteries*.

Often, a test item readily lends itself to only one domain. We would have trouble using the question "Do you like yourself?" on other than a personality test. Generally, however, particular test items are identified with particular domains as a function of a student's age or experience. For instance, the question "What is 3 and 5?" can be used to measure several different domains, depending on the particular student. If a child has just received systematic instruction in the addition of single-digit numbers, the question would be appropriate in an achievement test. If the question were asked of a child who had not received formal instruction in addition (a four-year-old, for instance), the question would be appropriate in an intelligence test. If the same question were given to a child who had received several years of systematic instruction, it would be appropriate in a math aptitude test. In short, the type of test in which an item is placed depends more on the characteristics of the person to be tested or on the intended use of the test than on the content of the particular item.

What Interpretative Data Are Desired?

The process of deciding what interpretative data the examiner wants to obtain necessarily includes answering several subquestions: (1) Is the examiner interested in the student's actual level of mastery or in an index of the student's relative standing? In other words, will the examiner use criterion-referenced or norm-referenced assessment? (2) Is the examiner interested in the student's maximum performance or in the level of performance the student can attain in a given amount of time? In other words, will the examiner use *power tests* (untimed tests) or *speed tests* (timed tests)?

Norm-Referenced vs. Criterion-Referenced Tests

Most noneducational tests are *norm-referenced devices,* which compare an individual's performance to the performance of his or her peers. In norm-referenced assessment, learning of particular content or skills is important only to the extent that differential learning allows the tester to rank individuals in order, from those who have learned many skills to those who have learned few. The emphasis is on the relative standing of individuals rather than on absolute mastery of content.

Norm-referenced tests are of two types: point scales and age scales. These differ in their construction. Age scales are less common today than in the past because of both statistical and conceptual limitations. Age scales are developed by scaling test items in terms of the percentages of children of different ages responding correctly to each test item. For example, an item would be placed at the 6-year level if 25 percent of five-year-olds responded to it correctly, 50 percent of six-year-olds responded to it correctly, and 75 percent of seven-year-olds responded to it correctly. When a test question is correctly placed in an age scale, younger 'children fail the item while older children pass it. The statistical and conceptual limitations of age scales are discussed in Chapter 5 in the sections dealing with developmental scores and quotients. The reader is cautioned that some tests, such as the 1972 revision of the Stanford-Binet, appear to be age scales but are more correctly considered point scales (compare Salvia, Ysseldyke, & Lee, 1975).

A point scale is constructed by selecting and ordering items of different levels of difficulty. The levels of difficulty are not associated with ages. In point scales, the correct responses (that is, points) are summed, and the total raw score is transformed to various derived scales (see Chapter 5).

Norm-referenced devices typically are designed to do only one thing: to separate the performances of individuals so that there is a distribution of scores. They allow the tester to discriminate among the performances of a number of individuals and to interpret how one person's performance compares to that of other individuals with similar characteristics. In norm-referenced testing, a person's performance on a test is measured relative to or in reference to the performances of others who are presumably like that person. Norm-referenced tests are standardized on groups of individuals, and typical performances for students of certain ages or in certain grades are obtained. The raw score that an individual student earns on a test is compared to the scores earned by other students, and a transformed score (for example, a percentile rank) is used to express the given student's standing in the group.

All norm-referenced and criterion-referenced tests are objective. Objective tests are tests that have predetermined answers and standards for scoring a response. They are objective in the sense that attitudes, opinions, and idiosyncrasies of the examiner do not affect scoring; any two examiners would score a response in the same way.[1] Objective scoring does not imply "fair" or justifiable scoring; it implies only predetermined criteria and standardized scoring procedures. Suppose a tester shows a child pictures of a ship, an automobile, the car of a passenger train, and a bus and then asks the child, "Which one is different?" The keyed response (the objective answer) is *ship;* the ship is the only water transport. If the child reasons that only an automobile is private transportation and gives the response *car,* the response would be scored as an incorrect answer. Similarly, if the child reasons that the car on the passenger train is the only vehicle that is not self-propelled—or the only one that requires tracks—and responds accordingly, the response is scored incorrect. "Being fair" has nothing to do with scoring objectively.

Norm-referenced devices have an advantage over criterion-referenced

---

1. A subjective test, by contrast, is a test for which a predetermined answer does not exist. Therefore, the examiner's subjective judgments, attitudes, and opinions can affect the scoring. Many people erroneously define an essay test as a subjective test. Such a test would be objective if there were predetermined, explicit criteria for correct responses; then the "same" response would be assigned the same score by two or more examiners.

devices when the purpose of testing is screening or program evaluation: they provide a means of comparing a student's performance to the performance obtained by others. Placement decisions, too, are most often made following the administration of norm-referenced devices, which enable the placement team to see where a student stands relative to other students. In fact, in most states evaluation with norm-referenced tests *must* play a part in any placement decision. In addition, norm-referenced tests are helpful in screening entire classes of students to identify those who demonstrate particular kinds of difficulties. Yet norm-referenced tests have many limitations.

Criterion-referenced tests are a relatively recent development in education and behavioral psychology. Rather than indicating a person's relative standing in skill development, criterion-referenced tests measure a person's development of particular skills in terms of absolute levels of mastery. Thus, criterion-referenced tests provide answers to specific questions such as, "Does Maureen spell the word *dog* correctly?"

When tests are administered for the purpose of assisting the classroom teacher in planning appropriate programs for children, criterion-referenced devices are recommended. When planning a program for an individual student, a teacher obviously should be more concerned with identifying the specific skills that the student does or does not have than with knowing how the student compares to others. In criterion-referenced measurement the emphasis is on assessing specific and relevant behaviors that have been mastered. Criterion-referenced tests treat the student as an individual rather than simply providing numerical indexes of where the student stands on a variety of subtest continua.

Items on criterion-referenced tests are often linked directly to specific instructional objectives and therefore facilitate the writing of objectives. Test items sample sequential skills, enabling a teacher not only to know the specific point at which to begin instruction but also to plan those instructional aspects that follow directly in the cirricular sequence.

Will a Commercially Prepared Test Be Used?

The preceding three sections can be applied to teacher-made and commercially prepared tests. Teacher-made tests are often termed "informal" tests. Yet teachers can prepare group or individually administered tests that measure single or multiple skills and that require speed or power. Such tests can be criterion-referenced or, if the teacher has a little statistical background, norm-referenced.[2] The only type of informal test your authors have not seen is an age scale.

2. Such norm-referenced devices would employ local norms. See Chapter 6.

Commercially prepared, or formal, tests may offer several advantages. They are often carefully constructed. The procedures for administering and scoring are standardized so that the test can be administered in a variety of settings. A description of the technical characteristics of the test (reliability, validity, norms) is often available. Finally, commercially prepared tests save the tester the time and effort required to develop a test.

In deciding whether to use a commercially prepared test as opposed to a homemade device, the domain of behaviors to be sampled is of prime concern. Informal achievement tests have one major advantage over commercially prepared achievement tests: teacher-made tests can correspond very closely to the content being taught and can therefore be superior for measuring the content of specific classroom experiences. Commercially prepared achievement tests may be useful in screening, program evaluation, and individual program planning. Moreover, because most people within the profession are familiar with standardized achievement tests, the results based on such tests are rapidly communicated to other professionals. In personality assessment, in cases when the test materials are used mainly as a device for eliciting a person's responses, either informal or standardized procedures can probably be used with equal effectiveness.

In areas other than achievement and personality testing, commercially prepared devices are usually superior to informal tests. In these areas (intelligence, readiness, and so on), a great deal of experimental work is necessary in order to develop accurate tests, and this is better done by the professional test maker.

CONSIDERATIONS SPECIFIC TO ASSESSMENT OF HANDICAPPED STUDENTS

Most commercially available standardized tests were developed for use with nonphysically and nonsensorily handicapped students. Later in this text we describe a number of tests designed specifically for use with handicapped students, but in this chapter on test selection we need to consider briefly some of the major problems encountered when professionals modify tests designed for use with nonhandicapped students and administer them to handicapped students.

Two kinds of test modifications are regularly made in assessment of handicapped students: modification of the stimulus demands and modification of the response requirements. Quite often, examiners modify *both* stimulus demands and response requirements. Very often diagnostic personnel change the way in which items are administered in an effort to accommodate the student's physical or sensory limitations. Verbal directions are often signed or pantomimed to hearing-impaired or deaf students; written items are read to visually impaired or blind students. Similarly, examiners often modify response requirements, such as by requiring multiple-choice pointing responses for students who evidence severe language disabilities and elimination of time requirements for motorically disabled students.

Modification of tests to facilitate their use with the handicapped has both good and bad points. By modifying stimulus demands and/or response requirements, examiners are able to obtain samples of behavior. However, the test is no longer a "standardized" test, since the conditions under which it was normed have been altered. Consequently, it is no longer appropriate for test users to attempt to make norm-referenced interpretations of the "scores" handicapped students earn. The norms are no longer relevant.

SUGGESTIONS FOR TEACHER ADMINISTRATION OF STANDARDIZED TESTS

When administering standardized tests to children, teachers must take a number of factors into consideration.

Group Size

Generally, when group tests are administered, the smaller the group the better. The optimal group size depends on the ages or grades of the test takers. For young children (kindergarten through grade 3) group size should not exceed fifteen. Young handicapped children should be tested in even smaller groups. When as many as fifteen children are tested at one time, it is advisable to have a monitor (another teacher, a teacher's aide, or some other informed adult) present to insure that directions are followed, broken pencils are replaced, and children do not dawdle or lose their place. Group size may be increased for older students, but, again, the presence of at least one additional monitor is advised. When handicapped children are tested, group size should probably not exceed five.

Adherence to Standardized Procedures

The examiner must at all times administer tests *exactly* according to directions. Standardized tests were meant to be given in exactly the same way each time. Departure from standardized procedures destroys the meaning of test scores by rendering the norms useless. Test users must not coach children on test items before administering the test; they must not alter time limits.

Length of Sittings

The length of testing sessions will vary with the age of the test takers and the extent of their handicaps. As a general rule, a testing session should not exceed 30 minutes in the primary grades, 40 to 60 minutes in the intermediate grades, and 90 minutes in junior and senior high school. However, the tester must exercise common sense. If children become restless, unruly, distracted, or disinterested, testing can be interrupted, the children given a brief break, and the testing resumed. If the test is timed, administration should be interrupted only *between* subtests and never during a subtest.

Elimination of Distractions

Tests should not be administered at times when children are regularly engaged in particularly pleasurable activities. Tests should not be administered at times when children regularly go to assembly, recess, gym, lunch, or art class. Care should be taken to avoid testing at times when other classes are having lunch, recess, and so on. Furthermore, it is usually not advisable to administer tests just before or after a long vacation, a special event, or a holiday.

While administering a group test, the tester should be as unobtrusive as possible. The tester should not move around the room and ask children how they are doing or make small talk. Likewise, conversations between the tester and the monitors should be minimized. Finally, the teacher should avoid publicly preparing an interesting activity to follow the test. Children will attend to the movie projector that is being set up, the novel apparatus for a lab experiment, the elephant that has just been brought into the classroom.

Providing Encouragement

Testers can use discretion in encouraging children taking tests. If a tester sees a child watching a bird building a nest outside the window, the child can be encouraged to pay attention to the test now and watch the bird later; the tester can also draw the window shades. The tester must use common sense so that the standard administration procedures are not violated.

Knowledge of the Tests

The tester should carefully study the manuals provided with the tests. The joint committee of the American Psychological Association, the American Educational Research Association, and the National Council on Measurement in Education stated that "it is appropriate to ask that any test manual provide the information necessary for a test user to decide whether the consistency, relevance, or standardization of a test makes it suitable for [the user's] purpose" (1974, p. 5). Users must study the actual content of a test carefully to make sure that the test adequately assesses the curricular content being taught and that the child has the skills necessary to take the test.

Using the Services of the Buros Institute of Mental Measurements

In addition to inspecting test manuals, all test users should be familiar with the resources available from the Buros Institute of Mental Measurements. The Buros Institute was founded by Oscar Krisen Buros and has one of the richest sources of data on tests in the world.

The institute provides three references that may be of use to educators and psychologists. First, the institute publishes *Tests in Print.* The latest in this series, *Tests in Print 3,* was published in Fall, 1983. This reference work contains a listing of every test that is registered with the institute. *Tests in Print* is cumulative, so it contains not only the most recent test but also tests from each of the previous *Tests in Print* as well as each volume of the *Mental Measurements Yearbooks,* which are also published by the institute. The Buros Institute attempts to acquire every commercially available test published in English throughout the world. *Tests in Print* simply lists all these tests and provides a short description of each.

The second and most notable reference work published by the Buros Institute is the *Mental Measurements Yearbook.* There are eight *Mental Measurements Yearbooks* and a ninth is scheduled for publication in 1985. Unlike *Tests in Print 3,* the *Mental Measurements Yearbooks* are not cumulative; instead, information in each yearbook pertains only to those tests that are new or revised at the time each volume is published. A listing of new or revised tests is typically accompanied by evaluative reviews written by qualified professionals.

Both *Tests in Print 3* and the *Mental Measurements Yearbooks* contain references. The institute has an ongoing policy of monitoring most major journals in psychology, business, and various other fields to find articles that reference tests. If a journal article does reference a test, the reference for the journal article is listed along with the test entry in *Tests in Print 3* and the *Mental Measurements Yearbooks.*

The third service provided by the institute is a computerized data base which is associated with bibliographic retrieval services and can be accessed through most major libraries. The data base is essentially a replication of the *Mental Measurements Yearbooks.* Currently, the entire *Eighth Mental Measurements Yearbook* has been read into the data base, and the institute provides monthly updates whereby all new information that will appear in the *Ninth Mental Measurements Yearbook* is blended into the data base. The major advantage of the data base is that it can be searched by means of the computer. The following questions could be answered easily using the computerized data base: (1) How many intelligence tests are designed for 3½-year-old children? (2) What tests are available that assess both reading recognition and reading comprehension for eighth-grade students? (3) Are there any behavior rating scales available for assessing hyperactivity?

Tests in Print and the *Mental Measurements Yearbooks* are available in the reference departments of most libraries. Information about the data base or any institute services may be obtained from the Buros Institute of Mental Measurements, 135 Bancroft Hall, University of Nebraska, Lincoln, Nebraska 68588-0348.

SUMMARY

Assessment is a complex process, and assessment data are used to make important decisions about individuals. Much can go wrong in the process of assessing students, and, when things go wrong, students and their life opportunities can be adversely affected. Several assumptions are inherent in assessing students. It is assumed that the person who gives tests is skilled in doing so, that error is always present, that the students we assess are like those to whom we compare them, that behavior sampling is adequate, and that only present behavior is observed. To the extent assumptions are not met or recognized, assessment is invalid.

Many factors must be considered in assessment. They include the student's current life circumstances, developmental history, and extrapersonal factors. We reviewed the many different kinds of assessment information typically collected on students, and we differentiated between formal and informal assessments.

There are three fundamentally different approaches to assessment. Many assessors focus their assessment efforts on finding out what is wrong with students, while others focus on diagnosing instruction. In yet a third approach, efforts are made to assess opportunity to learn.

In selecting and administering tests, users must evaluate the kinds of behaviors to be tested, the kinds of interpretative data they want, and the extent to which a commercially prepared test ought to be used. Several suggestions were made for teacher use and interpretation of standardized tests.

STUDY QUESTIONS

1. It is assumed that people who give tests to students are adequately trained to do so. What broad skills can you expect a qualified assessor to have? What happens when people who do not have these competencies assess students?

2. Differentiate between random error and systematic bias.
3. How might you evaluate the extent to which the students you assess have comparable acculturation to those in a test's norm group?
4. Differentiate between an observation and an inference and give two examples of each.
5. Identify three different ways to begin an assessment. Describe an optimal sequence of activities for assessing a student.
6. When and why might you want to administer a group test individually?
7. Differentiate between norm-referenced and criterion-referenced tests and give an advantage of each.
8. Identify two advantages and three disadvantages of informal (teacher-made) tests.

ADDITIONAL READING

Algozzine, B., & Ysseldyke, J. E. (1981). Special education services for normal students: Better safe than sorry? *Exceptional Children, 48,* 238–243.

Bersoff, D. N. (1973). Silk purses into sows' ears: The decline of psychological testing and a suggestion for its redemption. *American Psychologist, 28,* 892–899.

Bijou, S. W. (1970). What psychology has to offer education—now! *Journal of Applied Behavior Analysis, 3,* 65–71.

Boehm, A., & Weinberg, R. A. (1977). *The classroom observer: A guide for developing observation skills.* New York: Teachers College Press.

Carver, F. R. (1974). Two dimensions of tests: Psychometric and educative. *American Psychologist, 29,* 512–518.

Newland, T. E. (1973). Assumptions underlying psychological testing. *Journal of School Psychology, 11,* 316–322.

Newland, T. E. (1980). Psychological assessment of exceptional children and youth. In W. Cruickshank (Ed.), *Psychology of Exceptional Children and Youth.* Englewood Cliffs, NJ: Prentice-Hall.

Proger, B., & Mann, L. (1973). Criterion-referenced measurement: The world of the gray versus black and white. *Journal of Learning Disabilities, 6,* 72–84.

Semmell, M. I., & Thiagarajan, S. (1973). Observation systems and the special education teacher. *Focus on Exceptional Children, 5,* 1–12.

Ysseldyke, J. E., & Shinn, M. (1981). Psychoeducational evaluation: Procedures, considerations, and limitations. In D. Hallahan & J. Kauffman (Eds.), *The Handbook of Special Education.* Englewood Cliffs, NJ: Prentice-Hall.

CHAPTER 3

LEGAL AND ETHICAL CONSIDERATIONS IN ASSESSMENT

Much of the practice of assessing students is the direct result of legislation, guidelines, and court cases. If you were to interview directors of special education in your area and ask them why students are assessed, they might initially tell you that students are assessed to provide information on how best to teach them. Pressed harder, these directors would probably tell you that students are assessed because assessment is required by law. They might also tell you that specific kinds of students (for example, minority students) are *not* assessed because such assessments have been forbidden by the courts. Federal laws mandate that students must be assessed before they are declared eligible for special education services. Such laws also mandate that there must be an individualized education plan for every handicapped student and that instructional objectives for each of those students must be derived from a comprehensive individualized assessment.

In this chapter, we review Public Law 94-142, guidelines, and major court cases in which specific kinds of assessment activities have been prescribed. We then describe some of the ethical standards on assessment that have been developed by professional associations. We close the chapter by reviewing guidelines for the collection, maintenance, and dissemination of pupil records.

PUBLIC LAW 94-142

Education is a responsibility of state rather than federal government. No provision of the U.S. Constitution mandates education. Yet every state has compulsory education laws, laws that say that students must attend school. In

1975, the U.S. Congress passed a compulsory special education law, the Education for All Handicapped Children Act. Ballard and Zettel (1977) described that law (often known by its congressional number—Public Law 94-142) as designed to meet four major purposes:

1. To guarantee that special education services are available to children who need them
2. To insure that decisions about providing services to handicapped students are made in fair and appropriate ways
3. To set clear management and auditing requirements and procedures for special education at all levels of government
4. To provide federal funds to help states educate handicapped students

Much of what happens in assessment is directly mandated by one of the four provisions of Public Law 94-142. These provisions are described in the following sections.

Individualized Education Plan (IEP) Provisions

Public Law 94-142 specifies that all handicapped students have the right to a free, appropriate public education and that for each handicapped student schools must have an individualized education plan (IEP). In that document school personnel must specify the long-term and short-term goals of the instructional program. IEPs must be based on a comprehensive assessment by a multidisciplinary team. The team must specify not only goals and objectives but also plans for implementing the instructional program. They must specify how and when progress toward accomplishment of objectives will be evaluated.

IEPs are to be formulated by a multidisciplinary team meeting with the parents. Parents have the right to agree to the contents of the plan. We stress here the fact that assessment data are collected for the purpose of helping team members specify the components of the IEP. Figure 3.1 is an example of an IEP for a student in a Minnesota school district. Note that specific assessment activities that form the basis for the plan are listed as are specific instructional goals or objectives.

Protection in Evaluation Procedures (PEP) Provisions

Congress included a number of specific requirements in Public Law 94-142. These requirements were designed to protect students and help insure that assessment procedures and activities would be fair, equitable, and nondiscriminatory. Specifically, Congress mandated eight provisions.

1. Tests are to be selected and administered in such a way as to be racially and culturally nondiscriminatory.
2. To the extent feasible, students are to be assessed in their native language or primary mode of communication.
3. Tests must have been validated for the specific purpose for which they are used.
4. Tests must be administered by trained personnel in conformance with the instructions provided by the test producer.
5. Tests used with students must include those designed to provide information about specific educational needs, and not just a general intelligence quotient.
6. Decisions about students are to be based on more than performance on a single test.
7. Evaluations are to be made by a multidisciplinary team that includes at least one teacher or other specialist with knowledge in the area of suspected disability.
8. Children must be assessed in all areas related to a specific disability, including—where appropriate—health, vision, hearing, social and emotional status, general intelligence, academic performance, communicative skills, and motor skills.

Least Restrictive Environment (LRE) Provisions

In writing the Education for All Handicapped Children Act, Congress wanted to insure that, to the greatest extent appropriate, handicapped students would be placed in settings that would maximize their opportunities to interact with nonhandicapped students. Section 612(5)(B) states:

To the maximum extent appropriate, handicapped children . . . are educated with children who are not handicapped, and that special classes, separate schooling, or other removal of handicapped children from the regular educational environment occurs only when the nature or the severity of the handicap is such that education in regular classes with the use of supplementary aids and services cannot be achieved satisfactorily.

The least restrictive environment provisions arose out of court cases in which state and federal courts had ruled that when two equally appropriate placements were available for a handicapped student, the most normal placement was preferred.

Due Process Provisions

In Section 615 of Public Law 94-142, Congress specified the procedures that schools and school personnel would have to follow to insure due process in decision making. Specifically, when a decision affecting a student's educational

INDIVIDUAL EDUCATIONAL PLAN   11/11/82
<u>DATE</u>

STUDENT: Last Name   First   Middle

School of Attendance   Home School   Grade Level   Birthdate/Age

5.3   8-4-71

School Address   School Telephone Number

Child Study Team Members

LD Teacher

Case Manager

Name   Homeroom   Name   Parents
                Title   Title

Name   Facilitator   Name   Title
                Title

Name   Speech   Name   Title
                Title

Summary of Assessment results

IDENTIFIED STUDENT NEEDS: Reading from last half of DISTAR II — present performance level

LONG TERM GOALS: To improve reading achievement level by at least one year's gain. To improve math achievement to grade level. To improve language skills by one year's gain.

SHORT TERM GOALS: Master grade-level vocabulary and reading skills. Master math skills in basic curriculum. Master spelling words from Level 3 list. Complete units 1-9 from grade-level curriculum.

MAINSTREAM MODIFICATIONS _____

White Copy - Cumulative Folder   Golden Rod - Case Manager
Pink Copy - Special Teacher   Yellow Copy - Parent

FIGURE 3.1 Example of individualized education program

Description of Services to be Provided

Type of Service	Teacher	Starting Date	Amt. of time per day	OBJECTIVES AND CRITERIA FOR ATTAINMENT
SCD Level III	LD teacher	11-11-82	2½ hrs.	Reading: Will know all vocabulary through the "Honeycomb" level. Will master skills as presented through Distar II. Will know 123 sound-symbols presented in "Sound Way to Reading" Math: will pass all tests at Basic 4 level. Spelling: 5 words each week from Level 3 list. Language: will complete Units 1-9 of the 4th grade language program. Will also complete supplemental units from Language Step by Step.

Mainstream Classes	Teacher	Amt of time per day	OBJECTIVES AND CRITERIA FOR ATTAINMENT
		3½ hrs.	Out of seat behavior: sit attentively and listen during mainstream class discussions. A simple management plan will be implemented if he does not meet this expectation. Mainstream modifications of Social Studies: will keep a folder in which he expresses through drawing the topics his class will cover. Modified district social studies curriculum. No formal testing will be made. An oral reader will read text to him, and oral questions will be asked.

The following equipment, and other changes in personnel, transportation, curriculum, methods, and educational services will be made:

Distar II Reading Program, Spelling Level 3, "Sound Way to Reading" Program, Vocabulary tapes

Substantiation of least restrictive alternatives: The planning team has determined _____ academic needs are best met with direct SCD support in reading, math, language, and spelling.

ANTICIPATED LENGTH OF PLAN 1 yr. The next periodic review will be held: May 1983
DATE/TIME/PLACE

☒ I approve this program placement and the above IEP
☐ I do not approve this placement and/or the IEP
☐ I request a conciliation conference

_____
PARENT/GUARDIAN

Form 2011

_____
Principal or Designee

environment is to be made, the student's parents or guardians must be given the opportunity to be heard and the right to have an impartial due process hearing to resolve conflicting opinions.

Schools must provide opportunities for parents to inspect the records that are kept on children and to challenge material that they believe should not be included in those records. Parents have the right to have their child evaluated by an independent party and to have the results of that evaluation considered when psychoeducational decisions are made. In addition, parents must receive written notification before any education agency can begin an evaluation that might result in changes in the placement of students.

LITIGATION

Several major court cases preceded passage of Public Law 94-142, and it has been argued that the court cases led Congress to pass that law (Bersoff, 1979). Many issues were contested. In the mid-1960s, a suit was brought against the Washington, D.C., schools on behalf of black students who were assigned in disproportionate numbers to lower ability groups or tracks. The chief issue was the fairness of using ability and achievement tests to assign students to groups or tracks. Judge Skelly Wright ruled against tests.

The evidence shows that the method by which track assignments are made depends essentially on standardized aptitude tests which, although given on a system-wide basis, are completely inappropriate for use with a large segment of the student body. Because these tests are standardized primarily on and are relevant to a white middle-class group of students, they produce inaccurate and misleading test scores when given to lower-class and Negro students. (*Hansen* v. *Hobson,* 1967, p. 514)

After the ruling in *Hansen* v. *Hobson,* both ability grouping and standardized testing came under intense judicial scrutiny. Repeatedly, plaintiffs have argued that the use of standardized ability and achievement tests results in disproportionate placement of poor and minority students in both lower educational tracks and in special education. Judges have most often, although not always, ruled in favor of plaintiffs.

Another important court case, *Tinker* v. *Des Moines Independent Community School District,* set the stage for legislation and later litigation. This case had nothing to do with assessment. The issue it addressed was whether students had the right to wear black armbands to protest U.S. involvement in the Vietnam War. The court ruled that children are persons under the Constitution, have civil rights independent of their parents, and do not lose those civil rights when they attend school.

In 1972, in *Mills* v. *Board of Education,* the court asserted the rights of students to a due process hearing prior to exclusion from school, the right of handicapped students to an appropriate education, and the unconstitutionality of the exclusion of handicapped students to said education. Three other points are important.

1. Exclusion of students labeled as behavior problems, mentally retarded, emotionally disturbed, or hyperactive is unconstitutional.
2. Any handicapped child has the right to a "constructive education" including appropriate specialized instruction.
3. Due process of law requires a hearing prior to exclusion, termination, or classification into a special program.

Two major court cases addressed misclassification of students as handicapped. In both cases a consent agreement was reached: the cases were settled out of court when schools agreed to a number of actions. In *Diana* v. *State Board of Education* (1970), the California Department of Education agreed (1) to test all children whose primary language was not English in both their primary language and English, (2) to eliminate unfair verbal items from tests, (3) to reevaluate all Mexican-American and Chinese students enrolled in classes for the educable mentally retarded, using only nonverbal items and testing them in their native language, and (4) to develop IQ tests that reflect Mexican-American culture and are standardized only on Mexican-Americans. In *Covarrubias* v. *San Diego Unified School District* (1971) plaintiffs won the right to monetary damages as a result of being misclassified as handicapped.

In 1971, the Pennsylvania Association for Retarded Children sued the Commonwealth of Pennsylvania for excluding mentally retarded students from public school programs. The state agreed to engage in extensive efforts to locate and assess all mentally retarded students in the state; all students placed in public school classes for the mentally retarded were also reevaluated.

The best known court decision after passage of PL 94-142 was a 1979 decision in response to a case that began in 1971, *Larry P.* v. *Riles.* The result of that case was threefold.

1. The state of California was forced to stop using, permitting the use of, or approving the use of any standardized intelligence test for identification of black educable mentally retarded children, or to stop placing them in special classes for the educable mentally retarded.
2. Defendants were ordered to monitor or eliminate disproportionate placement of black students in such classes in California.
3. Defendants were ordered to reevaluate every black child currently identified as an educable mentally retarded pupil without using standardized intelligence tests.

The issue of bias in assessment was not settled in the *Larry P.* case; it continues to be debated in the nation's courtrooms. *PASE* v. *Hannon* (1980) was a class action suit brought by Parents in Action on Special Education on behalf of "all black children who have been or will be placed in special classes for the educable mentally handicapped in the Chicago school system" (p. 2). Plaintiffs observed that while 62 percent of the enrollment of the Chicago public schools was black, black students comprised 82 percent of the enrollment in classes for the educable mentally handicapped.

The judge ruled in favor of the defendants, stating that he could find little evidence that the tests were, in fact, biased. The ruling was clearly contrary to *Larry P.* Judge Grady addressed this fact.

As is by now obvious, the witnesses and the arguments which persuaded Judge Peckham [the judge in the *Larry P.* case] have not persuaded me. Moreover, I believe the issue in the case cannot properly be analyzed without a detailed examination of the items on the tests. It is clear that this was not undertaken in the *Larry P.* case. (p. 108)

Judge Grady found only eight items on the WISC–R and one item on the Stanford-Binet to be biased against black children. He further stated that poor performance on these items alone was not sufficient to result in the misclassification of black students as educable mentally handicapped.

One other court case, in Mississippi, also addressed assessment practices with minority students. In February 1979, U.S. District Judge Orma Smith approved a consent decree settling the four-year-old case, *Mattie T.* v. *Holladay* (Civil Action No. DC-75-31-S, N.D. Miss.). The case was filed on behalf of all schoolage children classified as handicapped in Mississippi and charged the Mississippi Department of Education with failure to meet the requirements of PL 94-142. Under this decree the following agreements were reached:

1. Specific criteria were established for determining when a school district can place handicapped children in classes and buildings separate from regular education programs.
2. The state must hire outside experts to evaluate and revamp the entire state procedure for classifying and placing handicapped students.
3. A timetable was set for the assessment process.
4. Each school district had to identify children misclassified as mentally retarded and give them an opportunity to enroll in a compensatory education program.
5. School districts were prohibited from removing students from school for more than three days.
6. The Mississippi Department of Education was required to monitor local school districts' compliance with the law.

The most farreaching requirement in this case was the one mandating a reworking of assessment procedures and timelines.

Clearly, courts can keep school personnel from testing students, or at least from giving specific kinds of tests to specific kinds of students. Moreover, the inverse is true: courts can require school systems to administer tests. This was one of the outcomes of the *Pennsylvania Association for Retarded Children (PARC)* v. *Commonwealth of Pennsylvania* case, as school personnel were required to engage in massive child-find activities. It also was an outcome of *Frederick L.* v. *Thomas* (1976, 1977). In that action, the Philadelphia public schools were charged with failure to provide an appropriate education to learning disabled students and with serving too few learning disabled students. The Philadelphia schools were required to engage in massive screening and follow-up individual psychoeducational evaluations to identify all learning disabled students in the system.

In a recent court case in Louisiana (*Luke S. & Han S.* v. *Nix et al.,* 1981)[1] attorneys sued the Louisiana Department of Education for failure to evaluate referred children in a timely fashion. In a consent decree the state agreed to increase the number of assessment personnel statewide and to assess larger percentages of students in accord with state assessment criteria and in a timely manner. In July 1983 a supplemental agreement was reached. It was found that students were being assessed in a timely manner, but state criteria for appropriate assessment were not being followed. The state agreed to implement statewide training of all assessment personnel.

ETHICAL CONSIDERATIONS

Professionals who assess students have the responsibility to engage in ethical behavior. Many professional associations have put together sets of ethical standards to guide the practice of their members; many of these standards relate directly to assessment practices. Here we cite a number of important ethical considerations, borrowing heavily from the *Ethical Standards of Psychologists* (American Psychological Association, 1979). The standards are not cited per se, but we have distilled from them a number of specific ethical considerations.

Responsibility for the Consequences of One's Work

The assessment of students is a social act that has specific social and educational consequences. Those who assess students use assessment data to make decisions about the students, and the decisions can significantly affect an

1. Luke S. and Han S. represent Luke Skywalker and Han Solo, characters from *Star Wars.* The attorneys for the plaintiffs selected these names because they felt they were taking on the Empire (the Louisiana Department of Education).

individual's life opportunities. Those who assess students must accept responsibility for the consequences of their work, and they must make every effort to be certain that their services are used appropriately.

For the individual who assesses students, this ethical standard means sometimes refusing to engage in assessment activities that are desired by a school system but that are clearly inappropriate. It means very careful decision making and assumption of responsibility for the decisions that are made.

Recognizing the Boundaries of One's Competence

Those who are entrusted with responsibility for assessing and making decisions about students have differing degrees of competence. Not only must professionals regularly engage in self-assessment to be aware of their limitations, but they should recognize the limitations of the techniques they use. For the individual this sometimes means refusing to engage in activities in areas in which one is not competent. It also means using techniques that meet recognized standards.

Confidentiality of Information

Those who assess students regularly obtain a considerable amount of very personal information about those students. It is expected that that information will be held in strict confidence. A general ethical principle held by most professional organizations is that confidentiality is broken only when there is clear and imminent danger to an individual or society. Results of pupil performance on tests must not be discussed informally with school staff. Formal reports of pupil performance on tests must be released only with the permission of the persons tested or their parents or guardians.

Adherence to Professional Standards on Assessment

A joint committee of the American Psychological Association, American Educational Research Association, and National Council on Measurement in Education publishes a document entitled *Standards for Educational and Psychological Tests.* These standards specify a set of requirements for test development and use. It is imperative that those who develop tests behave in accord with the standards and that those who assess students use instruments and techniques that meet the standards. In Parts 3 and 4 of this text we review commonly used tests and talk about the extent to which those tests meet the standards. We provide information to help test users make informed judgments about the technical adequacy of specific tests. There is no federal or state agency that acts to limit the publication or use of technically inadequate tests. Only by refusing to use technically inadequate tests will users force developers to improve inadequate tests. Think about this. If you were a test developer, would you spend considerable time and effort developing a test that few people purchased and used? Would you make changes in a technically inadequate test that people did buy and use and that yielded a large annual profit to you or your firm?

Test Security

Those who assess students are expected to maintain test security. It is expected that assessors will not reveal to others the content of specific tests or test items. At the same time, assessors must be willing and able to back up decisions that may adversely affect individuals with data on which those decisions are based.

PUPIL RECORDS: COLLECTION, MAINTENANCE, AND DISSEMINATION

Policies and standards for the collection, maintenance, and dissemination of information about children must balance two sometimes conflicting needs. Parents and children have a basic right to privacy; schools need to collect and use information about children (and sometimes parents) in order to plan appropriate educational programs. Schools and parents have a common goal, to promote the welfare of children. In theory schools and parents should agree on what constitutes and promotes a child's welfare, and in practice schools and parents generally do work cooperatively.

On the other hand, there have been situations where cooperation has been absent or schools have operated *against* the best interests and basic rights of children and parents. School personnel have often flagrantly disregarded the rights to privacy of parents and children. Educationally irrelevant information about the personal lives of parents as well as subjective, impressionistic, unverified information about parents and children has been amassed by the schools. Parents and children have been denied access to pupil records, and therefore they have effectively been denied the opportunity to challenge, correct, or supplement those records. At the same time, schools have on occasion irresponsibly released pupil information to public and private agencies that had no legitimate need for or right to the information. Worse yet, parents and children were often not even informed that the information had been accumulated or released.

Abuses in the collection, maintenance, and dissemination of pupil information were of sufficient magnitude that the Russell Sage Foundation convened a conference in 1969 to deal with the problem. Professors of education, school administrators, sociologists, psychologists, professors of law, and a juvenile court judge participated in the conference to develop voluntary guidelines for the proper collection, maintenance, and dissemination of pupil data. Since then, the guidelines (Goslin, 1969) that were developed at the Russell Sage Conference have been widely accepted and implemented.

In 1974, many of the recommended guidelines became federal law when the Family Educational Rights and Privacy Act (PL 93-380, commonly called the Buckley amendment) was enacted. The basic provisions of the act are quite simple. Any educational agency that accepts federal money (preschools, elementary and secondary schools, community colleges, and colleges and universities) must give parents the opportunity to inspect, challenge, and correct their children's records. (Students aged 18 or older are given the same rights in regard to their own records.) Also, educational agencies must not release identifiable data without the parents' written consent. Violators of the provisions of the Family Educational Rights and Privacy Act are subject to punishment; no federal funds are given to agencies found to be in violation of the law.

The remainder of this chapter deals with specific issues and principles in the collection, maintenance, and dissemination of pupil information. Our discussion draws on the issues raised by and the recommendations of the Russell Sage Foundation Conference Guidelines (hereafter referred to as RSFCG). The Buckley amendment is considered as it applies, as are specific provisions of Public Law 94-142.

Collection of Pupil Information

Schools collect massive amounts of information about individual pupils and their parents. As we said in Chapter 1, information can be put to several legitimate educational uses: referral, screening, and placement decisions, instructional planning decisions, and pupil guidance. A considerable amount of data must be collected if a school system is to function effectively in delivering educational services to children and in reporting the results of its educational programs to the various community, state, and federal agencies to which it may be responsible.

Classes of Information

The RSFCG delineated three classes of information that schools typically collect. The first class of information (category A) includes the basic, minimum information schools need to collect in order to operate an educational program. Category A data include identifying information (the child's and parents' name and address, the student's age, and so forth) as well as the student's educational progress (grades completed, achievement evaluations, attendance).

Category B data are test results and other verified information useful to the school in planning a student's educational program or maintaining a student "safely" in school. Some of the data that pertain to maintaining a student safely in school can be considered absolutely necessary. For example, available records of medical and pharmacological information about severe allergic reactions, such as a sensitivity to bee stings; special diets for children with certain chronic diseases such as diabetes; and unusual medical conditions such as hemophilia may mean the difference between life and death. Other category B data may not be absolutely necessary, but they are nonetheless clearly important in providing an appropriate educational program for a student. Intelligence test data are clearly relevant if the school places a student in a special program for the mentally retarded. Certain types of aptitude or ability data may be necessary if the school district attempts to differentiate instruction on the basis of differences in abilities. Systematic observations, counselor ratings, and various standardized test scores may be useful in cases where a student has problems that are thought to "interfere" with school progress. Certain types of information about a family's background may be important in selecting and interpreting tests used for guidance and placement or in individualizing instruction.

Category C data include information that may be *potentially* useful. When we are gathering information, we often do not know whether a particular bit of information is important or should be followed up. Category C can be considered as the repository for unevaluated but potentially useful information until it can be considered category B information or until it is removed from the student's records.

Consent

According to the RSFCG, no data should be collected without the consent of parents or their agents. The RSFCG accept the notion of representational consent for the collection of category A information and certain types of category B data (for example, intelligence or aptitude tests). *Representational consent* means that consent to collect data is given by appropriately elected officials, such as the state legislature.

The RSFCG recommend that individual informed consent be obtained for the collection of information *not* directly relevant and essential to the education of particular children. Individual informed consent should be obtained in writing prior to the collection of category C data. Informed consent means that the parent (or pupil) is "reasonably competent to understand the nature and consequences of his decision" (Goslin, 1969, p. 17). Individual consent usually should be required for the collection of family information (religion, income, occupation, and so on), personality data, and other noneducational information.

Public Law 94-142, in its section on procedural safeguards, mandates that written prior notice be given to the parents or guardians of a child whenever an educational agency proposes to initiate or change, or refuses to initiate or change, the identification, evaluation, or educational placement of the child or the provision of a free and appropriate education to the child. It is further required that the notice fully inform the parent, in the parent's native language, of all appeal procedures available. Thus, schools must inform parents of their right to present any and all complaints regarding the identification, evaluation, or placement of their child, their right to an impartial due process hearing, and their right to appeal decisions reached at a due process hearing, if necessary by bringing civil action against a school district.

The collection of research data requires individual informed consent of parents. Various professional groups, such as the American Psychological Association, consider the collection of data without informed consent to be unethical; according to the Buckley amendment, it is *illegal* to experiment with children without prior informed consent. Typically, informed consent for research-related data collection requires that the pupil or parents understand (1) the purpose and procedures involved in the investigations, (2) any risks involved in participation in the research, (3) the fact that all participants will remain anonymous, and (4) the option given any participant to withdraw from the research at any time.

Verification

While information is being collected, some distinctions must be made in terms of the quality of the information. Verification is a key concept. *Verifying information* means ascertaining or confirming the information's truth, accuracy, or correctness. Depending on the type of information, verification may take several forms. For observations or ratings, verification means confirmation by another individual. For standardized test data, verification can be equated with reliable and valid assessment.

Information that is not verified cannot be considered category A or B data. Unverified information can be collected, but every attempt should be made to verify such information before it is retained. For example, serious misconduct or extremely withdrawn behavior is of direct concern to the schools. Initial reports of such behavior by a teacher or counselor are typically based on unverified observations. The unverified information provides hints, hypotheses, and starting points for diagnosis. However, if the data are not confirmable, they should not be collected and must not be retained. Similarly, data from unreliable tests (for example, the Illinois Test of Psycholinguistic Abilities or the Developmental Test of Visual Perception) should, we believe, be considered unverified information unless other data are presented to confirm the results.

Maintenance of Pupil Information

Keeping test results and other information, once they are collected, should be governed by three principles. First of all, the information should be retained only as long as there is a continuing need for it. In any event, only category A and category B data—that is, verified data of clear educational value—should be retained. A pupil's school records should be periodically examined, and information that is no longer educationally relevant or no longer accurate should be removed. Natural transition points (for example, promotion from elementary school to junior high) should always be used to remove material from students' files.

The second major principle in the maintenance of pupil information is that parents have the right to inspect, challenge, and supplement student records. The Russell Sage Foundation Conference Guidelines recommended that "formal procedures should be established whereby a student or his parents might challenge the validity of any information contained in Categories 'A' or 'B' " (p. 23). This recommendation presupposes that parents have access to the data.

Parents of exceptional children have had the right to inspect, challenge, and supplement their children's school records for some time. The landmark right-to-education case *(Pennsylvania Association for Retarded Children* v. *Commonwealth of Pennsylvania)* not only won the guarantee of a free, public, appropriate educational program for *all* retarded children in Pennsylvania but it also guaranteed parents the right to inspect and challenge the contents of their children's school records. The consent agreement that terminated this suit, in addition to guaranteeing the right to education of all mentally retarded children in Pennsylvania, specified the right of parents to a due process hearing:

The notice of the due process hearing shall inform the parent or guardian of his right . . . to examine before the hearing his child's school records including any tests or reports upon which the proposed action may be based, of his right to present evidence of his own. (71-42, Sec. 2f)

In Pennsylvania, the right to education and the right to a due process hearing before changes in educational placement have been extended to all exceptional individuals, including the gifted. After 1972, several other right-to-education suits were brought against state departments of education.

Parents of all children won the right to inspect, challenge, and supplement their children's school records in 1974. The Buckley amendment brought the force of federal law to the RSFCG recommendations and the various right-to-education cases. No educational agencies receiving federal support may prevent parents (or persons 18 years of age or older) from (1) inspecting all official files and data related to their children or themselves, (2) challenging the content of such files, and (3) correcting or deleting inaccurate, misleading, or inappropriate information contained in the records.

In Public Law 94-142 the provisions of the Buckley amendment are again reiterated. Parents or guardians must be given the opportunity to examine all relevant records with respect to the identification, evaluation, and educational placement of the child and the free and appropriate public education of the child; and to obtain an independent evaluation of the child. Again, if parents have complaints, they may request an impartial due process hearing to challenge either the records or the school's decision regarding their child. The law specifies further that parents have the right to (1) be accompanied and advised by counsel and by individuals with special knowledge or training with respect to the problems of handicapped children, (2) present evidence and confront, cross-examine, and compel the attendance of witnesses, (3) a written or electronic verbatim record of such hearing, and (4) written findings of facts and decisions.

The third major principle in the maintenance of pupil records is that the records should be protected from snoopers, both inside and outside the school system. In the past, secretaries, custodians, and even other students have had access, at least potentially, to pupil records. "Curious" teachers and administrators, who had no legitimate educational interest, had access. Individuals outside the schools, such as credit bureaus, have often found it easy to obtain information about former or current students. To make sure that only individuals with a legitimate need have access to the information contained in a pupil's records, the RSFCG recommend that pupil records be kept under lock and key. Adequate security mechanisms are necessary to insure that the information in a pupil's records is not available to unauthorized personnel.

Dissemination of Pupil Information

Both access to information by officials and dissemination of information to individuals and agencies outside the school need to be considered. In both cases, the guiding principles are (1) the protection of pupils' and parents' rights of privacy and (2) the legitimate need to know of the person or agency to whom the information is disseminated.

Access Within the Schools

The Russell Sage Foundation Conference recommended that category A and category B data may be released within the school district to school officials with a legitimate educational interest. Those desiring access to pupil records should sign a form stating why they need to inspect the records; a list of people who have had access to their child's files and the reasons why access was sought should be available to parents (Goslin, 1969). The provisions of the Buckley amendment correspond to the Russell Sage Foundation Guidelines:

All persons, agencies, or organizations desiring access to the records of a student shall be required to sign a written form which shall be kept permanently with the file of the student, but only for inspection by the parents or student, indicating specifically the legitimate educational or other interest that each person, agency, or organization has in seeking this information. (Sec. 438, 4A)

When a pupil transfers from one school district to another, a pupil's records are also transferred. The Buckley amendment is very specific here as to the conditions of transfer. When a pupil's file is transferred to another school or school system in which the pupil plans to enroll, the school must (1) notify the pupil's parents that the records have been transferred, (2) send the parents a copy of the transferred records if the parents so desire, and (3) provide the parents with an opportunity to challenge the content of the transferred data.

Access to Individuals and Agencies Outside the Schools

School personnel collect information about pupils enrolled in the school system for educationally relevant purposes. There is an implicit agreement between the schools and parents that the *only* justification for collecting and keeping any pupil data is educational relevance. However, because the schools have so much information about pupils, they are often asked for pupil data by potential employers, credit agencies, insurance companies, police, the armed services, the courts, and various social agencies. To divulge information to any of these sources is a violation of this implicit trust, unless the pupil (if over 18) or the parents request that the information be released.

First, we must recognize the fact that the courts and various administrative agencies have the power to subpoena pupil records from schools. In such cases, the Buckley amendment requires that the parents be notified that the records will be turned over in compliance with the subpoena.

Except in the case of the subpoena of records or their transfer to another school district, the RSFCG recommend that no school personnel release *any* pupil information without the written consent of the parents. The Buckley amendment takes a similar position when it states that no educational agency may release pupil information unless "there is written consent from the student's parents specifying records to be released, the reasons for such release, and to whom, and with a copy of the records to be released to the student's parents and the student if desired by the parents" (Sec. 438, b2A). While the Buckley amendment lists exceptions, such as applications for financial aid, the thrust of the law and of the Russell Sage Foundation Guidelines is to control the dissemination of personal pupil information.

SUMMARY

The practice of assessing students takes place in a social, political, and legal context. Much of assessment takes place because it is mandated by law. School personnel are required to assess students before declaring them eligible for special education services. The major piece of legislation that currently serves as a guide for assessment activities is the Education for All Handicapped Children Act (Public Law 94-142). The law includes provisions specifying that schools must have individualized education plans for students, that students must be educated in least restrictive environments, and that students who are assessed have due process rights. The law also specifies a number of ways in which students who are evaluated are to be protected.

The practice of assessing students changes as courts define and set limits on that practice. We showed how assessment practices have changed as a function of specific court cases.

Those who assess students have certain ethical responsibilities. They are responsible for the consequences of their actions and for recognizing the limits of their competence. There are specific requirements for confidentiality of information obtained in assessment and for keeping the content of tests secure. Those who assess students should adhere to the professional standards outlined in *Standards for Educational and Psychological Tests.*

Schools are entrusted with the lives of children. Every day decisions are made that are intended to be in the children's best interests. These decisions are based on both objective information and professional interpretation of that information. The schools must exercise their power over the lives of children very carefully. When school personnel collect data, they must make sure that the data are educationally relevant; their authority does not include the power to snoop and pry needlessly. The schools need latitude in deciding what information is educationally relevant, but the parents must have the right to check and halt the school's attempts to collect some types of information. Parents' informed consent to the collection of information about their children is basic to the family's right to privacy.

The schools should periodically examine all pupil records and destroy all information that is not of immediate or long-term utility or that has not been verified. The information that is retained must be guarded. Parents, and students over 18, must be given the opportunity to examine records, to correct or delete information, and to supplement the data contained in files.

Sometimes the release of information that has been gathered could be damaging or embarrassing to children and their families. Schools must not release data to outside agencies except under subpoena or with the written consent of parents or a pupil who is over 18. As in all areas of testing and data maintenance, common sense and common decency are required.

STUDY QUESTIONS

1. What were the major purposes of Public Law 94-142, the Education for All Handicapped Children Act of 1975?
2. What four things must be specified in an individualized education plan (IEP)?
3. How might you go about deciding the extent to which a test was fair for use in making decisions about a specific student?
4. Identify two major court cases and describe the effect they have had on the practice of assessing students.
5. Describe differences in the conclusions judges Peckham and Grady reached in *Larry P.* v. *Riles* and *PASE* v. *Hannon.*
6. Under what circumstances is it ethically appropriate to divulge the scores that a client earned on a test?
7. What kinds of information on a student can one school send to another school? For which of these must the permission of the student or the student's parent or guardian first be obtained?

ADDITIONAL READING

Abeson, A., & Zettel, J. (1977). The end of the quiet revolution: The Education for All Handicapped Children Act of 1975. *Exceptional Children, 44,* 115–128.

Ballard, J., & Zettel, J. (1977). Public Law 94-142 and Section 504: What they say about rights and protections. *Exceptional Children, 44,* 177–185.

Bersoff, D. (1979). Regarding psychologists testily: Legal regulation of psychological assessment in the public schools. *Maryland Law Review, 39,* 27–120.

Ysseldyke, J. E., & Algozzine, B. (1984). *Introduction to special education* [Chapter 12: Legal factors in special education]. Boston: Houghton Mifflin.

PART 2

BASIC CONCEPTS OF MEASUREMENT

Part 2 begins with a chapter on basic measurement concepts. Chapter 4, designed for the person who has no background in descriptive statistics, presents the major concepts necessary for understanding the remaining chapters in this part and later parts of the book. Throughout Part 2 the emphasis is on the basic technical information that a consumer needs to understand and interpret tests adequately. Many nuances and niceties are not dealt with. No derivations or proofs are presented. We *do* include equations and computational examples to show how particular numbers are obtained as well as to provide material for the logical understanding of basic measurement concepts that is crucial to an understanding of tests and testing.

Basic statistics form the foundation of tests. The use of tests by those who do not understand basic statistics has caused considerable misuse and misinterpretation of tests in educational settings. The rationale of Part 2 is based on this fact. An individual who uses tests simply must understand basic statistics to use the tests intelligently. We realize that numbers often scare both beginning students and seasoned veterans. Yet the heart of testing is the quantification of behavior.

CHAPTER 4

DESCRIPTIVE STATISTICS

Descriptive statistics summarize data (information) for a particular group of people (a sample). This chapter deals with the basic concepts needed for an understanding of descriptive statistics. Specifically, it discusses scales of measurement, distributions, measures of central tendency, measures of dispersion, and measures of relationship.

SCALES OF MEASUREMENT

There are four scales of measurement: nominal, ordinal, ratio, and equal interval.[1] Ordinal and equal-interval scales are the most frequently used scales in norm-referenced measurement. Nominal and ratio scales are seldom used. The four scales are distinguished primarily on the basis of the relationship between adjacent or consecutive values on the measurement continuum. An *adjacent value* in this case means a potential or possible value rather than an obtained or measured value. In Figure 4.1, which depicts a portion of a yardstick, the possible values are any points between 2 inches and 6 inches, measured in intervals of eighths of an inch. Any two consecutive points (for instance, 3⅛ inches and 3¼ inches) are adjacent values. Any two points on the scale that have intervening values (for instance, 3⅛ inches and 4¼ inches) are *not* adjacent points. We could, of course, think of adjacent intervals larger than ⅛ inch. For example, adjacent 1-inch intervals could be considered, and the adjacent "points" would then be 1 inch, 2 inches, and so on.

1. For a more complete discussion see "Mathematics, Measurement, and Psychophysics" (p. 23) by S. S. Stevens, in *Handbook of Experimental Psychology,* edited by S. S. Stevens, 1951, New York: Wiley.

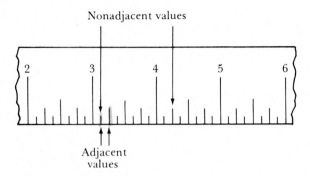

FIGURE 4.1   Adjacent and nonadjacent values

Nominal Scales

Generally, we think of variables as having numerical values. For example, a person's weight is a variable. The values that the variables take are the number of pounds or kilograms. Nominal scales do not use numbers; instead the values that variables take on nominal scales are *names*. More importantly, however, the names have no inherent relationship among themselves. Adjacent values have no inherent relationship. For example, at the local ice cream shop, ice cream flavor is a variable. The values that the variable can take are names: chocolate, strawberry, tutti-frutti, mocha almond fudge, and others. The first flavor listed is not better than the second flavor listed. Banana sherbet is not better than orange sherbet (although many may prefer one or the other). Ice cream flavors are just names.

Sometimes we use numbers as names. In such cases the numbers do not have mathematical properties. Two examples are common in everyday life: social security numbers are just number names for people and telephone numbers are just number names for the particular telephone units in particular locations. It would not make any sense to add up phone numbers and find the average or to compute the average social security number.

When numbers are used to name people or objects and when these numbers have no inherent relationship to one another in terms of their adjacent values, the scale of measurement is a *nominal scale*. An obvious illustration of a nominal scale is the assignment of numbers to football players. A number is used simply to identify an individual player. The player who wears the number 80 is not necessarily a better player than 70 or 77; 80 is just a different player. Numbers 68 and 69, which are typically thought of as adjacent values, have no relationship to each other on a nominal scale; there is no implied rank ordering in the numbers worn on the jerseys.

Ordinal Scales

Ordinal scales order things from best to worst or from worst to best. Several examples of ordinal scales are familiar from everyday life. Some ordinal scales may use names for the values of the variable; the names always imply a quantitative relationship. All comparisons of adjectives are ordinal: good, better, best; tall, taller, tallest; poor, worse, worst; and so forth. Ordinal scales also use numbers. Ordinal numbers—first, second, third, and so on—are, of course, an ordinal scale. Other examples include standing in the graduating class, the AP and UPI sports poll of the top twenty football or basketball teams, the winner and finalists in the Miss America contest, and so forth.

Ordinal scales order or rank information or scores on some kind of continuum. Adjacent numbers on an ordinal scale indicate higher or lower value. A simple example of an ordinal scale is a ranking of persons from first to last for some trait or characteristic, such as weights or test scores. Suppose Ms. Smith administers a test to her arithmetic class, in which twenty-five students are enrolled. The test results are reported in Table 4.1. Column 1 gives the name of each student, while column 2 contains each child's raw score. Column 3 contains the ranking of the twenty-five students; the children are listed in decreasing rank order from the student with the "best" performance to the student with the "worst" performance. It is important to note that the difference in raw-score points between adjacent ranks is not the same at each point on the rank (or order) continuum. For example, the difference between the "best" student and the next best student is not the same as the difference between the second-best and the third-best students. Column 4 contains the difference between each student's raw score and the raw score of the immediately preceding student. From this column, it is apparent that differences in adjacent *ranks* do not reflect the magnitude of differences in raw scores. The difficult concept to keep in mind is that although the difference between rank scores (first, second, third, and so on) is 1 everywhere on the scale, the differences between the raw scores that correspond to the ranks are not equal.

Ratio Scales

Ratio scales have all the characteristics of ordinal scales, but they have two additional characteristics. First, the magnitude of the difference between any two adjacent points on the scale is the same. For example, weight in pounds is measured on a ratio scale; the difference between 15 and 16 pounds is the same as the difference between 124 and 125 pounds. In Table 4.1, if we assume that each raw-score point that makes up the student's total score is of the same value, then the total test score is a ratio scale. This assumption requires that we accept the notion that the difference between 18 and 17 correct is the same as the difference between 11 and 10 correct (or between any other pair of adjacent scores).

TABLE 4.1   Ranking of Students in Ms. Smith's Arithmetic Class

Student	Raw-Score Total	Rank	Difference Between Score and Next Higher Score
Bob	27	1	0
Lucy	26	2	1
Sam	22	3	4
Mary	20	4	2
Luis	18	5	2
Barbara	17	6	1
Carmen	16		
Jane	16	8	1
Charles J.	16		
Hector	14		
Virginia	14		
Manuel	14		
Sean	14	13	2
Joanne	14		
Jim	14		
John	14		
Charles B.	12		
Jing-Jen	12	18	2
Ron	12		
Carole	11	20	1
Bernice	10	21	1
Hugh	8	22	2
Lance	6	23	2
Ludwig	2	24	4
Harpo	1	25	1

The second additional characteristic is that ratio scales have an absolute and logical zero. For instance, temperature on the Kelvin scale is a ratio scale. Absolute zero on that scale indicates the complete cessation of molecular action, or the absence of heat. The absolute zero of a ratio scale, then, allows one to construct ratios with scores. For example, if John weighs 200 pounds and Shawn weighs 100 pounds, John weighs twice as much as Shawn.

Equal-Interval Scales

Equal-interval scales are ratio scales without an absolute zero. Consequently, one cannot construct ratios with equal-interval data. Fahrenheit and Celsius scales are not ratio scales—zero on Fahrenheit has no particular meaning and zero on Celsius is the temperature at which water freezes under standard

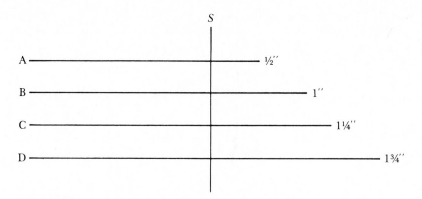

FIGURE 4.2   The measurement of lines as a function of the starting point

conditions. Neither zero is absolute or logical. Thus, 100 degrees Fahrenheit is not twice as hot as 50 degrees Fahrenheit.

Equal-interval scales are very useful nonetheless. It does not really matter where one starts measuring in order to tell the differences between scores. In Figure 4.2, the differences among lines A, B, C, and D are readily measured. We can start measuring from any point, such as from the point where line S intersects lines A, B, C, and D. Measured from S, line A is ½ inch long; line B is 1 inch long; line C is 1¼ inches long; and line D is 1¾ inches long. The lines are measured on an equal-interval scale, and the *differences* among the lines would be the same no matter where the starting point, S, was located. However, because S is not a logical and absolute zero, we cannot make ratio comparisons among the lines. Although we have begun measuring from S and found line A to measure ½ inch and found line B to measure 1 inch, the whole line B is obviously not twice as long as line A. In the same way that line B is not twice as long as line A, an IQ of 100 is not twice as large as an IQ of 50; IQ is not measured on a ratio scale.

DISTRIBUTIONS

Setting up a *distribution* is a way of summarizing a group or a set of scores. Distributions may be graphed to demonstrate visually the relations among the scores in the group or set. In such graphs, the horizontal axis *(abscissa)* is the continuum on which the individuals are measured; the vertical axis *(ordinate)* is the frequency (or the number) of individuals earning any given score shown on the abscissa. Three types of graphs of distributions are common in education and psychology: *histograms, polygrams,* and *curves.* To illustrate these, let us graph the examination scores already presented in Table 4.1. The scores earned on Ms. Smith's arithmetic examination can be grouped in three-point intervals (that is, 1 to 3, 4 to 6, . . . , 25 to 27). The grouped scores are presented as a histogram in the first part of Figure 4.3. In the second part of

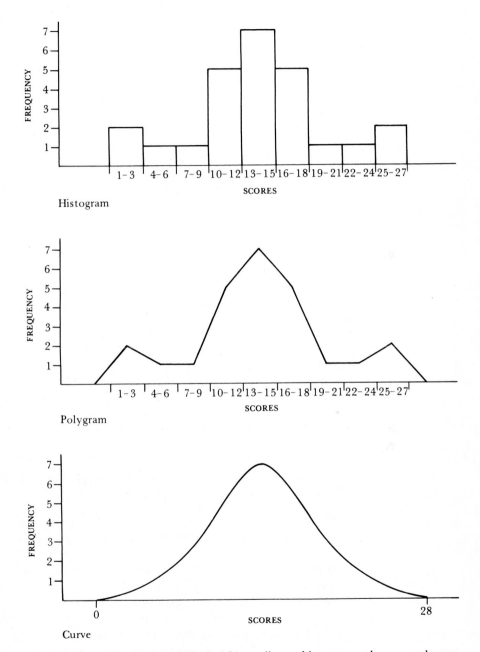

FIGURE 4.3 Distribution of Ms. Smith's pupils on a histogram, polygram, and curve

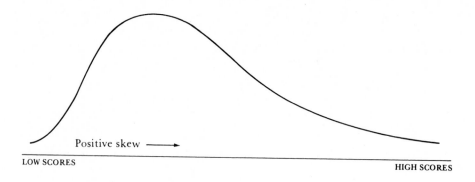

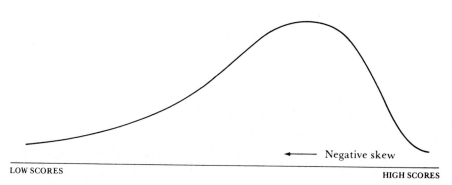

FIGURE 4.4   Positive and negative skew

that figure, the same data are presented as a polygram; note that the midpoints of the intervals used in the histogram are connected in constructing the polygram. The third part of Figure 4.3 contains a smoothed curve.

Distributions are defined by four characteristics: mean, variance, skew, and kurtosis. The *mean* is the arithmetic average of the scores and is the balance point of the distribution. The *variance* describes the "spread" or clustering of scores in a distribution. Both of these characteristics are discussed in greater detail in later sections.

Skew refers to the symmetry of a distribution. The distribution of scores from Ms. Smith's exam is not skewed; the distribution is *symmetrical.* However, if Ms. Smith had given a very easy test on which many students earned very high scores while only a few students earned fairly low scores, the distribution would have been skewed. In such a case, the distribution would have "tailed off" to the low end and would be called a *negatively skewed* distribution. On the other hand, if she had given a very hard test on which most of her students earned low scores and relatively few earned high scores, the

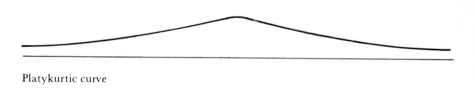

Platykurtic curve

Leptokurtic curve

FIGURE 4.5   A platykurtic and a leptokurtic curve

distribution of scores would have tailed off to the higher end of the continuum. Such a distribution is called a *positively skewed* distribution. Figure 4.4 contains an example of a positively skewed curve and a negatively skewed curve. The label assigned to a skewed distribution is determined by the direction of the tail of the distribution. Skewed distributions in which the tail is in the upper (higher-score) end are positively skewed, while those in which the tail slopes toward the lower end are negatively skewed.

Kurtosis, the fourth characteristic of curves, describes the "peakedness" of a curve or the rate at which a curve rises. Distributions that are flat and slow rising, such as the distribution formed by the scores on Ms. Smith's test, are called *platykurtic curves. (Plat*ykurtic curves are flat, just as a plate or a plateau is flat.) Fast-rising curves are called *leptokurtic curves.* Tests that do not "spread out" (or discriminate among) those taking the test are typically leptokurtic. Figure 4.5 illustrates a platykurtic and a leptokurtic curve.

The normal curve is a particular symmetrical curve. Many variables are distributed normally in nature; many are not. The *only* value of the normal curve lies in the fact that it is known exactly how many cases fall between any two points (ordinates) on the curve.

BASIC NOTATION

A number of symbols are used in statistics; these symbols are presented in Table 4.2. The summation sign Σ means "add the following," while X denotes any score. The number of scores in a distribution is symbolized by N, while f is used to denote the frequency of occurrence of a particular score. The arithmetic average *(mean)* of a distribution is denoted by $\bar{X}$. The variance of a distribution is symbolized by S^2, and the standard deviation by S.

TABLE 4.2   Commonly Used Statistical Symbols

Symbol	Meaning
Σ	Summation sign
X	Any score
N	Number of cases
f	Frequency
$\bar{X}$	Mean
S^2	Variance
S	Standard deviation

MEASURES OF CENTRAL TENDENCY

Three measures of central tendency are used: mode, median, and mean. The *mode* is defined as the score most frequently obtained. A mode (if there is one) can be computed for data on a nominal, ordinal, ratio, or equal-interval scale. Distributions may have two modes (if they do, they are called *bimodal* distributions) or they may have more than two. The mode of the distribution of raw scores obtained by Ms. Smith's class on the arithmetic test is readily apparent from an inspection of the data in Table 4.1 and the graphs in Figure 4.3. The mode of this distribution is 14; seven children earned this score.

A *median* is the score that divides the top 50 percent from the bottom 50 percent. It is that point on a scale above which 50 percent of the cases occur and below which 50 percent of the cases occur. Medians can be computed for ordinal, equal-interval, and ratio scales. Every distribution has a median. The median score may or may not actually be earned by a student. In Ms. Smith's arithmetic-test distribution, the median is 14. Seven children earned the median score.

The *mean* is the arithmetic average of the scores in a distribution. It is the sum of the scores divided by the number of scores. The formula for computing the mean, using statistical notation, is given in equation 4.1.

$$\bar{X} = \frac{\Sigma X}{N} \tag{4.1}$$

Using the scores obtained from Ms. Smith's arithmetic examination (Table 4.1), we find that the sum of the scores is 350 and that the number of scores is 25. The mean (average) score, then, is 14. The mean score was earned by seven children in the class. The mean, like the median, may or may not be earned by a child in the distribution.

The mode, median, and mean have particular relationships depending on the symmetry (skew) of a distribution. As Figure 4.6 shows, in symmetrical unimodal distributions the mode, median, and mean are at the same point. In positively skewed distributions, the median and mean are displaced toward the positive tail of the curve; the mode is a lower value than the median, and the median is a lower value than the mean. In negatively skewed distributions, the median and mean are displaced toward the negative tail of the curve; the mode is a higher value than the median, and the median is a higher value than the mean.

MEASURES OF DISPERSION

Four measures of dispersion are commonly computed: range, semi-interquartile range, variance, and standard deviation. The *range* is the distance between the extremes of a distribution, including those extremes; it is the highest score less the lowest score plus one. On Ms. Smith's test (Table 4.1), it is 27 ($27 = 27 - 1 + 1$). The range is a relatively crude measure of dispersion since it summarizes only two bits of information.

The *semi-interquartile range* is a more useful indication of the amount of dispersion in a distribution. It is one-half the distance between the top 25 percent of the scores and the bottom 25 percent of the scores.[2]

The variance and the standard deviation are of primary concern. The *variance* is a numerical index describing the dispersion of a set of scores around the mean of the distribution. Specifically, the variance (S^2) is the average squared-distance of the scores from the mean. Since the variance is an average, it is not related to the number of cases in the set or distribution. Large sets of scores may have large or small variances; small sets of scores may have large or small variances. Also, since the variance is measured in terms of distance from the mean, it is not related to the actual value of the mean. Distributions with large means may have large or small variances; distributions with small means may have large or small variances. The variance of a distribution may be computed with equation 4.2. The *variance* (S^2) equals the sum (Σ) of the square of each score less the mean [$(X - \bar{X})^2$], divided by the number of scores (N).

$$S^2 = \frac{\Sigma(X - \bar{X})^2}{N} \tag{4.2}$$

2. Technically, it is the average distance between the median and the score at the 25th percentile and the median and the score at the 75th percentile.

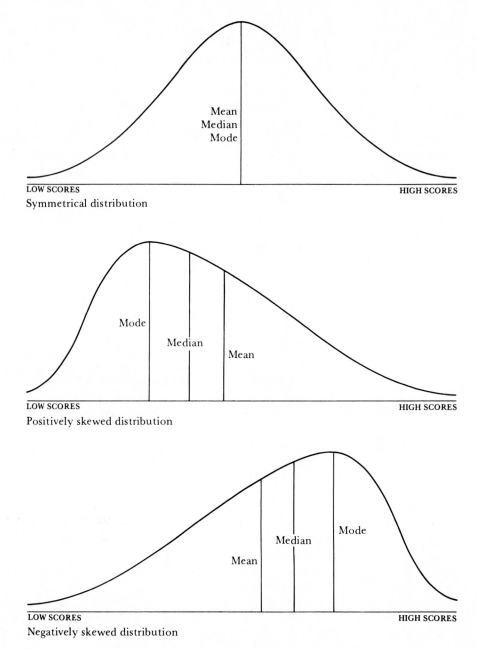

FIGURE 4.6   Relationships among mode, median, and mean for symmetrical and asymmetrical distributions

TABLE 4.3 Computation of the Variance of Ms. Smith's Arithmetic Test

Student	Test Score	$X - \bar{X}$	$(X - \bar{X})^2$
Bob	27	13	169
Lucy	26	12	144
Sam	22	8	64
Mary	20	6	36
Luis	18	4	16
Barbara	17	3	9
Carmen	16	2	4
Jane	16	2	4
Charles J.	16	2	4
Hector	14	0	0
Virginia	14	0	0
Manuel	14	0	0
Sean	14	0	0
Joanne	14	0	0
Jim	14	0	0
John	14	0	0
Charles B.	12	−2	4
Jing-Jen	12	−2	4
Ron	12	−2	4
Carole	11	−3	9
Bernice	10	−4	16
Hugh	8	−6	36
Lance	6	−8	64
Ludwig	2	−12	144
Harpo	1	−13	169
SUM	350	0	900

The scores from Ms. Smith's arithmetic test are reproduced in Table 4.3. The second column contains the score earned by each student. The first step in computing the variance is to find the mean. Therefore, the scores are added and the sum is divided by the number of scores. The mean in this example is 14. The next step is to subtract the mean from each score; this is done in column 3 of Table 4.3, which is labeled $X - \bar{X}$. Note that the scores above the mean are positive, the scores at the mean are zero, and the scores below the mean are negative. The differences (column 3) are then squared (multiplied by themselves); the squared differences are in column 4, labeled $(X - \bar{X})^2$. Note that all numbers in this column are positive. The squared differences are then summed; in this example, the sum of all the squared distances of scores from the mean of the distribution is 900. The variance equals the sum of all the squared distances of scores from the mean divided by the number of scores; in this case, the variance equals 900/25, or 36.

The variance is of little direct importance in measurement, but its calculation is necessary for the computation of the standard deviation (*S*), which is *very* important. The standard deviation is the positive square root ($\sqrt{}$) of the

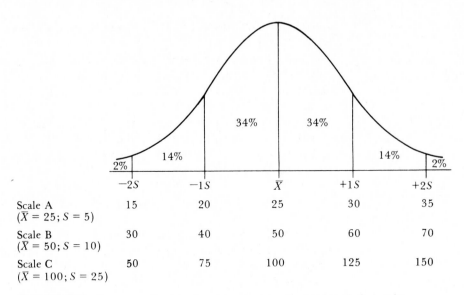

	−2S	−1S	$\overline{X}$	+1S	+2S
Scale A ($\overline{X} = 25$; $S = 5$)	15	20	25	30	35
Scale B ($\overline{X} = 50$; $S = 10$)	30	40	50	60	70
Scale C ($\overline{X} = 100$; $S = 25$)	50	75	100	125	150

FIGURE 4.7   Scores on three scales, expressed in standard deviation units

variance.[3] Thus, in our example, since the variance is 36, the standard deviation is 6. In later chapters, the standard deviation will be used in other computations such as standard scores and the standard error of measurement. It is also very important in the interpretation of test scores.

The standard deviation is used as a *unit of measurement* in much the same way an inch or ton is used as a unit of measurement. With *normal* distributions, scores can be measured in terms of standard deviation units from the mean; we know exactly how many cases occur between the mean and the particular standard deviation. As shown in Figure 4.7, approximately 34 percent of the cases always occur between the mean and one standard deviation (S) either above or below the mean. Thus, approximately 68 percent of all cases occur between one standard deviation below and one standard deviation above the mean (34% + 34% = 68%). Approximately 14 percent of the cases occur between one and two standard deviations below the mean *or* between one and two standard deviations above the mean. Thus, about 48 percent of all cases occur between the mean and two standard deviations either above or below the mean (34% + 14% = 48%). About 96 percent of all cases occur between two standard deviations above and two standard deviations below the mean. Appendix 2 lists the proportion of cases in a normal distribution occurring between the mean and any standard deviation above or below the mean. If we enter Appendix 2 at .44 (that is, .4 and .04), we find the number .1700. This

---

3. The square root of a particular number is the number that when multiplied by itself produces the particular number. For example: $\sqrt{144} = 12$, $\sqrt{25} = 5$, $\sqrt{4} = 2$. Appendix 1 contains a table of square roots for numbers between 1 and 100.

number means that 1,700/10,000 (17 percent) of the cases in the normal curve occur between the mean and .44 standard deviations from the mean, either below or above the mean. Thirty-three percent of the cases fall below .44 standard deviations below the mean. (Half of the cases, 50 percent, fall below the mean; 17 percent fall between $-0.44\ S$ and the mean; 50 percent less 17 percent equals 33 percent.)

As shown by the positions and values for scales A, B, and C in Figure 4.7, it does not matter what the values of the mean or standard deviation are. The relationship holds for various obtained values of the mean and the standard deviation. For scale A, where the mean is 25 and the standard deviation is 5, 34 percent of the scores occur between the mean (25) and one standard deviation below the mean (20) *or* between the mean and one standard deviation above the mean (30). Similarly, for scale B, where the mean is 50 and the standard deviation is 10, 34 percent of the cases occur between the mean (50) and one standard deviation below the mean (40) *or* one standard deviation above the mean (60).

It is extremely important that those who use tests to make decisions about students be aware of the means and standard deviations of the tests they use. Some tests, for example, have a mean of 100 and a standard deviation of 16. If scores on those tests are normally distributed, we would expect approximately 68 percent of the school population to have IQs between 84 and 116. Another test may have a mean of 100 and a standard deviation of 24. We would expect approximately 68 percent of the school population to have IQs between 76 and 124 if scores on the test are normally distributed. The meaning of a score in a distribution depends on the mean, the standard deviation, and the shape of that distribution. This is an obvious point, yet it is often overlooked. For example, some states use an absolute score in the school code for the placement and retention of mentally retarded children in special education programs; Pennsylvania uses a score of 75 ($\pm$5) for maintaining eligibility for placement. On the Stanford-Binet Intelligence Scale, a score of 80 is 1.25 standard deviations below the mean [(100 − 80)/16]; on the Slosson Intelligence Test, a score of 80 is 1.33 standard deviation below the mean [(100 − 80)/15]. If a single absolute score is specified, several *different* levels of eligibility for special education classes could be written into the school code unintentionally.

CORRELATION

Correlations quantify relationships between variables. *Correlation coefficients* are numerical indices of these relationships. They tell us the extent to which any two variables go together, the extent to which changes in one variable are reflected by changes in the second variable. These coefficients are used in measurement to estimate both the reliability and the validity of a test.

Correlation coefficients can range in value from .00 to *either* +1.00 or −1.00. The sign (+ or −) indicates the direction of the relationship while the number indicates the magnitude of the relationship. A correlation coefficient of .00 between two variables means that there is no relationship between the variables. The variables are independent; changes in one variable are not related to changes in the second variable. A correlation coefficient of either +1.00 or −1.00 indicates a perfect relationship between two variables. Thus, if you know a person's score on one variable, you can know that person's score on the second variable.

The Pearson Product-Moment Correlation Coefficient

The most commonly used correlation coefficient is the Pearson product-moment correlation coefficient (*r*). This is an index of the straight-line (*linear*) relationship between two variables measured on an equal-interval scale. Suppose Ms. Smith administered a second exam to her arithmetic class. The results of the first exam (the data from Table 4.1) are represented in column 2 of Table 4.4, while the results of the second exam are presented in column 3. (For the sake of simplicity, the example has been constructed so that the second test has the same mean and the same standard deviation—that is, 14 and 6—as the first test.) The two scores for each student are plotted on a graph (called a *scattergram* or *scatterplot*) in Figure 4.8. The scatterplot contains twenty-five points—one for each child. Inspection of the figure indicates that there is a pronounced tendency for high scores on the first test to be associated with high scores on the second test. There is a *positive* relationship (correlation) between the first and second tests. The line drawn through the scatterplot in Figure 4.8 is called a *regression line.* When the points corresponding to each pair of scores cluster closely around the regression line, there is a high degree of relationship. The points from Table 4.4 do cluster closely around the regression line; there is a high correlation (specifically, .89) between the first and second tests.[4] If all the points fell on the regression line, there would be a perfect correlation (1.00).

Figure 4.9 contains six scatterplots of different degrees of relationship. In parts a and b all points fall on the regression line so that the correlation between the variables is perfect. Part a has a correlation coefficient of +1.00; high scores on one test are associated with high scores on the other test. Part

4. The correlation coefficient can be computed with the following formula:

$$r = \frac{N\Sigma XY - (\Sigma X)(\Sigma Y)}{\sqrt{N\Sigma X^2 - (\Sigma X)^2} \; \sqrt{N\Sigma Y^2 - (\Sigma Y)^2}}$$

TABLE 4.4   Scores Earned on Two Tests Administered by Ms. Smith to Her Arithmetic Class

Student	Raw Score, Test 1	Raw Score, Test 2
Bob	27	26
Lucy	26	22
Sam	22	20
Mary	20	27
Luis	18	14
Barbara	17	18
Carmen	16	16
Jane	16	17
Charles J.	16	16
Hector	14	14
Virginia	14	14
Manuel	14	16
Sean	14	14
Joanne	14	12
Jim	14	14
John	14	12
Charles B.	12	14
Jing-Jen	12	11
Ron	12	12
Carole	11	10
Bernice	10	14
Hugh	8	6
Lance	6	1
Ludwig	2	2
Harpo	1	8

b has a correlation of -1.00; high scores on one test are associated with low scores on the other test (this negative correlation is called an *inverse* relationship). Parts c and d show a high degree of positive and negative relationship, respectively. Note that the departures from the regression lines are associated with lower degrees of relationship. Parts e and f show scatterplots with a low degree of relationship. Note the wide departures from the regression lines.

Zero correlations can occur in three ways, as shown in Figure 4.10. First, if the scatterplot is essentially circular (part a), the correlation is approximately .00. Second, if either or both variables are constant (part b), the correlation is .00. And third, if the two variables are related in a nonlinear way, the correlation is .00. In part c, for example, there is a very strong curvilinear relationship where all points fall close to a curved line, but the *linear* regression line would parallel one of the axes. Thus, while there is a curvilinear relationship, the coefficient of linear correlation is approximately .00.

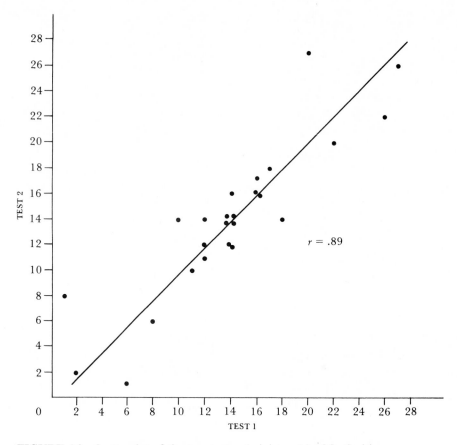

FIGURE 4.8   Scatterplot of the two tests administered by Ms. Smith

Variant Correlation Coefficients

Six variations of linear correlation are commonly found in test manuals and research literature dealing with reliability and validity. Four are members of the Pearson family of correlation coefficients and are computed by the same or by computationally equivalent formulas (see footnote 4). Two variations are not members of the Pearson family of coefficients and are calculated differently.

Pearson-Family Coefficients

Different names are typically given to the Pearson product-moment correlation coefficient depending on the scale of measurement used. The first member of the family of correlation coefficients is called the *Pearson product-moment* correlation coefficient and is symbolized by the letter *r*. This name

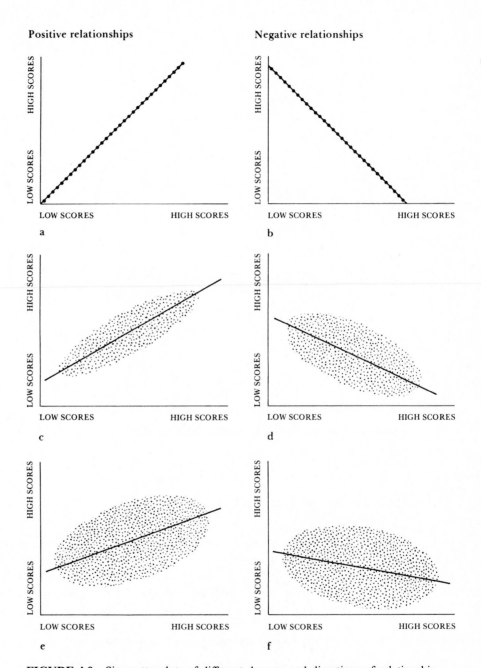

FIGURE 4.9 Six scatterplots of different degrees and directions of relationship

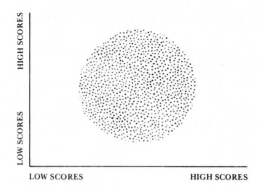

a. No relationship

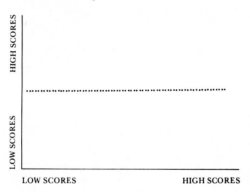

b. No relationship; one variable is constant

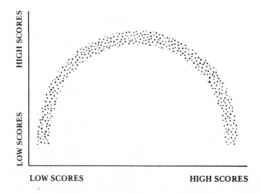

c. No linear relationship; relationship is curvilinear

FIGURE 4.10   Three zero-order, linear correlations

or symbol is used when the variables to be correlated are measured on an equal-interval (or ratio) scale. The second member of the Pearson family is called the Spearman rho (ρ). This coefficient is used when both variables are measured on an ordinal scale. The third and fourth members of the Pearson family are used when either or both of the variables to be correlated are naturally occurring dichotomous variables (for example, male/female). When a naturally occurring dichotomous variable such as sex is correlated with a continuous, equal-interval variable (height measured in inches for example), the correlation coefficient is called a *point biserial* correlation coefficient ($r_{pt.bis}$). When two sets of naturally occurring dichotomous variables (for example, male/female and dead/alive) are correlated, the correlation coefficient is called a *phi* coefficient (φ).

Non-Pearson-Family Coefficients

A continuous variable can be forced into a dichotomy. For example, the entire range of intelligence can be dichotomized into smart and dull at some arbitrary point on the continuum. If a variable that has been forced into an arbitrary dichotomy (for example, smart/dull) is correlated with a continuous equal-interval variable (for example, grade-point average), the resulting coefficient is called a *biserial* correlation coefficient (r_{bis}). If two arbitrarily dichotomized variables (for example, tall/short, smart/dull) are correlated, the coefficient is called a *tetrachoric* correlation coefficient (r_{tet}). These two correlation coefficients are computed differently than the Pearson-family coefficients are.

Relationship Among Correlation Coefficients

Figure 4.11 illustrates the different correlation coefficients commonly used in measurement that we have discussed.

In test manuals you will often see correlations between individual test items or between each test item and the total test score. Test authors typically report phi and point biserial correlation coefficients rather than tetrachoric and biserial coefficients in such cases. In selecting particular coefficients, an author assumes the nature of correct or incorrect response. An author who selects phi and point biserial correlations assumes that each response is either correct or incorrect; there are no "in-betweens." The author who reports tetrachoric and biserial correlations assumes that each test item represents a continuum ranging from totally correct to totally incorrect, even though the individual items are scored only as right or wrong. The differences between Pearson-family and non-Pearson-family coefficients should not cause a test administrator any difficulty. Modern tests rely almost exclusively on Pearson-family coefficients. But occasionally one sees r_{tet} or r_{bis}.

CHARACTERISTICS OF VARIABLE 1

	Pearson family			Non-Pearson family
	Ordinal	Equal interval	Natural dichotomy	Forced dichotomy
Ordinal	Spearman's rho(ρ)			
Equal interval		Pearson product-moment (r)	Point biserial ($r_{pt\,bis}$)	Biserial (r_{bis})
Natural dichotomy			Phi (ϕ)	
Forced dichotomy				Tetrachoric (r_{tet})

CHARACTERISTICS OF VARIABLE 2

FIGURE 4.11   Different kinds of correlation coefficients are used, depending on the scales of measurement for each variable. There are coefficients for some of the blanks in this figure (for example, biserial phi and rank biserial), but test users are not likely to encounter them in test manuals.

Causality

No discussion of correlation is complete without mentioning causality. Correlation is a necessary but insufficient condition for determining causality. Two variables cannot be causally related unless they are correlated. However, the mere presence of a correlation does not imply causality. For any correlation between two variables (A and B), *three* causal interpretations are possible: A causes B; B causes A; or a third variable, C, causes both A and B. For example, firemen (A) are often present at fires (B). Firemen do not cause fires (A does not cause B).[5] Fires cause firemen to be present (B causes A). As a second example, in a sample of children ranging from 6 months to 8 years of age, we might find a positive relationship between shoe size and mental age. Big feet do not cause intelligence (A does not cause B). Moreover, intelligence does not cause big feet (B does not cause A). More likely, as children grow older (C) they tend to increase in both shoe size and mental age; C causes both A and B.

5. Exceptions have been reported by Bradbury (1953).

Although the above examples illustrate fairly obvious instances of inappropriate reasoning, in testing situations the errors or potential errors are not so clear. For example, scores on intelligence tests and scores on achievement tests are correlated. Some argue that intelligence causes achievement; others argue that achievement causes intelligence. Since there are at least three possible interpretations of correlational data—and since correlational data do not tell us which interpretation is true—we must never draw causal conclusions from such data.

SUMMARY

Descriptive statistics provide summary information about groups of individuals. Data can be obtained on one of four scales of measurement: *nominal, ordinal, ratio,* and *equal-interval* scales. Collections of scores are called *distributions.* Distributions are defined by four characteristics: *mean, variance, skew,* and *kurtosis.* Depending on the scale of measurement, three indices may be used to indicate a distribution's central tendency: the *mode* (the most frequent score), the *median* (the score that separates the top 50 percent from the bottom 50 percent), and the *mean* (the arithmetic average). Depending on the scale of measurement, the dispersion of a distribution can be described by several indices: the *range* of scores, the *semi-interquartile range,* the *variance,* and the *standard deviation.* The quantification of the relationship between two variables is called *correlation.* When there is no relation between variables, the correlation is zero. When there is a perfect relationship between variables, the correlation is one. A plus or a minus sign indicates the type of relationship, not the magnitude of relationship. A positive correlation indicates that high scores on one variable are associated with high scores on the second variable. A negative correlation indicates an inverse relationship: high scores on one variable are associated with low scores on the other variable. There are several types of correlations that are often used in tests.

STUDY QUESTIONS

1. All third-grade pupils in a particular state took an achievement test. The superintendent of public instruction reviewed the test results and in a news conference reported concern for the quality of education in the state. The superintendent reported, "Half the third-grade children in this state performed below average." What is foolish about that?
2. What is the relationship among the mode, median, and mean in a normal distribution?

3. The following statements about test A and test B are known to be true:

Tests A and B measure the same behavior.

Tests A and B have means of 100.

Test A has a standard deviation of 15.

Test B has a standard deviation of 5.

2 s

    a. Following classroom instruction, the pupils in Mr. Radley's room earn an average score of 130 on test A. Pupils in Ms. Purple's room earn an average score on test B of 110. On this basis, the local principal concludes that Mr. Radley is a better teacher than Ms. Purple. Why is this inappropriate?

    b. Assuming the pupils were equal prior to instruction, what conclusions could the principal legitimately make?

4. On the Stanford-Binet Intelligence Scale, Harry earns an IQ of 52 and Ralph earns an IQ of 104. Their teacher concludes that Ralph is twice as smart as Harry. To what extent is this conclusion warranted?

PROBLEMS

1. Ms. Robbins administers a test to ten children in her class. The children earn the following scores: 14, 28, 49, 49, 49, 77, 84, 84, 91, 105. For this distribution of scores, find the following:
    a. Mode
    b. Mean
    c. Range
    d. Variance and standard deviation

2. Mr. Garcia administers the same test to six children in his class. The children earn the following scores: 21, 27, 30, 54, 39, and 63. For these scores, find the following:
    a. Mean
    b. Range
    c. Variance and standard deviation

3. Ms. Shumway administers a test to six children in her nursery school program. The children earn the following scores: 23, 33, 38, 53, 78, and 93. Find the mean and standard deviation of these six scores.

4. Using Appendix 2, find the proportion of cases that
    a. occur between the mean and the following standard deviation units: $-1.5, +.37, +.08, +2.75$.
    b. occur between + and $-1.7S$, between + and $-.55S$, and between + and $-2.1S$.
    c. occur above $-.7S, +1.3S$, and $+1.9S$.
    d. occur below $-.7S, +1.3S$, and $+1.9S$.

Answers

1. (a) 49; (b) 63; (c) 92; (d) 784 and 28.
2. (a) 39; (b) 43; (c) 225 and 15.
3. Mean = 53; standard deviation = 25.
4. (a) .4332, .1443, .0319, .4970; (b) .9108, .4176, .9642; (c) .7580, .0968, .0287; (d) .2420, .9032, .9713.

ADDITIONAL READING

McCollough, C., & VanAtta, L. (1965). *Introduction to descriptive statistics and correlation.* New York: McGraw-Hill.

CHAPTER 5

QUANTIFICATION OF
TEST PERFORMANCE

Most behaviors occur without systematic observation, quantification, and evaluation; the vast majority of behaviors do not occur in situations specifically structured to quantify and evaluate them. A test is an exception. A test is a structured, standardized situation in which standardized materials are presented to an individual in a predetermined manner in order to evaluate that individual's responses.

How the individual's responses are quantified depends on the test materials, the intent of the test author, and our intent in choosing the test. If we were interested only in a particular question and the response to it (that is, Can our student perform one particular task correctly?), we could simply classify the response as right or wrong. Essentially, we would have no need to quantify the test results. If the task were sufficiently complex, we could expand the classification of the response further (for example, correct, mostly correct, somewhat correct, totally wrong), but still there would be no need for quantification.

More often, though, we are interested in a particular item or question as a representative of a larger population of items, an item domain. For example, we might want to give a test that requires a child to add two single-digit numbers (including zero) whose sum is 10 or less. Since this is a very small domain, our test could well include all fifty-five possible problems. With larger domains of items, it is seldom either practical or desirable to select all the items in the domain. When we sample, particular items are important as representatives of the domain and tend to lose their individual importance. Consequently, we are more likely to be concerned with total scores, either the number correct or the number of partial-credit and full-credit points. We assume that a student's performance on all the items in the domain can be accurately inferred from the performance on the sample of items.

A raw score, or the number of problems correct, on a test that samples a domain of items is difficult to interpret. For example, if Carol earns a raw score of 17 on her spelling test, how good was her performance? Generally, we would first attempt to understand her performance by expressing her raw score as a percentage correct. If there were 50 spelling words, Carol spelled 34 percent of the words correctly. Typically, we would then evaluate Carol's performance by comparing it to the performances of her classmates on the same test. If the raw scores in Carol's class ranged from 17 to 3, we would conclude that Carol's performance was good.

A test performance is typically interpreted by comparing it to the performances of a group of subjects of known demographic characteristics (age, sex, grade in school, and so on). This group is called a *normative sample* or *norm group*. These comparison scores are called *derived scores* and are of two types: developmental scores and scores of relative standing.

Not only are derived scores useful in interpreting the score earned by an individual, they allow comparisons of several scores earned by one individual or one or more scores earned by several individuals. For example, it is not particularly helpful to know that George is 70 inches tall; Bill is 6 feet, 3 inches tall; Bruce is 1.93 meters tall; and Alan is 177.8 centimeters tall. To compare their heights, it is necessary to transform the heights into comparable units. In feet and inches, the four heights are: George, 5 feet, 10 inches; Bill, 6 feet, 3 inches; Bruce, 6 feet, 4 inches; and Alan, 5 feet, 10 inches. Derived scores put raw scores into comparable units.

DEVELOPMENTAL SCORES

Developmental Levels

Developmental scores are one method of transforming raw scores. The most common types of developmental scores are age equivalents (mental ages, for example) and grade equivalents. Suppose the average performance of 10-year-old children on an intelligence test was twenty-seven correct answers. Further, suppose that Horace answered twenty-seven questions correctly. Horace would have answered as many questions correctly as the average of 10-year-old children. He would have earned a mental age of 10 years. An *age equivalent* means that a child's raw score is the average (the median or mean) performance for that age group. Age equivalents are expressed in years and months; a hyphen is used in age scores (for example, 7-1). A *grade equivalent* means that a child's raw score is the average (the median or mean) performance for that grade. Grade equivalents are expressed in grades and tenths of grades; a decimal point is used in grade scores (for example, 7.1). Age-equivalent and grade-equivalent scores are interpreted as a performance equal to the average X-year-old's and average Xth grader's performance, respectively.

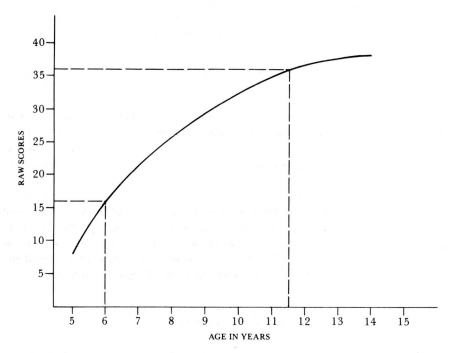

FIGURE 5.1   Mean number correct for eleven age groups: an example of arriving at age-equivalent scores

Suppose we gave a test to 1,000 children, 100 at each age (within two weeks of their birthdays) from 5 to 14 years. For each 100 children at each age, there is a distribution with a mean. These hypothetical means are connected in Figure 5.1. As the figure shows, a raw score of 16 corresponds exactly to the average score earned by children in the 6-year-old distribution. Thus, the child who earns a score of 16 has an age equivalent of 6 years, 0 months, or 6-0. A score of 36, by contrast, falls *between* the average of the 11-year-old distribution and the average of the 12-year-old distribution. A raw score of 36 would be estimated *(interpolated)* as an age score of 11-6; it would be awarded a score between 11 and 12, despite the fact that no children between 11 and 12 years of age were tested. A score of 4 would fall below the average of the lowest age group, the five-year-olds. If a child earned a raw score of 4, that child's age equivalent would be estimated *(extrapolated)* by continuing the curve in Figure 5.1. A raw score of 4 could be extrapolated to be the equivalent of an age score of 3-6 although *no* children that young are included in the sample. Similarly, a score greater than the average performance of the oldest children could also be extrapolated.

The interpretation of age and grade equivalents requires great care. Four problems occur in the use of developmental scores. The first problem is that children who earn an age equivalent of 12-0 have merely answered correctly as many questions as the average of children 12 years of age. They have not necessarily "performed as" a 12-year-old child would in the sense that they may well have attacked the problems in a different way or demonstrated a different performance pattern than many 12-year-old children. Similarly, a second grader and a ninth grader may both earn grade equivalents of 4.0. They probably have not performed identically. Thorndike and Hagen (1978a) have suggested that it is more likely that the younger child has performed lower-level work with greater accuracy (for instance, successfully answered thirty-eight of the forty-five problems attempted), while the older child has attempted more problems (for instance, successfully answered thirty-eight of the seventy-eight problems attempted).

The second problem inherent in the use of development scores is interpolation and extrapolation. Average age and grade scores are estimated for groups of children who are never tested. Consequently, a child can earn a grade equivalent of 3.2 when only children in the first and last tenth of third grade have ever been tested; or a child can earn a grade equivalent of 8.0 even though no children above the sixth grade have been tested.

The third problem is that the use of developmental scores promotes typological thinking. The average 12-0 child does not exist. That "average" child is a composite of all 12-0 children. Average 12-0 *children* more accurately represent a range of performances, typically the median 90 percent.

The fourth problem is that equivalent scores imply a false standard of performance. One expects a third grader to perform at the third-grade level or a nine-year-old to perform at the nine-year-old level. However, the arithmetic of equivalent scores insures that 50 percent of any age or grade group will perform below age or grade level.

The fifth problem with developmental scores is that such scales tend to be ordinal, not equal interval. The line relating the number correct to the various ages is typically curved, with a flattening of the curve at higher ages or grades. Figure 5.1 is a typical developmental curve.

Developmental Quotients

Before we try to interpret a developmental score, we must know the age of the person being evaluated. Knowing developmental age as well as chronological age (CA) allows us to judge an individual's relative performance. Suppose Horace earns a mental age (MA) of 120 months. If Horace is 8 years (96 months) old, his performance is above average. If he is 35 years old, however, it's below average. The relationship between developmental age and chronological age is often quantified as a developmental quotient. For example, a *ratio IQ* is:

$$IQ = \frac{MA \text{ (in months)}}{CA \text{ (in months)}} \times 100$$

All the problems that apply to developmental levels also apply to developmental quotients. There is one additional problem that is particularly bothersome. The variance of age scores within different chronological age groups is not constant. As a result, the same quotient may mean different things at different ages. For example, a developmental quotient of 120 at age five may mean that Billy performs better than 55 percent of five-year-olds. However, a developmental quotient of 120 at age eleven may mean that Billy performs better than 80 percent of eleven-year-olds. A related problem is that different quotients at different ages can mean the same thing. For example, a developmental quotient of 120 at age five may mean that Sally performs better than 55 percent of five-year-olds, but a developmental quotient of 110 at age ten may mean that Sally performs better than 55 percent of ten-year-olds. This problem engenders a great deal of unnecessary confusion.

Relationship Between Developmental Ages and Quotients

The developmental age is often interpreted as the level of functioning, whereas the quotient is interpreted as the rate of development. In any such scheme, a third variable, chronological age, is always involved. Of the three variables, only chronological age and the developmental quotient are independent of each other (that is, uncorrelated). The developmental age is related to both of the other two variables. In the case of intelligence, the developmental age is far more closely associated with chronological age than it is with the quotient (Kappauf, 1973). Developmental levels do not provide independent information. They only summarize data for age (or grade) and relative standing.

SCORES OF RELATIVE STANDING

Percentile Family

Percentile ranks (%iles) are useful for both ordinal and equal-interval scales. They are derived scores that indicate the percentage of people or scores that occur *at or below* a given raw score. The percentage correct is *not* the same as the percentage of people scoring below. Percentiles corresponding to particular scores can be computed by a four-step sequence.

1. Arrange the scores from the highest to the lowest (that is, best to worst).
2. Compute the percentage of cases occurring *below* the score to which you wish to assign a percentile rank.
3. Compute the percentage of cases occurring *at* the score to which you wish to assign a percentile rank.
4. Add the percentage of cases occurring below the score to one-half the percentage of cases occurring at the score to obtain the percentile rank.

TABLE 5.1 Computing Percentile Ranks for a Hypothetical Class of Twenty-five

Score	Frequency	Percent at the Score	Percent Below the Score	Percentile Rank				
				Percent Below the Score	+	½ of Percent at the Score	=	Percentile
50	2	8	92	92	+	(½)(8)	=	96
49	0							
48	4	16	76	76	+	(½)(16)	=	84
47	0							
46	5	20	56	56	+	(½)(20)	=	66
45	5	20	36	36	+	(½)(20)	=	46
44	3	12	24	24	+	(½)(12)	=	30
43	2	8	16	16	+	(½)(8)	=	20
42	0	—	—					
41	0	—	—					
40	2	8	8	8	+	(½)(8)	=	12
39	0	—	—					
38	1	4	4	4	+	(½)(4)	=	6
.								
.								
.								
24	1	4	0	0	+	(½)(4)	=	2

In Table 5.1, a numerical example is provided. Mr. Greenberg gave a test to his developmental reading class, which has an enrollment of twenty-five children. The scores are presented in column 1, and the number of children obtaining each score (the *frequency*) is shown in column 2. Column 3 gives the percentage of all twenty-five scores that each score obtained represents. Column 4 contains the percentage of all twenty-five scores that occurred below that particular score. In the last group of columns, the percentile rank is computed. Only one child scored 24; the one score is $\frac{1}{25}$, or 4 percent. No one scored lower than 24 so there is 0 percent ($\frac{0}{25}$) below 24. The child who scored 24 received a percentile rank of 2—that is, 0 plus one-half of 4. The next score obtained is 38, and again only one child received this score. Four percent of the total ($\frac{1}{25}$) scored at 38, and 4 percent of the total scored below 38. Therefore, the percentile rank corresponding to a score of 38 is 6—that is, 4 + (½)(4). Two children earned a score of 40, and two children have scored below 40. Therefore, the percentile rank for a score of 40 is 12—that is, 8 + (½)(8). The same procedure is followed for every score a child obtains. The best score in the class, 50, was obtained by two students. The percentile rank corresponding to the highest score in the class is 96.

The interpretation of percentile ranks is straightforward. The data from Table 5.1 provide a specific example. *All* students who score 48 on the test have a percentile rank of 84. These four students have *scored as well as or better than* 84 percent of their classmates on the test. Similarly, an individual who obtains a percentile rank of 21 on an intelligence test has scored as well as or better than 21 percent of the people in the norm sample.

Because the percentile rank is computed using one-half of the percentage of those obtaining a particular score, it is not possible to have percentile ranks of either 0 or 100. Generally, percentile ranks may contain decimals, so it is possible for a score to receive a percentile rank of 99.9 or .1. The fiftieth percentile rank is the median.

Deciles are bands of percentiles that are 10 percentile ranks in width; each decile contains 10 percent of the norm group. The first decile contains percentile ranks from .1 to 9.9; the second decile contains percentile ranks from 10 to 19.9; the tenth decile contains percentile ranks from 90 to 99.9.

Quartiles are bands of percentiles that are 25 percentile ranks in width; each quartile contains 25 percent of the norm group. The first quartile contains percentile ranks from .1 to 24.9; the fourth quartile contains the ranks 75 to 99.9.

Standard Scores

Standard scores are derived scores that transform raw scores in such a way that the set of scores always has the same mean and the same standard deviation. They are used appropriately only with equal-interval (or ratio) scales.

z-Scores

A *z-score* is defined as a standard score with a mean of 0 and a standard deviation of 1. A raw score is converted to a *z*-score by equation 5.1.

$$z = \frac{X - \bar{X}}{S} \tag{5.1}$$

A *z*-score equals the difference between the raw score less the mean of the distribution, divided by the standard deviation of the distribution. The *z*-scores are interpreted as standard deviation units. Thus, a *z*-score of $+1.5$ means that the score is 1.5 standard deviations *above* the mean of the group. A *z*-score of $-.6$ means that the score is .6 standard deviation *below* the mean. A *z*-score of 0 is the mean performance.

Since $+$ and $-$ signs have a tendency to "get lost" and decimals may be awkward to work with, *z*-scores often are transformed to other standard scores. The general formula for changing a *z*-score into a different standard score is given by equation 5.2. In the equation, *SS* stands for any standard score, as does the subscript *ss*. Thus, any standard score equals the mean of

TABLE 5.2   Converting z-Scores to T-Scores

	T-**Score** $=$ **50** $+$ **(10)**(z)
$z = +1.0$	$60 = 50 + (10)(+1.0)$
$z = -1.5$	$35 = 50 + (10)(-1.5)$
$z = -2.1$	$29 = 50 + (10)(-2.1)$
$z = +3.6$	$86 = 50 + (10)(+3.6)$
$z = \quad .0$	$50 = 50 + (10)(\quad .0)$

TABLE 5.3   Converting z-Scores to Deviation IQs $(\bar{X} = 100)$

z-**Score**	**IQ** $(S = 15)$	**IQ** $(S = 16)$
-2.00	70	68
-1.00	85	84
$.00$	100	100
$+1.00$	115	116
$+2.00$	130	132

the distribution of standard scores $(\bar{X}_{ss})$ plus the product of the standard deviation of the distribution of standard scores (S_{ss}) multiplied by the z-score.

$$SS = \bar{X}_{ss} + (S_{ss})(z) \tag{5.2}$$

T-Scores

A *T-score* is a standard score with a mean of 50 and a standard deviation of 10. In Table 5.2, five z-scores are converted to T-scores. A T-score of 60 is 10 points above the mean (50). Since the standard deviation is 10, a T-score of 60 is one standard deviation above the mean.

Deviation IQs

When the IQ was first introduced, it was defined as the ratio of mental age (MA) divided by chronological age (CA) multiplied by 100. Soon statisticians found that MA has different variances and standard deviations at different chronological ages. Consequently, the same IQ has different meanings at different ages; the same IQ corresponds to different z-scores at different ages. To remedy that situation, MAs are converted to z-scores for each age group, and z-scores are converted to deviation IQs. *Deviation IQs are standard scores with a mean of 100 and a standard deviation of 15 or 16* (depending on the test). A z-score can be converted to a deviation IQ by equation 5.2. In Table 5.3, five z-scores are converted to deviation IQs with standard deviations of 15 (column 2) and 16 (column 3).

Normalized Scores

Occasionally test authors will force obtained test scores into the form of a normal curve. The process, called transforming or normalizing a distribution, is discussed in detail in advanced measurement texts (for example, Ghiselli, 1964). A common method of transforming test scores is to compute percentile ranks for the obtained scores and then to *assign z*-scores to the percentile ranks based on the relationship between percentiles and *z*-scores in the normal distribution. The main advantage of such scores is that, after laborious calculations, percentile ranks can be quickly derived from the transformed scores. The major disadvantage is that the underlying distribution may not be normal. One example is the distribution of scores from a test of intelligence. Theory predicts a normal distribution; in practice, the distribution is skewed because of the excess of low-scoring individuals. In general, we feel that percentile ranks are more suitable than normalized scores for reporting purposes; for data analysis, we prefer raw scores, since *F*-distributions are relatively robust with respect to violations of normality (Box, 1953).

Stanines

Stanines are standard-score bands that divide a distribution into nine parts. The first stanine includes all scores that are 1.75 standard deviations or more below the mean, and the ninth stanine includes all scores 1.75 or more standard deviations above the mean. The second through eighth stanines are each .5 standard deviation in width with the fifth stanine ranging from .25 standard deviation below the mean to .25 standard deviation above the mean.

COMPARING DERIVED SCORES

Developmental scores, percentiles, and standard scores are interchangeable only under very restricted conditions. If one wishes to go from one derived score, such as deviation IQ, to another, such as mental age, one must ordinarily go to the raw score and then convert the raw score to the desired derived score. There is an exception to this generalization. If the distribution of raw scores is normal or if the scores have been normalized, there is a direct relationship between percentiles and standard scores. The relationships between developmental scores and both percentiles and standard scores vary with the ages of test takers and the particular tests being used. Figure 5.2 compares various types of scores when the distribution of raw scores is normal.

The selection of the particular type of score to use and to report depends on the purpose of testing and the sophistication of the consumer. In our opinion *developmental scores should never be used*. These scores are readily misinterpreted by both lay and professional people. In order to understand the

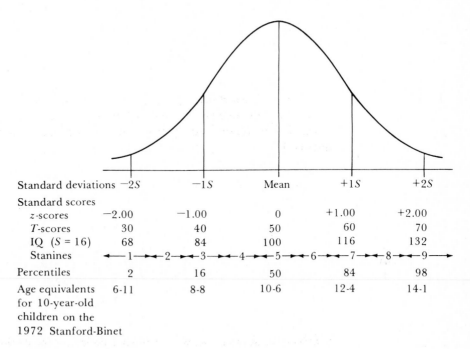

Standard deviations	−2S	−1S	Mean	+1S	+2S
Standard scores					
z-scores	−2.00	−1.00	0	+1.00	+2.00
T-scores	30	40	50	60	70
IQ (S = 16)	68	84	100	116	132
Stanines	←—1—►◄—2—►◄—3—►◄—4—►◄—5—►◄—6—►◄—7—►◄—8—►◄—9—►				
Percentiles	2	16	50	84	98
Age equivalents for 10-year-old children on the 1972 Stanford-Binet	6-11	8-8	10-6	12-4	14-1

FIGURE 5.2 Relationship among selected standard scores, percentiles, and *one* age score and the normal curve

precise meaning of developmental scores, one must generally know both the mean and standard deviation and then *convert* them to a more meaningful score, a score of relative standing. Various professional organizations (for example, the International Reading Association, the American Psychological Association, the National Council on Measurement in Education, and the Council for Exceptional Children) also hold very negative official opinions about developmental scores and quotients.

Standard scores are convenient for test authors. Their use allows the author to give equal weight to various test components or subtests. Their utility for the consumer is twofold. First, *if* the score distribution is normal, the consumer can readily *convert* standard scores to percentile ranks. Second, standard scores are very useful in profile analysis.

We favor the use of percentiles. These unpretentious scores require the fewest assumptions for accurate interpretation. The scale of measurement need only be ordinal, although it is very appropriate to compute percentiles on equal-interval or ratio data. The distribution of scores need not be normal; percentiles can be computed for any shape of distribution. They are readily understood by professionals, parents, and children. Most important, however, is the fact that percentiles tell us nothing more than what any norm-referenced derived score can tell us—namely, an individual's relative standing in a group.

Reporting scores in percentiles may remove some of the aura surrounding test scores, but it permits test results to be presented in terms users can understand.

SUMMARY

The number of correct answers or the number of errors a student makes on a test provides the examiner with relatively little information. One method of interpreting such raw scores is to compare them to the raw scores of a group of students of known characteristics called a norm group.

Two types of comparisons can be made—across ages and within ages. *Developmental scores* (that is, age and grade equivalents) compare students' performances across age or grade groups. Within a group, comparisons can be made using several different types of scores that have different characteristics. A *developmental quotient* (an age or grade equivalent divided by chronological age or actual grade placement, respectively) is the least desirable within-age comparison. Of greater value are *standard scores* (for example, *z*-scores, *T*-scores, and deviation IQs). Such scores have a predetermined mean and standard deviation that define them. The best derived scores for general use are percentile ranks.

STUDY QUESTIONS

1. Eleanore and Audrey take an intelligence test. Eleanore obtains an MA of 3-5 and Audrey obtains an MA of 12-2. The test had been standardized on fifty boys and girls at each of the following ages: 3-0 to 3-1, 4-0 to 4-1, 5-0 to 5-1, 6-0 to 6-1, and 7-0 to 7-1. The psychologist reports that Eleanore functions like a child aged 3 years and 5 months, while Audrey has the mental age of a 12-year-old child. Identify five problems inherent in these interpretations.
2. Differentiate between a *ratio IQ* (developmental quotient) and a *deviation IQ.* Why is a deviation IQ preferable?
3. Sam earned a percentile rank of 83 on a kindergarten admission test. What is the statistical meaning of his score? To what *decile* does the score correspond? To what *quartile* does the score correspond?
4. Marietta takes a battery of standardized tests. The results are as follows:
   Test A: Mental age = 8-6
   Test B: Reading grade equivalent = 3.1
   Test C: Developmental age = 8-4
   Test D: Developmental quotient = 103
   Test E: Percentile rank = 56
   What must the teacher do in order to interpret Marietta's performances on these five scales and compare the performances to each other?

5. Andrew earns a stanine of 1 on an intelligence test. To what *z-scores, percentile ranks,* and *T-scores* does his stanine score correspond?

PROBLEMS

Turn back to Table 4.4, which shows the results of the two tests Ms. Smith gave to her arithmetic class. For test 1, make the following computations.
1. Compute the percentile rank for each student.
2. Compute each student's *z*-score.
3. Convert Bob's, Sam's, Sean's, and Carole's *z*-scores to *T*-scores.
4. Convert Lucy's, Carmen's, John's, and Ludwig's *z*-scores to deviation IQs with a mean of 100 and a standard deviation of 15.

Answers

1. 98, 94, 90, 86, 82, 78, 70, 70, 70, 50, 50, 50, 50, 50, 50, 50, 30, 30, 30, 22, 18, 14, 10, 6, 2
2. 2.17, 2.00, 1.33, 1.00, .67, .5, .33, .33, .33, 0, 0, 0, 0, 0, 0, 0, −.33, −.33, −.33, −.5, −.67, −1.00, −1.33, −2.00, −2.17
3. 72, 63, 50, 45
4. 130, 105, 100, 70

CHAPTER 6

NORMS

It is seldom possible to test everyone in a particular population, since the membership of the population is constantly changing. Some children who are in the 6-year-old population today will be 7 years old tomorrow. Grade populations change at least once a year. However, testing an entire population is not only virtually impossible but also unnecessary. The characteristics of a population can be accurately estimated from the characteristics of a representative subset of the population (called a *sample*); inferences based on what one has learned from a sample can be extended to a population at large. Thus, the normative samples used in norm-referenced assessment are intended to allow inferences to be made about a population.

In norm-referenced assessment, norms are important for two reasons. First, the normative sample is often used to obtain the various statistics on which the final selection of test items is based. For example, Wechsler (1974, p. iii) states that "the final selection of test items and scoring procedures was fixed only after all the standardization data had been analyzed and evaluated." Consequently, measures of internal consistency, item-total correlations, and indices of item difficulties (*p*-values), as well as item selection and item scoring procedures, are all affected by the adequacy of the standardization sample.

The second reason that norms are important is more obvious. In norm-referenced assessment, an individual's performance is evaluated in terms of other people's performances. All the derived scores that were described in Chapter 5—percentiles, standard scores, and the rest—are based on the performance of the individuals in the normative sample. When we test individuals, we compare their performances to the performances of the individuals in the norm group. Even if a test is otherwise satisfactory, test scores may be misleading if the norms are inadequate. The adequacy of a test's norms depends on three factors: the representativeness of the norm sample, the number of cases in the norm sample, and the relevance of the norms in terms of the purpose of testing.

REPRESENTATIVENESS

In evaluating representativeness, particular attention must be paid to demographic variables because of their relationship—either theoretical or empirical —to what the test is intended to measure. Which demographic variables are significant for a particular test depends on the content of the test and/or the construct being measured. Representativeness hinges on two questions. The first is, Does the norm sample contain the same *kinds* of people as the population that the norms are intended to represent? "Kinds" of people usually refers to relative levels of maturation, levels of skill development, and degrees of acculturation. The second question of representativeness is, Are the various kinds of people present in the same proportion in the sample as they are in the population of reference?

When we compare a child's performance to a norm sample in order to predict future behavior, we assume that the child has had an opportunity to acquire skills, concepts, or experiences comparable to the opportunities of the children in the norm sample. When we compare a child's performance to a norm sample in order to understand better that child's current level of functioning, we need assume only that the norm sample is representative of the population. The distinction between understanding current level of functioning and predicting future behavior is part of the culture-free (or culture-fair) testing controversy. If a 10-year-old child has had no opportunity to learn to read (and consequently has not acquired the skills), the tester who notes that the child *currently* lacks skill is not being unfair or biased. On the other hand, if the child being tested and the children in the normative sample have not had comparable opportunities to acquire the behaviors sampled in the test, it may be misleading to use the child's test score to predict *future* behavior. When we predict future behavior, we assume that children have learned what they *can* learn. Children who have had no chance to learn have not been able to demonstrate what they *can* learn. Not knowing how well such children *will* learn given the opportunity, we cannot use their test scores to make predictions.

Kinds of People

Several factors are usually considered in the development of norms for psychoeducational tests. Following is a brief discussion of the most commonly considered factors, together with a rationale for the importance of each.

Age

A child's age is an excellent general indicator of several important factors. Physiological maturation is an important variable in motor and perceptual-motor tests, and age is directly related to maturation. It would be foolish to say that a 6-year-old child lacks physical stamina because that child can run for only as long a period of time as 2 percent of all ten-year-olds. Six-year-old children are not as big and strong as 10-year-old children. Consequently, we would not want to compare children of different ages on tests where there are physical, developmental effects.

A child's amount of experience with practically everything is a function of age. Indeed, age is an excellent indicator of the opportunity to acquire skills, information, and concepts. Mental growth (as measured by mental ages) and chronological ages are very highly correlated; Kappauf (1973) has empirically estimated the correlation to be in excess of .90. Again, it would usually be inappropriate to compare a six-year-old's fund of general information with that of a twelve-year-old. The six-year-old simply has not been around as long and therefore has not had the opportunity to acquire as much information.

There is a tendency for test authors to assume that some psychological traits stop developing after 16 or 18 years of age—and many traits do. In such instances, all individuals over a given age are treated as adults. For example, test users may be required to use 16 years in computation of the ratio IQ. The assumption of no growth after 16 may be tenable with supporting data. On the other hand, Wechsler (1955) provides adult norms that clearly indicate age is an important variable in interpreting IQ beyond 16. As shown in Figure 6.1, verbal ability continues to grow until 25 to 34 years of age; after 35 it slowly declines. Scores on the performance scale, however, peak between 20 and 24 years and then rapidly decline. Different abilities may be expected to have different growth curves (see Guilford, 1967, pp. 417–426).

Grade

All achievement tests and most intelligence tests measure the results of systematic academic instruction. Children of different ages are present in most grades. Consequently, grade norms are more appropriate than age norms for such tests when used with children of school age. Grade in school bears a more direct relationship to what is taught in school than does age. Some 7-year-old children may not be enrolled in school; some may be in kindergarten, some in first grade, some in second grade, and some even in third grade. The academic proficiency of seven-year-olds can be expected to be more closely related to what they have been taught than to their age.

Sex

Sex also plays an important role in a child's development. There are pronounced differences in typical patterns of physical development around puberty (Tanner, 1970). Personality differences have also been observed; boys

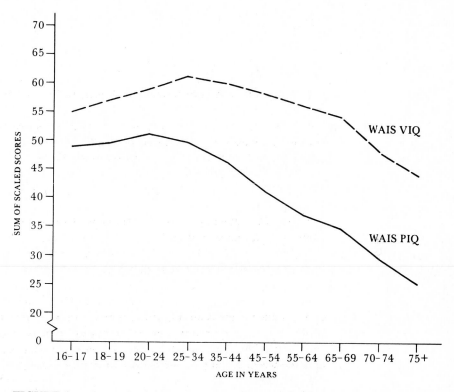

FIGURE 6.1 Sums of scaled scores on the WAIS for performance IQs and verbal IQs of 100, by ages

tend to be more aggressive than girls; girls tend to be more dependent and socially passive (Mischel, 1970).

Sex differences have also been reported in intellectual development. For example, Roberts (1971) reported that boys scored higher than girls on the Vocabulary and Block Design subtests of the Wechsler Intelligence Scale for Children. But the magnitude of sex differences on ability, achievement, and aptitude measures is nearly always very small; the male and female distributions overlap a great deal.

Although sex-role expectations seem to be changing, gender still may systematically limit the types of activities in which a child engages. This may result from such influences as modeling, peer pressure, or responsiveness to the attitudes of significant adults. For whatever reasons boys and girls differ systematically on tests, children of both sexes should be represented in the norm sample. Appropriate representation is especially important for behaviors on which there are known sex differences.

Acculturation of Parents

The level of acculturation of a child's parents or guardians has a direct impact on the child's performance on intellectual and academic tests. One can consider the academic or occupational attainment *(socioeconomic status)* of the parents as an indication of the child's acculturation as well as the level of acculturation in the home. There is a consistent relationship between these indices of acculturation and the performance of the child on various psychoeducational measures. Parental occupation and income have been consistently reported to be related to school achievement (for example, Schaie & Roberts, 1971) and intelligence (for example, Burt, 1959; Roberts, 1971). The causes of these consistent social class differences have been debated for years, and the debate continues today (see Gottesman, 1968). However, the causes of such differences are beyond the scope of this text. Whether one subscribes to a genetic interpretation, an environmentalist interpretation, or an interactionist interpretation, the fact of social class differences is undeniable. For this reason, test standardizations should include children of all social classes.

Geographic Factors

Different geographic regions of the United States differ in values and mores, and various psychoeducational tests reflect these regional differences. Children in the Midwest typically score better than children in the South on achievement tests (for example, Schaie & Roberts, 1971). During World War II rates of rejection for military service because of mental deficiency varied according to geographic region (Ginzberg & Bray, 1953); these differences reflected both intellectual and achievement differences. Community size is also related to academic and intellectual development; urban children typically score higher on achievement tests than rural children do (Schaie & Roberts, 1971).

Race

Race is a particularly sensitive issue, especially since the scientific community has often been insensitive to the issue and has even on occasion been blatantly racist (for example, Down, 1866/1969). With few exceptions children of minority races score lower than white children on intellectual measures (for example, Roberts, 1971) and academic achievement (for example, Coleman et al., 1966).

Most explanations for racial differences are beyond the scope of this text. Two are not. First, there has been a tendency to systematically *exclude* non-white children from standardization samples. For example, until the 1972 edition of the Stanford-Binet Intelligence Test, no blacks were included in the standardization sample. To the extent that children of different races undergo cultural experiences that differ even within social class and geographic region, norm samples that exclude them are biased. Also, to the extent that nonwhite children score lower than white children of equal social standing and from the same geographic region, test-score distributions that exclude nonwhites are unrepresentative of the total population.

The second argument deals with item selection. If nonwhites differ in acculturation and are excluded from the field tests of the test items, item difficulty estimates (p-values) and point biserial (item-total) correlations may be inaccurate. Hence, the test scaling may be in error. We believe that both these arguments have merit. It is important to include children of all racial and ethnic groups both in field tests of items and in the standardization of a test.

Intelligence

A representative sample of individuals, in terms of their level of intellectual functioning, is essential for standardizing an intelligence test—or any other kind of test. Intelligence is related to a number of variables that are considered in psychoeducational assessment. It is certainly related to achievement, since most intelligence tests were actually developed to predict school success. Correlations ranging between .60 and .80 are typical (for example, Tiegs & Clark, 1970). Since language development and facility are often considered an indication of intellectual development, intelligence tests are often verbally oriented. Consequently, one would also expect to find substantial correlations between scores on tests of intelligence and scores on tests of linguistic or psycholinguistic ability, as did Mueller (1965). Items thought to reflect perceptual ability appear on intelligence tests, and Thurstone (1944) found various perceptual tasks to be a factor in intelligence. Koppitz (1975) reports substantial correlations between scores on the Bender Visual Motor Gestalt Test and scores on intelligence tests. Thus, intelligence should be considered in the development of norms for perceptual and perceptual-motor tests.

In the development of norms for intelligence tests per se, it is essential to test the full range of intellectual ability. Limiting the sample to children enrolled in and attending school (usually regular classes) restricts the norms. Failure to consider the mentally retarded in standardization procedures introduces systematic bias into test norms. It has been estimated that 3 percent of the school-age population may be mentally retarded (Robinson & Robinson, 1976; Farber, 1968, pp. 46, 58). Dingman and Tarjan (1960) estimated that there is an excess frequency at the lower end of the intelligence distribution, probably as a result of pathological genetic conditions. They estimated that the mean IQ of this group was approximately 32, with a standard deviation approximately the same as that in the intellectually normal population. Exclusion of such a large portion of the school-age population seriously biases the estimate of the population mean and standard deviation. For example, let us assume that a test is standardized excluding mentally retarded children and that the scores of the children in the normative sample are converted to deviation IQs with a mean of 100 and a standard deviation of 16. Increasing the sample by including 3 percent more subjects whose scores have a mean IQ of 32 and a standard deviation of 16 would have the same effect as including the mentally retarded children who were excluded. The mean would be lowered from 100 to 98.[1] The standard deviation would be increased from 16 to 19.7.[2] A score that fell two standard deviations below the mean would be 68 without the retarded; it would be 59 if the retarded were included. Representative sampling would substantially reduce the ranks of the mentally retarded.

Date of Norms

An often overlooked consideration in assuring representativeness is the date the norms were collected. We live in an age of rapidly expanding knowledge and rapidly expanding communication of knowledge. Children of today know more than did the children of the 1930s or the 1940s. Children of today probably know less than will the children of tomorrow. For a norm sample to be representative it must be *current*.

Special Population Characteristics

Some characteristics of the sample and of the population are important only for particular types of tests. For example, test authors often caution test users to make sure the content of achievement tests reflects the content of the test

1. If the number of subjects in the norm group is 1,000 and the mean is 100, the sum of all scores is 100,000. If 30 children (3 percent of 1,000) whose mean is 32 are added to the 1,000 children, the sum of all scores is increased by 960 (30 × 32). The mean of the 1,030 children is 98 (100,960/1,030).
2. The variance is computationally equal to $\Sigma X^2/N - (\Sigma X/N)^2$. If the number of subjects (N) is 1,000 and the mean is 100, the sum of all scores is 100,000; if the standard deviation is 16, the variance is 256. By substituting these figures into the preceding formula, we obtain the sum of the squared scores, which is 10,256,000:

$$256 = \frac{\Sigma X^2}{1,000} - \left(\frac{100,000}{1,000}\right)^2$$

If we increase the sample by 30 children whose scores have a mean of 32 and standard deviation of 16, we increase the sum of the squared scores by 38,400:

$$256 = \frac{\Sigma X^2}{30} - \left(\frac{960}{30}\right)^2$$

The variance of the 1,030 children is 386.76:

$$386.76 = \frac{10,256,000 + 38,400}{1,030} - \left(\frac{100,000 + 960}{1,030}\right)^2$$

The standard deviation (the square root of the variance) is 19.67.

user's classroom curriculum. However, the test author must also make sure that the content is appropriate for the norm sample. Thus, for reading diagnostic tests, which often measure specific skills such as syllabication and sound blending, the author must specify the curriculum followed by the children in the norm sample. If a visual, sight-vocabulary orientation is used by children in the norm sample, the derived scores of children taught by a phonics method may be inflated; the children taught by the phonics method may earn relatively high scores when compared to the less skilled children in the norm group.

Tests used to identify children with particular problems should include such children in their standardization sample. For example, the Illinois Test of Psycholinguistic Abilities is often used to identify children with psycholinguistic dysfunctions that presumably underlie academic difficulties. Yet the norm sample included "only those children demonstrating average intellectual functioning, average school achievement, average characteristics of personal-social adjustment, sensory-motor integrity, and coming from predominantly English-speaking families" (Paraskevopoulos & Kirk, 1969, pp. 51–52). How can a test be used to identify children whose academic difficulties are caused by psycholinguistic dysfunction when such children are *excluded* from the normative sample? A child who earns the same score as any child in the norm sample has earned a score associated with school success.

Proportion of the Kinds of People

Implicit in the foregoing discussion of characteristics of the representative normative sample was the notion that the various kinds of people should be included in the *same proportion* in the sample as in the population. The development of systematic norms requires systematic data collection, which is both time-consuming and expensive. It is incumbent on the author of a test to demonstrate that its norms are in fact representative. Samples that are convenient, such as samples consisting of volunteers, are not necessarily representative; in fact, they are probably unrepresentative. Large numbers of subjects do not guarantee a representative sample. Roosevelt was re-elected president of the United States, even though predictions based on a large sample had proclaimed that Alf Landon would be the next president; the sample had been unrepresentative.

A test author demonstrates that a test is representative by presenting data to that effect. For example, French (1964) presented data to show that his stratification procedure was effective. He compared his norm sample to the 1960 census in order to ascertain the discrepancy between the population at large and his sample. As French's table (Table 6.1) shows, there was close agreement in the occupational strata. The norms of the Pictorial Test of Intelligence (French, 1964) are credible on all stratification variables (occupation of father, geographic region, and community size).

TABLE 6.1   Sample by Occupational Level

Occupational Class	Percent 1960 Census	Percent Tested	Percent Discrepancy
Professional and technical	16	16	0
Proprietary, manager, and officials	13	15	+2
Clerks and sales	15	15	0
Foremen and skilled	19	16	−3
Operatives and semiskilled	22	20	−2
Laborers, service workers, and unskilled	15	18	+3
	100%	100%	

SOURCE: From *Manual for the Pictorial Test of Intelligence* (p. 11) by J. L. French, 1964, Chicago: The Riverside Publishing Co. Copyright 1964. Reproduced by permission of the Publisher, The Riverside Publishing Company, 8420 Bryn Mawr Ave., Chicago, IL 60631.

NUMBER OF SUBJECTS

The number of subjects in a norm sample is important for several reasons. First, the number of subjects should be large enough to guarantee stability. "If the number of cases is small we cannot put much dependence on the norms, since another group consisting of the same number of persons might give quite different results. The larger the number of cases the more stable will be the norms" (Ghiselli, 1964, p. 49). Next, the number of cases should be large enough so that infrequent elements in the population can be represented. Finally, there should be enough subjects that the sizes of interpolations and extrapolations are relatively small. In a normally distributed array of scores, one hundred subjects are the minimum number for which a full range of percentiles can be computed and for which standard scores between ± 2.3 standard deviations can be computed without extrapolation. Consequently, we believe that one hundred should be the minimum number of persons in any norm sample. If the test spans a number of ages or grades, the norm sample should contain at least one hundred subjects per age or grade.

RELEVANCE OF THE NORMS

The major question regarding relevance of norms concerns the extent to which people in the norm sample will provide comparisons that are relevant in terms of the purpose for which the test was administered. For some purposes national norms are the most appropriate. If we are interested in knowing how a particular child is developing intellectually, perceptually, linguistically, or physically, national norms would be the most appropriate.

In other circumstances norms developed on a particular portion of the population may be meaningful. For example, if we wished to ascertain the degree to which a student had profited from his twelve years of schooling, norms developed for the particular school district he had been served by might be appropriate. Suppose the school district is providing such poor educational services that, as a district, it falls well below the national average. If this is the case, our twelfth grader could earn a percentile rank of 75 based on district norms and a percentile rank of only 35 based on representative national norms. Still, despite the fact that his score looks low in comparison to scores made nationwide, it's clear that our student has made comparatively good use of the inadequate services he has been getting. The same relationship between scores based on national and scores based on local norms might also be obtained if the school district were teaching materials not covered by the achievement test.

Local norms may be more useful in retrospective interpretations of a student's performance than in predictive interpretations. Thus, in the preceding example, if the content of the achievement test was appropriate in terms of what the schools were actually attempting to teach, we could conclude that the student had profited from instruction but nonetheless would probably be at a disadvantage if he entered college.

In addition, norms based on particular groups may be more relevant than those based on the population as a whole. Some devices are standardized on unusual populations: the Nebraska Test of Learning Aptitude is standardized on the deaf, the AAMD Adaptive Behavior Scale on institutionalized retardates, and the Blind Learning Aptitude Test on blind children. Aptitude tests are often standardized on individuals in specific trades or professions. The utility of special population norms is similar to the utility of local norms: they are likely to be more useful in retrospective comparisons than in future predictions. Without knowing how the special population corresponds to the general population, inferences may not be appropriate. Suppose a deaf child earns a learning quotient of 115 derived from norms based on deaf children. One knows only that the child scored better than the average deaf child. The basic question that must be addressed is, Does the score based on special population norms lead to correct interpretations? Thus, the test user must know how the change in norms affects predictive validity.

There are, however, specific instances in which special population norms have been misused. When a person's performance is similar to that of a special population, it does *not* mean the person belongs to or should belong to that population. Because Mary earns the same score as a typical lawyer on a test of legal aptitude does not mean Mary is or should become a lawyer. The argument that she should contains a logical fallacy, an undistributed middle term. (Clearly, if dogs eat meat and university professors eat meat, dogs are not university professors.)

Reasoning of this sort is often inferred when criterion groups are used in test standardization. Such inferences are valid if it can be demonstrated that *only* members of a particular group score in a particular manner. If some people who are *not* members of the particular group earn the same scores as members of that group, the relationship between group membership and scores should be quantified. For example, let us assume that 90 percent of brain-injured children make unusual—perhaps rotated, distorted, or simplified—reproductions of geometric designs. Let us also assume that 3 percent of the population is brain injured. If *only* non-brain-injured children made normal drawings, we could say with certainty that any child who makes normal drawings is not brain injured. However, since 10 percent of brain-injured children make normal reproductions, we cannot be so sure: .31 percent of the children who make normal drawings *are* brain injured.

In some instances, the "normal" population makes deviant responses. Assume that 20 percent of the normal population and all brain-injured children make unusual drawings. If 3 percent of the population is brain injured, 22.4 percent of the population will perform as brain injured (100% of 3% + 20% of 97% = 22.4%). A deviant performance on the test would mean only a 13 percent (.03/.224) chance that the child is brain injured.

USING NORMS CORRECTLY

The manuals accompanying commercially prepared tests usually contain a table that allows a tester to convert raw scores to various derived scores, such as percentile ranks, without laborious calculations. Occasionally, the tester is even confronted with several tables for converting raw scores. For example, it is not uncommon for the same manual to contain one set of tables for converting raw scores to percentile ranks on the basis of the age of the person tested and another set of tables for converting raw scores to percentile ranks on the basis of the school grade of the person tested. The tester must select tables based either on age or on grade. To select the appropriate table, the tester must determine the population to which the performance of the sample is inferred. This can be learned by examining how the norm group was selected. If the test author sampled by grades in school, then the population of reference is students in a particular grade; consequently, the grade tables should be used for converting raw scores to derived scores. Conversely, if the test author sampled by age, the age tables should be used, since the population of reference is a particular age group.

A problem arises when especially advanced or backward individuals undergo testing. Tests often lose their power to discriminate near the extremes of the distribution. For example, an intelligence test might be constructed in such a way that even if a person failed every item it might be impossible for that person to earn an IQ of less than 50. Since complete failure on a test provides little or no information about what a person *can* do, testers often administer tests based on a norm sample of people younger than the test taker. While such a procedure may provide useful *qualitative* information, norm-referenced interpretations are unjustified because the ages of the individuals in the norm group and the age of the person being tested are not the same.

Another serious error is committed when the tester uses a person's mental age to obtain derived scores from conversion tables set up on the basis of chronological age. The reasoning behind such practices, we suppose, is that if the person functions as an 8-year-old child intellectually, the use of conversion tables based on the performances of 8-year-old children is appropriate. Such practices are incorrect, since the norms were not established by sampling persons of a particular mental age. When assessing the reading skill of an adolescent or adult who performs below the first percentile, a tester has little need for further or more precise norm-referenced comparisons. The tester already knows the person is not a good reader. If the examiner wants to ascertain which reading skills a person has or lacks, a criterion-referenced (norm-free) device would be more suitable. Sometimes the most appropriate use of norms is no use at all.

To use norms effectively, the tester must be sure that the norm sample is appropriate both for the purpose of testing and for the person being tested.

Concluding Comment: Caveat Emptor

If the test author recognizes that the test norms are inadequate, the test user should be explicitly cautioned (APA et al., 1974). The inadequacies do not, however, disappear on the inclusion of a cautionary note; the test is still inadequate. It is occasionally argued that inadequate norms are better than no norms at all. This argument is analogous to the argument that even a broken clock is correct twice a day. With 86,400 seconds in a day, remarking that a clock is right twice a day is an overly optimistic way of saying that the clock is wrong 99.99 percent of the time. Inadequate norms do not allow meaningful and accurate inferences about the population. If poor norms are used, misinterpretations follow. The difficulty is that the test user seldom knows whether a particular test has an inflated or deflated mean or variance.

A joint committee of the American Psychological Association, the American Educational Research Association, and the National Council on Measurement in Education (1974) have prepared a pamphlet, *Standards for Educational and Psychological Tests and Manuals,* which outlines the standards to which test authors should adhere: *"Norms presented in the test manual should refer to defined and clearly described populations. These populations should be the groups with whom users of the test will ordinarily wish to compare the persons tested"* (p. 20). The pamphlet states that the test author should report how the sample was selected and whether any bias was present in the sample. The author should also describe the sampling techniques and the resultant sample in sufficient detail for the test user to judge the utility of the norms. "The description should include number of cases, classified by one or more of such relevant variables as ethnic mix, socioeconomic level, age, sex, locale, and educational status" (p. 21).

In the marketplace of testing, let the buyer beware.

SUMMARY

The normative sample is important because it is the group of individuals with whom a tested person is compared. Norms should be representative of the population to which comparisons are made. A number of variables typically considered important have been discussed: age, grade, sex, acculturation of the persons tested and of their parents, geographic factors, race, intelligence, the date of the norms, and special population characteristics. The norm sample should contain the same types of people in the same proportion as are found in the population of reference. The norm sample should be large enough to be stable and to provide a full range of derived scores. The norms should be relevant in terms of the purposes of testing, and they should be used correctly.

STUDY QUESTIONS

1. Identify two fundamental reasons that norms are important.
2. Willy Smith has only one leg. His teacher concludes that he cannot be tested in reading because no test demonstrates inclusion of one-legged children in its normative group. To what extent is the teacher's conclusion warranted?
3. Test X is standardized on fifty boys and fifty girls at each grade level from kindergarten through sixth grade. The children who made up the norm group were white, middle-class children living in Mount Pleasant, Michigan. Separate norm tables are provided for boys and girls in each grade. Danny, a third-grade black child residing in Oakland, California, is tested with test X, and the norm tables are used to interpret his score.
   a. To how many children is Danny being compared?
   b. To whose performance is Danny's performance being compared?
   c. What assumptions are being made about the relationship between Danny's acculturation and the acculturation of the normative sample?
4. Many tests were initially developed to discriminate between brain-injured and non-brain-injured adults. These same tests are now used to identify brain-injured children. Why is such a use inappropriate?
5. Under what conditions are local norms useful?
6. How might the author of a test demonstrate that its normative sample is representative of the population of children attending school in the United States?

ADDITIONAL READING

American Psychological Association, American Educational Research Association, & National Council on Measurement in Education. (1974). *Standards for educational and psychological tests,* Washington, DC: American Psychological Association, pp. 9–24.

CHAPTER 7

RELIABILITY

If test scores did not have meaning beyond themselves, they would not be of much importance or interest. Very few behaviors in which educators are interested, including test performances, occur only once or in very restricted circumstances. When we test, we are interested in *generalizing* what we see today under one set of conditions to other occasions. (For example, if we cannot generalize Billy's reading skills that are observed during testing to the classroom situation, then the test data are of little or no value.) To the extent that we can generalize from a particular set of observations (a test, for example), those observations are reliable.

Reliability is a major consideration in evaluating the psychometric characteristics of a test or scale. For example, when we give a person an individually administered test, we would like to be able to generalize the results in three different ways. We would like to assume that if another tester were to score the exam, the results would be the same; we would not usually be interested in behaviors that only some testers would note. We would also like to assume that the behavior we see today would be seen tomorrow (or next week) if we were to test again; behaviors that are stable are generally of interest in educational settings. Also, we would like to assume that slightly different test questions would give us similar results; we would like to be able to generalize to other similar test items. Thus, there are three kinds of reliability. Reliability for generalizing to different scorers is called interrater or interscorer reliability. Reliability for generalizing to different times is called stability or test-retest reliability. Reliability for generalizing to other test items is called alternate-form or internal-consistency reliability. If a test score is reliable and the tested trait or behavior is stable, then we can generalize the score. To the extent that a person's score cannot be generalized to other situations, the test score is not reliable. In education and psychology, we want reliable tests.

It is useful to describe just how one wishes to generalize observations and test scores. Suppose that Ms. Amig were interested in testing her kindergarten students on the upper- and lower-case letters of the English alphabet. She could assess the *domain*—all fifty-two upper- and lower-case letters—*or* she could sample from the domain. For example, she could ask each of her students to name the following letters: A, h, j, L, q, r, R, u, V, w. She would like to assume that another sample of letters (say, b, E, k, m, s, T, U, v, w, z) would lead to the same scores by her students. Specifically, she would like to assume that each student would earn the same score on any sample from the domain or on all the items in the domain. Thus, she wants to *generalize* from a sample of items to all the other items in the domain from which the sample was drawn. However, Ms. Amig wants more than that. Suppose that she tests her pupils on Monday morning at 9:30. She would like to assume that the students would earn the same scores if they were tested Tuesday at 1:45 P.M. There is a domain of times as well as a domain of items. Any one occasion is a sample from the time domain—all times. Ms. Amig would like to generalize the results found on one sample of time to the domain. Her pupils' knowledge of the alphabet would not be very useful if they knew the letters only on Monday at 9:30 A.M.

An easy way to think of reliability is to think of any measurement (any obtained score) as consisting of two parts: *true score* and *error*. Error is uncorrelated with true score and is essentially random. Error is best thought of as lack of generalizability that results from the failure to get a representative sample from the domain. For example, a sample of alphabet letters that consisted of *A, B, C, D,* and *E* would probably be much easier than other samples of letters. A systematically easier sample would inflate the scores earned by Ms. Amig's students. Similarly, a sample made up of the most difficult letters would probably deflate the scores earned by her students. Thus, error—failure to select a representative sample of items—can raise or lower scores. The average (mean) of error in the long run is equal to zero. In the long run, the samples balance out. True scores are the scores that are earned when the entire domain is assessed. It is also the mean of the scores on all possible samples from the domain. On achievement tests with elementary-level pupils, it is occasionally possible to assess the entire domain. Usually, however, such assessment is not possible.

As you may recall from the discussion of the assumptions underlying psychological assessment, error of measurement is always present. The important question is, How much error is attached to a particular score? Unfortunately, a direct answer to this question is not readily available. To estimate both the amount of error attached to a particular test score and a person's true score, two statistics are needed: (1) a reliability coefficient for the particular generalization, and (2) the standard deviation of the test.

THE RELIABILITY COEFFICIENT

The symbol used to denote a reliability coefficient is r with two identical subscripts (for example, r_{xx} or r_{aa}). The *reliability coefficient* is generally defined as the square of the correlation between obtained scores and true scores on a measure ($r_{xt}{}^2$). As it turns out, this quantity is identical to the ratio of the variance of true scores to the variance of obtained scores for a distribution. Accordingly, a reliability coefficient indicates the *proportion* of variability in a set of scores that reflects true differences among individuals. In the special case where two parallel forms of a test exist, the Pearson product-moment correlation coefficient between scores from the two forms is equal to the reliability coefficient for either form. These relationships are summarized in equation 7.1, where x and x' are parallel measures, and S^2 is, of course, the variance.

$$r_{xx'} = r_{xt}{}^2 = \frac{S^2_{\text{true scores}}}{S^2_{\text{obtained scores}}} = r_{xx'} \qquad (7.1)$$

If there is relatively little error, the ratio of true-score variance to obtained-score variance approaches a reliability index of 1.00 *(perfect reliability)*; if there is a relatively large amount of error, the ratio of true-score variance to obtained-score variance approaches .00 *(total unreliability).* [1] Thus, a test with a reliability coefficient of .90 has relatively less error of measurement and is more reliable than a test with a reliability coefficient of .50.

There are different methods of estimating a reliability coefficient that depend on what generalization one wishes to make. Test authors should always report the extent to which one can generalize to different times and the degree to which one can generalize to different samples of questions or items. If a test is difficult to score, the test author should also report the extent to which one can generalize to different scorers.

Generalizing to Different Times

Test-retest reliability is an index of *stability.* Educators are interested in many human traits and characteristics that, theoretically, change very little over time. For example, children diagnosed as colorblind at age five are expected to be diagnosed as colorblind at any time in their lives. Colorblindness is an inherited trait that cannot be corrected. Consequently, the trait should be perfectly stable. When a test identifies a child as colorblind on one occasion and not colorblind on a later occasion, the test is unreliable.

Other traits are less stable than color vision over a long period of time; they are developmental. A person's height will increase from birth through adulthood. The increase is relatively slow and predictable. Consequently, measurement with a reliable ruler should indicate little change in height over a one-month period. Radical changes in height (especially decreases) over short periods of time would cause us to question the reliability of the measurement device. Most educational and psychological characteristics are conceptualized

---

1. Although it is mathematically possible to obtain a negative reliability estimate, such an obtained coefficient is theoretically meaningless.

much as height is. For example, we expect reading achievement to increase with length of schooling but to be relatively stable over short periods of time, like two weeks. Devices used to assess traits and characteristics must produce sufficiently consistent and stable results if those results are to have practical meaning for making educational decisions.

The procedure for obtaining a stability coefficient is fairly simple. A large number of students are tested. A short time later (preferably two weeks, but the time interval can vary from one day to several months) they are retested with the same device. The students' scores from the two administrations are then correlated. The obtained correlation coefficient is the *stability coefficient.*

Estimates of the amount of error derived from stability coefficients tend to be inflated. Any change in the students' true scores attributable to maturation or learning is added to the error variance unless every student in the sample changes in the same way. Thus, if there is a "maturational spurt" between the two test administrations for only a few students, the change in the true score is incorporated into the error term. Similarly, if some of the students cannot answer some of the questions on the first administration of the test but learn the answers by the second administration, the learning (change in true score) is interpreted as error. The experience of taking the test once may also make answering the same questions the second time easier; the first test may sensitize the student to the second administration of the test. Generally, the closer together in time the test and retest are, the higher the reliability is, since within a shorter time span there is less chance of true scores changing.

Generalizing to Different Item Samples

There are two main approaches for estimating the extent to which we can generalize to different samples of items. The first approach requires that test authors develop two (or more) similar tests, called *alternate forms;* the second approach does not.

Alternate forms of a test are defined as two tests that measure the same trait or skill to the same extent and are standardized on the same population. Alternate forms offer essentially equivalent tests; sometimes, in fact, they're called *equivalent forms.* Let's look at a nonpsychometric example. At a local variety store counter, where several 12-inch rulers are sold, any ruler is thought to be the equivalent (or alternate form) of any other ruler. If one purchased a red ruler and a green ruler and measured several objects with both, one would expect a high correlation between the green measurements and the red measurements. This example is analogous to alternate-form reliability. There is one important difference, however. Alternate forms of tests do not contain the same items. Still, while the items are different, the means and variances for the two tests are assumed to be (or should be) the same. In the absence of error of measurement, any subject would be expected to earn the same score on both forms.

TABLE 7.1 Hypothetical Performance of Twenty Children on a Ten-Item Test

Child	1	2	3	4	5	6	7	8	9	10	Total Test	Evens Correct	Odds Correct
					Items							Totals	
1	+	+	+	−	+	−	−	−	+	−	5	1	4
2	+	+	+	+	−	+	+	+	−	+	8	5	3
3	+	+	−	+	+	+	+	−	+	+	8	4	4
4	+	+	+	+	+	+	+	+	−	+	9	5	4
5	+	+	+	+	+	+	+	+	+	−	9	4	5
6	+	+	−	+	−	+	+	+	+	+	8	5	3
7	+	+	+	+	+	−	+	−	+	+	8	3	5
8	+	+	+	−	+	+	+	+	+	+	9	4	5
9	+	+	+	+	+	+	−	+	+	+	9	5	4
10	+	+	+	+	+	−	+	+	+	+	9	4	5
11	+	+	+	+	+	−	+	−	−	−	6	2	4
12	+	+	−	+	+	+	+	+	+	+	9	5	4
13	+	+	+	−	−	+	−	+	−	−	5	3	2
14	+	+	+	+	+	+	+	−	+	+	9	4	5
15	+	+	−	+	+	−	−	−	−	−	4	2	2
16	+	+	+	+	+	+	+	+	+	+	10	5	5
17	+	−	+	−	−	−	−	−	−	−	2	0	2
18	+	−	+	+	+	+	+	+	+	+	9	4	5
19	+	+	+	+	−	+	+	+	+	+	9	5	4
20	+	−	−	−	−	+	−	+	−	−	3	2	1

To estimate the reliability coefficient by two alternate forms (A and B), a large sample of students is tested with both forms. Half the subjects receive form A, then form B; the other half receive form B, then form A. Scores from the two forms are correlated. The correlation coefficient is a reliability coefficient.

Estimates of reliability based on alternate forms are subject to one of the same constraints as stability coefficients: the more time between the administration of the two (or more) forms, the greater the likelihood of change in true scores. Unlike stability coefficients, alternate-form reliability estimates are not subject to a sensitization effect since the subjects are not tested with the same items twice.

The second approach does not require that the authors develop more than one form of the test. This method of estimating a test's reliability, called *internal consistency,* is a little different.

Suppose we wanted to use this second method of estimating a test's reliability. To do so we construct a test containing ten items and administer the test to twenty children. The results of this hypothetical test are presented in Table 7.1. If the ten individual test items all measure the same trait or characteristic, we can divide the test into two five-item tests, each measuring the same trait or characteristic. Thus, *after* the test is administered, we can create two alternate forms of the test, each containing one-half of the total number of test items, or five items. We can then correlate the two sets of scores and obtain an estimate of the reliability of each of the two halves in the same way we would estimate the reliability of two alternate forms of a test. This procedure for estimating a test's reliability is called a *split-half reliability estimate.*

It should be apparent that there are many ways to divide a test into two equal-length tests. The ten-item test in Table 7.1 can be divided into 126 different pairs of five-item tests.[2] If the ten items in our full test are arranged in order of increasing difficulty, both halves must contain items from the beginning of the test (that is, easier items) and items from the end of the test (harder items). There are many ways of dividing such a test (for example 1, 4, 5, 8, 9, and 2, 3, 6, 7, 10). The most common way to divide a test is by odd-numbered and even-numbered items (see the columns labeled "Evens Correct" and "Odds Correct" in Table 7.1.

While odd-even divisions and subsequent correlation of the two halves of a test are a common method for estimating a test's internal-consistency reliability, they do not necessarily offer the best method. In fact, depending on how the test is divided into two parts, the estimated reliability will vary. A more generalizable method of estimating internal consistency has been developed by Cronbach (1951) and is called *coefficient alpha.* Coefficient alpha is the average split-half correlation based on all possible divisions of a test into two parts. In practice there is no need to compute all possible correlation coefficients; coefficient alpha can be computed from the variances of individual test items and the variance of the total test score as shown in equation 7.2 where k is the number of items in the test.

$$r_{aa} = \frac{k}{k - 1} \left(1 - \frac{\Sigma S^2_{\text{items}}}{S^2_{\text{test}}} \right) \qquad (7.2)$$

Coefficient alpha can be used when test items are scored pass-fail or when more than one point of credit is awarded for a correct response. An earlier, more restrictive method of estimating a test's reliability, a method based on the average correlation between all possible split halves, was developed by Kuder and Richardson. This procedure is called *KR-20* and *is* coefficient alpha for dichotomously scored test items (that is, items that can be scored only right or wrong). Equation 7.2 can be used with dichotomous data; however, in this case the resulting estimate of reliability is usually called a KR-20 estimate rather than coefficient alpha.[3]

There are two major considerations in the use of internal-consistency estimates. First, this method should not be used for timed tests or tests that are not completed by all those being tested. Second, it provides no estimate of stability over time.

2. $126 = 10!/(5!5!)$
3. Sometimes a test author will estimate KR-20 with a formula called KR-21. However, this is usually not a desirable shortcut.

TABLE 7.2   Judgment of Distorted Body Image in a Class of Emotionally Disturbed Children

Child Number	Ms. Hawthorne	Mr. Torrance
1	normal	normal
2	distorted	distorted
3	distorted	normal
4	normal	normal
5	normal	normal
6	distorted	distorted
7	distorted	distorted
8	distorted	normal
9	normal	normal
10	normal	distorted
11	distorted	distorted
12	normal	normal
13	normal	normal
14	normal	normal
15	distorted	distorted
16	normal	distorted
17	normal	normal
18	distorted	distorted
19	normal	distorted
20	normal	distorted

Generalizing to Different Scorers

There are two very different ways of estimating the extent to which we can generalize to different scorers. The first way is similar to the ways of estimating generalizability that we just discussed. Two testers score a set of tests independently. Scores obtained by each tester for the set are then correlated. The resulting correlation coefficient is a reliability coefficient for scorers. For example, suppose that a psychologist (Ms. Hawthorne) was interested in the distortion of body image in emotionally disturbed school children. Further suppose she decided to assess distortion by evaluating the human-figure drawings of such children. Even with explicit criteria for what constitutes distorted image, scoring of human-figure drawings is difficult. Would another, equally trained, tester—Mr. Torrance—arrive at the same conclusions as Ms. Hawthorne? Can Ms. Hawthorne's judgments be generalized to other testers and scorers? To quantify the extent to which this type of generalization is possible, the two testers could evaluate the human-figure drawings made by a class of emotionally disturbed pupils. As shown in Table 7.2 there would be two ratings of distortion of body image for each drawing, and these two scores could be correlated. The resulting correlation coefficient (phi =) would be an estimate of interscorer reliability or agreement.

The second method of estimating generalizability to different scorers is

TABLE 7.3 Summary of Agreements and Disagreements from Table 7.2

		Ms. Hawthorne	
		Distorted	Normal
Mr. Torrance	Normal	2	8
	Distorted	6	4

prevalent in behavioral assessment. Instead of correlating the two scorers' ratings, one can compute a percentage of agreement. A simple index of agreement is obtained by dividing the number of agreements by the number of disagreements and multiplying the quotient by 100. For the data in Table 7.2, the percentage of agreement is 70 percent [that is, $(\frac{14}{20})$ (100)]. Another way of computing the percentage of agreement is to compute the *percentage of agreement for the occurrence of the target behavior* (see Equation 7.3). In this example, since Ms. Hawthorne is interested in the occurrences of distortion of body image, it might make better sense to look only at how well the two raters agree on the occurrence. The eight nonoccurrences where both Ms. Hawthorne and Mr. Torrance agree are not of interest and are ignored. The data in Table 7.2 can be summarized in Table 7.3. The percentage of agreement for occurrence is 50 percent [that is, (100) (6)/(20 − 8)].

$$\% \text{ agreement occurrence} = \frac{(100) \text{ (number of agreements on occurrence)}}{\text{number of observations} - \text{number of agreements on nonoccurrence}} \quad (7.3)$$

WHAT METHOD SHOULD BE USED?

The first consideration is the type of generalization one wishes to make. One must select the method that goes with the generalization. For example, if one were interested in generalizing about the stability of a score or observation, the appropriate method would be test-retest correlations. It would be inappropriate to use interscorer agreement as an estimate of the extent to which one can generalize to different times. Additional considerations in selecting the method to be used include the following:

1. When estimating stability, the convention is to retest after two weeks. There is nothing special about two weeks. (If all test authors used the same interval, it would be easier to compare relative stability of tests.)

2. When estimating the extent to which we can generalize to similar test items, we subscribe to Nunnally's (1967, p. 217) hierarchy for estimating reliability. The first choice is to use alternate-form reliability with a two-week interval. (Again, there is nothing special about two weeks; it is just a convention.) If alternate forms are not available, divide the test into equivalent halves and administer the halves with a two-week interval, correcting the correlation by the Spearman-Brown formula given in equation 7.4. When alternate forms are not available and subjects cannot be tested more than once, use coefficient alpha.

3. When estimating the extent to which we can generalize among different scorers, we prefer computing correlation coefficients to percentages of agreement. Correlation coefficients bear a direct relationship to other indicators of reliability and other uses of reliability coefficients; percentages of agreement do not. We also realize that current practice is to report percentages of agreement and not to bother with the other uses of the reliability coefficient for generalizing to other scorers.

FACTORS AFFECTING RELIABILITY

Several factors that affect a test's reliability can inflate or deflate reliability estimates.

Test Length

As a general rule, the more items on a homogeneous test, the more reliable the test. Thus, long tests tend to be more reliable than short tests. This fact is especially important in an internal-consistency estimate of reliability, because in this kind of estimate the number of test items is reduced by 50 percent. Internal-consistency estimates of reliability actually estimate the reliability of half the test. Therefore, such estimates are often corrected by a formula developed by Spearman and Brown. As shown in equation 7.4, the reliability of the total test is equal to twice the reliability as estimated by internal consistency divided by the sum of one plus the reliability estimate.

$$r_{xx} = \frac{2r_{(\frac{1}{2})(\frac{1}{2})}}{1 + r_{(\frac{1}{2})(\frac{1}{2})}} \tag{7.4}$$

For example, if coefficient alpha were computed on a test and found to be .80, the corrected estimated reliability would be .89:

$$.89 = \frac{(2)(.80)}{1 + .80} = \frac{1.60}{1.80}$$

A related issue is the number of effective items for each test taker. Tests are generally more reliable in the middle ranges of scores (for example, ± 1.5 S). For a test to be effective at the extremes of a distribution, there must be a sufficient number of difficult items for very bright pupils as well as a sufficient number of easy items for backward pupils.

Test-Retest Interval

A person's true abilities can and do change between two administrations of a test. The greater the amount of time between the two administrations, the more likely the possibility that true scores will change. Thus, when employing stability or alternate-form estimates of reliability, one must pay close attention to the interval between tests. Generally, the shorter the interval, the higher the estimated reliability.

Constriction of Range

The reliability coefficient is directly related to the variability of the test.[4] The greater the variance of a test, the greater its reliability estimate. When samples with relatively small variances are used to estimate reliability, the resulting estimates will be lower.

Moreover, a test's reliability will be seriously underestimated if scores from only a limited range of the test are studied. In Figure 7.1 alternate forms of a test produce a strong positive correlation when the entire range of the test is used. However, within any restricted range of the test, as illustrated by the dark square outline, the correlation may be very low. (Although it is possible to correct a correlation coefficient for restriction in range, it is generally unwise to do so.)

A related problem is that *extension* of range seriously *overestimates* a test's reliability. Figure 7.2 contains alternate-form correlations of first, third, and fifth grades. The scatterplot for each grade, considered separately, indicates poor reliability. However, spelling-test scores increase as a function of schooling; students in higher grades earn higher scores. When test authors combine the scores for several grades (or from several ages), poor correlations may be combined to produce a spuriously high correlation.

4. The relationship is shown in the formula

$$r_{xx} = 1 - \frac{\text{SEM}^2}{S_{\text{test}}^2}$$

The SEM (standard error of measurement) is discussed later in this chapter.

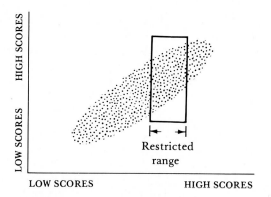

FIGURE 7.1 Constricting the range of test scores reduces the estimate of a test's reliability

SOURCE: From *Psychological Testing* (p. 115) by A. Anastasi, 1954, New York: Macmillan. Copyright 1954 by Macmillan Publishing Company, Inc. Copyright renewed 1982 by Anne Anastasi. Adapted by permission of the publisher.

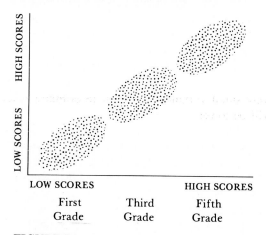

FIGURE 7.2 Extending the range of test scores may spuriously increase the estimate of a test's reliability

Guessing

Guessing is responding randomly to items. Even if a guess results in a correct response, it introduces error into a test score and into our interpretation of that score.

Variation Within the Testing Situation

The amount of error that variation in the testing situation introduces into the results of testing can vary considerably. Children can misread or misunderstand the directions for a test, get a headache halfway through testing, lose their place on the answer sheet, break the point on their pencil, or choose to watch a squirrel eat nuts on the windowsill of the classroom rather than taking the test. All such situational variations introduce an indeterminate amount of error in testing and, in doing so, lower reliability.

STANDARD ERROR OF MEASUREMENT

One of the primary reasons for obtaining a reliability coefficient is to estimate the amount of error usually associated with generalizing from a score obtained under a particular set of circumstances. The standard error of measurement (SEM) allows one to estimate the error associated with each type of error. One can compute standard errors of measurement for scorers, times, and item samples. However, SEMs are usually computed only on stability and item samples.

Earlier we discussed the generalization of performance on one sample of items to the mean of all possible samples of items drawn from the domain. This provides a convenient example of what the standard error of measurement means. Consider the alphabet recognition task again. There are so many samples of ten-letter tests that could be developed. If we constructed only one hundred of these tests and tested one kindergartner, we would probably find that the distribution of scores for that kindergartner was approximately normal. The mean of that distribution would be the student's true score. The distribution around the true score would be the result of imperfect samples of letters; some letter samples would overestimate the pupil's ability, and others would underestimate it. Thus, the distribution would be the result of error. The standard deviation of that distribution is the standard deviation of errors attributable to sampling and is called the standard error of measurement.

When we test a student, we typically test only once. Therefore, we cannot generate a distribution similar to the one depicted in Figure 7.3. Consequently, we do not know the test taker's true score or the variability of the measurement error that forms the distribution around that true score. However, we can use what we know about the test's reliability for items and standard deviation to estimate what that distribution would be.

Equation 7.5 is the general formula for finding the standard error of measurement. The standard error of measurement (SEM) equals the standard deviation of the obtained scores (S) multiplied by the square root of one minus the reliability coefficient ($\sqrt{1 - r_{xx}}$). The type of unit (IQ, raw score, and the like) in which the standard deviation is expressed is the unit in which the SEM is expressed. Thus, if the test scores have been converted to T-scores, the standard deviation is in T-score units and is 10; the SEM is also in T-score units. Similarly, if the reliability coefficient is based on stability, then the SEM is for times of testing. If the reliability coefficient is based on different scorers, then the SEM is for testers/observers.

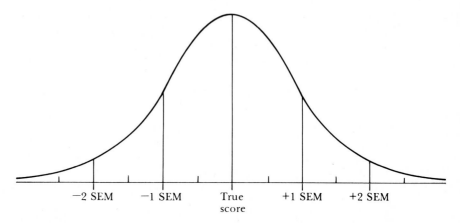

FIGURE 7.3 The standard error of measurement is the standard deviation of the error distribution around a true score for one subject

TABLE 7.4 Relationship Between Reliability Coefficient and SEM (Part A) and Relationship Between Standard Deviation and SEM (Part B)

Part A			Part B		
S	r_{xx}	SEM	S	r_{xx}	SEM
10	.96	2	5	.91	1.5
10	.84	4	10	.91	3.0
10	.75	5	15	.91	4.5
10	.64	6	20	.91	6.0
10	.36	8	25	.91	7.5

$$\text{SEM} = S\sqrt{1 - r_{xx}} \tag{7.5}$$

From equation 7.5 it is apparent that as the standard deviation increases, the SEM increases; and as the reliability coefficient decreases, the SEM increases. In Part A of Table 7.4 the same standard deviation (10) is used with different reliability coefficients. As reliability coefficients decrease, SEMs increase. When the reliability coefficient is .96, the SEM is 2; when the reliability is .64, the SEM is 6. In Part B of Table 7.4, different standard deviations are used with the same reliability coefficient (r_{xx} = .91). As the standard deviation increases, the SEM increases.

Because of the presence of measurement error, there is always some uncertainty about an individual's true score. The standard error of measurement provides information about the certainty or confidence with which a test score can be interpreted. When the SEM is relatively large, the uncertainty is large; we cannot be very sure of the individual's score. When the SEM is relatively small, the uncertainty is small; we can be more certain of the score.

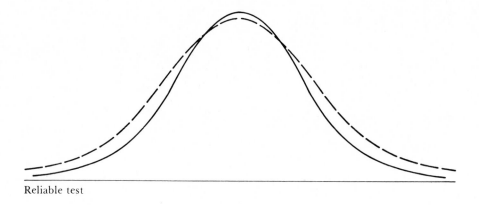

Reliable test

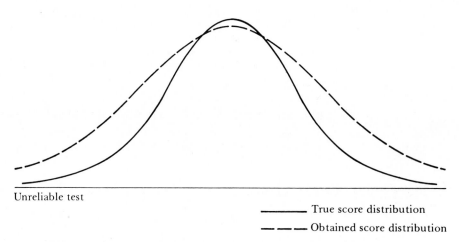

Unreliable test

——————— True score distribution

— — — Obtained score distribution

FIGURE 7.4 Relationship between true-score distribution and obtained-score distribution for reliable and unreliable tests

ESTIMATED TRUE SCORES

Unfortunately, we never know a subject's true score. Moreover, the obtained score on a test is not the best estimate of the true score. As mentioned in the previous discussion, true scores and errors are uncorrelated. However, obtained scores and errors *are* correlated. Scores above the test mean have more "lucky" error (error that raises the obtained score above the true score), while scores below the mean have more "unlucky" error (error that lowers the obtained score below the true score). An easy way to understand this effect is to think of a test on which a student guesses on half the test items. If all the guesses are correct, the student has been very lucky and earns a high grade.

TABLE 7.5 Estimated True Scores for Different Obtained Scores on Tests with Different Reliability Coefficients

Test Mean ($\bar{X}$)	Reliability Coefficient (r_{xx})	Obtained Score (X)	Estimated True Score (X')	Difference Between Obtained Score and Estimated True Score
100	.90	90	91.0	1.0
100	.90	75	77.5	2.5
100	.90	50	55.0	5.0
100	.70	90	93.0	3.0
100	.70	75	82.5	7.5
100	.70	50	65.0	15.0
100	.50	90	95.0	5.0
100	.50	75	87.5	12.5
100	.50	50	75.0	25.0

However, if all guesses are incorrect, the student has been unlucky and earns a low grade. Thus, obtained scores above or below the mean are often more discrepant than true scores. As can be seen from Figure 7.4, the less reliable the test, the greater the discrepancy between obtained scores and true scores. Nunnally (1967, p. 220) has provided an equation (equation 7.6) for determining the estimated true score (X'). The estimated true score equals the test mean plus the product of the reliability coefficient and the difference between the obtained score and the group mean.

$$X' = \bar{X} + (r_{xx})(X - \bar{X}) \tag{7.6}$$

The particular mean that one uses is the subject of some controversy. We believe the preferred mean is the mean of the demographic group that best represents the particular child. Thus, if the child is Asian and resides in a lower-class urban area, the most appropriate mean would be the mean of same-age Asian children from lower socioeconomic backgrounds who live in urban areas. In the absence of means for particular children of particular backgrounds, one is forced to use the overall mean for the child's age. As has been the case throughout this chapter, the choice of reliability coefficient depends on the type of generalization one wishes to make.

The discrepancy between obtained scores and estimated true scores is a function of both the reliability of the obtained score and the difference between the obtained score and the mean. In Table 7.5, a general case is illustrated where the mean in each example is 100; the obtained scores are 90, 75, and 50. The reliability coefficients are .90, .70, and .50. When the obtained score is 90 and the estimated reliability is .90, the estimated true score is 91 [91 = 100 + (.90)(90 − 100)]. However, when the obtained score is 50 and the reliability coefficient is .90, the estimated true score is 55 [100 + (.90)(50 − 100)]. Even when the reliability coefficient is constant, the farther an obtained score is from the mean, the greater will be the discrepancy between the obtained score and the estimated true score.

When the obtained score is 75 and the reliability coefficient is .90, the estimated true score is 77.5 [100 + (.90)(75 − 100)]. However, when the reliability coefficient drops to .50 and the obtained score doesn't change, the estimated true score rises to 87 [100 + (.50)(75 − 100)].

When the obtained score is below the test mean and the reliability coefficient is less than 1.00, the estimated true score is *always* higher than the obtained score. Conversely, when the obtained score is above the test mean and the reliability coefficient is less than 1.00, the estimated true score is *always* less than the obtained score. Note that the equation does not give the *true score,* only the *estimated true score.*

CONFIDENCE INTERVALS

Although we can never know a person's true score, measurement is not a hopeless activity. We can estimate a true score, and we can estimate the standard deviation of the error of measurement about the true score. With these two bits of information, we can construct a range within which we know the exact probability of including a person's true score. This range is called a *confidence interval.* A 50 percent confidence interval is a range of values within which the true score will be found 50 percent of the time. Of course, 50 percent of the time the true score will be outside the interval. A larger range—a greater confidence interval—could make us feel more certain that we have included the true score within the range. But it is impossible to construct an interval in which the true score will always be contained. However, if we construct 95 percent or 99 percent confidence intervals, then the chances are only 5 percent and 1 percent, respectively, that the true score will fall outside the confidence interval.

Establishing Confidence Intervals for True Scores

The characteristics of a normal curve have already been discussed. We can apply the relationship between *z*-scores and areas under the normal curve to the normal distribution of error around a true score. We can use equation 7.6 to estimate the mean of the distribution (the true score) and equation 7.5 to estimate the standard deviation of the distribution (the standard error of measurement). With these two estimates, we can construct a confidence interval for the *true score.* Since 68 percent of all elements in a normal distribution fall within one standard deviation of the mean, there is a 68 percent chance

TABLE 7.6 Commonly Used z-Scores, Extreme Areas, and Area Included Between $+$ and $-$ z-Score Values

z-Score	Extreme Area	Area Between $+$ and $-$
.67	25.0%	50%
1.00	16.0%	68%
1.64	5.0%	90%
1.96	2.5%	95%
2.33	1.0%	98%
2.57	.5%	99%

that the true score is within one SEM of the estimated true score. We can construct an interval with almost any degree of confidence except 100 percent confidence. Table 7.6 contains the extreme area for the z-scores most commonly used in constructing confidence intervals. The general formula for a confidence interval is given in equation 7.7. The lower limit of the confidence interval equals the estimated true score less the product of the z-score associated with that level of confidence and the standard error of measurement. The upper limit of the confidence interval is the estimated true score plus the product of the z-score and the SEM.

Lower limit of c.i. $= X' - (z\text{-score})(\text{SEM})$

Upper limit of c.i. $= X' + (z\text{-score})(\text{SEM})$ (7.7)

To construct a symmetrical confidence interval for a true score, a simple procedure is followed.

1. Select the degree of confidence, for example, 95 percent.
2. Find the z-score associated with that degree of confidence. (For example, a 95 percent confidence interval is between z-scores of -1.96 and $+1.96$.)
3. Multiply each z-score associated with the confidence interval (for example, 1.96 for 95 percent confidence) by the SEM.
4. Find the estimated true score.
5. Take the product of the z-score and the SEM, and both add it to and subtract it from the estimated true score.

For example, assume that a person's estimated true score is 75 and that the SEM is 5. Further assume that you wish to be 68 percent sure of constructing an interval that will contain the true score. Sixty-eight percent of the time, the true score will be contained in the interval of 70 to 80 [75 $-$ (1)(5) to 75 $+$ (1)(5)]; there is a 16 percent chance that the true score is less than 70 and a

16 percent chance that the true score is greater than 80. If you are unwilling to be wrong 32 percent of the time, you must increase the width of the confidence interval. Thus, with the same true score (75) and SEM (5), if you wish 95 percent confidence, the size of the interval must be increased; it would have to range from 65 to 85 [75 − (1.96)(5) to 75 + (1.96)(5)]. Ninety-five percent of the time the true score will be contained within that interval; there is a 2.5 percent chance that the true score is less than 65, and there is a 2.5 percent chance that it is greater than 85.

DIFFERENCE SCORES

In many applied settings, we are interested in discrepancies (differences) between two scores. For example, we might wish to know if a child's achievement age is commensurate (equal) to her mental age. In many definitions of educational disorders (for example, learning disabilities) a "significant" discrepancy is specified. In other disorders (for example, mental retardation) significant discrepancies are not expected. There are several major considerations in evaluating the "significance" of discrepancies (Salvia & Good, 1982): the reliability of the difference, the rarity of the difference, and the psychological meaningfulness of the difference. Here, the emphasis is on the reliability of the difference. The important thing to remember is that, usually, difference scores are less reliable than the scores on which the differences are based.

The reliability of a difference between two scores (A and B) is a function of four things: (1) the reliability of test A, (2) the reliability of test B, (3) the correlation between tests A and B, and (4) differences in norm groups. There are several approaches to evaluating the reliability of a difference. Two methods are particularly useful but rest on different assumptions and combine the data in different ways (that is, use different formulas).

One method uses a regression model and was originally described by Thorndike (1963). Within this model, one score is presumed to cause the second score. For example, intelligence is believed to cause achievement. Therefore, intelligence is identified as an independent (or predictor) variable, and achievement is identified as the dependent (or predicted) variable. When the predicted score (for example, the predicted achievement score) differs from the achievement score that is actually obtained, a deficit exists. The reliability of a predicted difference is given by equation 7.8. The reliability of a predicted difference ($\hat{D}$) is equal to the reliability of the dependent variable (r_{bb}) plus the product of the reliability of the independent variable (r_{aa}) and the square of the correlation between the independent variable and the dependent variable ($r_{aa}\,r_{ab}^2$) less twice the squared correlation of the independent and dependent variable ($-\,2r_{ab}$). This combination is divided by one minus the squared correlation between independent and dependent variables ($1 - r_{ab}^2$). The standard deviation of predicted differences (S), also called the standard error of estimate, is given in equation 7.9. The standard deviation of predicted differences is equal to the standard deviation of the dependent variable (S_b) multiplied by the square root of one minus the squared correlation between independent and dependent variables ($\sqrt{1 - r_{ab}^2}$).

$$\hat{D} = \frac{r_{bb} + (r_{aa})(r_{ab}^2) - 2r_{ab}}{1 - r_{ab}^2} \tag{7.8}$$

$$S_{\text{dif}} = S_b \sqrt{1 - r_{ab}^2} \tag{7.9}$$

The second method was proposed by Stake and Wardrop (1971). In this method, one variable is not assumed to be the cause of the other; neither variable is identified as the independent variable. However, this method does require that both measures be in the same unit of measurement (for example, T-scores or IQs). The reliability of a difference in *obtained scores* is given in equation 7.10.

$$r_{\text{dif}} = \frac{\frac{1}{2}(r_{aa} + r_{bb}) - r_{ab}}{1 - r_{ab}} \tag{7.10}$$

The reliability of an obtained difference equals the average reliability of the two tests [$\frac{1}{2}(r_{aa} + r_{bb})$] less the correlation between the two tests ($- r_{ab}$); this difference is divided by one minus the correlation between the two tests ($1 - r_{ab}$). The standard deviation for obtained differences is given in equation 7.11.

$$S_{\text{dif}} = \sqrt{S_a^2 + S_b^2 - 2r_{ab}S_aS_b} \tag{7.11}$$

The standard deviation of an obtained difference is equal to the square root of the sum of the variances of tests A and B ($S_a^2 + S_b^2$) less twice the product of the correlation of A and B multiplied by the standard deviations of A and B ($- 2r_{ab}S_aS_b$). The reliability of a difference and the standard deviation are combined in same manner for a difference score as for a single score. Substituting in equation 7.5, equation 7.12 is generated.

$$\text{SEM}_{\text{dif}} = \sqrt{S_a^2 + S_b^2 - 2r_{ab}S_aS_b} \; \sqrt{1 - \frac{\frac{1}{2}(r_{aa} + r_{bb}) - r_{ab}}{1 - r_{ab}}} \tag{7.12}$$

The standard error of measurement of a difference describes the distribution of differences between *obtained* scores. To evaluate difference scores, the simplest method is to establish a level of confidence (for example, 95%) and find the z-score associated with that level of confidence (1.96). We then divide the obtained difference by the SEM of difference. If the quotient exceeds the z-score associated with the level of confidence selected (1.96), the obtained difference is reliable. When a difference is assumed reliable at a particular level of confidence, we can estimate the true difference in the same manner as we estimate a true score on one test. In general, we assume that the group mean difference is .00. Thus, the formula for estimating the true difference for a particular student simplifies to equation 7.13.

$$\text{Estimated true difference} = (\text{obtained difference})(r_{xx(\text{dif})}) \qquad (7.13)$$

DESIRABLE STANDARDS

It is important for test authors to present sufficient information in test manuals for the test user to interpret test results accurately. Test results must be generalizable before they are useful. Whether a test measures what it purports to measure is a question of validity, the topic of the next chapter. However, for a test to be valid (to measure what its authors claim it measures), it must be reliable. Although not the only condition that must be met, reliability is a necessary condition for validity. No test can measure what it purports to measure unless it's reliable. No score is interpretable unless it's reliable. Therefore, test authors and publishers must present sufficient reliability data to allow the user to interpret test results accurately. Reliability indexes for each type of score (for example, raw scores, grade equivalents, and standard scores) must be reported. These should be reported for each age and grade. Furthermore, these indexes should be presented clearly in tabular form in one place. Test authors should not play hide and seek with reliability data. Test authors who recommend computing difference scores should provide, whenever possible, the reliability of the difference and the SEM of the difference. Once test users have access to reliability data, they must judge the adequacy of the test.

When a test score is reported, we strongly recommend that the estimated true score and a 68 percent confidence interval for that true score also be reported. How high must a reliability coefficient be before it can be used in applied settings? It depends on the use to which test data are put. A simple answer is to use the most reliable test available. However, such a response is misleading, for the "best" test may have a reliability coefficient too low for any application (for example, .12). We recommend that two standards of reliability be used in applied settings.

1. *Group Data* If test scores are to be used for administrative purposes and are reported for groups, a reliability of .60 should probably be the minimum.

2. *Individual Data*   If a test score is used to make a decision for one student, a much higher standard of reliability is demanded. When important educational decisions, such as tracking and placement in a special class, are to be made for a student, the minimum standard should be .90. When the decision being made is a screening decision, such as a recommendation that a child receive further assessment, there is still need for high reliability. For screening devices, we recommend a .80 standard.

read

SUMMARY

Reliability refers to the ability to generalize from a sample to a domain. The domains to which we usually want to generalize are other times (stability or test-retest reliability), other scorers (interrater or interscorer reliability), and other items (alternate-form or internal-consistency reliability). Reliability coefficients may range from .00 (total lack of reliability) to 1.00 (total reliability); .90 is recommended as the minimum standard for tests used to make important educational decisions for children. In diagnostic work with children the reliability coefficient has three major uses: It allows the user (1) to estimate the test's relative freedom from measurement error, (2) to estimate an individual subject's true score, and (3) to find the standard error of measurement. Knowledge of the standard error of measurement and the estimated true score allows the test user to construct confidence intervals for a subject's true score.

The discussion of estimated true scores, standard error of measurement, and confidence intervals can be extended to difference or discrepancy scores. The reliability of a difference score is affected by the reliability of the tests and by the correlation between the tests on which the difference is based. Differences in norm samples also affect difference scores, but this effect cannot be evaluated. Provided the two tests are correlated, difference scores are less reliable than the average of the reliabilities of the tests on which the difference is based.

There are several factors that affect reliability: the method used to calculate the reliability coefficient, test length, the test-retest interval, constriction of range, guessing, and variation within the testing situation.

STUDY QUESTIONS

1. Why is it necessary that a test be reliable?
2. Test A and test B have identical means and standard deviations. Test A has a standard error of measurement of 4.8; test B has a standard error of measurement of 16.3. Which test is more reliable, and why?

3. What is the greatest limitation of reliability estimates based on test-retest correlation?
4. List and explain five factors that affect the estimated reliability of a test.
5. The standard error of measurement is the standard deviation of what? Illustrate your answer with a drawing.

PROBLEMS

1. Mr. Treacher administers an intelligence test ($\bar{X} = 100$, $S = 16$, $r_{rx} = .75$) to his class. Five children earn the following scores: 68, 124, 84, 100, and 148. What are the estimated true scores for these children?
2. What is the standard error of measurement for the intelligence test in problem 1?
3. What are the upper and lower boundaries of a symmetrical confidence interval of 95 percent for the first child?
4. What are the upper and lower boundaries of a symmetrical confidence interval of 50 percent for the child who earns a score of 100?
5. Test A and test B have reliabilities of .90 and .80; the correlation between tests A and B is .50. What is the reliability of a difference between a score on test A and test B?

Answers

1. 76, 118, 88, 100, 136
2. 8
3. 92, 60
4. 105, 95
5. .70

ADDITIONAL READING

American Psychological Association, American Educational Research Association, & National Council on Measurement in Education. (1974). *Standards for educational and psychological tests.* Washington, DC: American Psychological Association. (Pp. 48–55.)

Coates, T., & Thoresen, C. (1978). Using generalization theory in behavioral observation. *Behavior Therapy, 9,* 605–613.

Cronbach, L., Gleser, G., Nanda, H., & Rajaratnam, N. (1972). *The dependability of behavioral measurement: Theory of generalizability of scores and profiles.* New York: Wiley.

Ghiselli, E. E. (1964). *Theory of psychological measurement.* New York: McGraw-Hill. (Chapter 8, pp. 207–253.)

Kazdin, A. (1982). *Single-case research designs.* New York: Oxford University Press. (Chapter 3: Interobserver agreement.)

Salvia, J., & Good, R. (1982). Significant discrepancies in the classification of pupils: Differentiating the concept. In J. T. Neisworth (Ed.), *Assessment in special education.* Rockville, MD: Aspen Systems.

CHAPTER 8

Read - important

VALIDITY

Validity refers to the extent to which a test measures what its authors or users claim it measures. Specifically, test validity concerns the appropriateness of the inferences that can be made on the basis of test results. A test's validity is not measured; rather, a test's validity for various uses is judged on a wide array of information, including its reliability and the adequacy of its norms. The process of gathering information about the appropriateness of test-based inferences is called *validation.* Three interrelated types of validity are usually considered in the validation of tests: content validity, criterion-related validity, and construct validity.

The valid use of tests is the responsibility of both the test author and the test user. A test author

should present the evidence of validity for each type of inference for which use of the test is recommended. . . .

If a user wants to use a test in a situation for which the use of the test has not been previously validated, or for which there is no supported claim for validity, he is responsible for validation. . . . He who makes the claim for validity is responsible for providing the evidence. (APA et al., 1974, pp. 31, 33)

To evaluate a test's validity, test users must have a clear understanding of what is to be measured. One must define what is to be measured before deciding how the measuring is to be done. Test authors should not start with a series of test items and then decide what those items might measure. Rather, they should first define what a trait (or characteristic or skill) is and what it is not and then select items to measure it. Selection of test items depends on a test author's own definition of and assumptions about the domain to be measured.

1. Three and six are _____.
   a. 4
   b. 7
   c. 8
   d. 9
2. What number follows in this series? 1, 2.5, 6.25, _____
   a. 10
   b. 12.5
   c. 15.625
   d. 18.50
3. Cuántos son tres y dos?
   a. 3
   b. 4
   c. 5
   d. 6
4. Ille puer puellas _____.
   a. amo
   b. amat
   c. amamus
   d. amant

FIGURE 8.1 Sample multiple-choice questions for an elementary-level (K–3) arithmetic achievement test

METHODS OF TEST VALIDATION

This section treats content, criterion-related, and construct validity separately. However, it is important to note that these three aspects of validity are not separable in the real world; they are interdependent.

Content Validity

Content validity is evaluated by a careful examination of the content of a test. Such an examination is judgmental in nature and requires a clear definition of what the content should be. Content validity is established by examining three factors: the appropriateness of the types of items included, the completeness of the item sample, and the way in which the items assess the content.

The first factor to examine in determining content validity is the appropriateness of the items included in the test. We must ask, "Is this an appropriate test question?" and "Does this test item really measure the domain?" Consider the four test items from a hypothetical elementary (kindergarten through grade 3) arithmetic achievement test presented in Figure 8.1. The first item requires the student to read and add two single-digit numbers whose sum is less than 10. This seems to be an appropriate item for an elementary arithmetic achievement test. The second item requires the student to complete a geometric progression. While this item is mathematical, the skills and knowledge required to complete the question correctly have not been taught in any elementary school curriculum by the third grade. Therefore, the question should be rejected as an invalid item for an arithmetic achievement test to be used with children in kindergarten through the third grade.

The third item also requires the student to read and add two single-digit numbers whose sum is less than 10. However, the question is written in Spanish. While the content of the question is suitable (this is an elementary addition problem), the methods of presentation require other skills. Failure to complete the item correctly could be attributed to the fact that the child does not know Spanish and/or to the fact that the child does not know "2 + 3 = 5." One should conclude that the item is not valid for an arithmetic test for children who do not read Spanish. The fourth item requires that the student select the correct form of the Latin verb *amare* ("to love"). Clearly, this is an inappropriate item for an elementary arithmetic test and should be rejected as invalid.

The second factor to examine in determining content validity is the completeness of the item sample. The validity of any elementary arithmetic test would be questioned if it included *only* problems requiring the addition of single-digit numbers whose sum was less than 10. One would reasonably expect an arithmetic test to include a far broader sample of tasks (for example, addition of two- and three-digit numbers, subtraction, and so forth).

The third factor to examine is how the test items assess the content—that is, the level of mastery at which the content is assessed. In the previous example, the child was expected to add two single-digit numbers whose sum was less than 10. However, one could evaluate a child's arithmetic skills in a variety of ways. The child might be required to recognize the correct answer in a multiple-choice array, supply the correct answer, apply the proper addition facts in a word problem, or analyze the condition under which the mathematical relationship obtains.

One way to insure content validity of a test is to construct a test that measures the desired content in the desired way. Bloom, Hastings, and Madaus (1971) have devoted several hundred pages to this topic in their book *Handbook of Formative and Summative Evaluation of Student Learning.* They have recommended that authors of achievement tests develop a *table of specifications* for the content to be tested. Such a table can be readily generalized to other types of tests. A table of specifications formally enumerates the particular contents of a test and the processes (or behaviors) it assesses. Content refers to the particular domains or subdomains the test author wishes to assess. The task of the test author is to specify the content as precisely as possible in order to convey clearly to both test author and test user what is being measured. The next step is to specify how the particular content objectives will be measured (the process by which the measurement will occur). Several levels of measurement are possible; they range from knowledge objectives to evaluation objectives. The definitions used by Bloom (1956) and Bloom, Hastings, and Madaus (1971) follow.

1. *Knowledge* is the "recall or recognition of specific elements in a subject area" (Bloom et al., p. 41).
2. *Comprehension* consists of three types of measurement: translation, interpretation, and extrapolation. Translation refers to rewording information or putting it into one's own words. Interpretation is evidenced "when a student can go beyond recognizing the separate parts of a communication . . . and can see the interrelationships among the parts" (Bloom et al., p. 149). Interpretation also is evidenced when a student can differentiate the essentials of a message from unimportant elements. Extrapolation refers to the student's ability to go beyond literal comprehension and to make inferences about what the anticipated outcome of an action is or what will happen next.
3. *Application* is "the use of abstractions in particular and concrete situations. The abstractions may be in the form of general ideas, rules of procedures, or generalized methods. The abstractions may also be technical principles, ideas, and theories which must be remembered and applied" (Bloom, 1956, p. 205).
4. *Analysis* is "the breakdown of a communication into its constituent elements or parts such that the relative hierarchy of ideas is made clear and/or the relations between ideas expressed are made explicit. Such analyses are intended to clarify the communication, to indicate how the communication is organized, and the way in which it manages to convey its effects, as well as its basis and arrangements" (Bloom, 1956, p. 205).
5. *Synthesis* refers to "the putting together of elements and parts so as to form a whole. This involves the process of working with pieces, parts, elements, etc., and arranging and combining them in such a way as to constitute a pattern or structure not clearly there before" (Bloom, 1956, p. 206).
6. *Evaluation* means "the making of judgments about the value, for some purpose, of ideas, works, solutions, methods, material, etc. It involves the use of criteria as well as standards for appraising the extent to which particulars are accurate, effective, economical, or satisfying. The judgments may be quantitative or qualitative, and the criteria may be either those determined by the student or those which are given to him" (Bloom, 1956, p. 185).

To illustrate how a table of specifications can be used, let us assume that we wish to develop a test to assess the understanding of reliability demonstrated by beginning students of psychoeducational assessment. The first step is to enumerate the *content areas* of the domain. Using Chapter 7 as a guide, we

TABLE 8.1 Table of Specifications for a Hypothetical Reliability Test

	Contents				
Processes	Reliability Coefficient	Standard Error of Measurement	Estimated True Scores	Confidence Intervals	Difference Scores
Knowledge	3 questions	2 questions	1 question	1 question	1 question
Comprehension	5 questions	2 questions	1 question	3 questions	1 question
Application	Not tested	2 questions	1 question	5 questions	Not tested
Analysis	Not tested	Not tested	Not tested	Not tested	Not tested
Synthesis	Not tested	Not tested	Not tested	Not tested	Not tested
Evaluation	Not tested	Not tested	Not tested	Not tested	Not tested

could assess the following areas: the reliability coefficient (meaning, methods of estimating it, and factors affecting it), standard error of measurement (meaning and computation), estimated true scores, confidence intervals (meaning and computation), and difference scores. One might reasonably expect a test user to have a better understanding of the meaning of the reliability coefficient and the construction and interpretation of confidence intervals. Therefore, these content areas could be stressed. The next step is to specify the *processes* by which the content areas are to be measured. One might expect beginning students to demonstrate understanding at the *knowledge, comprehension,* and *application* levels only. Therefore, the test might not contain items assessing analysis, synthesis, or evaluation. A table of specifications for this hypothetical test would resemble Table 8.1.

The number of questions used to assess each cell also is given in the table. The table of specifications shows that, of the twenty-eight questions in the test, eight deal with the reliability coefficient and nine deal with confidence intervals; eight questions assess knowledge, twelve questions assess comprehension, and eight assess application. Thus, while the hypothetical test assesses a student's understanding of reliability, it does so by emphasizing comprehension of the reliability coefficient and applications of confidence intervals.

Content validity is a major component of the validation process for any educational and psychological test. It is hard to imagine a valid test that lacks content validity. The best way for a test author and test user to establish a test's content validity is to examine the relationship among the test items, the domain of test content, and the methods of measuring that content.

The definition of the universe of tasks represented by the test scores should include the identification of that part of the content universe represented by each item. The definition should be operational rather than theoretical, containing specifications regarding classes of stimuli, tasks to be performed and observations to be scored. The definition should not involve assumptions regarding the psychological processes employed since these would be matters of construct rather than of content validity. (APA et al., 1974, p. 45)

Criterion-Related Validity - *going back to a certain standard*

A test's *criterion-related validity* refers to the extent to which a person's score on a criterion measure can be estimated from that person's test score. This is usually expressed as a correlation between the test and the criterion. The correlation coefficient is called a *validity coefficient.* Concurrent validity and predictive validity denote the time when a person's score on the criterion measure is obtained. *Concurrent* criterion-related validity refers to how accurately a person's current test score can be used to estimate the *current* criterion score. *Predictive* criterion-related validity refers to how accurately a person's current test score can be used to estimate what the criterion score will be *at a later time.* Thus, concurrent and predictive criterion-related validity of a test refer to the temporal sequence by which a person's score on some criterion measure is estimated on the basis of that person's current test score; concurrent and predictive validity differ as a function of the time at which scores on the criterion measure are obtained.

The nature of the criterion measure is extremely important. The criterion itself must be valid if it is to be used to establish the validity of another measure. Let's investigate this point by looking briefly at two examples of criterion-related validation, the first concurrent and the second predictive.

Concurrent Criterion-Related Validity

The basic concurrent criterion-related validity question is, "Does knowledge of a person's test score allow the accurate estimation of that person's performance on a criterion measure?" For example, if the Acme Ruler Company manufactures yardsticks, how do we know that a person's height as measured by the yardstick is that person's true height? How do we know that the "Acme foot" is really a foot? The first step is to find a valid criterion measure. The National Bureau of Standards maintains *the* foot (.3048 meter), and *the* foot is the logical choice for a criterion measure. We can take the Acme foot to the Bureau and compare Acme measurements with measurements made with *the* foot. If the two sets of measurements correspond closely (that is, are highly correlated and have very similar means and standard deviations), we can conclude that the Acme foot is a valid measure of length.

Similarly, if we are developing a test of achievement, we can ask, "How does knowledge of a person's score on our achievement test allow the estimation of that person's score on a criterion measure?" How do we know that our new test really measures achievement? Again, the first step is to find a valid criterion measure. However, there is no National Bureau of Standards for Educational Tests. Therefore, we must turn to a less-than-perfect criterion. There are two basic choices: other achievement tests that are presumed to be valid and teacher judgments of achievement. We can, of course, use both. If our new test presents evidence of content validity and elicits test scores corresponding closely (correlating significantly) to teacher judgments and scores from other achievement tests presumed to be valid, we can conclude that our new test is a valid measure of achievement.

Predictive Criterion-Related Validity

The basic predictive criterion-related validity question is, Does knowledge of a person's test score allow an accurate estimation of that person's score on a criterion measure administered some time in the future? For example, if Acme Ruler Company decides to diversify and manufacture tests of color vision, how do we know that a diagnosis of colorblindness made on the basis of the Acme test is accurate? How do we know that the Acme-based diagnosis will correspond to next month's diagnosis made by an ophthalmologist? We can test several children with the Acme test, schedule an appointment with an ophthalmologist, and compare the Acme-based diagnosis with the ophthalmologist's diagnosis. If the Acme test accurately predicts the ophthalmologist's diagnosis, we can conclude that the Acme test is a valid measure of color vision.

Similarly, if we are developing a test to assess reading readiness, we can ask, "Does knowledge of a child's score on our reading readiness test allow an accurate estimation of the child's actual readiness for subsequent instruction?" How do we know that our test really predicts reading readiness? Again, the first step is to find a valid criterion measure. In this case, the child's initial progress in reading can be used. Reading progress can be assessed by a reading achievement test (presumed to be valid) or by teacher judgments of reading ability or reading readiness at the time reading instruction was actually begun. If our reading readiness test has content validity and corresponds closely with either later teacher judgments of readiness or validly assessed reading skill, we can conclude that ours is a valid test of reading readiness.

Three aspects of criterion-related validity are extremely important. First, *"All measures of criteria should be described completely and accurately"* (APA et al., 1974, p. 33). Obviously, since the validity of the test is established by its relationship to a criterion, the criterion itself must be valid. The test author should present sufficient information to allow the test user to judge the adequacy of the criterion. *"A criterion measure should itself be studied for evidence of validity and that evidence should be presented in the* [test] *manual or report"* (APA et al., 1974, p. 34). Second, "The sample employed in a validity study and the conditions under which testing is done should be consistent with the recommended test use . . ." (APA et al., 1974, p. 36). The test authors must demonstrate that their test is valid not only for the recommended purposes of the test but also for the people who will be tested. Third, *"The* [test] *manual or research report should provide information on the appropriateness of or limits to the generalizability of validity information"* (APA et al., 1974, p. 35).

Construct Validity ✻

Construct validity refers to the extent to which a test measures a theoretical trait or characteristic. To validate a test of a construct, the test author must rely on indirect evidence and inference. The definition of the construct and the theory from which the construct is derived allow us to make certain predictions that can be confirmed or disconfirmed. In a real sense, one does not validate a test; one conducts experiments to demonstrate that the test *is not* a valid measure of the trait or construct. Continued inability to disconfirm the validity of a test, in effect, validates the test. For example, intellectual ability is generally believed to be developmental. One would hypothesize that, if we were to conduct an experiment, a test of intelligence would be correlated with chronological age. If a test of intelligence did not correlate with chronological age, it would cast serious doubt on the test as a measure of intelligence. (The experiment would disconfirm the test as a measure of intelligence.) However, the presence of a substantial correlation between chronological age and scores on the test does not confirm that the test is a measure of intelligence. Many other abilities correlate with chronological age (for example, achievement, perceptual abilities, and language skills). Gradually, one accumulates evidence that the test continues to act in the way that it would if it were a valid measure of the construct. As the research evidence accumulates, some claim to construct validity can be made.

Several types of evidence are generally brought to bear in research on construct validity. Correlation of test scores with chronological age is used with several types of tests. When tests claim to measure several different factors, factor analytic research is often conducted to learn if the test is really composed of different factors. Often, we expect differences in the behavior of individuals with different levels of the trait or characteristic. For example, a test to assess learning ability should be able to differentiate between fast and slow learners. One can predict, therefore, that the individuals who learn more in a given amount of time have more learning ability; that is, they would have higher scores on a measure of learning ability. If children with IQs of 125 on test X learn more material in one week than do children with IQs of 100 on test X, there would be a failure to disconfirm the test as a valid measure of learning ability. In that sense, there would be some evidence for the validity of the test. Other possible examples of this type of research are numerous. We would expect tests of intelligence to predict school achievement; the correlation between test X and school achievement does not mean that test X measures achievement. (Test X *could* measure achievement.) We would expect readiness tests to predict school achievement. If test Y does not predict school achievement, it probably is not a measure of readiness; if it does predict school achievement, it may be measuring any number of abilities or traits.

NONVALIDITY DATA

Information intended to document validity is often presented in test manuals and advertisements, but some of these data do not really establish the validity of the test. The following are examples of "nonvalidity" data—data that sound impressive but are not true indications of validity.

1. *Cash Validity*   Just because a test is a "big seller" does not imply that it is valid. The only thing that large sales guarantee is cash for the authors and publishers. Good tests may or may not sell well; poor tests may or may not sell well.
2. *Clinical Utility*   Unevaluated, uncontrolled clinical reports are simply testimonials. Testimonials about the practical utility of a test are not validity data. Only controlled experiments and evaluated investigations should be considered potentially useful in assessing a test's validity.
3. *Internal Consistency*   The internal consistency of a test (interitem or item-total correlations) is reliability information, not validity data. A high degree of internal consistency insures only that the test items are drawn from the same domain. That domain may or may not be the one the test is intended to measure. A reliable test may or may not be valid.

FACTORS AFFECTING VALIDITY

Whenever a test fails to measure what it purports to measure, validity is threatened. Consequently, any factor that results in measuring "something else" affects a test's validity. Unsystematic error (unreliability) and systematic error (bias) threaten validity.

Reliability

Reliability is a necessary but not a sufficient condition for valid measurement. The relationship between reliability and validity is expressed in equation 8.1. The empirically determined validity coefficient (r_{xy}) equals the correlation between true scores on the two variables ($r_{x(t)y(t)}$) multiplied by the square root of the product of the reliability coefficients of test X and test Y ($\sqrt{r_{xx}r_{yy}}$). Hence, the reliability of the test limits its potential validity. *All valid tests are reliable; no unreliable tests may be valid; reliable tests may or may not be valid.* Finally, the validity of a particular test can never exceed the reliability of that test. Unreliable tests measure error; valid tests measure the traits they are designed to measure.

$$r_{xy} = r_{x(t)y(t)}\sqrt{r_{xx}r_{yy}} \tag{8.1}$$

Systematic Bias

Method of Measurement

The method used to measure a skill or trait often determines what score a child will receive. A true score can be considered a composite of trait variance and method-of-measurement variance (Campbell & Fiske, 1959). To take just one example: Werner and Strauss (1941) conducted a series of experiments to study the figure-background perception of brain-injured and non-brain-injured retarded persons. They presented stimulus items tachistoscopically for a fraction of a second and asked their subjects to name what they saw. They found that brain-injured retarded persons responded more often to the background stimuli than did the non-brain-injured retarded persons. They concluded that brain injury results in figure-ground dysfunction. However, the method of testing (tachistoscopic presentation) and the trait to be tested (figure-ground perception) were confounded by the testing procedure. Rubin (1969) later demonstrated that under different testing procedures there were no differences between brain-injured and non-brain-injured retarded persons in figure-background responses. The differences between the findings of Strauss and Rubin are attributable to *how* figure-background perception was measured. It seems likely that Strauss was measuring perceptual speed because of his method of measurement. To the extent that trait or skill scores include variance attributable to method of measurement, these scores may lack validity.

Enabling Behaviors

Several behaviors are assumed in any testing situation. We must assume that the subject is fluent in the language in which the test is prepared and administered if there are any verbal components to the test directions or test responses. Yet in many states with substantial Spanish-speaking populations, students whose primary language is not English are tested in English. Intelligence testing in English of non-English-speaking children was sufficiently commonplace that a group of parents brought suit against a school district *(Diana* v. *State Board of Education).* Deaf children are routinely given the Performance subtests of the Wechsler intelligence scales (Levine, 1974) even though they cannot *hear* the directions. Children with extreme communication problems (speech impediments, for example) often are required to respond orally to test questions. Such obvious limitations or absences of enabling behaviors are frequently overlooked in testing situations even though they invalidate the test results.

Item Selection

Test items often presume that the subjects taking the test have had exposure to concepts and skills measured by the test. For example, standardized achievement tests presume that the students taking the tests have been exposed to similar curricula. If a teacher has not taught the content being tested, the results of the achievement test are invalid.

Administration Errors

Unless a test is administered according to the standardized procedures, the results are invalid. Suppose a teacher wished to demonstrate how effective her teaching was by administering an intelligence test and an achievement test to her class. She allows the children five minutes less than the standardized time limits on the intelligence test and five minutes more on the standardized achievement test. The result is that the children earn scores lower than their true intelligence (since they did not have enough time) and scores higher than their true achievement (since they had too much time). The apparent results, that slow children had learned more than anticipated, would not be valid.

Norms

Scores based on the performance of unrepresentative norms lead to incorrect estimates of relative standing in the general population. To the extent that the normative sample is systematically unrepresentative, in either central tendency or variability, the inferences based on such scores are incorrect and invalid.

SUMMARY

Validity is the only technical characteristic of a test in which we are interested. All other technical considerations, such as reliability, are subsumed under the issue of validity and are analyzed separately to simplify the issue of validity. We must know if a test measures what it purports to measure and if scores derived from the test are accurate. Adequate norms, reliability, and lack of bias are all necessary conditions for validity. None—separately or in total—is sufficient to guarantee validity.

When the necessary conditions for validity are met, systematic validation can proceed. The content may be inspected to see if each item is valid and to insure that all aspects of the domain are represented. If a standard or criterion of known validity is available, the test should be compared to that standard. In the absence of a known standard, construct validation should proceed. In this case, directional predictions are made based on the constructed trait; these predictions are empirically tested.

STUDY QUESTIONS

1. Why must test authors demonstrate validity for their tests?
2. What is the relationship between reliability and validity?

3. Identify three factors that must be considered in the establishment of content validity.

4. Ms. Wilson uses a new math curriculum to teach her class of third graders. She uses a traditional math test to assess pupil progress. All pupils score in the bottom quartile according to the test norms. What can Ms. Wilson legitimately conclude?

5. There are many tests whose manuals include absolutely no evidence as to validity. These tests are used in schools to make important educational decisions about children. Under what circumstances could such tests be used?

6. Test author G presents interitem correlation coefficients as evidence for the validity of his scale. To what extent are these coefficients evidence of validity?

7. Kim Ngo, a recent arrival from a Vietnamese orphanage, speaks no English. When she enrolls in a U.S. school, her intelligence is assessed by means of a verbal test that has English directions and requires English responses. Kim performs poorly on the test, earning an IQ of 37. The tester concludes that Kim is a trainable mentally retarded child and recommends placement in a special class. Identify two major errors in the interpretation of the test results.

8. Professor Johnson develops a test that he claims can be used to identify learning-disabled children who will profit from perceptual-motor training. What must he do to demonstrate that his test is valid?

ADDITIONAL READING

American Psychological Association, American Educational Research Association, & National Council on Measurement in Education. (1974). *Standards for educational and psychological tests.* Washington, DC: American Psychological Association.

Bagnato, S. (1982). Developmental scales and developmental curricula: Forging a linkage for early intervention. In J. T. Neisworth (Ed.), *Assessment in special education.* Rockville, MD: Aspen Systems.

Ghiselli, E. E. (1964). *Theory of psychological measurement.* New York: McGraw-Hill. (Chapter 11, pp. 335–369.)

Kazdin, A. (1982). *Single-case research designs.* New York: Oxford University Press. (Chapter 2: Behavioral assessment.)

PART 3

ASSESSMENT OF PROCESSES: DOMAINS SAMPLED AND REPRESENTATIVE TESTS

Part 3 is a description of the most common domains in which assessment of processes, or abilities, is conducted. In this part, we consider behaviors that represent one or more underlying hypothetical constructs, such as intelligence and oral language. The behaviors sampled by tests in the domains under consideration in this part allow educators to draw inferences about students' underlying abilities. Thus, for example, in assessment of processes, reading may be assessed to analyze a person's intellectual ability or expressive competence rather than to evaluate his or her word-recognition skills.

Each chapter focuses on a different process, and each is developed in a similar way. The chapter opens with an explanation of why the domain is assessed. We then provide a general overview of the components of the domain (that is, the behaviors that are usually assessed) and

discuss the more commonly used tests within the domain. Each chapter concludes with some suggestions for coping with problems in assessing the domain, followed by a general summary of chapter content.

We examine five factors in our evaluations of tests. First, we describe the general format of the test and the specific behaviors that the test is designed to sample. The descriptions allow the reader to evaluate the extent to which specific tests sample the domain. Second, we describe the kinds of scores that the test provides for the practitioner. This gives information about the meaning and interpretation of those scores. Third, we examine the standardization sample for each test. This enables the reader to judge—recalling the discussion in Chapter 6—the adequacy of the norm group and to evaluate the appropriateness of each test for use with specific populations of students. Fourth, we evaluate the evidence of reliability for each test using the standards set forth in Chapter 7. Fifth, for each device, we examine evidence of its validity and evaluate the adequacy of the evidence in light of the standards set forth in Chapter 8. Finally, there is a summary for each test.

Two principles guided our development of Part 3. First, we did not include all the available measures for each domain. Rather, we selected representative and commonly used devices in each area. Buros's *Mental Measurements Yearbooks* is an excellent source that provides reviews of standardized tests not reviewed here. These yearbooks are a compendium of critical test reviews by individuals who are authorities in assessment.

Second, in evaluating the technical adequacy of each test, we restricted our evaluation to information included in the test manuals. There were two major reasons for this decision. First, as stated in the *Standards for Educational and Psychological Tests,* test authors are responsible for providing all necessary technical information in their test manuals. The test authors must have some basis for claiming that their tests are valid. Therefore, we searched the manuals for the technical information that provides the support for the test authors' contentions. Second, an attempt to include the vast body of research literature on commonly used tests would have resulted in a multi-volume opus that would be impossible to publish as a current work. Entire books have been written on the subject of using and interpreting single tests. We urge our readers to peruse the literature and to examine the research that bears on tests in which they might be interested. We might add that test users also have a responsibility in this area.

CHAPTER 9

ASSESSMENT OF INTELLIGENCE: AN OVERVIEW

No other area of assessment has generated as much attention, controversy, and debate as "intelligence" testing. For centuries philosophers, psychologists, educators, and laymen have debated the meaning of intelligence. Numerous definitions of the term *intelligence* have been proposed, each definition serving as a stimulus for counterdefinitions and counterproposals. Several theories have been advanced to describe and explain intelligence and its development. The extent to which intelligence is genetically or environmentally determined has been of special concern. Genetic determinists, environmental determinists, and interactionists have all observed differences in the intelligence test performances of different populations of children. The interpretation of group differences in intelligence measurements and the practice of testing the intelligence of schoolchildren have been topics of recurrent controversy and debate, aired in professional journals, the popular press, and on television. In some instances the courts have acted to curtail or halt intelligence assessment in the public schools; in others the courts have defined what intelligence assessment must consist of. Debate and controversy have flourished about whether intelligence tests should be given, what intelligence tests measure, and how different levels of performance attained by different populations of children are to be explained.

No one, however, has seen a thing called intelligence. Rather, we observe differences in the ways people behave—either differences in everyday behavior in a variety of situations or differences in responses to standard stimuli or sets of stimuli; then we *infer* a construct called *intelligence.* In this sense, intelligence is an inferred entity, a term or construct we use to explain differences in present behavior and to predict differences in future behavior.

We have repeatedly stressed the fact that any test is a sample of behavior. So, too, intelligence tests are samples of behavior. Regardless of how an

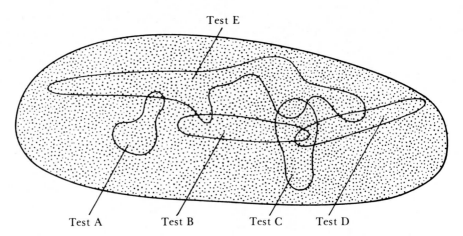

FIGURE 9.1   Intelligence tests as samples of behavior from a larger domain of behaviors

individual's performance is viewed and interpreted, intelligence tests and items on those tests simply sample behaviors. A variety of different kinds of behavior samplings are used to assess intelligence; in most cases, the kinds of behaviors sampled reflect a test author's conception of intelligence. In this chapter we review the kinds of behaviors sampled by intelligence tests with particular emphasis on the psychological demands of different test items as a function of pupil characteristics.

INTELLIGENCE TESTS AS SAMPLES OF BEHAVIOR

There is a hypothetical domain of items that could be used to assess intelligence. In practice, it is impossible to administer every item in the domain to a child whose intelligence we want to assess. The dots in Figure 9.1 represent different items in the domain of behaviors that could be used to assess intelligence. No two tests contain identical samples of behavior; some tests overlap in the kinds of behaviors they sample, and others do not. No test samples all possible behaviors in the domain. In Figure 9.1 we see that tests A and D sample different behaviors. Both tests assess some behaviors sampled by test E. None of the test samples all the possible behaviors in the domain.

The characterization of behaviors sampled by intelligence tests is complex. Some persons have, for example, argued that intelligence tests assess a student's capacity to profit from instruction, while others argue that such tests assess merely what has been learned; some have characterized intelligence tests as either verbal or nonverbal; some characterize intelligence tests as either culturally biased or culture fair. In actuality, nearly any contention regarding what it is that intelligence tests measure can be supported. The relative merit of competing opinions, theories, and contentions is primarily a function of the interaction between the characteristics of an individual and the psychological demands of items in an intelligence test. It is also a function of the stimulus and response requirements of the items.

There are many kinds of "nonverbal" behavior samples. A test might require children to point to objects in response to directions read by the examiner, to build block towers, to manipulate colored blocks in order to reproduce a design, or to copy symbols or designs on paper. Similarly, there are many kinds of "verbal" behavior samples. We could, for example, ask children factual questions, like "Who wrote *Huckleberry Finn*?" We could ask them to define words or to identify similarities and differences in words or objects. We could ask children to state actions they would take in specific social situations or ask them to repeat sequences of digits. Test items may be presented orally, or the test takers may have to read the items themselves.

Similar behaviors may be assessed in different ways. In assessing vocabulary, for example, the examiner may ask children to define words, to name pictures, to select a synonym of a stimulus word, or to point to pictures depicting words read by the examiner. All four kinds of assessments are called vocabulary tests, yet they sample *different* behaviors. The psychological demands of the items change with the ways the behavior is assessed.

In evaluating children's performances on intelligence tests, teachers, administrators, counselors, and diagnostic specialists must go beyond test names and scores to look at the kind or kinds of behaviors sampled on the test. They must be willing to question the ways test stimuli are presented to a child, to question the response requirements, and to evaluate the psychological demands placed on a child.

THE EFFECT OF PUPIL CHARACTERISTICS ON ASSESSMENT OF INTELLIGENCE

Acculturation is the most important characteristic in evaluating a child's performance on intelligence tests. *Acculturation,* as we have stated earlier, refers to a child's particular set of background experiences and opportunities to learn in both formal and informal educational settings. This, in turn, depends on the experiences available in the child's environment (that is, culture) and the length of time the child has had to assimilate those experiences. The culture in which a child lives and the length of time that child has lived in that culture effectively determine the psychological demands a test item presents. Simply knowing the kind of behavior sampled by a test is not enough, for the same test item may create different psychological demands for different children.

Suppose, for example, that we assess intelligence by asking children to tell how hail and sleet are alike. Children may fail the item for very different reasons. A child who does not know what hail and sleet are stands little chance of telling how hail and sleet are alike. He will fail the item simply because he does not know the meanings of the words. Another child may know what hail is and what sleet is but fail the item because she is unable to integrate these two words into a conceptual category (precipitation). The psychological demand of the item changes as a function of the children's acculturation. For the child who has not learned the meanings of the words, the item assesses vocabulary. For the child who knows the meanings of the words, the item is a generalization task.

In considering children's performance on intelligence tests, we need to know how acculturation affects test performance. Items on intelligence tests range along a continuum from items that sample fundamental psychological behaviors relatively unaffected by learning history to items that sample primarily learned behavior. To determine exactly what is being assessed, we need to know the essential background of the child. Consider for a moment the following item from the 11-year level of the 1972 Stanford-Binet Intelligence Scale:

Donald went walking in the woods. He saw a pretty little animal that he tried to take home for a pet. It got away from him, but when he got home his family immediately burned all his clothes. Why?[1]

For a student who knows what a skunk is and what a skunk does when approached by a person, the item can assess comprehension, abstract reasoning, and problem-solving skill. The student who does not know what a skunk is or what a skunk does may very well fail the item. In this case, failure is due not to an inability to comprehend or solve the problem but to a deficiency in background experience.

Similarly, we could ask a child to identify the seasons of the year. The experiences available in children's environments are reflected in the way they respond to this item. Children from central Illinois, who experience four discernibly different climatic conditions, may well respond, "Summer, fall, winter, and spring." Children from central Pennsylvania, who also experience four discernibly different climatic conditions but who live in an environment where hunting is prevalent, often respond, "Buck season, doe season, rabbit season, and squirrel season." Response differences are a function of experiential differences. Within specific cultures, both responses are logical and appropriate; only one is *scored* as correct.

Items on intelligence tests also sample different behaviors as a function of the age of the child assessed. Age and acculturation are positively related; older children in general have had more opportunities to acquire the skills assessed

1. From *Stanford-Binet Intelligence Scale, 1972 Norms Edition* (pp. 98–99) by L. Terman and M. Merrill, 1973, Chicago: The Riverside Publishing Co. Copyright 1973. Reproduced by permission of the Publisher, The Riverside Publishing Company, 8420 Bryn Mawr Ave., Chicago, IL 60631.

by intelligence tests. The performances of 5-year-old children on an item requiring them to tell how a cardinal, a bluejay, and a swallow are alike are almost entirely a function of their knowledge of the word meanings. Most college students know the meanings of the three words; for them the item assesses primarily their ability to identify similarities and integrate words or objects into a conceptual category. As children get older, they have increasing opportunity to acquire "the more abstruse elements of the collective intelligence of a culture" (Horn, 1965, p. 4).

The interaction between acculturation and the behavior sampled determines the psychological demands of an intelligence-test item. For this reason, it is impossible to define exactly what intelligence tests assess. *Identical test items actually place different psychological demands on different children.* Thirteen kinds of behaviors sampled by intelligence tests are described in the next section of this chapter. For the sake of illustration, let us assume that there are only three discrete sets of background experiences (this is a very conservative estimate; there are probably many times this number in the United States alone). To further simplify our example, let us consider only the thirteen kinds of behaviors sampled by intelligence tests rather than the millions of items that could be used to sample each of the thirteen kinds. With these very restrictive conditions, there are still $(mn)!/m!n!$ possible interactions between behavior samples and types of acculturation. This very restrictive estimate produces more than 1.35×10^{32} interactions! No wonder there is controversy about what intelligence tests measure. They measure more things than we can conceive of; they measure different things for different children.

BEHAVIORS SAMPLED BY INTELLIGENCE TESTS

Regardless of the interpretation of measured intelligence, it is a fact that intelligence tests simply sample behaviors. This section describes the kinds of behaviors sampled.

Discrimination

Intelligence test items that sample skill in discrimination usually present a variety of stimuli and ask the student to find the one that is different from all the others. Figural, symbolic, or semantic discrimination may be assessed. Figure 9.2 illustrates items assessing discrimination: items a and b assess discrimination of figures; items c and d assess symbolic discrimination; items e and f assess semantic discrimination. In each case, the student must identify the item that is different from the others. The psychological demand of the items, however, differs depending on the student's age and particular set of background experiences.

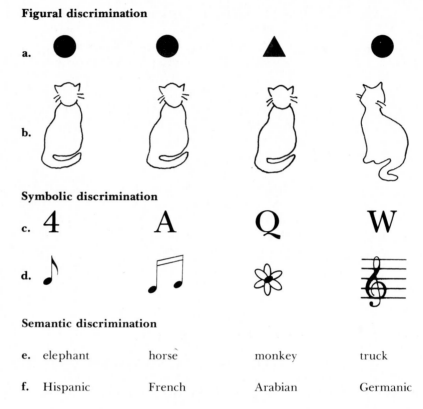

FIGURE 9.2   Items that assess figural, symbolic, and semantic discrimination

Generalization

Items assessing generalization present a stimulus and ask the student to identify which of several response possibilities goes with the stimulus. Again, the content of the items may be figural, symbolic, or semantic, while the difficulty may range from simple matching to a more difficult type of classification. Figure 9.3 illustrates several items assessing generalization. In each case, the student is given a stimulus element and required to identify the one that is like it or that goes with it.

Motor Behavior

Many items on intelligence tests require a motor response. The intellectual level of very young children, for example, is often assessed by items requiring them to throw objects, walk, follow moving objects with their eyes, demonstrate a pincer grasp in picking up objects, build block towers, and place

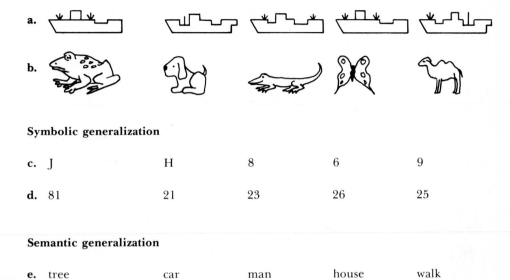

Figural generalization

Symbolic generalization

c. J   H   8   6   9

d. 81   21   23   26   25

Semantic generalization

e. tree   car   man   house   walk

f. salvia   flashlight frog   tulip   banana

FIGURE 9.3   Items that assess figural, symbolic, and semantic generalization

geometric forms in a recessed-form board. Most motor items at higher age levels are actually visual-motor items. The student may be required to copy geometric designs, trace paths through a maze, or reconstruct designs from memory. Obviously, since motor responses can be required for items assessing understanding and conceptualization, many items assess motor behavior at the same time that they assess other behaviors.

General Information

Items on intelligence tests sometimes require a student to answer specific factual questions, such as, "In what direction would you travel if you were to go from Poland to Argentina?" and "What is the cube root of 8?" Essentially, such items are like the kinds of items in achievement tests; they assess primarily what has been learned.

Vocabulary

Many different kinds of test items are used to assess vocabulary. The student must name pictures in some cases and in others must point to objects in

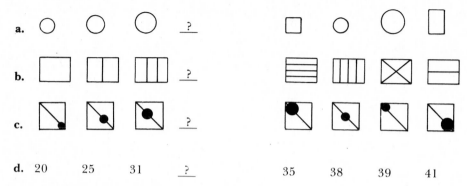

FIGURE 9.4 Items that assess sequencing skill

response to words read by the examiner. Some vocabulary items require the student to produce oral definitions of words, whereas others call for reading definitions and selecting one of several words to match the definition. Some tests score a student's definitions of words as simply pass or fail; others use a weighted scoring system to reflect the degree of abstraction used in defining words. The Wechsler Intelligence Scale for Children–Revised, for example, assigns zero points to incorrect definitions, one point to definitions that are descriptive (an orange is round) or functional (an orange is to eat), and two points to more abstract definitions (an orange is a citrus fruit).

Induction

Induction items present a series of examples and require the student to induce a governing principle. For example, the student is given a magnet and several different cloth, wooden, and metal objects and is asked to try to pick up the objects with the magnet. After several trials the student is asked to state a governing rule or principle about the kinds of objects magnets can pick up.

Comprehension

There are three kinds of items used to assess comprehension. The student gives evidence of comprehension of directions, printed material, or societal customs and mores. In some instances, the examiner presents a specific situation and asks what actions the student would take (for example, "What would you do if you saw a train approaching a washed-out bridge?"). In other cases, the examiner reads paragraphs to a student and then asks specific questions about the content of the paragraphs. In still other instances, the student is asked specific questions like "Why should we keep promises?"

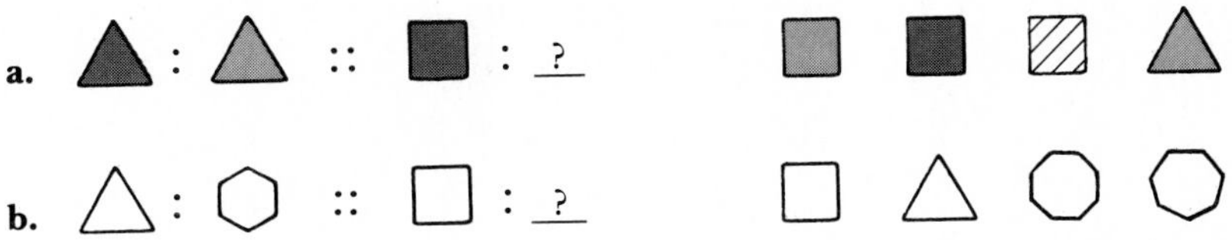

c. man : boy :: woman : ? — girl mother daughter aunt

d. tapeworm : platyhelminthes :: starfish: ? — echinoderm mollusca water porifera

e. variance : standard deviation :: 25 : ? — 4 5 625 747

FIGURE 9.5 Analogies items

Sequencing

Items assessing sequencing consist of a series of stimuli that have a progressive relationship among them, and the student must identify a response that continues the relationship. Four sequencing items are illustrated in Figure 9.4.

Detail Recognition

In general, not many tests or test items assess detail recognition. Those that do evaluate the completeness and detail with which a student solves problems. For example, certain drawing tests, such as the Goodenough-Harris, evaluate a student's drawings of a person on the basis of inclusion of detail. The more details in a student's drawing, the more credit the student earns. In other instances, items require a student to count the blocks in pictured piles of blocks in which some of the blocks are not directly visible, to copy geometric designs, or to identify missing parts in pictures. To do so correctly, the student must attend to detail in the stimulus drawings and reflect this attention to detail in making responses.

Analogies

"A is to B as C is to __" is the usual form for analogies items. Element A is related to element B. The student must identify the response that has the same relationship to C as B has to A. Figure 9.5 illustrates several different analogies items.

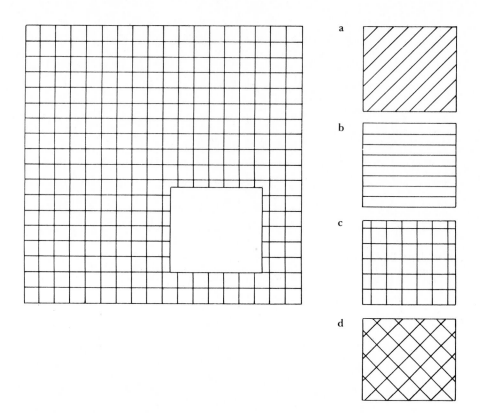

FIGURE 9.6   A pattern-completion item

Abstract Reasoning

A variety of items on intelligence tests sample abstract reasoning ability. The Stanford-Binet Intelligence Scale, for example, presents absurd verbal statements and pictures and asks the student to identify the absurdity. It also includes a series of proverbs whose essential meanings the student must state. In the Stanford-Binet and other scales, arithmetic-reasoning problems are often thought to assess abstract reasoning.

Memory

Several different kinds of tasks assess memory: repetition of sequences of orally presented digits, reproduction of geometric designs from memory, verbatim repetition of sentences, and reconstruction of the essential meaning of paragraphs or stories. Simply saying that an item assesses memory is too simplistic.

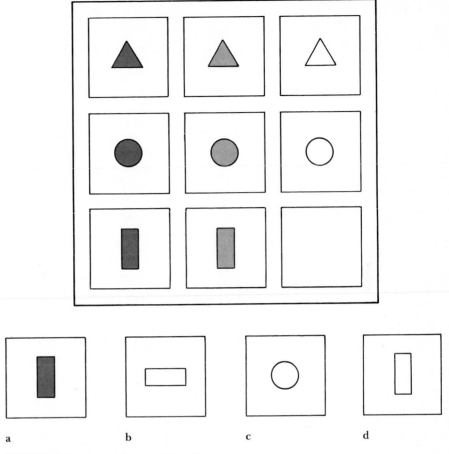

FIGURE 9.7   A matrix-completion item

We need to ask, "Memory for what?" The psychological demand of a memory task changes in relation to both the method of assessment and the meaningfulness of the material to be recalled.

Pattern Completion

Some tests and test items require a student to select from several possibilities the one that supplies the missing part of a pattern or matrix. Figures 9.6 and 9.7 illustrate two different completion items. The item in Figure 9.6 requires identification of a missing part in a pattern. The item in Figure 9.7 calls for identification of the response that completes the matrix by continuing the horizontal, vertical, and diagonal sequences.

SUMMARY

The practice of intellectual assessment of children is currently marked by controversy. However, much of that controversy could be set aside if intelligence tests were viewed appropriately. Intelligence tests are simply samples of behavior. And different intelligence tests sample different behaviors. For that reason, it is wrong to speak of a person's IQ. Instead, we can refer only to a person's IQ on a specific test. An IQ on the Stanford-Binet Intelligence Scale is not derived from the same samples of behaviors as an IQ on any other intelligence test. Because the behavior samples are different for different tests, one must always ask, "IQ *on what test?*"

The same test may make different psychological demands on test takers, depending on their ages and acculturation. Test results mean different things for different students. It is imperative that we be especially aware of the relationship between a person's acculturation and the acculturation of the norm group to which that person is compared.

Used appropriately, intelligence tests can provide information that can lead to enhancement of individual opportunity and protection of the rights of students. Used inappropriately, they can restrict opportunity and rights.

The next two chapters review commonly used group-administered and individually administered intelligence tests, with particular reference to the kinds of behaviors sampled by those tests and their technical adequacy.

STUDY QUESTIONS

1. How would you demonstrate that a particular test item measured intelligence?
2. Describe at least three kinds of behaviors sampled by intelligence tests.
3. Bill Jones fails an item requiring him to state the difference between an optimist and a pessimist. Give two explanations for Bill's failure.
4. The school psychologist tells you that Emily Andrews has an IQ of 89. What additional information do you need before you are able to know the meaning of the score?
5. Using the categorization of behavior samplings described in this chapter, identify the kind or kinds of behaviors sampled by the following test items.
   a. How many legs does an octopus have?
   b. In what way are *first* and *last* alike?
   c. Find the one that is different: (1) table (2) bed (3) pillow (4) chair
   d. Who wrote *Macbeth*?
   e. Window is to sill as door is to _____. (1) knob (2) entrance (3) threshold (4) pane
   f. Define: *hieroglyphic.*
   g. Identify the one that comes next: 3, 6, 9, __. (1) 12 (2) 11 (3) 18 (4) 15

6. Public Law 94-142 requires nondiscriminatory assessment of handicapped children. How can you demonstrate that a test is nondiscriminatory?

ADDITIONAL READING

Bersoff, D. N. (1973). Silk purses into sows' ears: The decline of psychological testing and a suggestion for its redemption. *American Psychologist, 10,* 892–899.

Cancro, R. (Ed.). (1980). *Intelligence: Genetic and environmental contributions.* New York: Grune and Stratton.

Cronbach, L. J. (1975). Five decades of public controversy over mental testing. *American Psychologist, 30,* 1–14.

McClelland, D. (1973). Testing for competence rather than for "intelligence." *American Psychologist, 1,* 1–14.

CHAPTER 10

ASSESSMENT OF INTELLIGENCE: INDIVIDUAL TESTS

In Chapter 9 we discussed the various kinds of behaviors sampled by intelligence tests, indicating that different tests sample different behaviors. In this chapter we will review the most commonly used individually administered intelligence tests with special reference to the kinds of behaviors they sample and to their technical adequacy.

Few individual intelligence tests can or should be administered by classroom teachers. Yet, over the last few years, test developers have developed intelligence tests with the specific intent that teachers or other nonpsychologists would be able to administer them. For example, the Test of Nonverbal Intelligence is specifically designed to be given by teachers. The Slosson Intelligence Test is described as equivalent to the Stanford-Binet Intelligence Scale, yet it can be given by people with no formal training in assessment. You will recall that one of the basic assumptions underlying psychoeducational assessment is that the person who uses tests is adequately trained to administer, score, and interpret them. The correct administration, scoring, and interpretation of individual intelligence tests is complex. Such tests should be used only by licensed or certified psychologists, who have specific training in their use.

Three kinds of individually administered intelligence tests are reviewed in this chapter. First, we review the most commonly used global measures of intelligence—the Stanford-Binet Intelligence Scale, the three Wechsler scales, the Slosson Intelligence Test, and the McCarthy Scales of Children's Abilities. In general, these tests sample the thirteen different kinds of behavior described in Chapter 9.

The second section of this chapter reviews the most commonly used picture vocabulary tests, instruments that assess receptive vocabulary but yield IQs.

Many children have handicaps (for example, blindness, deafness, and physical handicaps) that interfere with their capability to respond to traditional general intelligence tests. This fact has led several test authors to develop individually administered tests designed to assess the intelligence of blind, deaf, physically handicapped, and multiply handicapped persons. In a sense, the old adage "Necessity is the mother of invention" applies to these devices. The third section of this chapter is a review of individually administered tests designed for use with special populations of children.

WHY DO WE GIVE INDIVIDUAL INTELLIGENCE TESTS?

Individually administered intelligence tests are most frequently used for making educational placement decisions. State special education standards typically specify that the collection of data about intellectual functioning must be included in the decision-making process for placement decisions and that these data must come from individual intellectual evaluation by a certified psychologist.

GENERAL INTELLIGENCE TESTS

Stanford-Binet Intelligence Scale

The Stanford-Binet Intelligence Scale is the grandfather of all intelligence tests. The original Binet scales were developed by Alfred Binet in 1905 following a request by the minister of public instruction in Paris, France, to devise a method of differentiating between normal and mentally retarded children. Binet, in collaboration with Theodore Simon, constructed the Binet-Simon scale. In 1908 the scale was revised by grouping items according to age and the concept of *mental age* (MA) was introduced. The Binet-Simon scale was subsequently revised in 1911. In 1916 Louis Terman revised and extended the scale for use in the United States, entitling it the Stanford Revision and Extension of the Binet-Simon Intelligence Scale (Sattler, 1974).

The 1960 version of the Stanford-Binet Intelligence Scale was still an age scale; items were grouped according to age level (that is, an item at the 10-year level is typically answered correctly by the majority of ten-year-olds). The

1972 normative edition of the Stanford-Binet (Terman & Merrill, 1973) is the third revision of the test that was developed in 1916 and revised in 1937 and 1960. The 1972 edition of the Stanford-Binet was developed by renorming the 1960 edition.

In the process of renorming, a chief characteristic of the 1960 scale, placement of items in terms of the age of children passing the items, was lost. In the 1960 edition and in earlier editions, an item was placed, for example, at the 8-year level because the majority of 8-year-old children responded correctly to the item. In renorming the test, the placement of items was not changed, but the proportion of children passing the items did change. Salvia, Ysseldyke, and Lee (1975) discussed the potential difficulties for interpretation resulting from norm changes without changing test content. They illustrated that an average 10-year, 11-month-old child earned a mental age of 10 years, 11 months, on the 1960 Binet; but the "average" 10-year, 11-month-old child earned a mental age of 11 years, 5 months on the 1972 edition. In other words, renorming has produced a test in which children must perform above age level to earn average IQs; the items are no longer appropriately "age-placed."

The Stanford-Binet includes items ranging in difficulty from the 2-year level to the superior-adult level, but characterization of the kinds of behaviors sampled is difficult. Behavior samples change as a function of age; a variety of behaviors are sampled at each age level, and some behaviors are sampled at several age levels. In general, the Stanford-Binet stresses verbal skills and responses, although items at the early age levels require predominantly motor responses. The Binet probably represents the best cross-section of the behavior samples described and discussed in Chapter 9. Except for very young children (those 2 to 5 years of age), all thirteen behaviors discussed in Chapter 9 are sampled either singly or in combination in the assessment of intelligence. Several systems have been developed to classify the kinds of behaviors sampled by the Stanford-Binet. Meeker (1969) used Guilford's (1967) "Structure of the Intellect" model to classify items on the Stanford-Binet. Sattler (1965) presented a classification system that identifies seven types of items: language, memory, conceptual thinking, reasoning, numerical reasoning, visual-motor, and social intelligence. Valett (1964) classified Stanford-Binet items into six categories: general comprehension, visual-motor ability, arithmetic reasoning, memory and concentration, vocabulary and verbal fluency, and judgment and reasoning. The three classification systems were developed in an effort to simplify interpretation of the Stanford-Binet. Similarly, although never formally done, items could be classified on the basis of the thirteen kinds of behavior samplings described in Chapter 9.

The publishers of the Stanford-Binet have published three informative booklets regarding use of the test. These are entitled *How Should the Stanford-Binet Be Used?*, *How Did the Stanford-Binet Come About?*, and *Social Concerns and the Stanford-Binet* (Munday & Rosenberg, 1979).

Scores

Two scores, an MA and a deviation IQ ($\bar{X} = 100$, $S = 16$), are obtained from the Stanford-Binet. Only those items between a basal and a ceiling are administered to each individual. A *basal* is defined as "that level at which all tests are passed which just precedes the level where the first failure occurs" (Terman & Merrill, 1973, p. 60). A *ceiling* is defined as the maximal level of the test, the lowest age level at which an individual fails all items. A specified number of months' credit is earned for each item passed. It is assumed that an individual passes all items below the basal and fails all items above the ceiling. The number of months' credit is added to get a mental age. Tables in the test manual are used to convert MAs to deviation IQs.

Norms

The 1972 normative edition of the Stanford-Binet was standardized on approximately 2,100 subjects. A "representative sample" of approximately one hundred individuals was tested at each Stanford-Binet age level. The publisher of the Stanford-Binet had previously standardized the Cognitive Abilities Test. The scores earned on the Cognitive Abilities Test were used as the principal stratifying variable in selection of the standardization sample for the Stanford-Binet. The Cognitive Abilities Test was originally standardized on 20,000 subjects per grade, selected on the basis of community size, geographic region, and socioeconomic status. The Cognitive Abilities Test, however, had been standardized only on subjects in grades 3 through 12. In order to get subjects younger than 8 and older than 17 for the Binet standardization, siblings of those in the larger standardization group were selected.

There are no data in the 1973 Stanford-Binet manual identifying the demographic characteristics of subjects in the 1972 normative sample. The test was standardized in only seven communities.

Reliability

There are no data regarding the reliability of the 1972 Stanford-Binet. There is an implicit assumption that the 1972 normative edition is reliable because earlier editions of the test are reliable. Internal-consistency data are reported for the 1960 Stanford-Binet, a revision based on selection of items from the 1937 edition. Reliability of the Stanford-Binet is still based on the performances of individuals in 1937.

The Wechsler Scales

Three different measures of intelligence have been constructed by David Wechsler. Wechsler summarized his views on the concept of intelligence by stating that "intelligence is the overall capacity of an individual to understand and cope with the world around him" (Wechsler, 1974, p. 5). Wechsler states that his definition of intelligence differs from the conceptions of others in two important respects:

(1) It conceives of intelligence as an overall or *global* entity; that is, a multidetermined and multifaceted entity rather than an independent, uniquely defined trait.
(2) It avoids singling out any ability (e.g., abstract reasoning), however esteemed as crucial or overwhelmingly important. In particular, it avoids equating general intelligence with intellectual ability. (p. 5)

Validity

Validity data are also lacking for the 1972 normative edition. Once again, there is an assumption that the 1972 Stanford-Binet is valid because earlier editions were valid.

Summary

Although the Stanford-Binet has often been acclaimed as *the* intelligence test, the most recent edition of the test has questionable merit. The device has a long history and has been generally well accepted. However, the 1972 edition was standardized on subjects never adequately described in the manual. There are no reliability or validity data included in the manual for the 1972 normative edition. In our opinion, the authors of the Stanford-Binet need to provide sufficient data to warrant the continued faith that professionals place in this device.

The original Wechsler scale, the Wechsler-Bellevue Intelligence Scale (1939), designed to assess the intelligence of adults, was revised in 1955 and called the Wechsler Adult Intelligence Scale (WAIS). Its present form is called the Wechsler Adult Intelligence Scale–Revised (WAIS–R). In 1949, Wechsler developed the Wechsler Intelligence Scale for Children (WISC). This scale was revised and restandardized in 1974; its present form is called the Wechsler Intelligence Scale for Children–Revised (WISC–R). In 1967, Wechsler developed a downward extension of the WISC, the Wechsler Preschool and Primary Scale of Intelligence (WPPSI). Although the three scales are similar in form and content, they are distinct scales designed for use with persons at different age levels. The WAIS–R is designed for use

TABLE 10.1 Subtests of the Three Wechsler Scales

	WAIS–R	WISC–R	WPPSI
Verbal subtests			
Information	X	X	X
Comprehension	X	X	X
Similarities	X	X	X
Arithmetic	X	X	X
Vocabulary	X	X	X
Digit Span	X	S[b]	
Sentences			S
Performance subtests			
Picture Completion	S	X	X
Picture Arrangement	X	X	
Block Design	X	X	X
Object Assembly	X	X	
Coding[a]	X	X	X
Mazes		S	X
Geometric Design			X

[a]Called Digit Symbol on the WAIS–R and Animal House on the WPPSI.
[b]S's in the table indicate that although the subtest is included in the scale, it is considered a supplementary subtest and was not used in establishing IQ tables.

with individuals over 16 years of age; the WISC–R is designed to assess the intelligence of persons 6 through 16 years of age; the WPPSI is used with children ages 4 through 6½. All three scales are point scales; all three include both verbal and performance subtests. A special edition of the WISC–R, standardized on deaf and hearing-impaired students, is published by Gallaudet College. Subtests of the three Wechsler scales are summarized in Table 10.1.

Although the Wechsler scales differ in terms of age-level appropriateness, they sample similar behaviors. Descriptions of the behaviors sampled by each of the verbal and performance subtests follows; differences in format among the three scales are noted where appropriate.

Information The Information subtest assesses ability to answer specific factual questions. The content is learned; it consists of information that a person is expected to have acquired in both formal and informal educational settings.

Comprehension The Comprehension subtest assesses ability to comprehend verbal directions or to understand specific customs and mores.

Similarities This subtest requires identification of similarities or commonalities in superficially unrelated verbal stimuli.

Arithmetic This subtest assesses ability to solve problems requiring the application of arithmetic operations. Individual items range from relatively simple counting tasks on the WPPSI to conceptually and computationally more difficult problems on the WISC–R and the WAIS.

Vocabulary Items on the vocabulary subtest assess ability to define words.

Digit Span This subtest assesses immediate recall of orally presented digits.

Sentences   This subtest is included only in the WPPSI. It assesses ability to repeat sentences verbatim.

Picture Completion   This subtest assesses the ability to identify missing parts in pictures.

Picture Arrangement   The Picture Arrangement subtest assesses comprehension, sequencing, and identification of relationships by requiring a person to place pictures in sequence to produce a logically correct story.

Block Design   This subtest assesses ability to manipulate blocks in order to reproduce a visually presented stimulus design.

Object Assembly   This subtest assesses ability to place disjointed puzzle pieces together to form complete objects.

Coding   This subtest assesses the ability to associate certain symbols with others and to copy them on paper. The WPPSI uses the Animal House subtest in place of the Coding subtest. Instead of copying symbols on paper, the child must associate certain colored cubes with specific animals and match them.

Mazes   The Mazes subtest assesses ability to trace a path through progressively more difficult mazes.

Geometric Design   This subtest assesses ability to copy geometric designs. It appears on only the WPPSI.

Scores

Raw scores obtained on the three Wechsler scales are transformed to scaled scores with a mean of 10 and a standard deviation of 3. The scaled scores for verbal subtests, performance subtests, and all subtests combined are added and then transformed to obtain verbal, performance, and full-scale IQs. IQs for the Wechsler scales are deviation IQs with a mean of 100 and a standard deviation of 15. For the WPPSI and the WISC–R, but not for the WAIS–R, raw scores may be transformed to test ages. Test ages represent the average performance on each of the subtests by individuals of specific ages.

The Wechsler intelligence scales employ a differential scoring system for some of the subtests. Responses for the Information, Digit Span, Sentences, Picture Completion, and Geometric Designs subtests are scored pass-fail. A weighted scoring system is used for the Comprehension, Similarities, and Vocabulary subtests. Incorrect responses receive a score of zero, lower-level or lower-quality responses a score of one, while more abstract responses are assigned a score of two. The remainder of the subtests are timed. Individuals who complete the tasks in relatively short periods of time receive more credit. These differential weightings of responses must be given special consideration, especially when the timed tests are used with children who demonstrate motoric impairments that interfere with the speed of response.

Norms

All three Wechsler intelligence scales were standardized by selecting stratified samples and having individual examiners around the country administer the tests to specified kinds of individuals.

The WAIS–R was standardized "based on groups considered representative of the United States adult population" (Wechsler, 1981, p. 16). A stratified sampling plan based on age, sex, race, geographic region, occupation, education, and urban-rural residence was used. Proportions of specific kinds of individuals were

TABLE 10.2 Split-half Reliabilities for Subtests of the Three Wechsler Scales

	WISC–R	WPPSI	WAIS–R
Verbal subtests			
Information	.67–.90	.77–.84	.87–.91
Comprehension	.69–.87	.78–.84	.77–.90
Similarities	.74–.87	.82–.85	.78–.87
Arithmetic	.69–.81	.78–.86	.73–.87
Vocabulary	.70–.92	.72–.87	.94–.96
Digit Span	.71–.84[a]	—	.70–.89[a]
Sentences	—	.81–.88	—
Verbal IQ	.91–.96	.93–.95	.95–.97
Performance subtests			
Picture Completion	.68–.85	.81–.86	.71–.89
Picture Arrangement	.69–.78	—	.66–.82
Block Design	.80–.90	.76–.88	.83–.89
Object Assembly	.63–.76	—	.52–.73
Coding	.63–.80[a]	.62–.84[a]	.73–.86[a]
Mazes	.62–.82	.82–.91	—
Geometric Design	—	.77–.87	—
Performance IQ	.89–.91	.91–.95	.86–.94
Full-scale IQ	.95–.96	.96–.97	.96–.98

[a]Test-retest reliability.

included commensurate with their representation in the 1950 census. The WAIS–R was standardized on 1,880 adults, and extensive tables in the manual compare the percentage of the U.S. population to the percentage of specific kinds of individuals in the norms.

The WISC–R was standardized on 2,200 children ages 6½ to 16½. The standardization group was stratified on the basis of age, sex, race, geographic region, occupation of head of household, and urban-rural residence according to 1970 U.S. census information.

The WPPSI was standardized on 1,200 children stratified according to the 1960 census on the basis of age, sex, geographic region, urban-rural residence, "color," and father's occupation.

Reliability

Internal-consistency reliability is reported for the WAIS–R, WISC–R, and WPPSI in the forms of split-half reliability coefficients. The reliabilities differ for the specific subtests and the age levels on which the coefficients are based. Ranges of reliability are reported for the three scales in Table 10.2. Reliabilities for the separate subtests are reliabilities of scaled scores, whereas reliabilities for verbal, performance, and full-scale IQs are reliabilities for the IQs. Reliabilities for the Digit Symbol (coding) subtest on the WAIS–R, the Digit Span and Coding subtests of the WISC–R, and the Coding subtest (Animal House) of the WPPSI are test-retest reliabilities. Test-retest reliabilities are reported for all subtests of the WISC–R in the test manual and range from .63 to .95.

Validity

No evidence for the validity of the WAIS–R is included in the manual. Instead, the author argues that: (1) the WAIS–R and WAIS overlap considerably in content, (2) there are many studies of the validity of the WAIS, (3) the WAIS–R will no doubt correlate with other measures of global intelligence as well as the WAIS did. In fact, 20 percent of the items on the WAIS–R are new items. It cannot be asserted that the WAIS–R is valid because the Wechsler-Bellevue and WAIS were valid.

Three concurrent validity studies were used to ascertain the relationship between performance on the WISC–R and on other measures of intelligence. In the first study, fifty 6-year-old children were administered both the WISC–R and the WPPSI. The WISC–R full-scale IQ and the WPPSI full-scale IQ had a .82 correlation. Individual verbal subtests correlated more highly with the WPPSI verbal IQ than with the WPPSI performance IQ. Similarly, individual performance subtests correlated more highly with the WPPSI performance IQ than with the WPPSI verbal IQ. In a second study, forty children aged 16 years, 11 months, were given the WISC–R and the WAIS; the full-scale IQs on the two devices had a .95 correlation. Verbal IQs on the two devices were intercorrelated .96; performance IQs, .83. A third study was conducted to compare performance on the WISC–R with performance on the Stanford-Binet Intelligence Scale. Small samples of children (twenty-seven to thirty-three) at four ages were given both tests. Average correlations between Stanford-Binet IQs and WISC–R verbal, performance, and full-scale IQs were .71, .60, and .73, respectively.

Data on validity of the WPPSI are limited to one study of ninety-eight students in a single school in San Jose, California. WPPSI performance was correlated with performance on the Peabody Picture Vocabulary Test (old edition), the Pictorial Test of Intelligence, and the 1960 Stanford-Binet. Moderate correlations were reported. No other validity data are reported in the manual.

Summary

The three Wechsler intelligence scales (WAIS–R, WISC–R, WPPSI) are widely used individually administered intelligence tests. Although they are designed for different age levels, the three scales are similar in content and format. Evidence for the reliability of the three scales is good. Evidence for validity, as presented in the manuals, is either nonexistent (WAIS–R) or very limited (WISC–R and WPPSI).

Slosson Intelligence Test

The Slosson Intelligence Test (SIT) (Slosson, 1971) is a relatively short screening test used to estimate Stanford-Binet IQs. The test includes many items that appear in the Stanford-Binet, and the authors of the 1981 norms book for the SIT state that "the SIT and the SB are in most respects alternate forms of the same test instrument" (Armstrong & Jensen, 1981, p. 14). The test is merely designed to generate a number—an estimate of Stanford-Binet IQ. Whereas the Stanford-Binet is designed to give an examiner both a quantitative and qualitative picture of intellectual functioning, the SIT is designed merely to yield a score—a quantitative index of intellectual functioning.

The SIT is designed to be administered by teachers, guidance counselors, principals, psychologists, school nurses, and "other responsible persons who, in their professional work, often need to evaluate an individual's mental ability" (Slosson, 1971, p. iii). The author does not report an age range of individuals who may be tested with the Slosson. Items range from the .5 month level to the 27-year level; the 1981 standardization was on people from 27 months to 17 years, 2 months. Apparently, the author

(Slosson, 1971) believes the test is appropriate for nearly anyone, as there are directions in the manual for testing infants, those who have "reading handicaps" or "language handicaps," the blind, the hard of hearing, those with organic impairments, the emotionally disturbed, and the "deprived." There are, though, no data on the use of the test with these groups. Behaviors sampled by the SIT include most of the behaviors described and discussed in Chapter 9.

Scores

Raw scores for the SIT may be transformed to deviation IQs with a mean of 100 and a standard deviation of 16. To do so, the examiner does not use the procedures recommended in the manual, but uses the publication *Slosson Intelligence Test: 1981 Norms Tables* (Armstrong & Jensen, 1981). IQs may also be expressed as percentile ranks, normal curve equivalents, *T*-scores, or stanines.

Norms

The normative sample for the SIT consisted of a potpourri of individuals who are described by Slosson (1971) as follows:

The children and adults used in obtaining comparative results came from both urban and rural populations in New York State. The referrals came from cooperative nursery schools, public, parochial and private schools, from junior and senior high school. They came from gifted as well as retarded classes—white, negro, and some American Indian. Some came from a city Youth Bureau, some from a Home for Boys. The very young children resided in an infant home. The adults came from the general population, from various professional groups, from a university graduate school, from a state school for the retarded and from a county jail.

Many of these individuals were difficult to test as they were disturbed, negativistic, withdrawn, and many had reading difficulties. Some suffered from

neurological disorders or other defects. The only cases which were excluded from this study were individuals who could not speak English. (p. iv)

Items were selected on the basis of the performance of this group. Between 1968 and 1977 a sample of individuals was given both the Stanford-Binet Intelligence Scale and the SIT in order to develop a new set of norms for the SIT. The sample comprised 1,109 people, ages 27 months to 17 years, 2 months. All were from New England states and are not further described. Thus, in using the 1981 norms we know only that the individuals we test are being compared to an unspecified sample of people who live in the New England states.

Reliability

The only reliability data reported for the 1981 norms edition of the SIT are "parallel forms" reliability. The authors argue that since the Stanford-Binet and SIT are "parallel forms of the same instrument," they can use data on mean differences between scores on the two tests to estimate reliability. The reasoning is circular. The SIT norms were designed by equating scores on the two instruments. Then, the authors find they correlate highly. The two measures are not, in fact, parallel forms, and the arguments made for reliability are invalid.

Validity

Arguments for the validity of the scale are based on high correlations with the Stanford-Binet. The authors argue that since the Stanford-Binet and SIT correlate .975, the two can be used interchangeably.

Summary

The Slosson Intelligence Test is a screening instrument designed to give estimates of IQs on the Stanford-Binet. It was standardized on an unspecified sample of people in New England. Evidence for reliability and validity are based on correlations with the Stanford-Binet, a test to which it was statistically equated during development. Those who use the SIT to assess children are advised to use the Stanford-Binet, as it provides a more in-depth and qualitative evaluation than the SIT.

McCarthy Scales of Children's Abilities

The McCarthy Scales of Children's Abilities (MSCA) (McCarthy, 1972) were designed to evaluate the general intellectual level of children (ages 2½ to 8½) as well as their strengths and weaknesses in a number of ability areas. The test consists of eighteen subtests that make up six scales: Verbal, Perceptual-Performance, Quantitative, Memory, Motor, and General Cognitive. The General Cognitive scale is a composite of the Verbal, Perceptual-Performance, and Quantitative scales. The interrelationships among the eighteen separate subtests and the six scales are shown in Figure 10.1.

The behaviors sampled by the subtests are described by the author as follows.

Block Building   Children copy four structures that the examiner has constructed. The author suggests that these items provide an opportunity to observe children's manipulative skills and perception of spatial relations.

Puzzle Solving   In this subtest children are required to assemble puzzle pieces to form six common animals and foods. The items measure perceptual and motor skills as well as general cognition.

Pictorial Memory   In this subtest children are shown a card with six pictured objects on it. The objects are named by the examiner, and children are then asked to recall what they saw. The test measures immediate memory, general cognition, and verbal ability.

Word Knowledge   This subtest consists of two parts. In part 1 children are required to point to five common objects and name four additional objects shown to them on cards. Part 2 is an oral vocabulary test requiring children to define words.

Number Questions   Children are given twelve questions requiring quantitative thinking and involving solution of addition, subtraction, multiplication, and division problems.

Tapping Sequence   This subtest requires children to imitate the examiner's performance on a four-note xylophone. Memory, perceptual-motor coordination, and general cognition are said to be measured.

Verbal Memory   This is a two-part test. Part 1 requires children to repeat words and sentences. Part 2 requires them to recall the highlights of a paragraph read by the examiner.

Right-Left Orientation   Children are required to demonstrate knowledge of left and right with regard to their own bodies and then to demonstrate generalization of left and right to a picture of a boy. This subtest is not administered to children younger than 5.

Leg Coordination   Items requiring children to engage in a variety of exercises, such as walking backwards and on tiptoe, are used to assess the maturity of leg coordination.

Arm Coordination   Development of the arms is assessed in a variety of gamelike activities.

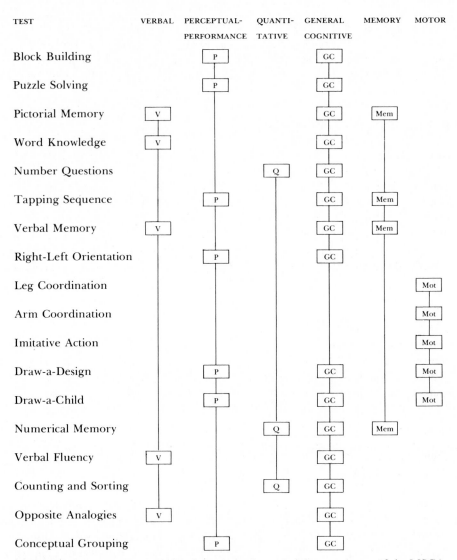

FIGURE 10.1   Interrelationship of the six scales and eighteen subtests of the MSCA
SOURCE: Reproduced by permission from the Manual for the McCarthy Scales of Children's Abilities. Copyright 1970, 1972 by The Psychological Corporation, Cleveland, Ohio. All rights reserved.

Imitative Action   Eye preference is assessed by requiring children to sight through a plastic tube.

Draw-a-Design   Children are required to copy various geometric designs.

Draw-a-Child   This subtest requires males to draw a boy and females to draw a girl.

Numerical Memory   This subtest assesses immediate recall by requiring children to repeat sequences of digits both forward and backward.

Verbal Fluency This subtest requires children to classify and think categorically. Children must name words that fall into each of four different categories within a time limit.

Counting and Sorting Children are required to count blocks and to sort them into quantitative categories (for example, two piles with *the same* number).

Opposite Analogies Children are required to provide opposites of key words in statements spoken by the examiner (for instance, "Milk is *cold,* but coffee is ____").

Conceptual Grouping Children must manipulate from one to three variables to discover classification rules for problems.

All directions for administering the test are extremely clear and specific. Procedures for scoring are clearly described; an eight-step procedure is outlined. Scores are described in language that teachers can easily understand.

Scores

Four kinds of scores are obtained on the MSCA: a general cognitive index, scale indexes, percentile ranks, and MA. The author states that the general cognitive index "is a scaled score; it is not a quotient" (p. 24). The score has a mean of 100 and a standard deviation of 16. Separate indexes are obtained for each of the other five major scales; they have a mean of 50 and a standard deviation of 10. Tables in the manual are used to transform scaled scores into percentile ranks and to provide estimated MAs for performance on the general cognitive scale.

Norms

The standardization of the MSCA was excellent. One hundred children at each of ten age levels participated in the standardization; the sample was stratified on the basis of sex, age, "color," geographic region, father's occupation, and urban-rural residence. Proportions in the normative sample approximate very closely the 1970 U.S. census data.

Reliability

Reliability data consist of internal-consistency coefficients for all but three subtests of the MSCA. For these three, internal-consistency estimates were viewed as inappropriate, and test-retest coefficients were computed. Reliability coefficients and standard errors of measurement for the six MSCA scales are reported in Table 10.3. Reliabilities for the Verbal and General Cognitive scales are excellent; coefficients for the other scales are lower.

Validity

Studies of both predictive and concurrent validity are reported in the manual. Thirty-one children were tested using the MSCA and then tested four months later using the Metropolitan Achievement Test. Correlations among the six scales of the MSCA and the six scales of the MAT were high for the Perceptual-Performance and Quantitative scales, mediocre for the General Cognitive Scale, and poor for the Verbal, Memory, and Motor scales. The last three MSCA scales had correlations averaging .15, .26, and .03 with the MAT. The author rightfully states that the results should be interpreted with caution because of the small size of the sample.

To establish concurrent validity, MSCA scores were correlated with scores obtained on the Stanford-Binet and the Wechsler Preschool and Primary Scale of Intelligence (WPPSI). The sample consisted of thirty-five white children (aged 6 to 6½) enrolled in a Catholic school in New York City. The obtained intercorrelations are reported in Table 10.4. The results lend some support to the concurrent validity of the MSCA.

TABLE 10.3 Reliability Coefficients and Standard Errors of Measurement of the Six MSCA Scales, by Age, for the Standardization Sample

Age in Years	N	Verbal		Perceptual-Performance		Quantitative		General Cognitive		Memory		Motor	
		r	SEM	r	SEM	r	SEM	r	SEM	r	SEM	r	SEM
2½	102	.90	3.2	.76	4.8	.77	4.9	.93	4.2	.78	4.6	.84	4.0
3	104	.89	3.2	.87	3.6	.82	4.2	.94	3.8	.73	5.0	.82	4.2
3½	100	.92	2.8	.90	3.2	.83	4.2	.96	3.4	.83	4.1	.84	4.1
4	102	.90	3.2	.86	3.6	.78	5.3	.91	4.7	.83	4.0	.78	4.6
4½	104	.88	3.5	.89	3.3	.79	4.6	.94	3.8	.74	5.0	.84	4.1
5	102	.87	3.6	.87	3.7	.86	3.7	.94	3.9	.78	4.9	.82	4.3
5½	104	.87	3.5	.84	3.9	.86	3.7	.93	4.2	.72	5.3	.80	4.5
6½	104	.84	3.9	.77	4.7	.80	4.3	.90	5.0	.84	4.0	.69	5.5
7½	104	.90	3.3	.84	4.1	.82	4.1	.94	3.9	.83	4.0	.75	5.1
8½	106	.86	3.7	.75	5.0	.83	4.2	.92	4.5	.82	4.3	.60	6.2
Average and SEM for the 10 Age Groups[a]		.88	3.4	.84	4.0	.81	4.3	.93	4.1	.79	4.5	.79	4.7

NOTE: The reliability coefficients presented here are based on split-half correlations corrected by the Spearman-Brown formula for the component tests, except for the Memory tests, Right-Left Orientation, and Draw-a-Child, for which that method was inappropriate. For these, test-retest correlations, based on smaller groups and corrected for restriction of range, were used in the computation of Scale reliability coefficients (Guilford, 1954, pp. 392–393).

The standard errors of measurement are in GCI units for the General Cognitive Scale, and in Scale Index units for the other five Scales. . . . Standard deviations . . . were used to compute the standard errors of measurement.

[a]The average coefficients were obtained by using Fisher's z transformation (Walker & Lev, 1953, p. 254).

SOURCE: Reproduced by permission from the Manual for the McCarthy Scales of Children's Abilities. Copyright 1970, 1972 by The Psychological Corporation, Cleveland, Ohio. All rights reserved.

TABLE 10.4 Coefficients of Correlation Between MSCA Scale Indexes and IQs Obtained on the Wechsler Preschool and Primary Scale of Intelligence (WPPSI) and Stanford-Binet

MSCA Scales	WPPSI IQ			Stanford-Binet (Form L-M) IQ	MSCA Scale Index	
	Verbal	Perform-ance	Full-Scale		Mean	SD
Verbal	.51	.43	.54	.66	52.5	8.2
Perceptual-Performance	.47	.59	.61	.70	53.4	10.3
Quantitative	.41	.27	.38	.41	50.0	8.4
General Cognitive	.63	.62	.71	.81	104.0	13.3
Memory	.42	.39	.46	.67	51.0	8.6
Motor	.02	.10	.07	.06	51.5	7.3
Mean	106.7	104.6	106.3	115.5		
Standard Deviation	10.9	12.4	11.1	14.2		

NOTE: Intervals between the administration of the MSCA and each of the other tests ranged from three to twenty days. Testing order was counterbalanced. $N = 35$ first-grade children aged 6 to 6½.

SOURCE: Data reproduced by permission from the Manual for the McCarthy Scales of Children's Abilities. Copyright 1970, 1972 by The Psychological Corporation, Cleveland, Ohio. All rights reserved.

Summary

In our opinion, it is only a matter of time before the MSCA becomes one of the most popular tests for assessing the abilities of preschool children. The tasks are interesting and enjoyable; the directions are clear; the standardization and reliability are excellent. Evidence about validity of the MSCA is still limited. Certain claims for the usefulness of the test with exceptional children appear unsubstantiated for two reasons: no exceptional children were included in the standardization, and there is no evidence for the validity of the scale with specific groups. The test does meet the majority of the standards of the American Psychological Association.

PICTURE VOCABULARY TESTS

A number of picture vocabulary tests are among the most widely used tests for assessment of children's intelligence. Before describing individual picture vocabulary tests, it is important to state what these devices measure. The tests are *not* measures of intelligence per se; rather, they measure only one aspect of intelligence, receptive vocabulary. Picture vocabulary tests present drawings to a child, who is asked to identify pictures corresponding to words read by the examiner. Some authors of picture vocabulary measures state that the tests measure receptive vocabulary; others equate receptive vocabulary with intelligence and claim that their tests assess intelligence. Because the tests measure only one aspect of intelligence, they should not be used to make placement decisions.

Full-Range Picture Vocabulary Test

The Full-Range Picture Vocabulary Test (Ammons & Ammons, 1948) is designed to assess the "intelligence" of individuals from 2 years of age through adulthood. Materials for the test consist of thirteen plates with four pictures on each plate, a one-page manual, and an answer sheet with norms printed on the back. Directions for administering the test are complex. For each plate, there are words representing levels of performance. Point levels are assigned to each of the words on a given plate and "represent approximately the mental age at which fifty percent of a representative population would fail the word" (Ammons & Ammons, 1948, p. 1). Test takers are given words for individual cards until they pass three consecutive levels and fail three. However, three plates have only three words, while two plates have only two words. Administration is complicated; while there may be only three words for certain plates, the words may represent levels that are very disparate. The examiner must assume "hypothetical levels" for certain plates.

Scores

Although administration is based on levels completed, scoring is based on number of *items* answered correctly. A table of norms is used to transform raw scores to MAs. Interpolation is often necessary because MAs are not specified for all possible raw scores. The authors state that a Wechsler-like scale of IQs accompanies each test kit. The scale was not included in our specimen kit.

Norms

The authors of the FRPVT state that "the present norms are based on 589 representative cases from two years of age to adult level" (p.

1). There is no specification or description of the population on whom this test was standardized.

Reliability

The one-page manual for the FRPVT does not include reliability data. In the manual for the Quick Test (Ammons & Ammons, 1962), the authors of the FRPVT state that

critics of the FRPV not familiar with its widespread use and our extensive research program have implied or stated that the FRPV is "poorly standardized," etc. Actually, this is not at all the case. Rather, since shortly after the FRPV was made available for use, there has been so much research with it that we have not been able to keep up with the findings. One of the consequences of this widespread use has been that we have been unable to prepare a comprehensive manual, although many separate articles reporting various aspects of work with the FRPV have been published. In order to make sure that a QT manual would be published, we deliberately refrained from releasing the QT until this manual was ready, reporting all experience and known research to date. If our experience with the FRPV is any indication, we may never get caught up again. (p. i)

Validity

There is no evidence for the validity of the FRPVT.

Summary

The FRPVT and its accompanying manual violate the majority of the standards for educational and psychological tests published by the joint committee of the American Psychological Association, the American Educational Research Association, and the National Council on Measurement in Education.

Quick Test

The Quick Test (Ammons & Ammons, 1962) is described by its authors as the "little brother of the Full Range Picture Vocabulary Test (FRPV), one of the most widely used brief tests of intelligence" (p. i). There are three forms of the Quick Test, each consisting of one plate of four drawings and a series of words that the examiner reads. The child or adult taking the test is required to point to the picture that most nearly represents the meaning of the word read by the examiner. The authors state that the single forms of the Quick Test can be given in 2 minutes or less, that "it can be seen that the three forms of the QT are 'short forms' of the FRPV, which itself is a very brief, but highly reliable and valid, test of intelligence" (p. i).

Scores

Raw scores for the Quick Test consist of the number of correct responses between the basal and the ceiling. Raw scores may be transformed to MAs and ratio IQs for children and to deviation IQs ($\bar{X} = 100$, $S = 15$) for adults. Actually, seven MAs and seven IQs are obtained (for form 1, form 2, form 3, forms 1 and 2 combined, forms 1 and 3 combined, forms 2 and 3 combined, and forms 1, 2, and 3 combined).

Norms

The Quick Test was standardized on 458 white children and adults from geographically restricted areas (parts of Montana and Louisville, Kentucky). The authors state that they attempted to control for age, grade, occupation of parents, and sex. They state, "We did not attempt any geographical control for practical reasons and because previous work with the FRPV had indicated such control was very likely not important" (p. 121).

Reliability

Ten studies are cited in the Quick Test manual to support the contention that the test is reliable. All ten studies are equivalent-form reliability studies. There are no reported investigations of either internal-consistency or test-retest reliability. Equivalent-form reliabilities range from .60 to .96. Apparently, very disparate scores are often earned on the three forms of the Quick Test. The authors state:

From time to time, FRPV or QT users have written to us, quite disturbed to find a testee who has shown a difference of two or three years in mental age on different forms of the test. Relatively inexperienced testers are inclined to say that the test is at fault, which of course it may be. However, in most instances, these discrepancies are well within the range which would be expected from the standard error of a test score. The tester only notices the few very large discrepancies, disregarding the far more numerous times when performances have been very similar. The tester should note that almost never has a large discrepancy been found for a good-sized group. Discrepancies are usually due to peculiar performance on a few (one to three) items and may very well have clinical significance. (p. 137)

Since reliability and standard error of measurement are inversely related, we wonder how the authors can claim that the test is highly reliable and still dismiss large discrepancies as "within the range which would be expected from the standard error of a test score."

Validity

Validity data for the Quick Test consist of both concurrent and predictive data. Concurrent validity was studied by correlating performance on the Quick Test with performance on the FRPVT. Since the Quick Test is the "little brother" of the FRPVT, the reported correlations of .62 to .93 are not surprising.

Predictive validity was established by correlating performance on the Quick Test with school grades and scores on achievement tests. Intercorrelations with subtests of the Iowa Tests of Basic Skills ranged from .32 to .59.

Summary

The Quick Test is a very brief measure of verbal intelligence that may be appropriate as a screening device but has many limitations for use in decision making. Standardization was carried out in a geographically circumscribed area, evidence regarding reliability is limited to equivalent-form reliability, and validity evidence is still limited.

Peabody Picture Vocabulary Test–Revised

The Peabody Picture Vocabulary Test–Revised (PPVT–R) (Dunn & Dunn, 1981) is an individually administered, norm-referenced measure of receptive (hearing) vocabulary designed to provide an index of achievement and/or scholastic aptitude. The authors of the test state that:

The PPVT–R is designed primarily to measure a subject's receptive (hearing) vocabulary for Standard American English. In this sense, it is an achievement test, since it shows the extent of English vocabulary acquisition.

Another function is to provide a quick estimate of one major aspect of verbal ability for subjects who have grown up in a standard English-speaking environment. In this sense, it is a scholastic aptitude test. It is not, however, a comprehensive test of general intelligence. Instead, it measures only one important facet of general intelligence: vocabulary. (Dunn & Dunn, prepublication copy of PPVT–R manual).

The PPVT–R, a revision of the Peabody Picture Vocabulary Test that originally appeared in 1959 and later in 1965, contains two-thirds new items. There are two parallel forms of the test (Forms L and M), and the test may be administered to persons between 2½ and 40 years of age.

The PPVT–R is administered in easel format, with the examiner showing an individual a series of plates on which four pictures are drawn. The examiner reads a stimulus word for each plate, and the person being tested points to the picture that best represents the stimulus word. The PPVT–R is an untimed power test, and it usually takes from 10–15 minutes to administer. The test is accompanied by both a manual and a technical manual, the latter providing extensive data on the development and technical characteristics of the test.

Scores

The student's raw score is the number of pictures correctly identified between basal and ceiling items. Because the test employs a multiple-choice format, the basal is the highest level at which a person makes eight consecutive correct responses; the ceiling is defined as that point at which a person makes six errors in eight consecutive items. Raw scores may be transformed to age equivalents, standard scores ($\bar{X} = 100$, $S = 15$), percentile ranks, and stanines. True score confidence bands are provided for obtained scores, and the authors use asymmetrical confidence intervals (see Chapter 7) for extreme scores.

Norms

The development of the PPVT–R began with a four-stage item tryout program between 1976 and 1978. A total of 9,099 persons were tested using 684 experimental items. This initial item tryout was followed by administration of 504 items (252 per form) to 5,717 persons as part of an item-calibration study. Subjects for this phase of test development were selected from a sample drawn on the basis of geographic region, rural-urban residence, socioeconomic status, and race (in preschool and grade 1 only). Both traditional item analysis and Rasch-Wright latent trait methods were used to select final items for the two forms of the test.

The PPVT–R was standardized on a representative national sample of 4,200 students, ages 2½ through 18, and on 828 adults. The 2½ to 18 sample was selected on the basis of geographic region, parental occupation, sex, race, and community size. Data in the technical manual illustrate close agreement between sample proportions and 1970 U.S. Census proportions. The adult sample was selected in proportion to the 1970 U.S. Census occupational data, and according to geographic region and sex. Again, the composition of the adult sample closely approximates census data.

Reliability

Extensive reliability data are provided in the technical manual for the PPVT–R. The section on reliability begins with a description of the relationship between performance on the 1965 and 1981 editions of the test. These data are of heuristic interest only, owing to extensive revision of the test.

Three kinds of reliability data are reported for the PPVT–R: split-half indices of internal consistency; immediate test-retest reliability using alternate forms; and delayed (9–31 day delay) test-retest reliability using alternate forms. Split-half reliability coefficients ranged from .67 to .88 with a median of .80 on form L, and from .61 to .88 with a median of .81 on form M for the younger (ages 2½ to 18) population, and from .80 to .85 with a median of .82 on form L for the adult population. Immediate test-retest data were collected on 642 children and adolescents. Reliabilities for raw scores for single-age groups ranged from .73 to .91 with a median reliability of .82. Reliabilities for standard scores for single-age groups ranged from .71 to .89 with a median of .79.

Delayed test-retest data were obtained by administering the test to 962 children and adolescents. Reliabilities for raw scores for single-age groups ranged from .52 to .90 (median = .78), and reliabilities for standard scores for single-age groups ranged from .54 to .90 (median = .77). The PPVT–R has satisfactory reliability for screening purposes, the intended use of the test.

Validity

There are no data in the PPVT–R manual on the validity of the test.

Summary

The PPVT–R is an individually administered, norm-referenced measure of hearing vocabulary. The test is well developed and adequately standardized. Data in the technical manual indicate adequate reliability for screening purposes, but there are no data on validity of the measure. Overall, the technical characteristics of this scale far surpass those of other picture vocabulary tests. Used properly and with awareness that it samples only receptive vocabulary, the PPVT–R can serve as an extremely useful screening device.

SCALES FOR SPECIAL POPULATIONS

As noted in the introduction to this chapter, a variety of devices have been developed to assess the intellectual capability of people who have difficulty responding to traditional devices. Assessment of special populations is usually carried out by one of the three following practices.

1. *Adapting Test Items.* In some cases, examiners change the procedures for administering an item to compensate for the handicaps of the person they are testing. Items normally timed are presented without time limits; verbal items are presented in pantomime; and so on. In such efforts, examiners often "forget" to consider the fact that the test is standardized using standardized procedures. If, as is usually the case, examiners use the published norms for the test, they may make inappropriate comparisons. The children on whom the test was standardized will have been tested using procedures *different* from those adapted procedures an examiner chooses to use.

2. *Using Response-fair Tests* In other cases, examiners select tests to which the person can respond with minimal difficulty. Some tests, for example, employ no verbal instructions and require no verbalized responses. Deaf persons *can* respond and items *can* be given to deaf persons. However, many of the tests that *can* be given are standardized on nonhandicapped persons. The acculturation of the handicapped differs from that of the nonhandicapped. In this instance the normative comparisons are unfair because the acculturation of those tested differs from the acculturation of those on whom the test is standardized.

3. *Using Tests Designed for and Standardized on Handicapped Populations* In still other cases, when examiners are required to test persons who demonstrate specific handicaps, they choose to use tests developed for use with and standardized on specific groups of handicapped individuals. A limited number of such devices are available, but they have the distinct advantages of appropriateness in both response requirements and normative comparisons.

In assessing special populations, examiners must be concerned with two restrictions. They must be sure that response requirements are fair and reasonable—that is, that the person being tested can reasonably be expected to be able to respond. They must be cautious also in the use of norms—in being reasonably certain that those they test have had comparable acculturation to those in the normative sample. The remainder of this chapter describes devices most often used with special populations.

The Nebraska Test of Learning Aptitude

The Nebraska Test of Learning Aptitude (NTLA) (Hiskey, 1966) is an individually administered test designed to assess the learning aptitude of deaf and hearing individuals between 3 and 16 years of age. The NTLA has twelve subtests with instructions for pantomime administration of the test to deaf persons and verbal directions for use with hearing children. To use the NTLA, the examiner must have considerable experience in individual intellectual assessment. To assess deaf children, the examiner should have specialized preparation and considerable experience working with the deaf. The manual for the NTLA includes suggestions about specific procedures to use in establishing rapport with deaf children, including suggested ways of correcting mistakes and of giving the child nonverbal reinforcement.

The NTLA may be administered either by pantomime or by verbal directions. The test was standardized using pantomime directions with deaf children and verbal directions with hearing children. For that reason, if pantomime directions are used, the scoring must be based on the norms for deaf children. If verbal directions are used, scoring must be based on the norms for hearing children.

Each of the twelve subtests is a power test beginning with very simple items designed to give the child practice in the kind of behavior being sampled. Response requirements in all subtests are nonverbal, requiring a choice (by pointing) of several alternatives or a motor response such as stringing beads or drawing parts of pictures. Some subtests are administered only to three- to ten-year-olds; some are administered to all ages; others are given only to those 11 years old or older. A description of the twelve subtests follows.

Bead Patterns (ages 3 to 10) This subtest assesses ability to string beads, copy bead patterns, and reproduce bead patterns from memory.

Memory for Color (ages 3 to 10) This subtest assesses ability to remember a visually presented series of colors after a short delay.

Picture Identification (ages 3 to 10) This subtest assesses ability to match identical pictures of increasing complexity.

Picture Association (ages 3 to 10) This subtest assesses the ability to match pictures to other picture pairs on the basis of perceptual and conceptual relationships.

Paper Folding (ages 3 to 10) This subtest assesses ability to fold pieces of paper to reproduce a sequence of folds previously made by the examiner.

Visual Attention Span (all ages) This subtest assesses ability to remember sequences of pictures after a short delay.

Block Patterns (all ages) This subtest assesses ability to build block patterns from pictorial representations including three-dimensional arrays. A person is allowed 2 minutes to build each pattern and receives bonus points for faster solutions.

Completion of Drawings (all ages) This subtest assesses ability to isolate missing parts in line drawings and to draw in missing parts with a pencil.

Memory for Digits (11 and above; omitted if mental retardation is suspected) This subtest assesses ability to reproduce sequences of visually presented digits. A sequence on a card is shown, the card is removed, and the person must reproduce the sequence using plastic digits.

Puzzle Blocks   (ages 11 and above)   This subtest assesses ability to assemble disjointed cubes into a whole. It employs varying time limits, and bonus points are given for rapid solutions.

Picture Analogies   (ages 11 and above)   This subtest assesses ability to solve visually presented analogies. Three pictures are shown and there is a relationship between the first two. The third picture bears the same relationship to a fourth picture that must be chosen from a response bank.

Spatial Reasoning   (ages 11 and above)   This subtest presents a whole figure and several samples of disjointed parts. It requires identification of the samples that could be put together to form the whole objects.

The NTLA is a point scale; that is, the child earns points on the specific subtests that are administered. Different subtests employ different ceiling rules. Criteria for stopping each of the subtests are adequately described in the test manual.

Scores

The kinds of scores obtained for the NTLA depend on how the test is administered. As noted earlier, the NTLA may be administered either in pantomime or verbally. When the test is administered in pantomime, the norms for deaf children are used to obtain a learning age (LA) and a learning quotient (LQ). When the test is administered verbally, the norms for hearing children are used to obtain a mental age (MA) and an intelligence quotient (IQ). Both scores and quotients are based on the median subtest learning ages and mental ages. Hiskey recommends that in interpreting the test performance

of hearing children, teachers and diagnostic specialists rely primarily on the MA. He advises that the learning age and learning quotient obtained for deaf children are not equivalent or comparable to MAs and IQs. He recommends that the learning age should be the only score used to interpret the performance of deaf children.

Norms

The NTLA was originally developed in 1941. Norms for hearing children were first published in 1957, and the revised edition of the test with norms for both deaf and hearing children was published in 1966 (Hiskey, 1966). The standardization sample for the 1941 edition included 466 children enrolled in state schools for the deaf in seven midwestern states and in one day school for the deaf in Lincoln, Nebraska.

In the revision and restandardization of the NTLA, Hiskey added one subtest (Spatial Relations) and many more difficult items. The revised NTLA was administered to 1,107 deaf children and 1,101 hearing children between the ages of 2-6 and 17-5 in ten "widely separate states." The deaf children were primarily from state schools for the deaf with no other data reported on the nature of the normative sample. The hearing children were selected on the basis of their parents' occupational levels with reference to the percentages found in the 1960 census. Hiskey states that "the samples included representatives from minority groups, although no effort was made to obtain a specified percentage of such children" (p. 10).

For the purpose of establishing age norms, the children from both samples were divided into fifteen age groups (all children between 2-6 and 3-5 were placed in the 3-year-old group, and so on). The number of children at each year level varied more for the deaf (25 to 106) than for the hearing (47 to 85). The 3- and 4-year-old samples of deaf children and the samples of older hearing children were limited in size. The final item placement was based on the performance of *deaf* children, and there are no comparisons reported in the manual between the performances of deaf children and hearing children. Thus, while evidence is reported on the increasing difficulty of items within subtests for deaf children, comparable data for hearing children are not reported.

The published norms are based on the performances of 1,079 deaf children and 1,074 hearing children. As noted earlier, both samples are inadequately described.

Reliability

The only reliability data presented in the manual for the NTLA are split-half reliabilities for the standardization groups. Hiskey reports split-half reliabilities of .95 for the 3- to 10-year-old deaf group, .92 for the 11- to 17-year-old deaf group, .93 for 3- to 10-year-old hearing children, and .90 for 11- to 17-year-old hearing children. No data about the standard errors of measurement are included in the manual.

Hiskey does report data on the internal consistency of the test but does so in an effort to demonstrate validity for the measure. In citing evidence of content validity, Hiskey reports subtest intercorrelations and correlations of each subtest learning age with the median learning age for the entire test. There are no data on the reliabilities of the individual subtests. Hiskey states that "studies in the near future will provide additional evidence of reliability based on re-test results after varying periods of time have elapsed" (p. 16). We have searched the literature and have failed to find these studies.

Validity

Hiskey states that "the best evidence of the validity of a test is to be found in its successful use over a period of years. Research reported during the past twenty years indicates that the original scale has been a valid instrument" (p. 12). He provides very little empirical evidence to support his contention. Data on validity consist of reported concurrent validity and evidence about correlation of subtest learning ages with median learning ages for the total test.

Hiskey reports correlations between subtest learning ages and the median learning age for the total test ranging from .55 to .89 for 3- to 10-year-old deaf children, from .59 to .67 for 11- to 17-year-old deaf children, from .51 to .77 for 3- to 10-year-old hearing children, and from .54 to .67 for 11- to 17-year-old hearing children.

Most data about the concurrent validity of the NTLA are based on the earlier edition of the test. Hiskey does, however, report the following concurrent validity coefficients for the 1966 revision of the NTLA: .86 for 99 hearing children (ages 3 to 10) between NTLA and Stanford-Binet IQs; .78 between the NTLA and Stanford-Binet IQs for fifty hearing children between 11 and 17 years of age; .82 between WISC and NTLA IQs for fifty-two hearing children between 5 and 11 years of age.

Summary

The NTLA is an individually administered measure of learning aptitude standardized on both deaf and hearing children. The test is administered by pantomime procedures for deaf children and by verbal instructions for hearing children. When administering the test, the examiner must be especially careful to use the appropriate set of normative data. The test was standardized using pantomime procedures for deaf children and verbal instructions for hearing children. The standardization samples are not described fully enough.

Reliability data for the NTLA are limited. No subtest reliabilities are reported; only split-half reliabilities for the entire scale are included in the manual. Validity data consist of reported correlations between subtest learning ages and the median learning age for the total test, data on the earlier edition of the test, and concurrent correlations of the NTLA scores with scores of hearing children on the Stanford-Binet and the WISC.

The Nebraska Test of Learning Aptitude is the best available device for the assessment of the learning aptitude of deaf children between 5 and 12 years of age. Because of limited technical data, results on the test must be interpreted with considerable caution.

Blind Learning Aptitude Test

The Blind Learning Aptitude Test (BLAT) (Newland, 1969)[1] was developed for assessing the learning aptitude of young blind children. Newland (1969) states that the BLAT was devised to give a clearer picture of the learning potential of young blind children than was possible using existent measures. He states:

While a certain amount and kind of light could be thrown on their basic learning capacities by means of more widely used individual tests, the kinds of behaviors sampled by such tests did not yield as full, and early, psychological information as is needed, particularly at the time such children entered upon formal educational programs—whether in residential or day schools. In a psychological sense, young blind children come into such programs from a much more diversified background of acculturation than do nonimpaired children. (p. 1)

In developing materials for the BLAT, Newland states, he used five guiding principles:

(1) the test items were to be bas-relief form, consisting of dots and lines; (2) the spatial discriminations to be made by the child among these dots and lines were to be greater than those called for in the reading of Braille; (3) no stimulus materials, other than the directions, were to be verbal in nature, (4) verbalization of response was not to be required in solving the items or in specifying the solutions to items. Pointing behavior was to be accepted although accompanying

verbalization could be accepted; (5) a variety of test-element patterns was to be developed, all of which would necessitate eduction of relationships and/or correlates by the child. (p. 1)

Newland designed the BLAT to sample "six discernibly different kinds of behavior." His description of the kinds of behaviors sampled is comparable to our descriptions of items assessing discrimination, generalization, sequencing, analogies, and pattern or matrix completion.

The BLAT was standardized on individuals from 6 to 20 years of age, but it is intended primarily for children between 6 and 12 years of age. There is a unique feature in the administration of BLAT subtests: training items are presented before the actual administration of subtest items. This allows the examiner to be certain that a child understands the kind of behavior required before being asked to demonstrate the behavior for a scored test item.

Scores

Two scores, learning-aptitude test age and learning-aptitude test quotient, are obtained from the BLAT. Newland (1969) describes the test age by stating that

a child who earns a given score on BLAT can be regarded as having earned a BLAT test age which is the midpoint of an age range. This is indicative of the level of his learning capability as a blind child, as reflected by his performance on the kinds of behavior being sampled by BLAT. (p. 19)

1. All quotations from the *Manual for the Blind Learning Aptitude Test* used in this discussion are copyrighted by T. Ernest Newland and reprinted by his permission.

The learning quotient is a deviation score with a mean of 100 and a standard deviation of 15.

Norms

The BLAT was standardized on 961 blind students in both residential and day schools. The standardization sample was stratified on the basis of geographic region, age, sex, race, and socioeconomic status. Extensive tables comparing standardization data to U.S. census data appear in the manual. In most instances BLAT sample proportions are closely comparable to the census proportions.

Reliability

Two kinds of reliability were ascertained for the BLAT. Internal consistency of the test for all 961 children in the standardization sample was .93. Test-retest reliability was reported as .87 for a sample of 93 children ranging in age from 10 through 16 who were retested seven months after the original testing. There was a median gain of 5.8 points between the original testing and subsequent retesting.

Validity

Validity for the BLAT was demonstrated in three ways. Newland states that estimates of concurrent validity would have limited value because "the 'intelligence' tests generally used with young blind children were regarded as having limited value in sampling learning potential—due to the nature of behavior samplings made and the very widely differing kinds and amounts of acculturation among blind children" (p. 10).

To establish validity for the BLAT it was demonstrated that performance on BLAT

(1) progressively improves across random samples of increasing chronological age levels;
(2) correlates well enough with performances on the Hayes-Binet and the WISC Verbal to suggest that the measurements are in a comparable domain, yet low enough to suggest differences in the behavior samplings; and
(3) correlates promisingly with measured educational achievement as compared with correlations between performances on the Hayes-Binet and WISC Verbal and measured educational achievement. (Newland, 1969, p. 10)

Summary

The Blind Learning Aptitude Test uses a bas-relief format and six different kinds of behavior samples to assess the intelligence of blind children between 6 and 12 years of age. The BLAT was standardized on blind children whose characteristics closely approximate census proportions. The test is sufficiently reliable to be used in making important decisions about children. Validity of the test is still based largely on theoretical postulates. The BLAT is currently the most adequate test for assessing the learning aptitude of young blind children.

Arthur Adaptation of the Leiter International Performance Scale

The Leiter International Performance Scale was first constructed by Russell Leiter in 1929 for the purpose of assessing the intelligence of children who might experience difficulty responding to a verbal test: the deaf, the hard of hearing, those who demonstrate speech difficulties, the bilingual, and those who do not speak English. The 1929 scale was an experimental edition; subsequent revisions were published in 1934, 1936, 1938, 1940, and 1948. In 1950, Grace Arthur published an adaptation (AALIPS) of the Leiter International Performance Scale.

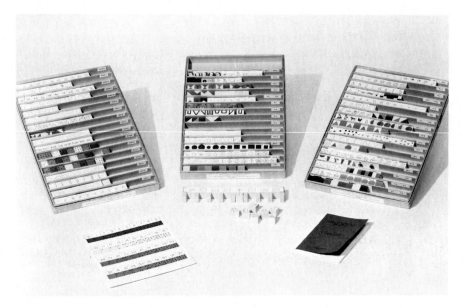

FIGURE 10.2 An item from the Arthur Adaptation of the Leiter International Performance Scale
SOURCE: Photo courtesy Stoelting Company.

The AALIPS is an untimed, nonverbal age scale containing sixty items ranging from the 2-year to the 12-year level. The 1948 edition of the LIPS contains additional items and can be used to assess the intelligence of persons 2 through 18 years of age. The test materials for the LIPS and the AALIPS are identical through the 12-year level.

Materials for the AALIPS consist of a response frame with an adjustable card holder and two trays of response blocks with corresponding stimulus cards (see Figure 10.2). All tests are administered by placing a stimulus card on the response frame and pantomiming the directions. The child responds by placing blocks in the response frame. The actual tasks range from matching colors and forms to completion of patterns, analogous designs, and classification of objects. Behaviors predominantly sampled, therefore, include discrimination, generalization, sequencing, analogies, and pattern comple-

tion. Most items require considerable perceptual organization and discrimination.

The directions for administering the scale that are included in the manual are confusing. They're illustrated by black and white pictures that, unfortunately, are of little assistance with items in which color is the discriminative feature in both administration and solution. Colored pictures would facilitate ease of administration; the use of black and white pictures necessitates reading an entire page of instructions in order to ascertain proper alignment of stimulus cards and pictures and to insure correct standardized administration.

Scores

A major shortcoming of the AALIPS is the fact that the correct answers (arrangements of blocks) to test questions are not included in the manual. Examiners must judge the correctness of a child's response on the basis of what they believe the correct response should be. We suggest that examiners solve the problems themselves before giving the test to children, that they obtain the consensus of others (preferably, reasonably "bright" persons) about the correctness of their responses, and that they then mark the blocks using a coding system to avoid scoring errors.

Two scores, MA and a ratio IQ, are obtained by administering the AALIPS. There are four subtests at each age level of the test. The child earns a certain number of months' credit for each subtest passed and the number of months are summed to produce a mental age. Only items between the child's basal and ceiling are administered. A basal is located by identifying the level at which a child answers all items correctly. A double ceiling is attained; the child must fail all items at two consecutive year levels before testing is discontinued. Comparisons of the AALIPS with other intelligence tests (that is, the WISC and Stanford-Binet) have consistently shown that scores on the AALIPS tend to be about five points lower than those earned on other scales. Arthur devised a bonus system that raises the basal and increases credit for subtests passed at the various year levels, thus bringing scores on the AALIPS into line with those on other tests.

Norms

Normative data for the LIPS are not included in the AALIPS manual. The AALIPS, on the other hand, was standardized on only 289 children. All 289 came from a homogeneous mid-dle-class, midwestern, metropolitan background. There were few children at either extreme of the socioeconomic scale and apparently few or none who were the kind of children for whom the scale was originally developed— that is, children who experience difficulty responding to a verbal scale.

Reliability and Validity

No reliability data are published in the manual for the AALIPS. Arthur reports a number of studies as evidence for the concurrent validity of the AALIPS. Correlations between performance on the AALIPS and on the Stanford-Binet Intelligence Scale for 4-, 5-, 7-, and 8-year-old children ranged from .69 to .93; for a sample of mentally retarded and brain-injured children these correlations were between .56 and .86. The AALIPS correlates more highly with the performance scale (from .79 to .80) than with the verbal scale (.40 to .78) of the WISC.

Summary

The AALIPS is, in theory and design, a test that holds considerable promise for the intellectual assessment of children who have difficulty responding verbally. It lacks the necessary technical characteristics to make it psychometrically adequate. The test is inadequately standardized, and few data about its reliability and validity are given in the manual. Until this test is made technically adequate, its use should be restricted to procurement of qualitative information by only the most experienced examiners.

Pictorial Test of Intelligence

The Pictorial Test of Intelligence (PTI) (French, 1964) was designed "to provide an easily administered, objectively scored individual testing instrument to be used in assessing the general intellectual level of both normal and handicapped children between the ages of three and eight" (p. 1). The test employs an objective, multiple-choice format and requires no verbal response; children respond either by pointing or, in the case of those who cannot point, by focusing their eyes on specific response items.

The PTI includes six subtests designed to assess general mental ability. All items are administered by showing the child a large picture card containing four response possibilities. The child points to or focuses on one of the four drawings in response to orally presented directions. According to the author, the six subtests sample the following behaviors.

Picture Vocabulary   This subtest assesses verbal comprehension. The child must identify the response that best fits the meaning of a stimulus word read by the examiner.

Form Discrimination   This subtest assesses perceptual organization. The child is shown increasingly complex stimulus drawings on a second card and must match these to one of four response drawings.

Information and Comprehension   The child must demonstrate a "range of knowledge, general understanding, and verbal comprehension" by pointing to pictures in response to verbal statements read by the examiner.

Similarities   This subtest requires the child to identify which of four pictures does not belong in either a perceptual or conceptual category with the other three.

Size and Number   This subtest assesses quantitative language (for example, *bigger*), enumeration, and word problems that require skills ranging from the addition of single-digit numbers to those needed to perform multiple arithmetic operations in the same problem.

Immediate Recall   This subtest assesses "ability to retain momentary perceptions of size,

space, and form relationships." The examiner presents a stimulus card for five seconds, removes it, and then asks the child to identify the identical stimulus on the four-choice response card.

Scores

Raw scores for the PTI are obtained by objective scoring of the multiple-choice responses. Raw scores may be transformed to MAs, percentiles, and deviation IQs ($\overline{X} = 100$, $S = 16$). All children take every item of the test; there are no basal and ceiling rules. A short form of the test, which may be administered to 3- and 4-year-old children, provides the same kinds of scores as the long form.

Norms

As we mentioned in Chapter 6, the PTI is a most adequately standardized device. The standardization sample consisted of 1,830 children selected as representative of the population of children ages 3 through 8 living in the United States. 1960 census data were used, and the sample was stratified on the basis of geographic region, community size, occupational level of head of household, and sex. Race was not employed as a specific stratification variable, since the author believed that "the most appropriate procedure would be to include all races with socioeconomic status as the prime control variable" (p. 12). Extensive tables in the manual compare proportions of individuals in the normative sample with proportions in the population of the United States. All children who participated in the normative sample were individually tested by experienced psychologists.

Reliability

Both internal-consistency and test-retest reliability data are reported in the PTI manual. Internal-consistency coefficients were computed

TABLE 10.5 Summary of Studies on Test-Retest Reliability for the PTI

Age	Time Lapse	r	N
3, 4; 8, 9	54–56 mos.	.69[a]	49
3, 4, 5	3–6 wks.	.96	27
5	2–6 wks.	.91	31
6	2–4 wks.	.90	30
7	2–4 wks.	.94	25

[a]NCITMA (ages 3 and 4) vs. PTI (ages 8 and 9).
SOURCE: *Manual for the Pictorial Test of Intelligence* (p. 19) by J. L. French, 1964, Chicago: The Riverside Publishing Co. Copyright 1964. Reproduced by permission of the Publisher, The Riverside Publishing Company, 8420 Bryn Mawr Ave., Chicago, IL 60631.

separately for each age level and ranged from .87 to .93. Separate internal-consistency estimates for the short form were .86 at age 3 and .88 at age 4.

Five studies investigated the test-retest reliability of the PTI. The results of these studies, time intervals between testings, and the age levels of the children are reported in Table 10.5. The PTI has the necessary reliability to be used in making important educational decisions.

Validity

Content validity for the PTI was inferred on the basis of item selection and test development.

Predictive validity for the test is based on studies of its predecessor, the North Central Individual Test of Mental Ability (NCITMA). Concurrent validity of the PTI was established by correlating performance on the scale with performance on the Stanford-Binet, WISC, and Columbia Mental Maturity Scale. Correlations obtained for a sample of thirty-two first graders are reported in Table 10.6. However, for this same sample the means and standard deviations differed considerably (PTI: $\bar{X} = 114.5, S = 8.2$; Stanford-Binet: $\bar{X} = 113.6, S = 17.6$; and WISC: $\bar{X} = 101.5, S = 10.1$).

The performance of thirty-two first graders on the PTI correlated .61 with their performance on the Lorge-Thorndike Intelligence Scale (now the Cognitive Abilities Test), while the PTI performance of thirty first graders correlated .62 with their earlier scores on the California Test of Mental Maturity.

Construct validity was established by demonstrating increasing scores with chronological ages and occupational level of children's parents.

Summary

The Pictorial Test of Intelligence is an individually administered device composed of six

TABLE 10.6 Correlations of PTI Total Test and Subtests with Other Intelligence Tests (32 First Graders)

Subtests	Stanford-Binet MA	WISC Scores			CMMS IQ	PTI Total
		Full-Scale	Verbal	Perform-ance		
Picture Vocabulary	.45	.38	.38	.33	.42	.55
Form Discrimination	.53	.56	.52	.49	.45	.68
Information and Comprehension	.41	.56	.23	.16	.22	.48
Similarities	.55	.25	.41	.23	.40	.63
Size and Number	.52	.50	.53	.42	.38	.74
Immediate Recall	.22	.14	.10	.14	.26	.38
Total raw scores	.77	.67	.71	.55	.61	—

SOURCE: *Manual for the Pictorial Test of Intelligence* (p. 21) by J. L. French 1964, Chicago: The Riverside Publishing Co. Copyright 1964. Reproduced by permission of The Riverside Publishing Company, 8420 Bryn Mawr Ave., Chicago, IL 60631.

separate subtests designed to assess general mental ability. The test does not require the child to respond verbally and is thus suitable for administration to children who experience difficulty making verbal responses (young children with speech and language difficulties, with cerebral palsy, and so on). The test is adequately standardized and has the necessary reliability to be used in making important educational decisions.

Columbia Mental Maturity Scale

The Columbia Mental Maturity Scale (CMMS) (Burgemeister, Blum, & Lorge, 1972) is an individually administered device that assesses general reasoning ability by requiring a child to make visual-perceptual discriminations in order to classify and relate series of pictures, colors, forms, and symbols. The ninety-two figural and pictorial classification items that make up the scale are arranged in eight overlapping levels and may be used with children between 3 years, 6 months, and 9 years, 11 months, of age. Children take the level of the test appropriate for their chronological age. The authors describe administration of the scale as follows.

Each item consists of a series of from three to five drawings printed on a 6-by-19-inch card. . . . The objects depicted are, in general, within the range of experience of most American children, even those whose environmental backgrounds have been limited. . . . For each item the child is asked to look at all the pictures on the card, select the one which is different from, or unrelated to, the others, and indicate his choice by pointing to it. In order to do this, he must formulate a rule for organizing the pictures so as to exclude just one. The bases for discrimination range from the perception of rather gross differences in color, size, or form, to recognition of very subtle relations in pairs of pictures so as to exclude one from the series of drawings. (p. 7)

Administration of the CMMS takes from 15 to 20 minutes. The child is taught the task by three training items and then takes the appropriate age level of the test.

Scores

The raw score for the CMMS is simply the number of items answered correctly. Raw scores may be converted to age-deviation scores, percentile ranks, stanines, and a maturity index. The age-deviation score is a standard score with a mean of 100 and a standard deviation of 16. Maturity indexes are essentially comparable to MAs, although they are more global, encompassing ranges rather than being specific MAs. A maturity index of 4U, for example, indicates that the child earned the same score on the test as did those in the standardization group who were in the range from 4 years, 6 months, to 4 years, 11 months. The symbols U and L are used to depict upper and lower ranges of a given year level.

Norms

The CMMS was standardized on 2,600 children stratified on the basis of geographic region, race, parental occupation, age, and sex. Proportions of children in each of the demographic groups closely approximate 1960 U.S. Census data, with one exception. Figures reported for community size indicate that a greater proportion of children in the normative sample were from large cities (43.74 percent) than is true of the general population (28.5 percent). The selection of the normative sample was in all other ways exemplary.

Reliability

Both internal-consistency (split-half) and test-retest reliability are reported in the CMMS manual. Internal-consistency coefficients ranged from .85 to .91. Test-retest reliability for three different age groups ranged from .84 to .86. Children gained an average of 4.6 age-deviation score points between administrations.

Validity

Validity for the CMMS is based on two kinds of data: data indicating that scores on the test correlate substantially with scores on the Stanford Achievement Test (.31 to .61) and with scores on other intelligence tests. The CMMS scores of 353 children in grades 1 through 3 in a single school system correlated .62 to .69 with their scores on the Otis-Lennon Mental Ability Test and .67 with their scores on the Stanford-Binet.

Summary

The CMMS is an easily administered individual intelligence test designed to assess children's "reasoning ability." The test is adequately standardized and appears technically adequate. The instrument may be used to assess children who have difficulty responding verbally. It does, however, sample only two kinds of intellectual behavior, discrimination and classification; users must be careful not to overgeneralize the test results.

Test of Nonverbal Intelligence

The Test of Nonverbal Intelligence (TONI) (Brown, Sherbenou, & Dollar, 1982) is a language-free intelligence test designed to be used in both screening and diagnosis with individuals between 5-0 and 85-11 years of age. The test is administered in pantomime, and those tested point to one of several responses presented in multiple-response array. Because no listening, speaking, reading, or writing is required in either the administration or scoring of this test, the test is especially useful with those who are unable to read or write or who may have impaired language abilities (for example, aphasic, non-English-speaking, culturally disadvantaged, mentally retarded, learning disabled, or deaf students). The test is designed to be administered individually, though the authors claim it can be group administered. They state: "Although the TONI should be administered individually, it is possible for a trained and experienced examiner to administer the test to a small group of two to five subjects with no loss of accuracy or stability" (p. 20). The authors provide no evidence to support this latter contention, so the test is best restricted to individual administration. The test is untimed and takes about 15 minutes.

There are two forms of the TONI; each has fifty items arranged in order of difficulty. The test is designed to assess one aspect of intelligence—problem solving. This aspect was selected because it was thought to be a general component of intelligence as well as a basic prerequisite of functional independence. All TONI items require test takers to solve problems by identifying relationships among abstract figures. The subject must point to the one response among several alternatives that best fits a missing part in a pattern or matrix. The test item shown in Figure 9.7 is an example of the kind of item used in the TONI.

In developing the TONI, the authors wanted to put together a set of items that could be administered in pantomime and responded to by pointing. They also wanted items that were both abstract (nonmeaningful) and figural. An initial pool of 307 test items was developed by reviewing the content and format of other nonverbal and performance tests of intelligence. These items were reviewed by an unspecified number of professors, graduate students, school psychologists, psychometrists, and special education teachers. Items that these experts thought were too ambiguous, that were symbolic, or that involved language were eliminated from the item pool. This left 183 items. These items were further reduced by giving the test to an unspecified sample of 322 students in grades K, 1, 3, 5, 7 and 9, and to young adults ages 18–35 and older adults ages 65–86. The number of items was reduced on the basis of indices of item difficulty and item discriminating power, and 50 items were assigned to each of the two forms of the test.

Scores

Two kinds of scores, percentile ranks and TONI quotients, may be obtained. TONI quotients are standard scores with a mean of 100 and a standard deviation of 15. Thus, they are like the IQs earned on other intelligence tests. In fact, in some tables in the manual they are called "TONI quotient deviation IQs."

Norms

The authors report that the TONI was standardized on 1,929 subjects from twenty-eight states, ages 5-0 to 85-11, stratified on the basis of sex, race, ethnicity, domicile (urban, rural), geographic location, parental occupation and education (for children), and occupation and education (for adults). Close inspection of tables provided in the manual shows, however, that 45 percent of the norm sample lived in two states (25 percent from Texas, 20 percent from Kansas). No other state was represented by more than 9 percent of the sample; only 13 percent of the sample was from the Northeast. In fact, 89 percent of the sample came from seven states. Data on racial, ethnic, sex, and domicile indicate close approximation to 1980 census figures.

Reliability

Data on internal consistency and alternate-form reliability are reported in the test manual. No data are presented on test-retest reliability. Internal consistency was evaluated in two ways. First, the authors used coefficient alpha to ascertain internal consistency on 400 cases drawn randomly across the age range from the standardization sample. All correlation coefficients exceeded .90. The authors also used a KR-21 procedure to examine internal consistency, and all coefficients except those for 5- and 6-year-old children exceeded .80. Most exceeded .90. The authors shade scores for five- and six-year-olds in their norm tables to remind users that reliabilities are lower at this age level.

The authors also report alternate-form reliabilities for 1,888 subjects. These are in the .80 to .90 range, with only one coefficient (at age range 8-6 to 10-11) below .80. This coefficient is .78. In addition, data on the reliability of the test are presented for four groups of handicapped students: 10 educable mentally retarded students, 30 deaf students, and two groups ($N = 11$ and 16) of learning disabled students. Internal consistency was at least .80. The authors present sufficient data to demonstrate that the TONI is a reliable measure.

Validity

Data from eight concurrent validity studies are presented. Three studies were conducted with normal students, the other five used groups of handicapped students. All validity coefficients exceeded .35; 41 percent exceeded .80. The number of students in groups on whom validity data was collected was small. One troublesome feature is that correlations of the TONI with other measures of intelligence were nearly the same as correlations with measures of achievement.

To establish the construct validity of this measure—that is, to show that the test measures intelligence—the authors demonstrated that the test discriminates well between normal and mentally retarded students.

Summary

The TONI is an individually administered non-verbal measure of problem-solving ability. The test is adequately standardized and there is good evidence that this is a reliable measure. Evidence on validity is presented in the test manual, but that evidence is limited. The TONI should be especially useful in screening the intellectual functioning of students in instances when it is unwise or not feasible to use a verbal measure.

COPING WITH DILEMMAS IN CURRENT PRACTICE

The biggest difficulty encountered in trying to use individual intelligence tests is a problem of definition. What is intelligence? We noted in Chapter 9 that intelligence is an inferred construct. No one has seen a thing called *intelligence.* Yet, there are many tests of this thing that no one has seen, and assessors are regularly required to assess it. Most of the definitions of conditions requiring or eligible for special education include reference to cognitive functioning, intelligence, or capability. Mentally retarded students are said to have too little of it, gifted students have an oversupply. Learning disabled students are said to have average intelligence but to fail to demonstrate school performance commensurate with the amount of it they have.

Those who assess intelligence, and most diagnostic personnel are required to do so, must recognize that they can only infer intelligence from a sample of behavior derived through testing. Assessors must pay special attention to the kinds of behaviors sampled by intelligence tests. Two considerations are especially important. First, intelligence tests are usually administered for the purpose of making a prediction about future academic performance. In selecting an intelligence test, one must always ask, "What is the relationship between the kind(s) of behavior sampled by the test and the kind(s) of behavior I am trying to predict?" The closer the relationship, the better the prediction. It is wise to try to select tests that sample behaviors related as closely as possible to the behaviors one is trying to predict.

Second, one must always consider the psychological demand of intelligence test items. In particular, when different kinds of intelligence tests are used to assess handicapped students, it is very important to be aware of the stimulus and response demands of the items. The descriptions of kinds of behaviors sampled by intelligence tests provided in the last chapter should be helpful. When we assess students' intelligence we want the test results to reflect intelligence, not sensory dysfunction.

It is important to remember that intelligence is not a fixed thing that we measure. Rather, it is an inferred entity, one that is understood best by evaluating the ways in which individuals, who have different kinds of acculturation, perform several different kinds of tasks. Intelligence tests differ markedly;

individuals differ markedly. Evaluations of the intelligence of an individual must be understood as a function of the interaction between the skills and characteristics the individual brings to a test setting and the behaviors sampled by the test.

SUMMARY

Many different individually administered tests are currently used to assess intelligence. The tests differ considerably in their basic design, the kinds of behaviors they sample, and their technical adequacy. In evaluating performance on intelligence tests, it is especially important that teachers and examiners go beyond obtained scores to consider the specific tests on which the scores were obtained and the kinds of behaviors sampled by those tests. The information in this chapter will facilitate that evaluation.

Special attention was given in this chapter to individually administered tests designed to assess the intelligence of special populations. Individual intellectual assessment of children with specific handicaps should be carried out using tests designed to minimize the effects of the handicaps on their performances.

STUDY QUESTIONS

1. The Stanford-Binet Intelligence Scale and the Wechsler Intelligence Scale for Children–Revised are the two intelligence tests most frequently used with schoolage children. Identify similarities and differences in the domains of behavior sampled by these two tests.
2. Why is it inappropriate to use the same intelligence tests with sensorily or physically handicapped children as with children who do not have such handicaps?
3. Identify the major advantages of using the Stanford-Binet Intelligence Scale instead of the Slosson Intelligence Test.
4. In Chapter 9, we stated that IQs earned on different intelligence tests are not comparable. Using the Peabody Picture Vocabulary Test–Revised, the Quick Test, and the Wechsler Intelligence Scale for Children–Revised, support the statement.
5. The Performance sections of the Wechsler scales are the tests most commonly used today to assess the intelligence of deaf children. What are the major shortcomings of this practice? What alternatives exist?
6. Using the manual for any of the individual tests described in this chapter, characterize the domain or domains of behaviors sampled by any ten *items*. Use the domains described in Chapter 9.
7. For what reasons would school personnel give individual intelligence tests?

ADDITIONAL READING

Buros, O. K. (Ed.) (1978). *Eighth mental measurements yearbook.* (2 vols.) Highland Park, NJ: Gryphon Press. (Reviews of individual intelligence tests, pp. 291–356.)

Gerweck, S., & Ysseldyke, J. E. (1974). Limitations of current psychological practices for the intellectual assessment of the hearing impaired. A response to the Levine survey. *Volta Review, 77,* 243–248.

Sattler, J. (1981). *Assessment of children's intelligence and other special abilities* (2nd ed.). Boston: Allyn & Bacon. (Chapter 4: Issues related to the measurement and change of intelligence; Chapter 5: The examination process; Chapter 8: Interpreting the Stanford-Binet Intelligence Scale; Chapter 11: Interpreting the WISC–R.)

Sattler, J., & Tozier, L. (1971). A review of intelligence test modifications used with the cerebral palsied and other handicapped groups. *Journal of Special Education, 4,* 391–398.

CHAPTER 11

ASSESSMENT OF INTELLIGENCE: GROUP TESTS

Group intelligence tests differ from one another in three ways. First, they differ in format. Whereas some group tests consist of a single battery to be administered in one sitting, others contain a number of subscales or subtests and are administered in two or more sittings. Second, they differ in the kinds of scores they provide. Some provide IQs and/or mental ages based on a global performance; others provide the same kinds of scores, but they are differentiated into subscale scores (for example, verbal, performance, and total; language, nonlanguage, and total). Third, some group intelligence tests are speed tests (timed), and others are power tests (untimed).

WHY DO WE GIVE GROUP INTELLIGENCE TESTS?

Group intelligence tests are used for one of two purposes. Most often, they are routinely administered as screening devices to identify those who are different enough from average to warrant further assessment. Their merit, in this case, is that they can be administered relatively quickly by teachers to large numbers of students. Their drawback is that they suffer from the same limitations as any group test: they can be made to yield qualitative information only with difficulty, and they require that students can sit still for about twenty minutes, that they can mark with a pencil, and, often, that they can read.

Group intelligence tests are also used to provide descriptive information about the level of capability of students in a classroom, district, or even state. They are, on occasion, used in place of or in addition to achievement tests to track students. When used in this way, they set expectations; they are thought to indicate the level of achievement to be expected in individual classrooms or districts.

SPECIFIC GROUP TESTS OF INTELLIGENCE

Culture Fair Intelligence Tests

Three different scales comprise the Culture Fair Intelligence Tests. Scale 1 (Cattell, 1950) is used with students between 4 and 8 years of age. Scale 2 (Cattell & Cattell, 1960a) is used with those who are between 8 and 14 years of age; scale 3 (Cattell & Cattell, 1963) is used with those who are over 14 years of age. The Culture Fair Intelligence Tests are unique among group intelligence tests, and it is helpful to note the rationale for the tests and the theoretical orientation of their author.

According to Cattell (1962), the motivation for construction of the Culture Fair Intelligence Tests "was originally the need for a test which would fairly measure the intelligence of persons having different languages and cultures, or influenced by very different social status and education" (p. 5). Cattell (1973a) states that "the Culture Fair Intelligence Tests measure individual intelligence in a manner designed to reduce, as much as possible, the influence of verbal fluency, culture climate, and educational level" (p. 5).

Cattell believes culture-fair intelligence tests are more adequate measures of learning potential than are traditional intelligence tests. The latter, he argues, are contaminated by the effects of prior learning. Many have argued that scores on the Culture Fair Intelligence Tests do not effectively predict academic achievement. Cattell (1973b) states that the tests have been criticized because "within the same year and among students all in the same kind of school, the Culture Fair does not correlate with ('predict') achievement quite so highly as the traditional test" (p. 8). Cattell (1973b) states that

this is not only admitted, but treasured by the exponent of the newer tests. The reason that the traditional test gives a better immediate "prediction" is

that it already contains an appreciable admixture of the school achievement it is supposed to predict. If all we want to do is predict, in March, children's school achievement in, say, July, we can do better than any intelligence test by predicting from their school achievement scores in March. The very object of an intelligence test, however, is to be *analytical*. As we study any individual child we are interested in the *discrepancy* between his native intelligence and his school achievement, and the more clearly and reliably this is brought out, the better the test. The claim of the Culture Fair Tests is that it will make a more fair selection for future performance when the passage of some years has given a chance for the present accidental inequalities of achievement opportunity to be ironed out. (p. 8)

The Culture Fair Intelligence Tests are designed to measure general mental ability and, with the exception of some parts of scale 1, consist entirely of figural analogies and figural reasoning items. Time limits are 22 minutes for scale 1 and 12½ minutes each for scales 2 and 3. Only parts of scale 1 can be group administered; the scale consists of eight different subtests; some are individually administered, while others are group administered. Only four of the subtests make up the group test, and only four are judged by Cattell to be culture fair. Subtests of scales 1, 2, and 3 are listed in Table 11.1. As we noted earlier, scale 1 contains eight subtests. Four of these make up the group-administered version of the scale; the behaviors they sample are as follows.

Substitution   This subtest is a coding task that requires the student to associate symbols with pictures and to copy them on paper.

Mazes   The student is required to trace paths out of increasingly complex mazes.

TABLE 11.1 Subtests of the Three Scales of the Culture Fair Intelligence Tests

Scale 1	Scales 2 and 3
Substitution[a,b]	Series
Classification[b]	Classification
Mazes[a,b]	Matrices
Selecting Named Objects[a]	Conditions (Typology)
Following Directions	
Wrong Pictures	
Riddles	
Similarities[a,b]	

[a]Group-administered form.
[b]Fully culture-fair form.

Selecting Named Objects   This subtest is essentially a picture vocabulary task requiring the student to identify pictures of words read aloud by the examiner. This is one of the subtests that, according to the author, is not culture fair.

Similarities   The student is required to identify which of several response pictures is just like a stimulus picture.

Scales 2 and 3 are made up of the same four subtests. Behaviors sampled by these subtests are as follows.

Series   The student is given a sequence of figures having some progressive relationship to each other and is required to choose from four possible responses the figure that continues the progressive relationship. The first item in Figure 11.1 is a Series item.

Classification   The student is given five figures and is required to identify which picture is different from the other four. The second item in Figure 11.1 is a Classification item.

Matrices   The student is given a matrix and is required to identify the response that is the missing element in the matrix. The third item in Figure 11.1 is a matrix-completion item.

Conditions (Typology)   The student is given a stimulus figure in which a dot is placed in a certain relationship (that is, inside the circle, but outside the square). The student must identify that response element in which the dot is in the same relationship to the other elements as in the stimulus figure (that is, *inside* the circle, but *outside* the square). The fourth item in Figure 11.1 is a Conditions item.

Scores

In taking scale 1, students mark their responses in consumable test booklets, and the booklets are hand scored. Raw scores may be transformed to mental ages or to ratio IQs. The ratio IQs have a mean of 100, but a standard deviation of approximately 20. Cattell believes the higher standard deviations obtained from culture-fair tests are more nearly correct values than those obtained from traditional intelligence tests because "the reduced scatter in traditional intelligence tests is probably due to a contamination of intelligence with achievement" (1962), p. 14). One must remember, therefore, that an IQ of 120 on scale 1 is the standard-score equivalent of an IQ of 116 on the Stanford-Binet Intelligence Scale. Similarly, an IQ of 60 on scale 1 is the standard score equivalent of an IQ of 68 on the Stanford-Binet. Ratio IQs obtained for scale 1 may be transformed to percentiles on an IQ distribution with a standard deviation of 20.

On scales 2 and 3 of the Culture Fair Intelligence Tests, students respond on answer sheets that may be machine scored or scored by hand using a stencil. Raw scores on these scales may be transformed to mental ages and to three different IQs, each having a mean of 100 but standard deviations of 24.4, 24, or 16. The first two distributions are recommended for use when doing research on practical application of the tests and when one wishes to obtain the full spread of IQs typically obtained in administration of the device. The third distribution is a

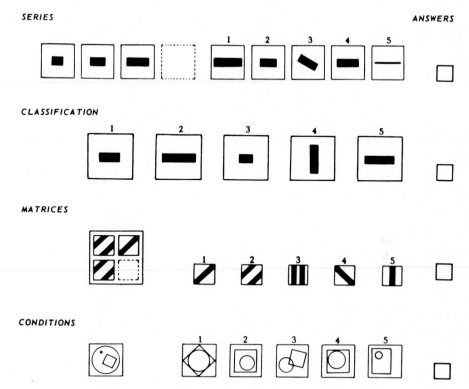

FIGURE 11.1   Items representative of subtests of the Culture Fair Intelligence Tests
SOURCE: Copyright 1949, 1957 by the Institute for Personality and Ability Testing, Inc. Reproduced by permission.

distribution of normalized standard scores with the standard deviation set at the standard deviation of "attainment-contaminated" tests. The distribution is used when one wishes to compare the results obtained on the Culture Fair Intelligence Tests with those obtained on more traditional intelligence tests.

Norms

The populations on whom the Culture Fair Intelligence Tests were standardized are inadequately described in the manuals. Cattell states that scale 1 was standardized on "more than 400 cases combining American and British samples" (1962, p. 12). He states that scale 2 was standardized on 4,328 boys and girls from var-

ied regions of the United States and Great Britain. The sample was apparently not stratified on the basis of any population characteristics. Norms for scale 3 were based on "3,140 cases, consisting of American high school students equally divided among freshmen, sophomores, juniors, and seniors, and young adults in a stratified job sample" (Cattell, 1973a, p. 21). There are no data in the manuals regarding the specific characteristics of the standardization samples.

Reliability

Data about reliability and validity of the three scales are reported in a separate Technical Supplement for scales 2 and 3 (Cattell, 1973b). Both internal consistency and test-retest data are reported for scale 1 on the basis of the test performance of 113 elementary school children of unspecified ages. Test-retest reliability based on the performances of 57 Head Start children over an unspecified time interval was reported to be .80 for the total test and to range from .57 to .71 for the subtests.

Three kinds of reliability data—internal-consistency, equivalent-form, and test-retest—are reported for scale 2. Based on the performances of 102 female Job Corps applicants, internal consistency for scale 2 was reported to range from .77 to .81 for form A and from .71 to .76 for form B. Split-half reliability, ranging from .95 to .97, was computed from a sample of 200 Mexican and American subjects. Equivalent-form reliability for scale 2 ranged from .58 to .72 with individuals of various ages. Test-retest reliability over an unspecified time interval was .82 for 200 American high school students and .85 for 450 eleven-year-old British secondary school students. There are no reliability data for the use of scale 2 with those under 11 years of age.

Reliability for scale 3 is reported in terms of internal-consistency and equivalent-form reliability for 202 high school students. Internal-consistency coefficients ranged from .51 to .68 for form A and from .53 to .64 for form B. Equivalent-form reliability ranged from .32 to .68.

Reliability for the Culture Fair Intelligence Tests sometimes approaches the necessary values for use of the test in screening. However, reliability data are incomplete.

Validity

The majority of evidence for the validity of the scales rests on a series of factor-analytic studies conducted by Cattell. Essentially, Cattell extracted a general ability factor ("g") and then correlated performance on each of the subtests with that factor. According to Cattell

TABLE 11.2   Correlations of Scores on Scale 2 of the Culture Fair Intelligence Tests with Scores Earned on Other Intelligence Tests

Test	Correlation with Scale 2
Otis Beta	.49
Pintner General Ability	.69
WISC Verbal	.62
WISC Performance	.63
WISC Full Scale	.72

and Cattell, "The real basis of validity of an intelligence test is its correlation with the 'construct' or concept of intelligence in the general ability factor" (1960b, p. 5). Cattell reports that correlations of the subtests with "g" range from '53 to '99.

Additional evidence for the validity of scale 1 consists of reported correlations with the Stanford-Binet ($r = .62$ for 25 "underprivileged children") and the Goodenough-Harris ($r = .46$ for 72 unspecified children). Scale 2 has been correlated with a number of other tests, and the correlations are reported in Table 11.2. Samples ranged in size from 186 to 1,000 and came from both the United States and Hong Kong. Validity for scale 3 is based on studies conducted with individuals in Taiwan and mainland China. Cattell reports that the scale correlated .29 with a critical thinking test, .22 with teacher ratings of intelligence, .23 with total grade average, .32 with math test scores, and .31 with math grades.

In addition, a number of studies are cited in the manual for scale 2 of the Culture Fair Tests that provide evidence, according to the author, of immunity of the tests from specific cultural influences.

Summary

The Culture Fair Intelligence Tests provide the examiner with a nontraditional approach to the assessment of intelligence. The tests assess intelligence with relatively little contamination by formal instruction. In evaluating how much meaningful information for one's own setting the tests provide, one must examine both the kind of information sought and one's own theoretical approach to intelligence testing. In interpreting the scores students earn on the scales, one must be especially aware of the large standard deviations of obtained scores. A major shortcoming of the Culture Fair Intelligence Tests is the inadequate description of the standardization group.

Cognitive Abilities Test

The Cognitive Abilities Test (CAT) (Thorndike & Hagen, 1978b) is a further development of the Lorge-Thorndike Intelligence Tests, which first appeared in 1954. There are ten levels of the CAT. Primary I is appropriate for use in kindergarten and grade 1; Primary II is to be used in grades 2 and 3. The multilevel edition of the CAT includes the remaining eight levels of the test in a single booklet. Items in the multilevel edition range from easy third-grade items to very difficult items at the twelfth-grade level. Examinees start and stop at different points, depending on the level being administered. The inclusion of eight levels of the test in a single multilevel edition allows teachers to administer levels of difficulty appropriate to the ability of their students. The scales increase in difficulty in very small steps. For students who attain little more than chance-level performance, the next easier level of the scale may be administered; whereas for those who get nearly every item correct, the next more difficult level may be administered. Practice tests are available for all subtests in the scale.

The CAT was constructed to provide a variety of tasks using verbal, numerical, and spatial symbols. The test requires the student to abstract and use relationships among the symbols. Whereas the original Lorge-Thorndike Intelligence Test included a verbal and nonverbal scale, the CAT consists of three batteries: Verbal, Quantitative, and Nonverbal. The *Verbal* battery has four subtests that sample the following behaviors.

Vocabulary This subtest assesses skill in selecting synonyms of words read by the student.

Sentence Completion The student reads a sentence with a missing word and must select the response word that most appropriately fills the blank.

Verbal Classification The student is given three or four words that are members of a conceptual category and must identify which response word best fits into the same category as the stimulus words.

Verbal Analogies The student must complete verbal analogies of the nature A : B :: C : ?.

The *Quantitative* battery is made up of three subtests:

Quantitative Relations Given two quantities (one might be $2\sqrt{4}$ and the other $\sqrt{2} \times 4$), the student must identify which one is greater.

Number Series Given a series of numbers that have a progressive relationship to one another, the student must select that number that best completes the relationship.

Equation Building The student must use numbers and symbols for mathematical operations to construct correct equations.

A *Nonverbal* battery that requires no reading has three subtests:

Figure Analogies   The student must complete figural analogies of the nature $\triangle : \triangle :: \bigcirc : \underline{\hspace{1em}}$.

Figure Classification   Given three figures that are alike in some way, the student must identify the response that best fits into the same conceptual category.

Figure Synthesis   The student is given parts of figures and must identify the whole figure that could be formed by placing the parts together.

Scores

Transformed scores obtained from the CAT include standard scores by ages (IQs with a mean of 100 and a standard deviation of 16); percentiles, normal curve equivalents, and stanines by age; and percentiles and stanines by grade. Separate scores may be obtained for the Verbal, Quantitative, and Nonverbal batteries. No total score for the combination of the three batteries is provided, and the authors rightly recommend that no total score be used.

Norms

The CAT was standardized concurrently with the Iowa Tests of Basic Skills (Hieronymus, Lindquist, & Hoover, 1978) and the Tests of Achievement and Proficiency (Scannell, 1978). The tests were administered to 18,000 students per grade (a total of about 235,000 students) in the fall, and again to about 3,600 pupils per grade in the spring. Some schools participated in both the fall and spring standardizations. A five-step procedure was used to stratify the standardization sample.

The initial step in sample selection was strat-ification of school districts throughout the nation according to the size of their enrollment. They were then sorted on the basis of geographic region. Third, the socioeconomic status of the communities represented was ascertained using 1970 census data, taking into account the median years of education in the districts and the median incomes of families. Districts were then selected at random from the stratified sample and invited to participate in standardization. Once districts agreed to participate, schools within districts were selected. The final step was review of both demographic data on the schools and indexes of achievement in those schools.

Several tables in the preliminary technical manual for the tests report correspondence of sample proportions with U.S. population proportions based on district enrollment, geographic region, and socioeconomic status. A weighting system was used to achieve closer correspondence between sample proportions and national population proportions.

Reliability

The authors report internal-consistency coefficients for subtests ranging from .91 to .96 based on the performance of students in the standardization sample. In addition, they report test-retest reliability coefficients ranging from .78 to .93 based on the performance of an unspecified number of students who participated in both fall and spring normative testing. Reliabilities of the CAT are listed in Table 11.3.

Validity

The authors of the CAT present reliability data, data on the long-term stability of the test, as evidence for construct validity. Not only are the data *not* validity data, but they are on an earlier edition (the 1971 edition) of the test.

In addition, the authors report several sets of

TABLE 11.3   Internal-Consistency and Test-Retest Reliability of the Cognitive Abilities Test

	Verbal Battery	Quanti-tative Battery	Nonverbal Battery
Level A (Grade 3)			
KR-20 Reliabilities*	.96	.92	.94
Test-Retest Reliabilities†	.85	.78	.81
Level B (Grade 4)			
KR-20 Reliabilities*	.95	.92	.93
Test-Retest Reliabilities†	.89	.83	.85
Level C (Grade 5)			
KR-20 Reliabilities*	.94	.92	.93
Test-Retest Reliabilities†	.91	.85	.85
Level D (Grade 6)			
KR-20 Reliabilities*	.94	.91	.93
Test-Retest Reliabilities†	.93	.86	.88
Level E (Grade 7)			
KR-20 Reliabilities*	.94	.92	.93
Test-Retest Reliabilities†	.92	.87	.89
Level F (Grade 8)			
KR-20 Reliabilities*	.94	.92	.93
Test-Retest Reliabilities†	.93	.88	.88
Level F (Grade 9)			
KR-20 Reliabilities*	.95	.93	.93
Test-Retest Reliabilities†	.93	.87	.87
Level G (Grade 10)			
KR-20 Reliabilities*	.95	.93	.93
Test-Retest Reliabilities†	.91	.83	.85
Level G (Grade 11)			
KR-20 Reliabilities*	.95	.93	.93
Test-Retest Reliabilities†	.90	.88	.85
Level H (Grade 12)			
KR-20 Reliabilities*	.96	.93	.92
Test-Retest Reliabilities†	.91	.88	.82

*The KR-20 reliabilities are uncorrected for possible speededness. Some degree of speededness can be expected for Level A.

†These data are based on test administrations spaced about 6 months apart. The reliabilities were adjusted to Standard Age Scores with a standard deviation of 16 in each grade.

SOURCE: From *Preliminary Technical Summary of the Cognitive Abilities Test, Form 3* (p. 12) by R. Thorndike and E. Hagen, 1978, Chicago: The Riverside Publishing Co. Copyright 1978. Reproduced by permission of the Publisher, The Riverside Publishing Company, 8420 Bryn Mawr Ave., Chicago, IL 60631.

data indicative of the criterion validity of the test. They report the relationship of scores on the *earlier edition* to reading and math grades, the relationship of scores on the *earlier edition* to scores on the Stanford-Binet, and the relationship of scores on the 1978 edition to scores on the Iowa Tests of Basic Skills. These latter correlations range from .54 to .89, within the expected range.

Summary

The Cognitive Abilities Test consists of three batteries (Verbal, Quantitative, and Nonverbal) designed to measure the intelligence of students in kindergarten through grade 12. The test is adequately standardized and evidence for reliability is good, but evidence for validity is meager.

Educational Ability Series

The Educational Ability Series (EAS) (Thurstone, 1978) is a group-administered ability test available only as an option with the SRA Achievement Series. The test cannot be separately purchased and administered. There are eight levels (A through H) of the test, matched to the eight levels of the SRA Achievement Series. The test comprises both a verbal and a nonverbal battery. The subtests that make up the verbal and nonverbal battery at each level of the test are listed in Table 11.4. Behaviors sampled by the subtests are as follows.

Picture and Word Vocabulary   This subtest measures a student's knowledge of word meanings by requiring the student to match a stimulus word with a response word or picture.

Number   This subtest measures a student's skill in understanding quantitative concepts.

Picture Grouping   This subtest assesses a student's ability to classify pictured objects. The student is required to identify which of four pictured objects differs from the other three.

Spatial   This subtest assesses development of skill in identifying spatial relationships. Early levels of the test require students to visualize relationships among shapes; at later levels students are required to identify which of four given pieces could be formed by putting four shapes together.

Number and Series   This subtest assesses pupils' skills in computation and sequencing.

Word Groupings   This subtest assesses skill in identifying the one of four words that does not fit a conceptual category.

Scores

Several different derived scores are obtained for the EAS. The first is a quotient score with a standard deviation of 16 and a "sliding mean" that begins at 100 at kindergarten and increases by 0.5 each grade year until grade 10, where it is 105. Users may obtain Growth Scale Values (GSVs), standard scores ranging from 20 to 780, that make it easier to contrast change (growth or loss) over time with that of the standardization sample. Users may also obtain percentile and stanine scores.

Norms

The EAS was standardized concurrently with the SRA Achievement Series (Naslund, Thorpe, & Lefever, 1978) on 83,681 students in 383

TABLE 11.4   Levels and Subtests of the Educational Ability Series

Test Level	Verbal	Nonverbal
A, B	Picture Vocabulary	Number Picture Grouping Spatial
C, D	Picture Vocabulary Word Vocabulary	Number Picture Grouping Spatial
E, F, G, H	Vocabulary Word Grouping	Number and Series Spatial

SOURCE: From User's Guide, *SRA Achievement Series.* © 1979, Science Research Associates, Inc. Reprinted by permission.

schools in eighty-one districts in spring 1978. An additional standardization was completed on 129,900 students in 457 schools in ninety-two districts in fall 1978. A three-stage sampling design was used; stratification of school districts on the basis of geographic region was followed by random sampling of schools within districts and a random sampling of classes within schools. Sample weighting procedures were used to improve the representativeness of the standardization sample. Specific demographic data on the standardization sample are included in Technical Report #1.

Reliability

The authors report internal-consistency reliabilities based on scores earned by those who participated in both fall and spring standardization of the scale. Reliabilities are reported separately by grade level and range from .77 to .93. Most exceed .80. There are no data on test-retest reliability.

Validity

Data on validity of the EAS are limited to correlations of scores on the measure with scores earned on subtests of the SRA Achievement Series. These are reported separately by grade level and range from .28 to .80.

Summary

The Educational Ability Series is a norm-referenced ability measure developed for use with the SRA Achievement Series. The test includes both a verbal and a nonverbal battery. The test is adequately standardized, though data on reliability and validity are limited.

Goodenough-Harris Drawing Test

The Goodenough-Harris Drawing Test (G-H) (Harris, 1963) is designed to measure *intellectual maturity,* which, according to the author, consists of "the ability to form concepts of increasingly abstract character" (p. 5). Harris states that intellectual maturity requires the ability to perceive, to abstract, and to generalize. The student is required to complete three drawings: one of a man, one of a woman, and one of himself or herself. Drawings can be scored by two methods, qualitative or quantitative. In quantitative scoring, points are awarded on the basis of the amount of detail in the drawing. For example, a student receives points for including a neck, indicating fingers, styling hair, and so forth. Artistic merit does not earn points, but smooth and well-controlled lines do. Harris states that "the literature on children's drawings shows quite clearly that the nature and content of such drawings are dependent primarily upon intellectual development" (1963, p. 68). The device may be administered individually or to groups of students age 3 through 15.

Scores

As noted above, scoring of the G-H is both quantitative and qualitative. A point scale is used to assign points for inclusion of specific features in drawings. A student's drawings of a man and of a woman are scored separately, but the self-drawing is never formally scored. Examples of criteria used in assigning points are illustrated in Figure 11.2.

The quality of the student's drawing is scored on a twelve-point scale. Figure 11.3 contains illustrations of drawings of a man that earn one, four, eight, and twelve points. The Quality scale was constructed and standardized for convenient and rapid scoring of the man and woman drawings. It was constructed on the basis of the opinions of a group of judges who were asked to sort 240 drawings (completed by twenty children at each age level) into twelve categories, with category 1 representing drawings of the "least excellence," category 6 those of "median excellence," and category 11 those of "greatest excellence." Categories 0 and 12 were included to sort out drawings that were outstandingly poor or outstandingly good. According to Harris (1963), "These scales are not as sensitive measures of development as the Point scales, especially after age eight or nine. Moreover, the Quality scales tend to magnify the sex differences observed on the Point scales" (p. 227).

Two kinds of scores are obtained for the G-H. Raw scores on the Point scale and on the Quality scale may be transformed to standard-score IQs (mean = 100, standard deviation = 15), which in turn may be transformed to percentile ranks. Scoring is in terms of whole-year intervals, so the same normative data are used for children who are 4 years, 1 month, and those who are 4 years, 11 months.

Norms

The G-H is a revision of the original Goodenough Draw-a-Man Test. In revising the scale, it was administered to "several thousand" children in four geographic areas. Harris reports that the final normative data were based on a selection of seventy-five children at each age level from this initial pool of subjects, stratified on the basis of the occupations of their parents. An equal number of boys and girls were selected at each age level. The manual does not include sufficient detail to demonstrate the extent to which the sample is adequate.

Reliability

Harris reports that studies of interscorer reliability have produced reliability coefficients ranging from the low .80s to as high as .96. Interscorer reliability for the Quality scale ranges from .71 to .91. Thus, the device can be scored with adequate reliability. Harris also summarizes several studies of the test-retest reliability of the scale, reporting that test-retest reliability coefficients are in the .60s to .70s over a time interval as long as three months.

Validity

Harris reports the results of a number of studies demonstrating indirect evidence for the validity of the G-H. In addition, he reports the results of twenty investigations correlating performance on the G-H with scores on other intellec-

18. **Hair I**   Any indication of hair, however crude.

19. **Hair II**   Hair shown on more than circumference of head and more than a scribble. Nontransparent, unless it is clear that a bald-headed man is portrayed. A simple hairline across the skull on which no attempt has been made to shade in hair does *not* score. If any attempt has been made, even in outline or with a little shading, to portray hair as having substance or texture, the item scores.

Credit

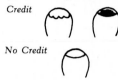

No Credit

20. **Hair III**   Any clear attempt to show cut or styling by use of side burns, a forelock, or conformity of base line to a "style." When a hat is drawn, credit the point if hair is indicated in front as well as behind the ear, or if hairline at back of neck or across forehead suggests styling.

21. **Hair IV**   Hair shaded to show part, or to suggest having been combed, or brushed, by means of *directed* lines. Item 21 is never credited unless Item 20 is; it is thus a "high-grade" point.

Credit

No Credit

22. **Ears present**   Any indication of ears.

23. **Ears present: proportion and position**   The vertical measurement must be greater than the horizontal measurement. The ears must be placed somewhere within the middle two-thirds of the head.

Full Face: The top of the ear must be separated from the head line, and *both* ears must extend from the head.

Credit

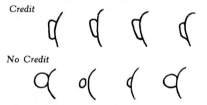

No Credit

Profile: Some detail, such as a dot, to represent the aural canal must be shown. The shell-like portion of the ear must extend toward the back of the head. (Some children, especially retarded boys, tend to reverse this position, making the ear extend toward the face. In such drawings this item is never credited.)

Credit

No Credit

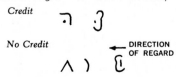

← **DIRECTION OF REGARD**

FIGURE 11.2   Examples of scoring criteria for the Draw-a-Man scale of the Goodenough-Harris Drawing Test

SOURCE: From *Children's Drawings as Measures of Intellectual Maturity* by Dale B. Harris, 1963, Orlando, FL: Harcourt Brace Jovanovich. Copyright 1963 by Harcourt Brace Jovanovich, Inc. Reproduced by permission.

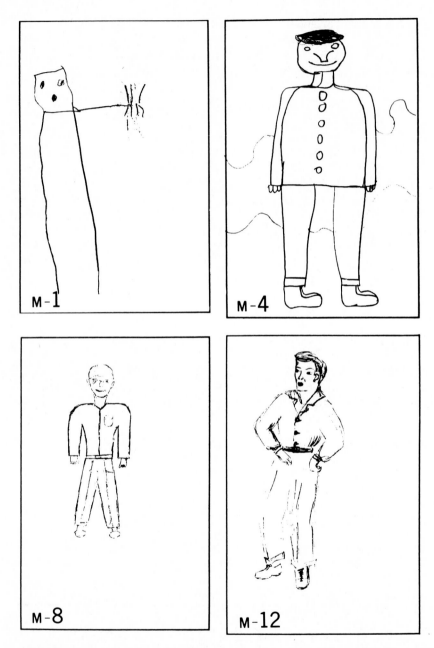

FIGURE 11.3   Examples of drawings that earn one, four, eight, and twelve points on the Goodenough-Harris Quality scale; the letter M indicates that the drawings are of males, and the numbers give the point values assigned

SOURCE: From *Children's Drawings as Measures of Intellectual Maturity* by Dale B. Harris, 1963, Orlando, FL: Harcourt Brace Jovanovich. Copyright 1963 by Harcourt Brace Jovanovich, Inc. Reproduced by permission.

tual measures. The correlations range from .05 to .92, with the majority in a range from .50 to .80. Correlations of performance on the revised G-H and the original 1929 scale ranged from .91 to .98. To establish validity for the Quality scale, Harris reports that it correlates .76 to .91 with the Point scale.

Summary

The Goodenough-Harris Drawing Test is either a group-administered or individually administered scale designed to assess students' intellectual development on the basis of their drawings of men, women, and themselves. In using the scale, one must be careful to remember that the test measures only one aspect of intelligence, detail recognition. In addition, the scale was standardized and scoring criteria developed during the 1950s. To the extent that dress styles change, students may be at a disadvantage. This is especially evident in the scoring of the Draw-a-Woman scale. On this scale, students receive credit if they draw a "skirt modeled to indicate pleats or draping: an irregular hemline is not sufficient; lines, shading, or sketching must appear" (Harris, 1963, p. 228). With contemporary styles of dress changing, the likelihood that students will draw a woman in a pleated skirt will also change.

Henmon-Nelson Tests of Mental Ability

The Henmon-Nelson Tests of Mental Ability (Lamke, Nelson, & French, 1973; Nelson & French, 1974) are "designed to measure those aspects of mental ability which are important for success in school work" (p. 3). There are four levels of the test, designed for assessment of children in grades kindergarten through 2, 3 through 6, 6 through 9, and 9 through 12. The Primary form, for kindergarten through grade 2, contains eighty-six items and is published as a consumable test booklet in which pupils record their responses directly. The other three levels each contain ninety items and have an accompanying self-scoring answer sheet so that the test booklets may be reused. Each level takes approximately 30 minutes to administer. The Primary form (kindergarten through grade 2) includes three subtests: Listening, Vocabulary, and Size and Number. These are designed to measure the following behaviors.

Listening   This subtest assesses knowledge of factual information, reasoning ability, and understanding of logical relationships. In each case, information is read to the student, who is then required to identify pictures.

Vocabulary   This subtest assesses understanding of words by requiring the student to identify which of four pictures best matches a word read by the examiner.

Size and Number   This subtest assesses understanding of basic spatial and numerical concepts by measuring "perception and recognition of size, number comprehension, ability to count, and ability to solve simple arithmetic problems"(1974, p. 4).

The remainder of the Henmon-Nelson levels do not include subtests but sample several different behaviors that are combined in a global score. A description of the kinds of behaviors sampled follows.

Vocabulary   The student is required to identify synonyms for stimulus words.

Sentence Completion The student is required to select which of five response choices best completes a sentence.

Opposites The student is required to identify antonyms for stimulus words.

General Information The student is required to answer specific factual questions.

Verbal Analogies The student is required to complete verbal relationships of the nature A : B : : C : ?.

Verbal Classification The student is required to identify which of five response possibilities does not belong with the other four.

Verbal Inference The student is given verbal information and must solve problems by inference.

Number Series The student is given a sequence of numbers having some relationship to one another and must identify the number or numbers that continue the relationship.

Arithmetic Reasoning The student is required to solve arithmetic problems employing one or more computational operations.

Figure Analogies The student is required to solve analogies that employ symbols as stimuli.

Scores

Raw scores that students earn on the Henmon-Nelson may be transformed to deviation IQs (mean = 100, standard deviation = 16), percentile ranks, and stanines.

Norms

The levels of the Henmon-Nelson for grades 3 through 12 were standardized on 48,000 pupils (4,000 from each grade plus an additional 4,000 per grade in grades 6 and 9). The Primary form was standardized on 5,000 children from the same schools as those used in the standardization of the other levels. The standardization was completed in regular classes, and the sample was stratified only on the basis of community size and geographic region. The authors provide descriptive tables for community size and geographic region, comparing sample proportions to U.S. population proportions. They do not provide descriptive data about individual students in the standardization sample.

Reliability

Reliability data for the Henmon-Nelson consist of internal-consistency coefficients (split-half reliability estimates corrected by the Spearman-Brown formula) for each of the levels by grade. These coefficients are reported in Table 11.5. The reported reliabilities are satisfactory for the use of the test as a screening instrument. No test-retest reliabilities are reported.

Validity

Validity data are reported separately in the Primary manual and the manual for grades 3 through 12. The authors of the Henmon-Nelson report concurrent validity for the Primary form based on correlations of scores earned on the Henmon-Nelson and scores earned on the Metropolitan Achievement Test (MAT) by thirty disadvantaged children (the author's definition of *disadvantaged* is not given) and thirty nondisadvantaged children. For the combined groups, the total score on the Henmon-Nelson correlated .72 with the total score on the MAT, while subtest correlations ranged from .41 to .73.

Two sets of validity data are reported for the levels of the test for grades 3 through 12, but they cover specifically grades 3, 6, and 9 only. The Lorge-Thorndike Intelligence Test (grades 3 and 6), the Otis-Lennon Mental Ability Test

TABLE 11.5 Odd-Even Reliability Coefficients for the Henmon-Nelson Tests of Mental Ability

Level	Grade	r (Corrected)
Primary	K	.84
Primary	1	.89
Primary	2	.88
3–6	3	.95
3–6	4	.96
3–6	5	.96
3–6	6	.97
6–9	6	.95
6–9	7	.94
6–9	8	.95
6–9	9	.95
9–12	9	.93
9–12	10	.95
9–12	11	.95
9–12	12	.96

SOURCE: From *Examiner's Manual for the Henmon-Nelson Tests of Mental Ability, 1973 Revision* (p. 38) by T. Lamke, M. Nelson, and J. French, 1973, Chicago: The Riverside Publishing Co. Copyright 1973. *Examiner's Manual for the Henmon-Nelson Tests of Mental Ability, Primary Form 1* (p. 31) by M. Nelson and J. French, 1974, Chicago: The Riverside Publishing Co. Copyright 1974. Reproduced by permission of the Publisher, The Riverside Publishing Company, 8420 Bryn Mawr Ave., Chicago, IL 60631.

(grade 9), and the Iowa Tests of Basic Skills were administered to three hundred pupils "representative of those enrolled in grades 3, 6, and 9 in Clearfield, Pennsylvania," during the spring of the year. The following fall, the Henmon-Nelson was given. Correlations between the Henmon-Nelson and the Lorge-Thorndike ranged from .78 to .83; those between the Henmon-Nelson and the Otis-Lennon from .75 to .82. Correlations between scores earned on the Henmon-Nelson and scores earned on subtests of the ITBS ranged from .60 to .86. Predictive validity requires that the predictor test be given first. What the authors have done, in fact, is to establish predictive validity for the other tests using the Henmon-Nelson as a criterion. There are no validity data on other grades or samples of pupils. The authors state that "since the 1973 Revision retains the essential characteristics of the earlier Henmon-Nelson forms, it is reasonable to expect that Form I [for grades 3–6] will show similar patterns of relationships with achievement tests" (p. 41).

Summary

The Henmon-Nelson Tests of Mental Ability are quickly administered group tests of mental ability. Levels of the scale for grades 3 through 12 are revisions of the earlier forms of the test. The level appropriate for use in kindergarten through grade 2 is a new downward extension of the test. While data about the reliability of the scale indicate adequate reliability for use of the test in screening, there are some serious questions about the adequacy of standardization of the scale. Data regarding validity are inadequate.

Otis-Lennon School Ability Test

The Otis-Lennon School Ability Test (OLSAT) (Otis & Lennon, 1979) is the fifth edition in the Otis Series. The original Otis test, the Otis Group Intelligence Scale, was the first group intelligence test designed for use in American schools. The test represented an effort to develop a paper-and-pencil test similar to the individually administered Stanford-Binet Intelligence Scale. The Otis Self-Administering Tests of Mental Ability were published between 1922 and 1929, while the Otis Quick Scoring Mental Ability Tests were developed later. The most recent edition is a revision of these earlier scales.

The OLSAT was designed "to provide an accurate and efficient measure of the abilities needed to acquire the desired cognitive outcomes of formal education" (Otis & Lennon, 1979). The authors identify this complex of abilities as "scholastic aptitude" or "school ability." The test measures this set of abilities by assessing students' skills in detecting similarities and differences, defining words, following directions, classifying, sequencing, solving arithmetic problems, and completing analogies.

The OLSAT is organized in five levels from grades 1 through 12. Primary I, intended for use in grade 1, requires 80 minutes to administer and assesses students' abilities in identifying analogies, classifying objects, and following directions. Primary II, intended for use in grades 2 and 3, measures similar skills and requires 80 minutes to administer. The content of Primary I and Primary II requires no reading. The Elementary (Grades 4 and 5), Intermediate (Grades 6 through 8), and Advanced (Grades 9 through 12) levels of the test sample verbal, figural, and quantitative reasoning and verbal comprehension ability. The tests require 40 to 45 minutes to administer, and all items are read by the student. There are two parallel forms of the test, forms R and S, at each level.

Scores

Three kinds of scores may be obtained using the OLSAT: a school ability index (SAI) and percentile ranks and stanines by age and grade. The school ability index is statistically equivalent to a deviation IQ with a mean of 100 and a standard deviation of 16. The authors state that "those who prefer to designate this score an IQ and feel that they can use this term without misinterpretation may, of course, do so."

Norms

The OLSAT was standardized in October 1977 on approximately 130,000 pupils in seventy school systems stratified and selected on the basis of geographic region, school system enrollment, socioeconomic status, and ethnic enrollment. Tables in the manual compare kinds of students with those in the national population.

Reliability

Both internal-consistency and test-retest reliability are reported in the test manual by both grade and age. All internal-consistency coefficients exceed .90. Test-retest reliability was ascertained by studying the test performance of students in grades 1, 2, 4, 7, and 10 over a 6-month interval. Summary data are reported in Table 11.6. Test-retest reliabilities ranged from .84 to .92.

Validity

Two kinds of validity data are reported on the OLSAT: correlations of performance on the test with teacher-assigned grades, and correlations of OLSAT scores with scores earned on the Metropolitan Achievement Test (MAT). Correlations of performance on the OLSAT and teacher grades ranged from .40 to .60 with a median of .49 in four school districts. Correlations between performance on the OLSAT and on the MAT ranged from .55 to .89. The pattern of relationships differs in grades 1 through 3, where the mean correlation is .70, and in grades 4 and up, where the median is .82.

Summary

The Otis-Lennon School Ability Test is a group-administered measure of scholastic aptitude or school ability. The test was adequately standardized and demonstrates the necessary technical adequacy to be used as a screening device.

TABLE 11.6 Test-Retest Reliability of the OLSAT over a 6-month Interval

Level	Grade	Sample Size	October 1977 Raw Score		April 1978 Raw Score		Fall-Spring Correlation
			Mean	SD	Mean	SD	
Primary I	1	378	36.1	11.0	42.5	10.5	.84
Primary II	2	348	39.1	14.8	48.1	15.5	.84
Elementary	4	302	34.9	15.1	40.6	15.5	.86
Intermediate	7	275	39.7	18.5	43.5	18.9	.92
Advanced	10	209	35.7	15.5	37.8	16.6	.84

SOURCE: Reproduced by permission from Manual for Administering and Interpreting the Otis-Lennon School Ability Test (p. 23). Copyright 1979 by The Psychological Corporation. All rights reserved.

Short Form Test of Academic Aptitude

The Short Form Test of Academic Aptitude (SFTAA) (Sullivan, Clark, & Tiegs, 1970) was derived from the earlier California Test of Mental Maturity. Three different publications contain information regarding the SFTAA: the technical report that contains research data for 1973, the Test Coordinator's Handbook for the series of tests, and the examiner's manuals that accompany each level of the test. The SFTAA, designed to assess the intellectual maturity of students in grades 1 through 12, has five levels. The levels and their corresponding grades are reported in Table 11.7.

Each level of the SFTAA contains two sections: language and nonlanguage. The language section includes two subtests, Vocabulary and Memory, and the nonlanguage section includes Analogies and Sequencing. Behaviors sampled by the respective subtests are as follows.

Vocabulary This subtest differs at each level of the test. Level 1 employs a picture-vocabulary format to assess the extent to which children are able to identify pictures of words read by the teacher. Levels 2 through 5 require students to identify synonyms of words that they must first read.

Memory This subtest assesses the recall of factual information as well as comprehension and interpretation of the content of stories. Levels 1 and 2 use pictured responses, while the other levels employ a printed-question format. The teacher reads the content of the stories, then administers the other subtests before administering the Memory subtest. In this way, there is a 30-minute delay with a considerable amount of interpolated material before the student is asked to recall information.

Analogies Pictures are employed at all levels to assess the extent to which the student is able to solve analogies of an A : B : : C: ? format.

Sequencing In this subtest the student looks at a sequence of stimuli having some progressive relationship to one another and then must identify a missing element in the sequence. Numerical and figural stimuli are employed at all levels.

Scores

Raw scores earned on the SFTAA are transformed to what the authors label *reference scale scores*, standard scores with a mean of 600 and a standard deviation of 100. These scores may be converted to deviation IQs with a mean of

TABLE 11.7 Levels of the Short Form Test of Academic Aptitude

Level	Grades
1	1.5–3.4
2	3.5–4.9
3	5.0–6.9
4	7.0–9.9
5	9.0–12.9

100 and a standard deviation of 16. Deviation IQs may be transformed into either age percentile ranks, grade percentile ranks, or grade stanines. Mental ages may also be obtained for scores on the SFTAA. Separate scores are obtained for the language, nonlanguage, and total scores.

Norms

The SFTAA was standardized jointly with the California Achievement Test on a national sample of 197,912 students in first through twelfth grade. In the selection of students for the normative sample, the authors selected schools rather than individual students. A stratification based on "1967 census figures" for geographic region, community type (urban, suburban, and so on), and district size was used to select 108 school *districts;* 60.1 percent agreed to participate. Replacements were selected for those districts that did not wish to participate, and the final sample was made up of 397 public and 42 Catholic schools. Although these variables were not used to select the sample, the manual does include a description of the normative sample in terms of student mobility, PTA attendance of parents, employed mothers, racial characteristics, kindergarten attendance, number of students with only one parent, number of students for whom English was a second language, occupational level of parents, and characteristics of the physical plant and administration of the school.

Reliability

Internal-consistency and test-retest reliability coefficients are reported by grade and level of the test for a subsample of those who made up the standardization sample. Internal-consistency coefficients ranged from .70 to .91 for individual subtests, from .85 to .93 for the language section, from .84 to .92 for the nonlanguage section, and from .90 to .96 for the total test.

Test-retest reliabilities over a two-week interval ranged from .82 to .94 for the language section, from .83 to .94 for the nonlanguage section, and from .89 to .96 for the total test. Over a fourteen-week interval, test-retest coefficients ranged from .73 to .89 for the language section, from .49 to .83 for the nonlanguage section, and from .68 to .91 for the total test. In general, the test demonstrates adequate reliability for screening purposes.

Validity

Validity was established by means of three correlational studies. A concurrent validity study compared pupil performance on the SFTAA with performance on the Short Form of the California Test of Mental Maturity, its parent test. Correlations between the language sections of the two scales ranged from .64 to .86, between the two nonlanguage sections from .38 to .74, and between total scores on the two devices from .63 to .84.

A second concurrent validity study looked at the relationship between performances of pupils in grades 2, 4, 6, 8, and 10 on the SFTAA and their performances on a measure of academic achievement, the Comprehensive Test of Basic Skills. Correlations between language, nonlanguage, and total scores and area totals on the CTBS ranged from .40 to .86.

A third concurrent validity study was completed by ascertaining the degree of relationship between performances on the SFTAA and on the California Achievement Test for students at every grade level. Twelve tables reporting the results of this investigation are in the technical manual. Although these tables must be examined carefully to get a true picture of the kinds and degrees of relationships identified, in general the correlations are adequate.

Summary

The SFTAA is a group-administered device designed to provide an index of general mental ability. The test consists of both a language and a nonlanguage section. The standardization of this test was based on a stratification of school districts, with only 60.1 percent of the originally chosen sample participating. The reliability of the scale is adequate for use in screening. Reliabilities for the subsections of the test are lower than reliabilities for the total, as is usually the case. Validity information is, at this time, limited. The only evidence the authors report to support the contention that the test measures general mental ability or intellectual maturity is a comparison of scores on the SFTAA and its parent test, the Short Form of the California Test of Mental Maturity. The items for the two tests are different.

COPING WITH DILEMMAS IN CURRENT PRACTICE

A number of specific limitations are inherent in the construction and use of group intelligence tests. The first limitation is that most tests have a number of levels designed for use in specific grades (for example, level A for kindergarten through third grade, level B for third through sixth grade). Tests are typically standardized by grade. Students of different ages are enrolled in the same grade; students of the same age are enrolled in different grades. Test authors use interpolation to compute mental ages for students based on grade sampling. In earlier discussions, an age score was defined as the average score earned by individuals of a given age. Let us now consider a problem.

Suppose that an intelligence test has a level Q, which is designed to measure the intelligence of students in grades 6 through 9. As is typical of group intelligence tests, the test is standardized on students in grades 6 through 9, students who range in age from approximately 10 to 15 or 16 years. Norms are based on this age range. The test is later administered to Stanley, age 10-8, who earns a mental age of 7-3. How can this be? Stanley, who is 10 years, 8 months old, could not possibly earn the same score as is typically earned on the test by students who are 7 years, 3 months old, since no 7-year, 3-month-old students were included in the normative sample. The score is based on an extrapolation.

The second limitation is that most group intelligence tests, while standardized on large numbers of students, often are not standardized on representative populations. Most are standardized on districts, not on individual students. An effort is made to select representative districts, but not necessarily a representative population of individuals. Yet, the normative tables for group intelligence tests typically provide scores for individuals, not for groups.

The third limitation is that most group intelligence tests are standardized on volunteer samples. In the process of standardizing the test, representative districts are selected and are asked to participate. Those districts refusing, for any number of reasons, are replaced by "comparable" districts. This process of replacement may introduce bias into the standardization.

Finally, it must be remembered that when tests are standardized in public schools, those students who are excluded from school are also excluded from the standardization population. Severely retarded students, severely disturbed students, and dropouts are excluded from the norms. Similarly, most authors of group intelligence tests do not describe the extent to which they included students enrolled in special-education classes in their standardization samples. Exclusion of students with low IQs biases the norms; the range of performance of the standardization group is reduced, and the standard deviation is decreased. It is extremely important for the authors of group tests to provide tables in test manuals illustrating the composition of the standardization sample. In doing so, it is preferable to include descriptions of the kinds of individuals on whom a test was standardized rather than descriptions of districts.

Many school districts have done away with the use of group intelligence tests for several reasons. The tests have been alleged to discriminate against members of racial and cultural minorities, so school personnel in some districts have simply stopped using them. Other schools no longer use the tests because they provide teachers with limited information for instructional planning. Because the administration of group intelligence tests produces scores, and because teachers may form unrealistic or inaccurate expectancies or stereotypes based on the scores, some schools have discontinued their use.

In spite of limitations and problems, group intelligence tests are still used. Those who use the tests must recognize that they are sampling behaviors and must be aware of the behaviors sampled by the test. School personnel give group intelligence tests to predict future performance, usually future achievement. It is, therefore, wise to use group intelligence tests and group achievement tests that have been standardized on the same population. We recommend that school personnel first select the group achievement test to be used and then choose the group intelligence test that has been standardized on the same population. The following pairs of tests have been standardized on identical groups of students: Otis-Lennon School Ability Test and Stanford Achievement Test, Cognitive Abilities Test and Iowa Tests of Basic Skills, Otis-Lennon School Ability Test and Metropolitan Achievement Tests, and Educational Ability Series and SRA Achievement Series.

SUMMARY

Group intelligence tests are used primarily as screening devices; they are designed to identify those whose intellectual development deviates significantly enough from "normal" to warrant individual intellectual assessment. Many different group intelligence tests are currently used in the schools. This chapter reviewed the most commonly used group tests in order to illustrate the many kinds of behaviors sampled in the assessment of intelligence. When teachers evaluate students' performances on group intelligence tests, they must go beyond obtained scores to look at the kinds of behaviors sampled by the tests. When selecting group intelligence tests, teachers must evaluate the extent to which specific tests are standardized on samples of students to whom they want to compare their pupils and the extent to which the tests are technically adequate for their own purposes.

STUDY QUESTIONS

1. Obtain a copy of any group intelligence test and identify the domains of behaviors sampled by at least ten *items*. Use the domains described in Chapter 9.
2. Identify at least four major factors a teacher must consider when administering a group intelligence test to students.
3. Why would school personnel give group intelligence tests to students?
4. Suppose you had to decide which group intelligence test to give in your school. What factors would you consider in selecting a test? Which test might you select. Justify your answer.
5. Of what value to classroom teachers are scores from group-administered intelligence tests?

ADDITIONAL READING

Buros, O. K. (1978). *Eighth mental measurements yearbook.* Highland Park, NJ: Gryphon Press (Reviews of group intelligence tests, pp. 249–290).

CHAPTER 12

ASSESSMENT OF SENSORY ACUITY

The *first* thing to check when a child is having academic or social difficulties is whether that child is receiving environmental information adequately and properly. In efforts to identify why children experience difficulties, we too often overlook the obvious in search of the subtle. Vision and hearing difficulties do interfere with the educational progress of a significant number of schoolchildren. The teacher's role in assessment of sensory acuity is twofold. First, the teacher must be aware of behaviors that may indicate sensory difficulties and thus must have at least an embryonic knowledge of the kinds of sensory difficulties children experience. Second, the teacher must know the instructional implications of sensory difficulties. Informed communication with vision and hearing specialists is the most effective way to gain such information. The teacher must have basic knowledge about procedures used to assess sensory acuity in order to comprehend and use data from specialists. This chapter, therefore, differs from previous chapters. It provides basic knowledge about the kinds of vision and hearing difficulties pupils experience as well as an overview of procedures and devices used to assess sensory acuity.

WHY DO WE ASSESS SENSORY ACUITY?

Difficulties in seeing or hearing are among the most obvious reasons that students experience academic and behavorial difficulties in school. They also generally are the kinds of difficulties most easily corrected or compensated for. We state that vision and hearing difficulties may cause academic *and* behavior problems. The link between sensory difficulties and academic problems is easy to appreciate. The fact that sensory difficulties may cause behavior problems, while not so obvious, is also true.

VISUAL DIFFICULTIES

There are three ways in which vision may be limited: visual acuity may be limited; the field of vision may be restricted; or color vision may be imperfect. Visual acuity refers to the clarity or sharpness with which a person sees. You probably have heard it said that a keen-sighted person has "perfect" vision—20/20 in both eyes.[1] The person might more accurately be described as demonstrating "normal" vision; the numbers 20/20 simply indicate that the person is able to see a standard-sized object from a standard number of feet away. This method of measuring visual acuity is derived from the use of the Snellen Wall Chart. A person is described as having 20/20 vision who at 20 feet is able to distinguish letters an average person can distinguish at 20 feet. A rating of 20/200 means that the person can distinguish letters at 20 feet that the average person can distinguish at 200 feet. Conversely, 20/10 vision means the person is able to distinguish letters at 20 feet that the average person can only distinguish at 10 feet. The former demonstrates limited vision, while the latter demonstrates better than average distant visual acuity.

The field of vision may be restricted in two ways. A person may demonstrate normal central visual acuity with a restricted peripheral field; this is usually referred to as *tunnel vision.* Or a person may have a *scotoma,* a spot without vision. If the spot occurs in the middle of the eye, it may result in central vision impairment.

Color vision is determined by the discrimination of three qualities of color: hue, saturation, and brightness. The essential difference between colorblind and normal persons is that hues that appear different to normal persons look the same to a colorblind person. Colorblind persons frequently do not know they are colorblind unless they have been tested and told so. They see the same things that other individuals see, and they usually have learned to call them by the same color names. Colorblindness is not an all-or-nothing thing. Most colorblindness is partial; the person has difficulty distinguishing certain colors, usually red and green. Total colorblindness is extremely rare. Colorblindness is an inherited trait found in about one out of twelve males and one out of two hundred females. There is no cure for colorblindness, but the condition is not usually regarded as a handicap.

Few people are totally blind; many have at least light perception and some light projection, either of which helps for mobility. Blindness, for legal purposes, is defined as

central visual acuity of 20/200 or less in the better eye, with correcting glasses, or central visual acuity of more than 20/200 if there is a field defect in which the peripheral field has contracted to such an extent that the widest diameter of visual field subtends an angular distance no greater than 20 degrees. (Hurlin, 1962, p. 8)

1. It is also said that hindsight is always 20/20.

Blindness may be either congenital or acquired. Congenital blindness or blindness acquired prior to age 5 has the most serious educational implications.

It has been said that more people are blinded by definition (the legal definition cited above) than by any other cause (Greenwood, 1963). According to Barraga (1976, p. 13)[2]

the term *visually handicapped* is being used widely at present to denote the total group of children who have impairments in the structure or functioning of the visual sense organ—the eye—irrespective of the nature and extent of the impairment. This term has gained acceptance because the impairment causes a limitation that, even with the best possible correction, interferes with incidental or normal learning through the sense of vision (Taylor, 1973, p. 156).

When we deal with children, we are concerned primarily with visual handicaps that require special educational provisions. Barraga differentiates among three categories of visual handicaps; these are as follows.

Blind. This term [is] used to refer to children who have only light perception without projection, or those who are totally without the sense of vision (Faye, 1970). . . . Educationally, the blind child is one who learns through braille and related media without the use of vision (Halliday, 1970), although perception of light may be present and useful in orientation and movement.

Low Vision. Children who have limitations in distance vision but are able to see objects and materials when they are within a few inches or at a maximum of a few feet away are another subgroup. Most low-vision children will be able to use their vision for many school learning activities, a few for visual reading perhaps, whereas others may need to use tactual materials and possibly even braille to supplement printed and other visual materials. . . . Under no circumstances should low-vision children be referred to as "blind."

Visually Limited. This term refers to children who in some way are limited in their use of vision under average circumstances. They may have difficulty seeing learning materials without special lighting, or they may be unable to see distant objects unless the objects are moving, or they may need to wear prescriptive lenses or use optical aids and special materials to function visually. Visually limited children will be considered for all educational purposes and under all circumstances as seeing children. (1976, p. 14)

Estimates of the number of schoolage children who experience visual difficulties range from 5 to 33 percent (U.S. Public Health Service, 1971). Obviously, estimates differ as a function of the definition used and the screening devices employed.

Teachers must be consistently on the lookout for signs of visual difficulty. When children complain of frequent headaches, dizziness, sensitivity to light,

2. Quotations from Barraga's *Visual Handicaps and Learning: A Developmental Approach* used in this discussion are copyright 1976 by Wadsworth Publishing Company, Inc., and reprinted by their permission.

or blurred vision, efforts must be made to evaluate the extent to which they are seeing properly. Obvious signs of possible visual difficulty include crossed eyes; turned-out eyes; red, swollen, or encrusted eyelids; constant rapid movement of the eyes; watery eyes or discharges; and haziness in the pupils. These, too, should receive special attention in the form of referral for vision screening (U.S. Public Health Service, 1971).

Certain behaviors indicate possible visual difficulties. According to the U.S. Public Health Service (1971), behaviors indicative of potential visual difficulties include holding books unusually close to or far from the eyes while reading; frequent blinking, squinting, or rubbing of the eyes; abnormal head tilting or turning; inattention in blackboard lessons; poor alignment in written work; unusual choice of colors in artwork; confusion of certain letters of the alphabet in reading (*o*'s and *a*'s, *e*'s and *c*'s, *b*'s and *h*'s, *n*'s and *r*'s); inability or reluctance to participate in games requiring distance vision or visual accuracy; and irritability when doing close work.

VISION TESTING IN THE SCHOOLS

Most schools now have vision screening programs, but the effectiveness of these programs is varied. Two fundamentally different kinds of tests are used: those that screen only central visual acuity at a distance and those that assess both central visual acuity and a number of other visual capabilities.

The Basic Test

The standard Snellen Wall Chart is the most commonly used screening test to assess visual acuity. The test consists simply of a wall chart of standard-sized letters that a child is asked to read at a distance of 20 feet. The test provides limited information about vision, assessing only central visual acuity at a distance of 20 feet. Specific difficulties may be encountered in using the test with some schoolage children. First, children may be unable to read the letters or to discriminate between letters like F and P. Second, children can often memorize the letters ahead of time. Third, the letters of the alphabet differ in legibility and lend themselves to guessing. The practical criterion for referral using this test is acuity of 20/40 or less in either eye for children in kindergarten through third grade, and 20/30 or less in either eye for those who are older (National Society for the Prevention of Blindness, 1961).

An adaptation of the Snellen Wall Chart, the Snellen E Test, is the most commonly used test with preschool children and those who are unable to read. The letter E is presented with its arms facing in one of four directions and the person being tested is asked either to name the direction, to point, or to hold up a letter E to match the stimulus. Again, this test assesses only central visual acuity.

More Comprehensive Tests

Several tests assess more aspects of vision than central visual acuity. The Massachusetts Vision Test, introduced in 1940, assesses (1) visual acuity using the Snellen E, (2) *accommodative ability* (the automatic adjustment of the eyes for seeing at different distances) using a plus lens, and (3) muscle imbalance.

Whereas the basic screening tests measure only visual acuity from a distance, the Keystone Telebinocular assesses fourteen different visual skills. The instrument measures the visual functioning of each eye separately and the functioning of both eyes together. In taking this test, students sit in front of a telebinocular instrument, view three-dimensional test slides, and tell the examiner what they see. Visual functioning is assessed at both near point (16 inches) and far point (20 inches); the distances are produced optically, and children remain seated in front of the instrument throughout testing.

Several alternative tests may be administered using the Keystone Telebinocular: a screening test, a comprehensive test battery, the Keystone Plus-Lens Test, the Keystone Primary Skills Test, and the Keystone Periometer Test. Skills tested in the screening test are as follows:

Far Point	*Near Point*
Simultaneous perception	Fusion
Fusion	Vertical eye posture
Color and depth perception	Usable vision
Usable vision	

Skills tested in the comprehensive test battery are as follows:

Far Point	*Near Point*
Simultaneous perception	Fusion
Fusion	Vertical eye posture
Vertical and lateral eye posture	Usable vision of each eye and both eyes together
Depth perception	
Color discrimination	
Usable vision of each eye and both eyes together	

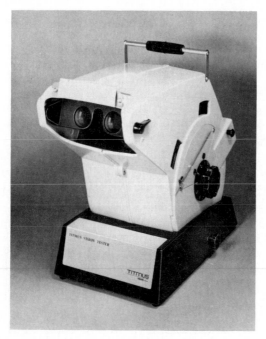

FIGURE 12.1 A Titmus Vision Tester
SOURCE: Courtesy Titmus Optical.

The Bausch and Lomb Orthorater is another instrument used for a more comprehensive assessment of visual functioning. The device assesses farsightedness, muscle balance at both near and far points, and visual acuity using the Snellen E. Like the Keystone Telebinocular, it is a relatively expensive instrument.

The Titmus Vision Tester, illustrated in Figure 12.1, is increasingly used for screening in public school settings. The device is used to assess both acuity and *phoria* (the tendency of the visual axis to turn in or out, up or down) at far and near points. In addition, slides are available to assess preschool children.

In selecting devices to screen visual functioning, it is imperative that the practitioner select devices that are diagnostically accurate, that is, devices that identify individuals who do indeed have visual difficulties. Error in the direction of overreferral to ophthalmologists and optometrists is better than missing anyone who has vision difficulties. Comparative studies of screening devices are difficult to locate. Studies summarized in bulletins published by the National Society for Prevention of Blindness (1961) and by the U.S. Public Health Service (1971) indicate that the Snellen Wall Chart continues to be a relatively effective screening test.

ASSESSMENT OF COLOR VISION

As we have indicated earlier, colorblindness is not usually an educationally handicapping condition. Nevertheless, it is important that color vision be assessed, primarily so that colorblind children and their parents can know that the children have this condition.

Colorblindness is a stable trait, and one we ought to be able to assess with considerable reliability and validity. However, current devices used to assess color vision are not as reliable and valid as would be expected. Adam, Doran, and Modan (1967) state that "it has repeatedly been stressed by experts in the field of color vision (e.g., Franceschetti, 1928; Wright, 1947, Waardenburg et al., 1963) that an accurate diagnosis of color vision can be attained only by the use of an anomaloscope" (p. 297). An *anomaloscope* is a scientific instrument that requires that a person indicate if two simultaneously presented light spots are of approximately equal brightness and if they are the same color. Salvia and Ysseldyke (1972) investigated the validity of measures of colorblindness as compared to the anomaloscope with mentally retarded boys. Validities were low; the tests misdiagnosed from 7 to 30 percent of the boys.

If measures of colorblindness are used with students, we recommend that at least two different tests be given. If a student is identified as colorblind on both tests, there is a strong likelihood that the student is colorblind.

A description of the tests most commonly used to assess color vision follows.

Farnsworth Dichotomous Test for Color Blindness

The Farnsworth Dichotomous Test for Color Blindness (Farnsworth, 1947) consists of fifteen colored caps that the student is asked to order with respect to a reference cap so that each cap is more like the preceding cap than any other. Diagnosis is made by plotting the order of the caps selected on a response sheet.

AO H-R-R Pseudoisochromatic Plates

The AO H-R-R Pseudoisochromatic Plates (Hardy, Rand, & Rittler, 1957) consist of twenty plates. Each plate is divided into four quadrants with background patterns and color (gray) identical for each quadrant and for each plate. In one or two of the quadrants, a symbol may appear, with no more than two symbols per plate. Subjects are asked to state what they see and where they see it.

Dvorine Pseudo-isochromatic Plates

The Dvorine Pseudo-isochromatic Plates (Dvorine, 1953) consists of fourteen number plates and seven trail plates with multicolor dots and a number (or trail) embedded in a contrasting color. Subjects are asked to read the number or trace the trail with a fine brush.

Ishihara Color Blind Test

The Ishihara Color Blind Test (Ishihara, 1970) consists of fourteen plates similar in composition to those in the Dvorine Test. There are seven number plates and seven trail plates. Subjects are asked to name the number or trace the trail with a fine brush.

ASSESSMENT OF HEARING DIFFICULTIES[3]

The early detection of hearing difficulties is imperative so that appropriate remedial or compensatory procedures can be instituted. Children with hearing problems characteristically fail to pay attention, give wrong answers to simple questions, hear better when watching the teacher's face, and ask frequently to have words or sentences repeated. Also, children with impaired hearing may function below their educational potential, be withdrawn, or exhibit behavior problems. Further, children who have frequent earaches, colds or other upper respiratory infections, or draining ears may also have a concomitant hearing problem. Children who fail to articulate clearly or who demonstrate other speech and language problems, as well as children who fail to discriminate between words with similar vowels but different consonants, may also have impaired hearing (Duffy, 1964).

Children with one or more of the symptoms listed above should be referred for a hearing test. Depending on the school system, this test will be given by a school nurse, speech-language therapist, hearing therapist, or trained technician. These professionals have received training for efficiently and accurately testing the hearing of children and can ascertain the extent to which the child's hearing sensitivity is within normal limits. If a hearing loss is detected, the child is then referred to an ear doctor (*otologist* or *otolaryngologist*) for an otological evaluation or to a specialist in hearing evaluation and rehabilitation *(audiologist)* for a complete audiological evaluation. The otologist and audiologist can supply the appropriate remediation and rehabilitation.

3. This section was specially written for this volume by Dr. Tom Frank, Associate Professor of Audiology, Division of Special Education and Communication Disorders, College of Education, The Pennsylvania State University.

The assessment of hearing difficulties is an exacting procedure that requires understanding of several basic concepts. As a prerequisite to a discussion of the assessment of hearing, the anatomy and physiology of the peripheral auditory system will be briefly described. This description will, it is hoped, provide a greater insight into assessment procedures.

The peripheral auditory system can be described as being divided into three parts: the outer, middle, and inner ear. Each part makes a specific contribution to the hearing process. The outer ear gathers sound from the environment and funnels it to the middle ear. The middle ear transmits and amplifies the sound and directs it to the inner ear. The inner ear analyzes the sound and initiates a neural response.

The sensation of hearing can be initiated in two ways. One is called *air conduction;* the other, *bone conduction.* These two modes of hearing serve as the basis for *pure-tone audiometry*—that is, hearing assessment employing pure tones as the test stimulus. When a sound passes through the complete peripheral mechanism (outer, middle, and inner ear), the sound is said to have been heard by *air conduction.* When sound is introduced by mechanically vibrating the skull, the sound waves will bypass the outer and middle ear and stimulate the inner ear. In this way, the sound is said to have been heard by *bone conduction.* Thus, air-conduction hearing depends on the function of the outer, middle, and inner ear and neural pathways beyond; bone-conduction hearing depends on the function of the inner ear and beyond. It is important to recognize that bone-conduction hearing represents the true (organic) sensitivity of the inner ear.

If a child has a hearing loss due to a wax *(cerumen)* buildup in the outer ear canal or fluid in the middle ear *(serous otitis),* bone-conduction hearing will be normal because the inner ear is not affected. However, hearing by air conduction will be abnormal because the dysfunction is due to a pathology in the outer ear or middle ear or both. This type of hearing loss (normal bone-conduction with abnormal air-conduction hearing sensitivity) is known as a *conductive hearing loss* because the pathology affects the sound-conducting mechanisms (the outer and middle ear).

If a child has a hearing loss due to a dysfunction of the inner ear, the bone-conduction as well as the air-conduction hearing will be abnormal. In fact, the bone-conducted tone and the air-conducted tone will be heard at about the same level (except in cases of a severe or profound hearing loss where bone-conducted responses cannot be obtained because of the bone-conduction output limits of the audiometer). This type of hearing loss (abnormal bone- and air-conduction hearing sensitivity usually occurring at about the same level) is known as a *sensorineural hearing loss.*

A hearing loss can also be a combined conductive and sensorineural hearing loss. This type of hearing loss (abnormal bone-conduction and even more abnormal air-conduction hearing sensitivity) is known as a *mixed hearing loss.* For example, a mixed hearing loss could arise from fluid in the middle ear and hair-cell dysfunction in the inner ear.

The main purpose of hearing assessment in a school situation is the identification of children with hearing problems. Experience has indicated that teachers may not identify a child with a hearing loss and that teachers may identify a child with normal hearing as having a hearing disorder. Thus, every child should have a hearing evaluation.

The identification of children with hearing problems and subsequent provisions for medical, surgical, audiological, educational, and related services fall within the realm of a hearing conservation program. The vast majority of schools have hearing conservation programs; in fact, most states have laws requiring hearing testing. Hearing conservation programs generally include regularly scheduled auditory screening tests, auditory-threshold tests for those who fail the screening test, and medical (otological) examination and treatment.

There are several auditory screening tests that can be used for hearing assessment. These tests can be divided into two types: group and individual. It should be kept in mind that the purpose of a screening test is to determine whether the child's hearing sensitivity is normal or abnormal.

Group hearing screening tests have lost popularity because of their low validity and reliability compared with individual screening tests. For the most part, screening tests in hearing conservation programs are performed on an individual basis. The assumption (probably a valid one) is that the additional time required to screen a large number of children on an individual basis will be more effective in identifying children with a hearing problem than will a group screening procedure.

Hearing sensitivity is assessed with an electronic instrument called an *audiometer.* Many types of audiometers are available. The type most commonly used in school settings is a portable unit known as a *pure-tone audiometer.* A photograph of a pure-tone audiometer is shown in Figure 12.2.

The pure-tone audiometer consists of an audio oscillator that generates pure tones of different frequencies (125, 250, 500, 750, 1,000, 1,500, 2,000, 3,000, 4,000, 6,000, and 8,000 Hz) covering the major portion of the auditory range (16 to 16,000 Hz). The term *Hertz* (Hz), after a German physicist, Heinrich Hertz, defines frequency in terms of number of cycles per second of a sound. Frequency can also be described by the subjective impression it creates, known as pitch. Within the audible range, as frequency increases so does the pitch. For example, a 125-Hz pure tone has a frequency of 125 cycles per second and is considered to be a low pitch compared with an 8,000-Hz tone, which is a high pitch.

The pure-tone audiometer also contains an amplifier and an attenuator system that can be adjusted in discrete steps to increase or decrease the intensity of a pure tone. Intensity can be described by a measurement unit

FIGURE 12.2   A portable pure-tone audiometer. Sitting on top of the audiometer are the earphones and the bone vibrator. The dial to the left is the hearing-level dial, which controls the intensity of the pure tone. The dial to the right controls the frequency of the pure tone. The output switch is in the top middle of the audiometer and can be manipulated to direct the pure tone to the right or left earphone or to the bone vibrator. The interrupter switch is the black bar in the bottom middle of the audiometer. When this bar is depressed, a pure tone is presented.
SOURCE: Courtesy of Beltone Electronics Corporation.

known as a *decibel* (dB). A decibel does not have a fixed absolute value; it is simply a ratio relating the proportion of one value to another. In hearing assessment the decibel scale is referenced to a normal *hearing level* (HL). Since the ear does not have the same hearing sensitivity at each frequency, the audiometer is internally calibrated. As a result, 0 dB HL on the audiometer dial represents normal hearing sensitivity for each pure tone frequency. The hearing level can usually be varied from—10 dB HL for all frequencies to a maximum of 110 dB HL in the middle frequencies.

The physical intensity of a sound creates the subjective reaction known as *loudness.* The relation between intensity and loudness is that as intensity increases loudness increases. For example, a 1,000-Hz tone at 60 dB HL will be louder compared with a 1,000-Hz tone of 40 dB HL.

The pure-tone audiometer is provided with a silent switch that is used to introduce or interrupt the pure tone. The output of the pure-tone audiometer can be routed to a right or left earphone or to a bone-conduction vibrator.

The American National Standards Institute has issued a detailed standard for the specifications of audiometers (ANSI, S3.6, 1969). Pure-tone audiometers manufactured in the United States conform to these standards. Thus, in general, American-made pure-tone audiometers are very similar except for the location of the external dials and switches.

In an individual screening test, the earphones of an audiometer are placed over the child's ears. The audiometer transmits pure tones, and the child is asked to raise a hand when the tone is heard. Because earphones are employed, the test tones stimulate the entire peripheral auditory system (outer, middle, and inner ear) so that the child's air-conduction hearing is being tested.

The most definitive work on identification audiometry was compiled by Darley (1961). It was suggested that hearing be screened at a hearing level of 20 dB at 500, 1,000, 2,000, and 6,000 Hz and at a hearing level of 30 dB at 4,000 Hz. That is, the hearing-level dial of the audiometer, which regulates the intensity of the pure tone, should be placed on 20 dB; the frequency dial should be adjusted to 500, 1,000, 2,000, and 6,000 Hz respectively; and a tone should be presented. At 4,000 Hz the hearing-level dial should be adjusted to 30 dB. This procedure is carried out for each ear. Needless to say, hearing testing should be carried out in a very quiet environment so that external noise does not mask perception of a tone.

A screening level of 20 dB HL, however, may not be realistic unless testing is done in a sound-treated environment, which most schools are not likely to have. Thus, more casual criteria are to screen hearing at 25 dB HL at 500, 1,000, 2,000, and 6,000 Hz and 30 dB HL at 4,000 Hz. Further, many states now require that 250 Hz be included in the hearing screening. If a child fails to hear a tone in one or both ears, a second screening is usually performed. The child who fails the second screening is referred for a pure-tone threshold test.

In the *pure-tone threshold test* the child's hearing sensitivity is obtained as a function of frequency. The purpose of this test is to find the hearing level at which the child just barely hears the tone for each frequency that is tested. The hearing level at which the child barely hears the tone is known as the child's *threshold of auditory sensitivity.* Because in this test earphones are again employed, the obtained thresholds are indicative of the child's air-conduction hearing sensitivity. Bone-conduction hearing should not be assessed in a school setting because of the many variables of this mode of testing. Rather, the child's bone-conduction sensitivity should be assessed by an audiologist or otologist who uses a sound-treated environment and more refined and elaborate equipment and procedures.

The pure-tone threshold test should always be done in a very quiet environment. The frequencies tested are usually 1,000, 2,000, 4,000, 8,000, 1,000 (recheck), 500, and 250 Hz (listed in the test sequence). One ear is tested completely before the other is tested. Initially, the tone (at each frequency) is presented at a normally adequate intensity, usually 40 dB HL, so that the child can respond. The tester then decreases the intensity of the tone in ten-dB steps, noting a response at each decrement, until the child does not respond. The intensity of the tone is then increased in five-dB steps until a response is noted. The tone is then decreased and increased in this bracketing manner until the threshold is found.

The results of the pure-tone threshold test are usually plotted on a graph called an *audiogram.* An audiogram is shown in Figure 12.3. Frequency in Hertz (Hz) is plotted along the top of the audiogram at intervals from 125 to 8,000 Hz. Approximately half-octave intervals of 750, 1,500, 3,000, and 6,000 Hz are also denoted. Hearing level in decibels (dB) is plotted along the side of the graph from − 10 to 110 dB in ten-dB steps. Symbols are plotted on the audiogram that depict the thresholds for each ear as a function of frequency and intensity. Each audiogram should contain an audiogram legend to define the meaning of the symbols. For example, an "O" indicates an air-conduction threshold for the right ear, and an "X" indicates an air-conduction threshold for the left ear. Also, it is common practice to depict thresholds for the right ear with red markings and for the left ear with blue markings. The American Speech and Hearing Association has issued guidelines for audiometric symbols (1974).

Figure 12.3 indicates that the sensitivity of air-conduction hearing is 30 dB HL for the right ear and 35 dB HL for the left ear from 250 to 8,000 Hz. The child whose audiogram this is could just barely hear the pure tone at (that is, her threshold was at) 30 dB HL for the right ear and 35 dB HL for the left ear.

The criteria for failing the pure-tone threshold test are the same as for the screening test: if the child's hearing level is 25 dB HL or more at any one of the frequencies 500, 1,000, 2,000, and 6,000 Hz or 30 dB HL or more at 4,000 Hz in one or both ears, the child has failed the pure-tone threshold test. The patient's hearing sensitivity shown on the audiogram in Figure 12.3 would be classified as a failure in each ear.

Even though the pure-tone screening test and the pure-tone threshold test are commonly used for the detection of hearing problems, they have a number of drawbacks that hinder accurate assessment. The amount of external noise in the testing situation and the rapport between the child and the tester will influence the results of pure-tone tests. Also, some children might fail these tests because of immaturity, inattention, or lack of comprehension of the instructions even though they have normal hearing. On the other hand, some children may pass these tests although they have a minor hearing problem or a fluctuating hearing loss, usually because of fluid in the middle ear. Consequently, several school and state hearing conservation programs have initiated another type of screening test in conjunction with the pure-tone tests. This screening test, called Acoustic Impedance Audiometry (Oto-admittance, or Middle Ear Screening Test or Immittance), is designed primarily to detect

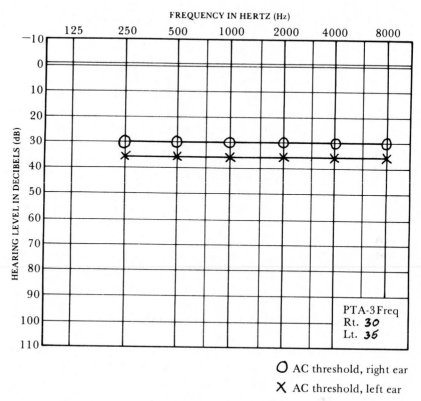

FIGURE 12.3 An audiogram showing a sensitivity of air-conduction hearing of 30 dB HL for the right ear and 35 dB HL for the left ear from 250 to 8,000 Hz

middle-ear disorders, which are the largest cause of hearing loss in children, especially in younger age groups.

The acoustic impedance screening test consists of a measurement of eardrum mobility called a *tympanogram* and a measurement of the presence or absence of the contraction of a muscle (stapedius) in the middle ear in response to a high-level acoustic stimulus called the *acoustic reflex.* The acoustic impedance screening test takes only about one minute per ear and is objective in the sense that the child does not have to give a voluntary response. If a child has a middle-ear disorder, which could affect hearing ability, the tympanogram will usually be abnormal and the acoustic reflex will be absent. If a child has a normal middle ear and normal (-10 to 25 dB HL) or abnormal (26 to 65 dB HL) hearing sensitivity, the tympanogram will be normal and the acoustic reflex will be present. For children with a sensorineural hearing loss greater than 70 dB HL, the tympanogram will be normal but the acoustic reflex will be absent.

Children who fail the pure-tone threshold test, have abnormal tympanograms, and have absent acoustic reflexes should be referred to an audiologist or to an otologist for further testing. Children who pass the pure-tone threshold test but have abnormal tympanograms and/or absent acoustic reflexes should be placed at risk and retested in two to three weeks. If they continue to demonstrate abnormal tympanograms and/or absent acoustic reflexes, they should be referred for further testing.

The actual diagnosis of a hearing problem in reference to the type of hearing loss (conductive, sensorineural, or mixed) and the severity must be completed by an audiologist or an otologist. Both audiologists and otologists are skilled in the administration and interpretation of various audiometric tests. Often the audiologist and otologist work as a team, since each has a particular area of expertise. For example, the otologist is trained from a medical standpoint and has expertise in the physical examination of the ear. If the child has a conductive or a mixed hearing loss, the otologist can usually provide the appropriate medical-surgical treatment. The audiologist is trained from an academic and paramedical standpoint and has expertise in the area of hearing assessment and rehabilitation. If a child has an educationally significant hearing loss due to a noncorrectable conductive or mixed hearing loss or a sensorineural hearing loss, the audiologist can usually provide rehabilitation by prescribing the appropriate hearing aid. Also, the audiologist can make suggestions to teachers, hearing therapists, and speech therapists concerning the child's hearing ability in different environmental situations. Further, the audiologist has expertise in testing the hearing of nonverbal children and those who are, in general, difficult to test.

The most common type of hearing loss in schoolage children is a conductive hearing loss. Remember that with a conductive loss the bone-conduction hearing sensitivity (true organic inner-ear hearing) is normal and that the air-conduction hearing sensitivity is abnormal. The pathology creating the hearing loss is located in the outer ear, in the middle ear, or in both areas. The most common pathologies of the external ear are due to impacted wax and infection of the outer ear canal. The most common pathology of the middle ear in schoolage children is due to a collection of fluid in the middle ear known as *serous otitis media.* The fluid usually forms when the middle ear does not receive proper aeration because of Eustachian tube dysfunction or hypertrophied adenoids obstructing the Eustachian tube. Serous otitis media is initially treated with decongestants and antihistamines. If the fluid remains after a month of medical treatment, it is usually removed surgically, and small tubes are placed in the *tympanic membrane* (ear drum) to ventilate the middle-ear space. The surgical procedure is called a *myringotomy and tubal insertion.* It should be noted that following the appropriate treatment for conductive hearing losses, the hearing can be restored to normal. In some cases, however, a conductive loss cannot be treated; and if the hearing loss is educationally significant (≥ 25 dB), a hearing aid should be considered.

The causes of sensorineural hearing loss are far too numerous to describe in this chapter. Usually, a significant sensorineural hearing loss will be detected before a child enters school. However, subtle hearing losses (abnormal hearing in one ear, abnormal high-frequency hearing, mild hearing losses) that are educationally significant are usually identified in kindergarten or first grade. A sensorineural hearing loss will not respond to medical-surgical treatment. In the vast majority of cases, a hearing aid will be extremely beneficial.

A mixed hearing loss is due to a pathology that causes a conductive and a sensorineural loss. The otologist can usually alleviate the conductive part of the hearing loss. However, in some cases the conductive pathology cannot be corrected. If the hearing loss is educationally significant, the use of a hearing aid is warranted.

The severity of a hearing loss is usually measured on the basis of the average air-conduction hearing sensitivity (threshold) for 500, 1,000, and 2,000 Hz. These frequencies are known as the *speech frequencies* because the vast majority of English speech sounds are contained in this frequency range. The decibel average for these three frequencies serves to predict the threshold for understanding speech. A scale of hearing impairment that shows the relations between the hearing threshold level and the probable handicap and needs has been devised by Goodman and Chasin (1976) (see Table 12.1). It should be noted that a child with a hearing loss of 25 dB HL or more has an educationally significant hearing loss.

A student with hearing difficulties should receive special assistance from the classroom teacher. Preferential seating close to the teacher can maximize the student's opportunity to hear the teacher's voice (and to lip-read). Of course, if the teacher moves around the room, the benefits of preferential seating will be lost.

In some individuals the hearing problem may be intermittent: on some days these students will have normal hearing, and on other days they will demonstrate a hearing loss. The teacher must be able to cope with these students and not become discouraged with their up-and-down hearing. Such students often pass the hearing screening because they are tested on a day when their hearing is good. If the teacher suspects a hearing loss, arrangements should be made to test these pupils on days when they demonstrate poor hearing.

Far too often a teacher has students with hearing problems in class and does not know the cause or severity of the problem. Sometimes these students may become educationally retarded because the teacher did not know how to handle them. The teacher should not be afraid to discuss the classroom management of these pupils with the attending speech therapist, hearing therapist, audiologist, or otologist.

COPING WITH DILEMMAS IN CURRENT PRACTICE

There are fewer difficulties in accurately assessing sensory acuity than there are in other kinds of assessment. Those who assess vision or hearing acuity are assessing relatively stable human characteristics. There are well-accepted ob-

TABLE 12.1 Scale of Hearing Impairment, Descriptive Term of Hearing Loss, and Relations Between the Hearing Threshold Level and Probable Handicap and Needs

Hearing Level in dB[a]	Descriptive Term of Hearing Loss	Probable Handicap and Needs
−10 to 26 dB[b]	Normal limit	*No significant handicap for most children.* Some at upper limits may have difficulty in sustained attention and may benefit from a hearing aid.
27 to 40 dB	Mild	*Slight handicap for some but significant handicap for many children.* Difficulty hearing faint speech and speech at a distance; needs preferential seating; may benefit from lip-reading instruction; benefits from the use of a hearing aid.
41 to 55 dB	Moderate	*Significant handicap.* Understands conversational speech at a distance of 3 to 5 feet; needs a hearing aid, auditory training, lip reading, speech correction, and preferential seating.
56 to 70 dB	Moderate to severe	*Marked handicap.* Conversation must be loud to be understood; difficulty in groups and classroom discussions even with a hearing aid; same needs as child with significant handicap; may be in a special class for the hearing impaired and integrated into a regular class.
71 to 90 dB	Severe	*Severe handicap.* May hear a loud voice 1 foot from the ear; may identify environment noises; same needs as child with significant handicap; may enter a regular class at a later time.
More than 90 dB	Profound	*Extreme handicap.* May hear some loud sounds; probably does not rely on hearing as a primary communication channel; needs a special class or school for the deaf; some of these children may be integrated into regular high schools.

[a]Average hearing levels for 500, 1,000, and 2,000 Hz (re: ANSI 1969 standards for pure-tone audiometers).

[b]Some children with hearing levels within a normal limit are not free from otologic abnormalities, but these abnormalities are not necessarily educationally handicapping.

SOURCE: Reprinted, with slight adaptations. From S. Gellis and Benjamin Kagan, *Current Pediatric Therapy,* 6, Philadelphia, W. B. Saunders Co., 1976. Reprinted by permission.

jective standards of performance for making decisions about the nature and extent of vision or hearing difficulties. With the exception of color vision, the relationship between sensory difficulties and performance in the curriculum is well understood and established. And there are known treatments (corrective lenses or hearing aids) for most mild vision or hearing problems. There are also known methods to cope with severe vision or hearing problems.

The major dilemma confronted in assessment of sensory acuity is that, with exception of routine screening, assessment is done by people outside the school. Students who have serious vision problems are assessed by optometrists or ophthalmologists. Those who have serious hearing problems are assessed by audiologists or ear, nose, and throat specialists. Communication between specialists outside the school and school personnel may be difficult—because specialists are not familiar with the curriculum, do not understand the educational relevance of their diagnoses, or do not take the necessary time to speak with school personnel about their findings for individual children. Difficulty may also come about when school personnel do not understand the vocabulary used by those who assess vision and hearing problems. Problems are most effectively overcome in situations in which there is very good communication and ongoing interaction among school personnel and out-of-school specialists.

SUMMARY

Vision and hearing difficulties can have a significant effect on the performance of children in educational environments. This chapter has provided a basic overview of the kinds of vision and hearing difficulties children experience and of the procedures used to assess sensory acuity. Screening tests of both visual and auditory acuity must be individually administered. Individually administered screening tests that are appropriate and reasonably effective have been reviewed. The actual diagnosis of sensory difficulties must be completed by specialists: ophthalmologists, optometrists, audiologists, and otologists.

STUDY QUESTIONS

1. Identify several characteristics (behaviors) that a student might demonstrate that would make you question whether that individual is seeing adequately.
2. Identify several characteristics (behaviors) that might make you question whether a student is hearing adequately.

ADDITIONAL READINGS

Bauman, M. K. & Kropf, C. A. (1979). Psychological tests used with blind and visually handicapped persons. *School Psychology Review, 8,* 257–270.

Sullivan, P. M. & Vernon, M. (1979). Psychological assessment of hearing impaired children. *School Psychology Review, 8,* 271–290.

Vernon, M., Bair, R. & Lotz, S. (1979). Psychological evaluation and testing of children who are deaf-blind. *School Psychology Review, 8,* 291–295.

CHAPTER 13

ASSESSMENT OF ORAL LANGUAGE

Language is any and all means a person uses to receive or give out information. In its widest sense, this can include identifying an object by touch alone, or even body language (the giving and receiving of information through body postures). However, our discussion will focus only on those aspects of language vital to the classroom teacher.

WHY DO WE ASSESS ORAL LANGUAGE?

There are two primary reasons for assessing oral language abilities. First, well-developed language abilities are desirable in and of themselves. The ability to speak fluently is a goal held for most individuals. Those who have difficulties with various aspects of language are often eligible for special services from speech and language specialists or from special educators (usually specialists in learning disabilities). The second reason for assessing oral language function is that various language processes and skills are believed to underlie subsequent development. Consequently, identification and remediation of language disorders is believed to have a broad, general, and positive effect on personal development.

Figure 13.1 presents a model of language that illustrates the abilities a child must have in order to perform the following classroom skills: understanding spoken language; reading, talking, or speaking; and writing (including spelling). What has only recently been appreciated is that language consists of four components: *phonology, morphology, syntax,* and *semantics.* Further, each of these components or language subskills is mediated through two channels of communication: *reception,* the input of information from another person or the environment, and *expression,* the output, or what is communicated to another

Note: The material in this chapter was written in collaboration with Edward S. Klein, Division of Special Education, Department of Speech Pathology and Audiology, The Pennsylvania State University.

person or the environment. Figure 13.1 crosses the components of language with the channels of communication, resulting in six boxes of skills prerequisite to language, each of which must be assessed in any complete evaluation of language competence.

THE FOUR COMPONENTS OF LANGUAGE

Phonology

Phonology—the study of the speech sounds of a language—is the foundation upon which other aspects of language (morphology, syntax, and semantics) are built (Klein, 1981). In the receptive channel, phonology refers to how well an individual can hear and discriminate, or hear the difference, among the different sounds of speech (upper left-hand cell in Figure 13.1). There has been some argument about the importance of teaching discrimination skill and its subskills (for example, letter-sound association or sound blending) in speaking or in reading. Van Riper (1963) argues that all training in articulation, or speech sound production, must be preceded by a long period of ear training, or the teaching of discrimination skills. Williams and McReynolds (1975), on the other hand, feel that speech training should be mostly concerned with teaching the production of the sounds, rather than listening skills. In reading, of course, the disagreement over whether to teach a child to read by training sound-letter associations or by increasing sight vocabulary is well known and of long standing. Those who believe in training discrimination, letter-sound association, sound blending, and other receptive skills have developed a number of assessment devices that purport to assess a child's abilities in those areas. A list of those tests, including tests that are discussed elsewhere in this book, can be found in Table 13.1.

In the expressive, or output, channel, phonology refers to the production or *articulation* of the speech sounds. Although formal assessments of articulation are most often conducted by speech pathologists, teachers do have a responsibility for screening and referring children with articulation dysfunctions. Also, teachers have over the years taken an increased responsibility for the training of speech and language within the classroom and thus should at least be familiar with the various assessment procedures.

In articulation, the units of speech assessed are called *phonemes,* which can be defined as the smallest units of sound that have no meaning by themselves but contribute to word meaning. For example, in the word *cane,* there are three phonemes: *c, a,* and *n;* the final *e* is silent and is not considered a phoneme. In American English, there are forty-four such speech sounds, or phonemes. Most devices that assess articulation attempt to survey a child's ability to produce all these sounds in all positions of a word. A number of methods are used to elicit this speech: imitation of an adult model, naming

	Phonology	Morphology and Syntax	Semantics	Ultimate Language Skill
Reception	Hearing and discrimination of speech sounds	Understanding grammatical structure of language	Understanding vocabulary meaning concepts	→ Understanding spoken language
Expression	Articulation of speech sounds	Using the grammatical structure of language	Using vocabulary meaning concepts	→ Talking

CHANNELS OF COMMUNICATION

FIGURE 13.1 A model of language subskills

TABLE 13.1 Tests Discussed Elsewhere in This Book That Provide Information About Auditory Discrimination, Letter-Sound Associations, Sound Blending, and Other Receptive Skills

California Achievement Tests
Criterion Reading
Diagnosis: An Instructional Aid: Reading
Diagnostic Reading Scales
Durrell Analysis of Reading Difficulty
Gates-McKillop-Horowitz Reading Diagnostic Tests
Iowa Tests of Basic Skills
Kaufman Assessment Battery for Children
Metropolitan Achievement Tests
SRA Achievement Tests
Stanford Achievement Test
Stanford Diagnostic Reading Test
Woodcock-Johnson Psychoeducational Battery

pictures whose labels contain the target sound, assessment of conversational speech, and reading sentences that present the target sound numerous times in varied word positions.

Obviously, a child either does or does not correctly produce a given sound. Thus, most testing of articulation is criterion-referenced. However, in deciding whether intervention is necessary, the developmental nature of articulation needs to be considered. For example, since some sounds develop at an earlier age than others, it is not unusual for a 3- or 4-year-old child to misarticulate some words. Wellman, Case, Mengert, and Bradbury (1931), Poole (1934), and Templin (1957) have studied the sequence in which children acquire speech sounds. These sources and others should be consulted if there is doubt as to whether a child's misarticulation is age appropriate.

Lately, there has been some disenchantment with assessing and training specific speech sounds in children. Many investigators [for example, Ingram (1976); Winitz (1975)] feel that children with articulation problems are having difficulty not with specific sounds, but with some of the features of sounds that distinguish groups of sounds from one another. For example, *s, f,* and *sh* might all be called "blowing sounds," in which the air is blown from the mouth in a continuous stream. In the sounds *p, t,* and *k,* on the other hand, there is a stoppage of air flow, followed by a burst of air. Perhaps the child who cannot articulate *s, f,* and *sh* has difficulty with the phonological rule of blowing versus nonblowing, rather than a generalized inability to produce these sounds. As a result of these recent developments in phonological theory, certain assessment devices have been developed that do not test the specific speech sounds, but instead test a series of phonological rules in the child's speech.

A list of the most frequently used articulation assessment devices can be found in Table 13.2.

TABLE 13.2 Listing of the Most Frequently Used Articulation Assessment Tests

Name of Test	Author	Publisher	Date of Publication
Arizona Articulation Proficiency Scale	J. Fudala	Western Psychological Services, Los Angeles, CA	1970
A Deep Test of Articulation	E. McDonald	Stanwix House, Pittsburgh, PA	1964
Fisher-Logemann Test of Articulation Competence	H. Fisher & J. Logemann	The Riverside Publishing Company, Chicago, IL	1971
Goldman-Fristoe Test of Articulation[a]	R. Goldman & M. Fristoe	American Guidance Service, Inc., Circle Pines, MN	1969
Phonological Process Analysis[a]	F. Weiner	University Park Press, Baltimore, MD	1979
Photo Articulation Test	K. Pendergast, S. Dickey, J. Selmar, & A. Soder	Interstate Printers & Publishers, Danville, IL	1969
Predictive Screening Test of Articulation, 3d ed.	C. Van Riper & R. Erickson	Continuing Education Office, Western Michigan University, Kalamazoo, MI	1973
Templin-Darley Tests of Articulation, 2d ed.	M. Templin & F. Darley	Bureau of Educational Research, University of Iowa, Iowa City, IA	1969

[a]Reviewed in this chapter.

Morphology

Morphology, the second level of language, is the study of how sounds are put together to have meaning and how words are composed of these units of meaning (Klein, 1981). In morphology, the unit studied is the morpheme, which is defined as the smallest combination of sounds that contributes to the meaning of the word. For example, the word *book* has one morpheme, but *books* has two because *s* is a separate morpheme that adds meaning to the word *book* by pluralizing it. Likewise, *booked* has two morphemes (*ed* is a morpheme signifying past tense), and *unbooked* has three (*un* is a morpheme indicating negation).

A child's abilities to understand and use morphemes are important prerequisites to language competence. However, only very recently have a child's morphological abilities received serious consideration in language assessment. In fact, many tests of listening and reading comprehension contain items that claim to assess grammatical competence (which should include morphology and syntax) but test only some of the components of grammar. Also, in most tests the samples used to assess any given linguistic structure are often inadequate to determine a child's competence with that structure. Finally, many of the tests are simultaneously assessing vocabulary performance, making it difficult to determine whether a child's error is due to considerations of grammar or vocabulary.

Syntax

Syntax refers to the way morphemes or words are strung together to form meaningful sentences. Together, morphology and syntax are the two elements of grammar, and both areas should be included in any valid language assessment. There are three components of syntax that must be assessed when determining a child's language competence.

Word Classes   The English language has a number of word types or categories, often called "parts of speech" (for example, nouns, conjunctions, adverbs). A child might have particular difficulty with a specific class of words. For example, John might leave out a whole class ("I chair" for "I see the chair"), or he might use a class incorrectly ("I going to the store"). It should be noted that this is the level where morphology overlaps with syntax. For example, in order for a child to use the past tense, *dressed,* the child not only must have some conception of the verb class (syntax) but must also be able to use the morpheme *ed* and connect it to the word *dress* (morphology).

Word Order   A child might be able to use all the parts of speech correctly but still not know how to put words together in a manner that conforms to the rules of English. The basic word order of English is illustrated by the classic subject-verb-object (s-v-o) sentence, "I wrestle bananas." The verb must follow the subject, and the object comes last. A child who did not know these rules might say something like "I pickles am eating." Here the word classes are used correctly, but the word order is inappropriate.

Transformations   The English language contains more than simple s-v-o sentences. In fact, there are rules of English that allow for variations of the basic s-v-o sentence. These rules that allow for changes and alterations to the s-v-o sentence are called *transformational rules,* and the changes themselves are called *transformations.* As an example of the use of transformations, consider the sentences, "Joe kissed the elephant" and "The elephant was kissed by Joe."

TABLE 13.3   Tests Discussed Elsewhere in This Book That Provide Information About Grammatical Usage

California Achievement Tests	Gilmore Oral Reading Test
Criterion Reading	Gray Oral Reading Test
Diagnosis: An Instructional Aid: Reading	Iowa Tests of Basic Skills
Diagnostic Reading Scales	Metropolitan Achievement Tests
Durrell Analysis of Reading Difficulty	Peabody Individual Achievement Test
Fountain Valley Teacher Support System in Reading	Stanford Achievement Test
	Stanford Diagnostic Reading Test
Gates-MacGinitie Reading Tests	Woodcock Reading Mastery Tests

Although both sentences have identical meaning, the former is an example of the basic s-v-o sentence, whereas the latter used transformational rules to vary the word order of the original sentence.

As is true with morphology, syntax has only recently received serious consideration in language assessment. Even those tests that purport to assess grammar usually test only one small part of it. For example, the Illinois Test of Psycholinguistic Abilities (ITPA) has a subtest entitled Grammatic Closure. When the items in this subtest are examined, it quickly becomes apparent that only morphology is being tested, and only a small sample of morphology at that. No syntactical rules are assessed. Some tests have been developed recently that include both morphology and syntax. Table 13.3 contains a list of tests that to some extent assess grammatical usage.

Semantics

Semantics refers to the meaning inherent in words and includes a wide variety of language elements such as vocabulary, categorizing, ability to define, identification of synonyms and antonyms, and detection of ambiguity or absurdity.

Vocabulary is perhaps the aspect of semantics that is most familiar and has received the most attention. As is true for the other components of language, vocabulary can be either receptive (listening and reading) or expressive (speaking and writing). Most devices measuring vocabulary are norm-referenced, and many are used for assessment of children's intelligence. The uses and limitations of these tests were discussed in Chapter 10. Table 13.4 lists a number of devices that measure a child's knowledge of word meanings and vocabulary.

Measures of other elements of semantics have been inadequate at best. The problem is that most devices that assess such areas as definitions or synonyms and antonyms have been designed, not as measures of language, but as measures of intelligence. Thus, the items presented are not organized so as to permit a valid conclusion about a child's semantic ability.

TABLE 13.4 Tests Discussed Elsewhere in This Book That Provide Information About a Child's Vocabulary

Boehm Test of Basic Concepts	Kaufman Assessment Battery for
California Achievement Tests	Children
Cognitive Abilities Test	Lee-Clark Reading Readiness Test
Criterion Reading	McCarthy Scales of Children's Abilities
Culture Fair Intelligence Tests	Metropolitan Achievement Tests
Diagnosis: An Instructional Aid:	Metropolitan Readiness Tests
Reading	Otis-Lennon School Ability Test
Diagnostic Reading Scales	Peabody Individual Achievement Test
Durrell Analysis of Reading Difficulty	Peabody Picture Vocabulary Test
Educational Ability Series	Pictorial Test of Intelligence
Fountain Valley Teacher Support	SRA Achievement Series
System in Reading	Short Form Test of Academic Aptitude
Full-Range Picture Vocabulary Test	Stanford Achievement Test
Gates-MacGinitie Reading Tests	Stanford-Binet Intelligence Scale
Gates-McKillop-Horowitz Reading	Stanford Diagnostic Reading Test
Diagnostic Tests	Test of Adolescent Language
Gilmore Oral Reading Test	Tests of Basic Experiences
Gray Oral Reading Test	Test of Nonverbal Intelligence
Henmon-Nelson Tests of Mental Ability	Wechsler Intelligence Scale for
Iowa Tests of Basic Skills	Children–Revised
	Woodcock-Johnson Psychoeducational
	Battery

Summary

For a long time, only certain parts of language were included in most language assessments. Now, finally, investigators have realized that phonology, morphology, syntax, and semantics are all important elements of a normal language system. All four must be investigated if a valid picture of a child's language competence is to be drawn.

OTHER CONSIDERATIONS IN THE ASSESSMENT OF ORAL LANGUAGE

Certain factors outside of test content or construction must be considered when undertaking a valid assessment of a child's language competence. First, since language is environmentally determined, a child's *cultural background must be considered.* Although most American children learn English, the form of English that they learn depends on where they were born, who their parents are, and so on. For example, in central Pennsylvania, a child might say, "My hands need washed," rather than the more standard "My hands need to be washed." In New York City, a black child of low socioeconomic level might say "birfday" instead of the Standard American pronunciation "birthday." These and other culturally determined alternative pronunciations are not incorrect or inferior; they are just different. In fact, a number of studies of Black English have shown that it has its own rules of pronunciation, structure, and meaning—and that those rules are at least as complex as those of Standard American English (Wolfram, 1971).

For many years, all nonstandard American dialects were viewed as inferior. Children who did not speak or write in Standard American English were diagnosed as having language dysfunctions. This error has been recognized. Children should be viewed as having a language dysfunction only if their primary language or dialect is dysfunctional. If the latter is not the case, then they have an understandable language variation. This is not meant to imply that children with speech variations should not be taught Standard American English. Knowledge of Standard American English is vital if a person is to progress academically, socially, and economically. Thus, a child should be taught Standard American English, not because other dialects are inherently inferior, but because it allows that child greater access to the general American cultural community (Salvia & Ysseldyke, 1978).

The factor of cultural background becomes particularly important when considering the language assessment devices that are currently available, including those listed in Tables 13.1 through 13.4. Ideally, a child should be compared with others in the same language community in order to determine the existence or nonexistence of a language dysfunction. Again, ideally, there should be separate norms for each language community, including Standard American English. Unfortunately, the normative samples of most language tests are heterogenous. Thus, scores on these tests may not be valid indicators of a child's language ability. As a final example, consider plate 25 of the Peabody Picture Vocabulary Test (PPVT). This plate contains four pictures, and the examiner is supposed to say, "Show me wiener." There are many places in this country where the only word for that item is *hot dog* or *frankfurter.* Yet, since the test was standardized using *wiener,* the examiner is bound to use that term. If Jimmy has never heard the word *wiener,* he is penalized and receives a lower score, although his error is cultural and not a semantic deficiency. If there are a number of such items on a test, a child's score can hardly be considered a valid indicator of language ability.

A second major consideration in the assessment of language is the child's *age,* especially if the test being used is criterion-referenced rather than norm-referenced. It is important for a teacher to be aware that language is developmental; some sounds, linguistic structures, and even semantic elements are correctly produced at an earlier age than others. Thus, it is not unusual or dysfunctional for a 2-year-old child to say "Kitty house" for "The cat is in the house," although the same phrase *would* be dysfunctional in a 3-year-old. A teacher must be aware of the developmental norms for language acquisition and must use those norms when making judgments about a child's language competence.

Finally, it must be realized that language and intelligence are closely related. Unfortunately, as has been discussed in Chapter 9, it is impossible to determine where one ends and the other begins. Indeed, language cannot be measured without at the same time measuring intellectual abilities to some degree. It seems logical, then, to deemphasize the normative aspects of language assessment devices and concentrate instead on what language information those devices provide. Thus, a test such as the PPVT should be used as a qualitative measure of a child's receptive vocabulary, not as a normative test of a child's "language age or level" compared with other children. Finally, it is important for the teacher to be aware that a given language assessment device might be measuring intelligence *more* than language, as the ITPA seems to.

WAYS OF ELICITING LANGUAGE BEHAVIOR

There has been some disagreement among language professionals concerning the most valid method of evaluating a child's language performance, especially in the expressive channel of communication. In all, there are three procedures used to gather a sample of a child's language behavior: spontaneous, imitative, and picture stimulus.

Spontaneous Language

One school of thought holds that the only valid measure of a child's language abilities is one that studies the language that the child produces spontaneously (for example, see Lee & Canter, 1971). Using this procedure, fifty to one hundred consecutive utterances produced by a child as the child is talking to an adult or playing with toys are recorded. These utterances are then analyzed in terms of phonology, morphology, syntax, and semantics to give the examiner a fairly good idea of what language abilities the child does or does not have. Although the analysis of a child's spontaneous language production has often been confined to the speaking mode, some interest has been shown in assessing a child's handwriting and spelling skills in an uncontrived, spontaneous situation (for example, the Test of Written Language by Hammill and Larsen).

Imitation

To use imitation, an examiner simply says to the child, "Say what I say," then utters a word, phrase, or sentence containing the language elements being assessed. Intuitively, the reader might assume that the child's auditory memory skills or lack thereof would bias any results obtained by using imitation. However, this seems not to be the case. In fact, many investigators have demonstrated that children's imitative language is essentially the same in content and structure as their spontaneous language (Brown & Bellugi, 1964; Ervin, 1964; Slobin & Welsh, 1973). What happens is that the children translate the adult sentences into their own language system and then repeat the sentences to the examiner using their own language rules. Thus, a young child might imitate "The boy is running and jumping" as "Boy run and jump." Imitation seems to be a valuable tool for providing information about a child's language abilities. One caution should be noted, however. Features of a child's language systems can be obtained using imitation only if the stimulus sentences are long enough to tax the child's memory, since a child will imitate perfectly any sentence *if the length of that sentence is within memory capacity* (Slobin & Welsh, 1973).

Assessment devices that use imitation usually contain a number of grammatically loaded words, phrases, or sentences that children are asked to imitate. The examiner records and transcribes the children's responses and then analyzes their phonology, morphology, and syntax. (Semantics is rarely assessed using an imitative mode.) Finally, imitation generally is used only in oral language assessment of written language.

Picture Stimulus[1]

Using a picture stimulus to elicit language involves no imitation on the part of the child but cannot be classified as a totally spontaneous procedure. It lies somewhere in between. The child is presented with a picture or pictures (of objects or action scenes) and then asked to do one of the following: (1) point to the correct object (a receptive vocabulary task), (2) point to the action picture that best describes a sentence (receptive language, including vocabulary), (3) name the picture (expressive vocabulary), or (4) describe the picture (expressive language including vocabulary). Although there is no reason that stimulus pictures cannot be used for assessment of handwriting, spelling, or other areas, generally the use of these pictures has been confined to the assessment of oral language.

Spontaneous, Imitation, or Picture—Which Is Best?

There are advantages and disadvantages to all three modes of language elicitation, and it is up to the teacher to decide which mode utilized in a given assessment device is appropriate to the child. The use of spontaneous language samples has two major advantages. First, a child's spontaneous language is

---

1. Although only stimulus pictures are described in this section, some tests use concrete objects rather than pictures.

undoubtedly the best and most natural indicator of everyday language performance because spontaneous language is child-generated without any outside influence. Second, the informality of the procedure allows the examiner to assess all children quite easily, without the trauma and subsequent silence that sometimes accompanies formal testing atmospheres.

Unfortunately, there are some important disadvantages to the spontaneous approach, perhaps the most important of which concerns time. Most clinicians or teachers do not have the long period of time it takes to get fifty or one hundred spontaneous utterances from a child. Second, those utterances are only a sample of the child's speech and often may not be representative of the child's total language abilities. For example, if Kate does not use a past tense verb in the spontaneous language sample, is it because the past tense is not part of her language system or because she has had no opportunity during the session to use it? A skilled examiner can attempt to structure an informal language evaluation so that the child has opportunities to use many structures, but this is difficult and not always successful. A final disadvantage of using spontaneous language becomes evident when a child has many errors. If a child says, "I chair," how is the examiner to know what the child means to say? Is it "I am sitting on the chair," "This is my chair," or something else? Although the examiner might be able to infer from the setting what a severely language-disordered child meant to say, such an inference may be unreliable. Without knowing the child's intended language output, it is difficult to define the scope of the language dysfunction.

The use of imitation overcomes many of the disadvantages inherent in the spontaneous approach. A good imitation test will assess many different language elements and provide a representative view of a child's language system. Also, because of the structure of the test, the examiner knows at all times what elements of language are being assessed. Thus, even the language abilities of a child with a severe language dynsfunction can be quantified. Finally, imitation devices can be administered much more quickly than spontaneous language samples. Unfortunately, the advantages of the spontaneous approach become the disadvantages of the imitative method. First, a child's auditory memory may have some effect on the results. For example, an echolalic child who repeats everything that is said will score very high on an imitative test, without necessarily knowing the elements of language being tested. An imitative test is inappropriate for such a child. Second, part of a sentence may be repeated exactly because the utterance is too simple or short to place a load on the child's memory. A good rule of thumb to follow with imitative tests is this: If a child repeats a word or words correctly, it does not necessarily mean that the child knows the element being tested. However, if the child produces certain language elements incorrectly, one can be quite certain that the child does not know these elements. Thus, one should draw conclusions only about a child's errors from an imitative test. A third disadvantage to imitative tests is that they are often quite boring to the child. Not all children can sit still for the time required to repeat fifty to one hundred sentences without any other stimulation such as pictures or toys.

The use of picture stimuli is an attempt to overcome the disadvantages of both imitation and spontaneous language. Pictures are easy to administer, interesting to children, and require minimal administration time. They can be structured to test desired language elements and yet retain some of the spontaneity of spontaneous language samples, since children have to formulate the language on their own. Since there is no limitation, results are not dependent on the children's word retention skills. Despite these advantages, one major disadvantage limits the usefulness of picture stimuli in language assessment. It is difficult to create pictures guaranteed to elicit specific language elements. Even though it is probably easiest to create pictures for object identification, difficulties arise even in this area. One can imagine the difficulties of creating pictures to test other elements of language, such as past tense or action verbs. How would one test the pronoun "I" using picture stimuli?

In short, all three methods of elicitation have their uses as well as their shortcomings. The examiner must decide which elements of language should be tested, which method(s) of elicitation is (are) most appropriate for assessing those elements, and then which assessment devices satisfy these needs as well as the structural requirements of a good test. It should not be surprising that often more than one test is necessary to assess all aspects of language (phonology, morphology, syntax, and semantics), both receptively and expressively.

SPECIFIC TESTS—COMPREHENSION AND SPEAKING

Goldman-Fristoe Test of Articulation

Language Component Assessed   Phonology

Communication Channel   Expressive

The Goldman-Fristoe Test of Articulation (GFTA) (Goldman & Fristoe, 1972) is one of the more popular tools developed to assess a child's ability to produce the sounds of speech. It is an individually administered, criterion-referenced device in which most consonant sounds and eleven common consonant blends (*st,* for example) are elicited in differing levels of complexity (word, sentence) and in a variety of word positions (beginning, middle, and end of word). Although the device does not specifically measure vowels, the examiner can still get a fairly good idea of a child's vowel production, since all vowels and diphthongs are used at least once within the stimulus words. The GFTA is divided into three sections.

Sounds-in-Words   In this subtest, thirty-five pictures of familiar objects are presented to the child, who must either name the picture or answer questions pertaining to it. In all, forty-four responses are elicited, including eleven common consonant blends and all single consonant sounds except *zh;* medial position *h, w,* and *y;* and final position voiced *th* (as in writhe).

Sounds-in-Sentences   This subtest is designed to elicit a sample of a child's speech in a more complex, spontaneous context. The examiner reads two stories aloud to the child while presenting four or five pictures illustrating each story. After the story is read, the examiner again presents the pictures to the child, who recounts the story. The story is loaded with sounds most commonly misarticulated by children, and the examiner appraises the child's speech-sound production in this more complex context (sentences).

Stimulability   After the first two subtests are completed, the examiner returns to the sounds the child has misarticulated and tries to stimulate correct production by means of a three-step procedure explained in the instructions. The purpose of this subtest is to find out how stimulable a child is to intervention. This clinical information then leads to a decision regarding prognosis for and length of that intervention.

The GFTA differs from some other articulation tests by assessing more than one speech sound at a time. This places a greater load on the listening abilities of the examiner, although many individuals using this test seem to have no problem listening for more than one sound in a given word. The stimulus pictures are large and colorful, making the test very motivating for young children. However, older children might find the device too juvenile, especially compared with the black-and-white pictures of a test such as the Arizona Articulation Proficiency Scale (Fudala, 1970).

Although classroom teachers may administer the GFTA, they should score only the *number* of errors the child makes. An analysis of

these errors should probably be made by a speech-language pathologist.

Scores

Percentile ranks (based on the National Speech and Hearing Survey conducted by Hill in 1971) are available for the Sounds-in-Words subtest. However, the GFTA is better used as a criterion-referenced device to assess the child's ability to produce a given sound correctly.

Reliability

The percent-agreement method[2] is used in reporting three types of reliability. The ratings used to estimate reliability were provided by experienced speech clinicians. High test-retest reliability (1-week interval) for each speech sound was found, with the median reliability ranging from 94 percent for sounds-in-sentences to 95 percent for sounds-in-words. Different clinicians rating the same speech samples provided higher interrater reliability, with a median agreement of 92 percent for the absence or presence of an error and 80 percent for classification of the type of error. Finally, in order to determine intrarater reliability, six clinicians rescored the responses of the four children. The median agreement for number and type of errors for these clinicans was 91 percent.

Validity

Since the GFTA is mostly used as a criterion-referenced device, content validity is most important. The test does indeed seem to be content valid, although the user of the GFTA must decide whether the test assesses the desired elements.

2. The number of agreements divided by the number of total chances to agree (agreements plus disagreements).

Summary

The GFTA is a criterion-referenced device that is individually administered with the intent of assessing a child's production of speech sounds in a variety of word positions and in both simple and complex contexts. The reliability of the device is excellent, as is its validity.

Phonological Process Analysis

Language Component Assessed   Phonology

Communication Channel   Expressive

The Phonological Process Analysis (PPA) (Weiner, 1979) is one of the first attempts to assess a child's articulation abilities in a manner other than examining the child's isolated speech-sound production. Instead, the PPA assumes that there are speech production rules or patterns that cut across single sounds. These rules, or processes, "are based on such factors as sound environment, syllable structure" and differences in the distinctive features of sounds (Weiner, 1979, p. 1). The PPA is an individually administered, criterion-referenced device that assesses sixteen such phonological rules that might explain a child's speech production problems.

For each rule tested, there are four to eight stimulus words. Each word is elicited twice from the child. The first mode of elicitation used is delayed imitation, where the child is shown an action picture and read an incomplete sentence. For example, "Uncle George is running fast. Uncle George, be careful; you are running too ———." The child must complete the sentence. Then, the examiner elicits the same stimulus word a second time by asking, "What is Uncle George doing?" The desired response is "running too fast." If the child does not respond correctly to these modes of elicitation, immediate imitation might be required. The examiner transcribes both responses for each stimulus word tested onto a process profile and analyzes the data to determine whether a child is having particular problems with any specific phonolog-

ical rules. In addition, all responses should be tape-recorded for verification and better analysis of the live transcription.

Although the PPA takes 45 minutes to complete with a cooperative child, it is not necessary to administer the entire analysis in one session. In fact, the examiner might not want to assess all phonological rules with every child.

Scores

Because the PPA is an unnormed, criterion-referenced device, there is no attempt to attribute scores to a child's responses. The examiner does, however, indicate the percentage of times the child has correctly used the given rule. If the percentage is less than 100 percent, the examiner must determine the extent to which the misuse of that rule is contributing to the child's speech problems. If the examiner decides that the child's misuse of the rule is a significant factor, a program of intervention should be developed to teach the given rule to the child.

Reliability

No reliability data accompany the PPA.

Validity

The content validity of the PPA appears satisfactory. Weiner states that the 136 test items included in the PPA were those that most often assessed the desired phonological rules in a group of 100 children with phonological dysfunctions. It should be noted that neither the severity nor the type of these children's phonological problems were described. Also, there is no information concerning whether some of the language might be too difficult for younger children.

The types of items included seem an appropriate measure of the test domain. The sample of items seems extensive enough to measure satisfactorily the sixteen phonological rules. Finally, the items assess the rules using two elicitation modes, delayed imitation and recall. This provides a good picture of a child's phonological abilities under easier and more difficult conditions of production.

Summary

The PPA is an individually administered, criterion-referenced test intended to assess the child's use of the phonological rules inherent in the production of speech. No reliability data are provided, and validity seems quite satisfactory.

Auditory Discrimination Test

Language Component Assessed   Phonology
Communication Channel   Receptive

The Auditory Discrimination Test (ADT) (Wepman, revised 1973) is an individually administered, norm-referenced device intended to measure the auditory discrimination abilities of 5- to 8-year-old children. The procedure used to equate the two forms of the ADT is not specified in the technical information. Each form contains forty pairs of words, ten of which are identical and thirty of which differ from each other in only one phoneme. In the different-word pairs, the location of the differing phoneme is the medial position for vowels and the initial and/or final position for consonants. To administer the device, the examiner reads each word pair. The child must indicate whether the two words are the same or different.

Scores

The child receives one point for each correct recognition of different-word pairs, for a possible raw score of 30. The technical manual provides tables with which the examiner can convert raw scores to a five-point rating scale. The scale appears to be based on percentile ranks for those for whom the test is valid. The test is deemed invalid if the child scores below 10 on the different-word pairs, or below 7 on the same-word pairs.

Norms

No data are given concerning either the children in the normative sample or their characteristics.

Reliability

Two types of reliability data are presented in the ADT. Test-retest reliability was undertaken twice, with good stability coefficients of 0.91 and 0.95. In addition, alternate-form reliability was estimated as 0.92. Neither the sample used to estimate the reliability coefficients nor the time interval between test administrations is discussed in the manual.

Validity

Of eight studies presented in the manual that purport to establish the validity of the ADT, only seven are truly studies of validity. These seven studies provide information regarding construct validity.

Three of the seven validity studies indicate

that there is a significant relationship between age and auditory discrimination score. As children get older, their auditory discrimination scores increase.

Two studies attempt to establish a relationship between auditory discrimination (as measured by the ADT) and reading. In fact, these studies report significant differences in reading scores between those students with adequate auditory discrimination and those with inadequate auditory discrimination. However, when the data are studied closely, some curious facts emerge. The first graders showing adequate auditory discrimination had a mean reading score of 2.2, while the other group (inadequate) had a 1.9 reading grade level. Both of these groups are well above normal reading ability.

Another validity study compared the scores of students in grade 1 on the ADT and the Metropolitan Achievement Tests (MAT). Wepman reports significant correlations between subtests of the MAT and the ADT and implies a causative connection between school achievement and auditory discrimination. However, the correlations found were only between .235 and .348, statistically significant but trivial.

In a final study, Wepman reports a significant difference between the auditory discrimination abilities of children with articulation problems and those without. However, there have been many studies in this same area, and Rees (1973), in a thorough examination of research on this relationship, has not proven the connection between auditory discrimination and speech ability.

No evidence of content or criterion-related validity is presented in the manual. After assessing the content of the ADT, it is questionable whether the items appropriately and completely measure the domain. For example, the two words in the different-word pairs differ only in placement of the articulators. There is no pair that tests discrimination of (1) acoustic characteristics [such as a stop-burst sound *(t)* versus an affricate *(ch)*], or (2) voicing of the sound versus nonvoicing (*s* versus *z,* for example). Also, some of the more frequently misarticulated sounds *(r, l, w, y)* are not even included in the test. In fact, Winitz (1975) concludes that the Auditory Discrimination Test does not provide the information needed to validly assess a child's auditory discrimination abilities.

Summary

The purpose of the ADT is to assess the auditory discrimination skills of children 5 to 8 years of age. It is individually administered and norm-referenced, although the sample on which the norms are based is not described in the manual. Reliability is fine, although the sample used is not described and there is no information concerning the time interval between test administration. The validity of the ADT seems very questionable. Construct validity is open to question, and content validity seems quite poor. No mention is made of criterion validity. The ADT should be used only with caution and with a thorough knowledge of its shortcomings.

Test of Auditory Comprehension of Language

Language Components Assessed   Morphology, syntax, and some semantics

Communication Channel   Receptive

The Test for Auditory Comprehension of Language (TACL) (Carrow, 1973) was one of the first attempts to assess more of language comprehension than just receptive vocabulary. In fact, the TACL had two purposes: first, to measure the child's auditory comprehension abilities and thus assign the child to a developmental level of auditory comprehension; and second, to determine specific content areas of language difficulty so that educational planning and intervention could be implemented.

The TACL is an individually administered device that consists of 101 plates of three black-and-white drawings. For each plate, one of the drawings is the referent for the language element being tested, and the other two drawings are either contrasting language elements or unrelated decoys. For example, one of the stimulus sentences is "The boy is at the side of the car." The child is shown three line drawings, one of which shows the child inside the car (incorrect), one of which shows the child under the car (incorrect), and the last of which shows the child standing beside the car (correct). After four practice items, the examiner continues through the 101 test items by stating the stimulus sentence and having the child point to the correct picture. No verbalization is required on the part of the child. The test takes about 20 minutes to administer, and the entire test must be administered since the items are not arranged by level of difficulty but instead by the language elements being assessed. The vocabulary items included in the test are those generally learned early in normal language development. These vocabulary items are tested separately so that when they are later used in language structure items, the examiner can determine whether an error is semantic or structural.

The TACL is available in both English and Spanish versions, and a screening test (twenty-five items from the longer version) is also available.

Scores

For each correct response, the child is given one point, the sum of which indicates the child's total raw score. This total raw score can be transformed to an auditory comprehension age score by using a chronological age–raw score equivalency norm table. A child's score can also be compared with that of other children in the given age group by using a table that includes measures of central tendency (mean, standard deviation, and median) for each age group. Finally, total raw scores can be converted to percentile ranks for each of the age groups.

Further analysis of the child's performance can be accomplished by dividing the total raw score into three subscores: vocabulary, morphology, and syntax. Although norms for these subcategory scores are not available, the items within each subcategory can be analyzed qualitatively in order to delineate specific areas of difficulty.

Norms

The 1973 English edition of the TACL was standardized on a sample of 200 middle-class black, Anglo, and Mexican-American children of ages 3 through 6; 50 children were in each group. Studies comparing the three middle-class ethnic groups indicated no significant differences among the groups. Thus, test results from the three groups were collapsed, and norms refer to middle-class children from all three.

No normative data are reported for the Spanish version of the TACL.

Reliability

Carrow reports impressive reliability data for early English and Spanish editions of the TACL. However, no reliability information is provided for the present edition (1973, revised). In fact, more than a third of the items in the present edition are different from the earlier versions. Other aspects of the test, including the order in which items are presented have been changed in the present edition (Byrne, 1978). Finally, the mean age of the children tested in the reliability studies was approximately 7 years. The current edition of the TACL is meant to be used only for children 3 to 6 years old. Thus, the reliability data presented are inapplicable to the 1973 (revised) edition of the TACL.

Validity

Some evidence of construct validity is presented by the author. The test manual indicates that the TACL successfully separates normal children from children known to have language comprehension disorders. Also, Carrow reports that there is a statistically significant relationship between age and increased language comprehension development as measured by the TACL. However, as was the case with the reliability data, the statistical procedures designed to establish construct validity were performed only on the earlier editions of the TACL. Thus, these claims of construct validity must be viewed with caution.

As a criterion-referenced device, it appears that the TACL can claim some content validity. A wide variety of language elements is being assessed, and some valuable diagnostic information about a child's auditory comprehension abilities can seemingly be obtained when the test is administered by a cautious, skilled examiner. However, any interpretation of the test results must be made with caution for the following reasons. First, because there are only three foils for each item, the child has a 33 percent chance of guessing the correct answer. Thus, conclusions cannot be made concerning items that the child answers correctly. Conclusions should be attempted only when analyzing items that a child has answered incorrectly. In other words, if a child gives the correct response, the examiner can't be certain that the child knows the language element being tested. If the child gives an incorrect response, however, the ex-

aminer can make a stronger assumption that the child does not know the element being assessed and can formulate an intervention program around those missed items. Second, since the TACL is not arranged developmentally, no basals or ceilings can be determined. Most children, especially younger children or children with significant language problems, will miss many items before the test is completed. It is often more difficult to maintain children's attention and motivation levels when they are missing many items. Thus, some of the children's errors, especially as the test progresses, might be due to lack of attention. Finally, extreme care must be taken when using the Spanish version of the TACL. Besides the lack of norms for the Spanish edition, about one-third of the directions to children are ambiguous because of the Spanish words used or are different in meaning from the English version (Byrne, 1978).

Summary

The TACL is an individually administered device designed to measure receptive morphological, syntactic, and semantic abilities in children 3 to 6 years of age. Although some valid information about a child's receptive language abilities can be obtained by a trained examiner, certain shortcomings must be kept in mind. Reliability information for the present (1973) revised edition does not appear in the technical manual. Validity is subject to the many limitations enumerated above. Thus, the TACL should be used with care.

Carrow Elicited Language Inventory

Language Components Assessed Morphology and syntax

Communication Channel Expressive

The Carrow Elicited Language Inventory (CELI) (Carrow, 1974), is one of the few formal tests designed to give the examiner diagnostic information about a child's expressive grammatical competence. Although quantification of a child's abilities is possible and normative data are provided, the CELI is best used as a criterion-referenced device that allows the examiner to determine which specific elements of language the child is producing incorrectly.

The CELI is an individually administered device consisting of fifty-one grammatically loaded sentences and one phrase. The length of the stimuli range from two to ten words, with six words the average length. Within these sentences, the following grammatical forms are tested: 41 pronouns (including six different types), 14 prepositions (in four contexts), 7 conjunctions, 41 articles (in two contexts), 9 adverbs, 5 Wh questions, 13 negatives (in three contexts), 59 nouns (including singular and plural), 7 adjectives, 103 verbs (twenty types), 8 infinitives, and 1 gerund.

To administer the test, the examiner says a stimulus sentence and requests the child to imitate that sentence. Ideally, the child's responses should be taped so that there can be two levels of analysis: one immediate and one after relistening to the tape. The scoring sheet is in the form of a matrix, with the grammatical categories listed horizontally and the sentences listed vertically in the order in which they are read to the child. The examiner marks the elements in the sentence that the child has produced incorrectly and then analyzes them. In addition to this score sheet, another score sheet, called the verb protocol, allows for a detailed analysis of the verb errors a child is making. This is helpful since a large percentage of grammatical errors made by children involve verbs. The verb protocol is suggested if the child's verb score falls below the tenth percentile. However, it can be profitably used with children above that cutoff point also.

The test itself takes about 20 to 30 minutes to administer, depending on the child's attention span (which is sometimes a problem, since the only stimulus for the child is the verbal sentence). The analysis, however, can take up to 45 minutes. Detailed training of prospective examiners, including a training tape and "practice children" included within the kit, is recommended. Although the CELI was developed for use by speech-language pathologists, the manual states that any examiner with a language background will be able to administer and use the test.

Finally, the manual warns that the test should not be used with the following groups of children: (1) those with such severe misarticulation that the examiner cannot understand what is being said, and (2) those with echolalia.

Scores

The number of grammatical errors the child makes is added up to provide the total error score, from which other scores may be obtained. An error score in each of the grammatical subcategories can also be obtained. Percentile ranks are given that correspond to the child's total and subcategory error scores. Stanines have been provided for each age level and subcategory.

As has been stated, the CELI is best used as a criterion-referenced device. In fact, the normative scores provided seem to have some problems that the technical manual has not satisfactorily explained. For example, from age 36 months to 79 months, the expected error score decreases. This is unsurprising. However, from 79 months to 95 months, the error score begins to rise again. Although the manual claims that perhaps a test ceiling has been reached at 79 months and the increased error score is due to chance, this explanation is unconvincing. A second problem with the scores provided is the instability of both the subcategory error scores. The manual itself states, "With the exception of the verb subscore in the grammar categories . . . the performance of the five, six, and seven year old children in the subcategories was relatively homogenous within each age group. Consequently, the percentile scores must be interpreted with caution" (Carrow, 1974). As a result, a 7-year-old child who makes no contraction errors will be at the one-hundredth percentile, while one who makes just one error will be at the fifteenth percentile. Also, because the scores of each of the groups are so homogenous, a child can achieve a score of 31 at age 3-11 and be placed in the seventy-sixth percentile, and yet one month later, if the child achieves the same score at 4-0, the child is placed in the twenty-eighth percentile. It seems, then, that the range of the age groups used in computing the scores (1 year) is too long to trace the development of language adequately.

Norms

The CELI was standardized on a restricted group of 475 white middle-class children aged 3-0 to 7-11 coming from homes where only Standard American English was spoken. The technical manual acknowledges that this is a narrowly defined group and indicates the intent to gather additional data on language-disordered children and children speaking the major dialects of English. All children selected in the original norming group came from day-care centers and church schools in middle-income neighborhoods in Houston, Texas. Children who had any speech or language disorders were eliminated from the sample.

Reliability

Three measures of reliability are provided for the CELI. Test-retest reliability was determined for twenty-five children (five each across five age levels), selected at random and retested after two weeks. The same examiner performed both tests. The stability coefficient obtained was 0.98.

Two measures of interrater reliability were obtained. First, two examiners listened to and scored ten randomly selected tapes of children's responses, with a resulting reliability coefficient of 0.98. Second, two examiners administered the test to twenty children, ten of whom were diagnosed as having language disorders. Responses were transcribed live and scored, with a resultant correlation coefficient of 0.99.

Validity

Since the CELI is best used as a criterion-referenced test, much of its validity rests on its content validity. Although the author makes little reference to content validity in the test manual, the wide variety of language structures sampled appears to indicate a content-valid test. However, it also appears that certain structures are inadequately sampled; for these structures, more caution is desirable when making conclusions about a child's language abilities.

Some evidence of concurrent validity is presented in the technical manual. First, the CELI was compared with the Developmental Sentence Scoring (DSS) procedure by Lee and Canter (1971), a widely used procedure for analyzing children's language abilities. The correlation between the two measures was -0.79. (Since the CELI uses error scores and the DSS uses "correct" scores, a negative correlation is desirable.) On the second test of concurrent validity, scores on the CELI for twenty children were ranked according to severity and then compared with a ranking of these children according to the external clinical judgment of expert observers. (It was not indicated how many independent judges ranked the children.) The rank order correlation (rho) between the CELI and the rank of the children by the judges was 0.77.

Finally, Carrow presents some evidence of construct validity. The correlation coefficient between total error score and age was -0.62. Also, the manual presents some evidence that the CELI successfully separates children with language disorders from those with normal language.

Summary

The CELI is an individually administered device designed to measure the expressive morphological and syntactic abilities of children between 3 and 8 years of age. Although some more work can be done in these areas, reliability and validity data appear adequate, and more than adequate if the CELI is used as a criterion-referenced device.

Northwestern Syntax Screening Test

Language Components Assessed   Some syntax, some morphology

Communication Channels   Receptive and expressive

For many years, the only formal device commonly used to evaluate a child's language structure was the Northwestern Syntax Screening Test (NSST) (Lee, 1969). Although other tests are now on the market, the NSST is still very popular in many areas. The NSST is an individually administered device, essentially a screening instrument to separate children who may have problems in the area of receptive or expressive morphology or syntax. It consists of two parts, the first of which screens a child's comprehension abilities. In part one, the child is shown a page with four black-and-white drawings and then told, "I'm going to tell you about these pictures. When I'm done, you show me the right pictures." The examiner then reads a pair of sentences to the child in the order given on the test form. After reading the sentence pair, the examiner repeats the sentence that has an asterisk after it, and the child must point to the correct picture. Then the examiner repeats the other sentence, and the child must point to the picture that illustrates *that* sentence. This continues for twenty pages and sentence pairs, with the child pointing to the picture that illustrates the sentence.

Part two has a slightly different format and screens expressive language. In part two, the child is shown a page with two pictures on it. The examiner says, "I will tell you about these pictures. When I am done, you say just what I say." The examiner says the pair of sentences in the order that they appear on the test form, then points to the asterisked picture and asks, "What is this picture?" The child has to repeat the correct sentence from the sentence pair. The examiner then points to the other picture and asks the same question; the child responds. This continues until twenty sentence pairs have been repeated. In the receptive section, the response is judged correct if the child points to the correct picture. In the expressive section, the response is considered correct if either verbatim responses or responses using equivalent grammatical structures are spoken.

The NSST contains twenty sentence pairs for each communication channel and assesses the following grammatical elements: plurals, verb tenses, pronouns, prepositions, negatives, possessives, passives, subject-verb agreement, Wh questions, and question-statement differences.

Scores

The child receives a score of 1 for each correct response. Thus, a child can score 0, 1, or 2 for each of the sentence pairs, for a total possible score of 40 for each part.

The total raw score on each part can be converted to percentile ranges (second, tenth, twenty-fifth, fiftieth, seventy-fifth, and ninetieth). If a child scores below the 2nd percentile (more than 2 standard deviations below the mean), the manual states that "the children are almost certain to be in need of interventional language teaching." If a child's score is between the 2nd and 10th percentile, further investigation is recommended before the child is enrolled in an intervention program.

Norms

The NSST was standardized on 344 children between the ages of 3 years and 7 years, 11 months. The number of children in each age group varied from 34 (at 7-0 to 7-11) to 160 (at 5-0 to 5-11). Normal nursery school or public school classes were used to provide the normative group, and the children's teachers reported on handicapping conditions that would contribute to inadequate language development. The children in the sample generally came from middle- and upper-middle-class midwestern communities from homes in which standard American English was spoken.

Reliability

No reliability information is provided in the manual.

Validity

The validity of the NSST rests on its content validity when used as instructed. Although the sample of test items measuring the various grammatical constructions is limited, the author appropriately warns against using the NSST as anything but as a screening device. No data are reported in the manual that correlate performance on the NSST with any other language measure, such as a child's spontaneous speech.

Summary

The NSST is a screening test of language comprehension and expression, with only a small sample of morphological and syntactic elements included for study. No reliability data are presented. In the manual, the author states best the uses of the NSST: "The NSST is intended to be used as a screening instrument only; it is, in no sense, to be considered a measurement of a child's general language skill nor even as an 'in depth' study of syntax."

Illinois Test of Psycholinguistic Abilities

Language Components Assessed Some morphology, some semantics; other "psycholinguistic" activities that theoretically underlie communication

Communication Channels Receptive and expressive

The revised edition of the Illinois Test of Psycholinguistic Abilities (ITPA) (Kirk, McCarthy, & Kirk, 1968) is an individually administered, norm-referenced test that has norms for children between the ages of 2 years, 4 months and 10 years, 3 months. The ITPA was designed to measure a child's relative ability to understand, process, and produce both verbal and nonverbal language and was theoretically based on an adaptation of the Osgood (1957a, 1957b) model of communication. The test contains ten regularly administered and two optional subtests, each designed to minimize the demands of any factor other than that being measured. For example, the auditory reception and visual reception subtests attempt to minimize response demands for the child by requiring only yes-no or pointing responses.

The format of the ITPA includes three hypothetical components of communication: (1) the channels of communication, including sensory input and verbal or motor response; (2) psycholinguistic processes, including reception, association, and expression; and (3) levels of organization, which encompass representational and automatic activities. At the representational level, some form of mediation is required, in contrast to the automatic level, where "the individual's habits of functioning are less voluntary but highly organized and integrated" (Paraskevopoulos & Kirk, 1969, p. 14). The twelve subtests of the ITPA and the behaviors sampled by each follow.

Auditory Reception (AR) This subtest presents a series of yes-no questions such as, "Do dogs eat?" The syntactic form of the question remains constant until the upper level of the scale, where adjectives are inserted before the noun ("Do wingless birds soar?"). The child responds by nodding or saying *yes* or *no*. This subtest seems to measure receptive vocabulary, a small part of semantics.

Visual Reception (VR) In this subtest, the child is shown a stimulus picture (a German Shepherd dog, for example). After this picture is removed, the child is shown a card having four pictures and instructed to point to one similar to the original picture. Among those four pictures might be another dog (for example, a Chihuahua). This subtest is meant to parallel the auditory reception subtest, while using a different sensory modality.

Auditory Association (AA) This subtest measures another aspect of semantic comprehension, verbal analogies. The child is presented with, for example, the following incomplete statement: "Brother is a boy. Sister is a ____." The child has to complete the unfinished phrase orally.

Visual Association (VA) In this subtest, the child is presented with a picture surrounded by four other pictures, one of which goes with the picture in the center. For example, the center picture might be a hammer, surrounded by four pictures, one of which is a nail. The child is then asked to point to the surrounding picture that goes with the picture in the center. At the upper level of the subtest, the task changes so that the child is presented with three pictures (tennis ball, tennis racket, baseball bat) and a blank. The child is instructed to find a picture out of an array of four pictures that goes with the third (baseball bat) as the first goes with the second.

Verbal Expression (VE) In this subtest, the child is shown an object, like a block, and is instructed to tell the examiner everything about it. Scoring is based on the number of correct, discrete statements the child makes about the object.

Manual Expression (ME) This subtest measures a child's understanding of the use of some common objects. After being shown a picture object (for example, a telephone), the child must gesturally show how to use it (that is, the child must dial).

Grammatic Closure (GC) In this subtest, the child is presented with a picture such as that depicted in Figure 13.2 and an incomplete statement such as "Here is one die; here are two ____." The child must complete the statement by supplying the correct word (in this case,

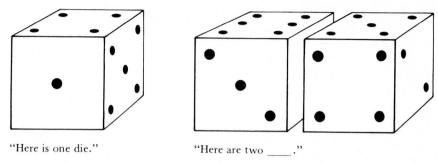

"Here is one die."   "Here are two ____."

FIGURE 13.2 An example of the format used in the Grammatic Closure subtest of the Illinois Test of Psycholinguistic Abilities

"dice"). This subtest is essentially a test of morphology.

Auditory Closure (AC) This is an optional subtest requiring that a child complete a word that has been presented orally with one or more missing phonemes. For example, the examiner says "olli-op" and asks the child, "What am I talking about?" The child must repeat the entire word (lollipop). The authors claim that this function "occurs in everyday life situations such as understanding foreign accents, speech defects, or poor telephone connections" (p. 21).

Sound Blending (SB) Also optional, this subtest requires the examiner to say a word, but pause for one-half second between syllables ["type-(pause)-wri-(pause)-ter"]. The child must put the syllables together and say the word as a whole.

Visual Closure (VC) In this subtest, the child must recognize familiar objects when only part of the object is pictured. For example, the child is shown a pictured object like a dog and then a complex scene with many objects in it. Within that scene are many partially depicted dogs (for example, just a tail). The child is given 30 seconds to find as many incomplete target objects as possible.

Auditory Sequential Memory (ASM) This subtest requires the examiner to present a sequence of digits orally to the child at half-second intervals. The child is expected to say the oral digit pattern correctly.

Visual Sequential Memory (VSM) In this subtest, the child is presented a card containing a sequence of two or more meaningless designs and given a number of chips, each containing one design. The child looks at the design sequence on the card for 5 seconds and then is requested to reproduce the design in correct order from memory, using the chips.

Scores

Various types of scores can be computed from the number of correct responses a child makes for each subtest and the total number of correct responses on the entire test.

Scaled Scores (SS) Raw scores can be changed to scaled scores (SS) having a mean of 36 and a standard deviation of 6. A composite SS is computed based on the total of raw-score points. Since the raw-score variances differ, the different subtests are not equally weighted. This means that in the total score, some subtests count more heavily than others.

Psycholinguistic Ages (PLAs) PLAs are available for the total score, as well as for each subtest. The authors obtained the PLAs by plotting a graph of mean CAs and mean raw scores for the eight age groups tested in the normative sample. After this, means were conducted and intermediate values were calculated. These values are the PLAs. Since Paraskevopoulos and Kirk (1969) present data showing that the "standard deviations of PLA vary from test to test and from age to age" (p. 91), PLAs for different subtests and ages are not comparable.

Psycholinguistic Quotients (PLQs) PLQs are essentially ratio scores (100 PLA/CA). Because of this, PLQs for different subtests, like PLAs, cannot be compared due to the unequal standard deviations. In addition, the technical manual states that "since the standardization sample was comprised of average children, *deviation* PLQs could not be computed without questionable extrapolations" (Paraskevopoulos & Kirk, 1969, p. 80). However, only fourteen pages later, the manual claims that the composite scaled score, "in contrast to the PLQ, is essentially comparable in nature to a *deviation* intelligence quotient" (p. 94). This seems strange in that the composite scaled score is based on the same sample as the PLQ. And the manual has already stated that the sample of average children was too restricted to be able to compute deviation scores without making questionable assumptions.

Percentage Score A percentage score that can be interpreted as a percentile rank for average deviations is also presented in the technical manual. The average deviation (AD) can be obtained by performing the following computations: (1) Subtract the *mean* of a given child's scaled scores from the child's scaled scores on each of the subtests. (2) Sum these differences (there will be twelve of them if twelve subtests are administered). Ignore the + and − signs.

(3) Divide this sum by the number of scores. The percentage of children in the normative group whose AD was greater than or equal to the computed AD is shown in the table.

Norms

The ITPA was standardized on a restricted group of children. It is interesting that although the test was designed "for use with children encountering learning difficulties" (Paraskevopoulos & Kirk, 1969, p. 51), children who were having problems in school were systematically excluded from the normative sample. In fact, the children included in the norm groups were "only those children demonstrating average intellectual functioning, average school achievement, average characteristics of personal-social adjustment, sensory motor integrity, and coming from predominantly English speaking families" (pp. 51–52). The norm sample included 962 children between the ages of 2-7 and 10-1. These children lived in Bloomington, Illinois; Danville, Illinois; Decatur, Illinois; Madison, Wisconsin; and Urbana, Illinois. These communities were selected because of "practical requirements of being middle-class communities" (Paraskevopoulos & Kirk, 1969, p. 57). Schoolage children were selected by sampling only schools that school administrators judged to be predominantly middle-class. In addition, only classes of normal children were sampled. In order to obtain the preschool sample, younger siblings of the school sample were tested, as were children referred "mostly by mothers of preschool siblings" (pp. 55–56).

The norm sample contains only about 4 percent black children, substantially less than the national average. This seems easily explained by the fact that schools in the communities selected were excluded from the sample if they had more than a 10 percent black enrollment. The technical manual attempts to show that the five communities making up the sample are representative of the entire U.S. population (1960 census), at least in terms of education, median family income, and occupation of residents. However, these comparisons are misleading in that the group of children selected was hardly a random sample representative of the five communities. Although the occupations of the sample children's fathers are presented and are said to correspond to countrywide data on occupations given in the 1960 census, these percentage figures are suspect. This is because of the median percentages reported for each group were computed as if each community sampled the same number of children, which was not the case. For example, 52 children were tested in Bloomington, while 273 were sampled in Danville. Instead, weighted medians should have been used in comparing the occupations of the sample fathers to the countrywide figures.

Finally, information is presented about the intelligence of the children in the normative sample, as measured by the Stanford-Binet (1960). Although the mean of the sample IQs was around 100, the standard deviation of the IQs in the sample was only approximately 8, indicating a severely restricted sample.

Reliability

A most adequate description of reliability data is provided in the technical manual accompanying the ITPA. For each of the eight age groups, and for each of the twelve subtests, internal-consistency estimates (generally KR-20) have been computed, yielding ninety-six reliability coefficients. Of these coefficients, only nine equal or exceed .90. In fact, only four of the twelve subtests have *any* reliability coefficients at or above .90. The composite reliability coefficients for each age level are better, with only two of the eight age levels having coefficients below .90. Unfortunately, however, most of the discussion on the uses and interpretation of the ITPA refers to the subtest scores and not to the

TABLE 13.5 Ranges of Reliability Estimates for Subtests of the ITPA

Subtests	Internal Consistency[a]	Test-Retest[a]
AR	.84–.91	.36–.56
VR	.73–.87	.21–.36
AA	.74–.85	.62–.71
VA	.75–.82	.32–.57
VE	.51–.79	.45–.49
ME	.77–.83	.40–.51
GC	.60–.74	.49–.72
AC	.45–.84	.36–.52
SB	.78–.91	.30–.63
VC	.49–.70	.57–.68
ASM	.74–.90	.61–.86
VSM	.51–.96	.12–.50
Composite	.87–.93	.70–.83

[a]Not corrected for restriction in intelligence range.

composite score, the only part of the test that has adequate internal consistency. Column one of Table 13.5 lists the ranges of internal-consistency estimates for each ITPA subtest.

Test-retest reliabilities are also reported in the technical manual and are quite a bit lower than the internal-consistency estimates. The test-retest coefficients were computed for the following three age levels, using a 5- to 6-month interval: four-year-olds ($n = 71$), six-year-olds ($n = 55$), and eight-year-olds ($n = 72$). Of the thirty-six subtest coefficients reported (twelve subtests at three age levels), twenty-seven, or 75 percent, had reported reliability coefficients below .60, and eighteen coefficients, or fully half, were below .50. Only two of the thirty-six coefficients were above .72. The estimate for composite test-retest reliability is predictably a bit better than the subtest estimates, but hardly impressive. The four-year-olds achieved an estimate of .83, but the reliability coefficients for the six- and eight-year-olds were only .70. Column two of Table 13.5 illustrates the range of test-retest reliabilities for the twelve subtests of the ITPA.

Finally, the technical manual provides other data, including SEMs for raw scores, scaled scores, and PLAs (in months). Also calculated are median reliability estimates for difference scores among subtests, based on the internal-consistency reliability estimates and median SEMs of scaled score differences. Coefficients indicating excellent interscorer reliability for the Verbal Expression subtest are presented.

In short, the reliability of the ITPA is far from adequate. However, the authors have presented all the reliability information in their manual, so that an informed decision regarding the stability of ITPA scores can be made.

Validity

Validity data presented in the ITPA manual is unconvincing. There are no estimates of predictive validity using teacher ratings or school achievement for the revised edition. As or more important, there is no evidence of validity with other measures of language for the revised edition. This leaves determination of content and/or construct validity up to the potential user. Unfortunately, the ITPA seems extremely weak in these areas also.

Although the communication model of Osgood, which is used as the rationale of the ITPA, is well respected among many speech and language professionals, there are three problems that make any attempt to turn the theoretical model into a concrete diagnostic device a questionable undertaking at best.

First, the model is theoretical and is observable only at the levels in which the person interacts with the environment. Thus, one can know that information is "going in" to the person, and can observe information "coming out." But what happens "in between" is open to much conjecture. In fact, there have been *many* adaptations of Osgood's model, and most of the differences between these adaptations involve the theorized activities "in between." The ITPA is only one more theoretical model, and there is no

reason to believe that this model explains the physiological activities within the nervous system better than any other. Certainly, Osgood never referred specifically to "sound blending," for example, in his original communication model. There is no evidence that proves that the construct of sound blending even exists, much less that it is causally related to language.

Second, even if one were to accept the author's interpretation of Osgood's theoretical model, people do not currently have sufficient technology to be able to measure these functions discretely, as even the authors admit (Paraskevopoulos & Kirk, 1969, p. 26). In fact, all the visual subtests require the child to have auditory comprehension abilities, if only to understand the directions. Moreover, the subtests of the ITPA rarely assess the behaviors that the authors claim they assess. For example, the Visual Reception subtest is said to assess the same elements as the Auditory Reception subtest, while using a different sensory modality. However, this seems questionable. Although the Auditory Reception subtest measures some semantic comprehension, the Visual Reception subtest seems little more than a visual discrimination task. No vocabulary ability seems necessary to answer items correctly in the visual test. In the auditory test, on the other hand, vocabulary is the main element being tested. As another example, consider the Visual Association subtest. Although the authors claim that the upper level items are comparable (though in a different sense modality) to the analogies of the Auditory Association subtest, this seems not to be true. In the auditory subtest, the elements paired are an item with its category (brother-boy) or an item with a verb (saw-cut). In the visual subtest, however, because the stimulus is a picture, an item must always be paired with another item (bat-ball). A child can correctly answer the latter type of analogy just by having seen the items paired in the past, without understanding the relationship. However, in the auditory items, some understanding of the relationship between the items is necessary before the child can give a correct answer. Also, it should be easy to realize that these two tests assess different elements of language, although the authors claim to be tapping the same psycholinguistic elements.

These problems contribute to very questionable content validity for the ITPA items as measures of language. Validity problems also arise when considering the use of ITPA profiles as an indication of pathology. Paraskevopoulos and Kirk state that "the larger the average deviation of individual scores from a child's mean score, the more discrepant the child's growth and the more likely it is that the child will have learning disabilities" (p. 142). In fact, users of the test are instructed to look for the child's profile of deviations from the mean as a possible factor in diagnosing learning disabilities (LD). However, the authors provide no data to support using the profiles in that manner. They have compared the average deviations of mentally retarded and normal children, but have not provided data for LD children. And practically all definitions of LD *exclude* retarded children, the only group they compared with normals. The authors are in essence using the results of one group to diagnose another. Moreover, even if LD children *do* have more dispersion in their scores, the reasoning behind the diagnosis of LD from those profiles is clearly faulty. Consider: LD children have disperse profiles; Jimmy has a disperse profile; therefore, Jimmy has a learning disability. It's easy to see where this reasoning is fallacious. The fact that all LD children have disperse profiles does not mean that all persons with disperse profiles have LD. To further explain, consider this example: All men are mortal; Jane is mortal; Jane is a man.

Although the content validity of the ITPA seems extremely weak, especially when it is considered as a measure of language, it must in all fairness be noted that there is a high correlation between the ITPA and the Stanford-Binet Intelligence Scale. Perhaps there would be more validity in regarding the ITPA as a psychometric measure much like the Stanford-Binet, rather than as a measure of language ability or as a diagnostic device for learning disabilities. Of course, for any test to be valid, it must first be reliable, and the ITPA as presently normed does not meet that criterion.

Summary

The ITPA seems to have inadequate norms, poor reliability, and questionable validity. One might wonder why so much space has been devoted to a test with so many shortcomings. The problem is that the ITPA is exciting and unique in format and purpose. And being exciting and different, it appeals to many individuals in the field who probably would be shocked to know that the test-retest reliability for eight-year-olds on the Visual Sequential Memory subtest is .12. Perhaps this extended discussion can at least persuade more individuals to read the manual for themselves. Following that, the test as currently used should speak for itself. Perhaps Paraskevopoulos and Kirk state it best: "characteristics of the ITPA . . . are based on data obtained primarily from average children. The psychometric characteristics of a test are a function not only of the test itself, but also a group of children to whom the test is applied. . . . It is necessary, therefore, to collect information on reliability, differential performance and validity on groups of children with whom the test is going to be used, such as retardates, culturally disadvantaged, learning disabilities, and other groups of deviant children." The unwritten next sentence is, "Perhaps, then, the ITPA can be validly used with those groups."

COPING WITH DILEMMAS IN CURRENT PRACTICE

Three issues are particularly troublesome in the assessment of oral language. We always want our assessments, often made in a highly structured assessment situation, to generalize to children's language performances in the real world. The extent to which we can assume that this will occur is affected by several factors. Two are especially noteworthy.

Low-functioning children are not very likely to generalize responses to situations beyond those in which responses were trained. Thus, we may teach social language to severely mentally retarded individuals in the classroom or the therapy room and find that it does not occur unprompted on the playground. Similarly, we may train one or two responses and find that we do not get response generalization. For example, we may train an individual to respond "hello" to waves or greetings from others. We cannot expect that more severely handicapped individuals will necessarily learn to respond "hi" or "how's it goin' guys" to greetings from acquaintances.

The generally recommended way to cope with this dilemma is to train specifically for generalization. What does this type of training specifically require? First, training should not be conducted on a continuous reinforcement schedule. Second, training should occur in a large variety of contexts—the classroom, playground, social situations, and so on. Third, a variety of stimulus conditions and response alternatives must be trained. This type of training is necessarily time consuming and complex.

The second problem is one of finding devices with adequate technical characteristics. Oral language tests, as a group, often have inadequate reliability, content validity, and norms. Assessors frequently need to assess a pupil's language ability and are not able to find a suitable language device. The only remedy that we know is to use criterion-referenced tests developed by a clinician and/or teacher or to use systematic observation procedures.

A final problem that is particularly difficult to cope with is the assessment of individuals who are not speakers of Standard American English. Diagnosticians must be thoroughly familiar with the language group to which the speaker belongs if they are to make an accurate assessment. Unless the diagnostician knows the dialectic and phonetic rules that govern the language group's speech, he or she cannot make an accurate diagnosis. Individuals who are members of the special language group can often help the clinician determine whether the student is speaking and comprehending in a way that is typical of the special language group.

SUMMARY

Language is a complex process made up of four interrelated elements: phonology, morphology, syntax, and semantics. These components of language are typically measured in each of the two channels of communication: reception and expression. All the language components must be assessed in both communication channels for a language assessment to be complete and valid. In addition to the aforementioned considerations, there are three important factors to consider when interpreting the results of a language assessment: (1) cultural background of the child, (2) age of the child, and (3) intellectual competency. Each factor will have an effect on language performance. Finally, there are three major procedures typically used to elicit a child's language behavior: (1) using the child's spontaneous language output, (2) eliciting language through imitation, and (3) using a picture or other stimulus to elicit language.

STUDY QUESTIONS

1. Identify and describe the four components of language.
2. What are the two channels of communication, and how do they relate to language assessment?
3. How do language tests differ from tests assessing other domains in terms of the requirements for adequate normative samples? In terms of validity considerations, which aspect of validity takes on major importance in language assessment?
4. A school district in San Diego, California, decides to screen preschool bilingual children using the ITPA, NSST, TACL, CELI, and the Goldman-Fristoe. The parents of these children protest the use of these tests. To what extent is the protest justified? How might the school district define its position? Consider in your answer the norms, reliability, and validity of *each* of the five tests.

ADDITIONAL READING

Bloom, L., & Lahey, M. *Language development and language disorders.* New York: Wiley, 1978.

CHAPTER 14

ASSESSMENT OF
PERCEPTUAL-MOTOR SKILLS

Educators and psychologists have operated for quite some time under the assumption that adequate perceptual-motor development is important both in and of itself and as a prerequisite to the development of academic skills. A wide variety of devices designed to assess children's perceptual-motor functioning are in use in the public schools today. While many measures of learning aptitude include items designed to assess perceptual or motor skills and while many readiness tests assess aspects of perceptual-motor development, this chapter focuses on those devices designed specifically and exclusively to assess perceptual-motor skills.

WHY DO WE ASSESS PERCEPTUAL-MOTOR SKILLS?

Perceptual-motor assessment typically takes place for one of several purposes. In some cases, the perceptual-motor skills of entire classes of students are assessed in an effort to identify those with perceptual-motor difficulties so that training programs can be instituted to prevent incipient learning difficulties. Students who perform poorly on perceptual-motor devices are said to demonstrate perceptual-motor problems thought to contribute to or cause learning problems. In other cases, students having academic difficulties are assessed by means of perceptual-motor tests in an effort to identify the extent to which perceptual-motor difficulties may be causing the academic difficulties. In both instances, efforts are made to identify perceptual-motor problems so that training programs can be prescribed. Finally, perceptual-motor tests are widely used to diagnose brain injury.

THE INTERESTING PAST AND PROBLEMATICAL PRESENT OF PERCEPTUAL-MOTOR ASSESSMENT

The practice of perceptual-motor assessment, while relatively new, has an interesting history. In the early 1900s gestalt psychology was born with a paper by Max Wertheimer that reported the work of Wertheimer, Kurt Koffka, and Wolfgang Kohler on perceptual phenomena such as apparent movement and afterimages. In 1923 Wertheimer put together a set of empirical statements known as the *principles of perceptual organization.* Gestalt psychologists, while certainly concerned with other aspects of psychology, made perception their major study. The early work of Wertheimer and his associates is apparent even today in the assessment of perceptual-motor development.

More recently, Hallahan and Cruickshank (1973) traced the history of the study of perceptual-motor problems in mentally retarded, brain-injured, and learning-disabled children. According to Hallahan and Cruickshank, the historical roots of current practices in perceptual-motor assessment can be traced to the early work of Goldstein and of Werner and Strauss. Goldstein (1927, 1936, 1939) was engaged in the study of soldiers who had suffered traumatic head injuries during World War I. According to Hallahan and Cruickshank (1973), "Goldstein . . . found in his patients . . . the psychological characteristics of concrete behavior, meticulosity, perseveration, figure-background confusion, forced responsiveness to stimuli, and catastrophic reaction" (p. 59).

In the mid-1940s the two German psychologists Heinz Werner and Alfred Strauss began to study the behavioral pathology evidenced by brain-injured persons. In a series of studies at the Wayne County Training School in Detroit, Michigan, Werner and Strauss studied two kinds of brain-injured subjects: brain-injured retardates, and nonretardates who had experienced traumatic head injury from an automobile accident, a fall, a gunshot wound, or other similar incident. Their early research resulted in a list of behavioral characteristics said to differentiate brain-injured and non-brain-injured persons. The tests that were constructed to assess these behavioral characteristics are used today for that purpose.

Hallahan and Cruickshank state that "for Werner and Strauss it became a major concern to learn whether the psychological manifestations of brain injury found in adults by Goldstein would also be observable in children" (p. 60). Despite this interest in children, it must be remembered that the subjects studied in early investigations and on whom early tests were developed differ significantly from the children we currently assess using perceptual-motor tests. Subjects in early investigations were primarily adults who exhibited focal brain injury in the form of tissue damage, lesions, or tumors. To generalize characteristics of such persons to children with "diffuse brain injury" ignores neurological differences as well as developmental differences between children and adults. Many current perceptual-motor tests were developed using a criterion-group approach; they were developed to differentiate between *groups* of persons known to have sustained brain injury and non-brain-injured persons. They are currently used to differentiate between *individuals* whose problems may or may not be due to brain injury and who usually have no proven injury to the central nervous system.

While perceptual-motor tests have been used for some time to diagnose brain injury, recently there has been a dramatic and significant increase in the use of various perceptual-motor devices to diagnose learning disabilities. According to Hallahan and Cruickshank (1973), the contemporary leaders in the field of learning disabilities, who were responsible for its origin and development and for the development of the major perceptual-motor tests, were at one time associates or students of Werner and Strauss or were at least significantly influenced by their work. William Cruickshank, Samuel Kirk, and Newell Kephart were all associated with the Wayne County Training School at the time Werner and Strauss were engaged in their early investigations. Gerald Getman, an optometrist, later worked with Kephart at Purdue University, while Ray Barsch worked with both Getman and Strauss. Marianne Frostig, while not a direct associate of Werner and Strauss, has stated that she was significantly influenced by their early investigations (Hallahan & Cruickshank, 1973).

The associates of Werner and Strauss went on to apply their early work to the study of behavioral pathology in nonretarded children who were experiencing learning difficulty. While Kirk emphasized psycholinguistic disabilities and with his students constructed the Illinois Test of Psycholinguistic Abilities, the others stressed perceptual problems. Cruickshank focused on brain-injured children and children with cerebral palsy, and Kephart, Getman, Barsch, and Frostig focused on the academic correlates of perceptual-motor problems.

Out of the long history of interest in perception and perceptual problems among adults and brain-injured retardates has grown today a particular concern for the perceptual and motor problems of nonretarded children who fail academically. The thinking underlying this concern is illustrated by statements made by Frostig, Lefever, and Whittlesey (1966).

It is most important that a child's perceptual disabilities, if any exist, be discovered as early as possible. All research to date which has explored the child's general classroom behavior has confirmed the authors' original finding that kindergarten and first-grade children with visual perceptual disabilities are likely to be rated by their teachers as maladjusted in the classroom; not only do they frequently find academic learning difficult, but their ability to adjust to the social and emotional demands of classroom procedures is often impaired.

Identification and training of children with visual perceptual disabilities during the preschool years or at the time of school entrance would help prevent many instances of school failure and maladjustment *caused* [emphasis added] by visual perceptual difficulties. Although some children may overcome these difficulties at a later age, there is as yet no method to predict whether a child will be able to do so without help. . . . The authors' research has shown that visual perceptual difficulties, regardless of etiology, can be ameliorated by specific training. Pinpointing the areas of a child's visual perceptual difficulties and measuring their severity is helpful and is often necessary in designing the most efficient training program to aid in overcoming the disabilities. (p. 6)

The writers of the preceding paragraphs (they are also the authors of the Developmental Test of Visual Perception) do not cite empirical support for their contentions. We would argue that the claims made are unwarranted. The majority of the research does not support the contention that children with visual-perceptual disabilities are likely to be rated as maladjusted. At most, it can demonstrate simply that children who are rated as maladjusted also perform poorly on perceptual-motor tests. Furthermore, the authors recommend assessment of perceptual-motor difficulties under the assumption that remediation of identified disabilities will lead to greater academic success, and yet reviews of the efficacy of perceptual-motor training demonstrate that it is grossly ineffective in improving academic performance (Mann, 1971b; Hammill & Wiederholt, 1973; Ysseldyke, 1973).

What the majority of the research *has* shown is that most perceptual-motor tests are unreliable. We do not know what they measure, because they do not measure anything consistently. Unlike the majority of intelligence and achievement tests, the tests used to assess perceptual-motor skills in children are technically inadequate. And for the most part they are neither theoretically nor psychometrically sound. For example, they are designed to assess perceptual-motor abilities under the assumption that such abilities cause academic success or academic failure (see Ysseldyke & Salvia, 1974). Or they are designed to assess hypothetical constructs like figure-ground perception and body image and differentiation but do not do so with consistency (see Ysseldyke, 1973; Ysseldyke & Salvia, 1974). Or they may be based on criterion keying, an approach that can lead to logical fallacies of undistributed middle terms (all canaries eat birdseed; Esmeralda eats birdseed; therefore, Esmeralda is a canary).

In short, the devices currently used to assess children's perceptual-motor skills are extremely inadequate. The real danger is that reliance on such tests in planning interventions for children may actually lead to assigning children to activities that do them absolutely no good. While we believe that few currently available perceptual-motor devices approach either theoretical or psychometrical adequacy, we review those that are most often used.

SPECIFIC TESTS OF PERCEPTUAL-MOTOR SKILLS

Bender Visual Motor Gestalt Test

The Bender Visual Motor Gestalt Test (BVMGT), consisting of nine geometric designs to be copied on paper, was originally developed by Loretta Bender in 1938. The designs in the test were first used by Wertheimer in 1923 to illustrate the perceptual principles of gestalt psychology. Bender used the designs in a test to differentiate brain-injured from non-brain-injured adults and to detect signs of emotional disturbance. The test has gained widespread popularity among clinical psychologists and has become one of the most frequently administered psychometric devices.

Administration of the BVMGT consists simply of presenting nine geometric designs, one at a time, to a subject who is asked to copy each of them on a plain sheet of paper. Although Bender provided criteria for scoring the test, a variety of other scoring systems have been developed, the most common of which is the system developed by Elizabeth Koppitz in 1963. The impetus for Koppitz's work arose from her experience in a child guidance clinic, where she was reportedly impressed with the frequency of perceptual problems among children with learning or emotional difficulties.

The Koppitz scoring system, restricted to use with children between 5 and 11 years of age, is the system most often used by psychologists in school settings. In 1963, Koppitz published a text describing the scoring system, the various uses of the BVMGT with children, normative data for the scoring system, and limited information about reliability and validity. In 1975, Koppitz published volume 2 of *The Bender Gestalt Test for Young Children,* a compilation and synthesis of research on the BVMGT between 1963 and 1973. This latter text is a commendable effort that eliminates the need to search the literature for research on the test.

Our discussion of the BVMGT is based entirely on use of the Koppitz scoring system with the test.

Scores

When scoring according to the Koppitz system, the examiner records the number of errors on each of the nine separate geometric forms. Four kinds of errors are recorded.

Distortion of Shape   Errors are scored as distortion of shape when a child's reproduction of the stimulus design is so misshapen that the general configuration is lost. If a child converts dots to circles, alters the relative size of components of the stimulus drawing, or in other ways distorts the design, errors are recorded.

Perseveration   Perseveration errors are recorded when a child fails to stop after completing the required drawing—for example, a child is asked to copy eleven dots in a row and then copies significantly more than eleven.

Integration   Integration errors consist of a failure to juxtapose correctly parts of a design, as illustrated in Figure 14.1. In drawing a, the components of the design fail to meet. In drawing b, they overlap.

Rotation   Rotation errors are recorded when a child rotates a design by more than 45 degrees or rotates the stimulus card, even though the drawing is correctly copied. Reversals are 180-degree rotations and are scored as rotation errors.

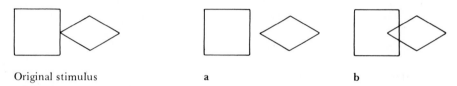

Original stimulus   a   b

FIGURE 14.1 Two integration errors in Koppitz's scoring of the Bender Visual Motor Gestalt Test

More than one error can be scored on each drawing. The total number of possible errors is twenty-five. The examiner adds the number of errors to obtain a total raw score for the test. The higher the total raw score, the poorer the performance.

The Koppitz manual (1963) contains a normative table reporting means and standard deviations of error scores for specific age levels in half-year intervals. This normative table, based on the 1963 standardization of the test, is used to transform error scores to developmental ages. The 1975 publication reporting research on the BVMGT from 1963 to 1973 includes two features. A new set of examples for scoring individual items has been included to eliminate the scoring difficulties that examiners reported to the author. It also includes a new set of normative tables based on a 1974 renorming of the test. This set of tables can be used to convert error scores to age equivalents and to percentile ranks.

Norms

Two sets of norms are now available for the Koppitz scoring system. The test was originally standardized on 1,104 children from forty-six classes in twelve public schools. The schools were reportedly selected from rural, urban, and suburban areas in unspecified proportions. The original normative sample included 637 boys and 467 girls. There are no data in the 1963 manual on the geographic areas the sample was drawn from or their demographic characteris-

tics. In volume 2 (1975), Koppitz reports that 98 percent of the original sample was white.

Koppitz renormed the test in 1974 in an effort to achieve a more representative sample of American schoolchildren. The 1974 normative sample included 975 children between the ages of 5 and 11. A geographic cross section was not attained: 15 percent of the children were from the West, 2 percent were from the South, and 83 percent were from the Northeast. Racial balance is more nearly representative; 86 percent of the sample was white, 8.5 percent black, 4.5 percent were either Mexican-American or Puerto Rican, and 1 percent was Oriental. There is no indication of the socioeconomic level of the sample; Koppitz states that research has demonstrated that socioeconomic status is not an important variable in children's performance on the BVMGT. Community size is adequately described; 7 percent were from rural communities, 31 percent were from small towns, 36 percent from suburbs, and 26 percent were from large metropolitan areas.

The sample sizes for half-year-interval age groups in both the 1963 and 1974 norms are unevenly distributed. For the 1963 norms, the norm group ranged in size from 27 children at ages 10-0 to 10-5 to 180 children at ages 6-6 to 6-11. For the 1974 norms, the norm group ranges in size from 47 children (at ages 5-0 to 5-5, 7-6 to 7-11, and 9-6 to 9-11) to 175 children at ages 6-0 to 6-5. Another major difficulty was present in the 1963 standardization: after age 8-6 the standard deviations for raw scores exceeded the means. For the 1974 norms, the standard deviations after age 8-6 are about equal to the means.

Reliability

Two kinds of reliability data are reported for the BVMGT. Koppitz (1975) summarizes twenty-three studies of the interscorer reliability for her scoring system. Interscorer reliabilities ranged from .79 to .99, with 81 percent exceeding .89. The revised set of scoring examples that Koppitz published in 1975 after test users reported scoring difficulties will probably facilitate interscorer agreement in scoring a child's performance.

In her 1975 addition to the 1963 manual, Koppitz reports research on factors she believes may affect performance on the scale. Her review of research on the effects of motivation, task familiarization, verbal labeling, tracing and copying, and specific perceptual-motor training led to the conclusion that the BVMGT does indeed serve mainly as a measure of children's level of maturation in integration of perceptual and motor functions. Only secondarily does it reflect their various learning experiences with specific perceptual-motor tasks.

The 1975 manual also summarizes the results of nine test-retest reliability studies with normal elementary schoolchildren. Reliability coefficients ranged from .50 to .90 (mean = 71.48; mode = .76). On the basis of her review, Koppitz made a claim for the essential reliability of the BVMGT scores for normal children. Yet five of the nine reliability studies she reports are on kindergarten children only; and only one of twenty-five reported coefficients exceeds the standard of .90 recommended for tests used to make important decisions. As Koppitz valuably cautions: "Certainly no diagnosis or major decision should ever be made on the basis of a single scoring point, nor for that matter on the basis of a youngster's total Developmental Bender Test score" (p. 29).

Validity

The construct of *visual-motor perception* is never adequately defined in either Koppitz manual. There is no evidence about the extent to which the test assesses visual-motor perception; the copying of nine designs is believed to be a measure of visual perception because some experts say it is one.

Koppitz (1975) cites several uses for the BVMGT and reports research on each of the suggested uses. She reports correlations of performance on the BVMGT and performance on measures of intelligence, academic achievement, and visual perception. She also cites evidence for use of the test in diagnosing minimal brain dysfunction and emotional disturbance. The paragraphs that follow describe some of her findings and recommendations.

In her 1963 manual, Koppitz reported results of tests of the relationship between scores earned on the BVMGT and scores earned on intelligence tests. She concluded that the BVMGT may be substituted "with some confidence" for a screening test of intelligence. She stated:

In clinical and school settings psychologists are constantly faced with the problem of how to use their limited time most economically. A full scale intelligence test usually requires so much time that only a brief period is left for other tests or an interview. The author has used the Bender test frequently with young children of normal intelligence who primarily seemed to show emotional problems and revealed no learning difficulties. The Bender test not only gives the examiner a rough measure of the youngster's intellectual ability, but also serves as a nonthreatening introduction to the interview. Children tend to enjoy copying the Bender designs, and in some cases the Bender figures evoke associations and spontaneous comments which can lead to further discussions. In most cases the Bender Test will suffice to rule out mental retardation or serious perceptual problems associated with neurological impairment and the examiner can use most of his/her time for projective tests and an interview rather than spending it on a lengthy intelligence test which offers little insight into the dynamics of the child's emotional problems. (p. 51)

In the 1975 addition to the 1963 manual, Koppitz continues to support the use of the BVMGT as a rough test of intelligence.

The statement "The Bender Gestalt Test can be used with some degree of confidence as a short nonverbal intelligence test for young children, particularly for screening purposes" (Koppitz, 1963, p. 50) has been supported by a number of recent studies. But as I previously suggested, the Bender Test should if possible be combined with a brief verbal test. (p. 47)

The BVMGT is *not* an intelligence test but a measure of a child's skill in copying geometric designs. It provides a very limited sample of behavior; in fact, of the thirteen kinds of behaviors described in Chapter 9 as being regularly sampled in intelligence tests, the Bender samples only one. In our opinion, the BVMGT should never be used as, or substituted for, a measure of intellectual functioning.

Koppitz (1975) reviews numerous investigations of the relationship between children's performance on the BVMGT and their academic achievement. Good students and poor students, she concludes, tend as groups to make significantly different total scores on the test. Furthermore, the scores normal children earn show a positive correlation with their academic achievement. Koppitz uses observed differences to conclude that scores earned on the BVMGT

appear to be most successful in predicting overall school functioning and rate of progress in total achievement. A child with a marked discrepancy between IQ and Bender Test scores usually has specific learning difficulties. LD pupils and slow learners mature at a significantly slower rate in visual-motor integration, as measured on the Bender Test, than do

well-functioning children. Scores from repeated administrations of the Bender Test are good indicators of progress a child is making, and they are helpful in planning an individualized educational program. (p. 70)

Children who perform well in school may well do better on the BVMGT than children who experience academic difficulty. But as Koppitz herself states, the test cannot be used to predict the academic performance of *individual* children (1975, p. 70). Moreover, Koppitz has not provided evidence to support the contention that the test facilitates individualization of instruction. To do so would require demonstration of an interaction between test performance and success under different forms (methods, techniques) of instruction—demonstration, in other words, of evidence for aptitude-treatment interactions.

Koppitz (1975) reviewed many studies of the use of the BVMGT to diagnose minimal brain dysfunction in schoolchildren. She concluded that the test is a valuable aid for this purpose but should never be used in isolation. Rather, she believes test results are valuable when combined with other medical and behavioral data.

Koppitz (1975) also claims that recent research gives additional validity to the ten indicators of emotional problems that she delineated in her 1963 text. Although she again provides notes of caution indicating that not all children with poor Bender protocols have emotional problems, she does state that "the presence of three or more emotional indicators on a Bender Test protocol tends to reflect emotional difficulties that warrant further investigation" (p. 92).

Koppitz (1975) provides evidence to support the contention that performance on the BVMGT is significantly related to performance on other visual-perceptual measures. She does not report the extent to which pupils who achieve low scores on the BVMGT perform well on these other tests or vice versa.

The BVMGT is, quite simply, a measure of skill development in copying geometric designs. It is *not* designed as a measure of intelligence, predictor of achievement, or measure of emotional disturbance or minimal brain dysfunction. Using it for any of these purposes is risky.

Summary

The BVMGT requires the child to copy nine geometric designs. The test was originally developed by Bender, who used designs developed earlier by Wertheimer. Koppitz has developed a scoring system for the test, and her system is designed for ages 5 to 11. The BVMGT is today one of the most widely used psychometric devices.

Reliability for the BVMGT is relatively low, at least too low for use in making placement decisions. Yet, performance on the test is used as a criterion in the differential identification of children as brain injured, perceptually handicapped, or emotionally disturbed. Validity for the BVMGT is currently not clearly established. The authors have not empirically demonstrated that the test measures visual-motor perception or that it discriminates *individual* cases of brain injury, perceptual handicap, or emotional disturbance. The test certainly provides a very limited sample of perceptual-motor behavior, and, for this reason if for no other, one would have to be extremely cautious in interpreting and using its results.

A statement by Koppitz is a fitting conclusion to our discussion of her test. "The very fact," she writes, "that the Bender Test is so appealing and is easy to administer presents a certain danger. Because it is so deceptively simple, it is probably one of the most overrated, most misunderstood, and most maligned tests currently in use" (1975, p. 2).

Developmental Test of Visual Perception

The Developmental Test of Visual Perception (DTVP) (Frostig, Maslow, Lefever, & Whittlesey, 1964; Frostig, Lefever & Whittlesey, 1966) is designed to measure "five operationally-defined perceptual skills" (Frostig et al., 1966, p. 5): eye-hand coordination, figure-ground perception, form constancy, position in space, and spatial relations. The areas were selected for assessment, according to the authors, because (1) they are critical for the acquisition of academic skills; (2) they affect the total organism to a greater extent than other functions such as color vision or tone discrimination; (3) they develop relatively early in life; (4) they are frequently disturbed in children diagnosed as neurologically handicapped; and (5) they are suitable for group testing.

The DTVP consists of a thirty-five-page consumable pupil response booklet. There are two manuals for the test, a standardization manual (Frostig et al., 1966) and an administration and scoring manual (Frostig et al., 1964). The test can be individually or group administered; it takes about 40 minutes. Behaviors sampled by each of the five subtests are described by the authors.

Eye-Hand Coordination This subtest assesses skill in drawing various kinds of continuous lines within boundaries and from point to point.

Figure-Ground Perception This subtest assesses skill in identifying figures as distinct from increasingly complex backgrounds and in discriminating intersecting and hidden geometric figures.

Form Constancy This subtest assesses skill in recognizing various geometric shapes regardless of size or orientation.

Position in Space This subtest assesses skill in discriminating reversals and rotations of figures in a series.

Spatial Relations This subtest assesses skill in copying patterns using dots as guide points. The child is shown a sample pattern and required to copy it by following the dots.

Scores

Scoring of the DTVP is objective. Ample scoring examples and in some cases scoring stencils are provided. Points earned depend on the quality of a child's responses to test items, and a raw score is earned for each of the subtests. Three kinds of derived scores are obtained for the DTVP: perceptual ages, scale scores, and perceptual quotients. Perceptual ages are age-equivalent scores and are derived separately for each subtest. The scale score is a ratio score obtained by dividing the perceptual age by the chronological age and multiplying by 10.[1] Thus, a child who is 6 years, 6 months old who has a perceptual age on the DTVP of 5 years, 3 months is given a scale score of 8.3. In the scoring procedures for the DTVP, the scale score is rounded to the nearest whole number. The perceptual quotient is a deviation score obtained by adding the subtest scale scores and using a table in the manual. The perceptual quotients are constructed so that a perceptual quotient of 100 is always at the fiftieth percentile; one of 90 is

1. The scale score obtained for the DTVP is *not* a scaled score. Scaled scores are standard scores and have a predetermined mean and standard deviation (see also the scaled scores for the Wechsler Intelligence Scale for Children—Revised). The scale scores for the DTVP are ratios. These ratios have different means and different standard deviations for children of different ages.

always at the twenty-fifth percentile; one of 110 is always at the seventy-fifth percentile; and so on.

Procedures recommended in the manual for the DTVP for transforming raw scores to scale scores and perceptual quotients are unnecessarily complex. Without really giving a rationale for doing so, the authors employ four different scoring procedures depending on the age of the child assessed. For children between the ages of 3 and 4, a table is used to convert raw scores to perceptual ages. These perceptual ages are then divided by chronological age to obtain scale scores. However, in all cases, regardless of the raw score, a constant score of 10 is assigned to a child's performance on the Spatial Relations subtest. For children between 4 and 8 years of age, different tables for different chronological ages are used to convert raw scores to scale scores and to obtain perceptual quotients.

A child between 8 and 10 years of age who receives the maximum perceptual age for any subtest is credited with a scale score of 10. It is, however, possible for a child who does *not* earn the maximum perceptual age to earn a higher scale score, and thus a higher perceptual quotient, than a child who earns the maximum score. Let us assume that two children, Amy and Christopher, who are both 8 years, 1 month old, take the DTVP. On subtest 1, Eye-Hand Coordination, Amy earns a raw score of 19, while Christopher earns a raw score of 20. Using Table 1 in the DTVP manual, Amy earns a perceptual age of 9-6, while Christopher earns a perceptual age of 10+. To obtain scale scores, the perceptual age is divided by the chronological age; the quotient is multiplied by 10; and the product is rounded to the nearest whole number. Amy earns a scale score of 12 ($114/97 \times 10 = 11.7$). Christopher, however, because he obtained the maximum perceptual age, is assigned a scale score of 10. A child who earns a maximum perceptual age on every subtest cannot earn a perceptual quotient greater than 100. Think for a moment what this must do to the reliability of the test. Raw scores and scale scores can actually be inversely related, and there is a ceiling effect.

Finally, the authors of the DTVP state that "any child of 10 years or more who does not receive the maximum Perceptual Age Equivalent for any subtest is presumed to have difficulty in the area measured" (1966, p. 31). *The transformed scores for the DTVP are not only confusing; they are questionably derived and therefore absolutely must not be used in making diagnostic decisions.*

The authors of the DTVP state that scale scores of less than 8 indicate perceptual-motor weaknesses in need of remediation. They further state that "it has been found very helpful to use a perceptual quotient of 90 as the cutoff point in the scores of kindergarten children, below which a child should receive special training" (1964, p. 479). Such interpretations simply cannot be made when the scores obtained on the DTVP do not have consistent meaning.

Norms

The 1963 edition of the DTVP was standardized on 2,116 children, between 107 and 240 children at each half-year level between the ages of 3 and 9. The authors (1964) do state, though, that the test was designed primarily for use with young children. The entire sample was drawn from nursery schools and public elementary schools in southern California. The sample was selected on the basis of the following considerations: (1) an attempt to get a stratified sample of children from different socioeconomic levels, (2) the willingness of schools to cooperate, and (3) the proximity to Frostig's research center. By Frostig's own admission the sample has some serious shortcomings. The sample was drawn from a geographically and socioeconomically restricted area. It was overwhelmingly

middle class (93 percent), despite the reported attempt to obtain a stratified sample of children from different socioeconomic backgrounds, and it had little minority representation (a few Chicanos, fewer Orientals, and no Blacks). Nowhere in the manual is there a report of the sex, grade level, or occupation and education of the parents of those in the normative group.

In Chapter 2, on the administration of tests, we discussed optimal group size for testing. The standardization of the DTVP was completed by testing *no fewer* than fifteen kindergarten and first-grade children at one time. Nursery schoolchildren were tested in groups of two to eight.

Reliability

Frostig et al. (1964) report the results of three test-retest reliability studies carried out in 1960 with a small sample of fifty children who were experiencing learning difficulties. The test-retest reliability for the perceptual quotient was reported as .98 using the full range of ages. In a second study of two groups of thirty-five first graders and two groups of thirty-seven second graders a reliability of .80 was obtained. Test-retest reliability for subtest scale scores, however, ranged from .42 (Figure-Ground) to .80 (Form Constancy).

A third study was conducted in 1962 to ascertain test-retest reliability when the device was administered by trained personnel who were not psychologists or psychometricians. The test was given to three kindergarten and three first-grade classes with a fourteen-day interval between test and retest. Obtained reliability coefficients for subtest scale scores ranged from .29 (Eye-Hand Coordination) to .74 (Form Constancy) for kindergarten children and from .39 (Eye-Hand Coordination and Figure-Ground) to .68 (Form Constancy) for first graders. The reliability coefficient for the total scale score was .69.

Split-half reliabilities obtained for the total scale score for the various age levels were .89 (5 to 6 years) to .68 (6 to 7 years) to .82 (7 to 8 years) to .78 (8 to 9 years). Reliabilities decreased with increasing age.

The low reliabilities for individual subtests certainly raise serious questions about their use in differential diagnosis, the very procedure Frostig recommends. You will recall that tests should have reliabilities in excess of .90 to be used in differential diagnosis and in making instructional decisions. Reliabilities for subtests of the DTVP come nowhere near this figure.

Validity

Frostig et al. (1964) report two validity studies in the manual for the DTVP. Correlations between total scale scores on the DTVP and teacher ratings of classroom adjustment, motor coordination, and intellectual functioning were .44, .50, and .50 respectively. The authors state that "the correlation found between teacher ratings of classroom adjustment and scores on the Frostig Test (1961 standardization) suggests the correctness of the hypothesis that disturbances in visual perception during the early school years are likely to be reflected in disturbances in classroom behavior" (p. 492).

In showing a moderate correlation between scores on the DTVP and teacher ratings the authors have demonstrated only a relationship, not necessarily a cause-effect relationship. The study does not provide validity evidence for the scale. It does not prove that the test measures what it is designed to measure. Such proof constitutes evidence of a test's validity. The DTVP was designed to assess visual-motor skills, not classroom adjustment or intellectual functioning.

The second validity study—based on the contention that the Goodenough-Harris Test is a measure of intellectual functioning, perceptual development, and personality—was designed to ascertain to what extent the DTVP and the Goodenough-Harris measured factors in common. Correlations between scores on the DTVP and the Goodenough-Harris were .46 for kindergarten, .32 for first-grade, and .36 for second-grade children.

As mentioned above, the test authors believe that for kindergarten children a perceptual quotient of 90 on the DTVP should be used as a cutoff point below which a child should receive visual-perceptual remediation. They also maintain that "a child's ability to learn to read is affected by his visual perceptual development" (1964, p. 493). To support these contentions, the authors conducted a study in a laboratory school classroom at UCLA. They report:

A group of 25 children between the ages of 4½ and 6½ were to be exposed to reading material but not forced to use it. All who used it were to be given training in word attack skills, phonics, observation of configuration, and use of contextual clues. The Frostig test was administered in July, 1962, and eight of the children were found to have visual perceptual quotients of 90 or below. It was predicted that these eight children would not attempt to learn to read because of their difficulties. This prediction proved to be highly accurate. In October, 1962, the children were rated for reading achievement. None of the children with a visual perceptual quotient below 90 had begun to read; of the two children with a perceptual quotient of 90, one had learned to read very well, while the other had not. Only one of the children with a PQ above 90 showed reading difficulties. (p. 495)

The authors simply cannot use the obtained data to support their contention. Such support would require a carefully controlled study accounting for the fact that the observed differences were not a function of intellectual level, some other variable, or teacher expectancy. The validity data reported in the manual for the DTVP do not support the authors' contention that the test measures five operationally defined perceptual skills.

Summary

The DTVP is a group-administered test designed to assess what the author has defined as five relatively independent components of visual perception. Data about the reliability of the scale obviously indicate that the five areas are not consistently assessed, and factor-analytic studies have pretty well dismissed the notion that the five areas are independently assessed.

Individual subtests of the DTVP lack the necessary reliability and validity to be used in diagnostic prescriptive teaching. We simply cannot put a great deal of faith in the accuracy (freedom from error) of the scores a child earns on the DTVP subtests.

In its composite form, as reflected by the perceptual quotient, the DTVP is a relatively reliable measure for theoretical and research purposes. The total test provides a global score indicative of overall visual-perceptual skill development. Performance on the DTVP must be interpreted with considerable caution.

Memory for Designs Test

The Memory for Designs Test (Graham & Kendall, 1960) assesses the ability of persons over 8 years old to copy geometric designs from memory. The express purpose of the test is to provide an instrument to use in research on organic impairment and to use as an adjunct test in a battery of tests administered to persons suspected of being brain injured. The Memory for Designs Test is administered by asking a person to copy fifteen geometric designs, each of which is individually exposed for a period of 5 seconds and then withdrawn. Administration time usually requires about 10 minutes.

Scores

Individual designs are scored in terms of the number and kinds of errors in the subject's drawing. The total score, the sum of scores for individual drawings, is used to judge the person's performance. Scores for each of the fifteen drawings are assigned on a four-point scale, described by the authors as follows.

0   A score of 0 is assigned to a satisfactory reproduction or to an omitted design.

1   A score of 1 is assigned when more than two easily identifiable errors are made but the general configuration of the design is retained.

2   A score of 2 is given when the general configuration of the design has been lost.

3   A score of 3 is given when the design is reversed or rotated.

According to the authors, the weight given to different types of errors was assigned on an empirical basis. Because rotation errors were observed to be more prevalent in brain-injured subjects, such errors are penalized more heavily. The assignment of a score of 0 for omitted designs is based on the observation that about as many brain-injured as non-brain-injured persons omit designs.

In addition to the raw score, a difference score is obtained for performance on the Memory for Designs Test. The difference score statistically controls for the effects of chronological age and vocabulary level. Older individuals and those of higher intellectual level are expected to make fewer errors on the Memory for Designs Test.

Raw scores are interpreted in such a way that for adults a score of 12 or greater is seen as indicative of "brain damage," a score of 5 to 11 is interpreted as "borderline" performance, and a raw score of 0 to 4 is interpreted as "normal" performance.

To obtain difference scores, values are assigned to both chronological age and vocabulary level (as assessed by the Vocabulary section of the Stanford-Binet or the Wechsler scales), and the score for Vocabulary level is subtracted from the score for chronological age. The difference score is used to ascertain the presence or absence of brain injury.

Norms

The norms for the Memory for Designs Test are based on eight groups of persons who participated in research on the test. The subjects were obtained from various clinics and hospitals in the St. Louis area. Some subjects took the test as part of a psychological examination or under the guise that it was a part of a routine medical examination. Others were informed that they were participating in research. To be included in the normative sample, subjects had to have had formal schooling to at least a third-grade level and a vocabulary equivalent to a Stanford-Binet IQ of at least 70; they had to complete at least eleven of the fifteen designs; and they had to demonstrate that they had no marked motor incoordination nor uncorrected defect in near vision. For child subjects, the educational restriction was dropped, but the child had to have an IQ of at least 70 on the Stanford-Binet or Wechsler-Bellevue scale.[2]

It is quite difficult to get a handle on the actual normative sample for the Memory for Designs Test. Those who participated in the

2. The Wechsler-Bellevue is an adult test.

standardization included persons with a variety of brain disorders including more than fifteen different classifications of both acute and chronic conditions, persons with idiopathic epilepsy and various forms of psychosis, and a "normal" group of persons. The test was normed on a total of 535 normal persons, 47 subjects who had idiopathic epilepsy, and 243 who suffered some form of brain injury. Subjects ranged in age from 8 to 70 years.

Reliability

Three kinds of reliability are reported in the Memory for Designs manual. Interscorer reliability, obtained by the two authors independently scoring 140 protocols, is reported as .99. Split-half reliabilities for the performance of the same 140 subjects is reported to be .92.

Test-retest reliabilities on readministrations within 24 hours to select groups of subjects are reported in Table 14.1. Reliability indexes are in the .80s with the exception of the group with low vocabulary scores. The average Memory for Designs score for all groups was 1.89 lower on the retest than on the original test. The authors attribute this improvement in performance to a practice effect.

Validity

Validity data consist primarily of criterion validity scores showing that brain-injured individuals earn lower scores on the test than do non-brain-injured persons. The test does differentiate between the groups, and the scores on the test do demonstrate little correlation with either age or intelligence. Just because the test differentiates between groups does not mean that it measures what it says it measures.

TABLE 14.1 Index of Reliability on the Memory for Designs Test, and Difference in Mean Raw Scores on Test and Immediate Retest for Various Samples

Sample	N	Reliability	Mean Diff.
Control children	(32)	.81	.41
Test score 8	22		−.41
Test score 8	10		1.60
Control adults	(45)	.85	2.22
Test score 8	17		1.82
Test score 8	28		2.46
Brain-disordered	(27)	.88	3.30
Special adult	(98)		
Mental deficiency diagnosis or low vocabulary	34	.72	2.32
Questionable diagnosis	41	.90	1.66
Over 60 years, mixed diagnosis	23	.86	1.44
Total	202	.89	1.89

SOURCE: Reprinted with permission of authors and publisher from Graham, F. K. & Kendall, B. S. Memory for designs test: revised general manual. *Perceptual and Motor Skills,* 1960, *11*, 147–188, Monograph Supplement 2-VII.

Summary

The Memory for Designs Test was originally constructed for the purpose of identifying brain-injured persons. Scores obtained on the device are reasonably reliable compared to those obtained on other perceptual-motor devices, and the test does discriminate between groups of brain-injured and non-brain-injured persons. The user of the test must, however, be cautious because it is very easy to make errors in logic. The test uses a criterion-group approach. A person who performs *like* a brain-injured person is not necessarily brain-injured. The Memory for Designs Test assesses skill in copying designs from memory; it does *not* assess brain injury. The diagnosis of an individual as brain-injured on the basis of relative difficulty in copying designs is quite clearly and simply an inference. As long as test results are viewed in this manner, there is little problem. To view the results as factual indicators of the extent of brain injury is simply inappropriate.

Developmental Test of Visual-Motor Integration

The Developmental Test of Visual-Motor Integration (Beery, 1982) is designed to assess visual perception and motor coordination in children ages 2 to 19. It is intended for use primarily with prekindergarten children and those enrolled in the early grades. The test may be administered individually or to groups. The test consists of twenty-four geometric designs of increasing difficulty to be copied with a pencil on paper. The test can be administered and scored by a classroom teacher and usually takes about 15 minutes. Scoring is relatively easy as the designs are scored pass-fail, and individual protocols can be scored in a few minutes.

Scores

The manual for the VMI includes one page of scoring information for each of the twenty-four designs. The child's reproduction of each design is scored pass-fail, and criteria for successful performance are clearly articulated. A raw score for the total test is obtained by adding the number of correct reproductions up to three consecutive failures. Normative tables provided in the manual allow the examiner to convert the total raw score to a developmental age equivalent.

Norms

The VMI was originally standardized on an unspecified sample of students in 1964. The test was renormed in 1982. A total of 3,090 persons ages 2-9 to 19-8 participated in the standardization. Data on the proportion of the sample from different ethnic groups, income levels, residence areas (urban, rural, suburban), and sex are reported in the manual. There are no data on the geographic areas from which the samples were drawn.

Reliability

The author summarizes the results of many different reliability studies conducted by others since initial publication of the VMI. Ten studies of interscorer reliability are listed, and it is reported that reliability coefficients ranged from .58 to .99 with a median of .93. Five studies of test-retest reliability are mentioned, and a range of .63–.92 is reported. Four studies of split-half reliability are reported, with coefficients ranging from .66 to .93 and a median of .79. The samples for these studies are not described.

Validity

The author summarizes studies by many different investigators but does not describe these studies specifically. He reports that scores on the VMI correlate .42 with a measure of handwriting, about .50 with readiness tests, .89 with chronological age, .41 to .82 with performance on the Bender Visual Motor Gestalt Test, and .37 to .59 with mental age. Studies of the relationship between performance on the VMI and later achievement show mixed results. Some investigators have found moderately strong relationships; others report little relationship.

Summary

The VMI is designed to assess the integration of visual and motor skills by asking the child to copy geometric designs. As is the case with other such tests, the behavior sampling is limited, although the twenty-four items on the VMI certainly provide a larger sample of behavior than is provided by the nine items on the Bender Visual Motor Gestalt Test or the fifteen items on the Memory for Designs Test. The VMI has relatively high reliability and validity in comparison to other measures of perceptual-motor skills.

Purdue Perceptual-Motor Survey

The Purdue Perceptual-Motor Survey (PPMS) (Roach & Kephart, 1966) was developed "to assess qualitatively the perceptual-motor abili- ties of children in the early grades" (p. 2). The survey, which consists of eleven subtests designed to measure some aspect of perceptual-motor development, includes twenty-two scorable items. The authors of the survey state that "the survey was not designed for diagnosis, per se, but to allow the clinician to observe perceptual-motor behavior in a series of behavioral performances" (p. 11).

Criteria used to include items in the PPMS are described by the authors in the test manual. Each item had to

(1) tap some perceptual-motor area; (2) be easy to administer and require a minimum of special equipment; (3) be representative of behavior familiar to all children; (4) have scoring criteria simple enough and clear enough that a minimum amount of training would be necessary for administration; and (5) not be over-structured so that it elicits a learned response. (p. 11)

Most items in the survey were chosen to be used with second, third, and fourth graders. The normative data are on children between 6 and 10 years of age. Items on the PPMS are grouped into five areas: Balance and Posture, Body Image and Differentiation, Perceptual-Motor Match, Ocular Control, and Form Perception. Each area samples certain behaviors.

Balance and Posture   Two activities, walking a balance beam and jumping, are used to assess balance and postural flexibility. The items are not precisely scored; rather, the examiner makes an effort to identify the extent to which children have "a general balance problem." The tasks assess the extent to which children use both sides of their bodies in a bilateral activity, shift from one side to the other in a smooth, well-coordinated fashion, and demonstrate rhythmic and coordinated control.

Body Image and Differentiation   Five tasks are used to assess body image and differentiation. These include (1) Identification of Body Parts,

(2) Imitation of Movement, (3) Obstacle Course, (4) Kraus-Weber, and (5) Angels in the Snow. In general, the tasks assess the extent to which children have knowledge of their body parts, can imitate movement, can avoid obstacles, have good physical strength, and can move their bodies as directed.

Perceptual-Motor Match   The match between perceptual information and motor response is assessed by two activities in which children are asked to draw several geometric forms on a chalkboard and to engage in rhythmic writing. Chalkboard activities include (1) drawing a circle, (2) drawing two circles simultaneously, one with each hand, (3) drawing a lateral line, and (4) drawing two straight vertical lines simultaneously. In the rhythmic writing task children reproduce on paper eight patterns drawn on the chalkboard by the examiner. They must reproduce the patterns accurately, with a free rhythmic flow, and must make certain "perceptual-motor adjustments" in doing so.

Ocular Control   The ability of children to establish and maintain contact with a visual target is assessed by means of four tasks requiring them to maintain eye contact with a penlight. The examiner evaluates the extent to which children are able to move their eyes (as opposed to the entire head) smoothly in following the movements of a flashlight. Ocular control for both eyes and for each eye individually is assessed. In addition, convergence of the eyes in focusing on objects is evaluated.

Form Perception   The extent to which children demonstrate adequate form perception and can reproduce geometric designs is assessed by asking them to copy seven simple geometric forms: circle, cross, square, triangle, horizontal diamond, vertical diamond, and divided rectangle.

Scores

Scoring for the PPMS is subjective and largely qualitative. While numbers are assigned as scores, they are used to designate the quality of a child's perceptual-motor behaviors. The record form for the PPMS includes a series of check lists for each task. The check lists enable the examiner to take note of the specific difficulties a child experiences on each of the tasks.

The authors of the PPMS stress the fact that the survey is not a test but a device for designating problem areas. They state that "the probable level of measurement is ordinal" (p. 13).[3]

Norms

The PPMS was standardized on fifty children at each of the first four grades. Only children known to be free of motor defect who had not been referred to an agency for evaluation of their academic achievement were included in the normative sample. By administering the Wide Range Achievement Test, the authors established the fact that all children studied were achieving at or above grade level. They report that

every child that participated in the study from the normative group was achieving at least within his assigned grade level. . . . Since the data were collected in midyear, this meant that children were achieving at various levels at or above grade placement. For example, some third graders were achieving at grade three, zero month, in spelling, while others were achieving at a much higher level. In all, the range of achievement was known to be varied. (p. 14)

The reader of the manual is led to believe that all children earned scores on the WRAT no lower than the lower limit of their grade level

3. *Ordinal* refers to rank order as discussed in Chapter 4.

(for example, no lower than 3.0). In the next sentence of the manual, however, the authors report that "it was assumed that intelligence, like achievement, was randomly distributed in the normative sample" (p. 14). The authors do not report data about the actual range of achievement and intelligence of children in the normative sample.

The authors do report the sex and socioeconomic status of children in the normative sample, but these data are reported only in the validity section of the manual. One needs to refer to validity tables to identify the numbers of children representing each specific socioeconomic group.

Reliability

The authors report a test-retest reliability of the PPMS of .95. They state that this coefficient was based on the performance of thirty children selected randomly from the normative sample and that the test-retest interval was one week.

Validity

To establish validity for the PPMS, the authors compared the performance of students in the normative sample to that of a clinic sample of ninety-seven nonachievers matched for grade level and age with the normative group. The items of the scale were validated by demonstrating that the nonclinic children performed at a significantly higher level than the clinic children on all but two items of the scale.

Additional validity studies were performed to illustrate that performance on items on the survey increases with higher grade level and with higher socioeconomic status. Performances on only two items increased significantly with grade level, while means for the six socioeconomic groups were in the order 5, 4, 1, 2, 3, 6. Thus, the authors' own research failed to support their contentions about grade and socio-economic status. The authors do not demonstrate that the survey measures what it says it measures.

Summary

The Purdue Perceptual-Motor Survey is designed to provide qualitative information regarding the extent to which children demonstrate adequately developed perceptual-motor skills. Because standardization was limited, the survey cannot be used for the purpose of making normative comparisons. Although good test-retest reliability has been demonstrated, validity of the scale is questionable. Individual teachers must judge whether they are willing to accept the authors' contention that the development of adequate perceptual-motor skills is a necessary prerequisite to the acquisition of academic skills. Such a claim is, to date, without support.

COPING WITH DILEMMAS IN CURRENT PRACTICE

The assessment of perceptual-motor skills is incredibly problematic. There are many obvious problems. First, it is very difficult to define perception, and therefore difficult to come up with measures of it. Yet school personnel assume, and in fact insist, that adequate perceptual-motor development is a necessary prerequisite to acquiring reading skills. Often, assessors are asked to find out whether students have perceptual-motor problems. Without adequate definition, with no technically adequate tests, and with no evidence that there are specific, effective interventions for students with perceptual-motor problems, the assessor is in a difficult bind.

We are of the opinion that if assessments cannot be done properly, they should not be done at all. This is one domain in which we believe that formal assessment using standardized tests is of little value. Rather, we encourage those who are concerned about development of perceptual-motor skills to engage in direct systematic observation in the natural environment in which these skills actually occur.

SUMMARY

Educational personnel typically assess perceptual-motor skills for one of three reasons: prevention, remediation, and differential diagnosis. The use of perceptual-motor tests to identify children who demonstrate perceptual-motor difficulties is based on the assumption that without special perceptual-motor training, these children will experience academic difficulties. They are used to try to ascertain whether perceptual-motor difficulties are causing academic difficulties and must therefore be remediated. Third, perceptual-motor tests are used diagnostically to identify brain injury and emotional difficulties.

This chapter reviewed the most commonly used perceptual-motor tests. Most lack the necessary reliability to be used in making important instructional decisions. Likewise, they lack demonstrated validity; we simply cannot say with much certainty that the tests measure what they purport to measure.

The practice of perceptual-motor assessment is linked directly to perceptual-motor training or remediation. There is a tremendous lack of empirical evidence to support the claim that specific perceptual-motor training facilitates the acquisition of academic skills or improves the chances of academic success. Perceptual-motor training will improve *perceptual-motor* functioning. When the purpose of perceptual-motor assessment is to identify specific important perceptual and motor behaviors that children have not yet mastered, some of the devices reviewed in this chapter may provide useful information; performance on individual items will indicate the extent to which specific skills (for example, walking along a straight line) have been mastered. There is no support for the use of perceptual-motor tests in planning programs designed to facilitate academic learning or to remediate academic difficulties.

STUDY QUESTIONS

1. Homer, age 6-3, takes two visual-perceptual tests, the Developmental Test of Visual Perception (DTVP) and the Developmental Test of Visual-Motor Integration (VMI). On the DTVP he earns a developmental age of 5-6, and on the VMI he earns a developmental age of 7-4. Give two different explanations for the discrepancy between the scores.

2. Original measures of perceptual-motor characteristics were shown to discriminate between brain-injured and non-brain-injured adults. Identify at least two major problems in the current use of these tests to diagnose brain injury in schoolage children.

3. Brairdale School decides to implement a preschool screening program to identify children with perceptual-motor problems. The decision is made to evaluate all four-year-olds in the community with the Memory for Designs Test, the Developmental Test of Visual Perception, and the Purdue Perceptual-Motor Survey. You are on the team charged with implementation of this screening project. Would you object to the proposed screening, and if so, why?

4. Identify at least three major problems in current perceptual-motor assessment practices.

5. A local school district in Boston, Massachusetts, uses the DTVP to screen kindergarten youngsters for potential perceptual-motor problems. To whom are these children being compared?

ADDITIONAL READING

Arter, J., & Jenkins, J. R. (1979). Differential diagnosis—prescriptive teaching: a critical appraisal. *Review of Educational Research, 49,* 517–556.

Buros, O. K. (Ed.). (1978). *Eighth mental measurements yearbook.* Highland Park, NJ: Gryphon Press. (Reviews of sensory-motor tests, pp. 1397–1420.)

Mann, L. (1971). Perceptual training revisited: The training of nothing at all. *Rehabilitation Literature, 32,* 322–335.

Yates, A. J. (1954). The validity of some psychological tests of brain damage. *Psychological Bulletin, 51,* 359–379.

Ysseldyke, J. E., & Algozzine, B. (1979). Perspectives on assessment of learning disabled students. *Learning Disability Quarterly, 2,* 3–15.

CHAPTER 15

ASSESSMENT OF PERSONALITY

Personality development is a nebulous concept, ill-defined, and subjectively measured. No one has seen a thing called personality. In fact, you could probably debate long and hard about the meaning of adequate personality development. Personality is never assessed. Rather, we observe and/or measure behaviors and infer a thing called personality. Inadequate or inappropriate personality functioning is inferred when a person does not behave according to social expectations. Behavior is evaluated in terms of the degree to which it is disturbing—either to the individual exhibiting the behavior or to people who come into contact with that individual.

Tests of personality and social-emotional behavior use items from several other domains of measurement (reading and writing, motor development, perceptual-motor integration, and so on). However, in the assessment of personality or social-emotional behavior, relative levels of skill development are *not* assessed. What is assessed is how skills are typically used and how that use is interpreted. In social-emotional assessment, we do not look at the level of oral vocabulary; we look at how a person uses words. For instance, a person might use words in an "aggressive" manner—swearing, threatening, and so on. We do not look at drawings to assess the completeness of a human figure or the integration of circles and squares; we interpret drawings as indicative of underlying feelings and emotions.

WHY DO WE ASSESS PERSONALITY?

In any social system there are individuals who exhibit behaviors that are disturbing to other people. Schools are social systems, and in schools the behavior of some students is bothersome to teachers or to other students. If such disturbing behaviors are exhibited often enough or strongly enough, the student can have significant difficulty profiting from instruction or can seriously disrupt the "orderly affairs" of the school. In its simplest sense, personality tests are used to decide what is wrong with the student so decisions can be made about him or her.

In the 1950s and 1960s, the use of personality tests was narrowly directed at making classification decisions about students. Students were classified as emotionally disturbed, behavior disordered, or socially maladjusted based on test-demonstrated evidence of pathology (Batsche & Peterson, 1983). Tests were used to identify "deep," "hidden," and "private" aspects of personality. Children were identified as normal or abnormal, as members of normal or clinical populations, based on their test performance. Elaborate systems of classifying students were developed, and elaborate classification manuals were designed to help assessors.

In recent years the use in schools of personality measures, especially projective measures, has diminished greatly. In part, this is due to changes in the theoretical beliefs of those who assess students—and to the ways in which assessors are educated. More importantly, it is due to a change in thinking about the purposes of assessment. When Public Law 94-142 was passed, the bottom line in assessment became establishment of instructional interventions for students. Personality measures provide very little information about what to teach or how to teach.

AN OVERVIEW OF PERSONALITY ASSESSMENT

Personality tests have been developed within the framework of "dynamic" psychology, including psychoanalysis and phenomenology. Various theorists hold that there are internal causes of behavior and that the identification of these causes will facilitate both an understanding of behavior and behavior change. In some cases, test authors design instruments to assess specific personality types, traits, or characteristics, such as aggression, withdrawal, dominance, paranoia, cyclothymia, and hysteria. Other test authors set out to identify needs, such as the need for affiliation and the need for nurturance, that allegedly motivate behavior.

Personality measures are usually constructed in one of two ways: a criterion-group approach or a factor-analytic approach.

The *criterion-group approach* is characterized by efforts to differentiate among certain groups of persons in the same way that tests of brain injury attempt to differentiate between brain-injured and non-brain-injured individuals. Thus, a test author might wish to develop a test to differentiate among hypochondriacs, hysterics, manic-depressives, and paranoid schizophrenics. Items are chosen that the author believes may distinguish personality types. They are then administered to individuals who have been previously diagnosed as hypochondriacs, and so on. Items that adequately discriminate among known groups are included in the scale. The scale is then applied to individuals who have not yet been classified, under the presumption that if the test can distinguish previously identified *groups* of individuals it can distinguish among unclassified *individuals*. An individual who responds like members of a criterion group is said to exhibit a "personality" characteristic of the criterion group.

The *factor-analytic approach* to personality test construction is a statistical procedure for developing tests. Items believed to assess personality are administered to many persons, and scores are then factor-analyzed to identify clusters of intercorrelated items. These clusters of items are examined for common features and then named. Items that do not fit into clusters are disregarded.

Methods of Measuring Personality

Walker (1973) provided a comprehensive guide to personality measures available for use with children. In it she identified five categories of measurement: attitude scales, measures of general personality and emotional development, measures of interests or preferences, measures of behavioral traits, and measures of self-concept. We have categorized the most commonly used personality tests according to Walker's system. These tests are listed in Table 15.1.

Walker also identified several different kinds of measurement techniques, originally described by Lindzey (1959), that are used to assess personality. A description of these techniques follows.

Projective Techniques

Projective personality assessment is accomplished by showing ambiguous stimuli such as pictures of inkblots, and then asking children to describe what they see. Projective techniques also include interpretations of drawings, word associations, sentence completion, choosing pictures that fit moods, and creative expression (puppetry, doll-play tasks, and so on). Theoretically, projective techniques allow children to assign their own thoughts, feelings, needs, and motives to ambiguous, essentially neutral stimuli. Children theoretically project aspects of their personalities in their responses.

Rating Scales

There are several types of rating scales; generally a parent, teacher, peer, or "significant other" in a child's environment must rate the extent to which that child demonstrates certain undesirable behaviors. Most rating scales are check lists designed to identify whether the child demonstrates certain behaviors

TABLE 15.1 Commonly Used Measures of Personality, Interests, and Traits

General Personality and Emotional Development

Bender Visual Motor Gestalt Test (Bender, 1938)
Blacky Pictures (Blum, 1967)
California Psychological Inventory (Gough, 1969)
California Test of Personality (Thorpe, Clark, & Tiegs, 1953)
Children's Apperception Test (Bellak & Bellak, 1965)
Draw-a-Person (Urban, 1963)
Early School Personality Questionnaire (Coan & Cattell, 1970)
Edwards Personal Preference Schedule (Edwards, 1959)
Edwards Personality Inventory (Edwards, 1966)
Eysenck Personality Inventory (Eysenck & Eysenck, 1969)
Family Relations Test (Bene & Anthony, 1957)
Holtzman Inkblot Technique (Holtzman, 1966)
House-Tree-Person (Buck & Jolles, 1966)
Human Figures Drawing Test (Koppitz, 1968)
Jr.-Sr. High School Personality Questionnaire (Cattell, Coan, & Belloff, 1969)
Minnesota Multiphasic Personality Inventory (Hathaway & McKinley, 1967)
Rorschach Inkblot Technique (Rorschach, 1966)
School Apperception Method (Solomon & Starr, 1968)
Sixteen Personality Factor Questionnaire (Cattell, Eber, & Tatsuoka, 1970)
Thematic Apperception Test (Murray, 1943)

Interests or Preferences

A Book About Me (Jay, 1955)
Kuder Personal Preference Record (Kuder, 1954)
School Interest Inventory (Cottle, 1966)
School Motivation Analysis Test (Sweney, Cattell, & Krug, 1970)

Personality or Behavior Traits

Burks' Behavior Rating Scale (Burks, 1969)
Devereux Adolescent Behavior Rating Scale (Spivack, Spotts, & Haimes, 1967)
Devereux Child Behavior Rating Scale (Spivack & Spotts, 1966)
Devereux Elementary School Behavior Rating Scale (Spivack & Swift, 1967)
Peterson-Quay Problem Behavior Checklist (Quay & Peterson, 1967)
Pupil Behavior Inventory (Vinter, Sarri, Vorwaller, & Schafer, 1966)
Walker Problem Behavior Identification Checklist (Walker, 1970)

Self-Concept

Piers-Harris Children's Self-Concept Scale (Piers & Harris, 1969)
Tennessee Self Concept Scale (Fitts, 1965)

believed to indicate some underlying pathology. Other rating scales require, in addition, that the rater estimate the frequency with which these behaviors are exhibited.

Self-report Measures

The self-report is a very common technique in personality assessment. It is used more frequently with adults than with children, however. Individuals being assessed are asked to reveal common behaviors in which they engage or to identify inner feelings. The devices used with children routinely ask them to identify feelings by checking happy or sad faces on a response form.

Situational Measures

According to Walker, "situational measures refer to a wide range of situations, ranging from highly structured to almost totally unstructured, that are designed to reveal to the tester something about an individual's personality" (1973, p. 31). Peer-acceptance scales and sociometric techniques are situational measures.

Observational Procedures

Most observational procedures used to assess personality or emotional characteristics are systematic. "Direct observation is the only procedure that allows one to observe the behavior as it occurs in the natural situation, thus reducing the chance of making incorrect assumptions" (Walker, 1973, p. 26).

Whatever technique is employed, it is only a vehicle for eliciting responses that are believed to represent a person's "true" inner state—feelings, drives, and so on. Responses are seldom interpreted at face value but are more often believed to be symbolic or representative. Consequently, the skill of the examiner is far more important than the device or vehicle for eliciting a person's responses.

Technical Characteristics

Scores

The particular kinds of scores obtained for personality measures vary with the kind of measure used. Scoring systems range from elaborate multifactor systems with profiles to nonquantifiable interpretive information. Entire books and manuals have been written to describe scoring and interpretation procedures (for example, Exner, 1966; Hutt & Briskin, 1960; Piotrowski, 1957). Some devices include very little information about scoring and interpretation.

Norms

Most personality assessment devices have inadequate norms. Walker states that "very few instruments have adequate standardization norms that are representative for a wide range of children of varying ethnic groups, intelligence levels, and socioeconomic backgrounds" (1973, p. 37).

Reliability

Many authors of personality measures do not report evidence of the reliability of their tests. When reliability data are reported, the reliabilities are generally too low to warrant use of the tests in making important educational decisions about individual children.

Validity

Definition of traits, characteristics, needs, and behaviors assessed by personality measures is not a common practice among test authors. Moreover, any effort to describe the specific behaviors sampled by the myriad of personality devices would be pointless, since the interpretation of the behaviors is of primary interest. Yet the absence of operational definitions creates a situation in which it is difficult to determine just what a test is designed to measure. Given this fact, it is impossible to assess how well the test measures what it purports to measure. According to Walker:

Underlying these inadequate socioemotional measures for young children is an inadequate and immature socioemotional developmental theory. No one theory to date satisfactorily describes the socioemotional aspects of man's development. More specifically, no theory is advanced enough to guide the development of a socioemotional measurement technology for young children. (1973, p. 40)

COPING WITH DILEMMAS IN CURRENT PRACTICE

School personnel are required to make decisions about eligibility of students for placement in classes for the "emotionally disturbed," "behavior disordered," and "socially maladjusted." Students often are said to be disturbed, disordered, or maladjusted based on their performance on personality measures. Despite this fact, there are no reliable and valid measures of specific personality traits or disorders and no reliable or valid measures of social or emotional maturity or development. We suggest that school personnel refrain from using personality measures, especially projective tests, in schools.

During the last fifteen to twenty years, there has been a shift in emphasis in psychology from "dynamic" psychology to a more objective study of behavior. There is an increased emphasis on the study of observable, operationally defined behaviors and deemphasis of unobservable thoughts, motives, drives, and traits that supposedly cause behavior. Most personality tests were originally designed to enable psychologists to get at those hidden aspects that supposedly cause persons to act in certain ways.

Along with a shift in theoretical orientation, there has developed an increased concern for accountability. Psychologists have been called on repeatedly to defend their activities and have had considerable difficulty defending the practice of personality assessment, both in terms of the psychometric adequacy of the devices and the educational relevance of the information provided by those devices. Psychologists today operate at nearly polar extremes. There are those who routinely administer personality tests as parts of larger assessment batteries, believing that by using the tests they will be able to pinpoint pathology. Others openly reject the use of personality tests, believing that the devices are psychometrically inadequate and educationally irrelevant. They rely instead on interviewing and on formal and informal observation to gather information about interpersonal functioning.

Along with a shift in orientation and an increased skepticism about the adequacy of personality devices and the relevance of information obtained, concern for the privacy of the individual has increased. Not long ago, congressional hearings debated the extent to which personality assessment constituted an invasion of privacy. Schools are now required by law to gain informed consent from parents before assessing children and may only maintain and disseminate *verified* information about a child. It has been increasingly difficult to convince parents that personality assessment *should* take place, and there is no way to verify the information gathered by personality tests.

Decisions about services to students who demonstrate behaviors that bother teachers are better made by collecting data through direct observation in classrooms. If school personnel document the frequency and duration of occurrence of behaviors that bother people, and if they also have data on extent of occurrence of those behaviors in students' agemates or grademates, then decisions about who should be served can be based on normative peer comparisons.

SUMMARY

In the assessment of personality, the *interpretation* of a person's behavior is of primary concern. Behaviors sampled by the tests and procedures discussed in this chapter may be the same as those discussed in earlier chapters; the interpretations of these behaviors are couched in different terms, however, since the purpose of assessment is no longer the mastery of skills and facts.

The assessment of personality takes different forms depending on the theoretical context in which the particular test or method was developed. Most often, the aim of personality assessment is to discover the underlying causes of behavior. The hypothetical causes vary with the theoretical orientation of the test authors. Five methods of assessing personality were discussed: projective techniques, rating scales, self-report measures, situational measures, and observational procedures. All of these techniques are best thought of as ways of eliciting responses, which the examiner then interprets.

STUDY QUESTIONS

1. Select any personality test and review the following:
   a. kinds of behaviors sampled
   b. adequacy of the norms
   c. evidence of reliability
   d. evidence of validity
2. For what reasons might personality tests be used in public school settings?
3. How might one validate a test of aggression?
4. Identify three major techniques for personality assessment.

ADDITIONAL READING

Anastasi, A. (1976). *Psychological testing.* New York: Macmillan. (Part 5: Personality tests, pp. 493–616.)

Buros, O. K. (Ed.). (1978). *Eighth mental measurements yearbook.* Highland Park, NJ: Gryphon Press. (Reviews of personality tests, pp. 684–1156.)

Buros, O. K. (Ed.). (1970). *Personality tests and reviews.* Highland Park, NJ: Gryphon Press.

Cronbach, L. J. (1970). *Essentials of psychological testing.* New York: Harper & Row. (Chapter 15: General problems in studying personality.)

Edelbrook, C. (1983). Problems and issues in using rating scales to assess child personality and psychopathology. *School Psychology Review, 12,* 293–299.

Fuller, G. B., & Goh, D. S. (1983). Current practices in the assessment of personality and behavior by school psychologists. *School Psychology Review, 12,* 240–243.

Knoff, H. M. (1983). Projective/personality assessment in the schools. *Special issue of the School Psychology Review, 12,* 375–451.

Walker, D. K. (1973). *Socioemotional measures for preschool and kindergarten children.* San Francisco: Jossey-Bass.

PART 4
_____

ASSESSMENT OF SKILLS:
DOMAINS SAMPLED AND
REPRESENTATIVE TESTS

Part 4 is an analysis of the most common domains in which assessment of skill attainment is conducted. In this part we consider the surface behaviors sampled by various tests, whereas in Part 3 we focused on the underlying hypothetical constructs, such as intelligence and oral language, that the behaviors are said to represent. Thus, for example, we are interested in a person's skill in reading in order to assess his or her ability to recognize words, rather than to examine that person's intellectual ability or expressive competence.

The chapters in Part 4 are organized in the same way as those in Part 3, but each chapter in this section focuses on a different domain of attainment. In order to refresh your memory of the chapter format and the approach we have taken in evaluating the tests covered in these chapters, we encourage you to review the introduction to Part 3 on page 143.

We do think, however, that our explanation of the two principles which guided our development of both Part 3 and Part 4 bears repeating here. First, we did not attempt to cover all available measures for each domain. Instead, we have selected representative and commonly used tests in each area. Buros's *Mental Measurements Yearbooks* provide an important resource for critical reviews of all currently available tests for readers who want information about devices that we have not evaluated in the text.

Second, our evaluation of the technical adequacy of each test is restricted to information contained in the test manual. We did not try to present a comprehensive review of the research literature for two reasons. First, as stated in the

Standards for Educational and Psychological Tests, test authors are responsible for providing all necessary technical information in their test manuals; they must have some basis for claiming that their tests are valid. Therefore, in evaluating the tests, we searched the manuals for the technical information that would support the test authors' contentions. Second, inclusion of the vast body of research on commonly used tests would have been beyond the scope and intent of this book. Again, we urge our readers to review the literature and to examine the research pertaining to tests in which they might be interested.

CHAPTER 16

ASSESSMENT OF ACADEMIC ACHIEVEMENT: SCREENING DEVICES

Achievement tests directly assess students' skill development in academic content areas. They are the most frequently used tests in educational settings. In contrast to aptitude tests, which are intended to assess a student's potential to profit from instruction in specific areas, achievement tests sample the products of past formal and informal educational experiences. They measure the extent to which a student has profited from schooling and/or life experiences compared to others of the same age or grade.

WHY DO WE ASSESS ACHIEVEMENT?

Various kinds of tests were described in Chapter 2. Figure 16.1 shows the different categories of achievement tests. Any achievement test is first of all either a screening or a diagnostic device. Screening devices are used to estimate a student's current level of functioning and the extent to which that individual has acquired the skills that most other students of the same age have acquired. Diagnostic achievement tests provide a much finer analysis designed to pinpoint strengths and weaknesses in skill development.

Achievement tests can be further categorized as either group-administered or individually administered devices. While group tests can be given to entire classes at one time, individual tests require a one-to-one student-examiner relationship. A group test, however, may be appropriately administered to one student at a time.

Achievement tests must reflect the content of the curriculum. If they do not, they provide misleading information. Most achievement tests are norm-referenced, although some more recent devices are criterion-referenced. The

Screening Devices

	Norm-referenced		Criterion-referenced	
	Single Skill	Multiple Skill	Single Skill	Multiple Skill
Group Administered	Gates-MacGinitie	California Achievement Test Iowa Tests of Basic Skills Metropolitan Achievement Tests (Survey Battery) SRA Achievement Series Stanford Achievement Tests	None	California Achievement Test Iowa Tests of Basic Skills Metropolitan Achievement Tests (Instructional Batteries) SRA Achievement Series Stanford Achievement Tests
Individually Administered	Test of Mathematical Abilities	Peabody Individual Achievement Test Wide Range Achievement Test Woodcock-Johnson Psychoeducational Battery Kaufman Assessment Battery for Children	None	None

FIGURE 16.1   Categories of achievement tests

former are designed by subject-matter experts, are thought to reflect national curricular trends, and are standardized on national samples. Criterion-referenced achievement tests, on the other hand, are designed to reflect the objectives of specific academic content areas and to assess the extent to which students have attained very specific skills.

Achievement tests assess skill development either in many areas or in a single subject-matter area. Some devices are multiple-skill batteries; others are specific to single content areas, such as reading, spelling, or math.

Figure 16.1 illustrates that the Stanford Achievement Test is, for example, both a norm and criterion-referenced (objective-referenced) group-administered screening test that samples skill development in many content areas. The Stanford Diagnostic Reading Test is both a norm-referenced, group-administered and a criterion-referenced, individually administered diagnostic test that

Diagnostic Devices

	Norm-referenced		Criterion-referenced	
	Single Skill	Multiple Skill	Single Skill	Multiple Skill
Group Administered	Stanford Diagnostic Reading Test Stanford Diagnostic Mathematics Test	None	Prescriptive Reading Inventory Diagnostic Mathematics Inventory Stanford Diagnostic Mathematics Test	None
Individually Administered	Gray Oral Reading Test Durrell Analysis of Reading Difficulty Diagnostic Reading Scales Gates-McKillop-Horowitz Reading Diagnostic Tests Gilmore Oral Reading Test Woodcock Reading Mastery Tests Test of Written Language Test of Written Spelling Test of Adolescent Language	None	KeyMath Diagnosis Criterion Reading Fountain Valley Stanford Diagnostic Reading Test	Brigance Diagnostic Inventories

FIGURE 16.1   (*cont.*)

samples skill-development strengths and weaknesses in the single skill of reading. The SDRT provides the classroom teacher with a detailed analysis of the student's strengths and weaknesses in reading, which is of assistance in program planning.

This chapter is addressed specifically to screening devices. Chapter 17 provides a detailed discussion of diagnostic achievement testing.

The very term *screening device* reflects the major purpose of these tests. Achievement tests are used most often to screen students in an effort to identify those who demonstrate relatively low-level, average, or high-level skills in comparison to their peers. Achievement tests provide a global index of academic skill development and may be used to identify individual students for whom educational intervention is necessary—either in the form of remediation (for those who demonstrate relatively low-level skill development) or in the form of academic enrichment (for those who exhibit exceptionally high-level skill development).

Although group-administered achievement tests are usually considered to be screening devices, they are occasionally used in classification or placement decisions. In principle, such a use is generally inappropriate, although it may be justifiable—or even desirable—under two circumstances. First, any group test may be administered individually. Considerably more qualitative information can be obtained during individual assessment. Second, some group tests (for example, the Stanford Achievement Test or the Metropolitan Achievement Tests) contain behavior samples that are more complete than those contained in some individually administered tests of achievement used for placement (such as the Wide Range Achievement Test). Use of an achievement test with a better behavior sample is desirable *if* the tester goes beyond the scores earned to examine performance on specific test items.

A third use of achievement testing, after screening and placement, is progress evaluation. Most school districts use routine testing programs at various grade levels to evaluate the extent to which pupils in their schools are progressing in comparison with some national standard. Scores on achievement tests provide communities, school boards, and parents with an index of the quality of schooling. Schools and, indeed, the teachers within those schools are often subject to question when pupils fail to demonstrate expected progress.

Finally, achievement tests are used to evaluate the relative effectiveness of alternative curricula. Brown School may choose to use the Scott, Foresman Reading Series in third grade, while Green School decides to use the Lippincott Reading Program. If school personnel can assume that children were at relatively comparable reading levels when they entered the third grade, then achievement tests may be administered at the end of the year to ascertain the relative effectiveness of the Scott, Foresman and Lippincott programs. There are, of course, many assumptions in such evaluations (for example, that the quality of individual teachers and the instructional environment are comparable in the two schools) and many research pitfalls that must be avoided if comparative evaluation is to have meaning.

The most obvious merit of achievement tests is the fact that they can provide teachers with data showing the extent to which their pupils have profited from instruction. By using group-administered multiple-skill batteries, teachers can obtain a considerable amount of information in a relatively short time. Norm-referenced devices allow teachers to evaluate pupil progress relative to a national sample of the same age or grade level.

OBTAINED SCORES

As in any form of norm-referenced testing, the raw scores obtained on achievement tests are of no direct value in interpretation. Scores must be transformed. All norm-referenced achievement tests provide the teacher with transformed scores of some kind. Most provide age- or grade-equivalent scores, percentile ranks within grades, and standard scores and/or stanines. In all cases, scores are reported by subtest, and the teacher is usually given a total achievement score. Procedures for and problems in the interpretation of the scores obtained from achievement tests used for screening purposes are discussed later in this chapter.

SPECIFIC TESTS OF ACADEMIC ACHIEVEMENT

The remainder of this chapter examines five popular group-administered multiple-skill batteries (the California Achievement Tests, the Iowa Tests of Basic Skills, the Metropolitan Achievement Tests, the SRA Achievement Series, and the Stanford Achievement Test Series), one group-administered reading test (the Gates-MacGinitie), two individually administered multiple-skill batteries (the Peabody Individual Achievement Test and the Wide Range Achievement Test), and one individually administered, criterion-referenced, multiple-skill battery (the Brigance Diagnostic Inventories).

In selecting an achievement test to be used in screening, teachers must consider several factors. First, they must evaluate the extent to which tests sample behaviors relevant to the content of the school's curriculum. Second, teachers must evaluate the adequacy of each test's norms, asking whether the normative group is composed of the kinds of individuals to whom they wish to compare their students. Third, for the tests reported in this chapter, teachers must examine the extent to which a total test and its subtests have the reliability necessary for use in screening. Finally, teachers must evaluate evidence for content validity, the most important kind of validity for achievement tests.

California Achievement Tests

The California Achievement Tests (CAT) (CTB/McGraw-Hill, 1977, 1978) are a series of norm-referenced and criterion-referenced tests used to assess skill development in six content areas in grades K through 12. The series includes measures of skill development in prereading, reading, spelling, language, mathematics, and the use of references. There are two forms of the test (CAT C and D), with ten overlapping levels (levels 10 to 19) in form C and seven in form D (levels 13 to 19). Two "locator tests" are available. These are used as pretests to determine the appropriate level of the test to be administered. Use of the lo-cator tests facilitates functional-level testing, that is, assessment of students at their functional level rather than their grade placement level.

Level 10 of this series is a prereading or readiness test, and is a revision of the earlier Comprehensive Test of Basic Skills. Although levels 11 to 19 are based on the tradition of the earlier California Achievement Test (Tiegs & Clark, 1970), the test is *not* a revision. It is entirely new, with a new structure and all new items.

Several materials accompany the CAT. There is an Examiner's Manual for each level at levels 10 to 13, and one Examiner's Manual for levels

14 to 19. A Test Coordinator's Handbook describes the development and content of the tests and provides a set of guidelines for supervision of testing programs and a set of guidelines for test interpretation. Norms Tables booklets are issued separately for each level; they provide directions both for hand scoring the tests and for obtaining derived scores. A Class Management Guide provides instructions for norm-referenced and criterion-referenced use and interpretation of the test results as well as selected instructional activities matched to the objectives assessed by the test. Two technical bulletins are available. Technical Bulletin 1 (CTB/McGraw-Hill, 1979) contains basic technical information on standardization, reliability, validity, and bias studies. Technical Bulletin 2 (CTB/McGraw-Hill, 1980) provides additional technical data, information about the validity of the locator tests, and guidelines for the use of the tests in Title I evaluation.

Administration time for the CAT varies from 1 hour, 53 minutes to 2 hours, 48 minutes depending on the level of the test being used. Recommended grade ranges and administration time for the levels of the CAT are summarized in Table 16.1. Subtests included in specific levels of the test are shown in Table 16.2. Specific behaviors sampled by the CAT are described below.

Prereading   There are six subtests in this content area:

1. *Listening for Information*   Assesses skill in gaining information from spoken words and expressions, focusing on school vocabulary, spatial and directional concepts, and an understanding of the relationships between facts and concepts.
2. *Letter Forms*   Measures skill in matching and discriminating between upper-case and lower-case letters.
3. *Letter Names*   An assessment of the student's skill in identifying letters named by the examiner.
4. *Letter Sounds*   An assessment of the student's skill in identifying letters that represent sounds at the beginning of an orally presented word.
5. *Visual Discrimination*   Measures skill in distinguishing similarities and differences in words and other visual stimuli.
6. *Sound Matching*   Assesses recognition of initial and final consonant sounds, initial and final consonant cluster and digraph sounds, and medial short vowel sounds by requiring students to discriminate among orally presented words.

Reading   This content area has four subtests:

1. *Phonic Analysis*   A measure of decoding that assesses skill in relating sounds to graphic illustrations of those sounds.
2. *Structural Analysis*   Assesses skill in identifying structural clues to identify the proper pronunciation and meaning of unfamiliar words. Skills assessed include recognition and understanding of compound words, syllables, contractions, base words, and affixes.
3. *Reading Vocabulary*   Assesses understanding of word meaning by requiring students to identify words that fit categories, that have the same meaning, or that have opposite meanings or to use context clues to identify the meaning of words that have multiple meanings.
4. *Reading Comprehension*   Assesses the student's skill in deriving meaning from written sentences and passages. Literal, inferential, and evaluative comprehension are assessed.

Spelling   The subtest in this content area assesses the student's skill in distinguishing correct from incorrect spellings of words used in sentences.

Language   This content area has two subtests:

1. *Language Mechanics*   Assesses capitalization and punctuation skills.
2. *Language Expression*   Assesses a student's

TABLE 16.1 Recommended Grade Range and Time Limits for Subtests of the California Achievement Tests

Complete Battery		
Grades K.0–K.9	Level 10	2 hours, 4 minutes
Grades 1.0– 1.9*	Level 11	1 hour, 53 minutes
Grades 1.6– 2.9	Level 12	2 hours, 33 minutes
Grades 2.6– 3.9	Level 13	2 hours, 35 minutes
Grades 3.6– 4.9	Level 14	2 hours, 48 minutes
Grades 4.6– 5.9	Level 15	2 hours, 48 minutes
Grades 5.6– 6.9	Level 16	2 hours, 48 minutes
Grades 6.6– 7.9	Level 17	2 hours, 48 minutes
Grades 7.6– 9.9	Level 18	2 hours, 48 minutes
Grades 9.6–12.9	Level 19	2 hours, 48 minutes

*Norms are available for end of kindergarten.
SOURCE: From Promotional Brochure for the California Achievement Tests, Forms C and D. Reprinted by permission of the publisher, CTB/McGraw-Hill, Del Monte Research Park, Monterey, CA 93940.

TABLE 16.2 Subtests at Each of the Ten Levels of the California Achievement Tests

Content Area	Test	Level									
		10	11	12	13	14	15	16	17	18	19
Prereading	Listening for Information	*									
	Letter Forms	*									
	Letter Names	*									
	Letter Sounds	*									
	Visual Discrimination	*									
	Sound Matching	*									
Reading	Phonic Analysis		*	*	*						
	Structural Analysis			*	*						
	Reading Vocabulary		*	*	*	*	*	*	*	*	*
	Reading Comprehension		*	*	*	*	*	*	*	*	*
Spelling	Spelling			*	*	*	*	*	*	*	*
Language	Language Mechanics			*	*	*	*	*	*	*	*
	Language Expression		*	*	*	*	*	*	*	*	*
Mathematics	Mathematics Computation		*	*	*	*	*	*	*	*	*
	Mathematics Concepts and Applications	*	*	*	*	*	*	*	*	*	*
Reference Skills	Reference Skills					*	*	*	*	*	*

SOURCE: From Test Coordinator's Handbook for the California Achievement Tests, Forms C and D. Copyright 1979 by McGraw-Hill, Inc. All rights reserved. Printed in the U.S.A. Reprinted by permission of the publisher, CTB/McGraw-Hill, Del Monte Research Park, Monterey, CA 93940.

skill in effective written expression, including word usage and understanding of sentence structure and paragraph organization.

Mathematics   Two subtests are included in this content area:

1. *Mathematics Computation*   Assesses skill development in the solution of addition, subtraction, multiplication, and division problems involving whole numbers, fractions, mixed numbers, decimals, and algebraic expressions.
2. *Mathematics Concepts and Applications* Measures the pupil's skill in understanding and applying a wide range of mathematical concepts.

Reference Skills   The subtest in the Reference Skills content area assesses skill development in ten areas: understanding of a title page, copyright page, table of contents, and index; skill in using a dictionary, maps, tables, diagrams, card catalogs, and the Reader's Guide; and skill in completing forms such as banking forms, job applications, and tax forms.

Scores

Five kinds of derived scores may be obtained for the CAT: percentile ranks, stanines, grade equivalents, normal curve equivalents (NCEs), and scale scores (ranging from 000 to 999). The tests may be hand-scored or submitted to the publisher for machine scoring. A variety of information systems are available, including individual test records, graphic frequency distributions, summary reports, and class test records. Schools may obtain criterion-referenced data on objectives mastered by individuals or by classes, norm-referenced data comparing pupil performance to national norms, or demographic norm reports comparing class or school performance to the performance of schools of comparable demographic makeup.

Norms

The CAT were standardized in such a way as to provide both fall and spring norms. The sample consisted of approximately 200,000 pupils from grades K through 12 drawn from public and Catholic schools using a stratified random sampling procedure.

The standardization sample was stratified on the basis of three variables: geographic region, school district size, and individual school demographic characteristics. The standardization took place in both fall 1976 and spring 1977. The same schools were used in both standardizations. Functional-level testing was employed throughout the standardization of the series of tests by using locator tests to identify the test levels appropriate for each student. In many of the districts in which standardization was carried out, the Diagnostic Mathematics Inventory, the Prescriptive Reading Inventory, and the Short Form Test of Academic Aptitude were administered. Each of these measures was given to 15 to 20 percent of the norm sample.

The public school norm sample for the CAT was selected by stratifying the national population of school districts. First, districts were stratified into seven geographic regions corresponding, with one exception, to the United States Office of Education (USOE) geographic regions. USOE regions 7, 8, and 9 (Rocky Mountain, Far West, and Noncontiguous) were combined into one region labeled "West." Within regions, school districts were selected on the basis of the size of their enrollment. The third stratification variable was a "demographic" index based on community characteristics believed to be related to district achievement. The characteristics are not specified in any of the manuals or materials that accompany the tests. After the selection of school districts, individual schools were selected. First specific high schools were chosen, then all students enrolled in a random sample of the elementary schools that served as feeder schools for the high schools were tested.

The Catholic school norm group was selected by stratifying on two variables. First, the national population of Catholic schools was divided into two geographic regions. Dioceses or archdioceses were selected on the basis of the size of their enrollments, and individual schools were selected randomly within each larger unit.

All schools participating in the norming of the CAT completed a demographic questionnaire; data are summarized in Technical Bulletin 1.

Reliability

Three kinds of reliability data for the CAT are reported in Technical Bulletin 1. Thirty pages of data report the internal consistency of raw scores and the standard errors of measurement for raw scores, scale scores, and grade equivalents for each subtest of the CAT at each of the ten levels. Internal-consistency coefficients for subtests range from .59 to .95, with most being between .75 and .90. Internal-consistency coefficients for total scores (for example, total reading, total mathematics) nearly always exceed .85.

Two sets of data are reported on the test-retest reliability of the CAT. The authors report test-retest reliability over a two- to three-week interval for grades K, 1, and 2 (levels 10 to 12). Subtest reliabilities ranged from .35 to .86, with most between .65 and .75. Test-retest reliabilities for most total scores exceeded .75. Data on test-retest reliability of forms C and D over six months are also reported. Reliabilities for individual subtests ranged from .23 to .81, with most being in the .60 to .70 range. Reliabilities for total scores ranged from .52 to .94, with most greater than .90.

Technical Bulletin 2 contains extensive reliability data on the criterion-referenced use of the CAT. Reliability estimates for category objectives are reported as mastery bands, and procedures for deriving estimated true scores are reported. The authors label the estimated true scores *derived objective mastery scores* and

report reliability coefficients for them. Reliabilities of these scores ranged from .36 to .87, with most greater than .70.

Validity

As for any achievement test, content validity of the CAT is of paramount importance. Although users must judge the relevance of this series of tests to their own classes, schools, or districts, the Technical Bulletins that accompany the CAT provide considerable support for content validity. The procedures for selection of objectives consisted of review of State Department of Education and large city curriculum guides in addition to the selection of objectives from two other tests (the Diagnostic Mathematics Inventory and the Prescriptive Reading Inventory) whose objectives were themselves selected after review of basal textbooks. Following item writing, items were reviewed for racial, ethnic, and sex bias by a panel of minority professionals. Item tryout and selection were completed during 1975 to insure adequate coverage of content within each category objective and adequate (statistical) discriminatory power.

Technical Bulletin 2 includes extensive additional data on this set of tests. Data on cross-validation of the locator tests and cross-validation of predicted scores based on the Short Form Test of Academic Aptitude, the Diagnostic Mathematics Inventory, and the Prescriptive Reading Inventory are reported and look favorable.

Summary

The California Achievement Tests are group-administered, norm- and criterion-referenced tests designed to assess skill development in grades K through 12. Skills are assessed in six content areas. The series is adequately standardized, and evidence for reliability and validity is very good.

Iowa Tests of Basic Skills and the Tests of Achievement and Proficiency

The Iowa Tests of Basic Skills (ITBS) (Hierony-mus, Lindquist, & Hoover) and the Tests of Achievement and Proficiency (TAP) (Scannell, 1978) are both norm- and criterion-referenced tests designed to assess broad general function-ing rather than specific facts and content. Both tests serve as continuous measures of growth in fundamental skills necessary to academic and later life success. The tests were designed to be used for multiple purposes, among which are (1) determination of students' developmental levels to assist in adapting instruction, (2) identifica-tion of specific qualitative strengths and weak-nesses, (3) identification of readiness both to begin instruction and to proceed to the next step in instruction, (4) provision of data to assist in grouping students, (5) evaluation of strengths or weaknesses in entire group performance, and (6) evaluation of individual pupil progress.

The ITBS measure skills in reading, lan-guage, listening, vocabulary, word analysis, work study, and mathematics. Two supplemen-tary subtests measure skills in science and social studies. The ITBS are used in grades K through 9. The TAP measure advanced skills of the high school curriculum, assessing achievement in reading comprehension, written expression, mathematics, use of information sources, sci-ence, and social studies. There are ten levels of the ITBS and four levels of the TAP. Levels 5 and 6 are the early primary battery used in kin-dergarten and first grade; levels 7 and 8 are the primary battery used in grades 1.7 to 3.5. Levels 9 to 14 make up the multilevel battery of the ITBS used in grades 3 through 9, while levels 15 to 18 comprise the TAP. Levels are essentially equivalent to chronological age and there are two forms at each level. There is a basic battery (nine of the fifteen subtests), which is a shorter version of the complete battery.

Subtests of the ITBS and the TAP are listed in Table 16.3. Specific behaviors sampled are as follows.

Listening   Listening subtests are included only at levels of the test used in kindergarten and first grade. Items of the test measure comprehension of orally presented information.

Word Analysis   This subtest measures skill in letter recognition, letter-sound correspondence, initial sounds, final sounds, and rhyming sounds. At higher levels (grades 2–3) more com-plex structural analysis is assessed.

Vocabulary   This subtest assesses knowledge of the meanings of words by requiring children to identify which of four response words is a synonym of a stimulus word, which they must read. At lower levels of the test, children dem-onstrate knowledge of word meanings by as-sociating words with pictures.

Reading   Lower levels of the ITBS assess word-analysis skills and require children to as-sociate pictures with sentences or stories they read. Upper levels of the test sample skill devel-opment in both literal and inferential reading comprehension by requiring students to read paragraphs and then answer specific questions about the content of the paragraphs.

Language   This subtest assesses skills in four subareas: spelling, capitalization, punctuation, and usage. The spelling subtest is a measure of recognition in which children identify one of four words as being the correct spelling of a word read by the teacher. Capitalization re-quires children to identify words that should be capitalized in sentences or paragraphs. The

TABLE 16.3 Content of the Basic Skills Assessment Program Achievement Tests

| | Iowa Tests of Basic Skills (Grades K–9) | | | Tests of Achievement and Proficiency (Grades 9–12) | |
| | Levels Available | | | | |
Subtest	Early Primary Battery	Primary Battery	Multilevel Battery	Subtest	Levels Available
Listening	5–6	7–8			
Vocabulary	5–6	7–8a	9–14a		
Word Analysis	5–6	7–8a			
Reading Skills					
Reading Comprehension	—	7–8	9–14	Reading Comprehension	15–18
Words	6	—	—		
Pictures	6	7–8a	—		
Sentences	6	7–8a	—	Written Expression	15–18
Word Attack	6	—	—		
Picture Stories	6	—	—		
Stories	—	7–8a	—	Using Sources of Information	15–18
Language Skills	5–6				
Spelling	—	7–8a	9–14a		
Capitalization	—	7–8	9–14		
Punctuation	—	7–8	9–14		
Usage	—	7–8	9–14		
Work Study Skills	—	7–8	9–14		
Visual Materials	—	7–8	9–14		
Reference Materials	—	7–8	9–14		
Mathematics Skills	5–6			Mathematics	15–18
Mathematics Concepts	—	7–8a	9–14a		
Mathematics Problems	—	7–8a	9–14a		
Mathematics Computation	—	7–8a	9–14a		
Science	—	—	9–14	Science	15–18
Social Studies	—	—	9–14	Social Studies	15–18

aSubtests in Basic Battery

SOURCE: From page 2 of the Preliminary Technical Summary for the Basic Skills Assessment Program. Copyright 1979. Reproduced by permission of the Publisher, The Riverside Publishing Company, 8420 Bryn Mawr Ave., Chicago, IL 60631.

punctuation subtest, on the other hand, requires children to identify those places in sentences that need specific punctuation marks. The usage subtest assesses knowledge of grammatical rules by requiring children to identify which of three alternative sentences employs correct usage.

Work Study This subtest assesses generalized skill development in three areas: map reading, reading graphs and tables, and knowledge and uses of references. The map-reading section requires children to answer specific questions by reading maps. The second section assesses similar skills by requiring children to answer specific questions by reading graphs and tables. The section on use of references requires children to demonstrate knowledge of how to alphabetize, read tables of contents, use a dictionary, classify information, and indicate reference sources for specific material.

Mathematics   Two kinds of math tests are included in the ITBS. The first assesses knowledge of mathematical concepts, while the second requires children to solve computational problems and written problems. At lower levels of the test, the directions are read to the children, at upper levels, children must read the directions themselves.

Specific behaviors measured by subtests of the TAP are as follows.

Reading Comprehension   This subtest assesses skill in comprehending both the kinds of written materials encountered in school and the kinds of materials (for example, labels and advertisements) encountered outside of school.

Mathematics   This subtest assesses both the understanding of mathematical principles and the use of basic mathematics in managing the quantitative aspects of everyday living.

Written Expression   Students' skill in expressing their ideas in writing; their skill in organizing ideas, letters, and themes; and their skill in word usage, word order, and punctuation are assessed in this subtest.

Using Sources of Information   This subtest assesses the extent to which students can act independently to locate and interpret information.

Social Studies   This subtest assesses students' knowledge of political science, geography, and other social sciences.

Science   Concepts and techniques of science are assessed in the content areas of biology, earth and space science, physics, and chemistry.

Three different testing plans may be used with the ITBS and the TAP. The first is graded testing, in which single levels of the tests are administered in each grade. Users may also employ functional-level testing, in which a single level is administered in a grade, but the level is selected on the basis of the average ability level of the students in the grade. Third, users may employ individualized testing by administering different levels to different students in the same classroom. This latter approach is especially useful in nongraded, continuous progress, and special education settings.

Total administration time for the complete battery of the ITBS or TAP ranges from 1 hour 55 minutes to 4 hours 4 minutes. When time is a consideration, the Basic Battery may be used to shorten administration time to about 2½ hours. Use of the Basic Battery, of course, decreases the number of subtests administered.

Scores

Various derived scores may be obtained for both the ITBS and the TAP. Raw scores may be converted to national grade percentiles and stanines, standard scores, grade equivalents, age equivalents (ITBS only), normal curve equivalents, and special percentile ranks and stanines (for large city school districts, private/parochial schools, and so on).

Tests may be submitted to the publisher's scoring service to obtain printouts, including lists of pupils' scores, profile narrative reports, student criterion-referenced skill analyses, and group item analyses. An extensive section in the teacher's guide for each test focuses on how the test results may be used to improve instruction in specific content areas.

Norms

The ITBS, the TAP, and the Cognitive Abilities Test (Thorndike & Hagen, 1978b) were standardized concurrently, a feature that controls for intellectual level in the development of the achievement measures. Initial selection of test items for the 1978 editions of the ITBS and the

TAP followed reviews of curricula, textbooks, and research to identify both skills to be tested and new ways of testing those skills. Initial items were edited after field testing on a sample of 300,000 students. Items were then edited for regional, sex, and racial balance. Following final review by a panel of experts representing five racial/ethnic groups, they were prepared in final form.

The tests were administered to 18,000 students per grade (a total of about 235,000 students). The standardization sample was stratified and selected in five steps. First, school districts throughout the nation were stratified according to the size of their enrollment. They were then sorted on the basis of geographic region. Third, the socioeconomic status of the communities represented was ascertained using 1970 census data, taking into account the median years of education in each district and the median income of families. Three districts were then selected at random from stratified samples and invited to participate in standardization. Once school districts agreed to participate, schools within the districts were selected. This final step involved review of both demographic data on the schools and indexes of achievement in those schools.

Several tables in the administrator's manual for the tests (Hieronymus, Lindquist, & Hoover, 1982) report correspondence of sample proportions with U.S. population proportions based on district enrollment, geographic region, and socioeconomic status. A weighting system was used to achieve closer correspondence between sample proportions and population proportions.

Reliability

Internal consistency reliabilities for the 1977, 1978, and 1979 standardizations of the ITBS are reported separately for fall and spring standardizations. Since major areas of the test (for example, language total and mathematics total) are most often used in norm-referenced interpretation, these are the reliabilities of greatest concern. Reliabilities range from .75 to .96 at the kindergarten and first-grade level and from .74 to .96 at the first- and second-grade level. Otherwise, reliabilities for major parts of the battery all exceed .87.

Equivalent-forms reliabilities are reported for the 1977–1978 standardization. These range from .82 to .96 for major skill areas assessed. The authors also report long-term stability of grade-equivalent scores over one-, two-, three- and four-year intervals. These data, however, are for earlier editions of the test.

Validity

The ITBS and TAP measure 264 skill objectives grouped in 96 categories. Content validity of the tests is addressed extensively, and the authors provide a taxonomy of skills assessed. They assert, correctly, that "the most valid achievement test for *your school* is the one that defines most adequately *your* objectives of instruction" (p. 7). They argue, again correctly, that the extent to which content validity is achieved is a matter of personal evaluation.

Predictive validity is reported for parts of the Early Primary Battery. In assessing the extent to which fall performance on the ITBS predicts spring reading achievement, the authors report validity coefficients ranging from .45 to .67. The same study with first graders produced validity coefficients ranging from .35 to .63.

All other validity data are useless, as they are based on earlier editions of the ITBS and TAP.

Summary

The Iowa Tests of Basic Skills and the Tests of Achievement and Proficiency are a comprehensive battery designed to assess broad functional skills in grades K through 12. Development and standardization of the scale appear adequate. Data on reliability are indicative of adequate reliability. Content validity of the ITBS and TAP are based on expert judgment, however, with the exception of limited data on the early Primary Battery, data relevant to criterion validity are for earlier forms of the test.

Metropolitan Achievement Tests

The 1978 Metropolitan Achievement Tests (MAT) are the fifth edition in a series that began in 1930. The most recent edition differs from traditional achievement tests in that it is a two-component system, including two "sets" of tests: Survey and Instructional. The authors moved to a two-component system in recognition of the multiple needs of test users. The MAT Survey Test (Prescott, Balow, Hogan, & Farr, 1978) is a group-administered test designed to provide a global evaluation of pupil skill development in five curricular areas: Reading Comprehension, Mathematics, Language, Social Studies, and Science. The MAT Survey Test provides both norm-referenced and criterion-referenced interpretation, is published in eight overlapping levels for grades K through 12, and requires from 1 hour 45 minutes to 3 hours 10 minutes to administer. Primary uses of the MAT Survey Test are screening, monitoring group performance, and evaluating the overall program.

The instructional component of the MAT is designed primarily for use by classroom teachers and curriculum specialists for the purpose of instructional planning and evaluation of specific parts of the curriculum. There are three Instructional Batteries, one each in Reading, Mathematics, and Language. The authors describe the instructional component as "an instructional planning tool that provides detailed prescriptive information on the educational performance of individual pupils in terms of specific instructional objectives" (Prescott, Balow, Hogan, & Farr, 1978, p. 2). Each Instructional Battery is a group-administered test that can be interpreted in either a norm-referenced or a criterion-referenced manner; each is published in six nonoverlapping levels from grades K.5 to 9.9; and each takes from 55 minutes to 2 hours 50 minutes to administer.

The MAT Reading Instructional Battery (Farr, Prescott, Balow, & Hogan, 1978) samples behaviors in eleven content areas: visual discrimination, letter recognition, auditory discrimination, sight vocabulary, recognition of consonant and vowel sounds, vocabulary in context, word part clues, rate of comprehension, skimming and scanning, and reading comprehension. The MAT Mathematics Instructional Battery (Hogan, Farr, Prescott, & Balow, 1978) samples behaviors in five content areas: numeration, geometry and measurement, problem solving, operations (whole numbers), and operations (law and properties). The MAT Language Instructional Battery (Balow, Hogan, Farr, & Prescott, 1978) samples behaviors in six content domains: listening comprehension, punctuation and capitalization, usage, grammar and syntax, spelling, and study skills. Teacher's manuals for both the Survey Test and each of the Instructional Batteries include detailed content outlines as well as lists of instructional objectives measured by each MAT item. The manuals provide extensive guidelines for interpretation of test results.

The MAT Survey Test is composed of items selected from the Instructional Batteries. The language and mathematics sections of the Survey Test were developed by selecting the most representative items from the respective Instructional Batteries. The reading section of the Survey Test is identical to the reading comprehension section of the Reading Instructional

Battery. The Survey Test and the three Instructional Batteries include practice tests for teachers to use in an effort to make sure that students understand the directions for the test.

Scores

Raw scores and six kinds of derived scores can be obtained for subtests and components of the MAT. Derived scores include scaled scores, percentile ranks (local and national), stanines (local and national), grade equivalents, normal curve equivalents, and instructional reading levels. Normal curve equivalents are z-scores used primarily for research purposes. Instructional reading levels are indexes of the highest level at which pupils can read without experiencing frustration. The manuals include, in addition to the derived scores, tables reporting the percentage of students in the national standardization sample who passed each item in the tests. Extensive discussion of both norm- and criterion-referenced interpretation is included in the manuals.

The MAT may be hand-scored or submitted to the publisher for machine scoring. The scoring service may be used to obtain class summary reports, norm-referenced analyses for classes and for individual pupils, and criterion-referenced analyses for classes and individuals.

Norms

Two phases were employed in developing norms for the MAT Survey Test and Instructional Batteries. Development began with item construction based on extensive analyses of contemporary curricula. Prior to actual field testing, items were reviewed by a minority panel in an effort to eliminate racial, ethnic, and sex bias.

In late 1975 and early 1976 a field-testing program was carried out in which 14,000 potential items were administered to 93,000 pupils from forty-four school systems. On the basis of an item analysis of pupil performance on the trial items, the Instructional Tests, comprising 7,500 items, were developed. The Survey Test was developed following development of the Instructional Tests.

During item tryout, the publishers of the MAT asked 3,000 teachers to complete a questionnaire that asked them, among other things, the extent to which their curricula included content relevant to each of the objectives listed for items of the MAT. Later, 9,000 additional teachers responded to the same questionnaire for the final versions of the tests. The authors claim, on the basis of this procedure, to have produced a set of "validated instructional objectives."

Both forms of the MAT Survey Test and Instructional Batteries were normed twice during the year, in April and October, on over 550,000 pupils. The tests were normed concurrently with the Otis-Lennon School Ability Test (Otis & Lennon, 1979) to control for the influence of intellectual level. Variables used in selecting the standardization sample included school system enrollment, public vs. nonpublic schools, geographic region, socioeconomic status, and ethnic background. Tables in the manuals contrast MAT sample proportions with national population proportions using data from the 1973 census and the National Center for Education Statistics (1976). Data from the National Center for Education Statistics are school system data. Thus, the authors were able to select their samples on data derived from school districts rather than other sampling units, a procedure they argue is advantageous.

Reliability

Manuals for each level of the MAT Survey Battery include internal-consistency estimates and standard errors of measurement for raw scores, scaled scores, and grade equivalents. Table 16.4

TABLE 16.4 Internal-Consistency Reliabilities of the Eight Levels of the MAT Survey Test

Level	Pre-primer	Primer	Primary I	Primary II
Grade	K.1	1.1	2.1	3.1
Reading	.94	.85	.96	.95
Mathematics	.77	.86	.86	.88
Language	.72	.81	.87	.91
Science	—	—	.74	.71
Social Studies	—	—	.72	.80
Basic Battery	.95	.93	.96	.97
Complete Battery	—	—	.96	.97

lists the internal-consistency reliabilities of the eight levels of the MAT Survey Battery.

Manuals at each level of the Reading, Mathematics, and Language Instructional Batteries also list internal-consistency estimates and standard errors of measurement for raw scores and scaled scores. Internal-consistency coefficients for the Reading Instructional Battery range from .88 to .95, those for the Mathematics Instructional Battery from .87 to .97, and those for the Language Instructional Battery from .85 to .91.

Validity

The authors of the MAT provide extensive data on the instructional objectives measured in this test in three special reports: Special Reports 1, 4, and 5. Special Report 6 includes a detailed cross-referencing of MAT Instructional Reading levels to thirty-one of the most widely used basal reading series. Additional evidence for validity is based on (1) demonstrated increasing difficulty of items with higher grade level and (2) a moderate to high relationship with previous editions of the MAT.

Special Report 21 presents equivalent scores between the 1978 MAT and the 1973 Stanford Achievement Test in grade-equivalent scores.

Summary

The Metropolitan Achievement Tests are of two types. A Survey Test is used to assess generalized skill development in academic content areas. Three Instructional Batteries are used in a criterion-referenced manner to assess skill development in reading, language, and mathematics. Data on standardization, reliability, and validity are indicative of technical adequacy.

SRA Achievement Series

The SRA Achievement Series (Naslund, Thorpe, & Lefever, 1978) is a group-administered, norm- and criterion-referenced battery of tests designed to assess skill development in basic curriculum areas in grades K through 12. The SRA series assesses skill development in reading, mathematics, language arts, social studies, sciences, and use of reference materials.

There are eight nonoverlapping levels of the series. Levels of the test, grade levels for which they are appropriate, and administration time in hours and minutes are summarized in Table

TABLE 16.4 (*cont.*)

Elemen-tary	Interme-diate		Advanced I			Advanced II		
4.1	5.1	6.1	7.1	8.1	9.1	10.1	11.1	12.1
.96	.95	.95	.93	.94	.94	.92	.93	.93
.90	.89	.90	.87	.89	.91	.90	.91	.91
.88	.90	.92	.89	.90	.91	.86	.88	.88
.90	.87	.88	.86	.88	.91	—	—	—
.90	.89	.91	.88	.90	.92	—	—	—
.97	.97	.97	.96	.97	.97	.95	.96	.96
.98	.98	.98	.97	.98	.98	—	—	—

16.5. Specific subtests and levels at which they appear are listed in Table 16.6.

Behaviors sampled by subtests of the SRA Achievement Series are as follows.

Reading: Visual Discrimination Requires pupils to match shapes and letters.

Reading: Auditory Discrimination Requires pupils to identify whether or not two words or letter sounds are alike.

Reading: Letters and Sounds Assesses skill in matching upper-case and lower-case letters, recognizing letters, identifying beginning or ending consonant sounds, identifying vowel sounds, and identifying letters or pictures that stand for ending consonant or vowel sounds.

Reading: Listening Comprehension Assesses skill in understanding directions, grasping details, summarizing, perceiving relationships, drawing conclusions, and understanding the vocabulary of material read to the student.

Reading: Vocabulary Assesses skill in identification of antonyms and synonyms, literal meanings of words, meanings of idioms, and meanings of figurative expressions.

Reading: Comprehension Assesses skill in understanding sentences, grasping details, summarizing, drawing conclusions, perceiving relationships, and understanding the author.

Mathematics: Concepts At the early levels (A to D), this subtest assesses skill in identifying numerals, sets, the meanings of operations and fractions, counting, place value, odd and even numbers, recognition of shapes, spatial relationships, patterns, relative size, time on a clock, money, and problem solving. At the later levels (E to H), this subtest measures conceptual understanding of whole numbers (including place values, factors, and multiples), fractions and

TABLE 16.5 Levels of the SRA Achievement Series, Grades for Which They Are Appropriate, and Administration Time

Level	Grades	Administration Time
A	K.2–1.1	2:00[a]
B	1.2–2.1	2:45
C	2.2–3.1	3:10
D	3.2–4.1	2:47
E	4.2–6.1	4:35
F	6.2–8.1	4:35
G	8.2–10.1	4:35
H	9.1–12.2	4:45

[a]Administration time is in hours and minutes.

TABLE 16.6 Subtests at the Eight Levels of the SRA Achievement Series

Subtests	Levels							
	A	B	C	D	E	F	G	H
Reading: Visual Discrimination	x	x						
Reading: Auditory Discrimination	x	x						
Reading: Letters and Sounds	x	x	x					
Reading: Listening Comprehension	x	x	x					
Reading: Vocabulary		x	x	x	x	x	x	x
Reading: Comprehension		x	x	x	x	x	x	x
Mathematics: Concepts	x	x	x	x	x	x	x	x
Mathematics: Computation		x	x	x	x	x	x	x
Mathematics: Problem Solving					x	x	x	x
Language Arts: Mechanics			x	x	x	x	x	
Language Arts: Usage			x	x	x	x	x	x
Language Arts: Spelling			x	x	x	x	x	x
Reference Materials					x	x	x	x
Social Studies					x	x	x	x
Science					x	x	x	x

decimals, geometry and measurement, and prealgebraic relationships.

Mathematics: Computation Assesses skill in addition, subtraction, multiplication, and division facts and algorithms; whole numbers, mixed numbers, and fractions; decimals; money; percents; and signed numbers.

Mathematics: Problem Solving Uses word problems to assess skill in solving whole-number problems; problems including fractions and decimals; multiple-step problems; rate, proportion, and percent problems; and problems involving the use of geometry, statistics, and probability.

Language Arts: Mechanics Assesses skill in capitalization, alphabetization, and punctuation.

Language Arts: Usage Assesses knowledge of correct usage of verbs, pronouns, adjectives, and adverbs; sentence structure; sentence transformation; and clarity.

Language Arts: Spelling Uses different formats at different levels to assess the development of spelling skills. At level C, the student must identify which of four alternative spellings of a word is correct. At level D, words are given in context so that context cues may be used to figure out the correct spelling. In levels D to H spelling words are given in phrases only.

Reference Materials Assesses skill in using such reference materials as dictionaries, books, encyclopedias, card catalogs, maps, tables, and graphs.

Social Studies Assesses major social studies concepts and skills rather than specific content.

Science Assesses science knowledge, comprehension of science concepts, and scientific inquiry.

The SRA Achievement Series is accompanied by a User's Guide that describes the series, includes overgeneralized teaching suggestions for improving skills in each subtest area, and lists skill areas matched to items assessing those skill areas. Three technical manuals are available for use with the SRA series. Manual 1 reports general data on development and standardization of Form 1; Manual 2 reports similar data on Form 2 and includes demographic data on the standardization sample; Manual 3 reports data on reliability and validity studies of the series.

Scores

A variety of transformed scores are reported for the SRA series. Grade equivalents, stanines, national and local percentiles, and national percentile bands are among the more traditional scores. In addition, users may obtain normal curve equivalents; special percentiles for Title I, large cities, and nonpublic schools; growth-scale values; and scores indicating percentage and ratio correct.

Normal curve equivalents are standard scores with a mean of 50 and a standard deviation of 20. Growth-scale values are standard scores ranging from 20 to 780, computed separately for each subtest. They enable the user to contrast change (growth or loss) over time in student performance with that of the norming sample. The percentage correct and ratio correct scores are simply indicative of the student's proportion of correct responses to total possible correct responses.

Norms

The SRA Achievement Series was standardized concurrently with the Educational Ability Series (EAS) (Thurstone, 1978). At level H the series was standardized concurrently with the EAS, the Iowa Tests of Educational Development (Lindquist & Feldt, 1980) and the Short Tests of Educational Ability (Chicago: Science Research Associates, n.d.).

A number of developmental steps preceded standardization of the series. Initial content planning was completed by searching textbooks, supplementary curricular materials, and other achievement tests. Item writing was carried out by teachers, educational writers, and curriculum specialists who were given content specifications, objectives, and format. Item editing for content and for sex and minority bias was completed before pretesting. Item pretesting consisted of administration of the preliminary test to 49,524 students from 979 classes in 226 schools for 154 cities in 38 states. Although the authors provide no data on procedures or criteria used to select the pretest sample, they do provide data on the grade level, minority representation, and community type and size from which the pretest sample was drawn. Following item analysis, the final test was selected.

Standardization was completed on 83,681 students in 383 schools in 81 districts in spring 1978 and on 129,900 students in 457 schools in 92 districts in fall 1978. A three-stage sampling design was used; stratification of school districts on the basis of geographic region was followed by random sampling of schools within selected districts and random sampling of classes within schools. Sample weighting procedures were used to improve the representativeness of the standardization sample. Specific demographic data on the standardization sample appear in Technical Manual 3.

Reliability

Three kinds of reliability data are reported in the technical reports that accompany the SRA Achievement Series. Internal consistency coefficients were reported for both fall and spring standardization samples. Reliability coefficients range from .54 to .94. Median reliabilities for subtests at each level of the test are listed in Table 16.7.

Alternate-form reliabilities are reported based on the performance of 1,300 students. They range from .87 to .94 for the composite score, with the majority of subtest reliabilities between .70 and .88. One-year test-retest reliabilities for the composite score ranged

TABLE 16.7 Median Internal Consistency Reliabilities for the SRA Achievement Series (Spring and Fall Standardization Samples)

Level	Grade	Spring	Fall
A	K	.85	.82
A	1	.79	.83
A	2	—	.71
B	1	.87	—
B	2	.87	.85
B	3	—	.78
C	2	.86	—
C	3	.85	.85
C	4	—	.84
D	3	.89	—
D	4	.89	.89
D	5	—	.90
E	4	.89	—
E	5	.91	.89
E	6	—	.91
F	5	.86	—
F	6	.89	.88
F	7	.90	.90
F	8	—	.91
G	7	.86	—
G	8	.88	.87
G	9	.88	.87
G	10	—	.88
H	9	.88	.87
H	10	.89	.89
H	11	.90	.90
H	12	.92	.91

from .88 to .94, while test-retest reliabilities for the majority of subtests were between .66 and .91.

Validity

Validity data consist of correlations between performance on the SRA Achievement Series and course grades, and between the test and other achievement tests. Correlations with course grades ranged from .43 to .79. The following correlations were reported with scores on other achievement tests: Iowa Tests of Basic Skills (.60 to .93), Metropolitan Achievement Tests (.71 to .82), California Test of Basic Skills (.45 to .90).

Summary

The SRA Achievement Series is a group-administered test assessing skill development in reading, mathematics, language arts, social studies, science, and the use of reference materials. Although its developers claim the test is both norm-referenced and criterion-referenced, the only criterion-referenced feature is a listing of items that sample objectives.

Data in technical reports that accompany this test indicate appropriate standardization. The test has adequate reliability and validity.

Stanford Achievement Test Series

The Stanford Achievement Test Series is made up of three separate measures. The Stanford Early School Achievement Test (SESAT) (Madden, Gardner, & Collins, 1983) is in its second edition and is intended for use in kindergarten and first grade. The Stanford Achievement Test (SAT) (Gardner, Rudman, Karlsen, & Merwin, 1982) is in its seventh edition and is used in first grade through ninth grade. The Test of Academic Skills (TASK) (Gardner, Callis, Merwin, & Rudman, 1983) is in its second edition and is used in eighth grade through community college. All forms and levels of the test are group administered. The test is both norm referenced and criterion referenced.

There are ten levels of the Stanford Achievement Test Series and five to eleven subtests at each level. Subtests at each level of the series as well as number of items per subtest and the administration time are listed in Table 16.8. No subtest occurs at all levels.

Assessors must decide whether to use a Basic Battery or a Complete Battery. The Basic Battery at all levels includes all subtests except the Science and Social Science subtests. Assessors may also decide to assess students in only reading, mathematics, or listening comprehension. The publishers have provided separate booklets including all reading tests, all mathematics tests, and the listening tests. Total administration time ranges from 2 hours, 15 minutes to 4 hours, 15 minutes for the Basic Battery. Administration time for the Complete Battery ranges from 2 hours, 10 minutes to 5 hours, 15 minutes. An optional Writing Test which assesses four types of writing—describing, narrating, explaining, and reasoning—is available with the Stanford Achievement Test.

Five reports called "Stanford Bulletins" are also available. These bulletins describe (1) reading assessment, (2) the Writing Test, (3) diagnosing comprehension, (4) testing in the secondary schools, and (5) assessment of effective listening. The bulletins include descriptions of ways in which the tests may be used to improve instruction.

Following is a description of subtests of the Stanford series and behaviors they sample.

Sounds and Letters This subtest is included only in SESAT 1 and 2. It is an assessment of the abilities to match beginning or ending sounds in words, to recognize letters, and to match sounds to letters.

Word Study Skills This is a measure of the student's skills in decoding words and identifying relationships between sounds and letters.

Word Reading This is a measure of the ability to recognize words by (1) matching spoken words to pictures, (2) identifying printed words that name particular illustrations, and (3) identifying printed words that describe or are associated with a picture.

Sentence Reading This subtest is at the SESAT 2 level only. It is an assessment of students' skill in identifying pictures that illustrate sentences they read.

Reading Comprehension Students are required to read passages that assess textual, functional, and recreational reading skills. Questions are asked at the end of each passage as an assessment of literal and inferential comprehension.

Vocabulary Students are asked to select words that best fit definitions read by the examiner. The measure thus provides an assessment of word knowledge independent of ability to read definitions.

Listening to Words and Stories This subtest is an assessment of ability to remember details, follow directions, identify cause and effect, identify main ideas, and understand aspects of language structure. Students must demonstrate knowledge of word meanings and skill in comprehending what is read to them.

Listening Comprehension This is an assessment of students' ability to process information that is read to them.

Spelling Students are given four words and must identify the one that is misspelled.

Language/English This subtest is organized into three parts: (1) language conventions including punctuation, capitalization, and so on, (2) language sensitivity including tasks such as recognition of complete sentences, and (3) reference skills.

Mathematics At the SESAT 1 and 2 levels there is a single mathematics measure. The test assesses skill in counting, knowledge of basic

TABLE 16.8 Subtests and Levels for the Stanford Achievement Test Series

Subtest	Test Levels and Recommended Grade Ranges							
	SESAT 1 K.0–K.9		SESAT 2 K.5–1.9		Primary 1 1.5–2.9		Primary 2 2.5–3.9	
	Items	Time*	Items	Time*	Items	Time*	Items	Time*
Sounds and Letters	44	30	45	25				
Word Study Skills					36	20	48	25
Word Reading	30	15	38	20	33	20	33	20
Reading Comprehension			30	20**	40	25	40	25
Vocabulary					35	20	38	20
Listening to Words and Stories	45	30	45	30				
Listening Comprehension					28	20	30	20
Spelling					30	20	30	20
Language/English†								
Concepts of Number					34	25	34	20
Mathematics Computation					45	45	38	30
Mathematics Applications							36	25
Mathematics	40	30	50	30				
Environment	38	25	40	20	27	20	27	20
Science								
Social Science								
TOTAL BASIC BATTERY								
TOTAL COMPLETE BATTERY	197	2 hrs. 10 min.	248	2 hrs. 25 min.	311	3 hrs. 35 min.	351	3 hrs. 45 min.

*Time for each subtest is in minutes.
**Sentence Reading at SESAT 2 level.
†An optional Writing Test is also available at levels Primary 3 through TASK 2.
SOURCE: Reproduced by permission from page 9 of the 1984 Test Catalog. Copyright © 1984 by The Psychological Corporation, Inc. All rights reserved.

number concepts, knowledge of geometric shapes and forms, understanding of comparative language of mathematics, and knowledge of basic addition and subtraction facts.

Concepts of Number A measure of understanding of basic number concepts.

Mathematics Computation Students are required to solve computation problems.

Mathematics Applications An assessment of students' ability to apply mathematics skills to the solution of problems.

Science A measure of students' understanding of the facts and concepts of the biological and physical sciences. The subtest also assesses inquiry skills in science.

Social Science A measure of skill development in geography, history, anthropology, sociology, political science, and economics.

Environment The Science and Social Science subtests are combined at the early levels of the test in an assessment of concepts about the social and natural environment.

In addition to the subtests listed, scores

TABLE 16.8 *(cont.)*

| Test Levels and Recommended Grade Ranges | | | | | | | | | | | |
| Primary 3 3.5–4.9 | | Intermediate 1 4.5–5.9 | | Intermediate 2 5.5–7.9 | | Advanced 7.0–9.9 | | TASK 1 8.0–12.9 | | TASK 2 9.0–13 | |
Items	Time*	Items	Time*	Items	Time*	Items	Time*	Items	Time*	Items	Time*
54	30	60	35	60	35						
60	30	60	30	60	30	60	30	50	30	50	30
38	20	36	20	36	20	40	20	37	20	37	20
40	30	40	30	40	30	40	30				
36	15	40	15	50	15	50	15	40	15	40	15
46	30	53	30	53	30	59	30	54	30	54	30
34	20	34	20	34	20	34	20				
42	35	44	40	44	40	44	40				
38	35	40	35	40	35	40	35				
								48	40	48	40
44	25	60	30	60	30	60	30	50	25	50	25
44	25	60	30	60	30	60	30	50	25	50	25
388	4 hrs. 5 min.	407	4 hrs. 15 min.	417	4 hrs. 15 min.	367	3 hrs. 40 min.	229	2 hrs. 15 min.	229	2 hrs. 15 min.
476	4 hrs. 55 min.	527	5 hrs. 15 min.	537	5 hrs. 15 min.	487	4 hrs. 40 min.	329	3 hrs. 5 min.	329	3 hrs. 5 min.

may be obtained for assessing skills in using information and writing. The using information score is obtained by separately scoring selected items from the Mathematics, Language, Science, and Social Science subtests. The score provides an index of a student's ability to use reference materials and to read graphs and charts. The writing score is obtained by administering the optional Writing Test.

There are two special editions of the Stanford Achievement Test: one for assessing blind or partially sighted students and one for assessing deaf students. The edition for use with blind or partially sighted students can be obtained in either braille or large print from the American Printing House for the Blind, and the edition for hearing impaired students may be obtained from Gallaudet College. Both special editions were standardized on the respective handicapped populations.

We noted earlier that the Stanford series is both norm referenced and criterion referenced. To facilitate criterion-referenced use of the tests, the authors have prepared a set of indexes of instructional objectives. These include a detailed listing of the behavior(s) sampled by each test item. Also indicated is the difficulty level of the item for students in particular grades at different times of the year.

Scores

A variety of transformed scores are obtained for the Stanford series: stanines, grade-equivalent scores, percentiles, age scores, and various standard scores. The tests may be scored by hand or submitted to the publisher for machine scoring. By submitting the protocols to the publisher's scoring service, it is possible to obtain record sheets for individual students, forms for reporting test results to parents, item analyses, class profiles, profiles comparing individual achievement with individual capability, analyses of each student's performance in attainment of specific objectives, local norms, and so forth.

Norms

Several factors were taken into account in the design of the national standardization for the Stanford series. Except for the SESAT 1 and 2 and the Primary 1 levels, the test was standardized in both the fall and the spring. So, separate norms are provided for schools whose students must be tested at specific times of the year. For the SESAT 1 and 2 and the Primary 1 levels, the test was standardized at midyear.

The Stanford series was standardized simultaneously with the Otis-Lennon School Ability Test. This enabled the authors to account for the ability levels of the students in the standardization population and also to develop a set of tables for comparison of ability level to achievement.

Sample selection was based on several variables including school district size, geographic region, socioeconomic status, and public/nonpublic status. About 450,000 students participated in the standardization of the series. Tables are included in the norms booklets showing the percentage of different types of students who participated and comparing those percentages to national census data. There is close correspondence between standardization sample makeup and the makeup of the 1970 census.

Reliability

Reliability data for the SESAT, SAT, and TASK consist of KR-20 internal consistency coefficients and alternate form reliability coefficients for each level of the test. Reliability coefficients range from .76 to .96. Most coefficients are between .85 and .90. Nearly all of the lower coefficients are for the listening comprehension subtest. Extensive tables listing reliability coefficients and standard errors of measurement are included in the norms booklets and technical manual for the test.

Validity

As for any achievement test, the validity of the Stanford series rests primarily on its content validity. Items for the series were originally written by the test authors and submitted to a group of subject-matter experts to establish the content accuracy. Several measurement experts edited the items for technical item-writing adequacy, and the items were then reviewed by general editors for writing clarity. The test items were submitted to a group of minority-group persons who screened the items in terms of the appropriateness of content for various cultural groups. Finally, a group of teachers were asked to evaluate the clarity of both the instructions and the items.

Empirical validity was established on the basis of two factors: an increasing difficulty of items with higher grade levels, and a moderate to high relationship with previous Stanford Achievement Tests and with the current and previous Metropolitan Achievement Tests. The authors state that three other factors were used to establish validity: (1) internal consistency, (2) correlation of obtained scores with scores expected on the basis of performance on the Otis-Lennon, and (3) "continuing reviews by representatives of minority and other groups." The first two are not necessarily validity data; the third we have previously discussed under content validity.

Summary

The Stanford Achievement Test Series is comprised of the SESAT, SAT, and TASK. The tests provide a comprehensive continuous assessment of skill development in critical content areas. Standardization, reliability, and validity are exceptionally good.

Gates-MacGinitie Reading Tests

The 1978 edition of the Gates-MacGinitie Reading Tests (MacGinitie, 1978) is the most recent in a series that began with publication of the Gates Silent Reading Test and the Gates Primary Reading Tests in 1926. The series consists of norm-referenced screening tests designed to assess skill development in reading from kindergarten through twelfth grade. There are seven levels of the tests, with at least two forms at each level; there are three forms for use in grades 4 through 9. Testing time is about 55 minutes for each level.

The specific subtests of the Gates-MacGinitie Reading Tests and the behaviors they sample follow.

Vocabulary   This subtest assesses reading vocabulary. The actual demand of the task varies with grade level. The Vocabulary subtest at grades 1, 2, and 3, for example, presents the child with four printed words and a picture illustrating one of the words. The child must circle the word that best corresponds to the picture. From grade level 4 and through grade level 12, the student is presented with a stimulus word and five additional words. The student must identify the response word that has the same meaning as the stimulus word.

Comprehension   This subtest assesses ability to read and understand whole sentences and para-

graphs. In grades 1 and 2 the child must read a selection and choose the picture that best describes its content. In grade 3, the child reads a paragraph and then selects, from among four response choices, the best answer to specific questions about the paragraph. In grades 4 through 12 the student is presented with paragraphs in which there are a number of blank spaces. The student must select from five response alternatives the word or phrase that best fits in the blank.

Scores

Raw scores for the Vocabulary and Comprehension subtests are simply the number of items correct. Raw scores are not obtained for the level of the test used in grades 1-0 to 1-9 (level R), because the subtests are very short. For level R, normative information is given descriptively (low, average, high). Raw scores for the other levels of the test may be transformed to normal curve equivalents, percentile ranks, stanines, grade equivalents, and extended scale scores.

Norms

The Gates-MacGinitie Reading Tests were standardized in October 1976, February 1977 (level A only), and May 1977. The sample was selected to correspond to 1970 census data: geo-

TABLE 16.9   Alternate-Form Reliabilities of the Gates-MacGinitie Reading Tests

Level	Vocabulary	Comprehension	Total
A	.88–.90	.89	.92–.94
B	.88–.90	.86	.92
C	.89–.90	.85–.86	.93
D	.86–.89	.83–.84	.91–.92
E	.86–.90	.82–.87	.89–.93
F	.86–.87	.77–.83	.89–.91

graphic region, district enrollment size, and the school district's socioeconomic status (median family income and median years of education completed by adults). A total of 65,000 students (approximately 5,000 per grade) were assessed. The author states that districts were selected to produce within each region a representative proportion of black and Hispanic students. There are no demographic data in the manuals that accompany this test describing the specific characteristics of the sample or contrasting sample proportions with population proportions.

Reliability

Three kinds of reliability data—internal-consistency, alternate-form, and test-retest—are reported in the technical manual for the Gates-MacGinitie Reading Tests. Internal-consistency coefficients based on the performance of pupils in the standardization sample are all greater than .85, with most being greater than .90.

Alternate-form reliabilities are reported for all levels. These are summarized for levels A to F in Table 16.9. Alternate-form reliability for the total test at level R was .91, but for subtests reliability ranged only from .57 to .78.

Test-retest reliability, based on correlations between pupils' performance in October and May, ranged from .77 to .89.

Validity

Two indexes of validity are reported for the Gates-MacGinitie Reading Tests. The author reports correlations ranging from .74 to .94 with the first edition of the test. He also reports correlations with corresponding subtests of the Metropolitan Achievement Test at grades 5-8 and 8-8. Correlations at grade 5-8 were .88 (Vocabulary), .83 (Comprehension), and .91 (Total); at grade 8-8 correlations were .86 (Vocabulary), .80 (Comprehension), and .88 (Total).

Summary

The second edition of the Gates-MacGinitie Reading Tests provides a comprehensive assessment of reading skills in two domains: vocabulary and comprehension. Data on the specific makeup of the standardization group are not provided. Evidence for reliability and validity of the tests is adequate.

Basic Achievement Skills Individual Screener

Basic Achievement Skills Individual Screener (BASIS) (Sonnenschein, 1983) is an individually administered achievement test that assesses pupil skills in reading, mathematics, spelling, and writing. The test takes less than one hour and provides both norm- and criterion-referenced interpretation. Normative scores are available for pupils in grades 1 to 12. Criterion-referenced use involves assessment of pupil performance on clusters of test items. Each cluster reflects the curriculum of a specific grade, and grade-referenced placement scores are obtained that describe achievement in basic skills. These scores are used to derive classroom and textbook placement suggestions.

BASIS may be administered by teachers, resource teachers, or school psychologists. They do not give all items of the test, but instead administer clusters of items appropriate to the student's developmental level. Clusters of items range from readiness to grade 8 in reading and mathematics, and from grade 1 to grade 8 in spelling. Testing starts with administration of relatively easy clusters and proceeds until the student fails to reach criterion on one of the more difficult graded clusters. Behaviors sampled by subtests of BASIS are as follows.

Reading A measure of comprehension of graded passages. The student supplies missing words in paragraphs. At early levels, students read words and sentences; at the readiness level, they must identify letters.

Mathematics This subtest measures computational skill by requiring the student to complete paper-and-pencil computation problems and word problems that are read to the student.

Spelling The student must write words dictated by the person giving the test.

Writing The student must write for 10 minutes on a subject that will elicit descriptive writing.

Scores

Both norm-referenced and criterion-referenced scores are obtained for BASIS. Both grade and age scores are expressed as standard scores, percentile ranks, stanines, grade equivalents, age equivalents, and normal curve equivalents. Cri-

terion-referenced scores, called grade-referenced placements, may also be obtained. These scores are used to recommend the grade or textbook level at which a student should be instructed in each subject.

Norms

In developing items for the test, the authors reviewed the most commonly used textbooks in each subject-matter area, selected those objectives that formed the essence of the curriculum, and developed items to measure those objectives. The authors focused on computation and problem solving in mathematics, on comprehension in reading, and on production from dictation in spelling. An item analysis was conducted in spring 1981 by administering the test to between 1,900 and 2,000 students. BASIS was standardized in the fall of 1972 on more than 3,200 students who were representative of students in grades 1–12. The sample was stratified on the basis of grade, sex, geographic region, socioeconomic status, and ethnic representation. The authors report characteristics of the sample in comparison to 1970 national census figures. Sample distribution was very close to population distribution on all characteristics.

Reliability

Several different indices of reliability were derived using the standardization group as a sample. Internal-consistency coefficients for the math, reading, and spelling subtest at each grade level all exceed .85. All but four coefficients exceed .90. Test-retest reliabilities were computed for a subsample (about 20 percent) of the standardization group. All test-retest reliabilities exceed .80.

Validity

Content validity was established by initial selection of items and later demonstration that items were matched appropriately to grade level; that is, item difficulty increased with grade level. Validity was also investigated by correlating performance on the BASIS with performance on unspecified achievement tests. Correlations ranged from .30 to .72. All correlations except one were greater than .43. Correlations between BASIS scores and report card grades consistently exceeded .40.

The authors of BASIS also conducted a number of studies on the validity of the test for use with special populations of children. First, the authors established correlations between performance on the BASIS reading subtest and scores on two reading achievement tests (Metropolitan Achievement Test and Degrees of Reading Power) using 49 mainstreamed students. Correlations were .61 and .64. Instructional reading levels (from MAT) were in consistent agreement with the Grade-Referenced Placements on BASIS. For 35 third-grade learning disabled students correlations between BASIS subtests and comparable content subtests of the MAT and WRAT ranged from .40

to .74. For 29 severely learning disabled seventh and eighth graders, BASIS reading correlated .60 with Woodcock Reading Mastery Test scores. BASIS correlated .44 to .57 with Metropolitan Achievement Test scores for 34 gifted fourth- and fifth-grade students. BASIS subtests correlated with WRAT subtests .44 (Math), .19 (Reading), and .90 (Spelling) for 26 educable mentally retarded junior high school students. Correlations between BASIS, WRAT, and California Achievement Test scores for 25 emotionally handicapped sixth, seventh, and eighth graders ranged from .51 to .81. For 22 hearing impaired students in grades 4, 5, and 6, correlations between BASIS scores and comparable content CAT scores ranged from .71 to .83.

Summary

BASIS is an individually administered achievement test that samples behaviors in reading, mathematics, spelling, and writing. The test is both norm referenced and criterion referenced. Technical adequacy is exemplary.

Peabody Individual Achievement Test

The Peabody Individual Achievement Test (PIAT) (Dunn & Markwardt, 1970) is a norm-referenced, individually administered test designed to provide a wide-range screening measure of academic achievement in five content areas. The test can be used with students in kindergarten through twelfth grade. PIAT test materials are contained in two easel kits—one for each volume of the test. Easel-kit volumes present stimulus materials to the student at eye level; the examiner's instructions are placed on the reverse side (see Figure 16.2). The student can see one side of the response plate, while the examiner can see both sides.

Behaviors sampled by the five subtests of the PIAT follow.

Mathematics This subtest contains eighty-four multiple-choice items ranging from items that assess such early skills as matching, discriminating, and recognizing numerals to items that assess advanced concepts in geometry and trigonometry.

Reading Recognition This subtest also contains eighty-four items ranging in difficulty from preschool level through high school level. Items assess skill development in matching letters, naming capital and lower-case letters, and recognizing words in isolation.

Reading Comprehension This subtest contains sixty-six multiple-choice items assessing skill

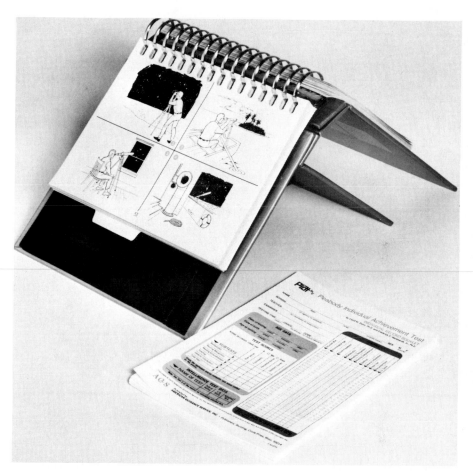

FIGURE 16.2 Easel kit for the Peabody Individual Achievement Test
SOURCE: Test by L. M. Dunn and F. C. Markwardt. Photo courtesy American Guidance Service, Inc.

development in understanding what is read. After reading a sentence the student must indicate comprehension by choosing the correct picture out of a group of four.

Spelling This subtest consists of eighty-four items sampling behaviors from kindergarten level through high school level. Initial items assess the student's ability to distinguish a printed letter of the alphabet from pictured objects and to associate letter symbols with speech sounds.

Items 15–84 assess the student's ability to identify, from a response bank of four words, the correct spelling of a word read aloud by the examiner.

General Information This subtest consists of eighty-four orally presented questions that the student must answer verbally. Items assess the extent to which the student has learned facts in social studies, science, sports, and the fine arts.

TABLE 16.10   Test-Retest Reliability Coefficients for PIAT Raw Scores by Selected Grade Levels

Grade	N	Mathe-matics	Reading Recognition	Reading Compre-hension[a]	Spelling	General Information	Total Test	Median
K	75	.52	.81	—	.42	.74	.82	.74
1	60	.83	.89	.78	.55	.70	.89	.80
3	54	.68	.94	.73	.78	.77	.91	.77
5	51	.73	.89	.64	.53	.88	.89	.80
8	68	.76	.87	.61	.75	.83	.89	.80
12	60	.84	.86	.63	.75	.73	.92	.79
Median		.74	.89	.64	.65	.76	.89	.78

[a]Kindergarten-level subjects did not take Reading Comprehension subtest.
SOURCE: From *Manual for the Peabody Individual Achievement Test* (p. 44) by L. M. Dunn & F. C. Markwardt, 1970, Circle Pines, Minn.: American Guidance Service. Reprinted by permission of American Guidance Service, Inc.

Scores

Four kinds of scores are obtained for each subtest of the PIAT and for the test as a whole: age equivalents, grade equivalents, percentile ranks, and standard scores. The standard scores are based on a distribution with a mean of 100 and a standard deviation of 15.

Norms

The population from which the standardization sample was drawn consisted of students enrolled in the "mainstream of education," attending regular classes in public day schools. The standardization sample was selected on the basis of geographic region and community size. Twenty-nine school districts participated in the standardization. A total of 2,899 children, at least 200 at each of thirteen grade levels, made up the normative sample. Approximately half the subjects were boys; 11.3 percent of the sample were black; and the percentages of the subjects' parents in various occupations were comparable to the percentages in the general U.S. population, as reported in the 1967 census.

Reliability

Reliability evidence for the PIAT consists of test-retest reliability on fifty to seventy-five subjects at selected grade levels (specifically, kindergarten and grades 1, 3, 5, 8, and 12). Table 16.10 contains test-retest reliability coefficients for raw scores by selected grade levels. Median reliabilities for the subtests range from .64 for Reading Comprehension to .89 for Reading Recognition. The authors include no data regarding internal consistency in the test manual, because they believe attempts to evaluate internal consistency would have resulted in spuriously high coefficients.

Validity

Two kinds of validity information, content validity and concurrent validity, are reported in the manual. Content validity is largely a matter of expert opinion and is based on "extensive reviews of curriculum materials used at each grade level" (p. 50).

Concurrent validity was said to be established by correlating scores on the PIAT, an achievement test, with scores on the Peabody Picture Vocabulary Test, an intelligence test. Obviously, the data cannot be considered a full and completely relevant estimate of the test's validity.

The authors of the PIAT essentially argue that because the correlations between the PIAT and the PPVT are similar to those between the PPVT and other achievement tests, the PIAT measures achievement. The logic of this argument contains an illicit step (the PPVT is a correlate of achievement; the PPVT is a correlate of the PIAT; therefore, the PIAT is a correlate of achievement). Although the conclusion *could* be correct, it cannot logically be derived from the premises. One other validity investigation (Sitlington, 1970) is reported in the manual. Sitlington compared scores earned by forty-five educable mentally retarded children on the PIAT and the 1965 edition of the Wide Range Achievement Test (WRAT) (Jastak & Jastak, 1965). Correlations were .58 between PIAT

Mathematics and WRAT Arithmetic, .95 between PIAT Reading Recognition and WRAT Reading, and .85 between PIAT Spelling and WRAT Spelling.

Summary

The Peabody Individual Achievement Test is designed to provide screening information on development of skills in five academic areas. Its standardization seems superior to that of most other individually administered achievement tests. While the reliabilities of the PIAT subtests are too low for use in making important educational decisions, the reliabilities of some subtests are adequate for screening purposes. Validity of the PIAT rests on its content validity. Teachers need to assess its appropriateness for the curricula they use.

Wide Range Achievement Test

The Wide Range Achievement Test (WRAT) (Jastak & Jastak, 1978) is an individually administered, norm-referenced, paper-and-pencil test that assesses performance in reading, arithmetic, and spelling. The 1978 edition is the fifth in a battery that was originally developed in 1936 and revised in 1946, 1965, and 1976. There are two levels of this test: level 1 for students younger than 12, and level 2 for those over 12. Three subtests at each level assess behavior as follows.

Reading Assesses skill in letter recognition, letter naming, and pronunciation of words in isolation.

Spelling Assesses skills in copying marks on paper, writing one's name, and writing single words from dictation.

Arithmetic Assesses skills in counting, reading numerals, solving orally presented prob-

lems, and performing written computation of arithmetic problems.

The authors of the WRAT list eleven specific uses for the test, ranging from "the accurate diagnosis of reading, spelling, and arithmetic disabilities in persons of all ages," to "the comparison between school achievement and other abilities in all individuals, especially those who are disturbed or maladjusted" (p. 1).

Included in the WRAT manual are extensive chapters on theoretical considerations, test criteria for learning abilities, case studies of learning abilities, and "new" and proper approaches to testing. Each of these is very dated, including only material prior to 1965.

Scores

Three types of scores are obtained for each of the subtests of the WRAT: grade ratings, percentile ranks, and standard scores by age, the latter having a mean of 100 and a standard deviation of 15. The authors appropriately caution users against adding or subtracting grade ratings as an index of gain or loss from one administration to another. Later in their manual, however, the authors use this procedure in an effort to establish validity.

Norms

The authors of the WRAT state explicitly that "No attempt was made to obtain a representative national sampling. Nor is such a sampling considered essential for proper standardization" (p. 43). We disagree with their position, as indicated in our statements in Chapter 6 regarding the development of norms.

When one uses norm-referenced scores obtained on the WRAT, one does not know the nature of the group to whom students are being compared. The test was standardized on a sample of individuals selected from only seven states. Norms were developed by administering the test to from 400 to 600 persons at each age level in half-year intervals through age 13, and in 1-year to 12-year intervals thereafter. All cases were given ability tests at the same time as the WRAT, though many different tests were used (WISC, WAIS, WRIPT, Lorge-Thorndike, Kuhlmann-Anderson, Stanford-Binet, and California Mental Maturity Scale), and there is no description of how these data were used.

The authors argue that they did not restrict the normative sample on variables like intelligence, socioeconomic status, and race. They report that these factors were distributed in the sample in proportions representative of their distribution in the population at large. No data are presented to support their contention.

Reliability

There are no data presented on the reliability of the 1978 WRAT. Data for the 1965 edition of the test are presented, and there are only split-half reliabilities on seven groups. While the reliability coefficients are greater than .94, there is no description of the nature of the seven groups.

Validity

As discussed earlier, the most important kind of validity for an achievement test is content validity. If the test does not assess the content of the curriculum, then interpretations based on obtained results may be very misleading. Although the subtests of the WRAT sample only very limited aspects of reading, spelling, and arithmetic curricula, the authors never question its content validity. A teacher who adjusted a student's reading curriculum on the basis of scores obtained on the Reading subtest of the WRAT would be on shaky ground indeed. The subtest assesses only skill in decoding isolated words, with no consideration of the student's skill in deriving meaning from those words, reading phrases and sentences, or comprehending what is read. Similarly, the Spelling subtest assesses only skill in writing dictated words, while the Arithmetic subtest is simply a measure of the student's computational skills.

The authors describe in the manual five kinds of evidence that can be used to establish validity, but provide insufficient data to establish the validity of the test. First, they observe that validity can be established by correlating test performance with performance on a criterion measure. They present data on the 1946 edition of the WRAT. Secondly, they demonstrate that raw scores increase with chronological age.

A third procedure described to establish validity is one of correlating performance with scores on intellectual measures. The authors present means and standard deviations for performance on the WRAT and various intellectual measures of five groups: adolescents and adults referred for vocational rehabilitation and evaluations, private school students, mentally retarded adolescents and adults, college adults, and "deprived" individuals. While the results of the comparisons are undated, it is apparent from the intelligence tests used that data were collected on pre-1976 editions of the WRAT.

The authors describe internal-consistency reliabilities as evidence for validity. Not only is the approach inappropriate, but the data presented are subtest intercorrelations. Finally, the manual includes a discussion of factor analysis and a poorly explained description of "Lobal factors" and "Obal integrations" with no data to support the discussion. Data from a 1973 U.S. Public Health Survey are reported and said to be self-explanatory. They are not.

The authors have demonstrated that subtest scores increase with chronological age. With this one exception, there is no evidence for the validity of the 1978 WRAT. Of particular concern is the lack of evidence for the validity of each of the eleven uses to which the authors state the test may be put.

As for any achievement test, users of the WRAT will have to judge its appropriateness based on the relevance of the behaviors sampled to the contents of their curricula. A serious shortcoming is the very limited behavior sampling. "Reading," for example, is assessed only by counting the number of words in isolation a student reads. The level 1 arithmetic subtest includes only three items, one oral and two written, assessing skill in addition of single-digit numbers.

Summary

The Wide Range Achievement Test is an individually administered device designed to assess academic achievement in three areas. The test has limited behavior sampling, inadequate standardization, and absence of reliability and validity data.

Brigance Diagnostic Inventories[1]

The Brigance Diagnostic Inventories consist of three batteries: the Diagnostic Inventory of Early Development (Brigance, 1978), which is intended for use with individuals with developmental ages less than 7 years, the Diagnostic Inventory of Basic Skills (Brigance, 1977), which is intended for use with children functioning from kindergarten through sixth grade, and the Diagnostic Inventory of Essential Skills (Brigance, 1980), which is intended for use in secondary programs. Each inventory is a criterion-referenced multiple-skill battery.

The three inventories are highly similar in purpose and format. Figure 16.3 illustrates an assessment from the early development inventory. The child's page contains the test stimuli. The examiner's page contains the suggested directions for administering the items, the rule for discontinuing the test, the criteria for scoring, the instructional objective for the item being assessed, and several other useful bits of information. Each inventory is intended to assess mastery of the skill or concept; consequently, testers are urged to adapt the testing procedures as necessary to insure valid assessment. Administering the inventories thus requires some professional judgment, although no special training is required. Each inventory assesses observable behavior or products and is scored objectively except for some rating forms in the essential skills inventory. Each inventory is comprehensive: the early development inventory assesses 98 skill sequences; the basic

1. *Brigance* is a trademark of Curriculum Associates, Inc., North Billerica, Mass. The Inventories and process are Patent Pending.

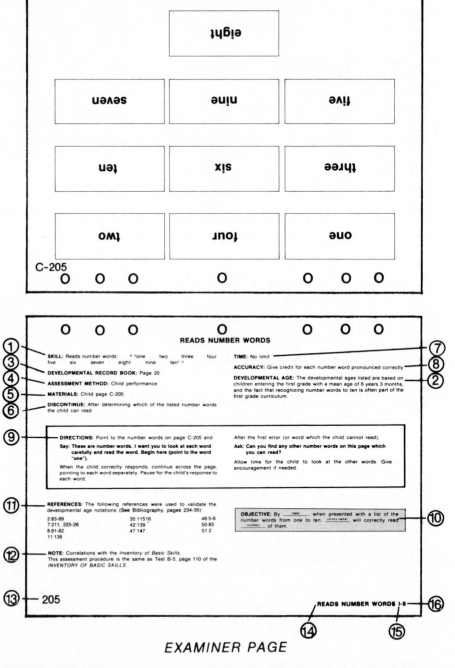

FIGURE 16.3 Sample from Brigance Diagnostic Inventory of Early Development
SOURCE: BRIGANCE® Diagnostic Inventory of Early Development, Copyright © 1978, Curriculum Associates, Inc. Reprinted by permission.

MODEL OF FORMAT

FOR AN ASSESSMENT PROCEDURE

WITH A CHILD PAGE

1. **SKILL:** A general statement of the skill being assessed. When appropriate, the skill sequence in the *Developmental Record Book* is also listed.

2. **DEVELOPMENTAL AGE NOTATION:** The numbers preceding a sequence indicate the year and month the child usually begins to learn or master that skill. Those following indicate when mastery is usually accomplished. Example: for 4-7, read 4 years and 7 months developmental age.

   In addition, the developmental ages are explained or discussed in a separate note where necessary.

3. **DEVELOPMENTAL RECORD BOOK:** The page on which this skill is listed in the *Developmental Record Book*.

4. **ASSESSMENT METHODS:** The means recommended for assessing.

5. **MATERIALS:** Materials which are needed for the assessment.

6. **DISCONTINUE:** Indicates the number of items the child may fail before you discontinue the assessment of skills in this sequence.

7. **TIME:** Time limits suggested for the child's response.

8. **ACCURACY:** Explanation of scoring criteria.

9. **DIRECTIONS:** The recommended directions for assessing the skills sequence. Recommended phrasing of instructions or questions is clearly labeled, indented and printed in bold face type.

10. **OBJECTIVE:** The objective for the skills being assessed is stated, and is a valuable resource for developing individualized education programs (IEP's).

11. **REFERENCES:** the numbers listed correspond to the sources used to establish and validate the skill sequences and developmental ages. References are found in the *Bibliography* on page 246-7.

12. **NOTES:** Helpful notes on observations, resources or diagnosing are listed here.

13. Examiner's page number.

14. Skill assessed.

15. The first letter, "I," indicates the section, where all basic reading skills are located.

16. This number indicates the ninth of the skills sequenced in the basic reading section of the *Inventory*.

FIGURE 16.3 (*cont.*)

skills inventory, 140 skill sequences; and the essential skills inventory, 165 skill sequences. As is true of most criterion-referenced systems, the inventories provide the educator with lists of mastered and unmastered skills from which strengths and weaknesses as well as potential instructional objectives can be inferred.

In addition to being criterion-referenced, the Diagnostic Inventory of Early Development is also "normative-referenced." Developmental skills are assigned developmental ages not by norming the items, but by consulting several

texts in which age norms for the skills are published. Moreover, the texts are referenced to each skill so that the user can check the sources for any skill of particular interest. Eleven subscales make up the early-development inventories.

1. Four preambulatory motor sequences (for example, supine, prone, sitting, and standing positions)
2. Thirteen gross motor sequences (for example, walking, catching, rhythm)

3. Nine fine motor sequences (for example, eye/finger/hand manipulations, painting)
4. Eleven self-help sequences (for example, eating, unfastening, toileting, household chores)
5. Three prespeech sequences (receptive language, gestures, and vocalization)
6. Ten speech and language sequences (syntax, social speech, singing)
7. Thirteen general knowledge and comprehension sequences (for example, body parts, colors, weather, community helpers)
8. Five readiness sequences (for example, response to and experience with books, lowercase letters)
9. Eleven basic reading sequences (for example, auditory discrimination, vowels, reading common signs)
10. Seven manuscript-writing sequences (for example, printing capital letters sequentially, printing simple sentences)
11. Twelve math sequences (for example, rote counting, writing dictated numerals, recognition of money)

In addition to being criterion-referenced, the Diagnostic Inventory of Basic Skills is "text-referenced." Grade levels are determined by the level at which the material is first taught, not by the level at which half of the students have learned the material. This inventory is composed of four subscales. The Readiness subscale contains twenty-four sequences ranging from developmental skills (such as color recognition, identification of body parts, articulation of sounds) to more academic enabling skills (among them, recognition of upper- and lower-case letters, number recognition, writing letters).

Reading   This subscale contains four subparts.

1. Six word-recognition sequences (for example, basic sight vocabulary)
2. Three reading sequences [oral reading comprehension, literal comprehension (recall), oral reading rate]
3. Nineteen word-analysis sequences (such as auditory discrimination, initial sounds auditorily and visually, prefixes and suffixes, syllabication)
4. Five vocabulary sequences (context clues, classification, analogies, antonyms, and homonyms)

Language Arts   This subscale contains four subparts.

1. Three handwriting sequences (cursive lower-case, cursive capitals, personal data)
2. Three grammar sequences (capitalization, punctuation, and parts of speech)
3. Four spelling sequences (initial consonants, initial clusters, suffixes, and prefixes)
4. Nine reference skills (such as dictionary use, maps)

Mathematics   This subscale has four parts.

1. Thirteen number sequences (for example, rote counting, writing numbers from dictation, decimals)
2. Seventeen operations sequences (such as addition combinations, division by decimals)
3. Twenty-five measurement sequences [four dealing with money, nine with time, four with the calendar, three with linear measurement, three with weight (including thermometer), and two with liquids]
4. Eight geometry sequences (for example, two-dimensional squares, three-dimensional cylinder)

The Diagnostic Inventory of Essential Skills focuses on "skills which have been identified as essential for mastery if the student is to be able to function successfully and with the greatest degree of independence as a citizen, consumer, worker, and family member" (Brigance, 1980, p. v). Unlike the other two inventories, this one has two forms (A and B) for several parts; it also contains nine rating scales to assess health practices and attitudes, self-concept, general attitude, personality, responsibility and self-discipline, job interview preparation, job interview, auto safety, and communication skills. The 165 skill sequences are divided into two parts: academic skills and applied skills. The academic skills include:

1. Oral reading (graded from second to eleventh grade)
2. Reading comprehension (graded from third to eleventh grade)
3. Functional word recognition (basic sight vocabulary, directions, abbreviations, signs, numbers)
4. Word analysis (such as vowel sounds, digraphs, and diphthongs, prefixes and suffixes)
5. Reference skills (for example, alphabetizing, using library card catalogue)
6. Graphic representations (TV schedule, graphs, and so forth)
7. Writing (including cursive letter formation, punctuation, letter writing)
8. Filling out forms
9. Spelling (for example, calendar words, initial consonants)
10. Numbers (such as recognition, writing from dictation)
11. Arithmetic functions (basic operations)
12. Computation of whole numbers
13. Fractions
14. Decimals
15. Percent
16. Measurement (money, time, metric and English linear, temperature, reading meters and gauges)
17. Metrics
18. Math vocabulary

The applied skills include:

1. Health and safety
2. Vocational
3. Food and clothing (for example, reading directions or labels, selection by best price for quantity)
4. Communication and telephone

Too comprehensive to be administered in its entirety, the essential skill inventory should be administered selectively. Grade placement tests are intended to provide a way to identify starting places for detailed assessments in word recognition, writing, spelling, and math.

Scores

The scores from the diagnostic inventories are mastered/unmastered on each skill sequence. These scores can be displayed on pupil record forms and class record forms. No summary scores are obtained. The normative-referenced and test-referenced features should not be thought of as scores.

Norms

The inventories are criterion-referenced, so norms are not required.

Reliability

No reliability data are provided. At a minimum, alternate-form reliability estimates should be provided on tests with two forms, and interrater agreement should be provided on the rating scales.

Validity

The content validity of the inventories is the overriding concern. Although there are subtle differences in the content validity of the three devices, they are highly similar. All were developed by review of appropriate literature, and all were submitted to field testing. A detailed description of these procedures is absent. Nonetheless, inspection of the content of the inventories indicates comprehensive coverage, careful preparation, and meticulous selection of items.

Summary

The Brigance Diagnostic Inventories offer comprehensive criterion-referenced assessment of important skills, concepts, and behavior. They are appropriately used with individuals ranging from infants through adolescents. The content validity of the devices is most acceptable. The devices should prove highly useful to teachers in planning and evaluating instruction for handicapped pupils.

GETTING THE MOST MILEAGE OUT OF AN ACHIEVEMENT TEST

The achievement tests described in this chapter provide the teacher with global scores in areas such as word meaning and work-study skills. While global scores can help us in screening children, they generally lack the specificity to help us in planning individualized instructional programs. Merely knowing that Emily earned a grade-equivalent score of 3.5 on the Mathematics Computation subtest of the Metropolitan Achievement Tests does not tell us what math skills Emily has. In addition, a teacher cannot rely on test names as an indication of what is measured by a specific test.

A teacher must look at any screening test—at *any* test for that matter—in terms of the *behaviors* sampled by that test. Let's take a case in point. Suppose Richard earned a grade score of 3.2 on a spelling subtest. What do we know about Richard?

We know Richard earned the same raw score on the test as the average of students in the second month of third grade. That is *all* we know without going beyond the score and looking at the kinds of behaviors sampled by the test. The test title tells us only that the test measures skill development in spelling. But we still do not know *what* Richard did to earn a grade score of 3.2.

First, we need to ask, "What is the nature of the behaviors sampled by the test?" Spelling tests can be of several kinds. Richard may have been asked to write a word read by his teacher, as is the case in the spelling subtest of the Wide Range Achievement Test. Such a behavior sampling demands that he recall the correct spelling of a word and actually produce that correct spelling in writing. On the other hand, Richard's grade score of 3.2 may have been earned on a spelling test that asked him to recognize the correct spelling of a word. For example, the spelling subtest of the Peabody Individual Achievement Test presents the student with four alternative spellings of a word (like *empti, empty, impty, emity),* and the teacher asks a child to point to the word "empty." Such an item demands recognition and pointing rather than recall and production. We need to look first at the nature of the behaviors sampled by the test.

Second, a teacher must look at these specific items a student passes or fails. This requires actually going back to the original test protocol to analyze the specific nature of skill development in a given area. We need to ask, "What kinds of items did the child fail?" and to look for consistent patterns among the failures. In trying to identify the nature of spelling errors, the teacher needs to ask such questions as, "Does the student consistently demonstrate errors in spelling words with long vowels? with silent *e*'s? with specific consonant blends?" and so on. The search is for specific patterns of errors, and the teacher tries to ascertain the relative degree of consistency in making certain errors.

Similar procedures are followed with any screening device. Quite obviously, the information achieved is not nearly as specific as the information we get from diagnostic tests. Administration of an achievement test that is a screening test gives the classroom teacher a general idea of where to start with any additional diagnostic assessment.

COPING WITH DILEMMAS IN CURRENT PRACTICE

Two limitations affect the use of achievement tests as screening devices. As was noted earlier, unless the content of an achievement test reflects the content of the curriculum, the obtained results are meaningless. If students are instructed in new math but tested with traditional math achievement tests, they may well perform poorly. Yet the obtained results cannot be said to reflect accurately and validly a student's level of skill development in math. Jenkins and Pany (1978) compared the contents of four separate reading achievement tests with the contents of five commercial reading series at grades 1 and 2. Their major concern was the extent to which students might earn different scores on different tests of reading achievement simply as a function of the degree of overlap in content between tests and curricula. Jenkins and Pany calculated the grade scores that would be earned by students who had mastered the words taught in the respective curricula and who had correctly read those words on the four tests. Grade scores are reported in Table 16.11. It is apparent that different curricula result in different performance on different tests. Those charged with the selection of achievement tests must go beyond a casual inspection of test items. They should construct a table of specifications for each area of the curriculum to be tested and compare prospective tests on that table.

TABLE 16.11   Grade Equivalent Scores Obtained by Matching Specific Reading Text Words to Standardized Reading Test Words

Curriculum	PIAT	MAT Word Knowledge	MAT Word Analysis	SDRT	WRAT
Bank Street Reading Series					
Grade 1	1.5	1.0	1.1	1.8	2.0
Grade 2	2.8	2.5	1.2	2.9	2.7
Keys to Reading					
Grade 1	2.0	1.4	1.2	2.2	2.2
Grade 2	3.3	1.9	1.0	3.0	3.0
Reading 360					
Grade 1	1.5	1.0	1.0	1.4	1.7
Grade 2	2.2	2.1	1.0	2.7	2.3
SRA Reading Program					
Grade 1	1.5	1.2	1.3	1.0	2.1
Grade 2	3.1	2.5	1.4	2.9	3.5
Sullivan Associates Programmed Reading					
Grade 1	1.8	1.4	1.2	1.1	2.0
Grade 2	2.2	2.4	1.1	2.5	2.5

SOURCE: From "Standardized Achievement Tests: How Useful for Special Education?" by J. Jenkins & D. Pany, 1978, *Exceptional Children, 44,* p. 450. Copyright 1978 by The Council for Exceptional Children, 1920 Association Drive, Reston, Virginia 22091. Reprinted by permission.

Only then will they be able to make valid judgments about the relative correspondence of test content and curriculum.

A second limitation is inherent in the way most achievement tests are administered. Most achievement tests are group administered, and teachers giving a group-administered test are unable to observe individual pupil performance. They may lose valuable information about how a student goes about solving problems, analyzing words, and spelling because they cannot observe individual behavior directly. Then, because most screening devices provide global scores by content areas, teachers must actually return to a student's test blank or answer sheet to investigate the kinds of errors made. Otherwise, teachers are left with a score but little information about how the score was obtained and no systematic analysis of skill-development strengths and weaknesses.

SUMMARY

This chapter has provided an intense look at screening devices used to assess academic achievement. Such devices provide a global picture of a student's skill development in academic content areas. The most commonly used screening tests have been discussed with an emphasis on the kinds of behavior each test samples, the adequacy of its norms, its reliability, and its validity. When selecting an achievement test or when evaluating the results of a student's performance on an achievement test, the classroom teacher needs to take into careful consideration not only the technical characteristics of the test but also the extent to which the behaviors sampled represent the goals and objectives of the student's curriculum. Our discussion also included suggestions for the teacher for administering group tests and for getting the most mileage out of the results of group tests.

STUDY QUESTIONS

1. State at least three different reasons for administering the screening tests described in this chapter.
2. Differentiate between screening tests and diagnostic tests.
3. Identify at least four important considerations in selecting a specific achievement test for use with the third graders in your local school system.
4. Identify similarities and differences in the domains of behavior sampled by the California Achievement Tests, the Iowa Tests of Basic Skills, and the Peabody Individual Achievement Test.
5. Ms. Epstein decides to assess the achievement of her fifth-grade pupils. She believes her pupils are unusually "slow" and estimates that, in general, they are functioning on about a third-grade level. She decides to use Primary Level III of the SAT. What difficulties will she face in doing so?
6. Mr. Spencer, a fourth-grade teacher in Bemidji, Minnesota, wants to group students in his class for reading instruction. He administers the reading recognition subtest of the Wide Range Achievement Test and assigns students to groups on the basis of the grade scores they earn on the test. Which of the basic assumptions underlying assessment has Mr. Spencer violated? How might he make this grouping decision?

ADDITIONAL READING

Buros, O. K. (Ed.). (1978). *Eighth mental measurements yearbook.* Highland Park, NJ: Gryphon Press. (Reviews of achievement batteries, pp. 1–124).

Gronlund, N. E. (1982). *Constructing achievement tests.* Englewood Cliffs, NJ: Prentice-Hall.

Gronlund, N. E. (1973). *Preparing criterion-referenced tests for classroom instruction.* New York: Macmillan.

Jenkins, J., & Pany, D. (1978). Standardized achievement tests: How useful for special education? *Exceptional Children, 44,* 448–453.

LaManna, J., & Ysseldyke, J. (1973). Reliability of the Peabody Individual Achievement Test with first grade children. *Psychology in the Schools, 10,* 437–439.

CHAPTER 17

DIAGNOSTIC ASSESSMENT
IN READING

In Chapter 16 we described achievement tests that are used for screening purposes. These tests provide relatively global information about a student's achievement. Often, school personnel need more specific information. Diagnostic tests provide such specific information. In this chapter we give you a detailed description of the kinds of behaviors sampled by diagnostic reading tests; we then describe commonly used diagnostic reading tests, both norm referenced and criterion referenced.

WHY DO WE ASSESS READING SKILLS?

Reading is thought to be the most fundamental skill students acquire through the process of schooling. Students who experience difficulty reading can be expected to have difficulty with nearly all academic curriculum content. It should not surprise you to learn that "difficulty reading" is the most frequently stated reason why students are referred for psychoeducational evaluation.

Criterion-referenced diagnostic reading tests are designed to help school personnel pinpoint students' strengths and weaknesses in reading and to help plan appropriate educational interventions for them. They are used to give teachers a systematic, relatively specific picture of where pupils stand in development of specific reading skills.

Another reason to use diagnostic reading tests is to spot common problems within groups of children. One of the authors recently consulted at a school in which pupils consistently performed above grade level in all areas of the curriculum but one: mathematics. Students in that school nearly all earned below-average scores on the mathematics subtest of the Metropolitan Achievement Test. A diagnostic mathematics test was used to pinpoint skill deficiencies that students consistently demonstrated. Once specific deficiencies were identified, teachers were able to explore alternative explanations for the deficiencies. Teachers learned that the skills were not systematically taught in the math curriculum used by the school. They then identified skills they thought were very important to teach and added those skills to the curriculum. In the example, a diagnostic math test was used. If the difficulties had been in reading, a diagnostic reading test could have been used.

Norm-referenced diagnostic reading tests provide information about relative standing in development of reading skills. This information might be used for making classification or placement decisions and for making program evaluation decisions. Norm-referenced diagnostic reading tests may be used in instructional planning, but when that is the case users must go beyond the derived scores to analyze pupil performance of the specific behaviors sampled by the test. Knowledge of grade scores, age scores, percentile ranks, and stanines is of limited value in instructional planning. For example, knowing where Heather stands relative to other students does not help a teacher decide how to teach Heather to read.

SKILLS ASSESSED BY DIAGNOSTIC READING TESTS

Reading is a complex behavior composed of many skills. No diagnostic reading test assesses all aspects of reading completely. Rather, the test samples specific reading or reading-related behaviors. The particular behaviors assessed by any one test are simply those behaviors that the test authors believe are most important to assess. In a broad sense, several different categories of behaviors are sampled by diagnostic reading tests. Specific tests or subtests assess oral reading skills, comprehension skills, word-attack skills, and rate of reading. A variety of supplementary subtests are included in a number of diagnostic reading tests.

Assessment of Oral Reading Skills

A number of tests or parts of tests are designed to assess the accuracy and fluency of a student's oral reading. Oral reading tests consist of series of paragraphs arranged sequentially from very easy paragraphs to relatively difficult ones. The student reads aloud while the examiner notes both the kinds of errors made and the behaviors that characterize the student's oral reading. Two commonly used tests, the Gray Oral Reading Test and the Gilmore Oral Reading Test, are designed specifically to assess skill development in oral reading. Two other commonly used tests, the Gates-McKillop-Horowitz

Reading Diagnostic Tests and the Durrell Analysis of Reading Difficulty, include oral reading subtests.

Different oral reading tests record different behaviors as errors in oral reading. The kinds of errors recorded on the different tests and subtests are summarized in Table 17.1. A description follows of the behaviors demonstrated as each specific kind of error takes place.

Aid   If a student either hesitates for a time without making an audible effort to pronounce a word or appears to be attempting for 10 seconds to pronounce the word, the examiner pronounces the word and records an error. The error is recorded by an underlined bracket.

Gross Mispronunciation of a Word   "A gross mispronunciation is one in which the pupil's pronunciation of a word bears so little resemblance to the proper pronunciation that the examiner must be looking at the word to recognize it" (Gray & Robinson, 1967, p. 5). An example of a gross mispronunciation is one in which the pupil reads the word *encounters* as "actors." The examiner records the error phonetically above the mispronounced word.

Omission of a Word or Group of Words   Omissions consist of skipping individual words or groups of words. The examiner simply circles the word or group of words omitted.

Insertion of a Word or Group of Words   Insertions consist of the student's putting one or more words into the sentence being read. The student may, for example, read *the dog* as "the mean dog." Insertions are recorded by placing a caret (^) in the sentence and writing in the word or words inserted.

Substitution of One Meaningful Word for Another   Substitutions consist of the actual replacement of one or more words in the passage by one or more meaningful words. The student might read *is* as "it" or *dense* as "depress." Children often replace entire sequences of words with others as illustrated in the reading of *he is his own mechanic* as "he sat on his own machine." The examiner records substitutions by underlining the word or words substituted and writing in the substitutions.

Repetition   Repetition consists of repeating words or groups of words while attempting to read sentences or paragraphs. In some cases if a student repeats a group of words to correct an error, the original error is struck but a repetition error is recorded. In other cases such behaviors are recorded simply as spontaneous corrections. Repetitions are recorded by underlining the repeated word or words with a wavy line. Errors due to stuttering are not recorded as repetition errors.

TABLE 17.1   Kinds of Behaviors Recorded as Errors on Specific Oral Reading Tests or Subtests

	Gray Oral Reading Test	Gilmore Oral Reading Test	Gates-McKillop-Horowitz Reading Diagnostic Test	Durrell Analysis of Reading Difficulty
Aid	X	X		X
Gross mispronunciation	X	X	X	X
Omission	X	X	X	X
Insertion	X	X	X	X
Substitution	X	X		
Repetition	X	X	X	X
Inversion	X		X	
Partial mispronunciation	X			
Disregard of punctuation		X		X
Hesitation		X		X

Inversion, or Changing of Word Order   Errors of inversion are recorded when the child changes the order of words appearing in a sentence. Inversions are indicated as follows:
house the

Partial Mispronunciation   A partial mispronunciation can be one of several different kinds of errors. The examiner may have to pronounce *part* of a word for a student (an aid); the student may phonetically mispronounce specific letters by reading words like *red* as "reed"; the student may omit part of a word, insert elements of words, make errors in syllabication, accent, or inversion. Such errors are recorded phonetically and scored as partial mispronunciations.

Disregard of Punctuation   The student may fail to observe punctuation—that is, may not pause for a comma, stop for a period, or indicate by vocal inflection a question mark or exclamation point. These errors of disregard of punctuation are recorded by circling the punctuation mark.

Hesitation   The student hesitates for two or more seconds before pronouncing a word. The error is recorded as a check (✓) over the word. If the examiner then pronounces the word, it is recorded ✓ p.

In addition to making a systematic analysis of oral reading errors, the examiner can note the behaviors that characterize a student's oral reading. Although, certainly, any characteristics may be observed, the indicators of difficulty more frequently looked for include head movement, finger pointing, loss of place, word-by-word reading, poor phrasing, lack of expression, reading in a monotonous tone, and reading in a strained voice.

Assessment of Comprehension Skills

Diagnostic reading tests assess three kinds of comprehension skills: literal comprehension, inferential comprehension, and listening comprehension. Assessment of *literal comprehension* is usually accomplished by asking a number of factual questions based directly on the content of a paragraph or story the student has read. The answers to such questions appear directly in the story or paragraph. Such comprehension tests require specific recall of material read and for that reason are sometimes characterized as memory tests—appropriately, unless, of course, the passage is available for the student to refer to when responding to the questions.

Inferential comprehension tests require interpretation and extension of what has been read. The student must demonstrate an ability to derive meaning from printed paragraphs or stories.

Assessment of *listening comprehension* is accomplished by reading a story or paragraph to a student and then asking questions based on recall or understanding of the material read. Listening comprehension tests can measure both literal and inferential comprehension.

In the process of assessing the development of comprehension skills, it is absolutely necessary for the teacher or diagnostic specialist to examine critically how those skills are assessed. The method by which comprehension skills are assessed may muddy the waters, in that pupil performance may depend more on other traits or skills than on comprehension of what is read. When literal comprehension is assessed by asking the student to read a passage and recall, without observing the passage, what has been read, performance may depend more on memory than on reading comprehension. Similarly, asking students to infer meaning on the basis of what they have read probably requires as much cognition as comprehension. In our opinion, the best way to assess comprehension is to ask students to state or paraphrase what they have read.

Assessment of Word-Attack Skills

Word-attack or word-analysis skills are those used "to derive the meaning and/or pronunciation of a word through phonics, structural analysis, or context clues" (Ekwall, 1970, p. 4). Children must decode words before they can gain meaning from the printed page. Since word-analysis difficulties are among the principal reasons why children have trouble reading, a variety of subtests of commonly used diagnostic reading tests specifically assess word-analysis skills.

Subtests assessing skill in word analysis range from such basic assessments as analysis of a student's skill in associating letters with sounds to tests of blending and syllabication. Subtests that assess skill in associating letters with sounds are generally of a format in which the examiner reads a word aloud and the child

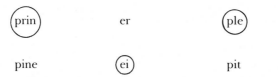

FIGURE 17.1   An item that assesses blending skill

must identify the consonant, vowel, consonant cluster, or digraph that has the same sound as the beginning, middle, or ending letter in the words. Syllabication subtests present polysyllabic words, and the child must either divide the word into syllables or circle specific syllables. Blending subtests, on the other hand, are of three types. First, the examiner may read syllables out loud ("wa - ter - mel - on," for example) and ask the child to pronounce the word. Second, the child may be asked to read word parts and pronounce whole words. Third, the child may be presented with alternative beginning, middle, and ending sounds and asked to produce a word. Figure 17.1 illustrates the third method used with the Stanford Diagnostic Reading Test.

Assessment of Word-Recognition Skills

Subtests of diagnostic reading tests that assess a pupil's word-recognition skills are designed to ascertain what many call *sight vocabulary*. A person learns the correct pronunciation of letters and words through a variety of experiences. The more exposure a person has to specific words and the more familiar those words become, the more readily the person recognizes those words and pronounces them. Well-known words require very little reliance on word-attack skills. Most readers of this book immediately recognize the word *hemorrhage* and do not have to employ phonetic skills to pronounce it. On the other hand, words like *nephrocystanastomosis* are not a part of the sight vocabulary of most of us. The word slows us down; we use phonetics to analyze it.

Word-recognition subtests form a major part of most diagnostic reading tests. Some tests use paper tachistoscopes to expose words for brief periods of time (usually one-half second). Students who recognize many words are said to have good sight vocabularies or good word-recognition skills. Other subtests assess letter recognition, recognition of words in isolation, and recognition of words in context.

Assessment of Rate of Reading

Reading rate is generally played down in the diagnostic assessment of reading difficulties. There are, however, some exceptions. Level II of the Stanford

Diagnostic Reading Test has a specific subtest to assess rate of reading. On the other hand, tests such as the Gray Oral Reading Test are timed, with time affecting the score a pupil receives. A pupil who reads a passage on the Gray Oral slowly but makes no errors in reading can earn a lower score than a rapid reader who makes one or two errors in reading.

Assessment of Other Reading and Reading-Related Behaviors

A variety of subtests that fit none of the above categories are included in diagnostic reading tests as either major or supplementary subtests. Examples of such tests include oral vocabulary, spelling, handwriting, and auditory discrimination. In most cases such subtests are included simply to provide the examiner with additional diagnostic information.

ORAL READING TESTS

Gray Oral Reading Test

The Gray Oral Reading Test (Gray & Robinson, 1967) is designed to provide an objective measure of skill development in oral reading from early first grade through college. The test was specifically designed to facilitate the diagnosis of oral reading difficulties. The Gray Oral Reading Test is available in forms A, B, C, and D. All forms are similar in organization, length, and difficulty level; this enables periodic retesting with comparable but nonidentical forms of the test.

The Gray consists of a series of graded reading passages in a spiral-bound booklet. The student reads the passages aloud while the examiner records errors and notes reading characteristics on a separate student record booklet. Following the reading of each passage, the materials are removed and the examiner asks a series of questions designed to assess the student's literal comprehension of material contained in the passage.

The Gray Oral Reading Tests provide the teacher, reading specialist, or psychologist with an assessment of both the speed and accuracy of oral reading. The examiner records the length of time it takes a student to read each individual passage. Starting points differ for individual students. The test manual provides general guidelines, based on a student's grade level, about the point where the test should be started. Each form contains thirteen reading passages of increasing difficulty. Students begin with an easy passage that they can read without error and read to the point where they make seven or more errors in two consecutive passages. For each reading passage the examiner records the number and kinds of errors in oral reading, along with the time it took a student to read the passage.

Actual administration of the device is simple, but recording and scoring are so difficult that a tape recorder should be used regularly. Considerable training and practice must precede use of this device for making diagnostic decisions, and those decisions must take note of the fact that speed affects the scores earned. Errors recorded for the Gray include aids, partial mispronunciations, gross mispronunciations, omissions,

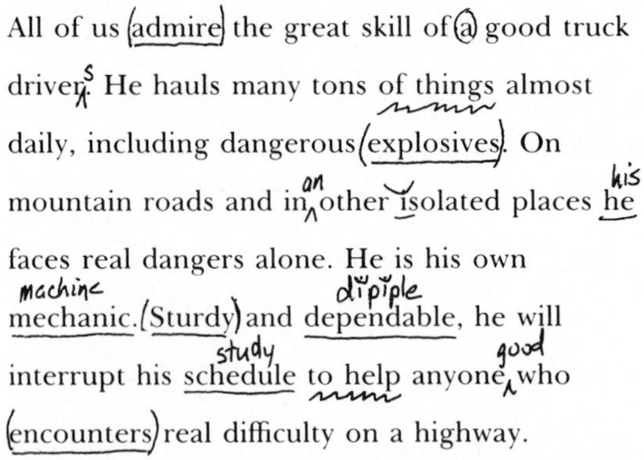

All of us (admire) the great skill of @ good truck
drivers. He hauls many tons of things almost
daily, including dangerous (explosives). On
mountain roads and in other isolated places he
faces real dangers alone. He is his own
mechanic. (Sturdy) and dependable, he will
interrupt his schedule to help anyone who
(encounters) real difficulty on a highway.

FIGURE 17.2   An illustration of errors on the Gray Oral Reading Test
SOURCE: Redrawn from the booklet of reading passages for *Gray Oral Reading Test* by W. S. Gray
and H. M. Robinson. Copyright 1967. Used by permission of Pro Ed, 5341 Industrial Oaks Blvd.,
Austin, TX 78735.

insertions, inversions, substitutions, and repetitions. The test has a convenient list of reading characteristics enabling examiners to check those they observe.

Figure 17.2 illustrates the kinds of errors made by Marjorie in the oral reading of a passage from the Gray. Marjorie made fifteen errors in reading the passage. The examiner had to pronounce four words *(admire, explosives, sturdy,* and *encounters)* for her. One gross mispronunciation ("dipiple" for *dependable)* and one omission *(a)* occurred. Marjorie inserted one word *(good)* and made three substitution errors ("his" for *he,* "machine" for *mechanic,* and "study" for *schedule).* On two occasions she repeated what she had read, as evidenced by the underlining of groups of words with wavy lines. Marjorie made three partial mispronunciation errors, one a phonetic mispronunciation *(isolated)* and two items consisting of partial insertions ("drivers" for *driver* and "another" for *other).*

Figure 17.2 illustrates Marjorie's reading of only one passage. From an analysis of errors made in all passages read, the examiner can get a picture of the kinds of difficulties Marjorie has in oral reading. Both the rate of reading and the number of errors affect the score a child earns.

The characteristics observed do not enter into scoring of the test as such, but they provide additional qualitative information to assist in planning developmental, corrective, or remedial strategies.

Scores

Two kinds of information are obtained from the Gray. The student earns a grade score that reflects in a global sense the speed and accuracy of oral reading. The most useful information, however, is the error analysis resulting from the administration of the Gray. Given a pattern of the kinds of errors individuals most frequently make, the teacher can at least begin to attempt differentiated instruction.

Norms

The Gray norms are described as "tentative" because they are based on the testing of only 502 children (256 boys and 246 girls), 40 at each grade, from schools in Florida and in Chicago and its suburbs. The test provides separate normative tables for boys and girls. The only information provided about the nature of the standardization population is information on sex, geographic location, and types of students excluded from the sample; students with speech problems, serious health problems, emotional problems, or students who had been held back or double promoted were excluded from the normative population. They do not identify the reading curriculum in which the students were enrolled.

It is important to note that since separate norms are provided for boys and girls and since normative data are based on forty children per grade, the population against whom we compare the performance of a specific boy or girl is twenty children at his or her grade level. While this normative sample is limited, the user of the Gray should remember that the test's real benefit is the systematic analysis of oral reading errors rather than the grade score obtained.

Reliability

Reliability data for the Gray consist of intercorrelations among grade scores on each of the four forms. Alternate-form reliability coefficients range from .97 to .98 for girls, and from .96 to .98 for boys. The standard error of measurement for the test is four raw-score points for the total score. No test-retest reliability data are reported.

Validity

The test authors devote two sentences in the manual to the issue of the validity of the test.

They state that the tests are valid primarily because of the procedures used in constructing them and because of the test's discrimination between students at different grade levels. Test construction was a matter of expert opinion based on data from a 1915 version of the test and a search of contemporary basal readers.

Summary

The Gray Oral Reading Test consists of series of passages the student reads aloud to the examiner. The examiner records both the kinds of errors the student makes and the student's oral reading characteristics. The test provides grade scores that indicate in a global sense the level at which a student is reading. The most useful information to a teacher, however, is the systematic analysis of oral reading errors.

Norms for the Gray are at this time both "tentative" and limited. The authors do not state whether more permanent norms will ever be provided. Original standardization occurred during 1959–1960. If more complete norms were to be provided, one would expect them to have appeared by now.

Reliability data presented in the manual are limited. Validity is based on expert opinion. The Gray will provide the teacher with estimates of the student's speed and accuracy in oral reading and will enable tentative hypotheses to be made about the nature of oral reading difficulties.

Gilmore Oral Reading Test

The Gilmore Oral Reading Test (Gilmore & Gilmore, 1968) is an individually administered test designed to assess skill development in oral reading from grades 1 through 8. The test consists of two forms, C and D, that assess the accuracy of oral reading, reading comprehen-

sion, and rate of reading. Each form of the test contains ten paragraphs of increasing difficulty. These ten paragraphs form a continuous story. Administration of the test generally takes 15 to 20 minutes.

The Gilmore is very much like the Gray Oral

TABLE 17.2 Performance Ratings for Accuracy and Comprehension on the Gilmore Oral Reading Test

Rating	Stanine	Percentile Band	Percentage of Pupils
Superior	9	Above 95	4
Above average	7, 8	77–95	19
Average	4, 5, 6	23–76	54
Below average	2, 3	4–22	19
Poor	1	Below 4	4

Reading Test with one major exception. A score earned on the Gray is a function of both the number of errors in oral reading and the rate of reading. The grade scores on the Gilmore are a function only of the errors made. Although the test is timed, rate is not used in arriving at the grade score.

The Gilmore provides a systematic analysis of the kinds of errors the student makes in oral reading. The kinds of errors recorded for the Gilmore include (1) substitutions, (2) mispronunciations, (3) words pronounced by the examiner (aids), (4) disregard of punctuation, (5) insertions, (6) hesitations, (7) repetitions, and (8) omissions. Substitution errors, aids, insertions, repetitions, and omissions are errors we discussed earlier and are scored identically to the errors of the same name on the Gray Oral Reading Test. Errors counted as gross mispronunciations and partial mispronunciations in the Gray are grouped into the category of "mispronunciations" on the Gilmore.

Errors scored as disregard of punctuation on the Gilmore consist of failures to observe punctuation, while a hesitation error is scored each time the pupil hesitates for at least two seconds before pronouncing a word. Whereas repetitions of words or phrases to correct other kinds of errors were counted as repetition errors in the Gray Oral, they do not count as repetition errors in the Gilmore. According to the Gilmore manual, a pupil who immediately corrects an error does not erase the error. The error is still counted.

There are quite obvious differences in the kinds of errors scored on the Gray and the Gilmore. It is imperative, therefore, that in using and interpreting the two tests the teacher look beyond the grade scores earned to note the kinds of errors the pupil has made.

Scores

Two kinds of scores, grade scores and performance ratings, are provided by the Gilmore. The student earns both grade scores and performance ratings (poor, below average, average, above average, and superior) for accuracy and comprehension. Performance ratings for accuracy and comprehension are based on stanines as shown in Table 17.2. Rate of reading is scored as slow, average, or fast. Within each grade, those whose rate of reading is within the top quartile are designated as fast readers, those in the bottom quartile as slow readers, and those in the two middle quartiles as average.

As in the Gray Oral Reading Test, grade scores—and in this case performance ratings, too—are global scores. The information of most use in designing programs of instruction is provided by the systematic analysis of errors in oral reading.

Norms

Standardization of the Gilmore was completed in 1967 in eighteen schools in six school sys-

TABLE 17.3 Alternate-Form Reliability Data for the Gilmore Oral Reading Test

Grade	N	Accuracy	Comprehension	Rate
3	51	.94	.60	.70
6	55	.84	.53	.54

tems selected to include students from a variety of socioeconomic backgrounds. The total normative sample included 4,455 pupils in grades 1 through 8. Form C was administered to 2,246 students, while form D was given to 2,209 students. There are no data in the test manual on the sex, ethnic background, or reading curriculum of the students in the normative sample.

Reliability

The only reliability data reported in the test manual are alternate-form reliabilities for fifty-one students in grade 3 and fifty-five students in grade 6. Reliabilities are reported in Table 17.3. There are no data on test-retest reliability for the Gilmore Oral Reading Test.

Validity

No validity was established for the current Gilmore. There are validity data in the manual, but these data are for an earlier edition (Form A) of the test.

Summary

The Gilmore Oral Reading Test is an individually administered test designed to assess oral reading skills, reading comprehension, and rate of reading. The student earns grade scores for accuracy and comprehension as well as performance ratings on all three scales.

The test was standardized on 4,455 children, who are inadequately described in the manual. Reliability data consist of alternate-form coefficients, all but one of which are considerably lower than the .90 standard. There are no data reported in the manual regarding the validity of forms C and D. The Gilmore Oral Reading Test may provide the experienced examiner with diagnostic information with which to construct instructional hypotheses. Its technical characteristics are such that one must use it with caution.

DIAGNOSTIC READING TESTS

Gates-McKillop-Horowitz Reading Diagnostic Tests

The Gates-McKillop-Horowitz Reading Diagnostic Tests (Gates, McKillop, & Horowitz, 1981) are a revision of the Gates-McKillop Reading Diagnostic Tests (Gates & McKillop, 1962). The tests consist of a battery of fourteen individually administered subtests and parts of subtests designed to assess skill development in reading. The tests are used with students in grades 1 through 6. No set battery of subtests must be given to each child; rather, the examiner is to select those measures thought necessary.

The manual for the Gates-McKillop-Horo-witz states no specific qualifications as necessary for administering the tests. Most subtests are easy enough for a classroom teacher with little testing experience to administer. Scoring and interpretation, are, however, complex and difficult for even the most experienced examiner.

Behaviors sampled by the tests follow.

Oral Reading The Oral Reading subtest of the Gates-McKillop-Horowitz is like the Gray and Gilmore oral reading tests. The errors recorded for this subtest include hesitations, omissions, additions, repetitions, and mispronunciations. Mispronunciations are scored in terms of the kind of error made, including directional errors (inversions), words with wrong beginnings, wrong middles, or wrong endings, words wrong in several parts, and accent errors.

Words: Flash This subtest purports to assess sight vocabulary. A cardboard tachistoscope is provided to the examiner to use to expose single words for one-half second. The student reads the words aloud.

Words: Untimed This subtest is said to be a measure of word-attack skills. The student is required to read words without time restriction.

Knowledge of Word Parts: Word Attack This subtest has six parts, all assessing skill development in word attack:

1. *Syllabication* The pupil is shown nonsense words divided into syllables and is asked to read the words aloud. The examiner records errors phonetically.
2. *Recognizing and Blending Common Word Parts* This part of the subtest is complex, both in administration and in scoring. The examiner asks the student to read nonsense words like *drack* and *glebe*. When the child reads a nonsense word incorrectly, the word is presented in two parts ("dr-ack") and the pupil is requested to pronounce the parts and to blend them to pronounce the nonsense word.
3. *Reading Words* The student is shown nonsense words and required to read them. The examiner records errors phonetically.
4. *Giving Letter Sounds* The pupil is shown letters and asked to give their sounds.
5. *Naming Capital Letters* The student is shown capital letters and asked to name them.

6. *Naming Lower-Case Letters* The student is shown lower-case letters and asked to name them.

Recognizing the Visual Form of Sounds This subtest contains one part called Vowels. The examiner reads nonsense words and the student is asked to identify the vowel that produces the vowel sound in each word.

Auditory Blending The examiner pronounces words part by part: "z-ip." The child must blend the parts to say the word.

Auditory Discrimination This subtest assesses skill in discriminating among common English phonemes.

Written Expression Two measures compose the Written Expression subtest:

1. *Spelling* The student writes words dictated by the examiner.
2. *Informal Writing Sample* The child writes on any topic. There are no formal criteria for scoring performance; rather, the examiner evaluates the pupil's performance on the basis of expression of ideas and handwriting.

Scores and Norms

A number of normative tables appear in the Gates-McKillop-Horowitz manual, but there is no information on the nature of the group on whom the test was standardized. Pupil performance is evaluated in two ways. For four subtests, grade scores are provided. These are, in turn, assigned a rating of high, medium, low, or very low relative to the student's grade. For the rest of the tests, there are no scoring standards. The authors simply provide guidelines for interpretation. Ratings for grade scores are based on the authors' opinion.

We commented earlier on the relative educational meaninglessness of scores that compare children to one another; transformed scores earned on the Gates-McKillop-Horowitz have little meaning. Normative comparisons provide very limited help in teachers' attempts to differentiate instruction. That process is further complicated by the use of grade scores—the kinds of scores that are most frequently misinterpreted. The value of the Gates-McKillop-Horowitz is limited to its clinical use. It may provide a skilled examiner with a sample of items that can be used to identify specific skill development strengths and weaknesses in reading; however, to accomplish this, the examiner will have to go beyond scores and look at performance on individual items.

Reliability

The authors report the results of two reliability studies. The first was completed on an unspecified group of twenty-seven students who took the Oral Reading subtest twice. Scores on the first administration correlated .94 with scores on the second administration. The other study was one of interscorer reliability. In our opinion, the reliability of this measure has not been established.

Validity

The authors report an investigation of the validity of the measure by correlating pupil performance on this test with performance on the Gates-McGinitie and the Metropolitan Achievement Tests. Only a range of coefficients is given (.68–.96) and the user is not told the number of coefficients for specific levels. The sample is not satisfactorily described. There is no evidence for the validity of the scale.

Summary

The Gates-McKillop-Horowitz Reading Diagnostic Tests are a widely used diagnostic instrument in spite of significant limitations. The manual provides normative tables without including a description of the population on whom the test was standardized. The many scores obtained on the tests are subject to misinterpretation. Evidence for reliability and validity is unsatisfactory.

Durrell Analysis of Reading Difficulty

The Durrell Analysis of Reading Difficulty (DARD) (Durrell & Catterson, 1980) is designed to assist diagnostic personnel in estimating general level of reading achievement and identifying specific strengths and weaknesses in reading. The test covers a range of reading ability from the nonreader or prereading level to the sixth-grade level. The 1980 edition of the test is the third edition in a series originally published in 1937.

The DARD is administered individually and is designed to be used by experienced teachers. The authors state that the administration of the test is best learned under the direction of a person who has had experience in analyzing and correcting reading difficulties. Test materials include a booklet of reading paragraphs to be used in the major subtests, a manual of directions, an individual record book, and a cardboard tachistoscope with accompanying test cards and word lists. Test administration takes about 30 to 90 minutes. The DARD samples several different reading and reading-related behaviors. The subtests and behaviors they sample follow.

Oral Reading   This subtest consists of eight paragraphs of increasing difficulty that the child is required to read aloud. The subtest is scored in much the same manner as the Gray, Gilmore, and the Oral Reading subtest of the Gates-McKillop-Horowitz. The child responds to literal comprehension questions following the reading of each paragraph.

Silent Reading   The Silent Reading subtest contains eight paragraphs of comparable difficulty to those in the Oral Reading subtest. The examiner tests and records voluntary memory (simple recall), prompted memory (responses to specific questions), and eye movement.

Listening Comprehension   The examiner reads the six paragraphs of this subtest aloud and asks specific comprehension questions. The most difficult paragraph in which the child misses no more than one comprehension question is identified, by grade and score, as the child's listening comprehension level.

Word Recognition and Word Analysis   This subtest contains several parts. The examiner uses a cardboard tachistoscope, exposing words for one-half second, to assess word-recognition skills. When the child reads a word unsuccessfully, the same word is presented in an untimed format. The student is then asked to name the letters seen and is given an opportunity to sound out the word.

Listening Vocabulary   This subtest contains the same words as those listed in the Word Recognition and Word Analysis subtest. The child must point to pictures to indicate an understanding of words read by the examiner. The examiner can compare performance on this subtest (a measure of words understood in speech) with performance on the Word Recognition and Word Analysis subtest (a measure of words understood in print).

Pronunciation of Word Elements   This subtest measures the child's skill in pronouncing sounds (letters, blends, digraphs, phonograms, and affixes) in isolation.

Spelling   This subtest measures the pupil's skill in writing and spelling correctly words read by the examiner.

Visual Memory of Words   The student is required to remember the visual pattern of words long enough to circle them (for students whose oral reading level is grade 3 or below) or to write them down.

Auditory Analysis of Words and Elements   The student is required to identify sounds in words (children whose oral reading is at or below third-grade level) or to spell words phonetically.

Prereading Phonics Abilities Inventories   Two new measures (syntax matching and identifying letter names in spoken words) have been added to three subtests—identifying phonemes, naming letters, and writing letters—from previous editions of the DARD. Together they form a measure of prereading abilities. These measures are designed to help evaluate prereading phonics skills necessary for success in learning to read.

Scores

Most subtests of the DARD provide raw scores that can be converted to grade scores. However, in interpreting pupil performance, the greatest emphasis is placed on the check list of instructional needs that follows each subtest. The comprehensive check lists are completed by the examiner following administration of each subtest.

Norms

The DARD was standardized on "carefully selected populations in six school systems in different geographic regions" (Durrell & Catterson, 1980, p. 8). The names of the school districts are listed in the test manual, but we know little more than that about the normative population. A total of 1,224 students participated in standardization of the test. Students were selected because they were enrolled in districts chosen by university personnel in graduate reading programs. The authors state that "factors such as language backgrounds, socioeconomic status, ethnic characteristics, and curriculum emphasis were taken into consideration in choosing the particular schools and classrooms from which the children were selected for testing" (p. 56).

Students in the six school districts were given the Metropolitan Achievement Tests. Forty children in each grade who earned average scores (4th, 5th, or 6th stanine) on the MAT were given the Durrell. The authors do not provide data on the sex, ages, socioeconomic status, or nature of reading curriculum for the standardization group.

Reliability

Reliability was assessed in several ways. For the Oral Reading and Silent Reading subtests, the authors correlated reading time for adjacent paragraphs. Correlations were .85 for oral reading and .80 for silent reading. These are not reliability data. What is needed is information on consistency over time on the same, similar, or parallel levels of passages. For each of the additional subtests, the authors computed internal consistency using the Kuder-Richardson 21 formula. Reliabilities ranged from .63 to .97.

Reliabilities exceeded .80 for eight of the thirteen subtests. No data are reported on test-retest reliability.

Validity

The section on validity in the DARD manual consists primarily of a discussion of the concept of validity, with little actual validity data presented. Initially, the authors make the case for expert opinion, stating that the device has been used and modified since 1937 and that the "stability of the content of the test from revision to revision attests to current professional confidence in its general validity." Stability of test content, of course, reflects only the fact that the authors have not made major changes in the test.

The authors do report one validity study. They correlated September measures of first-grade pupils' scores on the prereading inventory with their reading achievement at the end of first grade. Correlations ranged from "about .55" to "about .65." The authors do not say how many students participated in the study, they do not describe those who participated, they do not say what test was used to measure reading achievement.

Summary

The DARD is designed to assist classroom teachers delineate specific skill-development strengths and weaknesses in reading. As long as the examiner and user of the test data place little emphasis on scores obtained and look instead at the qualitative information afforded by the test, the results may be useful in making tentative hypotheses about the nature of a child's reading difficulties. The norm-referenced use of the test is hindered by inadequate standardization, absence of a description of the norm group, limited data on reliability, and limited validity.

Stanford Diagnostic Reading Test

The Stanford Diagnostic Reading Test (SDRT) (Karlsen, Madden, & Gardner, 1974, 1977) consists of a series of measures of specific reading skills. There are four overlapping levels of the test, with two parallel forms (A and B) at each level. Levels of the test are identified by color. The Red level is designed to be used at the end of grade 1, in grade 2, and with low-achieving pupils in grade 3 and succeeding grades, while the Green level is intended for use in grades 3 and 4 and with low-achieving pupils in grade 5 and succeeding grades. Children in grades 5 through 8 and low achievers in higher grades are assessed using the Brown level. The Blue level, also known as the SDRT III, was published before the other three (Karlsen, Madden, & Gardner, 1974) and is intended for use in grades 9 through 12. Whereas the diagnostic reading tests described thus far must be individually administered, the SDRT can be group administered by classroom teachers.

Four skill domains are sampled by the SDRT, though not all domains are sampled at all levels. Subtests and skill domains sampled are reported in Figure 17.3. Behaviors sampled by the subtests of the SDRT are as follows.

Auditory Vocabulary This subtest assesses skill in identifying synonyms of words read by the examiner. Initial items in the Red level require the child simply to associate words with pictures. The subtest is included at the Red, Green, and Brown levels of the SDRT.

Auditory Discrimination This subtest assesses skill in hearing similar and different sounds in words. At the Red level, the pupil must identify whether two words begin with or end with the same sound. The Green level assesses identification of similar and different beginning, middle, and ending sounds. The subtest is not included at the Brown and Blue levels.

Phonetic Analysis The Phonetic Analysis subtest assesses skill in identifying letter-sound relationships. Easier items assess skill in identifying letters that represent the beginning or ending sounds in words. More difficult items assess similar behaviors using both common and variant spellings of sounds. The subtest is included at all four levels.

Structural Analysis The Structural Analysis subtest is included only in the Green, Brown, and Blue levels. Behaviors sampled include the use of syllables, prefixes, root words, and blends. This subtest replaces the Syllabication and Blending subtests of the previous edition of the SDRT.

Word Reading The Red level of the SDRT includes a Word Reading subtest, which measures skill in word recognition. The child must identify which of several response words most closely represents a picture.

Reading Comprehension Behaviors sampled by this subtest vary at the different levels. At the Red level, the children must read sentences and identify the pictures that best represent what they have read; they must also complete sentences and paragraphs that use a modified cloze format.[1] At the Green level, two formats are used to assess comprehension: the modified cloze format and a paragraph-comprehension

---

1. The "cloze" procedure is a technique in which words are omitted from a sentence. To close the sentence correctly, the student must comprehend the story. Many programmed texts, for example, use a cloze format. The modified cloze format used in the SDRT gives the student a choice of several words. The following is an illustration:

Elephants are well known as animals that never forget. But Henry was a strange elephant who, unlike other elephants, always _____ things.

(a) wanted (b) forgot (c) remembered (d) liked

Decoding			
RED LEVEL	GREEN LEVEL	BROWN LEVEL	BLUE LEVEL (SDRT III)
TEST 2: Auditory Discrimination Consonant Sounds (24 items) Vowel Sounds (16 items) TEST 3: Phonetic Analysis Consonant Sounds (24 items) Vowel Sounds (16 items)	TEST 2: Auditory Discrimination Consonant Sounds (18 items) Vowel Sounds (18 items) TEST 3: Phonetic Analysis Consonant Sounds (18 items) Vowel Sounds (18 items) TEST 4: Structural Analysis Word Division (30 items) Blending (30 items)	TEST 3: Phonetic Analysis Consonant Sounds (18 items) Vowel Sounds (18 items) TEST 4: Structural Analysis Word Division (48 items) Blending (30 items)	TEST 3: Phonetic Analysis Consonant Sounds (15 items) Vowel Sounds (15 items) TEST 5: Structural Analysis Blending (24 items)

Vocabulary			
RED LEVEL	GREEN LEVEL	BROWN LEVEL	BLUE LEVEL (SDRT III)
TEST 1: Auditory Vocabulary (36 items)	TEST 1: Auditory Vocabulary (40 items)	TEST 1: Auditory Vocabulary (40 items)	TEST 2: Word Meaning (30 items) TEST 3: Word Parts (30 items)

Comprehension			
RED LEVEL	GREEN LEVEL	BROWN LEVEL	BLUE LEVEL (SDRT III)
TEST 4: Word Reading (42 items) TEST 5: Reading Comprehension Sentence Reading (32 items) Paragraph Comprehension (16 items)	TEST 5: Reading Comprehension Literal Comprehension (30 items) Inferential Comprehension (30 items)	TEST 2: Reading Comprehension Literal Comprehension (30 items) Inferential Comprehension (30 items)	TEST 1: Reading Comprehension Literal Comprehension (30 items) Inferential Comprehension (30 items)

Rate			
RED LEVEL	GREEN LEVEL	BROWN LEVEL	BLUE LEVEL (SDRT III)
		TEST 5: Reading Rate (34 items)	TEST 7: Fast Reading (30 items) TEST 6: Scanning and Skimming (32 items)

FIGURE 17.3   Subtests and skill domains of the Stanford Diagnostic Reading Test

format requiring literal comprehension of what has been read. The Brown and Blue levels assess both literal and inferential comprehension using a paragraph-reading format.

Rate   The subtest on rate of reading is included only at the Brown and Blue levels. It assesses skill in reading easy material quickly.

Scores

The SDRT is both norm-referenced and criterion-referenced. It can be used to assess a pupil's performance relative to the performance of others, and it can be used to pinpoint individual pupils' strengths and weaknesses in specific reading skills.

Students respond either directly in the test booklets or on machine-readable answer sheets. The test can, therefore, be either hand scored or machine scored. Six kinds of scores can be obtained; which scores are useful depends on the purpose for which the test has been administered.

Raw scores are obtained for each subtest and can be transformed to "Progress Indicators," percentile ranks, stanines, grade equivalents, and scaled scores. Progress Indicators are criterion-referenced scores, whereas the other four scores are norm-referenced. Progress Indicators are "+" or "−" indications as to whether a pupil achieved a predetermined cutoff score in a specific skill domain; they show whether a pupil demonstrates mastery of specific skills important to the various stages in the process of learning to read effectively. It is reported that

in setting the Progress Indicator cutoff scores, the SDRT authors were guided by the relative importance of the skills to the reading process, by the location of these skills in the developmental sequence of the reading process, and by the performance of pupils at different achievement levels on the items measur-

ing these skills. (Karlsen, Madden, & Gardner, 1977, p. 33)

The manual for each level of the SDRT includes an appendix that lists specific instructional objectives assessed by each level of the test.

The norm-referenced scores obtained by administering the SDRT can be used for a variety of purposes. The authors suggest that comparisons to national norms be made using percentile ranks, stanines, or grade equivalents. Detailed procedures for the use of stanines to group students for instructional purposes are included in the manuals. Scaled scores, because they are comparable across both grades and levels, are most useful in evaluating pupil growth and in interpreting the performance of pupils who are tested out of level (for example, the scores of a fifth grader who has taken the Red level).

Norms

In selecting the standardization sample for the SDRT, the authors used a stratified random-sampling technique. Socioeconomic status, school-system enrollment, and geographic region were the stratification variables. School-system data were obtained from the United States Office of Education's 1970 census tapes. The tapes were used to generate a random sample of 3,000 school districts. A composite socio-economic-status index for each system was determined by weighting family income twice and averaging it with the median years of parental schooling. Age and sex were not controlled in standardizing the SDRT.

Within each of the stratified cells, school districts were invited to participate in standardization of the test. A random sample of consenting districts within each cell was selected. The test was standardized in 55 school districts; approximately 31,000 pupils participated in the standardization. The manual includes detailed tables illustrating that the demographic characteristics of the school districts sampled closely parallel those indicated in the 1970 census.

Reliability

Two types of reliability information are available for the SDRT: reliability of raw scores and reliability of Progress Indicators. Reliability of raw scores earned on the test was ascertained by assessing both internal-consistency and alternate-form reliability. Internal-consistency coefficients for all subtests at all levels exceed .90 with the exception of coefficients for Auditory Vocabulary (these consistently range from .85 to .90). Alternate-form reliability coefficients range from .75 to .94. Standard errors of measurement in both raw-score and scaled-score units are tabled in the manuals.

The reliability of the Progress Indicators was determined by administering both forms to the same pupils and establishing each pupil's Progress Indicator on each form. Contingency tables provided in the manual enable the user to estimate the probability that a student would obtain a different Progress Indicator if she or he took the alternate form of the test. Data reported in the manuals indicate that the SDRT is a reliable measure of specific reading skills.

Validity

Limited space in the SDRT manuals is devoted to the issues of content validity and criterion-related validity. The authors state that the test's content validity, like the content validity of any other measure of academic achievement, must be based on an evaluation of the extent to which test content reflects local curricular content. Criterion-related validity was established by correlating performance on each of the SDRT subtests with performance on the reading subtests of the Stanford Achievement Test. These correlations range from .61 to .98 for the Red and Green levels, and from .39 to .94 for the Brown level.

Summary

The Stanford Diagnostic Reading Test is a group-administered device that is both norm- and criterion-referenced. The device was exceptionally well standardized and is reliable enough to be used in pinpointing specific domains of reading in which pupils demonstrate skill-development strengths and weaknesses. Validity for the SDRT, as for any achievement measure, must be judged relative to the content of local curricula.

Diagnostic Reading Scales

The Diagnostic Reading Scales (Spache, 1981) are a series of individually administered tests designed to provide standardized evaluations of oral and silent reading skills and of auditory comprehension. The tests consist of three lists of words to be recognized, twenty-two reading passages of graduated difficulty, and twelve supplementary word analysis and phonics tests. The scales can be used with students in grades 1 through 7 and, according to the author, with junior and senior high school students who are functioning below normal in reading.

The word lists are administered as an assessment of a child's skill in pronouncing words in isolation. According to the author, the word lists serve three purposes: to estimate the instructional level of reading, to reveal the child's methods of word attack and word analysis, and to evaluate sight vocabulary. The reading passages are used to assess literal and inferential comprehension of material read orally or silently by the child and of material read to the child. The author states that the passages are useful in identifying suitable reading material for the student and in determining the nature and extent of a student's reading errors and the student's reading speed and reading potential.

The twelve word analysis and phonics tests are: initial consonants, final consonants, consonant digraphs, consonant blends, initial consonant substitution, initial consonant sounds recognized auditorily, auditory discrimination, short and long vowel sounds, vowels with *r*, vowel diphthongs and digraphs, common syllables, and blending. The subtests are designed to give the examiner a detailed analysis of phonic knowledge and word analysis skills. Total administration time for the Diagnostic Reading Scales is about 60 minutes and all student responses are oral.

Scores

The word lists are administered to determine which of the several reading passages should be used as a starting point for the assessment of oral, silent, and auditory comprehension skills. The author states that on the basis of a child's score in oral reading the teacher can ascertain the child's instructional level, that is, the level at which instruction in reading should be given. Performance in comprehension of passages read silently is used to ascertain the child's independent level, the grade level at which the child can read recreational and supplementary reading materials. Performance in auditory comprehension is used as an assessment of the child's "potential reading level."

As is the case with most diagnostic reading tests, the most valuable information is obtained by careful analysis of the kinds of errors the child makes in oral reading and on the six supplementary subtests.

Norms

The Diagnostic Reading Scales were originally standardized in 1963 on an unspecified population of students. The test was revised in 1972 and again in 1981. As part of each revision the author conducted a study and used results of pupil performance to rearrange the items on the test. The 1981 version of the Diagnostic Reading Scales is not identical to the 1963 edition. As part of revising the scale, in 1981 the test was given to a sample of 534 students. The norm group is not described sufficiently in the manual.

In a section of the manual entitled "Validity," the author describes 534 students. He says that the students attended grades 1 through 8 in sixty-six school districts in thirty-two states, that there were approximately equal numbers of males and females, and a representative number of black and Hispanic students. The norms are not described in such a way as to enable a user to know the nature of those to whom an examinee is being compared.

Reliability

Data on reliability of the Diagnostic Reading Scales are reported in a separate technical manual. With minor exceptions, reliability data are on earlier versions of the test. The author does say that alternate-form reliabilities were computed on an unspecified number of students in grades 1 through 8. He does not report correlation coefficients by grade level, but says they averaged .89.

Data on test-retest reliability are reported only for grades 1 and 2, and only for the word analysis and phonics subtests. Data are on an unspecified number of students. Correlation coefficients ranged from .09 (initial consonant sounds recognized auditorily) to .93. Only half of the twenty-four coefficients exceed .80.

Data on internal consistency are reported

only for an unspecified number of students in grades 1 and 2. All but three of the twenty-four coefficients reported exceed .80. No data on reliability are reported for students in upper grades. The author argues that these students earn a ceiling too easily.

Validity

Much space in the technical manual is devoted to a discussion of validity. Again, though, nearly all data reported are on the 1963 and 1972 editions of the test. One validity study is reported on the 1981 scale. The author reports that test scores are higher with increases in grade level, teacher estimates of reading level, level of classroom reader, and scores on reading tests. The latter information is derived from a number of different reading tests. Data on validity are not convincing. The author reports that

the sample on whom validity and reliability data were based included far more older than younger students and an excessive number of cases scoring at the high end of the scale.

Summary

The Diagnostic Reading Scales are an individually administered series of scales designed to assess oral and silent reading skills and auditory comprehension. The manual includes normative tables, but it does not provide an adequate description of the nature of the group on whom the test was standardized. A separate technical manual includes data on reliability and validity, though most of this information is on earlier versions of the test. Evidence for the technical adequacy of the 1981 scales is very limited. At best, the scales are useful for screening purposes.

Woodcock Reading Mastery Tests

The Woodcock Reading Mastery Tests (Woodcock, 1973) are a battery of five individually administered tests used to assess skill development in reading with students in kindergarten through grade 12. The complete materials for the test are contained in an easel kit similar to the easel kit illustrated earlier for the Peabody Individual Achievement Test (Figure 16.2). There are two alternate forms of the battery, each of which can be administered in 20 to 30 minutes. The five subtests and the behaviors they sample follow.

Letter Identification   Assesses skill in naming letters of the alphabet. Assesses identification of both manuscript and cursive letters.

Word Identification   Assesses ability to pronounce words in isolation.

Word Attack   Assesses ability to use phonic and structural analysis skills in the identification of nonsense words.

Word Comprehension   Assesses knowledge of word meaning.

Passage Comprehension   Uses a modified cloze procedure in which the student's task is to read silently a passage that has a word missing and then tell the examiner an appropriate word to fill the blank space.

Scores

Raw scores for subtests of the Woodcock Reading Mastery Tests can be converted to grade scores, age scores, percentile ranks, and standard scores. Separate scores are earned in each of the subtests, and the test also provides a total score for reading based on a combination of the performances on the five subtests. Although the author states that the total score is the most reliable index of skill development in reading, it must be remembered that the total score is a global, undifferentiated score based on an average of several different kinds of behavior samplings.

In addition to the more traditional scores, the Woodcock provides "mastery scores." The author states that

the Mastery Scale is an equal interval scale that directly reflects changes in an individual's proficiency with a task. Any given difference between two points on the Mastery Scale has the same meaning at any level and in any of the five skill areas measured by the test. (p. 28)

Tables in the test manual facilitate conversion of raw scores to mastery scores. Essentially, the purpose of the mastery score is to provide an index of a student's reading proficiency at different levels of difficulty. A student may be reading at a fourth-grade level with 75 percent accuracy while reading third-grade material with 96 percent accuracy.

By using a Mastery Scale, the examiner can chart an individual's range of reading behaviors, from the level at which the student reads with ease to the level at which he or she fails to read.

Norms

The standardization of the Woodcock took place over a two-year period in fifty school districts throughout the United States. A total of 5,252 subjects in kindergarten through grade 12 were tested. The manual includes a detailed description of the normative sample in terms of community size, race, years of schooling, occupation, and income. The sample appears to be representative of the U.S. population, and in those cases where it is not, the author clearly

says so. The normative sample and its description in the test manual are superior to those of other norm-referenced diagnostic reading tests.

Reliability

Two kinds of reliability data are included in the Woodcock manual. The author reports split-half reliabilities for forms A and B for second-grade and seventh-grade populations. Alternate-form test-retest data are reported for three second-grade and three seventh-grade classes. Split-half reliability coefficients are reported for a prepublication form of the test, but because this form differs from either form A or B, the data have limited meaning. Split-half reliability coefficients for forms A and B are summarized in Table 17.4, while alternate-form test-retest reliability coefficients are reported in Table 17.5. Reliability for the test is lower in grade 7 than in grade 2. The extremely low reliabilities reported for the Letter Identification subtest at grade 7 are the result of most students' correctly identifying all letters.

In view of the reliability standards suggested in Chapter 7, some subtests of the Woodcock Reading Mastery Tests must be used with a degree of caution.

Validity

Data regarding content validity, construct validity, and predictive validity are reported in the Woodcock manual. Evidence for content validity, as in most diagnostic tests, is based on the procedures used to select test items. The author states that items were selected to assess identification, word attack, and comprehension.

The test author uses a sophisticated statistical procedure for establishing construct validity, the multitrait-multimethod matrix (Campbell & Fiske, 1959). Not only was this method overly sophisticated for the purpose of establishing validity, but, as the author states, the use of the

TABLE 17.4 Split-half Reliabilities for Subtests of the Woodcock Reading Mastery Tests

	Grade Level (Test Form)			
	2.9 (A)	2.9 (B)	7.9 (A)	7.9 (B)
Letter Identification	.79	.86	.02	.20
Word Identification	.99	.98	.96	.97
Word Attack	.97	.98	.94	.94
Word Comprehension	.88	.93	.86	.83
Passage Comprehension	.95	.93	.93	.93
Total Reading	.99	.99	.98	.98

SOURCE: From table 7 (p. 57) in *Woodcock Reading Mastery Test* by R. W. Woodcock, 1973, Circle Pines, Minn.: American Guidance Service. Adapted by permission of American Guidance Service, Inc.

procedure may well overestimate the validity of the separate tests.

Intercorrelations between subtests of the Woodcock range from −.04 to .92 depending on both the subtests considered and the grade level of the population of concern.[2] The intercorrelations are highly variant, but this is expected, given the hierarchical nature of the development of reading skills.

Predictive validity for the Woodcock was established by predicting performance on an alternate form of the test from scores on the first form. Using test-retest data on 205 subjects, the author was able to predict with from 30 to 80 percent accuracy the scores on an alternate form of the test. These are reliability, not validity, data.

Summary

The Woodcock Reading Mastery Tests are an individually administered battery of tests used to assess skill development in five areas. The author states that the tests can be used in either a norm-referenced or a criterion-referenced

2. Subtest intercorrelations, in general, range from .35 to .92. The lower intercorrelations all include the Letter Identification subtest at grade 7, a grade at which most students demonstrate 100 percent mastery of the task.

manner. The test was adequately standardized and provides both traditional scores and mastery ratings. The Mastery Scale, a unique feature of the Woodcock, provides an index of a student's reading proficiency at different levels of difficulty. For instance, a student may show 75 percent mastery of fourth-grade material and 96 percent mastery of third-grade material.

Reliability data are limited, and the reliability of specific subtests is below desirable standards. The author has gone to great lengths to demonstrate the validity of the tests.

TABLE 17.5 Alternate-Form Test-Retest Reliabilities for the Woodcock Reading Mastery Tests

	Grade Level (Test Sample Size)	
	2.9 (103)	7.9 (102)
Letter Identification	.84	.16
Word Identification	.94	.93
Word Attack	.90	.85
Word Comprehension	.90	.68
Passage Comprehension	.88	.78
Total Reading	.87	.83

SOURCE: From *Woodcock Reading Mastery Test* (p. 58) by R. W. Woodcock, 1973, Circle Pines, Minn.: American Guidance Service. Reprinted by permission of American Guidance Service, Inc.

The Woodcock Reading Mastery Tests provide diagnostic data that may help a classroom teacher pinpoint skill-development strengths and weaknesses in order to plan remedial programs. How much the test can help in doing so depends largely on the interpretative skill of the individual classroom teacher.

CRITERION-REFERENCED DIAGNOSTIC TESTING IN READING

The tests we have discussed to this point are norm-referenced tests, which are designed to provide diagnostic data and compare individuals to their peers. Criterion-referenced diagnostic testing in reading is a relatively new practice, dating from the late 1960s. Criterion-referenced diagnostic reading tests are designed to analyze systematically an individual's strengths and weaknesses without comparing that individual to others. The principle objective of criterion-referenced tests is to assess the specific skills a pupil does and does not have and to relate the assessment to curricular content. Criterion-referenced assessment is tied to instructional objectives, and individual items are designed to assess mastery of specific objectives.

While all criterion-referenced reading tests are based on task analyses of reading, the particular skills assessed and their sequences differ from test to test. This is because different authors view reading in different ways and see the sequence of development of reading skills differently. For this reason, it is especially important with criterion-referenced tests, as with norm-referenced tests, that teachers pay special attention to the behaviors and sequences of behaviors sampled by the tests.

Because normative comparisons are not made in criterion-referenced assessment, no derived scores are calculated. For that reason, many authors of criterion-referenced tests downplay the importance of reliability for their scales. But reliable assessment *is* important in criterion-referenced assessment. For criterion-referenced tests we are not concerned with the consistency of derived scores. We are concerned with the consistency of responses to items when all items in the domain are assessed. If a different pattern of item scores is obtained each time an individual takes the test, we begin to question the reliability of the device. Because criterion-referenced devices generally contain relatively limited samples of behavior, it is important that test authors report the consistency with which their tests assess each specific behavior. Test authors *can* and should report test-retest reliabilities for each item. We are concerned with the consistency with which the test samples the domain of possible test items when the domain is not exhausted. When alternate forms of a criterion-referenced test are available, the authors should report correlations between performances on the two forms.

Most currently available criterion-referenced reading tests are part of entire reading systems. The remainder of this chapter looks at four criterion-referenced reading systems: Diagnosis, Criterion Reading, the Fountain Valley Teacher Support System in Reading, and the Prescriptive Reading Inventory.

Diagnosis: An Instructional Aid

Diagnosis: An Instructional Aid (Shub, Carlin, Friedman, Kaplan, & Katien, 1973) is designed both to assess specific reading skills and to assist the classroom teacher in the systematic planning of appropriate instruction. There are two levels of Diagnosis: level A, which is appropriate for those whose reading skills are at a kindergarten to third-grade level, and level B, which is appropriate for those whose skill development in reading is at a fourth- to sixth-grade level. Each level contains a number of specific components including survey tests, probes, cassettes, a prescription guide, and a class progress chart. Each level is called a classroom laboratory. The heart of the diagnostic-instructional system is the set of thirty-four probes, each a criterion-referenced diagnostic test. Each of the items in the probes is related specifically to instructional objectives. The thirty-four probes measure skill in phonetic analysis (letter recognition, consonant identification, blends and vowels), structural analysis (compound words, contractions, prefixes, suffixes, and so on), comprehension, vocabulary, and use of sources (alphabetizing, dictionary use, and so on). Each area assessed is subdivided into specific skills.

The procedures employed in using Diagnosis are illustrated in Figure 17.4. The teacher begins systematic instructional planning for an individual student by administering a survey test, which assesses, in a limited fashion, the development of specific reading skills. The survey test is scored by a key in the teacher's handbook, and the results provide a global overview of strengths and weaknesses in reading. From results of the survey test the teacher or other examiner determines which of the

thirty-four probes should be administered. The probes are self-scoring, and each item administered is paired with a specific instructional objective. Once the particular pattern of a child's performance is known, instructional objectives appropriate for the child are provided.

The program does not quit at this point. Teachers frequently complain that even when they have written or have been provided with an instructional objective, they do not know what materials to use or how to teach to the objective. Diagnosis provides a prescription guide with each of the specific objectives cross-referenced to six basal reading programs: Ginn; Harper and Row; Houghton Mifflin; Scott, Foresman (the New Basic Reading Program and the Open Highways Program); Macmillan; and Science Research Associates. The prescription guide identifies the pages in the teacher's manual for a given series that tell how to teach to a particular objective, the specific pages in the series that teach to that objective, and appropriate spirit masters to use (see Figure 17.5).

The classroom teacher (or other examiner, for that matter) administers a survey test to learn what skills need to be further assessed by the use of probes. One or more probes are given, and the child's performance enables the teacher to pinpoint skill-development strengths and weaknesses and to specify instructional objectives relevant to skill development. The teacher uses the prescription guide to suggest appropriate materials and then, after teaching to a specific objective, readministers the probe to ascertain the extent to which the child has achieved the objective.

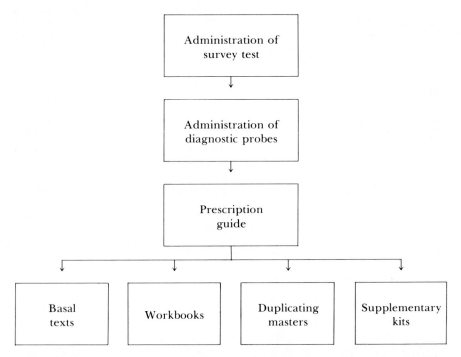

FIGURE 17.4   Flow chart of activities in using Diagnosis: An Instructional Aid
SOURCE: From Diagnosis: An Instructional Aid—Reading, Level 1, Teacher's Handbook.
© 1973, Science Research Associates, Inc. Reprinted by permission.

Scores and Norms

No norm-referenced scores are obtained by administering Diagnosis. The system is comprehensive, based on a task analysis of reading skills in kindergarten through grade 6. The student is not compared to others; the emphasis is on subject-matter content mastered. There are, for that reason, no norms for the test.

Reliability and Validity

No reliability data are reported for Diagnosis. There are two alternate forms of the survey test, both of which provide relatively limited samples of behavior. Alternate-form reliabilities are not reported. We advise that the examiner administer both forms of the survey test to increase reliability.

At the lower levels, the probes are pretty ex-

haustive, in many cases sampling the entire domain of behaviors. In assessing skill in naming lower-case letters, for example, skill in naming *all* lower-case letters is assessed. At the upper levels, behavior sampling is necessarily more limited.

Validity for Diagnosis is based on expert opinion. As is the case with any criterion-referenced system, the skills assessed and the sequence in which they are assessed depend on the authors' viewpoints about reading.

Summary

Diagnosis: An Instructional Aid is a criterion-referenced system used to assess skill-development strengths and weaknesses in reading. Use of the system allows teachers to assess specific skill-development weaknesses, the program pro-

PHONETIC ANALYSIS
Initial Consonants

Index Code	Teaching Guide	Workbook	Spirit Masters
2-Q	A: 25–41, 50–57, 74–102 B: 16–66	A: 6–17, 24–30, 45–72 B: 1–62	A: 3–8, 12–15, 24–43 B: 1–32

Medial Consonants

Index Code	Teaching Guide	Workbook	Spirit Masters
3-A	E: 16–33	E: 1–10	E: 1–6
3-B			
3-C	E: 16–33	E: 1–10	E: 1–6
3-D	E: 16–33	E: 1–10	E: 1–6
3-E	E: 16–33	E: 1–10	E: 1–6
3-F	E: 16–33	E: 1–10	E: 1–6
3-G	E: 16–33	E: 1–10	E: 1–6
3-H	E: 16–33	E: 1–10	E: 1–6
3-I	E: 16–33	E: 1–10	E: 1–6
3-J	E: 16–33	E: 1–10	E: 1–6
3-K	E: 16–33	E: 1–10	E: 1–6

Final Consonants and Blends

Index Code	Teaching Guide	Workbook	Spirit Masters
4-A	A: 58–65, 117–121 B: 54–66	A: 31–37, 87–94 B: 47–62	A: 16–19, 53–56 B: 25–32
4-B	B: 83–96	B: 79–94	B: 41–48
4-C			
4-D	A: 15–32, 88–95 B: 40–53	A: 1–11, 59–65 B: 31–46	A: 1–5, 34–38 B: 17–24
4-E	A: 74–80 B: 67–82	A: 45–51 B: 63–78	A: 24–28 B: 33–40
4-F	A: 50–57, 81–87 B: 16–28	A: 24–30, 52–58 B: 1–15	A: 12–15, 29–33 B: 1–8
4-G			
4-H	A: 66–73, 110–116 B: 67–82	A: 38–44, 80–86 B: 63–78	A: 20–23, 48–52 B: 33–40

PHONETIC ANALYSIS
Final Consonants and Blends

Index Code	Teaching Guide	Workbook	Spirit Masters
4-I	A: 33–41, 103–109 B: 54–66	A: 12–17, 73–79 B: 47–62	A: 6–8, 44–47 B: 25–32
4-J	A: 74–80	A: 45–51	A: 24–28
4-K	C: 61–70	C: 42–51	C: 29–35
4-L	C: 49–60	C: 32–41	C: 22–28
4-M	C: 38–48	C: 22–31	C: 15–21
4-N	C: 38–48	C: 22–31	C: 15–21
4-O	C: 40–61	C: 17–31	C: 12–21
4-P	C: 49–60	C: 32–41	C: 22–28

Consonant Blends I

Index Code	Teaching Guide	Workbook	Spirit Masters
5-A	C: 71–84, 114–138	C: 52–61, 84–94	C: 36–42, 57–63
5-B	C: 71–84, 114–138	C: 52–61, 84–94	C: 36–42, 57–63
5-C	C: 71–84, 114–138	C: 52–61, 84–94	C: 36–42, 57–63
5-D	C: 71–84, 114–138	C: 52–61, 84–94	C: 36–42, 57–63
5-E	C: 71–84, 114–138	C: 52–61, 84–94	C: 36–42, 57–63
5-F	C: 71–84, 114–138	C: 52–61, 84–94	C: 36–42, 57–63
5-G	C: 97–138	C: 73–94	C: 50–63
5-H	C: 97–138	C: 73–94	C: 50–63
5-I	C: 97–138	C: 73–94	C: 50–63
5-J	C: 97–113	C: 73–83	C: 50–56
5-K	C: 97–138	C: 73–94	C: 50–63
5-L			
5-M	C: 97–138	C: 73–94	C: 50–63

Consonant Blends II

Index Code	Teaching Guide	Workbook	Spirit Masters
6-A	C: 85–96, 114–138	C: 62–72, 84–94	C: 43–49, 57–63
6-B	C: 85–96, 114–138	C: 62–72, 84–94	C: 43–49, 57–63
6-C	C: 85–96, 114–138	C: 62–72, 84–94	C: 43–49, 57–63

FIGURE 17.5 Sample of prescription guide page correlating learning objective 5-A with the SRA Basic Reading Program

SOURCE: From Diagnosis: An Instructional Aid—Reading, Level 1, Teacher's Handbook. © 1973, Science Research Associates, Inc. Reprinted by permission.

vides instructional objectives, and the prescription guide can be used to select materials to teach to the objectives.

The use of criterion-referenced diagnostic devices such as Diagnosis enables the classroom teacher to go about individualized reading instruction in a very systematic manner. Much of the hit-or-miss of norm-referenced approaches is avoided, producing considerably more efficiency in assessment.

Criterion Reading

Criterion Reading (Hackett, 1971) is both a diagnostic system designed to assess skill-development strengths and weaknesses in reading and a learning-management system designed to facilitate systematic individualized instruction in reading. The system is criterion-referenced to a hierarchy of 450 reading skills that are divided into five levels and tied to eight areas of competence. The self-contained system provides pupil workbooks; it is not cross-referenced to basal readers.

Criterion Reading has its basis in a task analysis of reading, provides performance objectives for each specific reading skill, and provides tests to assess mastery of the performance objectives. The system is appropriate for use from kindergarten through junior high school and may be used in adult basic education courses.

Eight areas of competence are assessed in Criterion Reading. These are described by the author as follows.

Motor Skills Skills in such motor activities as holding a pencil, tying a shoelace, and walking on a balance beam are assessed.

Visual Input—Motor Response Competence in matching symbols, objects, and colors is assessed.

Auditory Input—Motor Response Competence in such skills as matching beginning sounds and repeating initial consonants is assessed.

Phonology Skill development in identifying, classifying, using, and producing alphabet-letter names, consonants, vowels, and their combinations is assessed.

Structural Analysis Competence in such skills as classifying singular possessive nouns, using rules for forming singulars and plurals, and using rules to divide words into syllables is assessed.

Verbal Information Identification, classification, use, and production of concepts and facts are assessed.

Syntax Skill development in classification of verbs, subject-predicate function, and the use of rules for sentence punctuation is assessed.

Comprehension Competence in analyzing, synthesizing, and evaluating language is assessed.

The first three competence areas listed above are assessed only at level I of Criterion Reading and generally pertain only to children in kindergarten and grade 1.

The use of Criterion Reading involves several procedures. The examiner administers one or more of the major tests assessing diagnostic outcome skills. The examiner continues to administer diagnostic outcome tests until the student encounters difficulty. The student is assessed using measures of "process skills" related to the diagnostic outcome tests that she or he has failed. In this way, diagnosis of the nature of the student's skill development in reading becomes increasingly refined. Figure 17.6 illustrates the hierarchy of activities in Criterion Reading.

Figure 17.7 illustrates that reading is assessed and taught in terms of pupil mastery of certain motor, listening/speaking, reading, and writing skills. Areas of competence are spelled out and each student's competence is assessed using measures of diagnostic outcome skills. For each diagnostic outcome skill there are a number of process skills, essentially related to enabling objectives. Having assessed a student using measures of the enabling objectives, the teacher knows to what extent the student demonstrates specific skill competencies. The program provides specific instructional objectives and includes workbooks designed to help the student achieve those objectives. Objectives are written in such a way that the behaviors can be observed. For example, the examiner can observe that, given rows of consonants, the student identifies initial single-consonant sounds with 95 percent accuracy.

The absence of a survey test for Criterion Reading means that teachers or other examiners have to spend considerable time assessing indi-

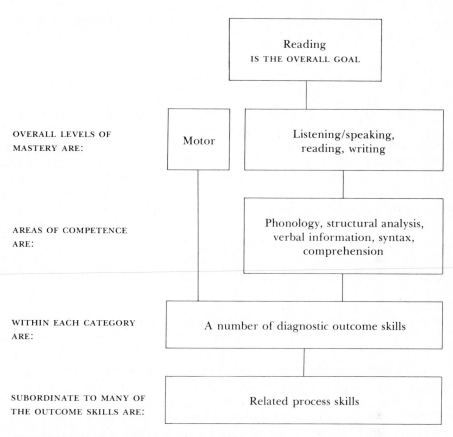

OVERALL LEVELS OF
MASTERY ARE:

AREAS OF COMPETENCE
ARE:

WITHIN EACH CATEGORY
ARE:

SUBORDINATE TO MANY OF
THE OUTCOME SKILLS ARE:

FIGURE 17.6   The Criterion Reading hierarchy
SOURCE: Redrawn from *Criterion Reading Teacher's Guide* (p. 10) by M. G. Hackett, 1971, New York: Random House, Inc. Copyright 1971 by Random House, Inc. Used by permission.

vidual children. Teachers must use their own judgment in deciding where to start with a particular child. The administration of each diagnostic outcome test (there are a total of twenty-three) takes about 20 minutes. If teachers misjudge the starting point, then assessment can take an inordinately long time.

Scores and Norms

Diagnostic Outcome Assessments are scored by students for the most part. For very young children, the teacher must score the Diagnostic Outcome Assessments, but since 95 percent

mastery is required and because most Diagnostic Outcome Assessments have twenty or fewer items, the scoring is pretty much pass-fail.

Criterion Reading is a criterion-referenced system and for that reason no traditional norm-referenced scores are obtained. The student is not compared to others in a normative sense.

Reliability and Validity

As is the case for most criterion-referenced devices and systems, there are no data regarding reliability and validity. There is an extensive listing of skills in the manual, and individual teachers will have to use their own judgment to decide whether the program is appropriate for specific uses.

Summary

Criterion Reading is an individualized, performance-based, criterion-referenced reading program designed to facilitate assessment of skill-development strengths and weaknesses in reading. The program is structured around 450 specific reading skills and includes a series of Diagnostic Outcome Assessments to assess mastery of the skills. While Criterion Reading has possibilities, and while the major objective of the program is a noble one, the program at this time is probably too complex for the average school system to adopt.

Criterion Reading is a very expensive program. It is doubtful that a school system could afford to adopt the program on a mass basis without considerable expense in both materials and time necessary to conduct in-service training sessions for teachers.

Criterion Reading is a refreshing switch from the typical norm-referenced test. It provides specific direction as opposed to simple scores. The system appears to be embryonic; yet it should be of considerable use to remedial specialists.

Fountain Valley Teacher Support System in Reading

The Fountain Valley Teacher Support System in Reading (Zweig, 1971) consists of seventy-seven separate self-scoring criterion-referenced tests measuring 367 behavioral objectives in reading. Fountain Valley is more than a series of tests, however, as it includes continuous pupil profiles designed to keep a record of individual pupil achievement and a cross-referenced prescription guide designed to help the teacher locate the pages in specific basal reading series appropriate to teaching to the instructional objectives.

Reading skills are evaluated in five areas: phonetic analysis, structural analysis, vocabulary development, comprehension, and study skills. The tests are arranged in order of difficulty and are color coded. Students may take the tests independently, in small groups, or as total classes.

Scores and Norms

Because Fountain Valley is a criterion-referenced system, there are no scores and no norms. After taking the criterion-referenced tests, the student has either passed or failed items related to specific instructional objectives. Rather than providing the teacher with certain scores such as grade scores, age scores, or percentiles, the system facilitates delineation of specific skill-development strengths and weaknesses in reading.

Reliability and Validity

Since Fountain Valley is a criterion-referenced system, there are no data about reliability and validity in the test manual. The tests provide relatively limited samples of specific reading behaviors, so test results must be interpreted cautiously. Validity of the system is based largely on expert opinion, but the system is flexible enough that teachers can adjust the sequence of objectives to fit the idiosyncrasies of nearly any classroom arrangement or instructional system.

Summary

The Fountain Valley Teacher Support System in Reading is designed to provide teachers with more than test scores. By using the criterion-referenced tests, classroom teachers, school psychologists, resource teachers, and other examiners can pinpoint where a student stands in the developmental sequence of reading. It enables teachers to pinpoint appropriate instructional objectives and to select from a variety of sources the particular methods, materials, and teaching strategies they want to use. The pupil record form enables teachers to monitor individual pupil progress and thus to engage in systematic instruction. The system is both diagnostic and prescriptive.

Prescriptive Reading Inventory

The Prescriptive Reading Inventory (CTB/McGraw-Hill, 1972) is a criterion-referenced test designed as an inventory of desired reading behaviors at the elementary school level. According to its developers, the PRI measures mastery or nonmastery of specific reading objectives "typical of reading curricula across the nation." The PRI consists of 568 items measuring mastery of ninety objectives at four levels. Some objectives are assessed at successive levels; hence a total of 155 objectives are assessed. The four levels of the PRI, each used to assess reading objectives appropriate to a range of age and grade levels, are listed in Table 17.6 along with the number of items and objectives at each level.

Two prereading measures, identified as Levels I and II, are included in the PRI. These test skill development in auditory and visual discrimination, alphabet knowledge, language experience, comprehension, attention skills, and initial reading. Specific skill areas assessed by levels A through D include sound and symbol recognition, phonic analysis, structural analysis, translation, and literal, interpretive, and critical comprehension.

Development of the PRI followed a careful sequence of activities. The publisher initially employed a staff of reading specialists who wrote 1,248 objectives based on a study of the five most widely used reading series. Then, to avoid having a very long, unmanageable test, they selected objectives that were introduced in a minimum of three of the five reading series across pairs of grade levels; they omitted objectives that could not be measured by a paper-and-pencil test, that required a vocabulary higher than the test level at which they were included, that would be affected by regional pronunciations, that were subsumed by or implicit in other objectives, or that were more appropriately in the language-arts domain. Following these editorial activities, from three to twenty items were developed to measure mastery of the remaining 220 objectives, and the test was field-tested on an unspecified national sample of 18,000 students in grades 1 through 6. Selection of the final test followed this field testing.

Scores and Norms

Traditional derived scores such as grade equivalents and age scores are not provided for the PRI. Because the device is criterion-referenced, scores consist of relatively detailed analyses of objectives mastered. Five kinds of reports are used for the purpose of interpreting pupil and class performance on the PRI.

1. *Individual Diagnostic Maps* Show the extent to which a student has mastered specific reading objectives at age and grade level
2. *Class Diagnostic Maps* Summarize the performance of each pupil in a class on items assessing each of the specific objectives
3. *Class Grouping Reports* Identify groups of students who share common reading difficulties and who may be grouped together for instructional purposes

TABLE 17.6 Levels, Items, and Objectives for the Prescriptive Reading Inventory

Level	Number of Items	Number of Objectives
Red	123	34
Green	153	41
Blue	162	42
Orange	148	38

4. *Individual Study Guides* Cross-reference reading objectives assessed in the PRI with page numbers in basal reading series where the objectives are taught
5. *Program Reference Guides* Cross-reference each basal reading series in its entirety to each of the objectives assessed by the PRI

While this battery is cross-referenced to basal readers, an *Interpretive Handbook* is also provided, identifying numerous specific instructional exercises that can be used to teach to areas of deficiency.

Reliability and Validity

No data on consistency of student performance are provided for the PRI. The developers do report a study of the validity of the device. The PRI and the Reading section of the 1970 edition of the California Achievement Test were administered to the 18,000 students who participated in the field testing. This procedure was used in an effort to check the extent to which the performance of the sample of 18,000 students was comparable to that of a representative national sample. Although no specific data are reported on the relationship of pupil performance on the two tests, the developers stated that no adjustments to the PRI were seen to be necessary. Validity rests largely on expert opinion. There are no data in the manual on the validity of the recommended grouping of students for instructional purposes.

Summary

The Prescriptive Reading Inventory is a criterion-referenced test designed to assess mastery of prereading behaviors and desired reading behaviors at the elementary school level. Five kinds of reports are available that should be of considerable assistance in pinpointing individual pupil strengths and weaknesses, evaluating individual pupil progress, grouping students for instructional purposes, and evaluating program effectiveness.

The cross-referencing of this system to the most widely used basal readers has two specific advantages: those who use the test do not have to purchase an entire curriculum, and teachers can readily shift materials for individual students who experience difficulty learning in specific curricula.

COPING WITH DILEMMAS IN CURRENT PRACTICE

There are three major problems in the diagnostic assessment of reading strengths and weaknesses. The first is the problem of curriculum match. Students enrolled in different reading curricula have different opportunities to learn specific skills. Reading series differ in the skills that are taught, in the emphasis placed on different skills, in the sequence in which skills are taught, and the time at which skills are taught. Tests differ in the skills that are assessed. Thus, it can be expected that pupils studying different curricula will perform differently on the same diagnostic reading test. It can also be expected that pupils studying the same curriculum will perform differently on different reading tests. Diagnostic personnel must be very careful to examine the match between skills taught in the student's curriculum and skills tested on the test. Most teacher's manuals for reading series include a listing of the skills taught at each level in the series. Many authors of diagnostic reading tests now include in test manuals a list of the objectives measured by the test. At the very least, assessors should carefully examine the extent to which the test measures what has been taught. Ideally, assessors would select specific parts of tests to measure exactly what has been taught. To the extent that there is a difference between what has been taught and what is tested, the test is not a valid measure.

A second problem is the selection of tests that are appropriate for making different kinds of educational decisions. We noted that there are different types of diagnostic reading tests. In making classification decisions, tests must be individually administered. One may either use an individually administered test or give a group test to one individual. In making instructional planning decisions, the most precise and helpful information will be obtained by giving individually administered criterion-referenced measures. One can, of course, systematically analyze pupil performance on a norm-referenced test, but the approach is difficult and time-consuming. It may also be futile since norm-referenced tests usually do not contain a sufficient number of items on which to base a diagnosis.

When evaluating individual pupil progress, the assessor must consider carefully the kinds of comparisons he or she wants to make. If one wants to compare pupils to others their age, norm-referenced measures are useful. If, on the other hand, one wants to know the extent to which individual pupils are mastering curriculum objectives, criterion-referenced measures are the tests of choice.

The third problem in reading is that there are few technically adequate tests. We have noted that for very many "norm-referenced" reading tests there is no description, or an inadequate description, of the groups on which the tests were standardized. Others were inadequately standardized. There is no evidence on the reliability and/or validity of many diagnostic reading tests. For others, reliability is not sufficient for use in making decisions about individuals. Diagnostic personnel should refrain from using technically inadequate measures. At the very least, they must operate with full awareness of the technical limitations of the devices they use.

The fourth problem is one of generalization. Assessors are faced with the very difficult task of describing or predicting pupil performance in reading. Yet, reading itself is difficult to describe. Reading is a complex behavior composed of subskills. Those who engage in reading diagnosis will do well to describe pupil performance in terms of specific skills or subskills (like recognition of words in isolation, listening comprehension, specific word-attack skills, and so on). They will do well also to limit predictions to making statements about probable performance of specific reading behaviors, not probable performance in reading.

SUMMARY

In this chapter we have reviewed the kinds of behaviors sampled by diagnostic reading tests. Several specific norm-referenced and criterion-referenced tests have been evaluated in terms of the kinds of behaviors they sample and their technical adequacy. Most of the norm-referenced devices clearly lack the technical characteristics necessary for use in making specific instructional decisions. Many do not present evidence of reliability and validity. In fact, some tests (Gates-McKillop-Horowitz, Durrell, and Diagnostic Reading Scales) present the consumer with numerous normative tables for interpreting test data without even describing the nature of the normative population.

The criterion-referenced tests described in this chapter are components of comprehensive systems designed to pinpoint skill-development strengths and weaknesses, provide teachers with instructional objectives, and direct teachers to materials that help teach to those objectives. We do not yet have sufficient empirical evidence to judge the extent to which criterion-referenced tests meet their stated objectives. Teachers need to judge for their own purposes the adequacy of the behavior samplings and the sequences of behaviors sampled. The systems still contain many rough spots that must be smoothed out.

How, then, do teachers and diagnostic specialists assess skill development in reading and prescribe developmental, corrective, or remedial programs? Reliance on scores provided by diagnostic reading tests is indeed precarious. Teachers and diagnostic specialists must rely on the qualitative information obtained in testing. Some tests provide checklists of observed difficulties, and these may be of considerable help in identifying individual pupils' reading characteristics.

In assessing reading strengths and weaknesses, teachers must first ask themselves what kinds of behaviors they want to assess. Specific subtests of larger batteries may then be used to assess those behaviors. Teachers should choose the subtests that are technically most accurate. Interpretation must be in terms of behaviors sampled rather than in terms of subtest names.

STUDY QUESTIONS

1. For what purpose are diagnostic reading tests given?
2. What are the relative merits and limitations in using criterion-referenced diagnostic reading tests? In using norm-referenced tests?

3. Several shortcomings have been noted for each of the specific norm-referenced diagnostic reading tests described in this chapter. What shortcomings do most of the tests have in common?

4. Dierdre, a student in Mr. Albert's fifth-grade class, has considerable difficulty reading. Mr. Albert wants to know at what level to begin reading instruction. Given the state of the art in diagnostic testing in reading, describe some alternative ways for Mr. Albert to identify a starting point?

5. You are teaching reading to a third-grade class. The school psychologist assesses one of the children in your class and reports that the child earned a grade score of 1.6 in reading. What additional information would you ask the psychologist to give you?

6. When teachers use criterion-referenced reading tests, they often find that the sequence in which specific individuals learn reading skills differs from the sequence of skills assessed by the test. How might this be explained?

7. It has been argued that norms are more important for screening tests than for diagnostic tests. Why?

ADDITIONAL READING

Buros, O. K. (Ed.). (1968). *Reading tests and reviews.* Highland Park, NJ: Gryphon Press.

Buros, O. K. (Ed.). (1978). *Eighth mental measurements yearbook.* Highland Park, NJ: Gryphon Press. (Reviews of reading tests, pp. 1157–1364.)

Guthrie, J. T. (1973). Models of reading and reading disability. *Journal of Educational Psychology, 65,* 9–18.

CHAPTER 18

DIAGNOSTIC ASSESSMENT IN MATHEMATICS

Diagnostic testing in mathematics is designed to identify specific strengths and weaknesses in skill development. We have seen that all major achievement tests designed to assess multiple skills include subtests that measure mathematics skills. These tests are necessarily global and attempt to assess a wide range of skills. In most cases, the number of items assessing specific math skills is insufficient for diagnostic purposes. Diagnostic testing in mathematics is more specific, providing a detailed assessment of skill development within specific areas.

There are fewer diagnostic math tests than diagnostic reading tests, but math assessment is more clear-cut. Because the successful performance of some mathematical operations clearly depends on the successful performance of other operations (for instance, multiplication depends on addition), it is relatively easier to sequence skill development and assessment in math than in reading. Diagnostic math tests generally sample similar behaviors. They sample various contents or mathematical concepts, various operations, and various applications of mathematical facts and principles.

WHY DO WE ASSESS MATHEMATICS?

There are several reasons to assess mathematics skills. First, we are often interested in evaluating a person's *attainments* in math. We may use diagnostic tests in mathematics to assess a person's readiness for instruction (in mathematics and other subjects) or to determine eligibility for employment. Second, all public school programs, with the exception of programs for the profoundly retarded, teach mathematical facts and concepts. Thus, teachers need to know if pupils have mastered particular facts and concepts. Diagnostic math tests are intended to provide sufficiently detailed information so that teachers can plan and evaluate instructional programs. Finally, diagnostic math tests are occasionally used to make classification decisions. Individually administered tests are usually required for classification and placement decisions. Therefore, we often see diagnostic math tests used to establish eligibility for programs for children with learning disabilities in mathematics.

BEHAVIORS SAMPLED BY DIAGNOSTIC MATHEMATICS TESTS

Behaviors sampled by diagnostic math tests have been classified by Connolly, Nachtman, and Pritchett (1971). A description of those behavior samples follows.

Content

A number of content areas are assessed by diagnostic math tests. Facts, knowledge, and concepts necessary for the successful performance of mathematical operations and for meaningful applications of math are assessed in each of the following content areas.

Numeration   Diagnostic math subtests assess knowledge of the number system. Items include those that assess identification of quantities and set value, rounding, identification of missing numbers in sequences, and counting.

Fractions   In nearly all cases and especially in tests designed to be used with students who are beyond fourth grade, understanding of basic concepts about fractions, decimals, and percentages is assessed.

Algebra   Some diagnostic math tests include subtests or items designed to assess knowledge and understanding of principles involved in the solution of linear and quadratic equations.

Geometry   Items that assess knowledge of geometry typically measure skill in recognizing specific shapes and, in some cases, understanding of theorems.

Operations

Subtests and items designed to assess children's skill in carrying out fundamental arithmetic operations include measures of counting, computation, and arithmetic reasoning.

Counting   Items designed to assess skill in counting usually require the student to count dots or objects and to select or write numerals to represent the number of objects counted.

Computation   Items and subtests designed to assess computational skills range from those that sample the traditional arithmetic operations of addition, subtraction, multiplication, and division to those that require the student to complete as many as four computational operations in problem-solving tasks. Items designed to assess specific operations generally range from those that require performance of the operation in the form of word problems to those that require the written solution of relatively complex computational problems.

Arithmetic Reasoning   Arithmetic reasoning subtests require the solution of problems with missing number facts.

Applications

Diagnostic math tests assess students' skills in applying mathematical facts and concepts to the solution of problems. Tasks generally include the following kinds of behavior samplings.

Measurement   Items assessing measurement require the recognition and application of common measurement units and the practical application of length, weight, and temperature measures.

Problem Solving   Problem-solving tasks require students to solve "story problems" that are read to them or that they read themselves. Four kinds of problems are generally included: (1) those requiring only a one-step mathematical operation, (2) those requiring more than one computational operation, (3) those requiring the student to differentiate between essential and nonessential information in solving problems, and (4) those requiring the student to demonstrate logical thinking by solving problems with missing elements.

Reading Graphs and Tables   The application of mathematical skills and concepts may be assessed by requiring the student to read graphs and tables in the solution of problems.

Money and Budgeting   The application of mathematical skills and concepts may be assessed by requiring the student to solve money problems. Items include those that assess the extent to which the student can make value judgments about purchasing articles, can interpret budgets, and can comprehend checks and checking accounts.

Time   The application of mathematical facts and concepts to the solution of problems involving time includes test items requiring the student to read clocks and to identify time intervals, holidays, and seasons.

SPECIFIC DIAGNOSTIC MATHEMATICS TESTS

This chapter reviews five diagnostic mathematics tests: the KeyMath Diagnostic Arithmetic Test, the Stanford Diagnostic Mathematics Test, the Test of Mathematical Ability, Diagnosis: an Instructional Aid in Mathematics, and the Diagnostic Mathematics Inventory.

KeyMath Diagnostic Arithmetic Test

The KeyMath Diagnostic Arithmetic Test (Connolly, Nachtman, & Pritchett, 1971) is an individually administered diagnostic test designed to assess math skill development in kindergarten through the eighth grade. The test, which is contained in an easel kit similar to those used with the Peabody Individual Achievement Test and the Woodcock Reading Mastery Tests, includes fourteen subtests organized into three areas: content, operations, and applications. The test gives four levels of diagnostic information: total test performance, area performance, subtest performance, and item performance. Examiners can use differing degrees of specificity in interpreting children's performances. An appendix contains a description of the specific behaviors sampled by each item included in the test.

Administration of KeyMath is relatively simple, and the authors state that no formal training is required to administer the test. The efficiency and meaningfulness with which the test is interpreted are a function of the expertise of the person who interprets a child's performance. According to the authors, maximum diagnostic meaningfulness will be achieved by those who have a background in teaching math. Each of the fourteen subtests is administered by assessing pupils' performances on a range of items. A basal (three consecutive correct responses) and a ceiling (three consecutive failures) are established for each subtest.

Subtests included in KeyMath, grouped according to the three areas measured by the test, are reported in Table 18.1.

Scores

Detailed directions for computing raw scores are included in the KeyMath manual. Four kinds of interpretation can be employed in evaluating a student's performance on the test. Total test performance can be evaluated by transforming raw scores to grade equivalents. A second way of interpreting a child's performance on KeyMath is to look at the performance pattern across the three areas. Area scores provide some indication of relative strengths and weaknesses in content, operations, and application of mathematical knowledge.

Third, the user of KeyMath can interpret a student's test performance by looking at relative performance on the fourteen subtests. The authors suggest that a student who is performing at a lower grade level on one subtest than on the other thirteen is demonstrating a weakness in that area. No evidence is presented to support the contention that discrepant scores represent significant deficiencies. Errors in interpretation could well result from use of the suggested procedures for interpreting subtest scores.

The fourth way of interpreting performance on KeyMath is as a criterion-referenced device. The authors have included a description of the specific behaviors sampled by each of the test items and have written behavioral objectives to correspond to each particular sampling. The classroom teacher or other diagnostic specialist interested in developing an educational program for children taking the test can analyze a student's performance on specific items. In this

TABLE 18.1 Subtests of KeyMath

Content	Operations	Applications
Numeration	Addition	Word Problems
Fractions	Subtraction	Missing Elements
Geometry and Symbols	Multiplication	Money
	Division	Measurement
	Mental Computation	Time
	Numerical Reasoning	

manner, the teacher receives specific information about the behaviors that individual students do and do not demonstrate. Although normative data are available for making both interindividual and intraindividual comparisons, these data have some real shortcomings, as we shall see.

Norms

The original item pool for KeyMath evolved from the doctoral dissertations of three authors. The studies were coordinated with each other and involved field testing of 1,400 educable mentally retarded children. Later, math curricula were searched, and additional items were written for inclusion in the test. The test was then administered to 950 children in kindergarten through grade 8 in four midwestern and one northwestern school districts in a "calibration study" designed to ascertain item difficulty and select final items for the scale. Actual standardization of the test was done by administering it to 1,222 children in kindergarten through grade 7 in forty-two school systems. On the basis of the calibration study conducted earlier, the authors stated that standardization could be completed by administering only *five items* to each child. Allegedly, the five would be representative of the total range of item difficulty. Nineteen items were selected as representative of the total 209 items included in this test. Each child in the standardization group took five of the nineteen items.

The description of the normative sample is post hoc and incomplete. Apparently, the normative sample was not systematically selected on the basis of traditional normative variables. The manual does report comparisons of community size and racial representation with census figures. No information is included regarding socioeconomic status, parental occupation, or parental education. More important, the authors do not report the kinds of math curricula in which the children were enrolled.

While standardization of KeyMath was certainly less than desirable, it must be remembered that the real value of this test is in the specific diagnostic information it provides. If KeyMath is used as a criterion-referenced test, normative comparisons are unnecessary.

Reliability

The authors report internal-consistency reliability coefficients for children included in the calibration study. Reliability coefficients, reported by subtest and grade level (kindergarten through grade 7), range from .39 to .90. Standard errors of measurement for each subject are reported in both the record booklet and the manual. The inclusion of these data should help the test user to establish confidence intervals and to interpret pupil performance. The authors do not report test-retest reliability, a feature that would have been of considerable value in such a heterogeneous test. Also, they do not include data on significance of differences between subtest scores, data that are necessary if the use of the diagnostic profile is to be meaningful.

Validity

KeyMath's ultimate utility must be judged on the basis of its content validity. As with any achievement test, the content of the test must match the content of the curriculum. KeyMath provides no data about the extent to which it samples any curricula.

Concurrent validity was investigated by comparing the KeyMath performance of twenty-eight "normal" fifth graders to their performance on the Iowa Tests of Basic Skills (ITBS) arithmetic subtests. A correlation of .38 was obtained between KeyMath performance and performance on the composite of arithmetic test scores. The authors admit that the data are inadequate for demonstrating concurrent validity.

Summary

KeyMath is an individually administered test designed to provide diagnostic analysis of skill development in mathematics. The device is best used as a criterion-referenced screening measure. Reliability is generally too low to use KeyMath for important educational decisions. Evidence of validity is quite limited, and the description of the normative sample is inadequate.

Stanford Diagnostic Mathematics Test

The Stanford Diagnostic Mathematics Test (SDMT) (Beatty, Madden, Gardner, & Karlsen, 1976) is a group-administered test designed to be both norm- and criterion-referenced. The test measures competence in the basic mathematical concepts and skills that are important in daily affairs and are prerequisite to the continued study of mathematics. The primary purpose of the SDMT is to identify specific areas in which a pupil is having difficulty. There are four levels of the test: the Red level (grades 1.5 to 4.5), the Green level (grades 3.5 to 6.5), the Brown level (grades 5.5 to 8.5), and the Blue level (grades 7.5 to high school). Each level consists of three subtests: Number System and Numeration, Computation, and Applications. A description of the kinds of behaviors sampled by each of the subtests follows.

Number System and Numeration Items included in this subtest range from samples of skill in identifying numerals and comparing sets to samples of competence in fractions and the more complex arithmetic operations. The items are noncomputational and are designed to assess pupils' understanding of numbers and their properties.

Computation The Computation subtest assesses knowledge of the primary facts and algorithms of addition, subtraction, multiplication, and division and the methods for solving simple and compound number sentences.

Applications This subtest assesses skill in applying basic mathematical facts and principles. Items range in difficulty from those that require students to solve simple story problems and select correct models for solving one-step problems to those that require students to solve multiple-step problems and measurement problems and to read tables and graphs.

The SDMT is norm-referenced in the sense that it was standardized on a sample representative of the United States public school population. It is criterion-referenced in the sense that groups of items have been assigned a "passing" score called by the authors a "Progress Indicator cutoff score." Pupils who reach or exceed the Progress Indicator cutoff on the group of items that measure a particular objective are said to be competent in that objective. The cutoffs were set by the authors of the test on the basis of a number of factors, including (1) the skills prerequisite to attaining the objective, and (2) the performance of pupils on the test items measuring the objective. The criteria were not set according to a strict norm-referenced procedure but are based primarily on expert opinion.

Item selection for the SDMT was based on a number of factors. Items initially were written to produce four complete test forms that would measure each of the objectives at the four levels of the test. Each item was reviewed and edited for content, style, and appropriateness in measuring a stated objective. A major concern in editing was, reportedly, the elimination of ethnic, cultural, racial, and sexual bias. The items were assembled into four forms and administered to a nationwide sample. Each level of the test was item analyzed in the grades for which the test was intended as well as in one grade lower and one grade higher. For each level, two forms (judged equivalent after content and item analysis) were assembled from the four experimental forms. Items were assigned to forms in such a way that the tasks required by the items, the statistical characteristics of the items, and the context of the items were balanced for each objective across the two forms.

Scores

The SDMT yields raw scores, scaled scores, grade equivalents, percentile ranks, stanines, and "Progress Indicators." The Progress In-

dicators are simply "+" or "−" indications as to whether the child reached or exceeded the predetermined Progress Indicator cutoff score for a specific skill domain. The derived scores (scaled scores, grade equivalents, percentile ranks, and stanines) are available on the subtests and the total.

Norms

The standardization sample for the SDMT was selected by means of a stratified random-sampling technique, with socioeconomic status, school-system enrollment, and geographic region as the stratification variables. School-system data were obtained from the United States Office of Education's 1970 census tapes. The tapes were used to generate a random sample of 3,000 school districts. A composite socioeconomic-status index for each system was determined by weighting family income twice in comparison to median years of schooling of parents. Age and sex were not controlled in the standardization of the SDMT.

Within stratified cells, school districts were invited to participate in standardization of the test. A random sample of consenting districts within each cell was selected. The test was standardized in thirty-seven school districts on approximately 38,000 pupils. The manual includes detailed tables illustrating that the demographic characteristics of the school districts sampled closely parallel those indicated in the 1970 census.

Reliability

Two types of reliability information are available for the SDMT: reliability of test scores and reliability of the Progress Indicators. Reliability of the raw scores for the test was determined by assessing internal consistency (using Kuder-Richardson 20): alternate-form reliability was computed by correlating performance of the same pupils on both forms of the test. Internal-consistency coefficients range from .84 to .97 for the four levels of the test; alternate-form coefficients range from .64 to .94, with most exceeding .80. Standard errors of measurement in both raw-score and scaled-score units are tabled in the manuals.

The reliability of the Progress Indicators was determined by administering both forms to the same pupils and establishing each pupil's Progress Indicator on both forms. Contingency tables provided in the manual may be used to estimate the probability of a student's obtaining a different Progress Indicator on taking the alternate form of the test.

Validity

Limited space in the SDMT manual is devoted to the issue of content validity and criterion-related validity. The authors state that the content validity of the SDMT, like that of any other achievement test, must be based on an evaluation of the extent to which the content of the test reflects the local curriculum. Criterion-related validity was established by correlating performance on the subtests of the SDMT with performance on the mathematics subtests of the Stanford Achievement Test. Correlations ranged from .64 to .94.

Summary

The Stanford Diagnostic Mathematics Test is a group-administered device that is both norm-referenced and criterion-referenced. The device was exceptionally well standardized and demonstrates enough reliability to be used in pinpointing specific domains of skill-development strengths and weaknesses in mathematics. Validity must be judged relative to the content of local curricula.

Test of Mathematical Abilities

The Test of Mathematical Abilities (TOMA) (Brown & McEntire, 1984) is a norm-referenced device intended for use with students in grades 3 through 12 or between the ages of 8-6 and 18-11. The TOMA provides information about a student's skills in computation and in solving word problems as well as about attitudes toward mathematics, mathematical vocabulary, and general cultural application of information. It is intended to identify students who are significantly ahead of or behind their age mates in mathematical ability, to determine strengths and weaknesses of the students, to document progress, and to serve as a useful research tool. Four of the subtests may be group administered; general information must be individually administered. The 107 test items are grouped into five subtests.

Attitude Toward Math   The 15 items in this subtest are based on the Estes Attitude Scales. Students use a three-point scale to rate their feelings about mathematics.

Vocabulary   The student must define 20 terms in writing.

Computation   Students solve 25 problems in their answer booklets.

General Information   Each of the 30 questions in this subtest requires an oral response to "cultural-social-practical applications of mathematics."

Story Problems   Students solve 17 word problems in their answer booklets.

Scores

Derived scores are reported by ages (half years from 8-0 to 10-0, then one-year intervals from 10 to 18-11), not by grades. Standard scores have a mean of 10 and a standard deviation of 3. A *math quotient* is obtained by adding the standard scores from each subtest. Math quotients have a mean of 100 and a standard deviation of 15. Percentile ranks as well as age and grade equivalents are also available.

Norms

The TOMA was standardized on 1,560 students living in five states. Although the five states seems rather few, the final sample is within 7 percent of the 1980 census proportions for urban-rural residence, race, and region of residence. However, no data are presented for socioeconomic status (education or income) of the parents of the students in the sample.

Reliability

The subtest scores are of considerably greater interest than total scores (which do not seem to us to be readily interpretable). Coefficient alpha for each of the 50 combinations of age-group (10) and subtest (5) ranged from .57 for computation at age 11 to .97 for computation at age 8-6 to 8-11. Only twelve of the fifty coefficients equaled or exceeded .90. Two studies examined the stability of TOMA. One used twenty-three normal 11-year-old students; reliabilities ranged from .71 (Attitude Toward Math) to .81 (General Information). In the second study, learning disabled students between ages 9 and 17 were tested. However, crossing so many age levels tends to inflate seriously estimates of reliability. (Indeed, for the norming sample, age correlated with test scores about .60). SEMs based on internal consistency estimates are also reported.

Validity

No evidence of content validity is presented.

Criterion-related validity was established by correlating the TOMA scores with the math subtests of the PIAT and the WRAT as well as with the KeyMath Diagnostic Arithmetic Test. Using these three tests as the criterion, the TOMA subtests of computation and story problems are of particular interest since their behavior samples are similar. The TOMA computation correlates .45 with the PIAT, but is nonsignificant with the WRAT. Story problems correlate .36 with the PIAT, but .37 with the WRAT despite the fact that there are no word problems on the WRAT. None of the criterion measures seems appropriate for attitude toward math. (Indeed, correlations between math attitudes and achievement might better be construed as construct validity.) All of the TOMA subtests correlate modestly with KeyMath total score.

Construct validity was established by showing that the TOMA scores increased with age, that the four subtests requiring cognitive skills were correlated with the WISC–R and the Slosson IQs, and that learning disabled students earned significantly lower scores than normal students on the TOMA.

Summary

The TOMA is an individually administered, norm-referenced test that assesses several aspects of mathematical ability. The quality of the norms is difficult to assess. They appear representative on the dimensions of urban-rural residence, geographic region, and race. No data are presented on social status of the parents of the children in the normative sample or on the curricula in which the students were enrolled. The internal-consistency reliability is adequate for screening decisions and occasionally adequate for important educational decisions. Stability is unknown for all but one subtest. No evidence of content validity is presented, and only limited evidence of criterion-related and construct validity is provided.

Diagnosis: An Instructional Aid in Mathematics

Diagnosis: An Instructional Aid in Mathematics (Guzaitis, Carlin, & Juda, 1972) is a counterpart to Diagnosis: An Instructional Aid, which tests reading; it is designed both to assess specific mathematical skills and to help the classroom teacher in the systematic planning of appropriate instruction. There are two levels of the system, level A, for those whose math skills are at a kindergarten to third-grade level, and level B, for those whose math skills are at a third- to sixth-grade level. Each of the levels contains a number of specific components including survey tests, probes, a prescription guide, a teacher's handbook, and a class progress chart.

Diagnosis is not a self-contained instructional system; rather, it is cross-references to basic elementary school mathematics curricula. The system helps teachers pinpoint instructional weaknesses and teach to specific objectives using materials already available in their classrooms.

The heart of this diagnostic-instructional program is the set of thirty-two probes, each of which is a criterion-referenced diagnostic device. Each item in the probes is related specifically to an instructional objective. The thirty-two probes measure competence in whole-number computation (addition, subtraction, multiplication, and division), fractional computation, decimal computation, numeration, mathematical operations, problem solving, measurement, and geometry.

The teacher or diagnostic specialist begins systematic instructional planning by administering a survey test that assesses, in a limited manner, the development of specific math skills. The survey test is scored by use of a key included in the teacher's handbook to obtain a global assessment of strengths and weaknesses in math. The teacher or other examiner uses the results of the survey test to determine which of the specific probes should be administered.

The probes are self-scoring; by simply tearing off a face sheet, teachers can identify items answered correctly. Each item is matched to a specific instructional objective. Teachers can identify specific instructional weaknesses and specify instructional goals to alleviate each weakness. The prescription guide directs teachers to the sections of several basic math curricula where the instructional objective is taught and to appropriate instructional materials.

Scores and Norms

No norm-referenced scores are obtained for Diagnosis. The system is comprehensive, based on a task analysis of math skills in kindergarten through grade 6. The child is not compared to others; the emphasis is on subject-matter content mastered.

Reliability and Validity

No reliability data are reported for Diagnosis. There are two alternate forms of the survey test, both of which provide very limited samples of each of the math skills assessed. Alternate-form reliabilities are not reported; we advise concurrent administration of both forms to insure reliability.

Validity for the system is based on expert opinion. As with any criterion-referenced system, the skills assessed and the sequence in which they occur depend on the authors' view of the development of math skills.

Summary

Diagnosis is a criterion-referenced system used to assess skill-development strengths and weaknesses in mathematics. The system allows teachers to assess specific skill-development weaknesses, to specify instructional goals, and to select materials to teach to those goals. The use of a system like this enables the teacher to individualize math instruction in a systematic manner. Much of the hit-or-miss of traditional diagnostic-instructional intervention is avoided, providing considerably more efficiency in instruction.

Diagnostic Mathematics Inventory

The Diagnostic Mathematics Inventory (DMI) (Gessell, 1977) is a criterion-referenced test designed to measure mastery or nonmastery of specific learning objectives in mathematics in grades 1.5 to 8.5. The test was designed for the purpose of helping educational personnel design individual educational programs, evaluate individual pupil progress, diagnose strengths and weaknesses in terms of specific objectives, group students for instructional purposes, and evaluate programs and instructional materials.

The DMI is a series of multiple-choice tests that assess 325 mathematics objectives. The series consists of seven levels, A through G, each assessing a grade level in half-year intervals (for example, 2.5–3.5, 4.5–5.5). In addition to the tests there are practice exercises for each level. Interim evaluation tests are available for use throughout the year to monitor student progress. A highlight of the series is the provision of three Learning Activities Guides that match specific test items and objectives to specific learning activities designed to teach to those objectives. Also provided are a Guide to Ancillary Materials that correlates the DMI objectives with more than seventy different nontextbook materials and a set of Master Reference Guides providing references to pages in mathematics textbooks where specific objectives are taught. Clearly, this series of tests and accompanying materials should assist the teacher who needs to plan individualized and very specific educational programs in mathematics.

Scores and Norms

Norms and norm-referenced scores per se are not available for the DMI. Rather, the test and the materials that accompany it are designed to be used in a criterion-referenced manner. The tests may be machine-scored, or students may respond on a self-scoring answer sheet. Three specific reports are available for the DMI.

Premastery Analysis This report provides information on behaviors exhibited by students before they demonstrate mastery of an objective. It tells the teacher specifically what went wrong in the students' efforts to answer test items (for example, did the students misadd, fail to carry, carry the wrong digit, multiply rather than add, add left to right, or subtract rather than add).

Objective Mastery Report This report, provided for the class, identifies for each student those objectives mastered and not mastered.

Individual Diagnostic Report This report, provided for the individual, indicates objectives mastered and not mastered.

Reliability and Validity

The DMI is a criterion-referenced mathematics test. Traditional reliability and validity data are not presented in the manuals that accompany the DMI.

Summary

The DMI is one of the most complete diagnostic-prescriptive inventories we have seen. The test assesses skill development relative to 325 specific objectives. Objectives are cross-referenced to mathematics textbooks and supplementary materials. In addition, specific learning activities are provided for each objective. The DMI should be extremely useful to teachers and other educational personnel in planning specific individualized instructional programs in mathematics.

COPING WITH DILEMMAS IN CURRENT PRACTICE

There are three major problems in the diagnostic assessment of mathematical skills. The first problem is the recurring issue of curriculum match. There is considerable variation in math curricula. This variation means that the diagnostic math tests will not be equally representative for all curricula—or even appropriate for some commonly used ones. As a result, great care must be exercised in using diagnostic math tests to make various educational decisions. Diagnosticians must be extremely careful to note the match between test content and curriculum. This usually involves far more than a quick inspection of test items by someone unfamiliar with the specific classroom curriculum. For example, a diagnostician could inspect the teacher's manual to insure that the test only assesses material that has been taught and that there is reasonable correspondence between the relative emphasis placed on teaching the material and testing the material. To do this, the diagnostician may have to develop a table of specifications for the math curriculum and compare test items to that table. However, once a table of specifications has been developed for the curriculum, a better procedure would be to select items from a criterion-referenced system to fit the cells in the table exactly.

The next problem is selecting an appropriate test for the type of decision that needs to be made. School personnel are usually required to use individually administered norm-referenced devices in classification decisions. Decisions about a pupil's eligibility for special services, however, need not be based on detailed information about a pupil's strengths and weaknesses, as provided by diagnostic tests; diagnosticians are interested in a pupil's relative standing. In our opinion the best achievement survey tests are subtests of group-administered tests. A practical solution is not to use a diagnostic math test for classification decisions but to administer individually a subtest from one of the better group achievement tests.

The third problem is that most of the diagnostic tests in mathematics do not test a sufficiently detailed sample of facts and concepts (although the DMI may be an exception). Consequently, one must generalize from a student's performance on the items tested to performance on the items that are not tested. The reliabilities of the subtests on diagnostic math tests are often not high enough for educators to make such a generalization with any great degree of confidence. As a result, these tests are not too useful in assessing readiness or in assessing strengths and weaknesses in order to plan instructional programs. We believe that the preferred practice in diagnostic testing in mathematics is for teachers to develop criterion-referenced achievement tests that exactly parallel the curriculum being taught.

SUMMARY

In this chapter we have reviewed the kinds of behaviors sampled by diagnostic mathematics tests and have evaluated the most commonly used tests in terms of the kinds of behaviors they sample and their technical adequacy. The five tests reviewed in this chapter are designed essentially to provide teachers and diagnostic specialists with specified information on those math skills that pupils have and have not mastered. Compared to diagnostic testing in reading, diagnostic testing in math puts less emphasis on the provision of scores.

The tests described in this chapter differ in their technical adequacy for use in making instructional decisions for students. Knowledge of pupil mastery of specific math skills as gained from administration of one or more of the tests, along with knowledge of the general sequence of development of math skills, can help teachers design curricular content for individuals.

STUDY QUESTIONS

1. Identify four ways a teacher can interpret the performance of a pupil on the KeyMath Diagnostic Test.
2. The Stanford Diagnostic Mathematics Test is both norm-referenced and criterion-referenced. Under what circumstances would a teacher want to use the norms for the SDMT?
3. Given the state of the art in diagnostic assessment in math, identify at least two ways a classroom teacher can pinpoint a starting place for teaching math to an individual pupil.
4. You are teaching arithmetic to a third-grade class. The local school psychologist assesses one of the children in your class and reports that the child earned a grade equivalent of 5.6 in arithmetic. What additional information would you ask the psychologist to give you?

ADDITIONAL READING

Ashlock, R. (1976). *Error patterns in computation* (2nd ed.). Columbus, OH: Charles E. Merrill.

Buros, O. K. (Ed.). (1978). *Eighth mental measurements yearbook.* Highland Park, NJ: Gryphon Press. (Reviews of mathematics tests, pp. 385–458).

Reisman, F. (1982). Strategies for mathematics disorders. In C. Reynolds and T. Gutkin (Eds.), *Handbook of school psychology.* New York: Wiley.

CHAPTER 19

ASSESSMENT OF
WRITTEN LANGUAGE

Written expression is the end product of a considerable amount of intellectual activity: the formation of ideas, their elaboration, their sequencing, and so forth. Much of what we consider to be writing is a creative endeavor. One's ability to use words to excite, to depict vividly, to imply is far more than a mechanical set of skills that can be taught, although they can be polished and honed. However, several aspects of written language can be thought of as skills that can be taught and mastered. These skills have been separated from those in Chapter 13 on oral language because they are routinely taught in school. The written encoding of language requires that we observe certain conventions —rules. These conventions are taught in school and learned by students. Several components of written language are assessed: spelling, punctuation and capitalization, grammar, word usage, penmanship, and, occasionally, outlining and organizing.

Spelling is often assessed as part of several standardized tests: the California Achievement Tests, the Iowa Tests of Basic Skills and Tests of Achievement and Proficiency, the Metropolitan Achievement Tests, the SRA Achievement Series, the Stanford Achievement Test, the Wide Range Achievement Test, the Peabody Individual Achievement Test, the BRIGANCE Diagnostic Inventory of Basic Skills, the Durrell Analysis of Reading Difficulty, and the Woodcock-Johnson Psychoeducational Battery. However, the spelling words that students are to learn vary considerably from curriculum to curriculum. For example, Ames (1965) examined seven spelling series and found that they introduce an average of 3,200 words between the second and eighth grades.

However, only about 1,300 words were common to all the series; about 1,700 words were taught in only one series. Moreover, the words taught in several series varied considerably in their grade placement, sometimes by as many as *five* grades.

Mechanics (capitalization and punctuation) are also assessed on several achievement batteries: the California Achievement Tests, the Iowa Tests of Basic Skills and Tests of Achievement and Proficiency, the Metropolitan Achievement Tests, the SRA Achievement Series, the Stanford Achievement Test, the BRIGANCE Diagnostic Inventory of Basic Skills, and the Woodcock-Johnson Psychoeducational Battery. Again, standardized tests are not well suited to measuring achievement in these areas since the grade level at which these skills are taught varies so much from one curriculum to another. To be valid, the measurement of achievement in these areas must be closely tied to the curriculum being taught. In capitalization and punctuation, for example, pupils may learn that a sentence always begins with a capital letter in kindergarten, first grade, second grade, or later. They may learn that commercial brand names are capitalized in the sixth grade or several grades earlier. Students may be taught that the apostrophe in "it's" makes the word a contraction of "it is" in the second or third grade but may still be studying "it's" in high school. Finally, in assessing word usage, organization, and penmanship we must take into account the emphasis that individual teachers place on these components of written language and when and how students are taught.

The more usual way to assess written language is to conduct an informal evaluation of a student's written work and to develop vocabulary and spelling tests that parallel the curriculum. In this way teachers can be sure that they are measuring precisely what has been taught. Most teacher's editions of language arts series contain scope and sequence charts that specify fairly clearly the objectives that are taught in each unit. From these charts teachers can develop appropriate criterion-referenced tests.

WHY DO WE ASSESS WRITTEN LANGUAGE?

Written language and spelling are regularly taught in school, and these areas are singled out for assessment in PL 94-142. Consequently, we assess written language and spelling for the same reasons we assess any achievement area. We may use tests to screen for pupils who exhibit difficulties in various aspects of written language. We may use tests to ascertain eligibility for special educational services for the language impaired or learning disabled. We may use language tests as an aid in planning instructional programs. Finally, we may use language tests to evaluate the progress of individual pupils.

TESTS OF WRITTEN EXPRESSION AND SPELLING

Test of Written Language

The Test of Written Language (TOWL) (Hammill & Larsen, 1983) is a norm-referenced device that can be administered to individuals or to groups of students. The TOWL is intended to assess a pupil's skill in word usage, punctuation and capitalization (style), spelling, handwriting, vocabulary, and sentence production (Hammill & Larsen, 1983, p. 5). For the subtests Vocabulary, Thematic Maturity, and Handwriting, the student is given an answer booklet that contains three pictures. The student is instructed to "write a complete story using all three pictures" (p. 21). For the Vocabulary score, the student receives a point for each word containing seven letters or more. Thematic Maturity is scored by noting the presence of twenty characteristics (for example, the student writes in paragraph format; the student notes objects from the pictures shown). Handwriting is scored on a scale from 0 to 10. Only penmanship is considered; scoring guides are provided, but the criteria are not clearly elaborated. The Spelling subtest consists of twenty-five words that are read aloud and used in a sentence by the examiner; the student spells from dictation. Word Usage is a separate subtest that requires the student to supply a word in the correct grammatical form in twenty-five sentences. The subtest assesses such forms as internally changing past tense (threw), internally changing plurals (children), and comparatives. The Style subtest requires the student to punctuate and to capitalize twenty-five stimulus sentences.

Scores

The manual provides tables to convert raw scores to percentiles and standard scores for subtests with a mean of 10 and a standard deviation of 3 and for the total score, called the Written Language Quotient having a mean of 100 and a standard deviation of 15. Stanines, T-scores, and z-scores are also available for the Written Language Quotient (WLQ). Twenty-two pages of the TOWL manual are devoted to the informal assessment of written language. Scope and sequence charts are presented for many of the skills assessed on the TOWL.

Norms

The authors provide no description of the procedures used to select the standardization sample. The TOWL was standardized on 3,418 students between the ages of 7-0 and 18-11 years of age who resided in fourteen states. The sample is intended to parallel the 1980 census and is within 6 percent of the population figures for sex, residence, and geographic region. The authors fail to provide data on socioeconomic status, a most important variable, and the ethnic composition of the sample is not described.

Reliability

It must first be noted that it is very difficult to estimate reliability for a test that requires the pupil to create an essay. The primary generalizations that one wishes to make are to other essays and to other scorers. Computing interscorer agreement is straightforward. To estimate generalizability to other essays requires the analysis of several essays written by the same students.

Three types of reliability data are considered

in the TOWL manual. Internal consistency (split-half corrected by the Spearman-Brown formula) was obtained at each age for three subtests (Style, Spelling, and Word Usage) except that estimates were inexplicably omitted for Spelling and Word Usage for the 14- to 15- and 16- to 18-year-old groups. The twenty-three obtained coefficients ranged from .80 to .96; the median corrected split-half reliability was .88. Eight coefficients equaled or exceeded .90. Stability was estimated by inappropriately combining several age groups; even so, stability for combined elementary and secondary pupils was less than .90 for four of the six subtests. Standard errors of measurement, based on stability coefficients combining all stability studies, are also reported. To estimate interscorer agreement one essay (a space story) was rated by fifteen experienced teachers. However, an unorthodox procedure was used to compute agreement: if a teacher awarded a score that was within one point of the mean (of all fifteen teachers) for the essay being judged, an agreement was scored; if a score was more than one point from the mean, a disagreement was scored. (The more usual procedure would be to compute agreement between all pairs of scorers and report the median and range of agreement.) In any event, percentages of agreement were reported for thematic maturity (.93), handwriting (.76), and vocabulary (.98).

Validity

Some degree of content validity is claimed by the rationale for test development. Several points about the TOWL's content should be made. The Style subtest is scored with one point for each correctly punctuated sentence although a sentence may require several marks of punctuation. Teachers will probably wish to look at each error made by the student. Moreover, the number of constructions that must be punc-

tuated is necessarily limited, but some constructions appear repeatedly while others never appear. Similarly, the Word Usage subtest contains far too few items to be considered diagnostic. Teachers must exercise considerable care in using the Spelling subtest to insure that the content of the spelling test and the content of their curriculum match.

Criterion-related validity was investigated by correlating the TOWL with various standardized and nonstandardized measures. Several of these studies computed correlation coefficients across several ages or grades; this procedure probably overestimates validity since all the TOWL subtests, except Handwriting, correlate .3 to .4 with chronological age. In one study where adolescents were the subjects, the WLQ from the TOWL correlated substantially with scores from the Picture Story Language Test. In another study with fourth graders as subjects, the TOWL subtests correlated highly with teachers' overall ratings of essays.

Construct validity was established by demonstrating that writing ability is developmental in nature, increasing with chronological age. Evidence is also provided that the TOWL is moderately correlated with oral and aural language.

Summary

The TOWL is a norm-referenced device intended to assess comprehensively the written language of schoolage individuals. The content of the test, while reasonable, does not offer the depth of assessment necessary to plan instructional programs. Reliabilities of the subtests and total score are generally not adequate for making decisions about classification. Evidence for the validity of the device is modest. Normative data are incompletely reported. The TOWL seems best suited for experimental work and screening.

Test of Written Spelling

The Test of Written Spelling (TWS) (Larsen & Hammill, 1976) is a norm-referenced, individually administered device developed to assess a child's spelling competency. (Although there are instructions for administering the TWS to groups, the authors recommend, and refer extensively to, individual administration in the technical manual.) The TWS is based on the idea that a child learns to spell in two ways. First, rules and generalizations relating to English spelling are learned. Second, for those words that do not conform to the rules, the child must learn "in a fashion that relies primarily upon memorization" (Larsen & Hammill, 1976, p. 9). The TWS has been designed to test spelling skills relating to both methods of learning and is divided into two subtests.

Predictable Words   This is a list of thirty-five words whose spellings are consistently rule-governed, according to the rules of English spelling.

Unpredictable Words   This is a list of twenty-five words that could not be spelled correctly by computer even after more than 2,000 rules of English spelling were applied (see Hanna, Hodges, & Hanna, 1971).

A three-step process is used to administer the TWS. The examiner (1) says the word in isolation, (2) uses the word in a sentence, and (3) says the word a second time in isolation. The child is required to write the words dictated by the tester, who must carefully monitor the child's responses in order to watch for errors. Because the words are sequenced according to difficulty, a performance ceiling can be obtained; testing should end when the child has made five consecutive errors on each of the two subtests. There is no basal; all children begin with item 1.

Although most discussion in the technical manual refers to the TWS as an individually administered device, it can also be utilized as a group-administered tool, and alternative directions are available to the examiner for using the test this way.

Scores

The examiner totals the number of words spelled correctly on each subtest, providing a *raw score* for both predictable and unpredictable words. From this breakdown of scores into predictable and unpredictable words, the teacher can get some diagnostic information regarding the "types" of words the child is having problems spelling, as well as some ideas for intervention. The sum of the raw scores for each subtest is the *total raw score,* and all three scores are entered on the score sheet.

Each of the raw scores can be converted into three other scores using tables provided in the manual: *spelling ages* (SAs), *grade equivalents* (GEs), and *spelling quotients* (SQs), which are ratio scores:

$$SQ = \frac{100 \times SA}{CA}$$

Norms

The TWS was standardized on an "unselected" sample of 4,544 children living in twenty-two states. Although procedures for picking the sample children are not specified, a breakdown of children indicates representativeness, at least in relation to geographical location of the communities sampled (Northeast, North Central, South, West), type of communities sampled (rural, urban), and sex of the children.

The number of children in each age group varied from 1,897 (at ages 6 to 8) to 745 (at ages 12 to 13). No information was given about the ethnic origin, class placement (regular or special), or other characteristics of the children, although one would hope that an "unselected" sample would be representative of the population in these areas as well. Most of the norm group (78 percent) were from middle social-status families, with 15 percent from upper and 8 percent from lower social-status units. The absence of comparisons of these figures to national norms is both striking and curious in light of those same comparisons for the other variables.

Reliability

Internal-consistency estimates of reliability are provided for each of the eight grade levels and for predictable, unpredictable, and total scores, yielding twenty-four reliability coefficients. Of the twenty-one coefficients between grades 2 and 8, only one is below .82. At grade 1, however, reliability estimates are .78 for the predictable words, .50 for the unpredictable words, and .78 for the total score. Because of the low reliability for the Unpredictable Words subtest, the authors suggest "that the results of the Unpredictable Words subtest not be interpreted separately" for first graders.

It should be noted that the KR-21 formula was applied to the sample scores in order to compute reliability. The KR-21 only approximates the true reliability score, and theoretically it should be used only when items are of equal difficulty (Guilford, 1956), which cannot be said of the items on the TWS. Thus, it is puzzling that this formula has been used for the TWS.

No other reliability data have been presented by the authors.

Validity

In an attempt to establish concurrent validity, the authors of the TWS have measured the relationships between the TWS and four other tests of spelling: The Durrell Analysis of Reading Difficulty, Wide Range Achievement Test, California Achievement Tests, and SRA Achievement Series. Correlation coefficients depicting these relationships are impressive—from .90 for the Durrell to .69 to the SRA Series.

Careful consideration in the selection of test items contributes to very impressive content validity. The authors of the TWS, in order to select the best items, made an "intensive survey of the ten most commonly used basal spelling series." Words common to all the series were chosen in the initial "item pool." Thus, all the words used in the TWS appear in all ten of the most common basal spellers.

In order to classify a given word as predictable or unpredictable, the authors used the data by Hanna et al. (1971), who programmed a computer with over 2,000 rules of English spelling and made it "spell" 1,700 words. Fifty percent of those words were correctly spelled, that is, predictable, according to the rules of English spelling.

Summary

The TWS is a norm-referenced device, usually individually administered. However, some diagnostic information is possible as a result of breaking the spelling words into the predictable and unpredictable categories. The reliability is adequate; the validity information is excellent. In all, the TWS appears to be a valuable tool.

Slingerland Screening Tests for Identifying Children with Specific Language Disability

The Slingerland Screening Tests for Identifying Children with Specific Language Disability (Slingerland, 1970) are intended to identify those children "with potential language difficulties and those with already present specific language disabilities who are in need of special attention . . ." (Slingerland, 1970, p. xx). Although the title of the test and the promotional materials claim that the test identifies children with language disabilities, the test actually assesses visual, auditory, and kinesthetic abilities believed to form the foundation upon which later language learning is built. Neither theoretical nor empirical evidence is presented by Slingerland in the technical manuals to support the link between the test content and language disability.

The test is available at four levels: form A (end of first grade or beginning of second grade), form B (end of second grade or beginning of third grade), form C (end of third grade or beginning of fourth grade), and form D (beginning or end of grades 5 and 6). Separate manuals are available for forms A, B, and C (Slingerland, 1970) and form D (Slingerland, 1974). Eight subtests are regularly administered at all levels; a ninth subtest is administered on form D. The subtests can be given to groups of students. In addition, optional, individually administered subtests to assess auditory ability are available.

Descriptions of the nine regularly administered subtests follow.

Copying from a Wall Chart The student has the choice of copying a story in either manuscript or cursive writing.

Copying Words in Isolation The student copies ten words presented in manuscript style.

Recalling Words, Numbers, and Letters Students turn their answer booklets over and place their pencils on the floor. The teacher shows a stimulus (for example, "our") to the class for "approximately 10 seconds," withdraws the stimulus, pauses for "a few seconds," and instructs the students to find what they saw in a horizontal multiple-choice array. Students pick up their pencils, turn their answer sheets over, and mark their selection. The motor task is intended to interfere with recall.

Matching Words to Sample Students select from a vertical array of options the word that matches the word at the top of the column.

Drawing from Memory Students draw twelve stimuli (letters, words, numbers, and designs) from memory. Again, turning over their answer booklets and picking up their pencils from the floor are intended to interfere with recall.

Writing Letters, Numbers, and Words from Memory The teacher says the stimulus (for example, the letters "Ess," "Eye," "Wye"), pauses for "several seconds," and tells the students to pick up their pencils, turn over their booklets, and write what they heard. There are twelve stimuli. Students may use cursive or manuscript, but they can only use lower-case letters.

Writing the Initial and Ending Letter in Words The teacher says one word at a time, and students write the initial letter of the ten words. Then the students are told to write the last letter of the next six words.

Recalling Words, Letters, and Numbers The teacher reads the stimulus, pauses "for a few seconds," and asks the students to circle the one the teacher said. From a horizontal array of four options, the student selects the one read by the teacher. There are twelve items.

Writing Answers to Questions (form D)   The teacher requests that certain information be written (for example, first and last name, name of the student's school), and students write down the information.

Scores

Poor formations and self-corrections are summed, and, for unexplained reasons, both are treated as errors. Uncorrected errors, of course, are also treated as errors. Uncorrected errors include omissions, substitutions, insertions, reversals, inversions, transpositions, substitutions of capital letter for lower-case letter (or vice versa), poor integration of symbol parts (for example, failure to join the parts of a letter is an error), poor proportion (for drawings), misspellings, and poor spatial organization.

Scores on the first two subtests are summed and contrasted with the performance on the third through eighth subtests. Slingerland (1970) advocates the use of "break-off points" —twelve to fifteen consistent errors on the third through eighth subtests are considered significant.

Reliability

A report by Fulmer (1980) accompanies the test materials. She studied 804 children in six school districts and provided data on the reliability of the Slingerland. For forms A through D, coefficient alpha was computed for visual and auditory composites and for the total score. For the visual composite, alpha ranged from .88 to .92; for auditory composite, alpha ranged from .88 to .94. Coefficient alpha for total correct ranged from .93 to .96. Interscorer reliability was also computed for total errors for each form. Reliability ranged from .69 (form A) to .91 (form C); only form C had adequate interscorer reliability. Test-retest reliability for subtests and totals are also presented. The stabilities for subtests are generally dismal; of the thirty-three coefficients, only one exceeds .7, and only five exceed .59. Stabilities for the total scores range from .71 to .85. Fulmer also reported a study by Burns and Burns, who found generally higher stabilities for total scores (.86 to .96)

Also of interest is stability of the categorization of students as "regular," "SLD," or "unready." Fulmer (1980) reports that from 71 to 87 percent of the time (depending on the grade level of the students) students were reclassified consistently upon retesting thirty days later. However, the classifications were based on more than the scores from the Slingerland.

Validity

Close examination of the Slingerland tests indicates that the content assesses perceptual-motor and memory functions in students. It is not a direct measure of language nor is it a direct measure of language disability, although it is conceivable that it predicts language function.

The empirical validity information does little to demonstrate that the device is a measure of language disability. Fulmer (1980) presents correlations between Slingerland total scores and scores from the Comprehensive Tests of Basic Skills. The number of students on which the correlations are based range from nine to seventy-one; obtained correlations vary from −.53 to −.86. (The correlations are negative because errors are correlated with correct responses.) She also reports similar results from a study by Oliphant. Whatever the test measures, it correlates with achievement. Fulmer also conducted factor analyses of the Slingerland and found that the factor structure varied from age to age. This means that whatever the test is measuring differs at different ages. Finally, Fulmer reports a study that compared the performances of students recommended for placement in a SLD class with children who were not experiencing learning difficulties. "Generally, *t*-tests for the difference between mean errors on subtests for each group proved significant at the .05 level (except for some subtests on form C)" (Fulmer, 1980, p. 18).

The validity of the recommended interpretations of scores is not established in the manuals. No data are presented to demonstrate that a number of errors greater than the "break-off" might signal the possibility of specific language disability. Nor were data provided to show that a difference between errors and errors plus self-corrections and poor formations is "an indication in itself of possible specific language disability," as Slingerland asserts (1970, p. 78).

Summary

The Slingerland is an unnormed, group-administered screening device intended to identify children with specific language disabilities. The test has adequate consistency for screening, but it lacks adequate interscorer and test-retest reliability. The validity of the device has not been demonstrated. Indeed, the content of the test would lead one to assume that it is a test of perceptual abilities, not of language.

Test of Adolescent Language

The Test of Adolescent Language (TOAL) (Hammill, Brown, Larsen, & Wiederholt, 1980) is a norm-referenced device that can be used with adolescents between the ages of 11-0 and 18-5. Six of the subtests can be group administered while two must be individually administered. The TOAL manual presents a clear description of the domain that is sampled by the test. The following components of language are assessed: spoken and written language, receptive and expressive language, and vocabulary and grammar. These six elements of language are combined into eight subtests. A brief description of each follows:

1. *Listening/Vocabulary*   This is a picture vocabulary task in which students are asked to select from a four-choice array the picture that best illustrates the word read by the examiner. Twenty-eight words are tested.
2. *Listening/Grammar*   Three sentences are read aloud to students who are asked to indicate which two express the same thought. Thirty-five three-sentence items are tested.
3. *Speaking/Vocabulary*   A word is said aloud by the examiner and the student must use it correctly in a sentence. Twenty words are tested.
4. *Speaking/Grammar*   This is a sentence imitation task in which the examiner reads a sentence to the student and the student repeats the sentence verbatim. There are twenty-five items in this subtest.
5. *Reading/Vocabulary*   This is a relational (generalization) vocabulary task where the student reads three stimulus words then reads a response bank of four words. Some of the words in the response bank will be similar and should be selected. The TOAL manual uses the following example: "Students read the words 'red,' 'blue,' and 'green'; then they read the words in the response bank: 'yellow,' 'circle,' 'orange,' and 'light.' They should select 'yellow' and 'orange'." There are twenty-five items.
6. *Reading/Grammar*   This subtest requires the student to select from a five-sentence array the two sentences that have similar meaning. There are twenty items.
7. *Writing/Vocabulary*   The student reads a

word and then writes a sentence using the word correctly. There are twenty-four items in this subtest.

8. *Writing/Grammar*   The student is given several short sentences and requested to combine them into one sentence containing all the information. There are twenty-five items.

Scores

For the subtests, raw scores are converted to normalized scaled scores with a mean of 10 and a standard deviation of 3. Ten composite scores are available on the TOAL: listening, speaking, reading, writing, spoken language, written language, vocabulary, grammar, receptive language, and expressive language. For these composites, the scaled scores are summed and the sums converted to another standard score with a mean of 100 and a standard deviation of 15. However, the total standardization sample was not used to develop the standard scores for the composites. Instead, the scores of fifty students from each age group were randomly selected and used to develop the standard scores.

Norms

The TOAL was standardized on 2,723 students from seventeen states and three Canadian provinces. The distribution of students seems comparable with national characteristics for sex and place of residence (city versus rural). No data on socioeconomic background were gathered. No handicapped students were included in the norms.

Reliability

Coefficient alpha was computed for each of the eight subtests at each of the seven grades. For these fifty-six coefficients, thirteen equal .9 while none falls below .6. Coefficient alpha was also computed for each of the eleven composites at each of the seven grades. For these seventy-seven coefficients, sixty equal .9 while only one falls below .8. Thus, the composites are usually sufficiently reliable for making important educational decisions; the total language score always is sufficiently reliable.

Stability data were also obtained for a multi-age sample with the effects of age controlled. (Consequently, stability estimates for each score for each grade are not available; only stabilities for subtests and composites were obtained.) For the subtests, only the Writing/Vocabulary subtest stability exceeds .9; for the composites, only the listening quotient (.82) and the speaking quotient (.85) were less than .9.

Finally, interscorer reliability was ascertained for the three subtests. There was some degree of subjectivity in the scoring. Using six scorers, interscorer agreements ranged from .7 to .99; the mean of the correlation coefficients ranged from .87 (Writing/Vocabulary) to .98 (Writing/Grammar). The mean number of points awarded on each subtest was also comparable for each scorer.

Validity

Evidence for content validity for the TOAL seems clear from the information presented in the manual. There is a clear description of the domain to be sampled, and there are equally clear discussions of how the domain was sampled.

Some evidence for the criterion-related validity of TOAL is presented from a study of thirty-two junior high school students. In this study, moderate to high correlations were found with several appropriate criterion measures.

Evidence for the TOAL's construct validity

comes from four sources. Mean scores on the subtests increase with age; this indicates that the TOAL measures developmental skills. The TOAL subtest scores are moderately intercorrelated. The TOAL scores correlate moderately with scores from a group intelligence test; one expects language skills and intelligence to be correlated. Mentally retarded and learning disabled students earned lower scores on the TOAL than nonhandicapped students as would be predicted.

Summary

The TOAL is a norm-referenced test designed to assess language functioning on three dimensions. Data on the standardization sample for the test are insufficient to warrant acceptance of the sample as representative, but the data that are presented do not allow one to reject the sample as unrepresentative. Reliability of the composite scores is generally good. There is clear evidence for the validity of the device.

COPING WITH DILEMMAS IN CURRENT PRACTICE

The most serious problem in the assessment of written language is inserting a match between what is taught in the school curriculum and what is tested. The great variation in the time at which various skills and facts are taught renders a general test of achievement inappropriate. This dilemma also attends diagnostic assessment of written language. Commercially prepared tests have doubtful validity for planning individual programs and evaluating the progress of individual pupils. We recommend that teachers and diagnosticians construct criterion-referenced achievement tests that closely parallel the curricula that the students follow.

In those cases where normative data are required, there are three choices. Diagnosticians can select the devices that most closely parallel the curriculum, develop local norms, or select individual students for comparative purposes.

Care should be exercised in selecting *methods* of assessing language skills. For example, it is probably better to test pupils in ways that are familiar to them. Thus, if the teacher's weekly spelling test is from dictation, then spelling tests using dictation are probably superior to tests requiring the student to identify incorrectly spelled words.

SUMMARY

Written language and spelling are regularly assessed in the schools. Teachers routinely assess these skills with informal and criterion-referenced tests. Most standardized test batteries include subtests that assess language and spelling. Very few individually administered tests have been published that deal with these content areas. Three are reviewed in this chapter.

STUDY QUESTIONS

1. Why is it important to teach standard American English in the public schools?
2. List and explain five components of written language.
3. Why is it important for spelling tests to correspond closely to the spelling words that teachers assign to their students?
4. List and explain three limitations on analyzing a pupil's English composition to assess skill in spelling, grammar, and punctuation.

ADDITIONAL READING

Cooper, C., & Odell, L. (1977). *Evaluating writing: Describing, measuring, judging.* Urbana, IL: National Council of Teachers of English. (Chapter 1: Holistic evaluation of writing; Chapter 2: Primary trait scoring.)

Graves, D. (1981). A new look at research on writing. In S. Haley-James (Ed.), *Perspectives on writing in grades 1–8.* Urbana, IL: National Council of Teachers of English.

Moss, P., Cole, N., & Khampalikit, C. (1982). A comparison of procedures to assess written language skills at grades 4, 7, and 10. *Journal of Educational Measurement, 19,* 37–47.

CHAPTER 20

ASSESSMENT OF
ADAPTIVE BEHAVIOR

Adaptive behavior is an elusive, deceptively simple concept. It refers to the extent to which individuals adapt themselves to the expectations of nature and society. Infants and preschool children are expected to conform to the normal course of maturation and development in language and cognitive functioning. The assessment of schoolage children and adolescents relies on the development of behaviors that enable them to perform adult roles. Adaptive behavior in adults is the conformity to and fulfillment of the roles that particular societies set for their adults. Adaptive behavior may also include avoidance of maladaptive behavior. What constitutes maladaptive behavior is determined by several factors: the social tolerance for particular behaviors, the context in which those behaviors are demonstrated, the status of the individual exhibiting the behavior, and the theoretical orientation of the person making the assessment.

The assessment of adaptive behavior differs from the assessment of other domains. Usually we just test the person. For adaptive behavior, we do not test the subject directly. Instead, we rely on the observation of a third person who is very familiar with the subject of the assessment. The diagnostician interviews this third person, who describes the typical behavior patterns of the subject. The subject's behavior is evaluated on this basis.

WHY DO WE ASSESS ADAPTIVE BEHAVIOR?

There are two major reasons for assessing adaptive behavior. The first is that mental retardation is generally defined as a failure in adaptive behavior. In theory, in order to classify a pupil as mentally retarded, one needs to assess adaptive behavior. More important, however, there are federal regulations and state school codes requiring that adaptive behavior be assessed before a pupil can be considered mentally retarded.

The second reason for assessing adaptive behavior is for program planning. Educational objectives in the domain of adaptive behavior are frequently developed for moderately and severely retarded individuals. Scales of adaptive behavior are often the source of educational goals.

TESTS OF ADAPTIVE BEHAVIOR

The five devices reviewed in the pages that follow are used most often with handicapped individuals. In addition, the Adaptive Behavior Inventory for Children (ABIC), which is a component of the System of Multicultural Pluralistic Assessment (SOMPA), is reviewed in Chapter 22.

Vineland Social Maturity Scale

The Vineland Social Maturity Scale (VSMS) (Doll, 1953) is perhaps the most widely known and widely used device for the assessment of social competence. In 1953 Doll published *Measurement of Social Competence: A Manual for the Vineland Social Maturity Scale.* This work is a model of what a technical manual should contain. The 664-page manual contains a detailed rationale and description of the scale as well as the necessary descriptions of norms, reliability, validity, administration and scoring, and applications. Where possible, Doll interweaves the rich research history of the scale with the explanations of its construction.

The administration of the device is unlike that of any other device discussed thus far in this book. The VSMS is *not* administered to the person being assessed. Rather, an interview procedure is used whereby an interviewer asks questions of a third person, or respondent, who is very familiar with the person being assessed. The examiner must be skilled in the general techniques of conducting clinical interviews. The *respondent* (the person being interviewed) must be well acquainted with the subject of the interview. The interviewer must be skillful in

eliciting, integrating, and evaluating the respondent's observations of the subject. Based on the information provided by the respondent, the interviewer's task is to determine whether the subject *habitually and customarily* performs certain acts; the purpose is not to determine if the subject *can* perform these acts.

Doll defined social competence as "a functional composite of human traits which subserves social usefulness as reflected in self-sufficiency and in service to others" (1953, p. 2). The VSMS assesses eight aspects of social competence. Although the 117 behaviors rated on the VSMS are clustered into eight areas, these eight areas are not subtests. The VSMS is an age scale similar in construction to the earlier editions of the Binet intelligence scales; different items appear at different age levels. The VSMS assesses social competence from birth through 30 years of age. Consequently, the items show remarkable variation—from "balances head" through "performs responsible routine chores" to "advances general welfare." Because of the tremendous age span and the complexities of social maturity, the behaviors sampled by the VSMS are difficult to characterize. Representative types of items in each of the eight clusters follow.

Self-Help General The items under this general heading assess general self-help activities such as sitting and standing unsupported, avoiding simple hazards, and using the toilet unassisted.

Self-Help Eating The items under this heading assess an individual's increasing responsibility in eating. Included are such skills as drinking from a cup with assistance, using a spoon to eat, discriminating edible from inedible objects, getting a drink unaided, and being completely self-sufficient at the dinner table.

Self-Help Dressing The items under this heading measure an individual's responsibility in dress and personal hygiene. Included are such skills as putting on a coat, buttoning, washing, and dressing completely by oneself.

Locomotion The items under this heading include walking, going about the house and yard, going about town, and going to near and distant places unattended.

Occupation The items under this heading measure an individual's increasing orientation to gainful employment. At younger ages, occupation items assess occupying oneself while unattended, using vehicular toys, and doing routine chores. At older ages, items include being employed or continuing one's education, performing skilled work, engaging in beneficial recreation, and performing expert work.

Communication Items under this heading assess command of increasingly demanding forms of communication. At very young ages, an individual is expected to demonstrate the rudiments of language (imitation of sounds, comprehension of instructions, speaking in complete sentences). At older ages, an individual is expected to read and write, use the telephone, use the mails, and enjoy reading.

Self-Direction The items in this category deal with the use of money (for example, is trusted with money, makes minor purchases, buys for others) and assuming responsibility for oneself (for example, goes out in the daytime or at night unsupervised, looks after one's own health).

Socialization Items grouped in this category assess interpersonal relationships, including for early ages behaviors like playing increasingly difficult games, and at the adult level rather more imposing behaviors like contributing to the social welfare, inspiring confidence, and promoting the general welfare.

Scoring Procedures and Scores

The task of the interviewer is to determine if the subject of the interview *habitually and customarily* performs the act or skill assessed by an item. A subject who does is given a passing score on the item. A passing score (F+) is also given if the subject formerly performed a particular act or skill but has since outgrown the behavior or is now not allowed to perform that act because of circumstances unrelated to it. This is quite similar to another type of passing performance (NO+)—no opportunity but the ability to perform the act. Scores of plus-minus are awarded to emerging behaviors; plus-minus scores are counted as half-plus (that is, two plus-minus scores equal one plus). Items are scored as minus and not credited under several conditions. F− scores are awarded when the subject formerly performed the act but is no longer capable of doing so because of some impairment, such as senility or a physical handicap. NO− scores are awarded when a subject is restrained from participating in an activity because that subject gets into trouble; for example, certain adolescents may have no opportunity to go out at night unsupervised because when they do, they steal cars. Finally, a failing score is given if the subject usually does not perform the act. One other score, no information (NI), is awarded when the respondent cannot or does not provide adequate enough information for the interviewer to score the item.

The number of passing scores is summed and converted to a social age (SA), which is interpreted in the same manner as any other age score. A ratio social quotient (SQ) can also be obtained ($100 \times SA/CA = SQ$). As in the case of age scores in general, the standard deviations of SAs and SQs vary at different chronological ages. Doll (1953) has tabled the means and standard deviations for SAs and SQs at each age.

Norms

A total of 620 white subjects, 10 males and 10 females at each age level from birth to 30 years of age, make up the norm sample. All subjects in the norm group were selected from the greater Vineland, New Jersey, area in 1935. Thus, the norms are over forty years old. Children with educational or mental retardation were excluded, as were children with physical handicaps. According to Doll, the normative data "show normal middle-class sampling without inclusion of marked extremes" (1953, p. 356).

Reliability

No internal-consistency estimates of reliability are provided in the manual. Doll does present a considerable amount of stability (test-retest) data. Two hundred fifty subjects from the norm sample were retested (1.7- to 1.9-year interval); SAs were grouped in one-year intervals, and the resulting test-retest correlation was .98. For the same sample, SQs were grouped in ten-point intervals, and the resulting test-retest correlation was .57. Since the stability estimate of the SQs should not be affected as much by CA, they are probably a better estimate.

Doll also reports interinterviewer and interrespondent correlations. For a sample of 123 feeble-minded subjects, he had the following retest data: 12 subjects had the same interviewer and the same respondent; 68 subjects had the same interviewer but different respondents; 19 subjects had different interviewers and the same respondent; and 25 subjects had different interviewers and different respondents. When the four conditions were pooled, the test-retest correlation was .92 for SA.

Validity

The validity of the VSMS rests on content analysis and correlations of ratings of social competence made by persons familiar with the subject and social ages derived from the VSMS. These correlations tend to be quite substantial—over .80 typically. One of the major difficulties with the content of the VSMS is its age. The majority of items are as representative of social competence today as they were in the 1930s. However, the placement of the items in the scale may well be incorrect today. For example, using the telephone is placed at the 10.3-year level and going about town unattended is placed at the 9.4-year level. Our intuition tells us that children use the telephone at an earlier age now but that they may not go about town unattended until a later age.

Summary

The VSMS is a venerable instrument used to assess social competence. We believe it is badly in need of revision and updating. The item placement may no longer be appropriate, and the sample is very restricted.

Vineland Adaptive Behavior Scale[1]

The Vineland Adaptive Behavior Scale (VABS) (Sparrow, Balla, & Cicchetti, 1984) is an individually administered scale given to an individual (such as a parent or caregiver) who is very familiar with the person who is the subject of the structured interview. The VABS has been billed as the 1984 revision of the Vineland Social Maturity Scale (VSMS). As would be expected, the revision entailed converting the old VSMS from an age scale to a more modern point scale, introduction of much needed standard scores, and complete restandardization. However, the revision is far more sweeping; the new VABS might better be considered a new device.

The new VABS is available in three forms that vary in the number and type of items contained. The Survey Form of the Interview Edition (297 items) is intended to provide a general appraisal of the individual and requires about 20 to 60 minutes to administer to a parent or caregiver. The Expanded Form of the Interview Edition (577 items) is intended to provide a comprehensive appraisal suitable for planning educational treatment programs for individuals; it requires about 60 to 90 minutes to administer to a parent or caregiver. The Classroom Edition (244 items) requires about 20 minutes to administer to a teacher. The three editions can be given in English or Spanish. All three assess communication, daily living skills, socialization, and motor domains. The two interview editions also assess maladaptive behavior.

Each edition is divided into domains; domains are divided into subdomains; subdomains are divided into clusters that consist of items.

For example, the first *subdomain* in communication is the "receptive subdomain"; the first *cluster* within the subdomain is "beginning to understand"; the first *item* within the cluster is "turns eyes and head toward sound." The Communication domain assesses three subdomains: receptive language (from "beginning to understand" to "listening and attending"), expressive language (from "beginning affective expression" —for example, smiling—to "expressing complex ideas"), and written subdomain (from "identifying letters and words" to "writing letters and reports"). The Daily Living Skills domain assesses three subdomains: personal (from "eating" to "caring for fingernails"), domestic (from "beginning housecleaning" to "sewing"), and community (from "safety at home" to "managing money"). The Socialization domain also assesses three subdomains: interpersonal relationships (from "beginning responsiveness" to "dating"), play and leisure time (from "playing with toys" to "going places with friends independently"), and coping skills (from "following rules" to "making and keeping appointments"). The Motor domain assesses two subdomains: gross (from "sitting" to "riding tricycle and bicycle") and fine (from "using both hands" to "using scissors"). The Maladaptive Behavior domain consists of thirty-six behaviors that were not listed in the advance materials.

Scores

Within domains, items between basal and ceiling are scored "yes" or "usually" (2 points), "sometimes" or "partially" (1 point), "no" or "never" (0 points), and "no opportunity" or "don't know" (1 point). Raw scores from domains of communication, daily living skills, socialization, and motor skills can also be added

1. At the time this chapter was being prepared, the Vineland Adaptive Behavior Scale had not been published. American Guidance Service was kind enough to allow us to review a prepublication version of the Sampler of the scale.

to form an "Adaptive Behavior Composite." Because the raw scores are simply added to form this composite, the subdomains are not weighted equally. Domain and composite totals can be converted to standard scores (mean = 100, standard deviation = 15), percentile ranks, stanines, and age equivalents. Descriptive categories for scores are also provided.

Norms

Several sets of norm groups are available. For the interview editions, a national sample of 3,000 individuals who ranged in age from birth to 18 years, 11 months was tested. The sample compares favorably to the 1980 census for region, race and ethnic group membership, parental education, and community size. For the classroom edition, 2,984 children between the ages of 3 and 12 years, 11 months were tested. The sample compares favorably to the 1980 census for race and ethnic group membership. It appears unrepresentative for geographic region (overrepresenting the North Central region and underrepresenting the others), parental education (overrepresenting college educated and underrepresenting those with a high school education or less schooling), and community size (overrepresenting central city and underrepresenting rural areas). Supplementary samples are also available: institutionalized and noninstitutionalized mentally retarded adults and institutionalized children who were either emotionally disturbed, visually handicapped, or hearing impaired. The supplementary norms are not carefully described.

Reliability

Only information on median split-half reliabilities (based on the standardization sample) for each domain and composite were available. For the Survey Form of the Interview Edition,

medians for the domains ranged from .83 (Motor Skills) to .90 (Daily Living Skills). For the Expanded Form of the Interview Edition, medians for the domains ranged from .86 (Maladaptive Behavior) to .95 (Daily Living Skills). For the Classroom Edition, medians for the domains ranged from .82 (Motor Skills) to .91 (Daily Living Skills). If the range of coefficients is too low, the reliabilities appear adequate for screening on the Survey Form and for assessment on the Expanded Form. They do not appear adequate for assessment on the Classroom Edition. The materials available indicated that data on stability (test-retest correlations) and interrater agreement would be available for both the Survey Form and Expanded Form of the Interview Editions.

Validity

Although content validity is not specifically addressed in the materials available, the methods of item selection and the actual items selected give credence to claims of validity. Concurrent validity was established by correlation with other measures of adaptive behavior. Construct validity was established by showing developmental trends in student performance on the domains and subdomains and by factor analysis.

Summary

The Vineland Adaptive Behavior Scale is an individually administered, norm-referenced device intended to assess the adaptive and maladaptive behavior of individuals under 19 years of age. The reliability, validity, and norms of the Survey Form and Expanded Form of the scale appear adequate. For the Classroom Edition, the reliability is too low for making important individual decisions, and the norms appear to be unrepresentative of the general population.

Cain-Levine Social Competency Scale

The Cain-Levine Social Competency Scale (Cain, Levine, & Elzey, 1963) is a device intended to assess the independence of trainable mentally retarded children between the ages of 5 years and 13 years, 11 months. The scale is administered in a structured interview with someone who is very familiar with the subject; the subject is not interviewed. The interviewer introduces each item with a general question about the subject's behavior in a particular area and then probes the respondent's answers. The forty-four items that make up the scale are grouped into four subscales: Self-Help, Initiative, Social Skills, and Communication.

Self-Help This subscale contains fourteen items "designed to estimate the child's manipulative ability, or motor skills" (Cain et al., 1963, p. 2). More points are awarded when it is reported that the subject performs the task adequately. Skills assessed include dressing, washing, eating, and helping with simple chores around the house.

Initiative This subscale contains ten items designed to assess the extent to which the subject initiates activities or is self-directed. Skills assessed include dressing, toileting, completing tasks, hanging up clothes, and offering assistance.

Social Skills This subscale contains ten items designed to ascertain the extent to which the subject maintains or engages in interpersonal relationships. Typical items are table setting, answering the telephone, and playing with and helping others.

Communication This subscale contains ten items intended to ascertain the degree to which the subject's wants are communicated. Individual items range from the use of oral language

and clarity of speech to delivery of messages and relating objects to actions.

Scoring Procedures and Scores

Thirty-eight items are rated on a four-point scale, while six items are rated on a five-point scale. For each item, a score of 1 represents the lowest level, or the absence, of behavior. For example, the item assessing question answering on the Communication subscale is scored 1 if the subject does not respond to questions and scored 4 if the subject answers questions with a complete sentence. In those cases where the subject is not permitted by parents or guardians to participate in an activity or to demonstrate a skill, the subject receives a score of 1.

Raw scores on the forty-four items are summed. Since boys typically earn somewhat lower scores than girls earn, a constant (the magnitude of which depends on the age of the subject) is added to the total score earned by boys. Each subscale and the total raw scores can be converted to percentile ranks. Five age tables are provided for this purpose: 5-0 to 5-11, 6-0 to 7-11, 8-0 to 9-11, 10-0 to 11-11, and 12-0 to 13-11.

Norms

The Cain-Levine was standardized on 414 males and 302 females between the ages of 5-0 and 13-11. "The children aged 8-0 and older were enrolled in city and county public school programs in the state of California. The names of children aged 5-0 through 7-11 years were obtained from public school districts and from parent associations" (Cain et al., 1963, p. 8). IQ data from various sources are presented in the technical manual to demonstrate that the sample is "trainable." IQs ranged from 25 through 59. At the 5-0 to 5-11 age level, there is a large difference in mean IQs between boys ($\overline{X}$ = 30.09) and girls ($\overline{X}$ = 45.50). After age 8-0, the mean IQs stabilize in the low to mid-40s. Data provided by the test authors indicate that the occupational levels of the parents or guardians in the Cain-Levine sample tend to be biased toward overrepresentation of lower-class families. However, this difference may accurately reflect the frequency of mental retardation in the different social classes (see Farber, 1968).

Reliability

For the total score, odd-even internal consistencies, based on the standardization sample, range from .75 to .91. Internal consistencies for individual subtests tend to be lower, ranging from .55 to .95. Test-retest reliability estimates over a three-week interval for thirty-five children are quite high. Total raw-score stability is reported as .98, while three of the four subtests have stability coefficients that exceed .90. However, stability coefficients were apparently computed across ages.

Validity

The validity of the Cain-Levine rests on item selection and the correlation between social competence and MA and CA. Item selection was based on an examination of "all major curriculum guides developed for the trainable mentally retarded by public schools and institutions," "consultations with professional personnel," "discussions with parents," and "careful examination of existing scales and evaluational instruments" (Cain et al., 1963, p. 7). The scale correlates reasonably well (between .4 and .5) with CA and not very well with IQ (between .09 and .30).

Summary

The Cain-Levine is an interview-based device designed to assess social competence in self-help, initiative, social skills, and communication. The device is sufficiently reliable for screening purposes and appears to have adequate validity, although the normative sample was limited to children residing in California.

AAMD Adaptive Behavior Scale

The American Association on Mental Deficiency (AAMD) Adaptive Behavior Scale (Nihira, Foster, Shellhaas, & Leland, 1969) is intended to measure the behavior of three types of handicapped persons: retarded, disturbed, and developmentally disabled. Specifically, the scale is designed to provide a description "of the way an individual maintains his or her personal independence in daily living or of how he or she meets the social expectations of his or her environment" (Nihira, Foster, Shellhaas, & Leland, 1974, p. 5).

As is the case with other measures of social competence, the scale is administered to a third person who is asked about the subject's performance. The scale consists of two parts. Part 1 contains sixty-six items that rate skill use in ten domains. For each item there are several statements. Some items require that the respondent check the one statement that best describes the subject; other items require that all statements applying to the subject be checked. Items are grouped into areas, and areas are grouped into domains.

Part 1 consists of items grouped into ten domains that are described as follows.

Independent Functioning In this domain skills are measured in eight areas: (1) Four items relate to eating—from use of utensils to table manners. (2) Two items deal with toilet use. (3) Five items deal with cleanliness and range from bathing to menstruation. (4) Posture and clothing items are clustered under the more general area of Appearance. (5) A separate area is used to access care of clothing. (6) The area of Dressing and Undressing is measured by three items. (7) Two items (Sense of Direction and Use of Public Transportation) deal with travel. (8) The last area (Independent Functioning) is assessed by two items: Telephone Use and a miscellaneous item.

Physical Development   In this domain skills are measured in two areas: (1) Sensory Function (vision and hearing), and (2) Motor Development (balance, ambulation, motor control, and so on).

Economic Activity   In this domain skills are measured in two areas: (1) Money Handling (knowledge of money and budgeting), and (2) Shopping.

Language Development   In this domain skills are measured in three areas: (1) Expression is assessed by five items (Prelinguistic Communication, Articulation, Word Usage, Use of Complete and Progressively More Complex Sentences, and Writing). (2) Comprehension is assessed by two items: Understanding Complex Statements and Reading. (3) Social language development is assessed by Conversational and Miscellaneous Language Skills.

Numbers and Time   In this domain skills are assessed by items dealing with the understanding and use of numbers and time.

Domestic Activity   In this domain skills are measured in three areas: (1) Cleaning, (2) Food and Serving, and (3) Miscellaneous.

Vocational Activity   In this domain skills are assessed by three items related to performing complex jobs safely and reliably.

Self-Direction   This domain consists of three areas: (1) In Initiative, two items (Initiation of Activities and Passivity) are included. (2) In Perseverance, two items (Attention and Persistence) are assessed. (3) In Leisure Time, several items assess what subjects do in their free time.

Responsibility   In this domain skills are measured by two items: Care of Personal Belongings and General Responsibility.

Socialization   In this domain seven items sample both appropriate and inappropriate behaviors. For inappropriate behaviors points are subtracted.

Part 2 consists of forty-four items grouped into fourteen domains. All items in part 2 are scored in the same way. The respondent rates all statements in each item that apply to the subject as a 1 (occasionally) or a 2 (frequently). A description of the domains assessed in part 2 follows.

Violent and Destructive Behavior   Five items assess personal and property damage as well as temper tantrums.

Antisocial Behavior   Six items assess teasing, bossing, disruptive behavior, and inconsiderate behavior.

Rebellious Behavior   Six items assess disobedience and insubordination.

Untrustworthy Behavior   This domain contains two items, Lying and Stealing.

Withdrawal   This domain contains three items, Inactivity, Withdrawal, and Shyness.

Stereotyped Behavior and Odd Mannerisms
This domain contains the two items described by the domain title.

Inappropriate Interpersonal Manners This domain has one item.

Unacceptable Vocal Habits This domain contains one item.

Unacceptable or Eccentric Habits This domain contains four items.

Self-Abusive Behavior This domain contains one item.

Hyperactive Tendencies This domain is also one item.

Sexually Aberrant Behavior This domain contains four items dealing with masturbation, homosexuality, and socially unacceptable behaviors, such as rape.

Psychological Disturbance This domain contains seven items that explore possible emotional disturbance.

Uses Medication Use of medication for the control of hyperactivity, seizures, and so on is considered by the scale authors to be maladaptive.

Two aspects of the statements contained in each item on both parts are especially noteworthy. First, many statements are not only overly value-laden but are also unnecessarily subjective. For example, hugging "too intensely" in public is viewed as unacceptable sexual behavior. One wonders to whom the hugging is too intense. The huggee or the observer? Second, the scale lacks proportion. For example, rape carries as much weight as being overly seductive in appearance. Similarly, attempted

suicide is given the same number of points as acting sick after an illness.

Scores

Raw scores for each domain are summed. Tables in the manual accompanying the scale allow the examiner to convert raw scores to deciles only, although the tables are labeled *percentile ranks*. In part 1, the higher the decile rank, the better the development of the person. In part 2, however, the higher the decile rank, the more *maladaptive* is the person's behavior.

Norms

Deciles are based on evaluations by unspecified individuals of approximately 4,000 institutionalized persons in eleven age groups from a 3-year-old group to a 50-to-69-year-old group. The number of persons in each age group ranges from 528 at 10 to 12 years to 97 at age 3. Mean IQs (tests unspecified) for each age group range from 28 at age 3 to 45.8 at age 16 to 18.

Reliability

Only interrater reliability is considered in the manual. Pearson product-moment correlation coefficients were used to estimate interrater agreement by attendants for 133 institutionalized subjects. For part 1, the mean reliability estimates ranged from .71 (Self-Direction) to .92 (Independent Functioning). For part 2, the reliability estimates ranged from .37 (Unacceptable Vocal Habits) to .77 (Uses Medication).

Validity

Results of two factor-analytic studies conducted by one of the scale's authors with the previous edition of the scale are discussed. Three factors were found and were labeled *personal independence, social maladaption,* and *personal mala-*

daption. The results of two other studies are also mentioned briefly; these studies showed there was some correspondence between "clinical" judgment by undefined persons and ratings derived from the scale.

No evidence of content validity is presented. Examiners must judge for themselves the validity and appropriateness of the particular items.

Summary

The AAMD Adaptive Behavior Scale is a recent attempt to quantify adaptive behavior. Al-though expressly designed for use with various groups of handicapped persons, it is standardized only on institutionalized retardates. Estimates of interrater reliability are so low that although some domains can be considered accurate enough only for screening purposes, some are not even adequate for experimental work. Very limited validity data are presented for the previous edition of the scale. At its present stage of development, the scale does not appear adequate for making important educational decisions about individuals.

AAMD Adaptive Behavior Scale, School Edition

Separate manuals and norms for the AAMD Adaptive Behavior Scale were prepared for use in the schools by Lambert, Windmiller, and colleagues. Three domains (Domestic Activity, Self-Abusive Behavior, and Sexually Aberrant Behavior), not readily observed in or pertinent to school, were deleted. The AAMD Adaptive Behavior Scale, School Edition (ABS–SE) (Lambert & Windmiller, 1981) is the latest edition of the scale. The items remain essentially the same as those in the 1974 edition although some renaming has occurred. Teachers are the preferred respondents. The specimen kit includes an Administration and Instructional Planning Manual, a Diagnostic and Technical Manual, an Instructional Planning Profile, a Diagnostic Profile, and A Parent's Guide: Using the Adaptive Behavior Scale to Identify Children's Special Needs.

The scale is intended to provide information about students' "personal independence and social skills and to reveal areas of functioning where special program planning" is needed. (Lambert, Windmiller, Tharinger, & Cole, 1981, p. 3). Part 1 of the scale consists of nine domains intended to assess adaptive behavior; part 2 consists of twelve domains assessing personality and behavior disorders. If the scale is given as an adjunct in instructional planning or program evaluation, the authors recommend combining the domains from part 1 into clusters: physical development, cognitive development, personal independence, volitional skills, and socialization (Lambert et al., 1981). If a more general overview of adaptive behavior is desired, one can construct a "diagnostic" profile that consists of five clusters of domains (derived from factor analytic studies of adaptive behavior of adults and children):[2] personal self-sufficiency, community self-sufficiency, personal-social responsibility, social adjustment, and personal adjustment.

---

2. In the Diagnostic and Technical Manual, Lambert cites four studies to support her contention that there are five factors on the ABS–SE. Two studies were conducted with adults (Guarmaccia, 1976; Nihira, 1969a). Two studies were done with children and adolescents. Lambert and Nicoll (1976) found two factors in part 1 that they named functional autonomy and interpersonal adjustment; they also found two factors, named social responsibility and intrapersonal adjustment, in part 2. The second study by Nihira (1969b), using an earlier version of the AAMD Adaptive Behavior Scale with institutionalized retarded persons, found three factors: personal independence, social maladaption, and personal maladaption. It is unclear how these studies support the existence of five factors.

Scores

Raw scores are converted to scaled scores that have a mean of 10 and a standard deviation of 3. Raw scores are also converted to "converted factor scores," which are in turn converted to "comparison scores." Comparison scores can be converted to cumulative percentages (the percentage of the sample earning lower scores).

The guidelines for interpreting the scores offered in the manual are misleading. We are told that "Domain score percentiles provide information about the relative standing of a student" (Lambert, 1981, p. 10) although there are *no* tables for converting to percentiles. (Cumulative frequencies are not percentiles; cumulative frequencies will differ substantially from percentiles when the samples are small or when several individuals earn the same raw score.) We are also told that serious deficits in adaptive behavior are indicated by percentile ranks below the 10th percentile (except for four domains where the critical number is the 15th percentile) and factor scores more than one standard deviation below the mean (that is, less than 7).

Norms

The standardization sample consists of five samples and is inadequately described in the manuals. Sample 1 consists of 2,135 children from the 1974 standardization sample of 2,600 California children between the ages of 7 and 13 who were attending regular classes or classes for the educable or trainable mentally retarded in 1972–1973. Sample 2 consists of 3,220 children between the ages of 3 and 16 attending regular classes or classes for the educable or trainable mentally retarded in Florida. Sample 3 consists of 363 regular and trainable mentally retarded preschoolers (between the ages of 3 and 6) living in California and Florida. Sample 4 consists of 656 California Educable and trainable mentally retarded persons between the ages of 6 and 16

"whose reevaluations indicated continued special education placement" (Lambert, 1981, p. 22). Sample 5 consists of 149 California adolescents between the ages of 13 and 16. Frequencies of individuals in the normative samples are provided by ethnic status, urbanization (urban, suburban, rural), classification (regular class, educable mentally retarded, trainable mentally retarded), and socioeconomic status (high, middle, and low). No data are presented to demonstrate that the sample is representative of any population. Only about 34 percent of the sample is considered "regular."

Separate norm tables are provided for students attending regular programs, programs for the educable mentally retarded (EMR), and programs for the trainable mentally retarded (TMR). For children between the ages of 3 to 4 and 6 to 7, conversion tables for regular and TMR pupils are available. From 7 to 8 to 15 to 16 conversion tables are available for regular, EMR, and TMR students. Tables for EMR students and TMR students are available for ages 16 to 17. The number of pupils in each age for each classification group varies considerably. Eighteen of the thirty-seven norm tables are based on less than 100 individuals. For TMR students, the size of the norm group varies from 29 to 110; for EMR students, size varies from 88 to 608; for students in regular classes, size varies from 39 to 320.

Reliability

Coefficient alpha was used to compute the internal consistency of each factor score at each age for pupils in regular classes as well as for EMR students and TMR students. For regular-class pupils, reliabilities ranged from .96 to .38; forty-two of the sixty-five age $\times$ factor coefficients are less than .90. For EMR students, coefficients ranged from .95 to .34; thirty-five of the fifty age $\times$ factor coefficients are less than .90. For TMR students, coefficients ranged from .94 to .27; of the seventy age $\times$ factor coefficients, forty-eight are less than .90.

No reliability data for domain scores or for total or composite scores are reported. No data on stability are reported.

Validity

Construct validity was established by correlating IQs and domain scores. The obtained correlations ranged from .18 to .63 for part 1 and from .28 to $-$.23 for part 2. Domain scores are associated with regular or EMR placement. Factor scores were also correlated with achievement test scores for both regular and EMR students in the Florida sample. Although there is considerable mention of factors in the ABS–SE, no data are presented demonstrating that five factors are obtained when one analyzes the ABS–SE.

Of special interest is the comparison score. The statistical procedures used were designed to optimize discriminations among regular students and EMR students and TMR students. The difficulty, of course, is that adaptive be-

havior is only one of several criteria used to place pupils in special programs for the retarded.

No data are provided to demonstrate that critical scores (below the 10th or 15th percentile on domains or more than one standard deviation below the mean on factor scores) are indeed suggestive of unusual problems.

Summary

The school edition of the AAMD Adaptive Behavior Scale contains essentially the same items that are found on the institutional instrument from which it was derived. However, it contains three fewer domains and some minor changes in wording. The norms do not appear representative, and the number of children in some of the norm groups is too limited to provide stable interindividual comparisons. Although the avowed purpose of the instrument is to aid in placement and program-planning decisions, the reliability of the scale is not adequate for these purposes. Validity for the interpretation of the various scores is also suspect.

COPING WITH DILEMMAS IN CURRENT PRACTICE

There are three severe problems in the use of currently available instruments to assess adaptive behavior. The first problem is professional consensus about what constitutes adaptive behavior. Reading the definitions offered in the scientific literature and inspecting the behaviors sampled by the various devices indicate a lack of agreement about adaptive behavior. Indeed, there is a broad range of behaviors sampled and orientations toward measurement. Without better agreement on the concept of adaptive behavior, one must exercise great care in making definitive statements about a person's adaptive behavior based on any one scale. In our opinion, diagnosticians should specify clearly the various aspects of adaptive behavior they wish to assess with one or more scales. In the absence of appropriate scales, the only option may be to develop one's own scale with local norms.

The second problem is more technical. Scales of adaptive behavior require that pupils be rated by people who are very familiar with them. There are numerous possibilities for bias; they range from ignorance to inaccurate statements about the student. There are at least three ways to deal with this potential problem. It is important for diagnosticians to encourage respondents to admit freely that they do not know particular facts about the pupil. Another strategy that a diagnostician can use is actual observation of the pupil. Many of the skills and behaviors assessed on the various adaptive behavior scales are observable and are of sufficiently high frequency that an observer would be able to note them in a relatively short time. A final strategy would be to interview two respondents about one pupil. Although it is possible that both respondents would be mistaken in their evaluations of a pupil, the risk should be substantially reduced.

The third problem is that scales of adaptive behavior are typically inadequate from a technical point of view. They are poorly normed (sometimes only on handicapped populations) and have limited reliability—two very serious shortcomings. If the norm samples are unrepresentative, they should not be used. An alternative to unrepresentative norms is simply to isolate one or two students to use for comparison. Teachers or parents can be asked to nominate individuals of the same age and sex whom they believe have "adapted" successfully. The behavior of these adaptive peers can then be used to make rather simple comparisons. Although one or two children certainly are no substitute for a normative sample, they may prove adequate for some comparisons. Inadequate reliability poses a more serious problem. If interobserver agreement and internal consistency are inadequate, the definition of the domain and the particular behavior that is being observed will have to be reworked. For commercially prepared devices, this boils down to making up a new instrument. Until this is done, diagnosticians may be forced to rely on observations and more general appraisals of individuals within the peer group.

SUMMARY

In the assessment of adaptive behavior we are interested in what an individual regularly does, not what the individual is capable of doing. Ultimately, the behaviors of interest in adults are those that allow individuals to manage their affairs sufficiently well that they do not require societal intervention to protect them or others. The behaviors that are believed to be important vary from time to time and from theory to theory. In general, in the United States, adults are expected to exercise reasonable care of themselves (health, dressing, eating, and so on), to work, and to engage in socially acceptable recreational or leisure activities. In children and adolescents, the behaviors of interest are those that are believed to enable the desired adult behaviors and skills.

The assessment of adaptive behavior usually takes the form of a structured interview with a person (for example, a parent or teacher) who is very familiar with the person being assessed (the subject of the interview). The assessment of adaptive behavior has been plagued by inadequate instruments—scales that lack reliabiltiy and are poorly normed. One must select scales (or parts of scales) with great care.

STUDY QUESTIONS

1. How does the assessment of adaptive behavior differ from the assessment of academic achievement?
2. What criteria would be appropriate to classify a behavior as maladaptive?
3. With the introduction of computers and robots to American industry, what do you think will happen to current definitions of adaptive behavior?
4. Do you think adaptive behavior ranges from absent to highly developed, or does it range from absent to adequate? Why?

ADDITIONAL READING

Reschly, D. (1982). Assessing mild mental retardation: The influence of adaptive behavior, sociocultural status, and prospects for nonbiased assessment. In C. Reynolds and T. Gutkin (Eds.), *Handbook of school psychology* (pp. 220–236). New York: Wiley.

CHAPTER 21

SCHOOL READINESS

The format of this chapter differs from that of previous chapters for two reasons. First, in each of the preceding chapters tests of a particular domain were reviewed, but no particular domain of items can properly be called "readiness" items. Second, the uses to which readiness tests are put are different from the uses of the tests previously discussed.

WHY DO WE ASSESS READINESS?

We use readiness and developmental tests with young children much as we use achievement tests with students who are enrolled in schools. We often use them as measures of attainment before formal schooling. Since special education services are frequently available for preschoolers, some form of attainment testing is needed to ascertain whether a child needs or is eligible for some form of special service. When used with children about to enter school, readiness tests give school personnel some idea of what to expect from incoming students. Such information may actually be used to exclude unready students or to track pupils into various programs. For children who have been in school for some time, readiness tests may be used to assess beginning skills for particular curricula (music or math, for example). In recent years there has been systematic deemphasis of readiness assessment except as a measure of attainment for preschoolers.

GENERAL CONSIDERATIONS

Readiness is usually considered essential for initial entry into school, although the concept of readiness can be appropriately applied at all levels of instruction. For example, to be ready for algebra instruction, the student must have mastered more basic mathematical concepts and operations. Readiness for higher-level academic instruction is usually conceptualized as mastery of prerequisite material. Readiness for school entry is a more complex topic. Readiness for the first grade or even kindergarten is a generalized readiness and refers to both academic and social readiness. Academic readiness is most often thought of in terms of reading readiness but properly includes readiness for *all* academic instruction. We must also consider, however, a child's readiness for the social milieu of school. In school, children must follow the directions of an adult other than their parent or guardian, must enter into cooperative ventures with their peers, must not present a physical threat to themselves or others, must have mastered many self-help skills such as toileting, and so on.

Readiness for school entry is further complicated because there are two different orientations toward the topic. The first, a *skill orientation,* was implicit in the foregoing discussion. It holds that readiness involves the skill development and knowledge prerequisite to *beginning* instruction. Academic and social instruction is viewed as a program of sequential skills and knowledge that is built on previously mastered skills and knowledge. From this perspective, skills learned in school build on skills learned at home. The second orientation, a *process orientation,* is further removed from direct instruction. Here readiness is viewed in terms of underlying processes (intelligence, discrimination, and so on) that are believed to be necessary for the acquisition of skills and knowledge. If the processes are mature or developed, the child is ready to learn, to acquire skills.

Traditionally, formal readiness assessment has dealt with academic-process testing. For the most part, the tests have been norm-referenced and the abilities that are thought to underlie all, or at least most, academic skills are the most typically tested. Thus, intelligence or learning aptitude, which is believed to underlie all school subjects, is often a component of a readiness assessment. Indeed, intelligence tests were developed to predict school success and are often validated against achievement tests or teacher ratings. Entry into formal school programs is often predicated upon a mental age of 6 or more years. Intellectual readiness can be assessed by any of the better tests discussed in Chapters 10 and 11. Perceptual-motor development is also thought to underlie school achievement, particularly reading (see Chapter 14). Readiness tests often contain many items or subtests that are appropriately termed perceptual-motor. Although these items and tests are usually less predictive of school achievement than are intelligence tests, many people feel they are an important component of readiness. Language development (see Chapter 19) is obviously important for school success. Children must be fluent in the idiomatic English of their peers; they must also understand and use standard (formal) English.

The assessment of school readiness is not a unique kind of measurement. What makes a test a readiness test is *not* what the test measures or how the measuring is done; three distinctive features make a test a readiness test. First, readiness tests are typically administered before school entry or during kindergarten. Second, the tests are used to predict initial school success and to select those children who perform poorly—and thus are thought not to be ready for regular school experiences—for participation in remedial or compensatory educational programs or delayed school entry. Third, these tests often contain the word *readiness* in the test name.

TECHNICAL CONSIDERATIONS

School readiness is a deceptively simple concept. Knowledge of a child's readiness can provide the teacher with invaluable information that may insure that the child enters an instructional sequence at an appropriate level *or* it can provide the teacher with a destructive self-fulfilling prophecy that may actually hamper a child's development. Since decisions made on the basis of readiness tests are so important, the validity of the tests is crucial.

The purposes of readiness tests are

1. To predict who is not ready for formal entry into academic instruction
2. To predict who will profit from either remedial or compensatory educational programs in which readiness skills or processes are developed

It is apparent from these two purposes that the academic development of many children must be followed and documented. When the same children are followed and their progress recorded, the data are called *longitudinal.* Readiness data *must* be longitudinal in both standardization and validation. Specifically, to validate a readiness test, a large number of children must be tested before they enter school and then be retested after a specific period of time in school—generally one year. Only in this way can we determine if children with poor scores on the readiness test perform poorly during actual schooling.

If readiness tests do indeed accurately identify which children will do poorly in school, the educator is faced with a choice of whether to admit a child to the regular school program or take another action. If the child is admitted to the regular school program, the only justification for the test having been administered is that it gives the teacher sufficient information to take steps to overcome the deficits in the child's readiness. Such a use for readiness tests is not justified when one views readiness as physiological maturation. However, if readiness is viewed as depending on skills or processes susceptible to environmental manipulation, there is some justification.

If the child is not admitted to the regular school program, the educator can choose either to delay entry into the regular program or to provide remedial or compensatory preschool or kindergarten programs. Either of these alternatives should be considered only in light of research data indicating that readiness tests are effective predictors of differential programming. In essence, aptitude-treatment interaction research is required to validate these uses. As an illustration of how this research might be accomplished, let us assume that a school district chooses to delay school entry for children who score poorly on a readiness test. To validate this action, it would be necessary to administer the test to a large number of children before admission to school and then divide the children randomly into two groups, admitting one group to school and delaying the entry of the other for, say, one year. After *both* groups had completed their first year of regular schooling (kindergarten or first grade), the groups would be compared on some measure of school success. Two of several possible outcomes are presented in Figure 21.1. In part a, no matter what their readiness score, children perform better if their school entry is delayed. A child scoring fairly low on readiness would earn a performance score at point A if entered immediately into school but at point A′ if allowed to wait before entering; similarly, a child with high readiness would earn a higher performance score (B′ as compared to B) with delayed entry. In short, there is no *differential* advantage afforded by delaying children who score poorly on the readiness test. In part b, by contrast, there is a significant aptitude-by-treatment interaction: children who score poorly on the readiness test perform better in school (at A′ rather than A) when their entry is delayed; but children who score well on the readiness test perform better in school (at B rather than B′) when they are immediately enrolled. The same type of research could be used to evaluate compensatory or remedial programs when placement decisions are based on readiness tests.

From the foregoing discussion, it is apparent that the validation of readiness tests is not a simple or convenient task. Validation takes a minimum of one or two years. It must take place in a variety of schools where distinctive features of the curriculum are carefully noted. It is possible that a particular readiness test may predict well who would profit from one type of remedial or compensatory program but not who would profit from another program. Similarly, the predictive validity may vary according to curriculum; one test may predict well a student's progress in one reading program but not predict that student's progress in another program.

Standardization sample norms are generally gathered for four groups; beginning kindergarten (September), middle kindergarten (January), end of kindergarten (June), and beginning first grade. Children tested for the norm group should also be retested at the end of first grade to determine predictive validity. In the area of readiness, perhaps more than any other, local longitudinal norms are very important.

Although the foregoing discussion has stressed norms and predictive validity, reliability should not be overlooked. As can be recalled from Chapter 7, reliability has a definite effect on validity. An unreliable test must have poor predictive validity. Finally, readiness is an area where tests *are* routinely used to make important educational decisions about individual children. Consequently, readiness tests must meet the highest technical standards.

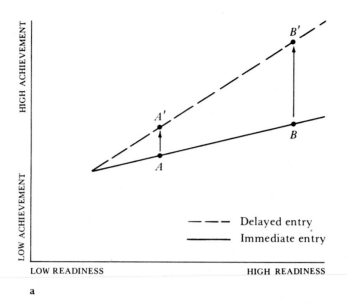

b

FIGURE 21.1   Possible interactions between readiness and delayed school entry

SPECIFIC TESTS OF SCHOOL READINESS

Denver Developmental Screening Test

The Denver Developmental Screening Test (DDST) (Frankenburg, Dodds, Fandal, Kazuk, & Cohrs, 1975) is an individually administered, norm-referenced, multiple-skill device designed for the early identification of children with developmental and behavioral problems. It is intended for use with children from birth to 6 years of age. No special training is needed to administer the screening test, which requires approximately 20 minutes to give, score, and interpret. Test forms and the test manual are available in Spanish.

One hundred five skills are clustered into four general developmental areas that must be administered in the order in which they are discussed here. The first area is *personal-social development.* It contains twenty-three items. These can be clustered into three subareas: responding to another person (for example, smiling), playing (playing pat-a-cake, joining in interactive games), and self-care (dressing, washing, feeding). The second area, *fine motor development,* contains thirty items. These assess grasping and manipulation, building towers of various heights with blocks, drawing (for example, scribbling, drawing a person), and copying increasingly difficult geometric designs. The third area is *language development.* The twenty-one items in this area assess the ability of younger children to produce and imitate sounds and require older children to demonstrate factual knowledge (for example, parts of the body and composition of familiar objects) as well as command of more traditional measures of language development such as vocabulary and syntax. The thirty-one items in the fourth area, *gross motor development,* can be classified as requiring body control (for example, lifting the head, rolling over), mobility (walking, jumping in place), coordination (kicking a ball, riding a tricycle), and balance (balancing on one foot).

Scores

All items are presented on the scoring sheet in the format shown in Figure 21.2. Across the top and bottom of the scoring sheet are age lines. The child's chronological age (CA) is computed, and a line at the appropriate age connects the top and bottom age lines. As shown in Figure 21.2, a child who is 3-6 has the age line drawn through skills 2 and 5. Each skill is enclosed in a rectangle with four discernible points along one of the horizontal sides. Vertical extensions of the four points intercept the age lines. For skill 1 in Figure 21.2, the vertical that goes from point A to the top age line intercepts the age line at about 2-1. This indicates that 25 percent of the children in the norm sample could perform skill 1 by the time they were about 2 years, 1 month old. Point B is the point at which 50 percent of the norm group could perform a skill. As shown in Figure 21.2, 50 percent of the children could perform skill 2 by age 3-4. Point C is the age at which 75 percent succeeded; 75 percent of the children could perform skill 4 by age 2-8. Point D is the age at which 90 percent successfully performed the skill. In Figure 21.2, 90 percent of the children in the norm group could perform skill 5 by age 4-1.

There is no formal basal rule for the scoring of the DDST.[1] Ceilings are not important since the purpose of the test is to determine developmental lags, not level of functioning. The exam-

1. A *basal age* is the age at which a child performs all tasks correctly and below which the tester can assume that all items will be passed. A *basal rule* states the number of items a child must pass before a basal age can be assumed.

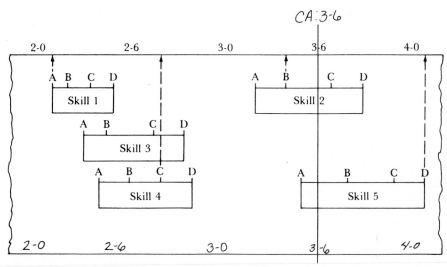

FIGURE 21.2 Sample scoring sheet for the DDST

iner should administer all test items through which the child's age line passes, and testing in each area should not be terminated until the child passes three items and fails three items.

Each item may be scored "pass," "fail," "passed by report," "refusal," or "no opportunity." Passed and failed items are observed directly by the examiner. Items passed by report (skills such as washing and drying the hands) are items that are difficult or time-consuming to administer but that can be observed reliably by the child's parents. If a parent reports that the child performs the particular task, the item is scored as a pass. Refusals are items to which the child *will not* respond whether the items are administered by the examiner or by the parents. If the examiner feels that the child *cannot* perform the task, the item is scored as failed. No-opportunity scores indicate that the child has not had the chance to learn the skill; such items are not included in the interpretation of the results.

Two types of scores are used. The first score

is called a *delay*. A delay is scored if the child fails an item that is passed by 90 percent of the children who are younger; thus, a delay is an item that is failed and lies to the left of the age-line vertical. The second score is the interpretation of the results as abnormal, questionable, untestable, and normal. An *abnormal* is scored when the child has (1) two delays in each of two sections or (2) one section with two delays and one section with one delay and in that same section "no passes intersecting the age line" (Frankenburg et al., 1975, p. 12). A *questionable* is scored (1) if the child has two or more delays in one section or (2) if the child has one delay and has not passed any items in that section through which the age line passes. An *untestable* is scored "when refusals occur in numbers large enough to cause the test result to be *questionable* or *abnormal if* they were scored as failures" (Frankenburg et al., 1975, p. 12). All other outcomes are scored as *normal*. If children earn scores other than normal, it is recommended that they be retested in two to three weeks. If the retest indicates other than normal and if the parents say the behavior is typical, the children should be referred for further assessment.

Norms

The DDST was standardized on 543 boys and 493 girls from 2 weeks through 6-4 years of age who (we presume, although the test is not clear on this point) lived in Denver, Colorado. Children with serious, known handicaps or difficult births were excluded. The standardization sample approximated the 1960 census in terms of racial-ethnic composition and occupations of the children's fathers.

The number of children in the sample at various ages is limited and is not evenly distributed. The number of children (in one-month intervals) from 1 month to 14 months ranges from thirty-six to forty-three, while the total number of children between 5 and 6 years of age is forty-seven.

Reliability

The authors report stability data (one-week interval) for the performance of twenty children who ranged in age from 2 months to 5 years, 6 months and who were tested by the same examiner. For each of the twenty children, there was at least 90 percent agreement[2] on the pass-fail decisions on the items administered. The specimen kit also contains a reprint of an article by Frankenburg, Goldstein, and Camp (1971). There the test-retest reliability (percentage-agreement method) of abnormal, questionable, and normal classifications for 186 children was reported to be .97.

2. Number of agreements divided by number of agreements plus disagreements.

Interrater agreement was also evaluated during the standardization of DDST, since it was important to know if two different examiners would elicit the same performances and score them in the same way. Using the percentage-agreement method, interrater reliability ranged from 80 to 95 percent agreement.

Validity

The authors can claim content validity by their method of item selection. They surveyed several intelligence and developmental tests and selected items from them. The authors also present data from the paper by Frankenburg, Goldstein, and Camp to demonstrate a strong relationship between classifications on the DDST (that is, abnormal, questionable, and normal) and scores on the Stanford-Binet Intelligence Scale or the Revised Bayley Infant Scales. This study also indicates low proportions of false positives and false negatives.[3]

Summary

The Denver Developmental Screening Test is a quickly administered and scored device that assesses a child's development in four general areas: personal-social, fine-motor, language, and gross-motor. The device is intended to provide a gross estimate of delayed development and must be followed by a more intensive evaluation. The test's reliability and validity are adequate for a screening device, although the norms are questionable.

3. A false positive is a child who is diagnosed as abnormal but on subsequent evaluation it is determined that the child is normal. A false negative is a child who is diagnosed as normal, but on subsequent evaluation it is determined that the child is abnormal.

Boehm Test of Basic Concepts

The Boehm Test of Basic Concepts (BTBC) (Boehm, 1971) is a group-administered, norm-referenced device that measures abstract concepts occurring frequently in preschool and primary curricula. The BTBC is intended to identify both the children who have not mastered the tested concepts and the concepts that the teacher should systematically teach to the class. The test is available in two forms (A and B), which are assumed to be roughly equivalent. Each form contains two levels of twenty-five concepts each; the first level (booklet 1) contains simpler concepts that the second level (booklet 2).

All concepts are tested in a similar format. The child is shown a set of pictures; the teacher reads a statement illustrated by one of the pictures. The child marks the picture that is most appropriate to the statement read by the teacher. (For example, "Mark the one where the boy is *next to* the horse.") The fifty concepts all deal with relative relationships. They can be categorized into four groups: (1) space (for example, next to, nearest), (2) quantity (few, not first or last), (3) time (after, beginning), and (4) miscellaneous (different, alike). Approximately 15 to 20 minutes are required for the administration of the test.

Scores

Two scores are provided for either form of the BTBC. Raw scores obtained on either form A or form B are converted to percentiles using the same table, since Boehm feels the two tests are equivalent. The conversion tables are entered with the child's raw score, grade placement (kindergarten, 1, 2, or 3), and socioeconomic level (presumably of the child rather than of the class). Separate norm tables are provided for mid-year and beginning-year administrations.

Separate tables are provided for each form of the test for the percentage of children passing each concept. These tables are entered by the concept, by the child's grade in school, and by socioeconomic level. Since each concept is judged to be important in and of itself, these latter tables are judged to be especially helpful because they provide the teacher with some indication of the grade appropriateness of the concept.

Norms

Boehm considers her test to be most useful as a criterion-referenced device. Consequently, she states that "it was considered unnecessary to select standardization samples representative of . . . the nation as a whole" (Boehm, 1971, p. 19). Form A was standardized on children enrolled in kindergarten through grade 3 in sixteen U.S. cities. The volunteer sample was tested in either mid-November to late February for mid-year norms or in September to October for beginning-year norms. Although separate norms are provided for low, middle, and high socioeconomic levels, no description is provided of how pupils were categorized. A description of the method of sampling different socioeconomic levels was not provided either. Boehm indirectly hints at the methods she used, however. *"As with the standardization of Form A* [emphasis added], the sample of each grade was subdivided by socioeconomic level, based upon the judgments of the local school administrators" (Boehm, 1971, p. 19). Form B was not standardized but was constructed in such a way as to be equivalent in difficulty to form A. Correlations between the two forms (one day to one week) are generally too low for the two forms to be considered equivalent, although they do have comparable means and standard deviations.

Reliability

Reliability was established by common norm-referenced procedures. Eighteen split-half reliability coefficients corrected by the Spearman-Brown formula are reported by grade and socioeconomic level for forms A and B. Form A is generally more reliable than form B. Reliabilities from both forms range from .12 to .94; the median coefficient is .81. Standard deviations range from .9 to 8.4; the median is 5.25. The standard errors of measurement (in raw-score points) range from 0.9 to 3.4; the median SEM is 2.15.

Validity

Boehm relies solely on content validity, but she does not present evidence to document the frequency of the fifty concepts in educational materials or curricula. Nonetheless, the fifty words have intuitive appeal as important concepts for children to have mastered before they begin their formal education.

Summary

The BTBC is a norm-referenced, group-administered device intended to identify a child's mastery of fifty key concepts. The norms are inadequate, but this is not a major disadvantage, since the test is most effectively used to obtain information about a child's knowledge of each concept. Form A at the kindergarten level, where the test is perhaps most appropriately used, has marginal reliabilities (.86, .90, and .85) for the three socioeconomic levels.

Lee-Clark Reading Readiness Test

The Lee-Clark Reading Readiness Test (LCRRT) (Lee & Clark, 1962) is a group-administered, norm-referenced, multiple-skill device designed to predict which children in a classroom are ready for reading instruction and which children need a "special developmental program" or a "full year of maturation and prereading preparation" (Lee & Clark, 1962, p. 2). The test is appropriately used with children finishing kindergarten or children entering first grade.

The LCRRT is divided into four subtests. The letter-matching test consists of two columns of twelve letters each. The child is required to draw a line to connect the same letters in the two columns. Practice items are administered before the start of this 2-minute test. The second subtest, a letter-discrimination task, consists of a four- by twelve-letter matrix. Each row of letters contains three letters that are the same and one that is different. The child is required to draw a line through the letter "that is not the same as the other letters" (Lee & Clark, 1962, p. 13). The letters vary in size but not in print style. After four practice items are administered, the child has 2 minutes to complete the twelve test items. The third subtest, an untimed picture vocabulary test, consists of twenty sets of pictures; the sets range from two stimulus pictures to five stimulus pictures. The child must mark the picture that matches the description read by the teacher. Two practice items are administered. The fourth subtest is an untimed letter and word recognition test using a match-to-sample format. The stimulus, which can vary from a single letter to a seven-letter English word, is separated by a dotted vertical line from four response options. The child must mark the letter or word in the response options that is the same as the stimulus. One practice item is administered before testing.

The LCRRT requires approximately 14 minutes to administer. The test may be given in two sittings, in which case subtests 1 and 2 should be administered first. Group size should probably not exceed six to eight children without someone to aid the tester.

Scores

Raw scores from each of the first three subtests and the total raw score (four subtests) may be converted to grade equivalents and classification scores. The classification scores (high, high average, low average, low) appear to be simple transformations, with high average and low average divided at the median. Insufficient data are presented in the test manual to determine at what point in the distribution (for example, quartile or standard deviation) high and high average or low and low average are separated.

Norms

The LCRRT was standardized on over 1,000 children of unknown age, sex, and demographic characteristics. The children in the norm sample were either at the end of kindergarten or entering first grade. The performances of the children in the 1962 sample were equated, through an unspecified procedure, with the performances of the children in the 1951 norm sample.

Reliability

Four split-half reliability coefficients, based on the total raw score and corrected by the Spearman-Brown formula, are presented in the LCRRT manual; the two coefficients for unspecified kindergarten samples were .96, while the coefficient for an unspecified first-grade sample was .87. The split-half reliability based on one combined group was also .96. Thus, the reliability of the total test for kindergarten children appears most acceptable. Standard errors of measurement in both raw scores and grade

equivalents for these four groups are also presented. The test authors provide reliability coefficients for the subtests; we believe they are too low for individual decisions (that is, .56 to .88).

Validity

Lee and Clark report predictive validity coefficients (one- and two-year intervals) for the LCRRT and Lee-Clark reading tests that range from .42 to .56. They also report the results of studies done in Portland, Oregon, with the LCRRT. The readiness test was administered after two months of school, and teacher ratings were made in January, April, and May. The LCRRT correlated from .37 to .74 with teacher ratings of a child's ability to read. The Lee-Clark Reading Test was also administered three times to these children. Correlations between the reading readiness test and the reading achievement test ranged from .25 to .70.

The readiness ratings (high, high average, low average, low) are of particular concern. The validity of these ratings is based on the performances of 177 children of unknown demographic characteristics who were enrolled in an undescribed reading program. These children were given the LCRRT during the first month of first grade and then given the Lee-Clark Reading Test (Primer) in April or May. Of the children who were rated as having low readiness, 22 percent were successful (according to Lee and Clark), while 15 percent of the children who were rated as having high readiness were unsuccessful. Two-thirds of the children rated high average and half of the children rated low average were successful readers in first grade. Using Lee and Clark's data, more than 28 percent of the children were incorrectly predicted for success or lack of success. From the predictive validity coefficients and the classification data, it is apparent that the LCRRT lacks the validity necessary to use the test to make educational decisions for children.

Summary

The LCRRT is a reliable test with norms of unknown appropriateness. The data presented by the authors do not demonstrate that the test has adequate predictive validity.

Preschool Inventory

The Preschool Inventory Revised Edition (Caldwell, 1970) is an individually administered, untimed device designed to assess the various skills deemed necessary for the school achievement of children 3 to 6 years of age. The first form of the device was known as the Preschool Achievement Test. After the first revision, it was known as the Preschool Inventory. The revised edition of the Preschool Inventory contains sixty-four items that can be administered in less than 15 minutes by anyone familiar with the device. The inventory assesses a child's knowledge of a variety of personal facts (such as name, age, and body parts), of social roles (mother,[4] teacher, and so on), of number concepts, of colors, and of geometric designs. The inventory also assesses whether a child follows instructions and copies various geometric forms.

Scores

In the initial versions of the test, the author sampled items as though a criterion-referenced device were being developed. Subsequent revisions have followed more traditional norm-referenced psychometrics. It is difficult to consider the current revision as a criterion-referenced device for several reasons. First, many items tap multiple behaviors; for example, given the response blank with a circle, square, and triangle, the child is requested to color the circle yellow. Second, the items were selected on the basis of their correlations with total score and not on relative educational importance. Percentile ranks are provided for five age ranges: 3-0 to 3-11, 4-0 to 4-5, 4-6 to 4-11, 5-0 to 5-5, and 5-6 to 6-5.

Norms

National norms are based solely on the performance of 1,531 children attending Head Start classes. Only the performance of children who were tested in English was included. No formal sampling plan is discussed. The ethnic and sex compositions of the norm sample for each of the five age ranges are presented. The age samples are about equally divided between boys and girls and are predominantly black (68.2 percent). Regional norms are based on the responses of at least 100 children, but in such cases neither sex nor ethnic breakdown is provided. In addition, specialized norms are provided separately for 246 4-year-old children in Louisville, Kentucky; for 133 children in Phoenix, Arizona; and for 317 children in North Carolina. Thus, the normative sample can, at best, be considered circumscribed and voluntary.

Reliability

Two estimates of internal consistency, based on the performance of the standardization sample, are provided for each age group: KR-20 coefficients range from .86 to .92; split-half reliabilities (corrected by the Spearman-Brown formula) range from .84 to .93. Raw-score SEMs are also presented.

---

4. Curiously, if a child responds to the question "What does a mother do?" with "Has babies," the response is not correct.

Validity

The initial form of the device, the Preschool Achievement Test, could lay some claim to content validity by the procedures used to select items. The author drew on her personal observations of deficits exhibited by disadvantaged preschool children, on the observations of others who had worked with disadvantaged children, and on inspections of various kindergarten curricula. In subsequent revisions, the total number of items was reduced from 161 to 64. The deletion of items may have reduced the scope of the Inventory. Yet if the test user is interested in the behaviors sampled, there is still ample claim to content validity.

Empirical validity is generally lacking. Stanford-Binet IQs were available for 1,476 children in the standardization sample; the correlation between the inventory and the Binet ranged from .39 (at 3 years) to .65 (at 5 years). In discussing the North Carolina norms, the author noted that in that sample the Inventory did not distinguish between children from high socioeconomic backgrounds and children from low socioeconomic backgrounds.

Summary

The Preschool Inventory is a quickly administered device that can give a teacher a list of accomplishments for a pupil. The estimated reliability of the device is adequate for screening purposes, but the norms limit the interpretation of percentiles.

Tests of Basic Experiences 2

The Tests of Basic Experiences 2 (TOBE 2) (Moss, 1979) are a set of group-administered tests designed to assess important concepts that contribute to a child's preparedness for school and learning. The directions for testers are comprehensive and clear; best results are said to occur when group size is five or six. TOBE 2 has two levels, neither of which requires reading: level K (preschool and kindergarten) and level L (kindergarten and first grade). The battery consists of four tests of twenty-six items each: mathematics, language, science, and social studies. A practice examination is provided, and there are two demonstration items at the beginning of each test. Administration time is about 20 minutes for the practice test and about 45 minutes for TOBE 2.

The mathematics test assesses quantitative vocabulary and concepts, geometric shapes, and money. The language test assesses letter recognition, same-different, prepositions, letter-sound associations, and other vocabulary. The science test assesses basic facts of botany (for example, the one that grows in the driest place), physics (for example, falling objects, buoyancy), and zoology (for example, mark the bird's tracks). The social studies test assesses social interactions, knowledge of occupations, and knowledge of tools, among other things.

Scores

Scoring can be done by hand or by machine. Raw scores are summed for each subtest and the total; sums can be converted to percentile ranks, normal curve equivalents ($\bar{x} = 50$, $S \approx 21$), and stanines. A Class Evaluation Record is used to show for each child those concepts correctly identified as well as derived scores. The teacher can sum the columns for each concept to find the number of children in the class who correctly identify the concept.

Norms

The standardization sample consisted of approximately 14,000 children. Since fall and spring testings were conducted in the same schools, the norms to some extent are longitudinal. Midyear norms are interpolated.

The children were intended to represent public school districts with enrollments over eleven in 1970 and the Catholic schools in 1975. Public school districts were stratified by geographic region, elementary school population, and relevant (but unspecified) demographic characteristics. Schools within districts were somehow selected, and all children in the target schools who were enrolled in kindergarten and first grade were tested. Catholic schools were stratified by geographic region and enrollment. Selection procedures for preschoolers were not discussed. Although voluminous data are presented, one cannot ascertain the extent to which the sample is representative. The general procedures followed should result in an adequate normative sample, however.

Reliability

Internal-consistency estimates of reliability for each subtest and the total for each form are presented for both fall and spring scores. Reliability estimates range from .76 to .85 for subtests; estimates for total scores all exceed .9. Test-retest correlations, from fall to spring, for subtests range from .64 to .78; for the total

scores the range is from .84 to .87. Thus, the reliability of the subtests appears adequate for screening purposes.

Validity

Moss (1979) enumerates the components of each subtest and gives the number of items in each component. She also discusses the criteria used for including and excluding individual test items: effectively used in the first edition of TOBE, traditionally assessed on similar subtests, relevant, easily illustrated, free from ethnic-racial-sex bias, high item-total correlations (which are necessary for developing a reliable test), and item difficulties. Evidence for concurrent or predictive validity was not reported.

Summary

The Tests of Basic Experiences 2 are a series of group-administered devices designed to assess pupil skill development in several areas. There are two levels of the test, with separate tests assessing development in mathematics, language, science, and social studies.

Although TOBE 2 was standardized on many children, it is difficult to ascertain from the data in the test manual how representative the sample was. Reliability data are adequate for screening. Users of the tests should be able to evaluate the content validity, since the necessary information is so clearly presented.

Developmental Indicators for the Assessment of Learning–Revised

The Developmental Indicators for the Assessment of Learning–Revised (DIAL–R) (Mardell-Czudnowski & Goldenberg, 1983) is an individually administered screening test intended to assess the motor, conceptual, and language skills of children between the ages of 2 and 6. Although individual children are screened, the testing procedures are designed to handle large numbers of children sequentially with different examiners administering different portions of the test. There are no special qualifications for the tester or test interpreters other than familiarity with the testing materials and procedures and a demonstration of "expertise in any of the following areas: special education; early childhood education; psychology; language and speech; or other related area" (p. 1).

The three subtests each consist of eight items, and, in some places in the test manual, it is suggested that individual items be plotted as a profile.

Motor In this subtest, the eight items are (1) catching and throwing a beanbag; (2) jumping, hopping, and skipping; (3) building with blocks; (4) touching the fingers of each hand with that hand's thumb; (5) cutting with scissors; (6) matching to sample; (7) copying letters and shapes; and (8) writing first name.

Concepts In this subtest, the eight items are (1) naming nine colors; (2) pointing to various body parts; (3) making one-to-one correspondences; (4) letter naming; (5) comprehending positions (for example, on, under, at, between, middle); (6) identifying fourteen concepts (for example, biggest, night, cold, least); (7) letter naming; and (8) sorting after observing the tester's sorting.

Language In this subtest, the eight items are (1) articulating fifteen words; (2) giving personal data (for example, identifying one's own photograph, giving one's telephone number); (3) remembering a sequence of hand claps, repeating digits, and repeating sentences; (4) naming nine pictured nouns (for example, TV, phone, ambulance); (5) naming pictured verbs (for example, sleep, talk, comb); (6) naming foods eaten; (7) problem solving (that is, social comprehension questions); and (8) sentence length of the child's longest response.

Scores

Scaled scores are computed for each item. However, these scores are not really scaled scores in the sense that they have the same means and standard deviations. Rather, they are age scores, given in one year age ranges. These scores are summed for each area and converted to another scale: "potential problem," "OK," "potential gifted." Children earning scores of potential problem or potential gifted are to be followed up.

Norms

DIAL–R was standardized on 2,447 children living in six states. The manual states that the primary goal was to "produce norms that would be representative of the U.S. population of children two years through six years of age" and that the sample was stratified on the basis of "age, ethnicity, geographic region, and size of community" (p. 70). Noticeably missing is stratification on the basis of socioeconomic class, a variable that has been repeatedly shown to affect significantly the development of children. There are serious shortcomings in the variables that were actually used in stratification. For example, ethnicity is white or nonwhite; geographic region is sampled by two cities in each of four regions, and the cities are located in only six states. The cities were classified as large (over 50,000) and small (less than 50,000); the large cities are Freeport, New York; Joliet, Illinois; Jacksonville, Florida; and Honolulu, Hawaii. No 6-year-old children were included in the sample. Separate norms for whites and nonwhites are available.

Reliability

Test-retest reliabilities are not readily interpretable since they are computed across age groups. These coefficients range from .76 (Motor) to .90 (Concepts); the reliability of the total score is .87. No stability data are presented on the categorization of scores as potential problem, OK, and potential gifted.

Coefficient alpha was also computed for each subtest at each three-month age group. Thus, there were forty-eight coefficients that ranged from .41 (Language at age 5-6) to .88 (Language at age 2-0); thirty-six of the coefficients fall below .8, including Motor at all ages. For the total score, reliabilities range from .75 (5-3) to .944 (total at 2-0); 2 of the 16 coefficients fall below .8. Thus, low reliability makes about three-fourths of the subtest scores unsuitable for screening purposes, but, with two exceptions, the total scores are suitable.

No interscorer agreement is reported on the drawing items.

Validity

To select the content of the test, the test authors interviewed early childhood and kindergarten teachers to identify behavior believed necessary for school success. The resulting list of behaviors was reviewed by a group of consultants. Inspection of the individual items raises some questions. For example, many of the items in the Motor subtest have heavy intellectual demands. Indeed, one factor analytic study reported by Mardell-Czudnowski and Goldenberg indicates that the items on the DIAL–R actually cluster into only two factors: (1) motor-language and (2) concepts.

Predictive validity is more difficult to evaluate because the authors contend that it is "unethical, as well as illegal, to withhold services from children who appear to require them . . ." (p. 91). The logical problem with this assertion is that it begs the question of the test's validity. (It assumes that the test is valid and can identify children who need services; the test authors also assume that the services available can have a significant impact on the children.) Nonetheless, the test authors report a longitudinal study involving 249 children. The range of obtained multiple correlations are described between the DIAL–R and a variety of criterion measures (such as teacher ratings obtained at various times, standardized achievement tests, and readiness tests) for kindergartners and first graders. The results of this study are not readily interpretable because of the way in which they are presented.

Mardell-Czudnowski and Goldenberg also report a concurrent validity study using the Stanford-Binet as the criterion (although the DIAL–R is not intended as a test of intelligence). A total of 125 children, between the ages of 2 and 6, were tested. The correlations between each DIAL–R subtest and the Stanford-Binet ranged from .5 (Concepts) to .28 (Motor).

No data are presented to demonstrate that the recommended assessments by individuals without special training result in valid assessments of "social-emotional sets" (p. 49) as claimed by the test authors. No data are presented to indicate that children scoring below the various cutoff points will have learning difficulties in school.

Summary

DIAL–R is an individually administered screening device assessing development in domains of motor, conceptual, and language behavior. The norms are questionable, reliability is poor, and validity is not clearly established. At this time, the DIAL–R is best considered an experimental test.

Metropolitan Readiness Tests

The 1976 revision of the Metropolitan Readiness Tests (MRT) (Nurss & McGauvran, 1976a, 1976b) is a norm-referenced, group-administered, multiple-skill battery intended to assess several important skills needed for early school success. The 1976 revision is the fourth in the series, which began in 1933 and was revised in 1949 and 1964. The tests are untimed, but typically require a total of approximately 80 to 90 minutes' administration time spread over several sessions. The child responds directly on the record form, which may be scored by hand or machine. The directions to the teacher for administering the tests are very clear and well organized. The directions to the children are also clear. The practice test should be administered several days before the MRT is given. Key concepts and skills (place keeping, making rows, and so on) are taught and practiced. The test authors are very sensitive to the difficulties involved in testing young children, and they stress small groups, proctors, and testing in several sessions; moreover, they provide multiple cues and checks to insure that the children do not lose their places.

The MRT consists of two levels. Level 1 is intended for use with children in the beginning or middle of kindergarten. Level 2 is intended for use with children at the end of kindergarten and the beginning of first grade. The two levels differ somewhat in content in order to reflect different levels of skill development. Two forms (P and Q) are available at each level. All tests, except copying, which is an optional test, employ a multiple-choice format.

Level 1 contains six regularly administered subtests; a description of each follows.

Auditory Memory This subtest has twelve items. Each consists of four pictures of familiar objects. The teacher reads three or four nouns,

and the child marks the response that contains the same sequence of nouns.

Rhyming This subtest has thirteen items. Each item consists of four pictures, each representing a familiar word. The teacher names each picture in the response array and then reads a fifth word that rhymes with one of the four. The child marks the picture that has the name rhyming with the fifth word read by the teacher.

Letter Recognition This subtest has eleven items. The child is shown four letters (both upper and lower case). The teacher names one of the letters, and the child marks it.

Visual Matching This subtest has fourteen items using a match-to-sample format. Individual items consist of single letters, multiple letters, or nonsense symbols.

School Language and Listening This subtest has fifteen items. The teacher reads a sentence, and the child marks the one picture in the response array that describes what the teacher read. The sentences require the child to comprehend prepositions, verb forms (tense and voice), and conjunctions as well as to draw inferences and separate relevant and irrelevant information.

Quantitative Language This subtest has eleven items. The child is required to complete matrices, know cardinal and ordinal numbers, perform simple arithmetic operations, comprehend quantitative words such as *more,* and visually rearrange disjointed parts to form a familiar object.

Level 2 consists of eight subtests; a description of each follows.

Beginning Consonants   This subtest has thirteen items. The child is shown pictures of four familiar objects that the teacher names. The teacher then says a fifth word. The child must select the one word in the response array that begins with the same sound.

Sound-Letter Correspondence   This subtest has sixteen items. The child is shown a five-item array: a picture of a familiar object named by the teacher and four letters (or double letters, such as *gl*). The child marks the letter or letters with the same sound as the initial sound of the word read by the teacher.

Visual Matching   This subtest has ten items. The format is the same as that used at level 1, but the items are more difficult; that is, there are more elements in each item and greater similarity among the distractors (the incorrect response options).

Finding Patterns   This subtest has sixteen items. The child is presented with a stimulus and four response options. Stimuli and responses may be letters, numbers, or nonsense symbols. One of the response options contains the sequence presented in the stimulus item. See Figure 21.3 for an example of such an item.

School Language   This subtest has nine items. The teacher reads a passage, and the child selects the one picture of three that best represents what the teacher has read. The language demands, while more complex, are similar to those of the School Language and Listening subtest in level 1.

Listening   This subtest also has nine items. The teacher reads a passage, and the child selects the one picture of four that best represents what the teacher has read. The child must comprehend or infer the meaning of complex sentences with a considerable amount of distracting information.

Quantitative Concepts   The nine items on this subtest are similar to, but more difficult than, the items in Quantitative Language in level 1.

Quantitative Operations   In this subtest the child must demonstrate comprehension of cardinal and ordinal numbers, set meaning, single and double digits, simple arithmetic operations (addition, subtraction, and multiplication), and multiple operations (addition and then subtraction).

Scores

Raw scores can be converted to three types of derived scores: percentile ranks, stanines, and performance ratings. *Performance ratings* are ratings based on stanine intervals: a low rating consists of scores from the first three stanines, an average rating consists of scores from the middle three stanines (4, 5, 6) and a high rating consists of scores from the three highest stanines (7, 8, 9).

For level 1, beginning-of-kindergarten and middle-of-kindergarten norm tables for each form for various scores are available. Raw scores on each subtest may be converted to performance ratings. Letter Recognition and Visual Matching can be combined into a composite termed Visual Skill Area; School Language and Listening and Quantitative Language can be combined into a composite termed Language Skill Area. Each raw-score composite total can also be transformed into stanines or performance ratings. Finally, the raw scores for each of the six subtests may be summed; the total raw score, termed Prereading Skills, may be converted to both stanines and percentile ranks.

For level 2, two sets of norm tables are available for each form for various scores: end of kindergarten and beginning of first grade. No

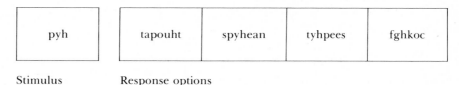

Stimulus Response options

FIGURE 21.3 An example of a test item from the Finding Patterns subtest of the MRT

norm-referenced scores or interpretations can be made for individual subtests. The eight subtests can be combined into five different composite scores: Beginning Consonants and Sound-Letter Correspondence into a composite termed Auditory Skill Area; Visual Matching and Finding Patterns into Visual Skill Area; School Language and Listening into Language Skill Area; Quantitative Concepts and Quantitative Operations into Quantitative Skill Area; and the Auditory, Visual, and Language Skill areas into Prereading Skills. Performance ratings and stanines are available for each subarea (for example, Visual Skill Area). Percentile ranks and stanines are available for the Prereading Skills composite.

Norms

The procedures used to develop the norms for both levels of the MRT were essentially the same. Data from the National Center for Education Statistics were used as a basis for a stratified random sampling plan. Six levels of school population and five levels of socioeconomic status (estimated by the median years of schooling of the adult population in the district) formed the thirty strata. In addition, data were obtained from parochial schools, very small schools (enrollments less than 300), and large urban districts (enrollments greater than 100,000).[5] A total of more than 66,000 children participated in the standardization program for each level;

5. No information is presented to indicate whether all the districts that were sampled agreed to participate.

approximately 50,000 children were used in developing the norm groups for each level. Sex, geographic, and ethnic data, as well as data indicating prior educational experience, are presented for each level. "Data from each school district were weighted so that the number of pupils in each stratum . . . [was proportional] . . . to the number of pupils in the U.S. population enrolled in school systems with similar characteristics" (Nurss & McGauvran, 1976a, p. 23). The norms appear representative; however, midyear norms for level 1 are interpolated. The two forms were statistically equated, and then the two levels were equated. The derived scores are based on smoothed curves of these equated data.

Reliability

Split-half reliability estimates (corrected by the Spearman-Brown formula), KR-20 estimates of internal consistency, and alternate-form reliability estimates are provided for each level. As shown in Table 21.1, the Prereading composites are sufficiently reliable to make educational decisions for children. The subtests in level 1 and the area scores in level 2 are generally not reliable enough for such decisions.

Validity

The validity of the MRT must rest on how well it samples behaviors necessary for school success and whether it predicts later school achievement. The content validity of the MRT

TABLE 21.1 Ranges of Reliability Estimates for MRT, by Level, Type of Score, Form, and Method of Estimation

	Form P		Alternate Form	Form Q	
	Split-Half	KR-20		Split-Half	KR-20
Level 1					
Subtests	.73–.88	.67–.88	.58–.81	.70–.90	.71–.90
Prereading composite	.93	.92	.85	.95	.95
Level 2					
Area scores	.72–.93	.72–.92	.67–.86	.73–.92	.68–.91
Prereading composite	.94	.93	.87	.94	.93

was established by "an analysis of the beginning reading process and an extensive review of the reading research literature"; and "a sequential list of the skills necessary for beginning reading was then prepared" (Nurss & McGauvran, 1976b, p. 25). Finally, test items to measure these skills were developed. The test items were constructed in such a way that their content was judged (presumably by the authors) "to be familiar to all kindergarten and Grade 1 pupils regardless of their sex, ethnic background, urban/rural residence, socioeconomic status, or geographic region" (Nurss & McGauvran, 1976a, p. 22). Minority-group consultants also screened test items, and those with possible ethnic bias were deleted. In addition the auditory items in level 2 were screened to guarantee that the sounds were "equally familiar to pupils who speak Spanish and to those who speak standard American English or a non-standard dialect" (Nurss & McGauvran, 1976a, p. 22). A major difficulty, however, is the limited number of items assessing various domains of the MRT. The authors are sensitive to this limitation and carefully caution test users:

The MRT does not provide in-depth diagnostic information about pupil strengths and weaknesses since each of the tests and skill areas contains a relatively small number of items. Scores should be viewed as suggestive of possible strengths and weaknesses subject to verification by other means suggested earlier. (Nurss & McGauvran, 1976a, p. 16)

Predictive validity for both levels was established by correlating MRT scores obtained in the fall with achievement scores from the Metropolitan Achievement Tests obtained in the spring. The prereading composite had a correlation of approximately .70 with both total reading and total math achievement scores for both levels. Level 2 was also used to predict Stanford Achievement Test (1973 edition) scores obtained *two* years later. The prereading composite was moderately to highly correlated with achievement: total reading, .69; total math, .65; total auditory, .68; basic battery, .75; and total battery, .78.

Summary

The MRT is a norm-referenced multiple-skill, group-administered device designed to assess a child's readiness for reading and other areas of school achievement. The device appears to be adequately normed and to have adequate reliability and substantial validity for a screening device. The MRT's major limitation is a relatively limited behavior sample. With judicious use, the 1976 revision of the MRT can provide very useful screening information.

Comprehensive Developmental Scale

The Comprehensive Developmental Scale (Quick, Little, & Campbell, 1974), developed as part of project MEMPHIS, is an individually administered, multiple-skill "age scale" intended for use with children who are handicapped or have developmental deficiencies. It can be used with children between 3 months and 6 years of age. Intended to assess skills "important to later school learning" (p. 13), it can be "administered by teachers in a classroom setting through information gained by personal observation of the child or information given to the teacher by others knowledgeable about the child" (p. 36).

The scale consists of five subscales. Personal-Social Skills contains sixty items that deal with eating, dressing, interpersonal relationships, following directions, self-concept, safety, and general self-help. Gross Motor Skills contains forty items mainly dealing with developmental mobility (for example, rolling over, standing, walking), balance, and stair walking. Fine Motor Skills contains forty items dealing mainly with drawing, grasping, depositing objects in containers, using scissors, manipulating paper (for example, unwrapping, folding, page turning), and tower building. Language Skills contains sixty items that assess vocabulary, grammar, morphology, and phonology. Perceptual-Cognitive Skills contains sixty items that in general resemble items found on tests of intelligence:

drawing, early language (for example, naming), quantitative concepts, memory, and so on.

Scores

Items on each scale are assigned to an age range. Raw scores are summed, and the age range to which the subtest total corresponds is the age score.

Norms

There is no mention of the procedures used to assign ages to scale items, nor is there any mention of norms in the technical materials.

Reliability

No evidence of any type of reliability is reported.

Validity

No evidence of validity is presented.

Summary

Project MEMPHIS's Comprehensive Developmental Scale is a device without technical data. It should be considered as an informal check list.

Developmental Profile

The Developmental Profile (Alpern & Boll, 1972) is a norm-referenced, multiple-skill inventory designed to screen individuals from birth through age 12. Administration is accomplished by an interview, and the test usually requires about 40 minutes to give and score. The Developmental Profile can also be self-administered. The 217 items are clustered in five areas. The Physical scale contains forty-one items that assess "large and small muscle coordination, strength, stamina, flexibility, and sequential control skills" (Alpern & Boll, 1972, p. 1). The Self-Help scale contains forty-eight items assessing eating, dressing, and working. The Social scale contains forty-five items assessing interpersonal relationships with family, peers, and adults. The Academic scale contains thirty-nine items measuring "intellectual abilities by evaluating, at pre-school levels, the development of skills prerequisite to scholastic functioning and, at the school age levels, actual academic achievements" (p. 1). The Communication scale contains thirty-nine items assessing expressive and receptive, verbal and gestural language.

The items are grouped in sixteen age intervals (for example, newborn to 6 months). There are usually three items in each interval on each scale. However, only two scales span the entire age range.

Scores

Age scores are derived on each of the five scales. However, items were placed on the basis of 70 to 80 percent of the age group passing (not the more usual and correct 50 percent). Consequently, the age equivalents must consistently overestimate a child's development. An IQ Equivalent can also be obtained by substituting academic age for mental age in the usual ratio IQ formula.

Norms

The scale was standardized on 3,008 children, 41 to 63 of each sex in each age interval. Only normal children were included in the sam-

ple. The children were drawn from geographically restricted areas: 91 percent lived in Indiana; 9 percent lived in Washington; 89 percent lived in large cities (Indianapolis and Seattle). Eighty-four percent of the sample was white, 14 percent black, and 2 percent Asian or "mixed." Social class, estimated by the occupation of the head of household, was distributed as follows: 9 percent lower class, 80 percent middle class, and 11 percent upper class.

Reliability

No data regarding internal consistency or stability are presented for the Developmental Profile. Tangential evidence of interscorer agreement (an interview concerning a $4\frac{1}{2}$-year-old) is presented for the "prestandardization version." Also, for the prestandardization version there is very limited evidence for interinterviewer agreement (in interviews concerning children ranging in age from 11 months to 9 years, 11 months).

Validity

Users will have to judge the content validity for themselves. An item pool was developed by unspecified procedures. These items were examined for racial, sex, or social-class bias; items showing racial and sex bias were either eliminated or balanced by items showing bias in the opposite direction. Social-class bias was reduced but not eliminated.

Criterion validity was established by comparing the results of interviews of mothers with the actual performance by their children for 197 of the scale items. The 100 children ranged in age from 3 months to 12 years. There was 84 percent agreement. However, the mothers all knew that their children were being tested while they were being interviewed.

Alpern and Boll present correlations with the Stanford-Binet as evidence that their IQ Equivalents are valid. In one sample, the IQE and Stanford-Binet correlated .85; in another, .49. The IQ and IQ Equivalent in the first sample differed by 10 points or less in 69 percent of the cases; in the other sample 50 percent of the cases differed by more than 10 points. Although the differences tended to average out when the samples were combined, we do not favor the use of IQEs. One other point needs to be made in conjunction with IQEs. Alpern and Boll note on page 29 of the technical manual that "while giving practice on specific items artificially inflates intelligence or academic achievement test scores, this is *not* the case with developmental tests, where teaching developmental task mastery helps the child without invalidating the evaluation." IQ Equivalents should *never* be based on test items that have been systematically taught.

Summary

The Developmental Profile is a norm-referenced screening device assessing attainment in the areas of physical development, self-help, social development, academic achievement, and communication. The norms were developed in geographically circumscribed areas but otherwise appear representative. Item scaling was unorthodox. Reliability is unknown, and evidence for validity is minimal.

COPING WITH DILEMMAS IN CURRENT PRACTICE

There are two major dilemmas in assessing readiness. The first is that the performances of preschoolers are so variable that there is relatively little long-term prediction (for example, one year). This inability to predict precisely is particularly pronounced with the shorter, quickly administered (and less reliable) measures of readiness. Since there is relatively poor predictive validity, most inferences about readiness must be drawn with great care. If individuals wish to use readiness measures to predict school success, they should recognize that the closer the predicted measure (that is, the criterion) is to the predictor measure (that is, the readiness test), the greater the accuracy of the prediction. For example, language tests predict later language skills better than perceptual-motor tests do.

The second problem occurs when one uses tests of readiness and development as measures of current functioning and current attainment. When used in this way, readiness tests must be viewed as achievement measures, and the content validity of the tests must be scrutinized. This is especially true when using developmental measures to document pupil progress at the preschool level. To use readiness and developmental measures in this way, one must make sure that there is appropriate linkage between the curriculum and the content of the test.

SUMMARY

Readiness is a construct used to explain why some people succeed in a sequence of instruction and others fail. There are two different perspectives on readiness that determine how it is assessed. First, it can be viewed as the presence of the behavior, skills, and knowledge that are prerequisites to the mastery of skills or information to be taught. Second, readiness may be viewed as the presence of certain processes (intelligence, discrimination, and so on) that are believed to underlie the acquisition of the behavior or information to be taught.

While readiness tests contain items that assess competence in several domains, these tests are used exclusively to predict a person's success or failure in an instructional sequence or program. Therefore, certain technical characteristics, such as predictive criterion-related validity, are extremely important. Moreover, since readiness tests are routinely used to make individual placement decisions, these tests must conform to the highest standards of technical excellence. Several devices, both general and specific (reading readiness tests, for example) were reviewed in this chapter.

STUDY QUESTIONS

1. Differentiate between a *process orientation* and a *skill orientation* toward readiness.
2. In Chapter 2 we stated that a fundamental assumption in assessment was that only present behavior can be observed; any statement about future performance is an inference. Discuss the use of readiness measures in light of this assumption.
3. In assessing the validity of readiness tests, what considerations are important?

ADDITIONAL READING

Bagnato, S., & Neisworth, J. (1979). Between assessment and intervention: Forging an assessment/curriculum linkage for the handicapped preschooler. *Child Care Quarterly, 8*(3), 179–195.

Boehm, A., & Sandberg, B. (1982). Assessment of the preschool child. In C. Reynolds and T. Gutkin (Eds.), *Handbook of school psychology.* New York: Wiley.

Buros, O. K. (Ed.) (1978). *Eighth mental measurements yearbook.* Highland Park, NJ: Gryphon Press. (Reviews of readiness tests, pp. 1148–1194.)

Lichtenstein, R., & Ireton, H. (1984). *Preschool screening.* New York: Grune & Stratton.

Meisels, S. (1978). *Developmental screening in early childhood.* Washington, DC: National Association for the Education of Young Children.

Paget, K., & Bracken, B. (1983). *The psychoeducational assessment of preschool children.* New York: Grune & Stratton.

CHAPTER 22

DIAGNOSTIC SYSTEMS

Earlier in this text we noted that tests are samples of behavior. Most tests sample behaviors from a single domain (for example, intelligence, achievement, or adaptive behavior). Two tests that sample behaviors from the same domain may actually differ significantly because they sample *different* behaviors from the same domain.

Within the last few years test publishers have begun to develop measures that sample behaviors from several domains. These super test batteries have been called diagnostic systems. Other chapters in Parts 3 and 4 of this text are restricted to specific domains (although achievement is a multiple domain). The newer measures reviewed in this chapter are actually entire diagnostic systems.

WHY DO WE HAVE ASSESSMENT SYSTEMS?

Diagnostic systems offer two major advantages. The first is technical. The same normative sample provides derived scores for all measures in the various domains assessed in the diagnostic system. As you recall from Chapter 7, differences between test scores may be a function of differences in normative samples. Thus, if Sam's IQ is 115 and his standard score (mean = 100, standard deviation = 15) on an achievement test is 106, part of the difference between 115 and 106 may be attributed to differences in the norms of the two tests. Diagnostic systems provide more accurate comparisons of a person's performances in different domains because the derived scores in the different domains are based on the same norm group. The second advantage is that diagnostic systems may be more convenient for the assessor to use than several tests of single domains. For example, the time necessary to administer tests may be reduced since redundancies in several domains may be lessened. In addition, it may take assessors less time to put together the necessary materials for testing.

SPECIFIC DIAGNOSTIC SYSTEMS

Kaufman Assessment Battery for Children

The Kaufman Assessment Battery for Children (K–ABC) (Kaufman & Kaufman, 1983) is an individually administered norm-referenced battery intended to provide a comprehensive assessment of intelligence (learning potential and preferred learning style) and achievement for children between the ages of 2-5 and 12-5. Kaufman and Kaufman claim that the test is useful for several purposes: (1) psychological and clinical assessment (including projective interpretation of personality and inferences about impulsivity-reflectivity, perseverative behavior, rigidity-flexibility, and tolerance for frustration); (2) psychoeducational evaluation of exceptional children, particularly the learning disabled; (3) educational placement and planning; (4) assessment of minorities (especially blacks, Hispanics, and bilingual children); (5) preschool assessment; and (6) neuropsychological assessment.

Sixteen subtests are combined into three regularly administered scales and one supplementary scale. Intelligence is assessed on three scales: the Simultaneous Processing Scale, the Sequential Processing Scale, and the optional Nonverbal Scale. Simultaneous and Sequential Processing scales are combined to form the Mental Processing Scale. Achievement is assessed with the Achievement Scale.

The K–ABC draws heavily on the information-processing theories of Das (for example, Das, Kirby, & Jarman, 1975) and Luria (1966) as well as neuropsychological research of Cohen (1972). The processing of information is viewed dichotomously. One may act upon information sequentially or simultaneously. Many examples of tasks that are essentially sequential in nature are provided in the K–ABC manuals and include the following: memorization of number facts, spelling, application of stepwise proce-dures in arithmetic (for example, the division algorithm), word-attack skills, and so on. The other method of acting on information is simultaneous processing. In many tasks separate elements are not handled sequentially; rather the elements are handled (processed) at once as a whole. For example, skilled readers seldom ponder individual letters in a word; they grasp the word as a whole.

Kaufman and Kaufman are also concerned with the assessment of culturally atypical children. The optional Nonverbal Scale combines subtests that can be administered gesturally and to which students can respond nonverbally. The Nonverbal Scale is believed to be "a good estimate of intellectual potential for . . . deaf, hearing-impaired, speech- or language disordered, autistic, and non-English-speaking children" (1983, p. 35).

Achievement is conceptualized as "the ability to integrate the two types of mental processing and apply them to real-life situations" (Kaufman & Kaufman, 1983, p. 33). The "Achievement Scale is intended to assess factual knowledge and skills usually acquired in a school setting or through alertness to the environment" (Kaufman & Kaufman, 1983, p. 33).

Brief descriptions of each subtest, based on the descriptions provided by Kaufman and Kaufman between pages 36 and 57 of the Interpretative Manual, follow. Unless otherwise indicated, each subtest can be administered to children between 2-5 and 12-5.

Sequential Processing Scale

1. *Hand Movements*   Requires a child to copy a sequence of taps made by the tester with the fist, palm, or side of the hand.

2. *Number Recall* Requires a child to repeat a series of digits read by the tester.
3. *Word Order* (CA 4-0–12-5) Requires a child to point to silhouettes of common objects in the order named by the tester.

Simultaneous Processing Scale

4. *Magic Window* (CA 2-6–4-11) Requires a child to identify a picture that the tester rotates behind a narrow slit, exposing only a part of the picture at any one time.
5. *Face Recognition* (CA 2-6–4-11) Requires a child to recall one or two faces that have been briefly presented by selecting the correct face(s), in a different pose, from a group photograph.
6. *Gestalt Closure* Requires a child to complete an inkblot drawing and to name or describe it.
7. *Triangles* (CA 4-0–12-5) Requires a child to assemble rubber triangles (one side blue, one side yellow) to match an abstract design.
8. *Matrix Analogies* (CA 5-0–12-5) Requires a child to select the picture or design that completes a 2-by-2 visual analogy.
9. *Spatial Memory* (CA 5-0–12-5) Requires a child to remember where pictures were arranged on a page.
10. *Photo Series* (CA 6-0–12-5) Requires a child to organize photographs that illustrate an event and to place them in proper chronology.

Achievement Scale

11. *Expressive Vocabulary* (CA 2-6–4-11) Requires a child to name objects from photographs.
12. *Faces & Places* Requires a child to name famous persons, fictional characters, or places from pictures.
13. *Arithmetic* (CA 3-0–12-5) Requires a child to name numbers, to count, to compute, and to understand mathematical concepts.

14. *Riddles* (CA 3-0–12-5) Requires a child to name a concrete or abstract concept when given several of its characteristics.
15. *Reading/Decoding* (CA 5-0–12-5) Requires a child to name letters and to read words orally.
16. *Reading/Understanding* (CA 7-0–12-5) Requires children to act out commands given in sentences that they read.

Nonverbal Scale The composition of the Nonverbal Scale varies with a child's age. For four-year-olds, the scale consists of Face Recognition, Hand Movements, and Triangles. For five-year-olds, the scale consists of Hand Movements, Triangles, Matrix Analogies, and Spatial Memory. For children 6 years and older, the scales consist of Hand Movements, Triangles, Matrix Analogies, Spatial Memory, and Photo Series.

Scores

A variety of transformed scores are used. Scaled scores (mean = 10; S = 3) are available by chronological age for the Mental Processing subtests. Mental Processing subtests are combined into Sequential Processing, Simultaneous Processing, Mental Processing Composite, and Nonverbal scales (mean = 100; S = 15). Raw scores on the Achievement Scale yield standard scores with a mean of 100 and a standard deviation of 15. Percentile ranks are available for each subtest and scale. Age equivalents are available for each subtest of the Mental Processing Scale, and grade equivalents are available for each of the Achievement subtests.

Norms

There are national norms and sociocultural norms available for comparisons. The *national norms* consist of 100 at each half year of age from 2-6 to 12-5. A representative sample was obtained by stratifying on sex, education of the parent, ethnic status (white, black, Hispanic, other), geographic considerations, and school placement. In addition, *sociocultural norms* are provided to compare a child to others of similar racial and ethnic background and socioeconomic status on the Mental Processing Scale and Achievement subtests (except Expressive Vocabulary).

Reliability

Both split-half and test-retest reliability coefficients, based on the standardization sample, are provided. Split-half coefficients, corrected with the Spearman-Brown formula, range from a high of .92 (Triangles at age 5) to a low of .62 (Gestalt Closure at age 7) on the Mental Processing *subtests*. Of the eighty coefficients reported, only one equaled or exceeded .90. Corrected split-half coefficients on the Mental Processing *Scale* (including the Nonverbal Scale) range from a high of .95 (several ages on the Composite Mental Processing Scale) to a low of .84 (ages 2 and 3 on the Simultaneous Processing Scale). As would be expected, the composites are more reliable than the subtests; of the forty-two coefficients, thirty equal or exceed .90. On the achievement *subtests,* corrected split-half reliabilities range from .97 (Reading/Decoding at age 6) to .70 (Faces & Places at age 3). Of the forty-eight age-subtest coefficients, twelve equal or exceed .90. The reliability of the composite Achievement *Scale* exceeds .90 at all ages.

Test-retest reliabilities (two- to four-week interval between tests) were obtained by retesting 246 children from the standardization sample. The correlations were, however, based on several combined ages. Stabilities for the Mental Processing *subtests* range from .86 (Gestalt Closure at age range 9-0 through 12-5) to .59 (Hand Movements at age range 9-0 through 12-5). Of the 23 stability coefficients, none equals or exceeds .90. Stabilities for the Mental Processing *Scale* range from .93 (the Composite at age

range 9-0 through 12-5) to .77 (Sequential Processing and Simultaneous Processing at age range 2-6 through 4-11). Of the twelve coefficients, two equal or exceed .90. Stabilities on the Achievement subtests range from .98 (Reading/Decoding at age range 5-0 through 8-11) to .72 (Riddles at age range 2-6 through 4-11). Of the fourteen age range–subtest coefficients, eight equal or exceed .90; the composite Achievement Scale exceeds .90 at the three age ranges.

Validity

Forty pages of the Interpretative Manual, describing numerous unpublished studies, are devoted to the validity of the K–ABC. To demonstrate construct validity, several types of evidence are presented. Scores on each subtest of K–ABC increase with age. The subtests are internally consistent (although this type of information is better considered as reliability). The results of several factor analyses that partially support the theorized factor structure of the K–ABC are also discussed. Convergent/discriminant validity is reported.

Criterion-related validity is also examined by correlating the K–ABC with several other tests. To support the contention that the K–ABC measures intelligence, correlations between the K–ABC scales and various intelligence scales were examined. Correlation with the WISC–R full scale IQ and the Mental Processing Composite was .70. WISC–R full scale IQ and the Mental Processing Scale were moderately correlated: Simultaneous Processing and Nonverbal Scale, in the .60s; Sequential Processing, .47. Correlations with the Stanford-Binet using various samples of children ranged from .36 to .72 for the Mental Processing Composite, from .15 to .65 for the Simultaneous Processing Scale, from .27 to .63 for the Sequential Processing Scale, and from .31 to .70 for the Nonverbal Scale. Other tests of intelligence that were used as criteria include the McCarthy Scales, Cognitive Abilities Test, Woodcock-Johnson

Cognitive Ability subtests, Columbia Mental Maturity Scale, and Slosson Intelligence Test. Finally, several studies examined the relationship of the the K–ABC with the Peabody Picture Vocabulary Test. The sixty coefficients ranged from .21 (Sequential Processing) to .75 (Mental Processing Composite).

K–ABC scores were also used to predict achievement. Generally the correlations were unimpressive. For example, correlations between the PIAT subtests and the Sequential Processing Scale ranged from .12 (spelling) to .64 (math); with the Simultaneous Processing Scale, from .02 (reading recognition) to .62 (math); with the Nonverbal Scale, from .12 (reading recognition) to .51 (math). Correlations with various subtests from the Iowa Tests of Basic Skills, California Achievement Tests, and SRA Achievement Series are comparable to the PIAT correlations.

Validation of the Achievement Scale is less persuasive, largely because of the definition of achievement employed: "factual knowledge and skills usually acquired in a school setting or through alertness to the environment" (p. 33). (Achievement is more usually defined as the consequence of direct instruction.) The issue is further complicated by the way in which achievement subtests are described. For example, "Expressive vocabulary is a direct adaptation of the Stanford-Binet Picture Vocabulary task" (Kaufman & Kaufman, 1983, p. 51) or "Riddles probably comes closest to a Wechsler or Stanford-Binet Vocabulary subtest in terms of what it measures" (p. 54). The problem is

that the Weschler scales and the Stanford-Binet are used by the Kaufmans to validate the *intelligence* components of their scale. This is not the same as proving that the scale measures achievement. In addition, the K–ABC provides no linkages to curricula; there is no table of specifications. Numerous correlations between the Achievement Scale and various achievement tests are presented. However, the composite achievement score is not meaningful because it mixes such disparate contents.

Although the manuals present considerable evidence to indicate the K–ABC assesses two different types of mental processing, there is little convincing evidence that the K–ABC can be substituted for more traditional measures of intelligence or achievement. No data are presented to validate the K–ABC as a measure of learning potential, for use in educational placement and planning, for clinical assessment, or for neurological assessment.

Summary

The K–ABC is designed to assess the way children process information and the amount of information they have obtained compared to others of similar age and background. The battery was adequately standardized. The composite scales are generally reliable; the subtests are not. Although there is considerable indication that the battery measures different mental processes, the validity of the battery for the purposes for which it is intended is not established.

System of Multicultural Pluralistic Assessment

The System of Multicultural Pluralistic Assessment (SOMPA) (Mercer, 1979) is intended to provide comprehensive, nondiscriminatory assessment of public school pupils between the ages of 5 and 11. SOMPA provides data on

children from three different viewpoints, called models: medical, social-system, and pluralistic. The medical model is intended to identify "biological anomalies, disease processes, sensory or motor impairment, or other pathological conditions in the organism" (Mercer, 1979, p. 42). The social-system model is intended to assess the extent to which the child meets the "expectations of the social systems in which he or she is participating" (p. 85). The pluralistic model is "essentially a redefinition of the traditional general intelligence model" (p. 52) and is intended to ascertain the child's "learning potential" or intelligence.

SOMPA offers two new things. First, it contains a new scale, the Adaptive Behavior Inventory for Children (ABIC), that offers considerable promise for valid measurement. Second, it offers a new score, the Estimated Learning Potential (ELP), that attempts to equalize the means of ethnic and social groups on the WISC–R. SOMPA stresses the requirement that, when intelligence is being assessed, a child should be compared only with children of comparable acculturation. This comparison is accomplished by locating the child's background in a two-dimensional matrix, ethnic group by sociocultural group. Three "ethnic" groups are included (black, Hispanic, and white). Sociocultural status is determined by administering the "Sociocultural Scales." Through multiple-regression techniques, separate norms are generated for each cell in the matrix. No group has a mean ELP of less than 100, although advantaged whites have means that are greater than 100.

Norms

There are eight different tests included in SOMPA, all standardized on the same sample of public school students. There are approximately 50 boys and 50 girls at each age from 5 to 11. The total sample consists of 2,085 children, with approximately equal numbers of blacks, Hispanics, and whites. A stratified cluster-sampling technique was used and appears to have provided a representative sample of *California* children. Great care should be exercised in using the norms in other areas of the country.

Sociocultural Scales

The sociocultural scales are of critical importance because they are used to (1) validate other measures within SOMPA and (2) transform WISC–R IQs into ELPs. The scales, administered to the child's mother in English or Spanish, are intended to measure the "extent to which the child's family background differs from the American core culture, and the socioeconomic status of the family within the ethnic group" (Mercer, 1979, p. 35). Although the concept of culture is a key one, little in the way of definition is offered: "language, values, customs, beliefs, and lifestyles" (p. 15). Current American core culture is never defined or described. Yet, the twenty-one questions on the sociocultural scales are supposed to pinpoint cultural differences. A description of the four scales follows.

Family Size

Number of full siblings
Number of persons living in household

Family Structure

Biological relationship between child and head of household
Biological relationship between child and respondent

Socioeconomic Status

Occupation of head of household
Sources of income

Urban Acculturation

Sense of efficacy (an assessment of three beliefs)
Community participation
Anglicization (education of mother and head of household, geographic area in which mother

and head of household were raised—deep South *or* foreign country versus the rest of the United States, and English usage of respondent)

Scores

Raw scores are weighted. Separate tables for blacks, Hispanics, and whites are used to convert weighted sums to scaled scores ($\overline{X} = 50$, $S = 15$).

Reliability

No reliability data are reported in the technical manuals.

Validity

Since culture is never defined, judging the content validity of the scales is problematic. Originally all members of the standardization sample were asked thirty-eight "sociocultural" questions. Responses were factor-analyzed to reduce the question pool to twenty-one. The criteria by which the thirty-eight original questions were selected are not mentioned. No rationale was offered for factor-analyzing the sociocultural scales (especially since they are ordinal). Mercer does present a large number of significant differences among blacks, Hispanics, and whites on the means of the Sociocultural Scales. Apparently she believes that the presence of ethnic/racial differences implies that the scales are valid:

From this analysis [mean comparisons] we reach this major conclusion: the Sociocultural Scales are measuring characteristics that do differentiate locations in sociocultural space. These locations differ sufficiently so that the white, black, and Hispanic children in our samples *cannot* be treated as a single population with a common lifestyle and a homogeneous cultural heritage. (1979, p. 37)

The conclusion that racial/ethnic differences must represent cultural differences is not logically valid. Finally, the Sociocultural Scales are supposed to "measure the extent to which the child's family background differs from the American core culture" (Mercer, p. 35). Yet, there was no reported effort to assess the responses of "core-culture Americans" unless *white* is taken to be synonymous with *core-culture* American. We conclude that these scales lack demonstrated validity for the purposes for which they were intended.

Medical Model

In SOMPA the medical model consists of five measures:[1] Physical Dexterity Tests, Bender Visual Motor Gestalt Test, Weight by Height, Visual Acuity, and Health History Inventories. Mercer assumes that performance on these measures is "caused by biological conditions in the organism" (1979, p. 59).

Physical Dexterity Tests   These consist of twenty-nine tasks clustered into six groups of activities.

1. *Ambulation*   The child has to move up and down a 6-foot (by 2-inch) strip of masking tape stuck to the floor. The child is to heel-and-toe forward the length of the tape, then to return heel-to-toe backward. For each item, the number of errors (up to twenty) are counted; 0 indicates no errors.
2. *Equilibrium*   The child is required to stand, with eyes closed and arms raised, and count to twenty. An error is scored if the child does not follow the directions, pauses during counting, changes the rate of counting, or fails to hold arms parallel to the floor, if the

---

1. Although Auditory Acuity is listed as a "measure" within the medical model, no provision or requirement is made for collecting such information.

child's hands tremble or touch, or if the child grimaces.

3. *Placement* Two basic movements must be performed with eyes open, with eyes shut, with the right side of the body, and with the left side. The first movement is nose-touch, and the second is touching the shin with the heel of the foot. Up to three errors are scored on each of the eight tasks.

4. *Fine-Motor Sequencing* This timed tapping task is done with the index finger of first one hand, then the other, then with the toes of one foot (heel on floor), then with the toes of the other foot. Up to three errors are scored per task.

5. *Finger-Tongue Dexterity* Four tasks are included in this group. The first two require the child to touch the thumb to each finger of the same hand, then to repeat the task with the other hand. The next task requires the child to open and close hands alternately. The last task requires the student to put the tongue on the left cheek, then the right cheek, and alternate between cheeks. Up to ten errors are scored.

6. *Involuntary Movement* This group includes six tasks, each of which requires that a position be maintained for 20 seconds. The first two tasks require the child to hold both arms straight from the shoulders with palms down. In the first task, the eyes are open, while in the second they are closed. The third and fourth tasks require that the child stand on one foot with hands at sides and eyes open. Standing on the left foot is one task; standing on the right foot, the other. The next task requires the child to stand with heels together, toes apart, hands at sides, and eyes closed. The last task requires the child to stand heel-to-toe with eyes closed and hands at sides. The scoring is based on the time the child holds each position: from 0 for 20 seconds to 3 for 9 seconds or less.

Bender Visual Motor Gestalt Test The Bender, with the Koppitz (1963) scoring system, is used. We have described this test in Chapter 14 and will not repeat it here except to note that the Bender cannot be considered a valid measure of organic pathology. SOMPA norms are used instead of Koppitz's.

Visual Acuity The Snellen Chart (see pp. 217 and 218 in this text) is used. For children who wear corrective lenses, measures are taken with and without glasses or contact lenses. Children whose uncorrected vision is 20/40 or poorer are classified as "at risk" even if they wear glasses that correct their vision to 20/20.

Weight by Height Each child is weighed and measured. Two scores are provided: (1) overweight or not, and (2) underweight or not.

Health History Inventories The inventories consist of forty-five items: ten dealing with pre- and postnatal factors, six dealing with injuries, eighteen dealing with disease and illness, eight dealing with vision, and three dealing with hearing. Mercer and Lewis (1977) believe that this information is useful in identifying students who may "need further medical follow-up or specialized educational services" (p. 60).

Scores

Mercer (1979) is particularly concerned with the shape of the distribution of scores within the medical perspective. Since she believes that measures within the medical model should not differentiate normal from superior status (and therefore should be negatively skewed), she developed scales with such characteristics, although such scales have undesirable statistical properties. On the Physical Dexterity Tests, the Bender Visual Motor Gestalt Test, and Weight by Height, raw scores at or below the mean are converted to scaled scores ($\overline{X} = 50$, $S = 15$);

scores above the mean are given a score of 50. Percentile ranks of 16 or less and scaled scores of 35 or less are considered "at risk," while scores above those points are considered "not at risk." Children scoring "at risk" on the medical measures should receive "an in-depth medical examination by a medical practitioner" (p. 44).

Reliability

The various measures in the medical portion of SOMPA are clearly intended as screening devices. Reliabilities of the six physical dexterity tasks at each age were estimated by internal consistency (that is, odd-even split-half correlations corrected by the Spearman-Brown formula). The estimates range from .61 (finger-tongue dexterity at age 11) to a high of .94 (placement at age 5). Only twenty of the forty-two estimates equal or exceed .80, the desirable minimum standard for screening devices. The reliabilities for each age for each ethnic group are reported also.[2] They range from .65 to .74, unsatisfactory for a screening device. Reliability estimates for the other medical measures were not reported.

Validity

Mercer claims that each model (that is, medical, social-system, and pluralistic) is validated differently and that it is inappropriate to extend validation procedures appropriate within one model to another.[3] For the medical model, Mercer admits two criteria for validity. First, "the validity of an instrument in the medical model will be determined by the extent to which it predicts scores on other biological measures" (Mercer, 1979, p. 44). Although the appropriate

2. Since Mercer (1979) insists that the medical measures are transcultural, we see no reason to report separate reliabilities for the three ethnic/racial groups.
3. We disagree.

data are never summarized, they are presented throughout the technical manual. Without considering average scores or scores at each age, there are fifteen separate scores in the medical model. Thus, there are 105 possible correlations. Of the 105, forty-two are not significant, fifty-five are significant but account for less than 5 percent of the common variation, and eight are significant and account for between 5 and 10 percent of the common variation. Indicative of the inconsequential but statistically significant correlations is the one between the vision questions on the Health History Inventories and visual acuity assessed by the Snellen Chart: $r = .14$. Moreover, the logic of this criterion escapes us. For example, we see no reason for a valid measure of visual acuity to be correlated with being overweight.

The second criterion Mercer holds appropriate for judging the validity of medical-model measures is that there be nonsignificant correlations with sociocultural measures. There are sixty correlations of interest among the four sociocultural variables and the fifteen medical-model measures. Twenty-seven are statistically significant. Small correlations may be statistically significant because of the large N on which they are based. Therefore, Mercer "established the rule that a correlation must not only be statistically significant but must account for at least 5 percent of the variance in a measure before we would consider the relationship of substantive importance" (1979, p. 59). We can readily accept the 5 percent rule, but we wonder why it was not applied to intercorrelations among medical-model measures. If it were applied, only eight of the 105 correlations would have "substantive importance." Moreover, Mercer waffles on the same point later in the technical manual: "The Vision Inventory is an equally good predictor of difficulties. Eight of the eleven correlations are significant beyond the .01 level" (p. 83). Unfortunately, the greatest correlation accounts for less than 2 percent of the variance, and all the rest account for less than ½ of 1 percent of the variance. The logic of such a criterion again escapes us.

When "regular" logic is applied to SOMPA, many difficulties are apparent. The placement of the Bender Visual Motor Gestalt Test in the medical model is particularly troublesome. Mercer asserts, "standardized tests are measures of acculturation to the Anglo core culture and, as such, fit within the social system model" (1979, p. 20). The Bender is, of course, a standardized test. Its directions and the skills it assesses are no less culture-specific than WISC–R block design, coding, or maze subtests. Koppitz, whom Mercer cites as an authority on the Bender, claims it can be used as an intelligence test (although we disagree with that claim).

The content validity of the various subtests is suspect. The physical dexterity tests are intended to provide tests of "the intactness and capability of the motor and sensory pathways." No evidence is offered that any of these measures are drawn from the appropriate domain. Some are very suspect (for example, follows directions, counts to 20). The weight-by-height measure is also of some interest. Medical tests are supposed to answer the question, "Is the child an intact organism?" or "to screen for biological abnormalities" or to find "pathological signs" (Mercer, 1979, p. 40). The relationship of the weight-by-height charts to these purposes is never specified.

One of the most severe shortcomings of the medical-model tests is that they are screening devices that have not been validated by further diagnosis. For example, the sixteenth percentile is the critical score selected by Mercer to indicate "at risk." There is no evidence offered that the sixteenth percentile isolates children determined by physicians to be at risk. Why should we believe that a child at, for example, the fifteenth percentile for underweight is at risk?

Social-System Model

Within the social-system model a child's performance is evaluated in terms of the adequacy with which the child fills various social roles and "the extent to which the child is able to negotiate entry, establish interpersonal ties with other group members, learn the skills required to play social roles, and achieve an adaptive fit in each social system" (Mercer, 1979, p. 46). To assess role performance, two tests are given: (1) the WISC–R (as a measure of "academic role performance in the public schools") and (2) the Adaptive Behavior Inventory for Children (ABIC).

WISC–R The WISC–R is reviewed in Chapter 10. Within SOMPA it is considered to be "a measure of how much the child has learned about the core culture of modern American society. . . . It is a measure of the child's adaptive fit to the student role" (Mercer, 1979, p. 114). The WISC–R is, moreover, an indirect measure of adaptive fit and its validity within the SOMPA scheme is "determined by its 'predictive power.' Other forms of validity, such as construct validity, face validity,[4] and content validity are not directly relevant and will not be considered further" (p. 116). Such a position is convenient, since there is a lack of content and construct validity for the WISC–R for this purpose. It was developed and validated as a test of intelligence and not as a measure of academic role performance. It is unclear to us how block design, coding, digit span, or mazes measure learning of the core culture.

To establish the predictive validity of the WISC–R for the purposes of SOMPA, two studies of the correlations between WISC–R and grade-point averages are reported. These correlations were generally .3 or less. Such cor-

4. Face validity is not generally considered as validity. It refers to the extent to which a test's content looks right on the face of it.

relations clearly indicate how poor the WISC–R is as a measure of academic role performance. Several studies with the old WISC are also reported; generally, the results are the same: unacceptably low correlations.

Adaptive Behavior Inventory for Children   The Adaptive Behavior Inventory for Children (ABIC) contains 242 questions organized into six scales: family (fifty-two questions), peer relations (thirty-six questions), nonacademic school roles (thirty-seven questions), earner/consumer (twenty-six questions), and self-maintenance (forty-nine questions). As with other measures of adaptive behavior, a respondent who is familiar with the child is interviewed. The interview may be conducted in English or Spanish. The first thirty-five questions are asked about all children; the last 207 use a basal and ceiling rule. "Questions were developed that would apply equally to both sexes, to all socioeconomic levels, and to all ethnic groups" (Mercer, 1979, p. 93). Other criteria used to include and exclude items are unclear. Subsequent analysis of the responses made by members of the standardization sample shows that questions favoring boys are approximately balanced by questions favoring girls, questions favoring high-status families by questions favoring low-status families. There are racial/ethnic differences.

Scores

Responses to the ABIC receive one of five scores: latent role (child has not performed the activity), emergent role (child is beginning to perform the role), mastered role, no opportunity/not allowed, and respondent doesn't know. Raw scores for each of the six subtests of the ABIC are converted to standard scores ($\bar{X}$ = 50, S = 15). The average scale score is the mean of the six subscales.

Reliability

Split-half estimates (with Spearman-Brown correction) were computed for each age level for each subscale of the ABIC. Reliabilities of the subscales are generally too low for use in making individual decisions (thirty-six of the forty-two estimates are less than .9). The reliabilities for the average scores are excellent, .97 or higher. Some evidence of interrater agreement is provided. The data are based on the responses of undescribed individuals completing training workshops. The standard deviations of scores are erroneously averaged;[5] this results in systematically underestimated variability. Nonetheless, it does appear that workshop completers score ABIC interviews consistently.

Validity

Mercer asserts that for "proper" validation of the ABIC scales, one must distinguish between indirect measurement and direct measurement. Direct measurement is an evaluation that comes "from members of the system, . . . such as a peer evaluating a child's performance in the peer group" (Mercer, 1979, p. 107). Indirect measurements are evaluations by persons not members of the system. Indirect measurements are to be validated by predicting direct measurements. Direct measurements are to be validated by interrater agreement. Using Mercer's own criteria, the ABIC scales are unvalidated.

From a more usual perspective, the ABIC scales appear to be measuring adaptive behavior. However, the technical manual does not delineate the contents that ought to be sampled to assure content validity. Users of the scales will need to judge their validity for themselves.

---

5. Variances, not standard deviations, are additive.

Pluralistic Measure

The central tenet of SOMPA is that differences in measured intelligence among social classes and ethnic groups are the result of different opportunities to learn materials tested because "the genetic potential for acquiring the cognitive skills needed to perform as a student is essentially the same in all ethnic and cultural groups" (1979, p. 135). To turn this admirable social belief into a scientific fact, a statistical procedure is used to develop separate means and standard deviations for each racial/ethnic group at each sociocultural level. Specifically, a multiple regression equation is developed to predict WISC–R scores from the sociocultural scales for each racial/ethnic group. The predicted WISC–R score is assumed to be the mean for the group and is subtracted from the child's obtained WISC–R score; this difference is divided by the standard deviation of predicted scores.[6] The score produced is treated as a *z*-score and is then converted to an ELP (Estimated Learning Potential), a score with a mean equal to 100 and a standard deviation equal to 15.

Reliability

The reliability of the ELP is not discussed in the SOMPA technical manuals. However, the ELP is essentially a difference score in which there is reliability associated with the estimated mean and with the obtained WISC–R score.

Validity

Mercer asserts that the "appropriate test of the validity [of the ELP] is the amount of variance in WISC–R IQs accounted for by the socio-

cultural variables in the regression equation" (1979, p. 141). Indeed, the sociocultural scales do not account for a modest proportion of the variation in WISC–R scores. Yet this seems a hollow criterion by which to judge a score as an indicator of a "child's probable potential for future learning" (p. 143). The unspoken criterion appears to be that the test must be considered a valid test of intelligence for members of the core culture. Its extension to other sociocultural groups is deemed permissible with "pluralistic" (that is, multiple) norms.

Two serious internal contradictions must also be noted. Mercer devotes four paragraphs to denying the appropriateness of correlating ELP scores with "social-system" measures. Six paragraphs later (p. 143) she urges that users focus their interpretations on Verbal ELPs "because it is more highly correlated . . . with both dimensions of the school role: academic performance and interpersonal relations." (Moreover, no correlations between ELPs and *any* measures are provided.) The second contradiction is most bothersome. Throughout the technical manuals, the SOMPA authors continually refer to discriminatory assessments as those that result in mean differences among ethnic/racial groups. After all the SOMPA adjustments are made, the mean for advantaged whites is still higher than the means for other groups. The reason is that SOMPA does not use the predicted WISC–R score as the mean when it is greater than 100. In these cases, ELP and WISC–R are interpreted to be the same. We believe that potential SOMPA users are deliberately misled into believing that racial/ethnic differences as well as social-class differences have been eliminated when in fact they have not been.

There are other fundamental problems with the validity of the ELP. SOMPA leads the reader to believe that once sociocultural factors are taken into account, genetic potential for learning will be assessed. Also, Mercer mis-

---

6. The *S* of predicted scores is the standard error or estimate (S_{EE}). The S_{EE} can be computed by the formula $S_{EE} = S\sqrt{1 - r^2}$

takenly calls the organism the genotype when she writes, "the genotype is modified by environmental factors such as the physical health and nutrition of the mother and, after birth, the nature of the physical environment" (1979, p. 52). Although the genotype is *not* altered,[7] the organism is indeed modified. However, the impact of this point was somehow missed: "inferences about a child's learning potential can be made *if* the child's performance is compared only with others who have come from similar sociocultural settings and presumably have had the same opportunity to learn the material in the test, the same motivation to learn that material, and the same test-taking experience" (Mercer, 1979, p. 53). Environment modifies *learning potential,* and to the extent that it does, SOMPA's ELPs are conceptually wrong. The most nurturing physical and psychological environments are not equally distributed among social groups (for example, the children of the rich do not usually suffer malnutrition). Another example of how the ELP may be in error involves rural and urban children. Mercer asserts that urban and rural children have equal potential to learn. However, there is selective migration to cities. Children who move from rural areas to urban areas have higher IQs than the children who remain (Roberts, 1971). Obviously this will produce different means for urban and rural

children. In short, SOMPA ignores a vast literature of the effects that environment can have on measured intelligence. There is much more than genotype and opportunity to learn the test materials.

Finally, it must be noted that the technical manual is most annoying. Factual errors are littered throughout. Critical information is absent (for example, intercorrelations of sociocultural scales). Standards for making decisions shift, so that the decision reached is consistent with dogma rather than data. Minor statistical misunderstandings crop up too often (for example, the WISC–R is called an ordinal scale and then used in analyses that require equal-interval data).

Summary

SOMPA is a system that attempts to provide data from multiple perspectives in order to understand a child's current level of functioning and potential for future learning. The norms are representative of public school students in California. Users outside of California should be extremely careful in using SOMPA's norms and regression equations. Except for the ABIC and WISC–R, reliabilities are either too low or unreported. Validities for various purposes are not established. At best, SOMPA should be considered experimental.

7. This thoroughly discredited theory is called the Lamarckian fallacy.

Woodcock-Johnson Psychoeducational Battery

The Woodcock-Johnson Psychoeducational Battery (WJ) (Woodcock, 1978) is an individually administered multiple-skill battery designed to assess cognitive ability, scholastic aptitude, academic achievement, and interests in individuals from 3 to 80 years of age. The complete battery contains twenty-seven subtests or-

ganized into three parts. Part 1 contains twelve subtests that may be used to assess both cognitive ability and specific scholastic aptitudes (for example, reading ability). Part 2, consisting of ten subtests, assesses academic achievement in seven content areas. Part 3 assesses specific scholastic and nonscholastic interests. Although administration time for the complete battery is more than 2 hours, portions of the battery may be administered to meet specific assessment needs. The complete battery is contained in two easel-format books. The authors describe at least twelve different uses for the battery, ranging from "diagnosis of strengths and weaknesses" to "evaluation of changes in performance following a certain interval of special services."

An adaptation of the Rasch model was used in constructing the battery. The Rasch model, also used in the development of the KeyMath Diagnostic Arithmetic Test, the Woodcock Reading Mastery Test, and the Goldman-Fristoe-Woodcock Test of Articulation, is one that produces an equal-interval scale of test items and enables standardization on fewer subjects. According to Woodcock (1978), the following three fundamental assumptions underlie the use of the Rasch model.

Unidimensionality   It is assumed that all items in a given subtest measure the same underlying ability. Underlying abilities are called "latent traits" because they are not directly measured.

Local Independence   It is assumed that performance on each test item is independent.

Equal Discrimination   It is assumed that items in the test have equal discrimination characteristics. It is assumed that the probability of a seven-year-old getting an item at the 7-year level correct is the same as the probability of a nine-year-old getting an item at the 9-year level correct.

When tests are developed using the Rasch model, items are analyzed to determine the extent to which they fit the model. Those that do not fit the model are dropped from the test. A special transformation of the Rasch model, the W scale, was used in developing the Woodcock-Johnson Psychoeducational Battery.

Several unique steps were used in developing this battery. The authors first decided which subtests would be included in the battery and selected items for each subtest. After initial field testing, items were edited and assembled into a calibration-norming form. This calibration norming form was administered to the standardization sample. The authors developed "clusters," weighted combinations of two or more subtests, to prevent interpretation of students' strengths and weaknesses on the basis of subtests.

Following assessment of the first half of the norming sample, the authors used several statistical analyses to identify those subtests of the cognitive ability scale that should be included in each of the cognitive clusters. They used the performance of the second half of the norming sample to assign relative weights to the subtests in each cluster. However, for the achievement and interest parts of the test, the authors state that the subtest composition for clusters "was known ahead of time." Weights for these clusters were assigned in proportion to the number of subtests in a cluster. Thus, if a cluster is composed of four subtests, each one gets a weight of .25.

Subtests in the three parts of the battery and a description of the behaviors sampled follow.

Cognitive Ability Subtests

Picture Vocabulary   This subtest assesses an individual's ability to identify pictured objects or actions.

Spatial Relations   This subtest assesses a person's ability to select from among several shapes the components of a complete shape.

Memory for Sentences   This subtest measures an individual's ability to repeat orally presented sentences.

Visual Auditory Learning   This subtest presents a miniature learning-to-read task in which a person is required to associate unfamiliar visual stimuli (rebuses) with familiar oral words and to translate sequences of rebuses into sentences.

Blending   This subtest assesses an individual's skill in integrating components of orally presented words into whole words.

Quantitative Concepts   This subtest measures the ability to answer specific questions assessing knowledge of quantitative concepts and vocabulary. No specific arithmetic calculations are required.

Visual Matching   This subtest is a timed assessment of skill in identifying two identical numbers in a row of six numbers.

Antonyms-Synonyms   This is a two-part subtest, requiring the subject to identify antonyms (by stating a word whose meaning is opposite to that of a presented word) and synonyms (by stating a word whose meaning is the same as that of a presented word).

Analysis-Synthesis   This subtest measures an individual's ability to analyze the parts of an equivalency statement and then put them back together to solve a novel equivalency statement. A practice pretest is included in which the examiner corrects subject errors.

Numbers Reversed   This subtest assesses a person's ability to repeat in reverse order a series of orally presented digits.

Concept Formation   In this subtest, a student must identify the rule for a concept given instances and noninstances of the concepts.

Analogies   This subtest assesses an individual's ability to solve problems of an A:B::C:? nature.

Achievement Subtests

Letter-Word Identification   This subtest assesses skill in recognizing letters and words in isolation.

Word Attack   This subtest measures word-attack skills achieved by requiring pronunciation of nonsense words.

Passage Comprehension   This subtest uses a cloze procedure to assess skill in comprehension of written material.

Calculation   The Calculation subtest measures skill in solving paper-and-pencil addition, subtraction, multiplication, and division problems.

Applied Problems   This subtest assesses skill in solving practical arithmetic problems.

Dictation   The Dictation subtest assesses skill in writing letters, spelling, punctuation, capitalization, and usage.

Proofing   This subtest assesses skill in punctuation, capitalization, spelling, and usage by requiring the individual to correct typewritten passages.

Science   This subtest measures knowledge of the content of the physical and biological sciences.

Social Studies   This subtest measures content knowledge in geography, history, government, economics, and other broad aspects of social science curricula.

Humanities   The Humanities subtest assesses knowledge in art, music, and literature.

Interest Subtests

Reading Interest This subtest measures a person's interest in reading activities.

Mathematics Interest This subtest assesses an individual's interest in participating in activities that require learning or applying math.

Written Language Interest This subtest measures interest in participating in activities that require written language.

Physical Interest This subtest assesses interest in group and individual physical activities.

Social Interest This subtest assesses preference for engaging in activities that involve other people.

Scores

Although the Woodcock-Johnson Psychoeducational Battery is composed of subtests on which students earn raw scores, the recommended unit of analysis is cluster scores, scores earned on clusters of subtests. Figure 22.1 lists the clusters for the battery and identifies the subtests included in each cluster. Note that for some clusters, subtests act as suppressor variables, that is, they have a negative weighting in deriving the cluster.

At the cluster level the authors have recommended several kinds of interpretation. Percentiles may be derived for clusters, and strengths and weaknesses may be identified using profile analyses of percentiles. One may also construct achievement-aptitude profiles and "instructional implications profiles."

This test is almost too sophisticated, and thereby potentially confusing, in the numbers of other kinds of derived scores that may be obtained, many of which are unconventional.

Users may derive grade equivalents for cluster scores. The battery provides "extended" grade-score scales, enabling the user to obtain percentile ranks for grade scores below 1.0 and above 12.9.

Age-equivalent scores may be obtained to age 34, after which percentile ranks are provided. Users may also convert scores to instructional ranges, indicative of levels between an "easy level" and a "frustration level." Instructional-range indexes allegedly provide the user with an index that has instructional implications.

Users of the Woodcock-Johnson Psychoeducational Battery may convert obtained aptitude scores to Expected Achievement scores. These scores are average achievement scores earned by participants in the norming sample who had the same aptitude scores as the student being assessed.

The authors of this battery state that cluster difference scores are obtained by computing the deviation of an individual's cluster score from the average cluster score earned by those in the reference group. These scores are, in turn, used to determine percentile ranks and Relative Performance Indexes (RPIs). Relative Performance Indexes employ a concept similar to that used with a Snellen chart. The Snellen index indicates visual acuity; persons with a Snellen index of 20/200 have to be at 20 feet to see what a person with normal visual acuity sees at 200 feet. An RPI of 80/90 means that an individual would be expected to demonstrate 80 percent mastery on tasks that average persons in the reference group perform with 90 percent mastery.

As noted earlier, despite the many kinds of derived scores that can be obtained, the recommended level of interpretation is cluster scores. The authors recommend that users construct percentile rank profiles for cluster scores, and use several "rules of thumb" to interpret differences in performance on clusters.

CLUSTERS	Picture Vocabulary	Spatial Relations	Memory for Sentences	Visual-Auditory Learning	Blending	Quantitative Concepts	Visual Matching	Antonyms-Synonyms	Analysis-Synthesis	Numbers Reversed	Concept Formation	Analogies	Letter-Word Identification	Word Attack	Passage Comprehension	Calculation	Applied Problems	Dictation	Proofing	Science	Social Studies	Humanities	Reading Interest	Mathematics Interest	Written Language Interest	Physical Interest	Social Interest
Broad Cognitive--Full Scale	●	●	●	●	●	●	●	●	●	●	●	●															
Broad Cognitive--Preschool Scale	●	●	●	●	●	●																					
Broad Cognitive--Brief Scale					●		●																				
Verbal Ability	●							●	−																		
Reasoning								−	●		●	●															
Perceptual Speed		●					●																				
Memory			●							●																	
Reading Aptitude				●	●			●				●															
Mathematics Aptitude								●	●	●	●																
Written Language Aptitude				●	●			●		●																	
Knowledge Aptitude			●		●						●																
Reading Achievement													●	●	●												
Mathematics Achievement																●	●										
Written Language Acheivement																		●	●								
Knowledge Achievement																				●	●	●					
Skills Achievement													●				●	●									
Scholastic Interest																							●	●	●		
Non-Scholastic Interest																										●	●

Note: A "—" denotes the fact that the subtest acts as a suppressor variable in derivation of the cluster score

FIGURE 22.1 Subtests included in clusters of the Woodcock-Johnson Psychoeducational Battery

Norms

All three parts of the Woodcock-Johnson Psychoeducational Battery were normed on the same 4,732 subjects in forty-nine communities. The majority of the subjects (3,900) made up the school sample. The other 832 individuals were either preschoolers or adults. Norms for preschoolers and adults are based on limited numbers of individuals.

Five stratification variables were used in selecting the norm sample for the battery: sex, race, occupational status, geographic region, and type of community (urbanized or nonurbanized). A three-stage sampling plan was used in which communities were selected first, then schools, and finally students. The test was normed in eighteen communities, on students selected at random within schools. Handicapped students were excluded from the norm sample unless they were being educated within regular education classes.

Tables in the manual contrast norm sample statistics with population statistics. A comparison of the sex, race, geographic region, and type of community of the sample illustrates disparity from 1970 U.S. Census data for the population. In several instances more than a 10 percent difference in proportions is evidenced. The sample included significant overrepresentation of individuals from nonurban north central communities, and significant underrepresentation of people from nonurban southern communities. Race, sex, and occupational status distributions closely approximate U.S. census data. The authors used an individual-subject weighting system to achieve "exact comparability" to census data.

Reliability

Split-half reliabilities for subtest scores and cluster scores are reported in appendices to the technical manual. Reliabilities were calculated for "standings," that is, for percentile ranks and standard scores, rather than for raw scores. For subtest scores, median reliability coefficients exceed .80 except for punctuation and capitalization (.78) and visual matching (.65). Median reliabilities for clusters exceed .85 except for the perceptual speed cluster (.70). Median reliabilities for achievement-aptitude differences are also reported; they are, as would be expected, lower, ranging from .62 to .95.

All reliability data were derived from the performance of the norm sample. There are no data on test-retest reliability.

Validity

Extensive data on validity are reported in the technical manual for the Woodcock-Johnson Psychoeducational Battery. The results of ten different validity studies are reported, and al-

though the locations in which the studies took place are identified, descriptive information on the subjects (for example, sex) is not provided.

Correlations of subject performance on the battery with preschool measures, cognitive measures, achievement tests, diagnostic tests, opinion questionnaires, and written language tests are reported.

While there is considerable evidence for the validity of the battery in a traditional sense, the authors do not provide validity data to support each of the twelve recommended uses they identify for the test.

Summary

The Woodcock-Johnson Psychoeducational Battery is a wide-age-range test designed to measure cognitive abilities, scholastic aptitude, achievement, and interest. The three parts of this test were standardized on the same population, and it is thus the only individually administered test with common norms on cognitive ability, achievement, and interest.

The authors recommend that scores earned on clusters, weighted combinations of subtests, should serve as the level of interpretation. Yet, at this time there is no evidence to support the generalization of the clusters from the norm sample to other populations. The extent to which evidence is found to support generalization will make this device either extremely helpful or largely useless.

The battery was adequately standardized, and data provided in the manual support both its reliability and its validity.

COPING WITH DILEMMAS IN CURRENT PRACTICE

The general problems that are raised by diagnostic systems are often the same as those raised in the measurement of the domains that are included in the systems. Methods for coping with the problems are also the same. For example, when a diagnostic system examines achievement, the question of curriculum match must be addressed.

One problem is noteworthy. The theoretical constructs on which the diagnostic systems are based often force the assessor to interpret behavior samples in novel and unusual ways. For example, SOMPA uses the Bender Visual Motor Gestalt Test (with Koppitz's scoring procedures) as a measure of organic pathology. From SOMPA's perspective, there is a need for such a measure. From a more traditional measurement standpoint, the Bender cannot be used in this way. The K–ABC provides another example. Simultaneous and sequential processing are proposed as measures of intelligence. However, such an orientation to intellectual assessment is quite revolutionary. For many diagnosticians, acceptance of the K–ABC's orientation will require a considerably larger base of research support. We believe that the way to cope with novel theoretical orientations is to defer acceptance until a firm base of research indicates their validity. Until such research is available, patience and skepticism may serve the tester well.

SUMMARY

Three diagnostic systems, assessment devices sampling behaviors in multiple domains, were reviewed. Devices like K–ABC, SOMPA, and Woodcock-Johnson are attractive and appealing; indeed, we might expect Ed McMahon on the *Tonight* show to say, "Here, in one handy package, are the necessary scales, subtests, and items to get at everything you ever wanted to know about a student." Wrong. The tests are simply samples of behavior with overly sophisticated interpretive systems built around them. These tests (which are very complex) require the investment of considerable time to administer, score, and interpret. When the user is finished, we believe he or she has *not* produced a nondiscriminatory assessment; we also believe he or she has little information of instructional relevance.

STUDY QUESTIONS

1. What instructional implications can you derive from the K–ABC?
2. To what extent does the SOMPA provide a nondiscriminatory assessment of students?
3. Identify three potential difficulties that users may face in using the SOMPA and the Woodcock-Johnson Psychoeducational Battery.
4. Earlier in this text we stated than one of the fundamental assumptions in assessment is that the student tested has comparable, although not necessarily identical, acculturation as the group on whom a test is standardized.

The SOMPA employs multiple norm groups to address this assumption. To what extent does the SOMPA succeed?

ADDITIONAL READING

School Psychology Review (1979), *8*(1). (The entire issue is a symposium on the SOMPA.)

Journal of Special Education, Fall 1984 issue. (The entire issue is a symposium on the Kaufman Assessment Battery.)

PART 5

APPLYING ASSESSMENT INFORMATION TO EDUCATIONAL DECISION MAKING

Assessment does not occur in a vacuum. It is a process whereby data are collected for the purpose of making decisions about students. In Part 5 we describe ways in which assessment data are collected and used. Specifically, we describe the use of assessment information in making referral, classification, and instructional planning decisions. We do so by showing how these different decisions are made for five students, each of whom has different kinds of problems.

The activities described in Part 5 are examples of ways in which assessment information is collected and used in schools. Frankly, the cases are simplified examples; assessment in schools is likely to be more complex.

In earlier parts of the text we have provided basic information about the how and why of testing and assessment, discussed basic measurement principles, and presented evaluations of the assessment devices used in schools. In Part 5 we show how all of this information is applied to the process of making important decisions about students.

CHAPTER 23

MAKING REFERRAL DECISIONS

Technically speaking, a referral is a request for help. A teacher or parent calls a student to the attention of a specialist when assistance seems to be needed to provide the student with an appropriate educational program. There is, frankly, much confusion about the act of referral, and much of that confusion can be traced directly to misinformation that has been dispensed to teachers as part of their training. For years teachers were trained to look for specific kinds of problems that would indicate the need to refer a student to some other person. Teachers learned lists of characteristics associated with specific kinds of disorders. They learned those lists so that they could spot problems early and spot specific students who should be referred to others. This practice has contributed to some problems.

A cursory look at referral practices in today's schools reveals a mixture of practices. In some settings, practice is still pretty traditional, and teachers refer students *to* other professionals. In such settings, the act of referral is often one in which the teacher abdicates responsibility for a student. The teacher learns to give up or is reinforced for giving up on specific students and sending them to other professionals in the school. Such traditional practices are encouraged when those to whom students are referred (counselors, school psychologists, speech and language pathologists, social workers) respond by testing students and trying to find out "what is wrong with them."

In other settings referral is viewed as a request for help in providing an appropriate educational program for a student. There is considerable emphasis on prereferral assessment for the purpose of verifying and specifying the nature of academic, behavior, or physical problems. Some teachers have always engaged in significant prereferral assessment. Recently, the practice has become more prevalent. In part this is due to efforts, in response to Public Law 94-142, to educate students in least restrictive environments.

THE PREREFERRAL ASSESSMENT PROCESS

Under ideal circumstances, a great deal of prereferral assessment and prereferral intervention takes place before students are ever considered for special education placement. The goal of prereferral assessment and intervention is twofold: (1) verification and specification of the nature of a student's difficulties, and (2) provision of services in the least restrictive environment.

Graden, Casey, and Bonstrom (1983) describe five stages in prereferral assessment and intervention. We think it is important to review these stages, as they illustrate nicely ideal practice.

Stage 1: Request for Consultation   The first step in the process ought to be a request for consultation rather than a request for testing. The classroom teacher asks for help, either from a resource teacher or from some other specialist. A form similar to that shown in Figure 23.1 may be used to initiate the request.

Stage 2: Consultation   The resource teacher or other specialist works with the classroom teacher to verify the existence of a problem, to specify the nature of a problem, and to develop strategies that might relieve the problem. The following steps occur during this initial consultation.

a. The referring teacher is asked to specify, in observable terms, the reason(s) for referral. For example, the teacher may specify a problem by saying that "Heather does not recognize the letters of the alphabet" or that "Matthew does not complete homework assignments."
b. Reasons for referral are ranked in order of importance for action. This act helps the consultant to identify specific problems to be addressed.
c. The referring teacher is asked to specify the ways in which the student's behavior affects the teacher and the extent to which the behavior is incongruent with the teacher's expectations.
d. An intervention is designed by the referring teacher. Graden, Casey, and Bonstrom (1983) find the form shown in Figure 23.2 useful in designing an intervention. In planning prereferral interventions, it is often helpful to involve the student, the parents, and other school personnel as appropriate.
e. Interventions are implemented and evaluated. These interventions will either succeed in alleviating the problem or will lead to additional teaching modifications.

On completion of this stage, those who educate the child will have verified the existence of a problem, specified the nature of the problem, tried to intervene to remove the problem, and collected data on the effectiveness of those interventions.

FIGURE 23.1 Request for consultation

Student _____ Sex _____ Date of Birth _____

Referring Teacher _____ Grade _____ School _____

_____

Describe specific educational/behavioral problems:

_____

_____

_____

_____

Current instructional level:

Reading _____ Math _____

What special services is the student receiving (e.g., speech, Title I, Reading Teacher)?

_____

_____

Results of vision, hearing, medical screening:

_____

_____

_____

Most convenient days/times to meet for consultation on referral:

_____

_____

THIS IS NOT A REFERRAL FOR TESTING

Stage 3: Observation Observation of pupil behavior in classroom settings makes it possible to document the specific nature of referral problems. It is one way to verify the existence of a problem or problems. The following kinds of activities may occur:

a. A designated person (resource teacher or school psychologist, for example) observes in relevant school settings, noting the frequency and duration of behaviors of concern and the extent to which the student's behavior differs from that of his or her classmates.
b. The observer describes (1) the curriculum being used with the student, the tasks the student is being asked to do, and the specific demands being placed on the student; (2) the way in which the teacher interacts with or responds to the student, specifically what the student does, grouping structure, and seating arrangements; (3) interactions between the student and his or her classmates; (4) causes and consequences of the student's behaviors.
c. The observer meets with the classroom teacher to provide feedback on what has been observed, and the two work together to verify the existence and specify the nature of the problem.
d. The observer and teacher develop prereferral interventions designed to address the problem. The form shown in Figure 23.3 can be used for this purpose.
e. Interventions are implemented and evaluated. Interventions will either alleviate the problem(s) or, perhaps, lead to additional instructional modifications.

The primary goal of stages 2 and 3 is the development of prereferral interventions and the evaluation of the extent to which those interventions alleviate problems that students show in classrooms. When interventions are implemented prior to formal referral and data are collected on the effectiveness of those interventions, school personnel develop a "track record." They can see the extent to which alternative instructional approaches work with a student. The form shown in Figure 23.4 can be used to document the effectiveness of interventions. When prereferral interventions are used, school personnel go through the following steps:

a. They plan several possible interventions based on data collected during consultation or observation.
b. For each intervention planned they specify (1) the behavior(s) to be changed (what); (2) the criterion for success; (3) the duration of intervention (how long); (4) the location of intervention (where); (5) the person(s) responsible for intervening (who); and (6) the methods to be used (how).
c. Intervention plans are ranks in terms of importance. They are then implemented, monitored, evaluated, and modified, continued, or terminated.

FIGURE 23.2   Consultation contacts

Student _____ Sex _____ Date of Birth _____

Teacher _____ Grade _____ School _____

Problem Identification Interview   Date _____

Behavioral description of problem(s):

Conditions under which behavior occurs:

Performance to be measured:

What:

How:

By whom:

Teacher _____ Consultant _____

Next contact _____

FIGURE 23.2   (*cont.*)

Problem Analysis Interview   Date _____

Discrepancy between actual/desired performance:

Performance goals/objectives:

Strategies:

Teacher _____   Consultant _____

Next contact _____

Implementation Contact   Date _____

_____ Implemented as planned

_____ Modifications to implementation plan (note): _____

_____

_____

Problem Evaluation Interview   Date _____

Evaluation of plan effectiveness:

_____ Follow-up contact to successful intervention.   Next contact _____

_____ Proceed to observation.   Next contact _____

Teacher _____   Consultant _____

FIGURE 23.3 Observation contacts

Student _____ Sex _____ Date of Birth _____

Teacher _____ Grade _____ School _____

Report on Observation   Date _____

Behavior observed:

Conditions of observed behavior:

Causes/consequences of observed behavior:

Teacher _____   Consultant _____

Next contact _____

FIGURE 23.3   (*cont.*)

                        Observation Contact   Date _____

Feedback on observation:

Intervention plan based on observation:

Goals/objectives:

Strategies:

Teacher _____   Consultant _____

                                        Next contact _____

                Follow-up on Observation Interventions   Date _____

Evaluation of plan effectiveness:

____ Follow-up contact to successful intervention.   Next contact _____

____ Proceed to interventions.   Next contact _____

Teacher _____   Consultant _____

FIGURE 23.4 Intervention contacts

Student _____ Sex _____ Date of Birth _____

Teacher _____ Grade _____ School _____

Intervention Plan Meeting Date _____

Prioritize intervention objectives:

Data needed to plan interventions:

Intervention goals/objectives:

Behavior to be changed:

Criterion for success:

Duration of intervention:

Context of intervention:

Who to implement:

Strategies:

Methods:

Materials

Teacher _____ Consultant _____

Next contact _____

FIGURE 23.4   (*cont.*)

<hr>

Intervention Monitoring Meeting   Date _____

____ Interventions implemented as planned.

____ Modifications to intervention plan (note):

Teacher _____   Consultant _____

Next contact _____

<hr>

Intervention Evaluation Meeting   Date _____

Outcomes of interventions:

____ Follow-up on successful intervention plan.   Next contact _____

____ Continued intervention.   Next contact _____

____ Case referred to child study team.

Teacher _____   Consultant _____

Next contact _____

d. The process may end if interventions are successful. The process may continue until school personnel reach a limit of tolerance in attempts to intervene.

Stage 4: Conference A conference may be held to review pupil progress and to decide whether formal referral is necessary. This meeting would involve appropriate school personnel and might also include the parents and/or the student. At this meeting; the following things occur:

a. Data on consultations, observations, and the effectiveness of interventions are shared.
b. Feedback from team members is solicited.
c. A decision is made to (1) continue interventions, (2) modify interventions, or (3) refer the student for formal psychoeducational assessment to consider her or his eligibility for special education services.

Stage 5: Formal Referral A formal referral is made for psychoeducational intervention. The student enters the formal child study process and two kinds of assessment occur:

a. Data collected during the first four stages are evaluated.
b. Tests are administered or behaviors are sampled in an effort to gather information needed to plan a specific instructional program.

CASE STUDY EXAMPLES

Referral has two meanings. It is a request for help. It is also a request for evaluation. We now describe referral information on five different students. In each instance we assume the students are being formally referred for psychoeducational evaluation and that consultation, observation, and prereferral intervention have already occurred. We provide you with information on how problems were verified and specified. In Chapter 24 we will follow four of these students through the classification process. In Chapter 25 we will show how instructional interventions were developed for the students. The cases illustrated are real, but students' names have, of course, been changed.

Phoebe

Phoebe was a 13-year-old eighth grader who was experiencing considerable difficulty with math problems. Phoebe came to the attention of school personnel when her parents asked the junior high school counselor to "have her tested for learning disabilities in mathematics." The counselor met with the eighth-grade math teacher (consultation) to discuss Phoebe's performance in math.

The counselor was told that Phoebe could not do beginning algebra and that her performance in science was poor. The teacher reported that Phoebe was becoming truant, often skipped math class, and often talked about quitting school. The teacher reported that he had held two meetings with Phoebe's parents and that the parents seemed to be exerting a lot of pressure for Phoebe to succeed in math and science. The father, an engineer, had stated specifically that he wanted Phoebe to go to college and that he thought math and science were the two most important subjects in school.

The counselor reviewed Phoebe's previous school records. She could find no evidence of prior academic, behavior, or physical problems. The counselor noted that Phoebe's progress in school had been simply adequate. Most grades were Bs and Cs, with a D+ earned in seventh-grade science. Phoebe had taken a standardized achievement test, the California Achievement Test, in seventh grade and had scored at the 55th percentile in both math computation and math concepts and applications. The protocol was not available since it was machine scored.

In order to verify and specify the nature of Phoebe's math problems, the counselor decided to interview the teacher, the student, and the parents and to observe Phoebe's behavior in math and English classes.

Teacher Interview

The counselor discussed Phoebe's performance with the eighth-grade math teacher in an effort to specify the nature of her difficulties. The teacher reported that Phoebe's performance was very slow and that she seldom completed math tests. The teacher said Phoebe seemed overly concerned with the correctness of her performance, and overly concerned with errors. The teacher could not sort out any particular kind of math problem that was posing difficulty for Phoebe. He reported that Phoebe's record of turning in completed homework assignments was getting worse. When asked how Phoebe's performance compared to that of other eighth graders, the teacher reported that Phoebe was among the poorest students in Algebra I, but far better than students enrolled in Basic Math.

Student Interview

The counselor met with Phoebe to talk about her academic progress. Phoebe reported that it was taking more and more time to complete her math assignments and that her parents were increasingly "getting on her case" about performance in math. She stated that no matter how hard she tried, her parents "kept bugging her" about math. She said she wanted to give up, because no matter how hard she tried, her parents were always too busy to help her. She stated that her father repeatedly scolded her for spending more time on the phone than on math.

Parent Interview

The counselor met with the parents to discuss Phoebe's performance in math, and school in general. It was reported that the parents were highly success oriented and placed considerable emphasis on math achievement. The parents reported having purchased a microcomputer in response to an ad on television about students with math problems. They reported that Phoebe initially used the math software but now prefers to play games. The father indicated little understanding of or sympathy for Phoebe's difficulties, stating that math always came easily for him.

Classroom Observation

On three occasions the counselor tried to observe Phoebe in math class. Yet on only one of those occasions was Phoebe present. When Phoebe was observed, it was noted that she appeared to listen to instructions and worked very hard at completion of an in-class assignment. Phoebe seemed to be working harder than several other students in the class, yet about half of her work was completed incorrectly. Observation of her behavior in English class indicated little difference from her behavior in math.

Action

The counselor verified the existence of a problem in math by consulting with the math teacher, the parents, and Phoebe. The problem could not be specified beyond general, across-the-board difficulties in math and a developing negative attitude toward math. The counselor further verified the existence of a problem by direct observation in the classroom. A decision was made to forgo prereferral intervention for two reasons: (1) Phoebe's poor attendance in math class, and (2) the general rather than specific nature of her difficulties. Formal referral was made to the school psychologist who was asked to determine (1) the specific nature of Phoebe's difficulties in math and (2) whether or not Phoebe was eligible for special education services.

Bill

Bill was an 8-year-old black student whose third-grade teacher initially asked for help because Bill was having reading difficulties. The resource teacher, Mr. Will, responded to this referral by meeting with the third-grade teacher. The first step used by the resource teacher was one of clarifying and specifying the nature of the problems Bill was experiencing. The third-grade teacher informed Mr. Will that Bill was having difficulty in recognizing and decoding the very simplest words. In addition, Bill was beginning to withdraw from classroom interactions and to show behavior problems, especially as evidenced in scribbling on other students' worksheets.

Observation

The resource teacher observed Bill in class on two separate occasions, once for 45 minutes and once for 10 minutes. It was observed that Bill's performance in reading was at the very lowest level. During reading instruction he simply did not read. Bill was in the lowest reading group in his class, and clearly was the poorest reader in that group. Worksheets requiring him to match pictures with words were completed sloppily; performance was at a chance level.

Parent Interview

Mr. Will and the third-grade teacher met with Bill's parents. The parents both worked and were from a middle-class background. They stated that Bill's development had been pretty much normal and that he had had few physical illnesses. There was no history of vision or hearing problems. The parents said that Bill gets along "just fine" with other children in his neighborhood and that he spends most of his time playing with two 9-year-old neighbor boys.

Prereferral Intervention

The resource teacher and classroom teacher together planned an intervention that involved Bill going to a reading tutor three times a week for 45 minutes. The tutor selected 20 words that Bill did not know. She used flash cards and a word-picture association method to teach five words, a phonic approach to teach five others, a kinesthetic approach to teach five other words, and a combination of the three approaches to teach the remaining five words. The word-picture association approach worked best, but the overriding result was that Bill learned to recognize only two words under this approach. The tutor recommended that the teacher try using computer-assisted instruction (CAI) in which Bill had to match words with pictures.

A two-week intervention using CAI to teach word-picture association proved fruitless. Bill performed at random in efforts to match pictures to words. The teacher met with the resource teacher, and they recommended formal evaluation for potential special education placement.

Luis

Luis was a 7-year-old Hispanic student who was attending kindergarten at the time he was referred for psychoeducational evaluation. His parents had held him out of school until age 7 because so many developmental problems were indicated. Luis was referred by the kindergarten teacher during the first week in September. She asked for assistance, stating that "Luis shows developmental delays in all areas."

Teacher Interview

The school psychologist met with the kindergarten teacher to specify the nature of the difficulties shown by Luis. The teacher reported that Luis was extremely immature compared to other kindergarten children, that he had difficulty walking, had many toilet accidents, and spoke seldom and with little intelligibility. The teacher reported that Luis sometimes spoke in Spanish, but most often used English.

Parent Interview

The kindergarten teacher and school psychologist met with Luis's mother. They learned that Luis had shown considerable immaturity in all areas since he was an infant. The mother reported that Luis was much slower to walk and talk than her other children and that he had only begun to talk at age 5. The mother reported that both parents were bilingual, but that Luis's vocabulary in both Spanish and English was very limited.

Classroom Observation

The school psychologist observed Luis in the kindergarten classroom. Luis did not respond to teacher directions; he simply sat at a table and crumpled papers. He did not interact with other children and did not speak during the time he was observed.

Action

The school psychologist completed a formal referral for psychoeducational evaluation for consideration of eligibility for special education services.

Matt

Matt was a 13-year-old eighth grader whose teacher, Ms. Brooks, made a request for consultation. The request was received by the resource teacher, Ms. Edwards. Information on the form indicated that Matt was demonstrating serious behavior problems in English and study hall, both classes taught by Ms. Brooks.

The resource teacher met with Ms. Brooks to verify the existence of a problem and to specify the nature of the difficulties evidenced by Matt. Ms. Brooks reported that Matt was using frequent negative verbalizations. He teased other students and called them names. For example, he would say things like "You're ugly," "You're a jerk," or "You're stupid." Sometimes these statements were also made to the teacher. Often, the statements included obscenities. Ms. Brooks reported that she could not identify anything that triggered the negative verbal statements, they just occurred. She reported that teasing and name calling were more frequent during independent work time than during group instructional activities.

Ms. Edwards asked Ms. Brooks how she typically responded to Matt's teasing and negative verbal statements. Ms. Brooks said she usually told Matt his behavior was inappropriate, sometimes raised her voice in speaking with Matt, and often told him his behavior would not be tolerated. She said that on two occasions she had sent him to the vice principal's office but Matt had simply wandered around the school until the next class started. Ms. Brooks had not reported this to the vice principal. When Ms. Edwards asked how students who were picked on reacted to Matt, she was told that Matt was much bigger than the other students and they either ignored him or complained to the teacher. In addition, Matt did participate in class and was earning a grade of C.

Ms. Brooks stated that she wanted to decrease the number of instances of negative verbalizations *without* decreasing the number of positive verbalizations and contributions to class. She said she would like to find out if Matt had serious emotional problems and if he would be better off in a class for emotionally disturbed students. Ms. Edwards asked Ms. Brooks about the frequency of the teasing and name calling. Matt was said to have "good days" and "bad days." On good days the frequency of negative verbalizations ranged from 8 to 10 per hour. On bad days there were often as many as 40 to 50 in a one-hour class. Matt was said to have two or three "bad days" per week.

Observation

The resource teacher, Ms. Edwards, observed Matt's behavior in English class for three hours and in study hall for one hour. During three hours of observation in English class there were 90 negative verbalizations. During the one-hour observation in study hall, there were 41 negative verbalizations. Ms. Edwards kept track of ways in which Ms. Brooks responded to the negative verbalizations. Ms. Brooks responded inconsistently. Usually she would ignore two or three instances of negative behavior and then become loud and scolding on the next.

Teacher Meeting

Ms. Edwards met with Ms. Brooks to review the findings of her observation and to design an intervention. She reported the number of negative verbalizations per hour in English as 37, 8, and 45, and the number of negative verbalizations per hour in study hall as 41.

Intervention Plan

Ms. Edwards and Ms. Brooks designed an intervention for English class. If it worked, they would use it in study hall as well. Ms. Brooks first reviewed classroom rules with all students. She then met with Matt to explain to him that she would be keeping a record of his negative verbal statements by placing a tally mark on the chalkboard each time a negative verbalization was observed. Matt was allowed up to 15 verbalizations per day (Intervention A). For any day he did not exceed 15 negative verbalizations in English class, he would be allowed to listen to his radio in study hall for 10 minutes. To keep Matt from exceeding 15 negative verbalizations and then engaging in an excess number, a second condition was instituted. If Matt had no more than 5 negative verbalizations over the limit, he would receive 20 minutes of free time on Friday of the week.

Ms. Brooks tallied negative verbalizations during English class for one week. During that time there was a steady decrease in negative verbalizations, and they averaged 9 per day (see Figure 23.5). Then, at Ms. Edwards's suggestion, the criterion was lowered to 10 negative verbalizations per day (Intervention B) and tallies were kept on a piece of graph paper at Ms. Brooks's desk. The record sheets were shared with Matt at the end of each day. After three more weeks, the frequency of negative verbalizations during English class decreased to an average of 3 per day. The intervention was then put in place in study hall (Intervention C) where, after three more weeks, negative verbalizations decreased to an average of 4 per day. (The number of instances of negative verbalizations was graphed. The graph for study hall and English class is shown in Figure 23.5.) The intervention was continued for the remainder of the school year and no formal referral for testing was made.

Marty

Marty was a 6½-year-old child who was coming to school for the first time. Although a preschool program for the handicapped and an integrated kindergarten were available within the district, Marty's parents had elected to hold him out of these programs.

Parent Interview

The school principal interviewed Marty's mother, Mrs. Webster, who brought Marty to school the first day. Marty is the only child of Mark and Danielle Webster. Mr. Webster is a loan officer at one of the local banks. Mrs. Webster works part-time in the editorial department of a small publishing company located in town.

Mrs. Webster informed the principal, Mr. Schmidt, that when Marty was

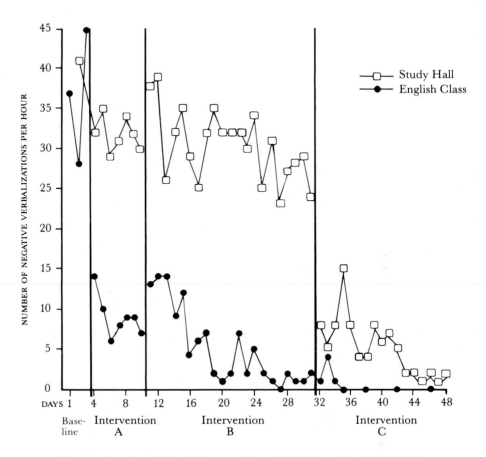

Intervention A = Tally of the negative verbalizations with a limit of 15 per day in English class only

Intervention B = Tally of the negative verbalizations with a limit of 10 per day in English class only

Intervention C = Tally of the negative verbalizations with a limit of 10 per day in both English class and study hall

FIGURE 23.5   Tally of Matt's negative verbalizations in English class and study hall

almost 2 years old, she learned that he was legally blind and had been from birth. She understood that he would require special education services, and the physician had told her that Mary would never learn to read. Mrs. Webster presented the principal with an ophthalmological report that confirmed Marty's severe myopia (he had less than 20/200 vision in his better eye with the best correction) and nystagmus. Marty's mother wanted him to enroll in school and was quite fearful that he would have to go to the state school for the blind. Mr. Schmidt assured her that the school district would do its best to provide services for Marty right in their home community and that he would get Marty into the kindergarten where three other handicapped youngsters were enrolled on a trial basis.

Teacher Interview

Two days later Mr. Schmidt checked with the kindergarten teacher, Ms. Hampton. She reported that Marty accompanied his mother to the kindergarten classroom each day. He appeared eager to come to school but was fearful that his mother would leave him. He talked freely with the other children but engaged in no gross motor activities; he expressed the fear that he would run into things. When the class lined up to go outside, Marty had trouble keeping in the line. On the playground, he was very hesitant to move away from the school building and stayed close to the school walls. When walking, Marty tended to shuffle his feet and had trouble when the surface on which he was walking changed from asphalt to grass.

Action

After observing Marty in the kindergarten for one week, Ms. Hampton prepared a referral. She noted that Marty was trying to use his vision. He did considerable head positioning—that is, tilting and turning his head to look indirectly at the chalkboard. She also noted that he pushed very close to her at story time. Ms. Hampton also mentioned that he became noticeably fatigued as the day wore on. He seemed a very agreeable child, but "a bit slow intellectually." Finally, she noted that the materials that were available in the classroom were just not suitable for Marty. Although the print size did not seem to be a major problem, all the printed materials were on glossy white paper.

SUMMARY

Assessment information is used for the purpose of making referral decisions. Under ideal circumstances, a considerable amount of assessment and diagnostic teaching will take place prior to formal referral. We have used several case studies to illustrate how school personnel collect data, consult, interview, and observe to gather information necessary in deciding whether to refer a student.

STUDY QUESTIONS

1. Why might it be better to think of referral as a request for help rather than a request for testing?
2. Why would one want to develop interventions in regular classroom settings before testing students? What would be gained by doing so?

3. Identify at least four things that could be documented specifically by observing in classrooms.
4. Several prereferral interventions were attempted with Bill. Identify one other intervention that might have been tried.

ADDITIONAL READING

Algozzine, B., Christenson, S., & Ysseldyke, J. E. (1982). Probabilities associated with the referral to placement process. *Teacher Education and Special Education, 5,* 19–23.

Christenson, S., Ysseldyke, J. E., & Algozzine, B. (1982). Institutional and external pressures influencing referral decisions. *Psychology in the Schools, 19,* 341–345.

Christenson, S., Ysseldyke, J. E., Wang, J. J., & Algozzine, B. (1983). Teachers' attributions for problems that result in referral for psychoeducational evaluation. *Journal of Educational Research, 76,* 174–180.

Ysseldyke, J. E., Christenson, S., Pianta, B., & Algozzine, B. (1983). An analysis of teachers' reasons and desired outcomes for students referred for psychoeducational evaluation. *Journal of Psychoeducational Assessment, 1,* 73–83.

CHAPTER 24

MAKING CLASSIFICATION DECISIONS

Assessment data are regularly used to make classification decisions about individuals. All of us are classified within several types of systems. Sociologists may assign us to particular social classes according to our education, occupation, and income. Individuals are classified in several ways under the legal systems of the federal and state governments: citizen or noncitizen, voter or nonvoter, felon, adjudicated delinquent, and so forth. When we are ill, our sickness may be classified by our physician: cold, sore throat, or herpes simplex. Psychiatrists may classify clients according to DSM-III *(Diagnostic and Statistical Manual of Mental Disorders)*.

One type of classification system is of particular importance—classification systems used to determine eligibility. Our society classifies individuals as eligible for various social services: social security benefits, food stamps, veterans' benefits, welfare, and so forth. Of importance for us is eligibility for special education services. One of the primary reasons for classifying students in the public schools is to ascertain their eligibility for special services.

There are several variables that can seriously affect a pupil's educational progress: chronic illness, ineffective instruction, lack of motivation, sensory or cognitive impairment, and so forth. It is very clear that society does *not* choose to help all students who fail to make adequate progress. Unmotivated students, students who receive inadequate or inappropriate instruction, and students living in a variety of disadvantageous conditions do not receive special help. Society has decided, when achievement is seriously impeded by a few select conditions, that government should come to the aid of the individuals affected. The federal and state governments extend special benefits to these individuals. For example, if Joey is mentally retarded, he may be excused from meeting certain educational requirements (for example, high school graduation requirements may be different); he may be taught by teachers who have had special coursework and practicum experiences and may have special certification; he may use special materials; he will probably be taught in smaller classes. These special services generally cost more than the educational services provided for most students in regular education. Part or all of the additional costs will be borne by state and federal government. Determining whether or not Joey is mentally retarded in essence determines whether or not part of his special education will be paid for under special provisions of federal and state law. Thus, in the schools, classification decisions usually are decisions about whether or not a child is eligible for additional help paid for by special funds earmarked for children with particular handicapping conditions.

DETERMINING ELIGIBILITY FOR SPECIAL SERVICES

Several classification systems are used in the United States today. Table 24.1 shows that, in different states, different terms are used to specify the handicapping conditions that are eligible for special education services. The most frequently used terms are those that are used for reporting under the regulations of PL 94-142.

Every definition of a handicapping condition requires that an assessment be made. [Many definitions (or parts of definitions) imply that testing be done; most state education codes *require* that testing be done.] When assessing for the purpose of classification, we gather information to clarify and to verify the relationship of a pupil's abilities and skills to the criteria for eligibility for special services used in a particular state. Sometimes school personnel do not gather the data; a physician or other professional may be required to perform the evaluation. In such cases, school personnel review the information and decide whether a pupil is eligible for services, and—if eligible—what services are to be provided. More often, school personnel themselves gather the information, decide about eligibility, and identify the particular services that will be delivered.

Classification Criteria

The process of classification begins with referral. Generally, a good referral contains some pertinent clues about the classification a student is likely to receive. All students who are classified as handicapped will probably demonstrate problem(s) in achievement unless some interventions have already been made.

Mentally retarded pupils are those who demonstrate "significantly subaverage intellectual functioning existing concurrently with deficits in adaptive behavior, and manifested during the developmental period" (Grossman, 1983). Students who are eventually labeled mentally retarded are often referred because of generalized slowness: they lag behind their agemates in most areas of

TABLE 24.1   Labels Used in the United States for Special Education

State	Blind	Deaf-blind	Early Childhood Special Education	Gifted, Talented	Hard of Hearing	Mentally Retarded	Multiple Handicapped	Orthopedically Impaired	Other Health Problems	Seriously Emotionally Disturbed	Special Learning Disabilities	Speech Impaired	Visually Impaired
Alabama	X	X	X	X	X	X	X		X	X	X	X	X
Alaska	X				X	X	X	X	X	X	X		X
Arizona	X				X	X	X		X	X	X	X	X
Arkansas	X	X			X	X		X	X	X	X	X	X
California	X				X	X	X	X	X	X	X	X	X
Colorado	X				X	X	X	X		X	X	X	X
Connecticut	X			X	X	X	X	X		X		X	X
Delaware	X				X	X		X	X	X	X	X	X
D.C., Wash.	X	X			X	X		X	X	X	X	X	X
Florida	X					X		X		X	X	X	X
Georgia	X	X	X	X	X	X	X			X	X	X	X
Hawaii	X				X	X	X			X	X	X	X
Idaho	X	X		X	X	X	X	X	X	X	X	X	X
Illinois	X				X	X	X	X	X	X	X	X	X
Indiana	X				X	X	X	X		X	X	X	X
Iowa	X				X	X		X		X	X	X	X
Kansas	X	X			X		X	X		X	X	X	X
Kentucky	X				X	X	X		X	X	X	X	X
Louisiana	X	X		X	X	X	X		X	X	X	X	X
Maine	X			X	X	X	X		X	X	X	X	X
Maryland	X			X	X	X	X		X	X	X	X	X
Massachusetts	Children in need of special services												
Michigan	X				X	X	X	X	X	X	X	X	X
Minnesota	X				X	X		X		X	X	X	X

SOURCE: From "Categories Used for Identification and Education of Exceptional Children" by J. E. Garrett and N. Brazil, 1979, *Exceptional Children,* 45, 291–292.

academic achievement, social and emotional development, language ability, and perhaps physical development. This slowness must be demonstrated on an individually administered test of intelligence that is appropriate for the student being assessed. Thus, the test must be appropriate not only for the age of the student but also for the pupil's acculturation as well as physical and sensory abilities. However, a test of intelligence is not enough. The pupil must also demonstrate slowness in adaptive behavior. An assessment for mental retarda-

TABLE 24.1 (*cont.*)

State	Blind	Deaf-blind	Early Childhood Special Education	Gifted, Talented	Hard of Hearing	Mentally Retarded	Multiple Handicapped	Orthopedically Impaired	Other Health Problems	Seriously Emotionally Disturbed	Special Learning Disabilities	Speech Impaired	Visually Impaired
Mississippi	X	X		X	X	X	X		X	X	X	X	X
Missouri	X			X	X	X	X	X	X	X	X	X	X
Montana	X				X	X		X		X	X	X	X
Nebraska	X				X	X		X	X	X	X	X	X
Nevada	X			X	X	X	X	X		X	X	X	X
New Hampshire	X				X	X		X	X	X			X
New Jersey	X				X	X	X	X	X	X			X
New Mexico	X			X	X	X	X	X		X	X	X	X
New York	X				X	X	X	X		X	X	X	X
North Carolina	X			X	X	X	X			X	X	X	X
North Dakota	X	X	X		X	X	X		X	X	X	X	X
Ohio	X	X	X	X	X	X	X	X	X	X	X	X	X
Oklahoma	X				X	X		X		X			X
Oregon	X				X	X		X		X	X	X	X
Pennsylvania	X	X		X	X	X			X	X	X	X	X
Rhode Island	X				X	X	X		X	X	X	X	X
South Carolina	X	X			X	X			X	X	X	X	X
South Dakota					Children in need of special services								
Tennessee	X	X	X	X	X	X	X	X	X	X	X	X	X
Texas	X	X	X		X	X	X		X	X	X	X	X
Utah	X	X			X	X	X		X	X	X	X	X
Vermont	X				X	X	X	X	X	X	X	X	X
Virginia	X		X		X	X	X	X		X	X	X	X
Washington	X				X	X	X	X	X	X	X	X	X
West Virginia	X	X		X	X	X		X		X	X	X	X
Wisconsin	X	X	X		X	X	X	X	X	X	X	X	X
Wyoming	X	X			X	X			X	X	X	X	X

tion should always contain an assessment of achievement, intelligence, and adaptive behavior.

Learning disabled pupils are those who demonstrate

a disorder in one or more of the basic psychological processes involved in understanding or in using language, spoken or written, which may manifest itself in the imperfect ability to listen, think, read, write, spell, or do mathematical calculations. The term [learning disabilities] includes such conditions as perceptual handicaps, brain injury, minimal brain dysfunction, dyslexia, and developmental aphasia. The term does not include children who have learning problems which are primarily the result of visual, hearing, or motor handicaps, of mental retardation, emotional disturbance, or environmental, cultural, or economic disadvantage. (USOE, 1977, p. 65083)

Students who are eventually labeled learning disabled are often referred because of inconsistent performance; they are likely to have pronounced patterns of academic and cognitive strengths and weaknesses. For example, Harry may grasp mathematics and social concepts quite well, but he may not learn to read no matter what his teacher tries; Joyce may be reading at grade level, be a good speller, have highly developed language skills, but not be able to master addition and subtraction facts. Criteria for eligibility for services for the learning disabled vary considerably from state to state. Generally, a pupil must demonstrate normal (or at least nonretarded) general intellectual development on an individually administered test of intelligence. The student must also demonstrate, on an individually administered test of achievement, some areas that are within the normal range while demonstrating significantly delayed development in other areas of achievement, and demonstrate (corrected) hearing and vision within normal limits. Eligible pupils would not have significant emotional problems or cultural disadvantage. Finally, the basic process disorder that causes the learning disability may or may not have to be tested, depending on the particular state's education code. If assessed, measures of visual and auditory perception as well as measures of linguistic and psycholinguistic abilities would be administered.

Emotionally disturbed pupils exhibit

one or more of the following characteristics over a long period of time and to a marked degree, which adversely affects educational performance: (a) an inability to learn which cannot be explained by intellectual, sensory, or health factors; (b) an inability to build or maintain satisfactory interpersonal relationships with peers and teachers; (c) inappropriate types of behavior or feelings under normal circumstances; (d) a general pervasive mood of unhappiness or depression; or (e) a tendency to develop physical symptoms or fears associated with personal or school problems. (Education of Handicapped Children, *Federal Register,* Section 121a5, 1977)

Students who are eventually labeled emotionally disturbed are often referred for problems in interpersonal relations (for example, fighting or extreme noncompliance) an/or unusual behavior (for example, unexplained episodes of crying or extreme mood swings). Requirements for establishing a pupil's eligibility for special education services for the emotionally disturbed vary markedly among the states. Some or all of the following sources of information may be used in determining eligibility: observational data, behavior rating scales, psychological evaluation, and examination by a board-certified psychiatrist or psychologist.

The standards applied to sensorily handicapped students are in some ways quite objective. *A blind person* has "visual acuity for distant vision of 20/200 or less in the better eye, with the best correction or visual acuity of more than 20/200 if the widest diameter of field of vision subtends an angle no greater than 20 degrees" (National Society for the Prevention of Blindness, 1966, p. 10). Visually impaired students have corrected visual acuity of 20/70 or less in the better eye. *A deaf person* has hearing acuity in the speech range of −90 decibels or less in the better ear while a *hard-of-hearing person* has hearing acuity of −35 decibels or less in the better ear. The standards applied to sensorily handicapped pupils can be complex and subjective, however, when one assesses sensorial functioning to decide about a particular placement and the extent to which vision or hearing may be used as a primary modality of instruction. Sensorily handicapped children often come to school already diagnosed. Sometimes they do not. Referrals for undiagnosed visually impaired students may indicate gross and fine motor problems, variable visual performance (for example, the size of print, amount of light, and fatigue all influence performance). Referrals for undiagnosed hearing-impaired students may indicate both expressive and receptive language problems, variable hearing performance, problems in attending to aural tasks, and perhaps problems in peer relationships. Assessment to establish eligibility for programs for sensorily impaired students is generally conducted by health professionals. Visual acuity and visual field are usually assessed by an ophthalmologist. Functional visual assessment is usually done by a specialist through systematic observation of a child's responses to various types of paper, print sizes, lighting conditions, and so forth. Assessment of hearing acuity is performed by an audiologist. Functional hearing assessment may be conducted by an audiologist or a teacher of the hearing impaired.

The standards applied to *students with chronic physical and health problems* are seldom specified in state education codes. Rather, federal and state regulations typically require that the condition be so severe that education in the regular program is not possible and then enumerate the conditions that are eligible for special consideration (for example, spina bifida, muscular dystrophy, heart disease, and so forth). Physically handicapped pupils are generally identified prior to entering school. However, accidents and disease may impair a previously normal student. Medical diagnosis is necessary to establish the presence of the condition. The severity of the condition may be established in part by medical opinion and in part by systematic observation of the particular student.

Establishing Appropriate Classification

A word of caution is necessary. Sometimes the condition implied by the referral is *not* the handicapping condition. Those who are responsible for classification of pupils must adopt a point of view that is, in part, disconfirmatory—a point of view that looks to disprove the working hypothesis. Assessors must collect information that would allow them to reject the classification if a pupil proves not to be handicapped or to suffer from a different handicap. For example, if Harvey were referred for possible classification as a mentally retarded student, we would try to select tests of intelligence and adaptive behavior on which he would do well in order to disconfirm the working hypothesis. As another example, if Tom were referred for inconsistent performance in expressive language even though his other skills—especially math and science—were average, we might infer that he could have a learning disability. What would it take to reject the hypothesis that he is learning disabled? If we could show that his problem was caused by a sensorineural hearing loss, he would not be learning disabled; if his problem arose because his primary language is a dialect of English, he would not be learning disabled; if he suffered from recurrent bouts of *otitis media* (middle ear infections), he would not be learning disabled. Therefore, we should generate other possible causes of his behavior and collect data that would allow us to evaluate these other explanations.

Finally, in our attempt to establish that a student should be classified as handicapped, we often must choose among competing procedures and tests. There are different tests to *operationalize* the eligibility requirements. For example, to be mentally retarded in Pennsylvania, a pupil must earn a score of less than 80 on an individually administered test of intelligence. However, as we showed in Chapter 10 individual tests of intelligence are not interchangeable. They differ significantly in the behaviors they sample, significantly in the adequacy of their norms and reliability, and slightly in their standard deviations. A dull, but normal, person may earn an IQ of less than 80 on one or two tests of intelligence but earn scores greater than 80 on others. Thus, we can be caught in a terrible dilemma of conflicting information. The routes around and through the dilemma are easier to state than to accomplish. First, we should choose (and put the most faith in) objective, technically adequate (reliable and well-normed) procedures that have demonstrated validity for the particular purpose of classification. Second, we must consider the *specific* validity. For example, we must consider the culture in which the student grew up and how that culture interacts with the content of the test. Sometimes a test's technical manuals contain information about the wisdom of using the test with individuals of various cultures; sometimes the research literature has information for the particular cultural group to which a student belongs. Often theory can guide us in the absence of research. Sometimes it is just not possible to test validly, and we must also recognize that fact. Finally, when we find ourselves in a swamp of conflicting data, we must remember *why* we gathered the data. In this example, we gathered the data to learn if a student met the eligibility requirement of an IQ equal to or less than 80. (We did not give an intelligence test to see if the student needed help; we already knew that.)

CASE STUDY EXAMPLES

The remainder of this chapter provides four examples of classification. Here, we will follow Phoebe, Bill, Luis, and Marty who were discussed in the preceding chapter on referral. Please bear in mind that these cases are intended to illustrate the *process* of assessment for classification. The cases are very simple; in the schools, many will be far more complex.

Phoebe

Background

As you will recall, Phoebe's referral indicated that this thirteen-year-old was having problems in beginning algebra and science. She lived in a small Midwestern college town. Ninety-two percent of the high school graduates not only attended college, they graduate; over the past ten years, 67 percent earned advanced degrees. The mean IQ (Otis-Lennon) of the students in her high school was 119. It was apparent that her academic problems were beginning to cause behavioral problems (truancy) and to cause her to rethink her future education plans.

From the referral data, Phoebe did not appear to have general academic problems, although the presence of behavior problems might have had implications. The initial impression was that a specific learning disability in math might be producing problems in science and conflict at home. On the other hand, if Phoebe were to be considered handicapped, her problems might be caused by a beginning emotional disturbance that was first manifesting itself in math and science.

An assessment plan was developed to verify the presence of a specific problem in math attainment and not in other academic areas. It was also decided to administer a measure of intellectual development to verify normal intelligence. These two tests would allow the disconfirmation of the label, learning disabled. It was further decided to administer a diagnostic math test and to have the school psychologist interview Phoebe about her feelings toward school and her changed behavior. Three tests were selected. Since there were no indications of sensory or physical impairment and since there seemed nothing atypical in Phoebe's acculturation, the Weschler Intelligence Scale for Children–Revised (WISC–R), Wide Range Achievement Test (WRAT), and the Test of Mathematical Abilities (TOMA) were administered. The test results are presented in Table 24.2.

Results

The test results indicated that Phoebe was of normal intelligence (FSIQ = 104). The 10-point difference between performance IQ and verbal IQ was

TABLE 24.2 Summary of Phoebe's Test Performances[a]

WISC–R standard scores ($\bar{X}=100$, $S=15$)	
FSIQ	101–107
VIQ	105–112
PIQ	94–104
WRAT standard scores ($\bar{X}=100$, $S=15$)	
Reading	122–128
Spelling	121–127
Arithmetic	93–100
TOMA ($\bar{X}=10$, $S=3$)	
Attitude Toward Math	4– 6
Vocabulary	10–12
Computation	8–10
General Information	10–12
Story Problems	9–11

[a]In 50% confidence intervals around her estimated true scores.

neither reliable nor unusual. Her scores on the WRAT indicated above-average performances in reading and spelling and average performance in arithmetic computation. The TOMA results indicated a very poor attitude toward math, but average attainment of skills and concepts. Observations during testing indicated a slow and very careful approach to the test items. Moreover, she seemed anxious and unsure: she frequently asked if an answer was correct, said that she was dumb in math, said she hated math, and generally checked her work two or three times.

Decisions

In order to classify Phoebe as learning disabled, she would have to demonstrate a significant discrepancy between achievement and ability not attributable to other handicapping conditions or to environmental deprivation. Phoebe's test performance confirmed that her math skills were not as well developed as other skills. However, they were well within the average range. Her intellectual ability appeared average. If anything, she earned higher scores in some areas of achievement than would be expected. There were no indications of severe emotional problems, although Phoebe was obviously stressed. Given the data collected, Phoebe did not meet the eligibility requirements for learning disabled students. Furthermore, nothing in her records or from current assessment indicated any other handicapping conditions that would make her eligible for special education services. Phoebe was a normal student experiencing difficulties in math and science.

Recommendations

Several options within regular education were available for Phoebe. First, her math skills were adequate, and there did not appear to be any reason for her not to continue studying algebra. However, the pace of the instruction in the middle math track (regular algebra) did appear to be too fast. Therefore, it was recommended that Phoebe transfer to the slower (transitional) algebra track where first-year algebra is taught in two years. Next, the school counselor scheduled several conferences with Phoebe's father and mother in which the counselor tried to help the parents develop more reasonable expectations and better communication skills.

Bill

Background

Bill's referral—described in Chapter 23—indicated that this third grader was still having trouble with beginning reading and was experiencing some adjustment problems. He was now the poorest reader in the lowest reading group. In the referral information, there was no mention of generalized academic or intellectual problems. The behavior problems that were noted were just beginning to develop and were, therefore, considered a secondary problem, probably stemming from the reading problems. The initial impression was that Bill might have a specific learning disability (LD) in reading.

An assessment plan was developed that would provide data that could be used to decide whether Bill was eligible for services for LD students. To rule out sensory problems, the school nurse would use the Snellen Chart and the district hearing specialist would administer a pure-tone audiometric screening test. Since Bill was black and lived in a lower-class neighborhood, a home visit was scheduled to gather information on the family's acculturation prior to selecting standardized tests. (Intelligence and achievement testing would be the minimum testing required to determine eligibility for LD placement.)

Results

The results of the sensory screening tests indicated that Bill's vision and hearing were excellent. His parents were both interviewed at their home in the evening. Both parents worked, were high school graduates, and native speakers of Standard American English. Nothing in the interview indicated that Bill's home environment could be considered culturally different. Bill's parents also indicated that he had had no recent illnesses and had an unremarkable developmental history. Both parents were very concerned about Bill's lack of reading skill.

After the parental interview and sensory screening, it was decided to test Bill with the achievement portions of the Woodcock-Johnson Psychoeducational Battery, the WISC–R, and the Developmental Test of Visual-Motor Integration (VMI). The results of these tests, in 50 percent confidence intervals, appear in Table 24.3. Bill's full scale IQ was at the lowest end of the average

TABLE 24.3   Summary of Bill's Test Performances

WISC–R standard scores (50% confidence) ($\bar{X} = 100$, $S = 15$)	
FSIQ	89– 95
VIQ	89– 96
PIQ	91–100
Woodcock-Johnson percentile ranks (68% confidence)	
Reading	1
Mathematics	19–42
Written Expression	not administered
General Knowledge	23–48
VMI	age equivalent = 10-2

range and well within the normal range. Subscale and subtest variation were also within the normal range. Bill's scores on the Woodcock-Johnson were quite varied. His math ability and general knowledge were within the low average range. However, his score on the reading cluster was at the 1st percentile. Because of his poor performance on the reading cluster, the written language cluster was not administered. An analysis of Bill's performance on the subtests of the reading cluster indicated minimal letter recognition and no skill in letter-sound correspondences. Minor errors were noted on the VMI, but his performance was high average.

Finally, Bill was interviewed by the school psychologist. Of particular interest were Bill's feelings about school and his recent behavior problems. Bill was quite insightful. He said he had just given up. "They put me with the dumb kids. I just don't know how to read." When questioned about fighting and cursing, he said, "When they call me dumb, I punch 'em; they stop calling me dumb then." Bill expressed a willingness to try to learn to read again, and he promised that he would refrain from fighting unless "really provoked."

Decisions

Bill's normal intelligence precluded classification as mentally retarded. His behavior problems were too new and not severe enough to warrant classification as emotionally disturbed. His vision, hearing, and oral language skills all seemed quite normal. There were no signs of cultural deprivation. The only handicap that Bill could have had was a learning disability. He did have average intelligence; his reading skills were very discrepant. His teachers had tried (and had documented their efforts) to teach him to read. Bill met the eligibility requirements for LD.

Recommendations

There were several options available for Bill. The overriding concern was to improve his reading. Since he was already in the lowest reading group and was

TABLE 24.4 Summary of Luis's Test Performances

Stanford-Binet Intelligence Scale–Revised	41 (47)
Goodenough-Harris Drawing Test	62
ABIC ($\bar{X} = 50$; $S = 15$)	
Family	20
Community	18
Peer Relations	23
Nonacademic School Roles	10
Earner/Consumer	15
Self Maintenance	10
Boehm[a]	3rd percentile
Bender[a] (z-score)	−1.5 to −0.7

[a]Scores are given in 50 percent confidence intervals.

not making progress, it was decided to institute an intensive (40 minutes per day, five days per week) instructional program in an LD resource room. The rest of the day would be spent in the regular classroom.

Luis

Background

As will be recalled, Luis was referred because of generally delayed performance including preacademic skills, self-help skills (including toileting), and emotional development. Recent physical examinations indicated no physical or sensory impairments that might be causing his problems. Luis's parents are bilingual (Spanish and English); both languages are spoken in the home. The initial impression was that Luis was generally retarded and might be eligible for special services as a mentally retarded student.

An assessment plan was developed to gather data to see if Luis was, indeed, eligible for special education placement. However his low functioning and bilingual background made it difficult to select appropriate standardized tests —especially tests of intelligence. Measuring his adaptive behavior would also require the recognition that his acculturation probably differed from that of most Anglo-Americans.

Results

It was decided to administer the Adaptive Behavior Inventory for Children (ABIC), the revised Stanford-Binet Intelligence Scale, the Goodenough-Harris Drawing Test, the Boehm Test of Basic Concepts, and the Bender Visual Motor Gestalt Test. Luis's scores on these tests are reported in Table 24.4 using 50 percent confidence intervals when possible.

The parental interview that formed the basis of the ABIC administration was conducted in both Spanish and English. The interviewer and mother flowed back and forth between the two languages. Luis earned scores that were significantly subaverage on all subtests. The directions for the Goodenough-Harris Drawing Test were given in English, then in Spanish. Luis's drawing of a man was 2.5 standard deviations below the mean. The Stanford-Binet was given in accordance with the standardized procedures and scored. Luis's responses were scored regardless of the language in which they were given; he earned an IQ of 41. The items that Luis missed between his basal and the last item in the ceiling were readministered in Spanish and rescored. Luis earned an IQ of 47. Luis's performance on the Bender was also poor and was interpreted as exhibiting systematic immaturity. The Boehm produced similar results when given in Spanish and in English; Luis scored at the 3rd percentile.

Finally, the psychologist observed Luis in kindergarten and also engaged in diagnostic teaching. The kindergarten enrolled other bilingual Hispanic children. Luis did not engage in activities despite prompting by the teacher and the urging of the other children. His spontaneous language consisted of one- and two-word utterances. He soiled himself just before lunch. Attempts to teach him three concepts from the Boehm were time consuming; 17 five-minute sessions were necessary.

Decisions

Although Luis differed systematically in acculturation from the children in the norm group, English and Spanish administration of the tests of intelligence provided essentially the same results. Luis's intelligence test scores were clearly within the range of moderate mental retardation. Moreover, his adaptive behavior was significantly below what one would expect of a boy his age. Nothing in the systematic observations and parental interview contradicted these findings. Thus Luis met the two key criteria for classification as a mentally retarded student: significantly subaverage intellectual functioning and failure in adaptive behavior. Other measures (Boehm and Bender) implied the same conclusions: Luis was functioning at the very bottom of his age group. There was no evidence of severe emotional disturbance or physical/sensory problems that might account for his generalized developmental delays. Luis met the eligibility requirements for special education for the mentally retarded.

Recommendations

There were few options available for Luis. He lacked the self-help and preacademic skills necessary for enrollment in a program for educable mentally retarded (EMR) students. His level of functioning indicated placement in a program for trainable mentally retarded students with provisions to monitor his progress. It was thought that he might later prove capable of work in the EMR curriculum.

Marty

Background

The classification of Marty as visually handicapped was straightforward. As will be recalled, Mrs. Webster brought an ophthalmological report indicating that Marty met the state's standards for special education for the visually impaired. Even a brief observation of Marty in the kindergarten class would validate the impression that Marty did, indeed, have a severe visual impairment.

Since the school was not equipped to provide special services if Marty were also handicapped in other ways, a thorough assessment was desired to rule out the possibility of multiple handicaps. First, as a precaution, Marty would be screened audiometrically to make sure his hearing was within the normal range. Marty's limited vision should not present a problem in assessing his hearing so no special steps would be taken. Next, he would be tested to learn if he was developing cognitively at a normal rate, a rate that would allow the school to provide services on an itinerant basis. Clearly, Marty's vision was so poor that the use of many tests was ruled out. Any test requiring Marty to look at stimulus materials or write (or draw) a response would be inappropriate. However, several options were available since, except for his limited vision, he presented no special problems (that is, inability to hear testing instructions or different acculturation). It was decided to administer the verbal scale of the Weschler Intelligence Scale for Children–Revised. Finally, the school psychologist would observe Marty in kindergarten and interview him to form an impression of his freedom from emotional problems.

Results

Marty's hearing was well within the normal range in the speech frequencies. His obtained IQ was 115; a 50 percent confidence interval around his estimated true score was from 111 to 118. Clearly, this performance is within the normal range of intelligence. The interview by the school psychologist indicated no serious emotional problems although there was a tendency for Marty to express more than usual feelings of dependency on his parents.

Decisions

From the data in the ophthalmological report and direct observation, it was clear that Marty was blind and therefore eligible for services for visually handicapped students. Furthermore, Marty did not appear handicapped in other ways and he did attempt to use his residual vision.

Recommendations

It was decided to provide itinerant services to Marty directly and to provide consultative services to his teacher, Ms. Hampton. Initially Marty would need to be provided with mobility training and instruction in the functional use of his residual vision. Because Marty did use his residual vision, it was also recommended that, at least at the start of instruction, the teacher would make use of Marty's visual as well as auditory abilities. Special, large-print materials were not likely to be needed initially since the kindergarten materials were in large print already.

SUMMARY

Assessment data are collected for the purpose of making classification decisions. Classification is an administrative act. Federal and most state special education laws contain provisions specifying that students must be classified before they can be declared eligible for services. Criteria for establishing the existence of handicapping conditions are specified in rules or guidelines and tests are used to ascertain the extent to which the criteria are met. We have followed four of the cases introduced in Chapter 23 and have shown how assessment data are used in classifying students.

STUDY QUESTIONS

1. Why is it necessary for the government to set standards for providing services to certain types of handicapped students?
2. List and explain three benefits of classification of handicapped students.
3. How would you go about selecting an assessment battery to see if a boy (age 8) should be eligible for special education classes.

ADDITIONAL READING

Cromwell, R. L., Blashfield, R. K., & Strauss, J. S. (1975). Criteria for classification systems. In N. Hobbs (Ed.), *Issues in the classification of children* (Vol. 1). San Francisco: Jossey-Bass.

McDermott, P. (1982). Actuarial assessment systems for the grouping and classification of school children. In C. Reynolds and T. Gutkin (Eds.), *Handbook of school psychology*. New York: Wiley.

Ysseldyke, J. E., Algozzine, B., & Epps, S. (1983). A logical and empirical analysis of current practice in classifying students as handicapped. *Exceptional Children, 50,* 160–166.

CHAPTER 25

MAKING INSTRUCTIONAL PLANNING DECISIONS

A major purpose of assessment is to provide for instructional planning. Unless differential treatment can be based on assessment data, assessment in the schools serves only two major purposes: research and evaluation of instruction. Pupils are treated differentially when individualized education programs are provided for them. Most people would agree that it is desirable to individualize programs for students in special and remedial education since the regular education programs have not proved beneficial to them. Assessment data can be important for such planning. Numerous books and hundreds of articles in professional and scientific journals discuss the importance of using assessment data to plan instructional programs for students. PL 94-142 requires a thorough assessment that results in an individualized education plan (IEP). However, beyond the general agreement about using information gained from assessment to plan education programs, there are sharp divisions within the education community about the way to assess. School personnel must make two different kinds of decisions in instructional planning. They must decide *what* to teach, and they must decide *how* to teach.

DECIDING WHAT TO TEACH

Decisions about what to teach include three major areas: selection of goals, selection of algorithms, and selection of objectives. Perhaps the most fundamental distinction between special and regular education is that we hold different goals for students completing the programs. We do not expect all handicapped students to achieve the same goals as nonhandicapped students: we do not expect deaf individuals to pass courses in music appreciation; we do not expect educable mentally retarded students to master calculus; we do not expect trainable mentally retarded students to pass American history; we do not expect quadraplegics to pass a swimming test. When we do hold the same goals for handicapped and nonhandicapped students, we may not expect handicapped students to achieve the goals at the same level of proficiency. Thus, we might require both normal and educable mentally retarded adolescents to take three years of high school mathematics in order to graduate. However, what is actually taught in the special education mathematics courses and in the lowest track of the regular mathematics courses may not be comparable. In social studies, we might require mentally retarded students to learn where and how to get help with paying their taxes, whereas nonhandicapped students might be asked to write an essay explaining how a constitutional amendment was necessary before an individual income tax could be levied by the federal government.

Next, we often use different algorithms (the way we teach or the way we try to achieve an instructional goal) to teach the same goal. The most obvious examples come from the education of sensorily handicapped students where a sensory loss precludes certain types of instruction. However, we often change algorithms for nonsensorily handicapped pupils. For example, we may wish educable mentally retarded and learning disabled students to compute long division problems correctly. However, we might not use the typical "goes into" paradigm. We may instruct them in the correct use of a pocket calculator rather than the usual algorithm of long division. We might even use a cumulative subtraction algorithm. Thus, although the goal might be the same, the means by which we achieve the goal may differ considerably.

Finally, specific objectives may vary although the goals and algorithms do not differ. For example, in teaching learning disabled adolescents who have problems with written language, we might have objectives that require the students to "tell" rather than to "write." We might also lower the level of mastery of the objective. For example, we may require students in a regular American history class to *analyze* the causes of the Civil War, whereas students in special education may be required to explain "in their own words" how slavery was a cause of the war—a comprehension level of mastery.

Tests can be somewhat useful in helping parents and teachers agree on appropriate goals for handicapped students. When students are very far behind their peers, parents and teachers have two fundamental choices. The first choice might be to accelerate instruction in the retarded area—give more instruction—and pay less attention to a less important area. The second choice is to reduce substantially the importance of the goal in the area in which the pupil lags (in some cases, the area can actually be eliminated). In areas where instruction will continue, tests can be used to place pupils within the sequence of instruction. By learning what objectives the student has already mastered and knowing what objectives have yet to be mastered, teachers or caregivers can select the *next* objective in the sequence of objectives.

Thus, tests are useful for making decisions about what to teach in two ways:

first, in specifying goal areas in which instruction should take place; second, in specifying appropriate short-term objectives to teach.

DECIDING HOW TO TEACH

Several tests have been developed that are intended to tell teachers how to teach—for example, the Developmental Test of Visual Perception (Frostig, Maslow, Lefever, & Whittlesey, 1964), the Illinois Test of Psycholinguistic Abilities (Kirk, McCarthy, & Kirk, 1968), the Kaufman Assessment Battery for Children (Kaufman & Kaufman, 1983), and the Purdue Perceptual-Motor Survey (Roach & Kephart, 1966). These tests, while they are based on very different theories and have varying degrees of technical adequacy, have provided more publications and sales for their authors than innovations in effective teaching strategies for students in special and remedial education.

At present, the best way to teach handicapped learners is to rely on generally effective procedures. During acquisition, teachers can do several things to make it easier for their pupils to learn the material, skill, or behavior. They can model the desired behavior. They can break the terminal goal down into its component parts and teach each of the steps and their integration. They can teach the objective in a variety of contexts with a variety of materials to facilitate generalization. They can provide varying amounts of practice, and they can choose the schedule on which practice is done (in other words, distributed versus massed practice). Several techniques that are under the direct control of the teacher can be employed to teach any learner effectively. To help pupils recall information that has been taught, teachers have several strategies available. Organizing the material that a pupil is to learn is an effective strategy to facilitate recall. Providing rehearsal strategies is another effective way to help learners recall material. Overlearning facilitates recall of information that has been learned. Distributed practice also facilitates recall. There are also a number of things teachers can do to elicit responses that have already been acquired. Various reinforcers and punishers have been shown to be effective in the control of behavior.

At present, we recommend that teachers first reply on general principles that are known and demonstrated to be effective in facilitating learning for handicapped students. However, we can seldom find validated translations of these principles into actual classroom activities and procedures. Moreover, even if we did find studies that demonstrated that a particular application of a learning principle "worked" for a research sample, we still could not be sure that it would work for the students in a specific classroom. The odds are that it will, but we cannot be sure. Consequently, we must treat our translation of these principles, known to be effective, as tentative. In a real sense, we *hypothesize* that our treatment will work, but we need to verify that it has worked. Deno and Mirkin (1977) make this point cogently:

At the present time we are unable to prescribe specific and effective changes in instruc- tion for individual pupils with certainty. Therefore, changes in instructional programs which are arranged for an individual child can be treated only as hypotheses which must be empirically tested before a decision can be made whether they are effective for that child. (p. 11)

Teaching is experimental in nature. Generally, there is no data base to guide our selection of specific tasks or materials. Decisions are made about particular strategies, methods, and materials to use in instruction, but these decisions must be tentative. The decision maker makes some good guesses about what will work and then implements an instructional program. We do not know the extent to which decisions are correct until we gather data on the extent to which the instructional programs actually work. We only know the program works *after* it has worked; we never know it will work until it has worked.

Tests do provide some very limited information about how to teach. Tests of intelligence, for example, yield information that gives a teacher some hints about teaching. Generally, the lower a pupil's intelligence, the more practice the student will require for mastery. A score of 55 on the WISC–R does *not* tell the teacher that a pupil needs 25 percent or 250 percent more practice. It does alert the teacher to the likelihood that the pupil will need more practice than the average child. Other tenuous hints can be derived, but we feel that it is better to rely on direct observation of how a student learns in order to make adjustments in the learning program. Thus, we would observe Sally's recall of information to see if we had provided enough practice rather than looking at Sally's IQ to see that she would need a lot of practice. We cannot do anything about Sally's IQ, but we can do something about the amount of practice she gets.

CASE STUDY EXAMPLES

In previous chapters we have described the process of making referral and classification decisions about individual students. We now illustrate how in- structional decisions might be made for four of the students.

Phoebe

Phoebe was a 13-year-old student referred because she was experiencing diffi- culties in mathematics. No interventions were tried prior to referral because of Phoebe's poor attendance and the general rather than specific nature of her problems. Several tests were administered in an effort to make a classification decision: the WISC–R, the WRAT, and the TOMA. Phoebe was of normal intelligence and was functioning at an average level in mathematics. It was recommended that she be enrolled in the slower (transitional) algebra track.

No tests were administered in an effort to plan instruction. Rather, specific goals of the algebra curriculum were identified, and a system was set up by which Phoebe's teacher recorded the number of assignments she completed and the percentage of math problems she solved correctly on each assignment.

The counselor met with Phoebe to develop a contingency contract using the procedures of Homme (1969) in order to cut down on truancy. Phoebe earned points by attending all her classes in any school day. These points, in turn, could be exchanged for privileges. The privileges, therefore, were contingent on attending classes. Plans called for the contract to be rewritten over time so that criteria for class attendance increased.

Bill

Bill was referred because he was having difficulty in reading and was beginning to experience behavior problems. Several interventions were tried with Bill before referring him formally for evaluation. A tutor had tried several alternative approaches to reading instruction and had found that a word-picture association approach worked best. A two-week intervention using computer-assisted instruction to teach word-picture association proved fruitless.

Bill was classified as learning disabled, and it was recommended that he receive intensive intervention (40 minutes per day, five days per week) in reading in a resource room setting. In an effort to plan an instructional program for Bill and to decide specifically *what* ought to be taught, the resource teacher used a criterion-referenced measure of skill development in reading. She used Diagnosis: An Instructional Aid in Reading to pinpoint his skill development level.

Bill performed poorly on the survey measure of Diagnosis and all probes were administered. Bill demonstrated knowledge of letter names and letter sounds as long as the letters were at the beginning of words. He had considerable difficulty recognizing the sounds of consonants in the middle of words. Based on this knowledge, the resource teacher developed the following three short-term instructional objectives. For each objective the teacher used the Prescription Guide that accompanies the test to decide what instructional materials to use with Bill. Although the Lippincott Reading Series was used in Bill's school, the teacher decided to use a different series with Bill. The Lippincott series is a linguistic-phonics series, and data from the tutor who had intervened prior to referral indicated that Bill performed better when a "look-say" approach was used. The teacher decided to use the Scott, Foresman Open Highways Program. The following objectives and materials were specified:

1. When Bill has worked through the materials prescribed he will recognize the sound of the letter p in the middle of a word. To teach this the teacher decided to use pages 60–62 of Teachers' Manual 3-2, page 11 of workbook 3-2, and page 7 of workbook 4. She used duplicating master 4 from set 4 to provide practice in recognition of the letter p in medial position.

2. When Bill has worked through the materials prescribed he will recognize the sound of the letter *m* in the middle of a word. To teach this the teacher decided to use pages 60–62 of Teachers' Manual 3-2, page 11 of workbook 3-2, and duplicating masters 12 from set 3-2 and 5 from set 4.

3. When Bill has worked through the materials he will recognize the sound of the letter *d* in the middle of a word. To teach this skill the teacher decided to use pages 60–62 of Teachers' Manual 3-2, page 6 of workbook 4, and duplicating master 5 from set 4.

You may ask how the teacher decided to use the specific materials identified in the objectives. The Prescription Guide in Diagnosis lists for each skill assessed the place in specific reading series where the skill is taught. The decision to use the Scott, Foresman series was based on knowledge about how Bill learns which was obtained through actually teaching him (the prereferral intervention by the tutor). Only by monitoring Bill's progress and frequently testing the extent to which he accomplishes objectives will the teacher know whether the instructional choices she has made are appropriate.

Luis

Luis was referred because of generally delayed performance including preacademic skills, self-help skills, and emotional development. Assessment indicated that Luis was functioning as a trainable mentally retarded child. Special education was recommended to the parents, who agreed with the recommendation.

Initially, placement in a self-contained district classroom for trainable mentally retarded pupils was selected as the most appropriate (and least restrictive) environment for the boy. Luis's parents agreed to a program stressing language development, self-help skills, and play skills. However, they did not want the schools to work on toileting with Luis; they believed that was the responsibility of the parents. They were, however, willing to follow several suggestions offered by the school district. (The district recommended, essentially, that the parents follow the techniques of Foxx and Azrin.) Luis's parents also wanted to enroll in an evening program in behavior modification run by the school district for parents of handicapped students.

The school would stress social-emotional development (appropriate play and participation in small groups) and eating skills (Luis still could not use a fork or spoon). The school would also stress language. However, there was some concern about the language that Luis would learn. If Luis were expected to lead a semi-dependent life, he would not need the skills in English that he would need if he were expected to lead an independent life. The school district, however, was hesitant to agree to bilingual instruction in a class for trainable mentally retarded students. A compromise was struck whereby a bilingual teacher's aide would be employed in Luis's class. The aide would be responsible for repeating the language enrichment exercises with Luis in Spanish.

As an aid in instructional planning, the AAMD Adaptive Behavior Scale was administered to Luis's mother. His mother checked the following behaviors:

"Feeds self with fingers, or must be fed"

"Does not drink from a glass or cup unassisted"

"Chews food with mouth open"

"Uses napkin incorrectly"

Also as an aid in instructional planning, Luis's behavior during free time (recess, unstructured playtime, and so on) was observed to ascertain the level of interaction with other children. Roberto, another Hispanic retarded child, was observed for comparison purposes. Over a three-day time span with fifteen observation periods, Luis did not initiate conversation or activities with other children; Roberto initiated seven brief interchanges and played next to other children during eleven intervals, but he did not play cooperatively with the other children in the class.

Based on these observations and test data (including the data obtained during classification), the following long-term objectives were established:

1. Luis will feed himself with a spoon at lunch with not more than one spill per minute of eating time.
2. Luis will initiate play activities with classmates.
3. Luis will initiate brief conversation with classmates.
4. Luis will increase his oral language skills in both English and Spanish.

His teacher used a backward chaining paradigm to teach eating with a spoon. Initial observation indicated that Luis liked food (it was a natural reinforcer for him) and that he could (and would) hold a spoon. The teacher used a shaping program with a changing criterion design to increase play and conversation with classmates. In addition, the teacher and the aide used the Peabody Language Development Kit with Luis.

Marty

Marty was referred for psychoeducational evaluation at the time of initial school entrance because he was legally blind. Despite his classification, primary placement in a regular class setting was recommended. Marty and his teacher were to receive the help of an itinerant teacher who specialized in working with blind and partially sighted students. Initially, Marty would be provided with mobility training and receive instruction in functional use of his residual vision.

Marty was assigned preferential seating for all classroom activities. Usually, he was seated in the first row center seat for routine activities but was allowed (and encouraged) to move closer for demonstrations. Because Marty could use residual vision, special care was taken in encouraging him to use his vision in learning. The teacher was instructed to speak as she wrote material on the board. Marty was always given the first copy of dittoed worksheets and was taught to put dittoes and other worksheets in yellow acetate folders to increase contrast and reduce glare.

Several other suggestions were made to the regular classroom teacher. She was reminded that activities requiring near vision and far vision should be alternated to reduce visual fatigue. She was reminded to take special precautions to reduce glare from the windows in the classroom. It was suggested that she reduce requirements for written drill for Marty because it would take him considerably longer than his classmates to complete such assignments.

Marty received the services of an itinerant vision specialist who worked with him on mobility training. The specialist designed a set of procedures to evaluate the extent to which a cane was necessary for mobility.

Since Marty was just beginning school, it was decided that, initially at least, all educational objectives appropriate for nonhandicapped students would be considered appropriate for Marty. Compensatory teaching methodologies would be used to help him accomplish these objectives. Objectives for Marty included development of prereading skills, alphabet learning, numeration learning, and learning social skills.

SUMMARY

Assessment data are collected and used for the purpose of planning instructional programs. When teachers plan instructional programs, they must decide what to teach and how to teach. Tests are sometimes helpful in deciding what to teach. Experimentation with different methods is generally the best way to determine how to teach—the teacher selects and uses an approach that seems most suited to the student's needs and then gathers data on the effectiveness of the strategy. Adjustments are made or other approaches are tried until the teacher determines which strategy is most effective. We have followed cases introduced in earlier chapters to show how assessment data are used to make initial instructional decisions.

ADDITIONAL READING

Alper, T. C., & White, O. R. (1971). Precision teaching: A tool for the school psychologist and teacher. *Journal of School Psychology, 9,* 445–454.

Arter, J., & Jenkins, J. (1979). Differential diagnosis—prescriptive teaching: A critical appraisal. *Review of Educational Research, 49,* 517–559.

Ysseldyke, J. E., & Algozzine, B. (1983). Where to begin in diagnosing reading problems. *Topics in Learning and Learning Disabilities, 2,* 60–69.

Ysseldyke, J. E., & Mirkin, P. K. (1981). The use of assessment information to plan instructional interventions: A review of the research. In C. Reynolds & T. Gutkin (Eds.), *A handbook for school psychology.* New York: Wiley.

EPILOGUE

There are several ways of gathering the data we need to support the educational decisions we are called upon to make. Technically adequate norm-referenced devices have certain advantages over other assessment practices when we must make screening or placement decisions. Norm-referenced devices provide objective measurement, a method of comparing the performance of a particular student to the performance of similar students and require no test-construction time of the user. They provide the teacher or diagnostic specialist with content created and evaluated by experts in an already usable format. When appropriately administered, scored, and interpreted, norm-referenced devices can serve to protect children from haphazard and capricious decision making. Historically, tests were constructed to compensate for the inadequacies of observation and decision making based on subjective feelings about a student. Norm-referenced assessment adds a perspective to the making of placement decisions, a perspective that allows educators to say that a child with an IQ of 90 in a school district where the average IQ is 120 is normal—even though that child differs from the other children in the district.

Norm-referenced tests do have a place in educational decision making, provided they are used appropriately for the purposes for which they were designed. Two major difficulties confront both regular and special education: (1) the use of technically adequate devices for purposes other than those for which they were developed, and (2) the use of technically inadequate devices for any purpose. Reynolds (1975) describes the issue well:

Although there are legitimate and important uses for norm-referenced tests and institutionally-oriented decisions, it is argued . . . that they have been vastly overemphasized at levels of relatively early education where the orientation most properly should be to individual payoff. (p. 25)

Criterion-referenced assessment, observation, and diagnostic teaching are the preferred techniques for determining appropriate educational interventions for individual students or when evaluating the extent to which they have profited from instruction. Criterion-referenced devices may be selected from commercially available systems, or they may be teacher constructed. Teacher-constructed tests are developed by constructing items that assess the extent to which specific instructional objectives have been attained. Gronlund (1968, 1976) has written several texts on teacher-constructed tests. As Hofmeister (1975) states, "Criterion-referenced testing can reach its full potential only when it is so integrated into the day-by-day functioning of the classroom that it cannot easily be separated out as a 'testing activity" (pp. 77–78).

Observation is an essential element of all classroom practices and, similarly, of all assessment practices. *Observation* is a generic term that can be applied to a range of activities from relatively informal observation of an individual to systematic counting of an individual's behaviors. Entire manuscripts have been written on observation (Boehm & Weinberg, 1977; Cartwright & Cartwright, 1974; Weinberg & Wood, 1975), and these outline the variety of systematic procedures that are used to observe students. Systematic observation is an integral component in the implementation of behavior modification in school settings. Kazdin (1973) has developed in detail the assessment strategies (frequency counting, duration counting, and interval recording) used when behavior-modification techniques are employed in school settings. Observation is both an integral part of other assessment procedures and a separate alternative to them.

Diagnostic teaching is not a new concept; it is a practice in which any effective teacher engages. Simply put, the concept refers to the practice of systematic trial and evaluation of a variety of instructional strategies (including materials, methods of presentation, and methods of feedback) with individual students as part of their everyday educational program. Other assessment procedures can be used and are used within diagnostic teaching. Teaching strategies are modified according to whether specified techniques used in particular educational settings result in success or failure for the student.

Assessment is an integral part of the educational process and is engaged in for many educational purposes. The main question in obtaining assessment information is not, How can we use tests? Rather, the fundamental question is, How can we obtain the information necessary to make certain educational decisions? The recent and significant revisions in public policy relating to the education of handicapped children are reflected in the intent and provisions of Public Law 94-142, the Education for All Handicapped Children Act of 1975. PL 94-142 mandates zero exclusion within educational settings, appropriate educational programming for all handicapped children, placement of all children in "least restrictive environments," assurance of extensive identification procedures, and maintenance of individual educational plans for all handicapped children. Assessment data are used in making important decisions to implement the law. Different decisions require different kinds of information. Many of the convictions expressed in this book now have the force of law.

We have presented detailed information about tests in an effort to facilitate their intelligent use. We have attempted to be objective and yet critical in our review of contemporary assessment practices and devices. Used appropriately, tests can and do provide extremely useful information to facilitate decision making; used inappropriately, tests are worthless. As professionals, we must be constantly aware of the fact that our first responsibility is to children and that test-based decisions directly and significantly affect them.

Assessment is a very important activity that often has lifelong consequences for the students who are assessed. Few educational practices have aroused so much controversy as assessment, and few educational activities are so carefully prescribed. Federal and state regulations prescribe what types of tests will be administered to make certain educational decisions. For example, individual tests of intelligence must be administered to determine eligibility for services for the mentally retarded. Regulations sometimes prescribe who will administer the tests. For example, certified school psychologists must administer certain types of tests within the schools. Certification, accreditation, and licensure requirements prescribe standards of training for testers. All of these prescriptions are designed to improve and guarantee high standards of assessment services.

Nonetheless, we are often overwhelmed with descriptions of abuses that occur in testing. There have been so many—in the scientific community, in policy, and in educational practice. In education, the abuses that have occurred are the result of ignorance and overzealousness. The most crucial uses—and consequently the most serious abuses—of tests are those that involve decisions about individual students: referral and screening, classification, program planning, and evaluation of individual pupil progress. Inappropriate testing for these purposes can, at best, result in wasted time and wasted money. At worst, assessment can result in inappropriate classification and labeling and inappropriate educational programming.

Several errors are worth noting. Using the wrong test is more common than we would like to admit. Tests are used in assessment to specify and to verify problems in several domains. This statement sounds so simple, and yet assessment is one of the most complicated of human endeavors. The most difficult tasks facing assessors are the selection and interpretation of appropriate assessment procedures. Testers usually have a choice among several devices that all ostensibly assess the same domain. However, the devices never work in the same way for the individual being assessed. Slight differences in norms and validity can produce variations in scores for a student. As a result, in many cases the selection of a particular test will produce one decision, where as the selection of a different test would produce the opposite decision. Some tests are so poor that they should not be used for most purposes. Tests that inadequately reflect the domain to be assessed, that have unacceptable levels of reliability, and that are inadequately normed should not be used for making educational decisions. When inadequate tests are all that are available to verify or to specify problems in some domain, assessors will necessarily have to supplement their information with data from other forms of assessment (for example, systematic observation). They will also need to be far more tentative in their conclusions and recommendations since the data upon which they are relying are much less compelling.

Sometimes perfectly acceptable tests are used with children for whom those tests are inappropriate. Slight differences in acculturation and background experience can produce variations among students on scores on a test. If a pupil differs significantly in acculturation and background experience from the students for whom the test was developed and on whom the test was standardized, the test should not be used. Significant differences in age and language also preclude the use of an otherwise acceptable test with particular students.

Finally, test performances are sometimes misinterpreted. A good norm-referenced test, properly administered, scored, and interpreted can only rank order students. That rank is a very limited piece of information. Even a good norm-referenced test cannot explain why students have performed as they have. A good criterion-referenced test, properly administered, scored, and interpreted can show the teacher only what skills and knowledge a student has acquired. It cannot explain why a student has or has not acquired those skills and concepts. Furthermore, we can only observe behavior on any test. We cannot observe mental retardation or giftedness on an intelligence test; we cannot see a deficit in auditory processing on the ITPA; we cannot see brain damage on a Bender protocol.

It is easy to forget that the intentions of the testing establishment (testers and decision makers who use test data) are benevolent. However, we must not lose sight of the fact that good intentions are not enough.

Psychological and educational assessment is serious business. We've treated it that way in this textbook. It is serious business because the decisions professionals make about students have a significant effect on their life opportunities. We invite you to join us in the quest to improve the practice of assessing students.

APPENDIXES

Appendix 1   Square Roots

n	$\sqrt{n}$	$\sqrt{10n}$	n	$\sqrt{n}$	$\sqrt{10n}$
1.00	1.00000	3.16228	1.45	1.20416	3.80789
1.01	1.00499	3.17805	1.46	1.20830	3.82099
1.02	1.00995	3.19374	1.47	1.21244	3.83406
1.03	1.01489	3.20936	1.48	1.21655	3.84708
1.04	1.01980	3.22490	1.49	1.22066	3.86005
1.05	1.02470	3.24037	1.50	1.22474	3.87298
1.06	1.02956	3.25576	1.51	1.22882	3.88587
1.07	1.03441	3.27109	1.52	1.23288	3.89872
1.08	1.03923	3.28634	1.53	1.23693	3.91152
1.09	1.04403	3.30151	1.54	1.24097	3.92428
1.10	1.04881	3.31662	1.55	1.24499	3.93700
1.11	1.05357	3.33167	1.56	1.24900	3.94968
1.12	1.05830	3.34664	1.57	1.25300	3.96232
1.13	1.06301	3.36155	1.58	1.25698	3.97492
1.14	1.06771	3.37639	1.59	1.26095	3.98748
1.15	1.07238	3.39116	1.60	1.26491	4.00000
1.16	1.07703	3.40588	1.61	1.26886	4.01248
1.17	1.08167	3.42053	1.62	1.27279	4.02492
1.18	1.08628	3.43511	1.63	1.27671	4.03733
1.19	1.09087	3.44964	1.64	1.28062	4.04969
1.20	1.09545	3.46410	1.65	1.28452	4.06202
1.21	1.10000	3.47851	1.66	1.28841	4.07431
1.22	1.10454	3.49285	1.67	1.29228	4.08656
1.23	1.10905	3.50714	1.68	1.29615	4.09878
1.24	1.11355	3.52136	1.69	1.30000	4.11096
1.25	1.11803	3.53553	1.70	1.30384	4.12311
1.26	1.12250	3.54965	1.71	1.30767	4.13521
1.27	1.12694	3.56371	1.72	1.31149	4.14729
1.28	1.13137	3.57771	1.73	1.31529	4.15933
1.29	1.13578	3.59166	1.74	1.31909	4.17133
1.30	1.14018	3.60555	1.75	1.32288	4.18330
1.31	1.14455	3.61939	1.76	1.32665	4.19524
1.32	1.14891	3.63318	1.77	1.33041	4.20714
1.33	1.15326	3.64692	1.78	1.33417	4.21900
1.34	1.15758	3.66060	1.79	1.33791	4.23084
1.35	1.16190	3.67423	1.80	1.34164	4.24264
1.36	1.16619	3.68782	1.81	1.34536	4.25441
1.37	1.17047	3.70135	1.82	1.34907	4.26615
1.38	1.17473	3.71484	1.83	1.35277	4.27785
1.39	1.17898	3.72827	1.84	1.35647	4.28952
1.40	1.18322	3.74166	1.85	1.36015	4.30116
1.41	1.18743	3.75500	1.86	1.36382	4.31277
1.42	1.19164	3.76829	1.87	1.36748	4.32435
1.43	1.19583	3.78153	1.88	1.37113	4.33590
1.44	1.20000	3.79473	1.89	1.37477	4.34741

Appendix 1 (continued)

n	$\sqrt{n}$	$\sqrt{10n}$	n	$\sqrt{n}$	$\sqrt{10n}$
1.90	1.37840	4.35890	2.35	1.53297	4.84768
1.91	1.38203	4.37035	2.36	1.53623	4.85798
1.92	1.38564	4.38178	2.37	1.53948	4.86826
1.93	1.38924	4.39318	2.38	1.54272	4.87852
1.94	1.39284	4.40454	2.39	1.54596	4.88876
1.95	1.39642	4.41588	2.40	1.54919	4.89898
1.96	1.40000	4.42719	2.41	1.55242	4.90918
1.97	1.40357	4.43847	2.42	1.55563	4.91935
1.98	1.40712	4.44972	2.43	1.55885	4.92950
1.99	1.41067	4.46094	2.44	1.56205	4.93964
2.00	1.41421	4.47214	2.45	1.56525	4.94975
2.01	1.41774	4.48330	2.46	1.56844	4.95984
2.02	1.42127	4.49444	2.47	1.57162	4.96991
2.03	1.42478	4.50555	2.48	1.57480	4.97996
2.04	1.42829	4.51664	2.49	1.57797	4.98999
2.05	1.43178	4.52769	2.50	1.58114	5.00000
2.06	1.43527	4.53872	2.51	1.58430	5.00999
2.07	1.43875	4.54973	2.52	1.58745	5.01996
2.08	1.44222	4.56070	2.53	1.59060	5.02991
2.09	1.44568	4.57165	2.54	1.59374	5.03984
2.10	1.44914	4.58258	2.55	1.59687	5.04975
2.11	1.45258	4.59347	2.56	1.60000	5.05964
2.12	1.45602	4.60435	2.57	1.60312	5.06952
2.13	1.45945	4.61519	2.58	1.60624	5.07937
2.14	1.46287	4.62601	2.59	1.60935	5.08920
2.15	1.46629	4.63681	2.60	1.61245	5.09902
2.16	1.46969	4.64758	2.61	1.61555	5.10882
2.17	1.47309	4.65833	2.62	1.61864	5.11859
2.18	1.47648	4.66905	2.63	1.62173	5.12835
2.19	1.47986	4.67974	2.64	1.62481	5.13809
2.20	1.48324	4.69042	2.65	1.62788	5.14782
2.21	1.48661	4.70106	2.66	1.63095	5.15752
2.22	1.48997	4.71169	2.67	1.63401	5.16720
2.23	1.49332	4.72229	2.68	1.63707	5.17687
2.24	1.49666	4.73286	2.69	1.64012	5.18652
2.25	1.50000	4.74342	2.70	1.64317	5.19615
2.26	1.50333	4.75395	2.71	1.64621	5.20577
2.27	1.50665	4.76445	2.72	1.64924	5.21536
2.28	1.50997	4.77493	2.73	1.65227	5.22494
2.29	1.51327	4.78539	2.74	1.65529	5.23450
2.30	1.51658	4.79583	2.75	1.65831	5.24404
2.31	1.51987	4.80625	2.76	1.66132	5.25357
2.32	1.52315	4.81664	2.77	1.66433	5.26308
2.33	1.52643	4.82701	2.78	1.66733	5.27257
2.34	1.52971	4.83735	2.79	1.67033	5.28205

Appendix 1 (continued)

n	$\sqrt{n}$	$\sqrt{10n}$	n	$\sqrt{n}$	$\sqrt{10n}$
2.80	1.67332	5.29150	3.25	1.80278	5.70088
2.81	1.67631	5.30094	3.26	1.80555	5.70964
2.82	1.67929	5.31037	3.27	1.80831	5.71839
2.83	1.68226	5.31977	3.28	1.81108	5.72713
2.84	1.68523	5.32917	3.29	1.81384	5.73585
2.85	1.68819	5.33854	3.30	1.81659	5.74456
2.86	1.69115	5.34790	3.31	1.81934	5.75326
2.87	1.69411	5.35724	3.32	1.82209	5.76194
2.88	1.69706	5.36656	3.33	1.82483	5.77062
2.89	1.70000	5.37587	3.34	1.82757	5.77927
2.90	1.70294	5.38516	3.35	1.83030	5.78792
2.91	1.70587	5.39444	3.36	1.83303	5.79655
2.92	1.70880	5.40370	3.37	1.83576	5.80517
2.93	1.71172	5.41295	3.38	1.83848	5.81378
2.94	1.71464	5.42218	3.39	1.84120	5.82237
2.95	1.71756	5.43139	3.40	1.84391	5.83095
2.96	1.72047	5.44059	3.41	1.84662	5.83952
2.97	1.72337	5.44977	3.42	1.84932	5.84808
2.98	1.72627	5.45894	3.43	1.85203	5.85662
2.99	1.72916	5.46809	3.44	1.85472	5.86515
3.00	1.73205	5.47723	3.45	1.85742	5.87367
3.01	1.73494	5.48635	3.46	1.86011	5.88218
3.02	1.73781	5.49545	3.47	1.86279	5.89067
3.03	1.74069	5.50454	3.48	1.86548	5.89915
3.04	1.74356	5.51362	3.49	1.86815	5.90762
3.05	1.74642	5.52268	3.50	1.87083	5.91608
3.06	1.74929	5.53173	3.51	1.87350	5.92453
3.07	1.75214	5.54076	3.52	1.87617	5.93296
3.08	1.75499	5.54977	3.53	1.87883	5.94138
3.09	1.75784	5.55878	3.54	1.88149	5.94979
3.10	1.76068	5.56776	3.55	1.88414	5.95819
3.11	1.76352	5.57674	3.56	1.88680	5.96657
3.12	1.76635	5.58570	3.57	1.88944	5.97495
3.13	1.76918	5.59464	3.58	1.89209	5.98331
3.14	1.77200	5.60357	3.59	1.89473	5.99166
3.15	1.77482	5.61249	3.60	1.89737	6.00000
3.16	1.77764	5.62139	3.61	1.90000	6.00833
3.17	1.78045	5.63028	3.62	1.90263	6.01664
3.18	1.78326	5.63915	3.63	1.90526	6.02495
3.19	1.78606	5.64801	3.64	1.90788	6.03324
3.20	1.78885	5.65685	3.65	1.91050	6.04152
3.21	1.79165	5.66569	3.66	1.91311	6.04979
3.22	1.79444	5.67450	3.67	1.91572	6.05805
3.23	1.79722	5.68331	3.68	1.91833	6.06630
3.24	1.80000	5.69210	3.69	1.92094	6.07454

Appendix 1 *(continued)*

n	$\sqrt{n}$	$\sqrt{10n}$	n	$\sqrt{n}$	$\sqrt{10n}$
3.70	1.92354	6.08276	4.15	2.03715	6.44205
3.71	1.92614	6.09098	4.16	2.03961	6.44981
3.72	1.92873	6.09918	4.17	2.04206	6.45755
3.73	1.93132	6.10737	4.18	2.04450	6.46529
3.74	1.93391	6.11555	4.19	2.04695	6.47302
3.75	1.93649	6.12372	4.20	2.04939	6.48074
3.76	1.93907	6.13188	4.21	2.05183	6.48845
3.77	1.94165	6.14003	4.22	2.05426	6.49615
3.78	1.94422	6.14817	4.23	2.05670	6.50384
3.79	1.94679	6.15630	4.24	2.05913	6.51153
3.80	1.94936	6.16441	4.25	2.06155	6.51920
3.81	1.95192	6.17252	4.26	2.06398	6.52687
3.82	1.95448	6.18061	4.27	2.06640	6.53452
3.83	1.95704	6.18870	4.28	2.06882	6.54217
3.84	1.95959	6.19677	4.29	2.07123	6.54981
3.85	1.96214	6.20484	4.30	2.07364	6.55744
3.86	1.96469	6.21289	4.31	2.07605	6.56506
3.87	1.96723	6.22093	4.32	2.07846	6.57267
3.88	1.96977	6.22896	4.33	2.08087	6.58027
3.89	1.97231	6.23699	4.34	2.08327	6.58787
3.90	1.97484	6.24500	4.35	2.08567	6.59545
3.91	1.97737	6.25300	4.36	2.08806	6.60303
3.92	1.97990	6.26099	4.37	2.09045	6.61060
3.93	1.98242	6.26897	4.38	2.09284	6.61816
3.94	1.98494	6.27694	4.39	2.09523	6.62571
3.95	1.98746	6.28490	4.40	2.09762	6.63325
3.96	1.98997	6.29285	4.41	2.10000	6.64078
3.97	1.99249	6.30079	4.42	2.10238	6.64831
3.98	1.99499	6.30872	4.43	2.10476	6.65582
3.99	1.99750	6.31664	4.44	2.10713	6.66333
4.00	2.00000	6.32456	4.45	2.10950	6.67083
4.01	2.00250	6.33246	4.46	2.11187	6.67832
4.02	2.00499	6.34035	4.47	2.11424	6.68581
4.03	2.00749	6.34823	4.48	2.11660	6.69328
4.04	2.00998	6.35610	4.49	2.11896	6.70075
4.05	2.01246	6.36396	4.50	2.12132	6.70820
4.06	2.01494	6.37181	4.51	2.12368	6.71565
4.07	2.01742	6.37966	4.52	2.12603	6.72309
4.08	2.01990	6.38749	4.53	2.12838	6.73053
4.09	2.02237	6.39531	4.54	2.13073	6.73795
4.10	2.02485	6.40312	4.55	2.13307	6.74537
4.11	2.02731	6.41093	4.56	2.13542	6.75278
4.12	2.02978	6.41872	4.57	2.13776	6.76018
4.13	2.03224	6.42651	4.58	2.14009	6.76757
4.14	2.03470	6.43428	4.59	2.14243	6.77495

Appendix 1 (continued)

n	$\sqrt{n}$	$\sqrt{10n}$	n	$\sqrt{n}$	$\sqrt{10n}$
4.60	2.14476	6.78233	5.05	2.24722	7.10634
4.61	2.14709	6.78970	5.06	2.24944	7.11337
4.62	2.14942	6.79706	5.07	2.25167	7.12039
4.63	2.15174	6.80441	5.08	2.25389	7.12741
4.64	2.15407	6.81175	5.09	2.25610	7.13442
4.65	2.15639	6.81909	5.10	2.25832	7.14143
4.66	2.15870	6.82642	5.11	2.26053	7.14843
4.67	2.16102	6.83374	5.12	2.26274	7.15542
4.68	2.16333	6.84105	5.13	2.26495	7.16240
4.69	2.16564	6.84836	5.14	2.26716	7.16938
4.70	2.16795	6.85565	5.15	2.26936	7.17635
4.71	2.17025	6.86294	5.16	2.27156	7.18331
4.72	2.17256	6.87023	5.17	2.27376	7.19027
4.73	2.17486	6.87750	5.18	2.27596	7.19722
4.74	2.17715	6.88477	5.19	2.27816	7.20417
4.75	2.17945	6.89202	5.20	2.28035	7.21110
4.76	2.18174	6.89928	5.21	2.28254	7.21803
4.77	2.18403	6.90652	5.22	2.28473	7.22496
4.78	2.18632	6.91375	5.23	2.28692	7.23187
4.79	2.18861	6.92098	5.24	2.28910	7.23878
4.80	2.19089	6.92820	5.25	2.29129	7.24569
4.81	2.19317	6.93542	5.26	2.29347	7.25259
4.82	2.19545	6.94262	5.27	2.29565	7.25948
4.83	2.19773	6.94982	5.28	2.29783	7.26636
4.84	2.20000	6.95701	5.29	2.30000	7.27324
4.85	2.20227	6.96419	5.30	2.30217	7.28011
4.86	2.20454	6.97137	5.31	2.30434	7.28697
4.87	2.20681	6.97854	5.32	2.30651	7.29383
4.88	2.20907	6.98570	5.33	2.30868	7.30068
4.89	2.21133	6.99285	5.34	2.31084	7.30753
4.90	2.21359	7.00000	5.35	2.31301	7.31437
4.91	2.21585	7.00714	5.36	2.31517	7.32120
4.92	2.21811	7.01427	5.37	2.31733	7.32803
4.93	2.22036	7.02140	5.38	2.31948	7.33485
4.94	2.22261	7.02851	5.39	2.32164	7.34166
4.95	2.22486	7.03562	5.40	2.32379	7.34847
4.96	2.22711	7.04273	5.41	2.32594	7.35527
4.97	2.22935	7.04982	5.42	2.32809	7.36206
4.98	2.23159	7.05691	5.43	2.33024	7.36885
4.99	2.23383	7.06399	5.44	2.33238	7.37564
5.00	2.23607	7.07107	5.45	2.33452	7.38241
5.01	2.23830	7.07814	5.46	2.33666	7.38918
5.02	2.24054	7.08520	5.47	2.33880	7.39594
5.03	2.24277	7.09225	5.48	2.34094	7.40270
5.04	2.24499	7.09930	5.49	2.34307	7.40945

Appendix 1 (continued)

n	$\sqrt{n}$	$\sqrt{10n}$	n	$\sqrt{n}$	$\sqrt{10n}$
5.50	2.34521	7.41620	5.95	2.43926	7.71362
5.51	2.34734	7.42294	5.96	2.44131	7.72010
5.52	2.34947	7.42967	5.97	2.44336	7.72658
5.53	2.35160	7.43640	5.98	2.44540	7.73305
5.54	2.35372	7.44312	5.99	2.44745	7.73951
5.55	2.35584	7.44983	6.00	2.44949	7.74597
5.56	2.35797	7.45654	6.01	2.45153	7.75242
5.57	2.36008	7.46324	6.02	2.45357	7.75887
5.58	2.36220	7.46994	6.03	2.45561	7.76531
5.59	2.36432	7.47663	6.04	2.45764	7.77174
5.60	2.36643	7.48331	6.05	2.45967	7.77817
5.61	2.36854	7.48999	6.06	2.46171	7.78460
5.62	2.37065	7.49667	6.07	2.46374	7.79102
5.63	2.37276	7.50333	6.08	2.46577	7.79744
5.64	2.37487	7.50999	6.09	2.46779	7.80385
5.65	2.37697	7.51665	6.10	2.46982	7.81025
5.66	2.37908	7.52330	6.11	2.47184	7.81665
5.67	2.38118	7.52994	6.12	2.47386	7.82304
5.68	2.38328	7.53658	6.13	2.47588	7.82943
5.69	2.38537	7.54321	6.14	2.47790	7.83582
5.70	2.38747	7.54983	6.15	2.47992	7.84219
5.71	2.38956	7.55645	6.16	2.48193	7.84857
5.72	2.39165	7.56307	6.17	2.48395	7.85493
5.73	2.39374	7.56968	6.18	2.48596	7.86130
5.74	2.39583	7.57628	6.19	2.48797	7.86766
5.75	2.39792	7.58288	6.20	2.48998	7.87401
5.76	2.40000	7.58947	6.21	2.49199	7.88036
5.77	2.40208	7.59605	6.22	2.49399	7.88670
5.78	2.40416	7.60263	6.23	2.49600	7.89303
5.79	2.40624	7.60920	6.24	2.49800	7.89937
5.80	2.40832	7.61577	6.25	2.50000	7.90569
5.81	2.41039	7.62234	6.26	2.50200	7.91202
5.82	2.41247	7.62889	6.27	2.50400	7.91833
5.83	2.41454	7.63544	6.28	2.50599	7.92465
5.84	2.41661	7.64199	6.29	2.50799	7.93095
5.85	2.41868	7.64853	6.30	2.50998	7.93725
5.86	2.42074	7.65506	6.31	2.51197	7.94355
5.87	2.42281	7.66159	6.32	2.51396	7.94984
5.88	2.42487	7.66812	6.33	2.51595	7.95613
5.89	2.42693	7.67463	6.34	2.51794	7.96241
5.90	2.42899	7.68115	6.35	2.51992	7.96869
5.91	2.43105	7.68765	6.36	2.52190	7.97496
5.92	2.43311	7.69415	6.37	2.52389	7.98123
5.93	2.43516	7.70065	6.38	2.52587	7.98749
5.94	2.43721	7.70714	6.39	2.52784	7.99375

Appendix 1 (continued)

n	$\sqrt{n}$	$\sqrt{10n}$	n	$\sqrt{n}$	$\sqrt{10n}$
6.40	2.52982	8.00000	6.80	2.60768	8.24621
6.41	2.53180	8.00625	6.81	2.60960	8.25227
6.42	2.53377	8.01249	6.82	2.61151	8.25833
6.43	2.53574	8.01873	6.83	2.61343	8.26438
6.44	2.53772	8.02496	6.84	2.61534	8.27043
6.45	2.53969	8.03119	6.85	2.61725	8.27647
6.46	2.54165	8.03741	6.86	2.61916	8.28251
6.47	2.54362	8.04363	6.87	2.62107	8.28855
6.48	2.54558	8.04984	6.88	2.62298	8.29458
6.49	2.54755	8.05605	6.89	2.62488	8.30060
6.50	2.54951	8.06226	6.90	2.62679	8.30662
6.51	2.55147	8.06846	6.91	2.62869	8.31264
6.52	2.55343	8.07465	6.92	2.63059	8.31865
6.53	2.55539	8.08084	6.93	2.63249	8.32466
6.54	2.55734	8.08703	6.94	2.63439	8.33067
6.55	2.55930	8.09321	6.95	2.63629	8.33667
6.56	2.56125	8.09938	6.96	2.63818	8.34266
6.57	2.56320	8.10555	6.97	2.64008	8.34865
6.58	2.56515	8.11172	6.98	2.64197	8.35464
6.59	2.56710	8.11788	6.99	2.64386	8.36062
6.60	2.56905	8.12404	7.00	2.64575	8.36660
6.61	2.57099	8.13019	7.01	2.64764	8.37257
6.62	2.57294	8.13634	7.02	2.64953	8.37854
6.63	2.57488	8.14248	7.03	2.65141	8.38451
6.64	2.57682	8.14862	7.04	2.65330	8.39047
6.65	2.57876	8.15475	7.05	2.65518	8.39643
6.66	2.58070	8.16088	7.06	2.65707	8.40238
6.67	2.58263	8.16701	7.07	2.65895	8.40833
6.68	2.58457	8.17313	7.08	2.66083	8.41427
6.69	2.58650	8.17924	7.09	2.66271	8.42021
6.70	2.58844	8.18535	7.10	2.66458	8.42615
6.71	2.59037	8.19146	7.11	2.66646	8.43208
6.72	2.59230	8.19756	7.12	2.66833	8.43801
6.73	2.59422	8.20366	7.13	2.67021	8.44393
6.74	2.59615	8.20975	7.14	2.67208	8.44985
6.75	2.59808	8.21584	7.15	2.67395	8.45577
6.76	2.60000	8.22192	7.16	2.67582	8.46168
6.77	2.60192	8.22800	7.17	2.67769	8.46759
6.78	2.60384	8.23408	7.18	2.67955	8.47349
6.79	2.60576	8.24015	7.19	2.68142	8.47939

Appendix 1 (continued)

n	$\sqrt{n}$	$\sqrt{10n}$	n	$\sqrt{n}$	$\sqrt{10n}$
7.20	2.68328	8.48528	7.60	2.75681	8.71780
7.21	2.68514	8.49117	7.61	2.75862	8.72353
7.22	2.68701	8.49806	7.62	2.76043	8.72926
7.23	2.68887	8.50294	7.63	2.76225	8.73499
7.24	2.69072	8.50882	7.64	2.76405	8.74071
7.25	2.69258	8.51469	7.65	2.76586	8.74643
7.26	2.69444	8.52056	7.66	2.76767	8.75214
7.27	2.69629	8.52643	7.67	2.76948	8.75785
7.28	2.69815	8.53229	7.68	2.77128	8.76356
7.29	2.70000	8.53815	7.69	2.77308	8.76926
7.30	2.70185	8.54400	7.70	2.77489	8.77496
7.31	2.70370	8.54985	7.71	2.77669	8.78066
7.32	2.70555	8.55570	7.72	2.77849	8.78635
7.33	2.70740	8.56154	7.73	2.78029	8.79204
7.34	2.70924	8.56738	7.74	2.78209	8.79773
7.35	2.71109	8.57321	7.75	2.78388	8.80341
7.36	2.71293	8.57904	7.76	2.78568	8.80909
7.37	2.71477	8.58487	7.77	2.78747	8.81476
7.38	2.71662	8.59069	7.78	2.78927	8.82043
7.39	2.71846	8.59651	7.79	2.79106	8.82610
7.40	2.72029	8.60233	7.80	2.79285	8.83176
7.41	2.72213	8.60814	7.81	2.79464	8.83742
7.42	2.72397	8.61394	7.82	2.79643	8.84308
7.43	2.72580	8.61974	7.83	2.79821	8.84873
7.44	2.72764	8.62554	7.84	2.80000	8.85438
7.45	2.72947	8.63134	7.85	2.80179	8.86002
7.46	2.73130	8.63713	7.86	2.80357	8.86566
7.47	2.73313	8.64292	7.87	2.80535	8.87130
7.48	2.73496	8.64870	7.88	2.80713	8.87694
7.49	2.73679	8.65448	7.89	2.80891	8.88257
7.50	2.73861	8.66025	7.90	2.81069	8.88819
7.51	2.74044	8.66603	7.91	2.81247	8.89382
7.52	2.74226	8.67179	7.92	2.81425	8.89944
7.53	2.74408	8.67756	7.93	2.81603	8.90505
7.54	2.74591	8.68332	7.94	2.81780	8.91067
7.55	2.74773	8.68907	7.95	2.81957	8.91628
7.56	2.74955	8.69483	7.96	2.82135	8.92188
7.57	2.75136	8.70057	7.97	2.82312	8.92749
7.58	2.75318	8.70632	7.98	2.82489	8.93308
7.59	2.75500	8.71206	7.99	2.82666	8.93868

Appendix 1 *(continued)*

n	$\sqrt{n}$	$\sqrt{10n}$	n	$\sqrt{n}$	$\sqrt{10n}$
8.00	2.82843	8.94427	8.40	2.89828	9.16515
8.01	2.83019	8.94986	8.41	2.90000	9.17061
8.02	2.83196	8.95545	8.42	2.90172	9.17606
8.03	2.83373	8.96103	8.42	2.90345	9.18150
8.04	2.83549	8.96660	8.44	2.90517	9.18695
8.05	2.83725	8.97218	8.45	2.90689	9.19239
8.06	2.83901	8.97775	8.46	2.90861	9.19783
8.07	2.84077	8.98332	8.47	2.91033	9.20326
8.08	2.84253	8.98888	8.48	2.91204	9.20869
8.09	2.84429	8.99444	8.49	2.91376	9.21412
8.10	2.84605	9.00000	8.50	2.91548	9.21954
8.11	2.84781	9.00555	8.51	2.91719	9.22497
8.12	2.84956	9.01110	8.52	2.91890	9.23038
8.13	2.85132	9.01665	8.53	2.92062	9.23580
8.14	2.85307	9.02219	8.54	2.92233	9.24121
8.15	2.85482	9.02774	8.55	2.92404	9.24662
8.16	2.85657	9.03327	8.56	2.92575	9.25203
8.17	2.85832	9.03881	8.57	2.92746	9.25743
8.18	2.86007	9.04434	8.58	2.92916	9.26283
8.19	2.86182	9.04986	8.59	2.93087	9.26823
8.20	2.86356	9.05539	8.60	2.93258	9.27362
8.21	2.86531	9.06091	8.61	2.93428	9.27901
8.22	2.86705	9.06642	8.62	2.93598	9.28440
8.23	2.86880	9.07193	8.63	2.93769	9.28978
8.24	2.87054	9.07744	8.64	2.93939	9.29516
8.25	2.87228	9.08295	8.65	2.94109	9.30054
8.26	2.87402	9.08845	8.66	2.94279	9.30591
8.27	2.87576	9.09395	8.67	2.94449	9.31128
8.28	2.87750	9.09945	8.68	2.94618	9.31665
8.29	2.87924	9.10494	8.69	2.94788	9.32202
8.30	2.88097	9.11043	8.70	2.94958	9.32738
8.31	2.88271	9.11592	8.71	2.95127	9.33274
8.32	2.88444	9.12140	8.72	2.95296	9.33809
8.33	2.88617	9.12688	8.73	2.95466	9.34345
8.34	2.88791	9.13236	8.74	2.95635	9.34880
8.35	2.88964	9.13783	8.75	2.95804	9.35414
8.36	2.89137	9.14330	8.76	2.95973	9.35949
8.37	2.89310	9.14877	8.77	2.96142	9.36483
8.38	2.89482	9.15423	8.78	2.96311	9.37017
8.39	2.89655	9.15969	8.79	2.96479	9.37550

Appendix 1 (continued)

n	$\sqrt{n}$	$\sqrt{10n}$	n	$\sqrt{n}$	$\sqrt{10n}$
8.80	2.96648	9.38083	9.20	3.03315	9.59166
8.81	2.96816	9.38616	9.21	3.03480	9.59687
8.82	2.96985	9.39149	9.22	3.03645	9.60208
8.83	2.97153	9.39681	9.23	3.03809	9.60729
8.84	2.97321	9.40213	9.24	3.03974	9.61249
8.85	2.97489	9.40744	9.25	3.04138	9.61769
8.86	2.97658	9.41276	9.26	3.04302	9.62289
8.87	2.97825	9.41807	9.27	3.04467	9.62808
8.88	2.97993	9.42338	9.28	3.04631	9.63328
8.89	2.98161	9.42868	9.29	3.04795	9.63846
8.90	2.98329	9.43398	9.30	3.04959	9.64365
8.91	2.98496	9.43928	9.31	3.05123	9.64883
8.92	2.98664	9.44458	9.32	3.05287	9.65401
8.93	2.98831	9.44987	9.33	3.05450	9.65919
8.94	2.98998	9.45516	9.34	3.05614	9.66437
8.95	2.99166	9.46044	9.35	3.05778	9.66954
8.96	2.99333	9.46573	9.36	3.05941	9.67471
8.97	2.99500	9.47101	9.37	3.06105	9.67988
8.98	2.99666	9.47629	9.38	3.06268	9.68504
8.99	2.99833	9.48156	9.39	3.06431	9.69020
9.00	3.00000	9.48683	9.40	3.06594	9.69536
9.01	3.00167	9.49210	9.41	3.06757	9.70052
9.02	3.00333	9.49737	9.42	3.06920	9.70567
9.03	3.00500	9.50263	9.43	3.07083	9.71082
9.04	3.00666	9.50789	9.44	3.07246	9.71597
9.05	3.00832	9.51315	9.45	3.07409	9.72111
9.06	3.00998	9.51840	9.46	3.07571	9.72625
9.07	3.01164	9.52365	9.47	3.07734	9.73139
9.08	3.01330	9.52890	9.48	3.07896	9.73653
9.09	3.01496	9.53415	9.49	3.08058	9.74166
9.10	3.01662	9.53939	9.50	3.08221	9.74679
9.11	3.01828	9.54463	9.51	3.08383	9.75192
9.12	3.01993	9.54987	9.52	3.08545	9.75705
9.13	3.02159	9.55510	9.53	3.08707	9.76217
9.14	3.02324	9.56033	9.54	3.08869	9.76729
9.15	3.02490	9.56556	9.55	3.09031	9.77241
9.16	3.02655	9.57079	9.56	3.09192	9.77753
9.17	3.02820	9.57601	9.57	3.09354	9.78264
9.18	3.02985	9.58123	9.58	3.09516	9.78775
9.19	3.03150	9.58645	9.59	3.09677	9.79285

Appendix 1 (continued)

n	$\sqrt{n}$	$\sqrt{10n}$	n	$\sqrt{n}$	$\sqrt{10n}$
9.60	3.09839	9.79796	9.80	3.13050	9.89949
9.61	3.10000	9.80306	9.81	3.13209	9.90454
9.62	3.10161	9.80816	9.82	3.13369	9.90959
9.63	3.10322	9.81326	9.83	3.13528	9.91464
9.64	3.10483	9.81835	9.84	3.13688	9.91968
9.65	3.10644	9.82344	9.85	3.13847	9.92472
9.66	3.10805	9.82853	9.86	3.14006	9.92975
9.67	3.10966	9.83362	9.87	3.14166	9.93479
9.68	3.11127	9.83870	9.88	3.14325	9.93982
9.69	3.11288	9.84378	9.89	3.14484	9.94485
9.70	3.11448	9.84886	9.90	3.14643	9.94987
9.71	3.11609	9.85393	9.91	3.14802	9.95490
9.72	3.11769	9.85901	9.92	3.14960	9.95992
9.73	3.11929	9.86408	9.93	3.15119	9.96494
9.74	3.12090	9.86914	9.94	3.15278	9.96995
9.75	3.12250	9.87421	9.95	3.15436	9.97497
9.76	3.12410	9.87927	9.96	3.15595	9.97998
9.77	3.12570	9.88433	9.97	3.15753	9.98499
9.78	3.12730	9.88939	9.98	3.15911	9.98999
9.79	3.12890	9.89444	9.99	3.16070	9.99500
			10.00	3.16228	10.000

SOURCE: Presentation of data used in the present volume is from *Statistics: An Intuitive Approach,* Third Edition, by G. H. Weinberg and J. A. Schumaker. Copyright © 1962, 1969, 1974 by Wadsworth Publishing Company, Inc. Reprinted by permission of the publisher, Brooks/Cole Publishing Company, Monterey, California.

Appendix 2 *Areas of the Normal Curve*

Area equals the proportion of cases between the z-score and the mean; extreme area equals .5000 less the proportion of cases between the z-score and the mean.

z	.00	.01	.02	.03	.04	.05	.06	.07	.08	.09
0.0	.0000	.0040	.0080	.0120	.0160	.0199	.0239	.0279	.0319	.0359
0.1	.0398	.0438	.0478	.0517	.0557	.0596	.0636	.0675	.0714	.0753
0.2	.0793	.0832	.0871	.0910	.0948	.0987	.1026	.1064	.1103	.1141
0.3	.1179	.1217	.1255	.1293	.1331	.1368	.1406	.1443	.1480	.1517
0.4	.1554	.1591	.1628	.1664	.1700	.1736	.1772	.1808	.1844	.1879
0.5	.1915	.1950	.1985	.2019	.2054	.2088	.2123	.2157	.2190	.2224
0.6	.2257	.2291	.2324	.2357	.2389	.2422	.2454	.2486	.2517	.2549
0.7	.2580	.2611	.2642	.2673	.2704	.2734	.2764	.2794	.2823	.2852
0.8	.2881	.2910	.2939	.2967	.2995	.3023	.3051	.3078	.3106	.3133
0.9	.3159	.3186	.3212	.3238	.3264	.3289	.3315	.3340	.3365	.3389
1.0	.3413	.3438	.3461	.3485	.3508	.3531	.3554	.3577	.3599	.3621
1.1	.3643	.3665	.3686	.3708	.3729	.3749	.3770	.3790	.3810	.3830
1.2	.3849	.3869	.3888	.3907	.3925	.3944	.3962	.3980	.3997	.4015
1.3	.4032	.4049	.4066	.4082	.4099	.4115	.4131	.4147	.4162	.4177
1.4	.4192	.4207	.4222	.4236	.4251	.4265	.4279	.4292	.4306	.4319
1.5	.4332	.4345	.4357	.4370	.4382	.4394	.4406	.4418	.4429	.4441
1.6	.4452	.4463	.4474	.4484	.4495	.4505	.4515	.4525	.4535	.4545
1.7	.4554	.4564	.4573	.4582	.4591	.4599	.4608	.4616	.4625	.4633
1.8	.4641	.4649	.4656	.4664	.4671	.4678	.4686	.4693	.4699	.4706
1.9	.4713	.4719	.4726	.4732	.4738	.4744	.4750	.4756	.4761	.4767
2.0	.4772	.4778	.4783	.4788	.4793	.4798	.4803	.4808	.4812	.4817
2.1	.4821	.4826	.4830	.4834	.4838	.4842	.4846	.4850	.4854	.4857
2.2	.4861	.4864	.4868	.4871	.4875	.4878	.4881	.4884	.4887	.4890
2.3	.4893	.4896	.4898	.4901	.4904	.4906	.4909	.4911	.4913	.4916
2.4	.4918	.4920	.4922	.4925	.4927	.4929	.4931	.4932	.4934	.4936
2.5	.4938	.4940	.4941	.4943	.4945	.4946	.4948	.4949	.4951	.4952
2.6	.4953	.4955	.4956	.4957	.4959	.4960	.4961	.4962	.4963	.4964
2.7	.4965	.4966	.4967	.4968	.4969	.4970	.4971	.4972	.4973	.4974
2.8	.4974	.4975	.4976	.4977	.4977	.4978	.4979	.4979	.4980	.4981
2.9	.4981	.4982	.4982	.4983	.4984	.4984	.4985	.4985	.4986	.4986
3.0	.4987	.4987	.4987	.4988	.4988	.4989	.4989	.4989	.4990	.4990

SOURCE: Presentation of data used in the present volume is from *Statistics: An Intuitive Approach,* Third Edition, by G. H. Weinberg and J. A. Schumaker. Copyright © 1962, 1969, 1974 by Wadsworth Publishing Company, Inc. Reprinted by permission of the publisher, Brooks/Cole Publishing Company, Monterey, California.

Appendix 3 Percentile Ranks for z-Scores of Normal Curves

z	Area[a]	z	Area[a]	z	Area[a]
−4.0	.000	−1.0	.159	2.0	.977
−3.9	.000	−0.9	.184	2.1	.982
−3.8	.000	−0.8	.212	2.2	.986
−3.7	.000	−0.7	.242	2.3	.989
−3.6	.000	−0.6	.274	2.4	.992
−3.5	.000	−0.5	.308	2.5	.994
−3.4	.000	−0.4	.345	2.6	.995
−3.3	.001	−0.3	.382	2.7	.996
−3.2	.001	−0.2	.421	2.8	.997
−3.1	.001	−0.1	.460	2.9	.998
−3.0	.001	0.0	.500	3.0	.999
−2.9	.002	0.1	.540	3.1	.999
−2.8	.003	0.2	.579	3.2	.999
−2.7	.004	0.3	.618	3.3	.999
−2.6	.005	0.4	.655	3.4	1.000
−2.5	.006	0.5	.692	3.5	1.000
−2.4	.008	0.6	.726	3.6	1.000
−2.3	.011	0.7	.758	3.7	1.000
−2.2	.014	0.8	.788	3.8	1.000
−2.1	.018	0.9	.816	3.9	1.000
				4.0	1.000
−2.0	.023	1.0	.841		
−1.9	.029	1.1	.864		
−1.8	.036	1.2	.885		
−1.7	.045	1.3	.903		
−1.6	.055	1.4	.919		
−1.5	.067	1.5	.933		
−1.4	.081	1.6	.945		
−1.3	.097	1.7	.955		
−1.2	.115	1.8	.964		
−1.1	.136	1.9	.971		

[a]Move decimal two places to the right for the percentile rank. Values are rounded to three places.

SOURCE: Presentation of data used in the present volume is from *Statistics: An Intuitive Approach*, Third Edition, by G. H. Weinberg and J. A. Schumaker. Copyright © 1962, 1969, 1974 by Wadsworth Publishing Company, Inc. Reprinted by permission of the publisher, Brooks/Cole Publishing Company, Monterey, California.

Appendix 4 List of Equations Used in the Text

Location in Text	Term Defined	Equation
(4.1)	Mean	$\bar{X} = \dfrac{\Sigma X}{N}$
(4.2)	Variance	$S^2 = \dfrac{\Sigma(X - \bar{X})^2}{N}$
		or
		$S^2 = \dfrac{\Sigma X^2}{N} - \left(\dfrac{\Sigma X}{N}\right)^2$
p. 72	Pearson product-moment correlation coefficient, where X and Y are scores on two tests	$r = \dfrac{N\Sigma XY - (\Sigma X)(\Sigma Y)}{\sqrt{N\Sigma X^2 - (\Sigma X)^2}\sqrt{N\Sigma Y^2 - (\Sigma Y)^2}}$
		or
		$r = \dfrac{\Sigma Z_x Z_y}{n}$
p. 86	Percentile rank for a particular score	%ile = percent of people scoring below the score + ½ percent of people obtaining the score
(5.1)	z-score	$z = \dfrac{X - \bar{X}}{S}$
(5.2)	Any standard score	$SS = \bar{X}_{ss} + (S_{ss})(z)$
(7.2)	Coefficient alpha	$r_{aa} = \dfrac{k}{k-1}\left(1 - \dfrac{\Sigma S^2_{items}}{S^2_{test}}\right)$
p. 114	Simple agreement	$\dfrac{100 \text{ (number of agreements)}}{\text{number of observations}}$
(7.3)	% agreement occurrence=	$\dfrac{100 \text{ (number of agreements on occurrence)}}{\text{number of observations} - \text{number of agreements on nonoccurrence}}$

Appendix 4 (continued)

Location in Text	Term Defined	Equation
(7.4)	Spearman Brown, correction for test length	$r_{xx} = \dfrac{2r_{(1/2)(1/2)}}{1 + r_{(1/2)(1/2)}}$
(7.5)	Standard error of measurement	$\text{SEM} = S\sqrt{1 - r_{xx}}$
(7.6)	Estimated true score	$X' = \bar{X} + (r_{xx})(X - \bar{X})$
(7.7)	Lower and upper limits of a confidence interval, where z-score determines level of confidence	Lower limit $= X' - (z)(\text{SEM})$ Upper limit $= X' + (z)(\text{SEM})$
(7.8)	Reliability of a predicted difference	$\hat{D} = \dfrac{r_{bb} + (r_{aa})(r_{ab}^2) - 2r_{ab}}{1 - r_{ab}^2}$
(7.9)	Standard deviation of a predicted difference	$S_{\text{dif}} = S_b\sqrt{1 - r_{ab}^2}$
(7.10)	Reliability of a difference	$r_{(\text{dif})} = \dfrac{\frac{1}{2}(r_{aa} + r_{bb}) - r_{ab}}{1 - r_{ab}}$
(7.11)	Standard deviation of a difference	$S_{\text{dif}} = \sqrt{S_a^2 + S_b^2 - 2r_{ab}S_a S_b}$
(7.12)	Standard error of measurement of a difference	$\text{SEM}_{\text{dif}} = \sqrt{S_a{}^2 + S_b{}^2 - 2r_{ab}S_a S_b} \times$ $\sqrt{1 - \dfrac{\frac{1}{2}(r_{aa} + r_{bb}) - r_{ab}}{1 - r_{ab}}}$
(7.13)	Estimated true difference	$d' = (\text{obtained difference})(r_{xx(\text{dif})})$

Appendix 5   List of Publishers

Individuals wishing to purchase test specimen kits or secure additional test materials can write to the test publisher. The following is a list of the publishers whose tests are reviewed in this book.

American Association on Mental Deficiency, 5101 Wisconsin Ave. N.W., Washington, DC 20016

American Guidance Service, Inc., Publishers' Building, Circle Pines, MN 55014

American Orthopsychiatric Association, 1775 Broadway, New York, NY 10019

American Printing House for the Blind, 1839 Frankfort Ave., P.O. Box 6085, Louisville, KY 40206-0085

American Psychological Association, Inc., 1200 17th St. N.W., Washington, DC 20036

Bausch & Lomb, Inc., Rochester, NY 14602

Bobbs-Merrill Co., Inc., 4300 West 62nd St., P.O. Box 7080, Indianapolis, IN 46206

California Test Bureau/McGraw-Hill, Del Monte Research Park, Monterey, CA 93940

Campus Publishers, 713 W. Ellsworth Rd., Ann Arbor, MI 48104

Childcraft Education Corporation, 20 Kilmer Rd., Edison, NJ 08818

Consulting Psychologists Press, Inc., 577 College Ave., P.O. Box 11636, Palo Alto, CA 94306

Counselor Recordings and Tests, Box 6184, Acklen Station, Nashville, TN 37212

C.P.S., Box 83, Larchmont, NY 10538

Curriculum Associates, Inc., 5 Esquire Rd., North Billerica, MA 01862

The Devereux Foundation Press, 19 South Waterloo Rd., Devon, PA 19333

Educational and Industrial Testing Service, P.O. Box 7234, San Diego, CA 92107

Educational Testing Service, Rosedale Rd., Princeton, NJ 08541

Grune & Stratton, Inc., 111 Fifth Ave., New York, NY 10003

Harcourt Brace Jovanovich, Orlando, FL 32887

Harvard University Press, 79 Garden St., Cambridge, MA 02138

Marshall S. Hiskey, 5640 Baldwin, Lincoln, NB 68507

Institute for Personality and Ability Testing, P.O. Box 188, Champaign, IL 61820-0188

Jastak Associates, 1526 Gilpin Ave., Wilmington, DE 19806

Ladoca Project and Publishing Foundation, Inc., East 51st Ave., and Lincoln St., Denver, CO 80216

Language Research Associates, 175 East Delaware Pl., Chicago, IL 60611

Learning Concepts, 2501 N. Lamar, Austin, TX 78705

Charles E. Merrill Publishing Co., 1300 Alum Creek Drive, Box 508, Columbus, OH 43216

Appendix 5 *(continued)*

Modern Curriculum Press, 13900 Prospect Rd., Cleveland, OH 44136

T. Ernest Newland, 1004 Ross Dr., Champaign, IL 61820

NFER-Nelson Publishing Company Ltd., Darville House, 2 Oxford Rd. East, Windsor, Berkshire SL4 1DF, England

Northwestern University Press, 1735 Benson Ave., Evanston, IL 60201

Personnel Press, 20 Nassau St., Princeton, NJ 08540

Pro-Ed, 5341 Industrial Oaks Blvd., Austin, TX 78735

Psychodynamic Instruments, University of California, Santa Barbara, CA 93106

The Psychological Corporation, 7500 Old Oak Blvd., Cleveland, OH 44130

Psychological Test Specialists, Box 9229, Missoula, MT 59807

Psychologists and Educators Press, Inc., 211 West State St., Jacksonville, IL 62650

Random House, Inc., 201 East 50th St., New York, NY 10022

The Riverside Publishing Company, 8420 Bryn Mawr Ave., Chicago, IL 60631

Science Research Associates, 155 North Wacker Dr., Chicago, IL 60606

Slosson Educational Publications, 140 Pine St., P.O. Box 280, East Aurora, NY 14052

C. H. Stoelting Co., 1350 S. Kostner Ave., Chicago, IL 60623

Teachers College Press, 1234 Amsterdam Ave., New York, NY 10027

Teaching Resources Corporation, 50 Pond Park Rd., Hingham, MA 02043

The University of Illinois Press, 54 E. Gregory Dr., Box 5081, Station A, Champaign, IL 61820

Western Psychological Services, 12031 Wilshire Blvd., Los Angeles, CA 90025

Richard L. Zweig Associates, Inc., 20800 Beach Blvd., Huntington Beach, CA 92648

Appendix 6   How to Review a Test

We have often been asked how we go about analyzing and reviewing tests for this book—and in general. So we have decided to include a how-to section. Before starting an analysis of a test, you must first assemble the materials. We find that it is best to order a specimen kit and any supplementary manuals available. Be prepared to experience difficulty obtaining material from some test publishers. When you request a specimen kit and supplementary materials, you will occasionally receive all materials. More often, when you review specimen sets, you'll learn that additional materials must be ordered separately. Sometimes, it takes a very long time to figure out just what is published where. Sometimes, it takes up to six months to acquire all the material on a test. Sometimes, you just never obtain materials. Patience and perseverance are almost always required.

When materials arrive, you must prepare yourself properly. The right setting is very important. A well-ventilated, well-lit room (preferably a bit on the chilly side) and a hard, straight-backed chair are essential.

Next, and more important, reviewers must adopt a "show me" attitude. Do not expect test authors to admit in the manuals that the test was poorly normed because there was no money to pay testers or that the test has inadequate reliability because they didn't develop enough test items. Test authors put the best possible face on their tests, as might be expected. You simply cannot accept the claims made by test authors and their colleagues who write the technical manuals. If you accepted them at their word, they would only have to say that they had a "good, reliable, valid, and well-normed test." Test authors must *demonstrate* that their tests are reliable, valid, and well-normed.

After assembling the relevant materials and finding a suitable place in which to ask "Where's the proof?" we usually follow these procedures. First, we skim through the material to get a general idea of what the test is intended to do and what is included in each document that accompanies it. We generally keep several separate sheets of paper—one for each topic that we consider: background and purposes, behavior sampled, scores, norms, reliability, and validity.

Then we reread the manuals. You might expect that test authors would organize test manuals neatly so that you could turn to the table of contents, find the section on, for example, reliability, and turn to the pages indicated for the proof. Sometimes, yes; more often, no. If manuals do not have section headings or chapters, we just begin reading and making notes under our headings. If the manuals are sectioned, we start with the behaviors sampled by the test. It doesn't matter too much where you start except that validity is best left until last. We often start with the behaviors sampled. Test manuals frequently contain a useful description of the behaviors sampled but more often they merely name the domains sampled. For example, a test may be said to assess reading, but that does not tell you if it assesses reading recognition, reading comprehension, or oral reading. Look at the test directions (especially directions on how to score student responses) and the protocol (the answer form). These sources generally give you a pretty good idea of what behaviors are actually measured. Then, try to describe the behavior in straightforward terms—avoiding psychological and educational jargon.

Next, we generally look at the section on norms. When evaluating a test's norms, first note the ages (or grades in the case of achievement tests) of the students on whom the test was normed. Next, look for statements describing the students. Also, anticipate quantification of the norm groups. For example, you should anticipate that the test author will tell you how many boys and how many girls and how many persons from various ethnic or racial groups were tested at each age or grade. Also expect geographic information. For example, what percentage of the sample lived in big cities? in the Northwest? Finally, expect socioeconomic information about the students: parents' occupations, parents' educational attainment, income of the household. Next, look for an explicit comparison of the characteristics of the norm group with the most recent census before publication of the test. Sometimes, test authors include all the data and all the comparisons in neat tabular form, but you may find substantial discrepancies between the norm sample and the population. Generally, we look for correspondence between the sample and the population within about 5 percent. Thus, if 31 percent of the sample lived in the Southwest and only 26 percent of the U.S. population lived in the Southwest, we would not be overly concerned about the discrepancy. We realize that this is an arbitrary margin of error. If you prefer a different one, that's fine.

Information on scores is apt to be located in many places: in the section on scoring the test, in the description of the norms, in a separate section on scores, in the section dealing with the interpretation of scores, or in the norm tables themselves. Generally, the best place to find information on the types of scores available is the norm tables. These tables allow the conversions of raw scores to derived scores and subtest scores to total scores. The next best place to look is in the section on scoring the test. There you find the directions for crediting responses and combining raw scores into derived scores. In the norms section, you may find phrases such as "percentile norms" or "grade-equivalent norms," sure tip-offs that percentiles and grade equivalents will be available. In the sections on interpretation, you may find information on the proper interpretation of derived scores. For example, many test authors will tell you the mean and standard deviation of standard scores and how they are to be interpreted. However, it pays to double check against the norm tables themselves because test authors occasionally err in their descriptions.

Finding reliability data may be more difficult. If there is a section on reliability, the task is fairly simple. You wish to see if there is evidence of each appropriate type of reliability. Demand numbers; do not settle for statements as to the test's reliability. Make the authors show you the proof. Read the tables. You should usually anticipate finding estimates of generalization across items (split-half, KR-20, coefficient alpha, alternate-form, and so on) and across time (test-retest reliability). If the scoring is difficult, you should also anticipate finding a section on interscorer agreement. (Data on the extent to which one can generalize across scores can often be found in the section on scoring.) You should expect to find reliability estimates for each subtest at each grade or age. In addition, tables giving the standard error of measurement for each subtest at each grade or age are occasionally provided.

The next step is very important: you must determine the scores that are to be interpreted, because those are the ones you must judge for adequacy. In the sections dealing with score interpretation, you will often find the scores that the test authors think are most important. Many tests have subtests that are combined into a total score. Sometimes the subtest scores are stressed over the total score (for example, the Illinois Test of Psycholinguistic Abilities), whereas other test stress the total score or part scores over subtest scores (for example, the Wechsler Intelligence Scale for Children–Revised). The scores that are stressed as important and that are to be interpreted must meet the minimum desirable standards of reliability. Consequently, different tests are held to different standards. For example, the subtests on the ITPA must meet a higher standard of reliability than the subtests of the WISC–R because we are urged to interpret the ITPA subtests but not the WISC–R subtests.

If there is no section on reliability, check the table of contents to see if there are tables for standard errors of measurement or reliability coefficients. You can usually find all the information that you need in the tables without reading the text. If there are no tables and no section on reliability, there may be no data on reliability in the manuals; it happens frequently. However, reliability information may be hidden in the section on validity or in the section on scores or in the section on interpretation. Keep a look out for it as you skim and read.

The evaluation of a test's validity is the most difficult aspect of reviewing a test. You have already considered the adequacy of the norms and the reliability. If they are inadequate, there will be severe problems with validity. Even if they are adequate, the authors must still prove to you that the test is valid for each recommended use. This means that you must learn how the authors recommend using the test. Do not expect to find this information in a section labeled validity. More often you will find such statements in the beginning of the test manuals or in the promotional materials.

You will always find a statement to the effect that the test measures some domain. How do the test authors prove this? Data on content validity is often included in a section called "the development of the test" or "selection of items." In these sections, the authors will explain to you how they chose the items in the test. For other tests, the information will be buried in the manual. For still others, there will be no mention—no proof.

Depending on the particular type of test, you may also find information on concurrent and predictive validity and on construct validity. Again, you must remember that the purpose of presenting these data is to demonstrate to us that the test measures the domain its authors claim it measures. The data should logically bear on the issue of validity.

Beyond claims that the test assesses a particular domain, you may find assertions that the test can be used in particular ways. This is especially true for tests of achievment where we are often told the test can be used in program planning. When we see such assertions, we expect to find a large number of test items appropriate for each grade. We look at the test items, and we often look at the norm tables to get an idea of the difference in the number of test items at each grade. All you have to do is find the raw score at the 50th percentile at two adjacent grades. For example, suppose 17 points correct was the 50th percentile at the second grade and 21 points correct was the 50th percentile at the third grade. Then, only 4 raw-score points would separate second and third grade work. This is probably too few items on which to base an educational plan, although it may well discriminate among test takers. Sometimes we are told that scores can be used in particular ways. Such assertions are often found in the interpretation sections of the manuals. For example, you may find information on critical levels of performance; the authors may tell you that scores below a particular value are indicative of potential problems or that students earning such scores require special instructional interventions. Check out each assertion for the use of the test and expect to find proof.

Finally, we tend to be suspicious of strange formulations of reliability, validity, or scores. You should be, too. Remember, if you are an intended user of the test, the test author should provide all the necessary data in clear and usable form. If it isn't there, it isn't your fault.

REFERENCES

Adam, A., Doran, D., & Modan, R. (1967). Frequencies of protan and duetan alleles in some Israeli communities and a note on the selection of relaxation hypotheses. *American Journal of Physical Anthropology, 26,* 297–306.

Algozzine, B., Christenson, S., & Ysseldyke, J. E. (1982). Probabilities associated with the referral to placement process. *Teacher Education and Special Education, 5,* 19–23.

Alpern, G. D., & Boll, T. J. (1972). *Developmental Profile manual.* Aspen, CO: Psychological Development Publications, 1972.

American National Standards Institute. (1969). *Specifications for audiometers.* ANSI S3.6. American National Standards Institute, Inc., New York.

American Psychological Association. (1954). *Technical recommendations for psychological tests and diagnostic techniques.* Washington, DC: American Psychological Association.

American Psychological Association. (1966). *Standards for educational and psychological tests and manuals.* Washington, DC: American Psychological Association.

American Psychological Association. (1979). *Ethical standards of psychologists.* Washington, DC: American Psychological Association.

American Psychological Association, American Educational Research Association, & National Council on Measurement in Education. (1974). *Standards for educational and psychological tests.* Washington, DC: American Psychological Association.

American Speech and Hearing Association. (1974).

Guidelines for audiometric symbols. *American Speech and Hearing Association Journal, 16,* 260–263.

Ames, W. (1965). A comparison of spelling textbooks. *Elementary English, 42,* 146–150, 214.

Ammons, R. B., & Ammons, C. H. (1948). *The Full Range Picture Vocabulary Test.* New Orleans: R. B. Ammons.

Ammons, R. B., & Ammons, C. H. (1962). The Quick Test (QT): Provisional model. *Psychological Reports, 11,* 111–161.

Anastasi, A. (1976). *Psychological testing.* New York: Macmillan.

Anderson, R. (1963). *Kuhlmann-Anderson Intelligence Tests* (7th ed.). Princeton: Educational Testing Service.

Armstrong, R. J., & Jensen, J. A. (1981). *Slosson Intelligence Test: 1981 norms tables application and development.* East Aurora, NY: Slosson Educational Publications.

Arter, J. A., & Jenkins, J. R. (1979). Differential diagnosis—prescriptive teaching: A critical appraisal. *Review of Educational Research, 49,* 517–556.

Arthur, G. (1950). *The Arthur Adaptation of the Leiter International Performance Scale.* Chicago, IL: C. H. Stoelting.

Ballard, J., & Zettel, J. (1977). Public Law 94-142 and Sec. 504: What they say about rights and protections. *Exceptional Children, 44,* 177–185.

Balow, I. H., Hogan, T. P., Farr, R. C., & Prescott, G. A. (1978). *Metropolitan Achievement Tests: Language Instructional Battery.* Cleveland: The Psychological Corporation.

Bangs, T. E. (1968). *Language and learning disabilities of the pre-academic child.* New York: Appleton-Century-Crofts.

Barraga, N. (1976). *Visual handicaps and learning: A developmental approach.* Belmont, CA: Wadsworth.

Batsche, G. M., & Peterson, D. W. (1983). School psychology and protective assessment: A growing incompatibility. *School Psychology Review, 12,* 440–445.

Beatty, L. S., Madden, R., Gardner, E. G., & Karlsen, B. (1976). *Stanford Diagnostic Mathematics Test.* Cleveland: The Psychological Corporation.

Beery, K. E. (1982). *Revised administration, scoring, and teaching manual for the developmental test of visual-motor integration.* Cleveland: Modern Curriculum Press.

Bellak, L., & Bellak, S. (1965). *Children's Apperception Test.* Larchmont, NY: C.P.S.

Belmont, J. M. (1966). Long-term memory in mental retardation. In N. R. Ellis (Ed.), *International review of research in mental retardation* (Vol. 1). New York: Academic Press.

Bender, L. (1938). *A visual motor Gestalt test and its clinical use* (Research Monograph, No. 3). New York: American Orthopsychiatric Association.

Bene, E., & Anthony, J. (1957). *Family Relations Test: An objective technique for exploring emotional attitudes in children.* Windsor, Berkshire, England: NFER-Nelson Publishing Company.

Bersoff, D. (1973). Silk purses into sows' ears: The decline of psychological testing and a suggestion for its redemption. *American Psychologist, 10,* 892–899.

Bersoff, D. N. (1979). Regarding psychologists testily: Legal regulation of psychological assessment in the public schools. *Maryland Law Review, 39,* 27–120.

Bijou, S. W. (1970). What psychology has to offer education—Now. *Journal of Applied Behavior Analysis, 3,* 65–71.

Bijou, S. W., Peterson, R. F., Harris, F. R., Allen, K. E., & Johnson, M. S. (1969). Methodology for experimental studies of young children in natural settings. *Psychological Record, 19,* 177–210.

Bloom, B. (Ed.). (1956). *Taxonomy of educational objectives: The classification of educational goals.* Handbook 1. *Cognitive domain.* New York: McKay.

Bloom, B., Hastings, J., & Madaus, G. (1971). *Handbook of formative and summative evaluation of student learning.* New York: McGraw-Hill.

Bloom, L. (1974). Talking, understanding and thinking. In R. Schiefelbusch and L. Lloyd (Eds.), *Language perspectives, acquisition, retardation and intervention* (pp. 193–296). Baltimore: University Park Press.

Blum, G. (1967). *Blacky Pictures: A technique for the exploration of personality dynamics.* Santa Barbara: Psychodynamic Instruments.

Boehm, A. E. (1971). *Boehm Test of Basic Concepts Manual.* Cleveland: The Psychological Corporation.

Boehm, A., & Weinberg, R. A. (1977). *The classroom observer: A guide for developing observation skills.* New York: Teachers College Press.

Box, G. (1953). Non-normality and tests on variance. *Biometrika, 40,* 318–335.

Bradbury, R. (1953). *Fahrenheit 451.* New York: Ballantine Books.

Brigance, A. (1977). *Brigance Diagnostic Inventory of Basic Skills.* North Billerica, MA: Curriculum Associates.

Brigance, A. (1978). *Brigance Diagnostic Inventory of Early Development.* North Billerica, MA: Curriculum Associates.

Brigance, A. (1980). *Brigance Diagnostic Inventory of Essential Skills.* North Billerica, MA: Curriculum Associates.

Brown, L., Sherbenou, R. J., & Dollar, S. J. (1982). *Test of Nonverbal Intelligence.* Austin, TX: Pro-Ed.

Brown, R., & Bellugi, U. (1964). Three processes in the child's acquisition of syntax. *Harvard Educational Review, 34,* 133–151.

Brown, V., & McEntire, E. (1984). *Test of Mathematical Abilities.* Austin, TX: Pro-Ed.

Buck, J., & Jolles, I. (1966). *House-Tree-Person.* Los Angeles: Western Psychological Services.

Burgemeister, B. B., Blum, L. H., & Lorge, I. (1972). *Columbia Mental Maturity Scale* (3rd ed.). Cleveland: The Psychological Corporation.

Burks, H. (1969). *Burk's Behavior Rating Scales.* Los Angeles: Western Psychological Services.

Burt, C. (1959). Class differences in general intelligence: III. *British Journal of Statistical Psychology, 12,* 15–33.

Byrne, M. C. (1978). Appraisal of child language acquisition. In F. L. Darley & D. C. Spriestersbach, *Diagnostic methods in speech pathology* (2nd ed.). New York: Harper & Row.

Cain, L., Levine, S., & Elzey, F. (1963). *Manual for the Cain-Levine Social Competency Scale.* Palo Alto: Consulting Psychologists Press.

Caldwell, B. (1970a). *Preschool Inventory Revised Edition.* Princeton, NJ: Educational Testing Service.

Caldwell, B. (1970b). *Preschool Inventory Revised Edition–1970: Handbook.* Princeton, NJ: Educational Testing Service.

Campbell, D., & Fiske, D. (1959). Convergent and discriminant validation by the multitrait-multimethod matrix. *Psychological Bulletin, 56,* 81–105.

Carrow, E. (1973). *Test of Auditory Comprehension of Language* (rev. ed.). Austin, TX: Learning Concepts.

Carrow, E. (1974). *Carrow Elicited Language Inventory.* Austin, TX: Learning Concepts.

Cartwright, C., & Cartwright, G. P. (1974). *Developing observation skills.* New York: McGraw-Hill.

Cassel, R. (1962). *Child Behavior Rating Scale.* Los Angeles: Western Psychological Services.

Cattell, R. B. (1950). *Culture Fair Intelligence Test: Scale 1.* Champaign, IL: Institute for Personality and Ability Testing.

Cattell, R. B. (1962). *Handbook for Culture Fair Intelligence Test: Scale 1.* Champaign, IL: Institute for Personality and Ability Testing.

Cattell, R. B. (1973a). *Measuring intelligence with the Culture Fair Tests: Manual for scales 2 and 3.* Champaign, IL: Institute for Personality and Ability Testing.

Cattell, R. B. (1973b). *Technical supplement for the Culture Fair Intelligence Tests scales 2 and 3.* Champaign, IL: Institute for Personality and Ability Testing.

Cattell, R. B., & Cattell, A. K. S. (1960a). *Culture Fair Intelligence Test: Scale 2.* Champaign, IL: Institute for Personality and Ability Testing.

Cattell, R. B., & Cattell, A. K. S. (1960b). *Handbook for the individual or group Culture Fair Intelligence Test: Scale 2.* Champaign, IL: Institute for Personality and Ability Testing.

Cattell, R. B., & Cattell, A. K. S. (1963). *Culture Fair Intelligence Test: Scale 3.* Champaign, IL: Institute for Personality and Ability Testing.

Cattell, R. B., Coan, R., & Belloff, H. (1969). *Jr.-Sr. High School Personality Questionnaire.* Indianapolis: Bobbs-Merrill.

Cattell, R. B., Eber, H., & Tatsuoka, M. (1970). *Sixteen Personality Factor Questionnaire.* Champaign, IL: Institute for Personality and Ability Testing.

Chomsky, N. (1965). *Aspects of the theory of syntax.* Cambridge, MA: M.I.T. Press.

Cleary, T. A., Humphreys, L. G., Kendrick, S. A., & Wesman, A. (1975). Educational uses of tests with disadvantaged students. *American Psychologist, 30,* 15–41.

Coan, R., & Cattell, R. B. (1970). *Early School Personality Questionnaire.* Champaign, IL: Institute for Personality and Ability Testing.

Cohen, G. (1972). Hemispheric differences in a letter classification task. *Perception and Psychophysics, 11,* 139–142.

Cohen, S. A. (1969). Studies in visual perception and reading in disadvantaged children. *Journal of Learning Disabilities, 2,* 498–507.

Coleman, J., Campbell, E., Hobson, C., McPartland, J., Mood, A., Weinfeld, F., & York, R. (1966). *Equality of educational opportunity.* Washington, DC: National Center for Education Statistics (F.S. 5.238:38001).

Connolly, A., Nachtman, W., & Pritchett, E. (1971). *Manual for the KeyMath Diagnostic Arithmetic Test.* Circle Pines, MN: American Guidance Service.

Cottle, W. (1966). *School Interest Inventory.* Chicago: The Riverside Publishing Company.

Cromwell, R. L., Blashfield, R. K., & Strauss, J. S. (1975). Criteria for classification systems. In N. Hobbs (Ed.), *Issues in the classification of children* (Vol. 1). San Francisco: Jossey-Bass.

Cronbach, L. (1951). Coefficient alpha and the internal structure of tests. *Psychometrika, 16,* 297–334.

Cronbach, L. J. (1960, 1970). *Essentials of psychological testing.* New York: Harper & Row.

CTB/McGraw-Hill. (1972). *Prescriptive Reading Inventory.* Monterey, CA: CTB/McGraw-Hill.

CTB/McGraw-Hill (1977, 1978). *The California Achievement Tests.* Monterey, CA: CTB/McGraw-Hill.

CTB/McGraw-Hill (1979). *The California Achievement Tests: Technical bulletin No. 1.* Monterey, CA: CTB/McGraw-Hill.

CTB/McGraw-Hill (1980). *The California Achievement Tests: Technical bulletin No. 2.* Monterey, CA: CTB/McGraw-Hill.

Darley, F. L. (Ed.). (1961). Identification audiometry. *Journal of Speech and Hearing Disorders,* Monograph Supplement Number 9.

Das, J., Kirby, J., & Jarman, R. (1975). Simultaneous and successive syntheses: An alternative model for cognitive abilities. *Psychological Bulletin, 82,* 87–103.

Davis, W. Q. (1968). *A study of test score comparability among five widely used reading survey tests.* Unpublished doctoral dissertation, Southern Illinois University.

Deno, S., & Mirkin, P. (1977). *Data-based program modification: a manual.* Reston, VA: Council for Exceptional Children.

Dingman, H., & Tarjan, G. (1960). Mental retardation and the normal distribution curve. *American Journal of Mental Deficiency, 64,* 991–994.

Doll, E. (1953). *Measurement of social competence: A manual for the Vineland Social Maturity Scale.* Princeton, NJ: Educational Testing Service.

Doll, E. (1965). *Vineland Social Maturity Scale.* Circle Pines, MN: American Guidance Service. (Originally published 1953.)

Down, A. L. (1969). Observations on an ethnic classification of idiots. In R. Vollman (Ed.), *Down's Syndrome (Mongolism), a reference bibliography.* Washington, DC: United States Department of Health, Education and Welfare. (The paper by Down that appears in this collection was originally published in 1866.)

Duffy, J. (1964). Report 5: *Hearing problems in school-age children.* In Maico Audiological Library Series I. Minneapolis: Maico Electronics.

Dunn, L., & Dunn, L. (1981). *Peabody Picture Vocabulary Test–Revised.* Circle Pines, MN: American Guidance Service.

Dunn, L. M. (1968). Minimal brain dysfunction: A dilemma for educators. In H. C. Haywood (Ed.), *Brain damage in school age children.* Reston, VA: Council for Exceptional Children.

Dunn, L. M., & Markwardt, F. C. (1970). *Peabody Individual Achievement Test.* Circle Pines, MN: American Guidance Service.

Durost, W. N., Bixler, H. H., Wrightstone, J. W., Prescott, G. A., & Balow, I. H. (1971). *Metropolitan Achievement Test.* Cleveland: The Psychological Corporation.

Durrell, D., & Catterson, J. (1980). *Durrell Analysis of Reading Difficulty.* Cleveland: The Psychological Corporation.

Dvovine, I. (1953). *Dvovine Pseudo-isochromatic Plates* (2nd ed.). Baltimore: Waverly Press.

Eaves, R. C., & McLaughlin, P. (1977). A systems approach for the assessment of the child and his environment: Getting back to basics. *Journal of Special Education, 11,* 99–111.

Edwards, A. (1959). *Edwards Personal Preference Schedule.* Cleveland: The Psychological Corporation.

Edwards, A. (1966). *Edwards Personality Inventory.* Chicago: Science Research Associates.

Ekwall, E. E. (1970). *Locating and correcting reading difficulties.* Columbus, OH: Merrill.

Engelmann, S., Granzin, A., & Severson, H. (1979). Diagnosing instruction. *Journal of Special Education, 13,* 355–365.

Ervin, S. M. (1964). Imitation and structural change in children's language. In E. H. Lenneberg (Ed.), *New directions in the study of language.* Cambridge, MA: M.I.T. Press.

Exner, J. E. (1966). *Workbook in the Rorschach technique.* Springfield, IL: Charles C Thomas.

Eysenck, H., & Eysenck, S. (1969). *Eysenck Personality Inventory.* San Diego: Educational and Industrial Testing Service.

Farber, B. (1968). *Mental retardation: Its social context and social consequences.* Boston: Houghton Mifflin.

Farnsworth, D. (1947). *The Farnsworth Dichotomous Test for Color Blindness.* Cleveland: The Psychological Corporation.

Farr, R. C., Prescott, G. A., Balow, I. H., & Hogan,

T. P. (1978). *Metropolitan Achievement Tests: Reading Instructional Battery.* Cleveland: The Psychological Corporation.

Faye, E. (1970). *The low vision patient.* New York: Grune & Stratton.

Fernald, C. (1972). Control of grammar in imitation, comprehension, and production, problems of replication. *Journal of Verbal Learning and Verbal Behavior, 11,* 606–613.

Finch, F. (1951). *Kuhlmann-Finch Tests.* Circle Pines, MN: American Guidance Service.

Fitts, W. (1965). *Tennessee Self Concept Inventory.* Nashville: Counselor Recordings and Tests.

Frankenburg, W., Dodds, J., Fandal, A., Kazuk, E., & Cohrs, M. (1975). *Denver Developmental Screening Test, Reference Manual, Revised 1975 Edition.* Denver, CO: LA-DOCA Project and Publishing Foundation.

Frankenburg, W., Goldstein, A., & Camp, B. (1971). The revised Denver Developmental Screening Test: Its accuracy as a screening instrument. *Pediatrics, 79,* 988–995.

French, J. L. (1964). *Pictorial Test of Intelligence.* Chicago: The Riverside Publishing Company.

Frostig, M., Lefever, W., & Whittlesey, J. (1966). *Administration and scoring manual: Marianne Frostig Developmental Test of Visual Perception.* Palo Alto: Consulting Psychologists Press.

Frostig, M., Maslow, P., Lefever, D. W., & Whittlesey, J. R. (1964). *The Marianne Frostig Developmental Test of Visual Perception: 1963 standardization.* Palo Alto: Consulting Psychologists Press.

Fudala, J. (1970). *Arizona Articulation Proficiency Scale.* Los Angeles: Western Psychological Services.

Fulmer, S. (1980). *Pre-reading screening procedures and Slingerland Screening Tests for Identifying Children with Specific Language Disability, technical manual.* Los Angeles: Western Psychological Services.

Gardner, E. F., Callis, R., Merwin, J. C., & Rudman, H. C. (1983). *Stanford Test of Academic Skills* (2nd ed.). Cleveland: The Psychological Corporation.

Gardner, E. F., Rudman, H. C., Karlsen, B., & Merwin, J. C. (1982). *Stanford Achievement Test* (7th ed.). Cleveland: The Psychological Corporation.

Garrett, J. E., & Brazil, N. (1979). Categories used for identification and education of exceptional children. *Exceptional Children, 45,* 291–292.

Gates, A. I., McKillop, A. S., & Horowitz, R. (1981). *Gates-McKillop-Horowitz Reading Diagnostic Tests.* New York: Teachers College Press.

Gerweck, S., & Ysseldyke, J. E. (1974). Limitations of current psychological practices for the intellectual assessment of the hearing impaired: A response to the Levine survey. *Volta Review, 77,* 243–248.

Gessell, J. K. (1977). *Diagnostic Mathematics Inventory.* Monterey, CA: CTB/McGraw-Hill.

Ghiselli, E. E. (1964). *Theory of Psychological Measurement.* New York: McGraw-Hill.

Gilmore, J. V., & Gilmore, E. C. (1968). *Gilmore Oral Reading Test.* Cleveland: The Psychological Corporation.

Ginzberg, E., & Bray, D. W. (1953). *The Uneducated.* New York: Columbia University Press.

Gold, M. W. (1968). The acquisition of a complex assembly task by retarded adolescents. Urbana: University of Illinois, Children's Research Center. (Mimeographed)

Goldman, R., & Fristoe, M. (1972). *Goldman-Fristoe Test of Articulation.* Circle Pines, MN: American Guidance Service.

Goldstein, K. (1927). Die lokalisation in her grosshirnrinde. *Handb. Norm. Pathol. Physiologie.* Berlin: J. Springer.

Goldstein, K. (1936). The modification of behavior consequent to cerebral lesions. *Psychiatric Quarterly, 10,* 586–610.

Goldstein, K. (1939). *The organism.* New York: American Book.

Goodman, A. C., & Chasin, W. D. (1976). Hearing problems. In S. S. Gellis and B. M. Kagan (Eds.), *Current Pediatric Therapy 6.* Philadelphia: W. B. Saunders.

Goslin, D. A. (1969). *Guidelines for the collection, maintenance and dissemination of pupil records.* Troy, NY: Russell Sage Foundation.

Gottesman, I. (1963). Genetic aspects of intelligent behavior. In N. Ellis (Ed.), *Handbook of mental deficiency.* New York: McGraw-Hill.

Gottesman, I. (1968). Biogenics of race and class. In

M. Deutsch, I. Katz, & A. Jensen (Eds.), *Social class, race, and psychological development.* New York: Holt, Rinehart and Winston.

Gough, H. (1969). *California Psychological Inventory.* Palo Alto: Consulting Psychologists Press.

Graden, J., Casey, A., & Bonstrom, O. (1983). *Prereferral interventions: Effects on referral rates and teacher attitudes* (Research Report #140). Minneapolis: Minnesota Institute for Research on Learning Disabilities.

Graham, F., & Kendall, B. K. (1960). Memory for Designs Test: Revised general manual. *Perceptual and Motor Skills, 11,* 147–188.

Gray, W. S., & Robinson, H. M. (1967). *Gray Oral Reading Test.* Austin, TX: Pro-Ed.

Greenwood, L. (1949). Shots in the dark. Cited by I. Schloss, *Implications of altering the definition of blindness* (Research Bulletin 3). American Foundation for the Blind.

Gronlund, N. (1968). *Constructing achievement tests.* Englewood Cliffs, NJ: Prentice-Hall.

Gronlund, N. (1976). *Measurement and evaluation in teaching* (3rd ed.). New York: Macmillan.

Grossman, H. (1983). *Manual of terminology and classification in mental retardation.* Washington, DC: American Association on Mental Deficiency.

Guarmaccia, V. (1976). Factor structure and correlates of adaptive behavior in noninstitutionalized retarded adults. *American Journal of Mental Deficiency, 80,* 543–547.

Guidelines for audiometric symbols. (1974). *American Speech and Hearing Association Journal, 16,* 260–264.

Guilford, J. (1954). *Psychometric methods.* New York: McGraw-Hill.

Guilford, J. (1956). *Fundamental statistics in psychology and education.* New York: McGraw-Hill.

Guilford, J. P. (1967). *The nature of human intelligence.* New York: McGraw-Hill.

Guskin, S., & Spicker, H. (1968). Educational research in mental retardation. In N. Ellis (Ed.), *International review of research in mental retardation* (Vol. 3). New York: Academic Press.

Guzaitis, J., Carlin, J. A., & Juda, S. (1972). *Diagnosis: An Instructional Aid (Mathematics).* Chicago: Science Research Associates.

Hackett, M. G. (1971). *Criterion Reading.* New York: Random House.

Hallahan, D., & Cruickshank, W. (1973). *Psychoeducational foundations of learning disabilities.* Englewood Cliffs, NJ: Prentice-Hall.

Halliday, C. (1970). *The visually impaired child— growth, learning, development—infancy to school age.* Louisville, KY: American Printing House for the Blind.

Halstead, W. C. (1947). *Brain and intelligence.* Chicago: University of Chicago.

Hammill, D., Brown, V., Larsen, S., & Wiederholt, J. (1980). *Test of Adolescent Language.* Austin, TX: Pro-Ed.

Hammill, D., & Larsen, S. (1983). *Test of Written Language.* Austin, TX: Pro-Ed.

Hammill, D., & Leigh, J. (1983a). *Basic School Skills Inventory, Diagnostic.* Austin, TX: Pro-Ed.

Hammill, D., & Leigh, J. (1983b). *Basic School Skills Inventory, Screen.* Austin, TX: Pro-Ed.

Hammill, D., & Wiederholt, J. L. (1973). Review of the Frostig Visual Perception Test and the related training program. In L. Mann & D. Sabatino (Eds.), *The first review of special education* (pp. 33–48). Philadelphia: Buttonwood Farms.

Hanna, P. R., Hodges, R. E., & Hanna, J. S. (1971). *Spelling: Structure and strategies.* Boston: Houghton Mifflin.

Hardy, L. H., Rand, G., & Rittler, M. C. (1957). *AO H-R-R Pseudoisochromatic Plates.* Buffalo: American Optical Company, Instrument Division.

Harris, D. (1963). *Children's drawings as measures of intellectual maturity.* Orlando, FL: Harcourt Brace Jovanovich.

Hathaway, S., & McKinley, J. (1967). *Minnesota Multiphasic Personality Inventory.* Cleveland: The Psychological Corporation.

Herrnstein, R. (1971). IQ. *Atlantic Monthly, 43,* 228.

Hieronymus, A. N., Lindquist, E. F., & Hoover, H. D. (1978). *Iowa Tests of Basic Skills.* Chicago: The Riverside Publishing Company.

Hieronymus, A. N., Lindquist, E. F., & Hoover, H. D. (1982). *Iowa Tests of Basic Skills.* Chicago: The Riverside Publishing Company.

Hiskey, M. (1966). *Hiskey-Nebraska Test of Learning Aptitude.* Lincoln, NB: Marshall S. Hiskey.

Hofmeister, A. (1975). Integrating criterion-referenced testing and instruction. In W. Hively & M. Reynolds (Eds.), *Domain-referenced test-*

ing in special education (pp. 77–88). Minneapolis: Leadership Training Institute/Special Education, University of Minnesota.

Hogan, T. P., Farr, R. C., Prescott, G. A., & Balow, I. H. (1978). *Metropolitan Achievement Tests: Mathematics Instructional Battery.* Cleveland: The Psychological Corporation.

Holtzman, W. (1966). *Holtzman Inkblot Technique.* Cleveland: The Psychological Corporation.

Horn, J. (1965). *Crystallized and fluid intelligence: A factor analytic study of the structure among primary mental abilities.* Unpublished doctoral dissertation, University of Illinois.

Hurlin, R. G. (1962). Estimated prevalence of blindness in the U.S.—1960. *Sight Saving Review, 32,* 4–12.

Hutt, M. L., & Briskin, G. J. (1960). *The Hutt Adaptation of the Bender Gestalt Test.* New York: Grune & Stratton.

Ingram, D. (1976). *Phonological disability in children.* New York: American Elsevier Publishing Co.

Jastak, J. E., & Jastak, S. R. (1965, 1978). *Wide Range Achievement Test.* Wilmington, DE: Jastak Associates.

Jay, E. (1955). *A book about me.* Chicago: Science Research Associates.

Jenkins, J., & Pany, D. (1978). Standardized achievement tests: How useful for special education. *Exceptional Children, 44,* 448–453.

Jensen, A. R. (1969). How much can we boost IQ and scholastic achievement? *Harvard Educational Review, 39,* 1–123.

Johnson, D., & Myklebust, H. (1967). *Learning disabilities: Educational principles and practices.* New York: Grune & Stratton.

Johnston, P. W. (1952). An efficient group screening test. *Journal of Speech and Hearing Disorders, 17,* 8–12.

Kamin, L. J. (1974). *The science and politics of I.Q.* Hillsdale: NJ: Lawrence Erlbaum Associates.

Kamin, L. J. (1975). Social and legal consequences of IQ tests as classification instruments: Some warnings from our past. *Journal of School Psychology, 13,* 317–323.

Kappauf, W. E. (1973). Studying the relationship of task performance to the variables of chronological age, mental age, and IQ. In N. Ellis (Ed.), *International review of research in mental retardation* (Vol. 6). New York: Academic Press.

Karlsen, B., Madden, R., & Gardner, E. F. (1974). *Stanford Diagnostic Reading Test: Level III.* Cleveland: The Psychological Corporation.

Karlsen, B., Madden, R., & Gardner, E. F. (1977). *Stanford Diagnostic Reading Test.* Cleveland: The Psychological Corporation.

Kaufman, A., & Kaufman, N. (1983). *Kaufman Assessment Battery for Children, interpretive manual.* Circle Pines, MN: American Guidance Service.

Kazdin, A. E. (1973). The effects of vicarious reinforcement in the classroom. *Journal of Applied Behavior Analysis, 6,* 71–78.

Kirk, S. A., & Kirk, W. D. (1971). *Psycholinguistic learning disabilities: Diagnosis and remediation.* Champaign: University of Illinois Press.

Kirk, S., McCarthy, J., & Kirk, W. (1968). *Illinois Test of Psycholinguistic Abilities.* Champaign: University of Illinois Press.

Klein, E. S. (1981). Communication dysfunctions. In R. M. Smith & J. T. Neisworth, *Exceptional child: A functional approach.* New York: McGraw-Hill.

Knoff, H. M. (1983). Justifying projective/personality assessment in school psychology: A response to Batsche and Peterson. *School Psychology Review, 12,* 446–451.

Koppitz, E. M. (1963). *The Bender Gestalt Test for Young Children.* New York: Grune & Stratton.

Koppitz, E. M. (1968). *Human Figures Drawing Test.* New York: Grune & Stratton.

Koppitz, E. (1975). *The Bender Gestalt Test for Young Children: Volume II: Research and application, 1963–1973.* New York: Grune & Stratton.

Kuder, R. (1954). *Kuder Personal Preference Record.* Chicago: Science Research Associates.

Lambert, N. (1981). *Diagnostic and technical manual, AAMD Adaptive Behavior Scale—School Edition.* Monterey, CA: CTB/McGraw-Hill.

Lambert, N., & Nicoll, R. (1976). Dimensions of adaptive behavior of retarded and non-retarded public-school children. *American Journal of Mental Deficiency, 81,* 135–146.

Lambert, N., & Windmiller, M. (1981). *Diagnostic*

and technical manual, revised AAMD Adaptive Behavior Scale—School edition. Monterey, CA: CTB/McGraw-Hill.

Lambert, N., Windmiller, M., Tharinger, D., & Cole, L. (1981). *Administration and instructional planning manual, AAMD Adaptive Behavior Scale—School edition.* Monterey, CA: CTB/McGraw-Hill.

Lamke, T., Nelson, M., & French, J. (1973). *Henmon-Nelson Tests of Mental Ability.* Chicago: The Riverside Publishing Company.

Larsen, S., & Hammill, D. (1976). *Test of Written Spelling.* Austin, TX: Pro-Ed.

Lee, J., & Clark, W. (1962). *Manual Lee-Clark Reading Readiness Test.* Monterey, CA: CTB/McGraw-Hill.

Lee, L. (1969). *Northwestern Syntax Screening Test.* Evanston, IL: Northwestern University Press.

Lee, L., & Canter, S. (1971). Developmental Sentence Scoring: A clinical procedure for estimating syntactic development in children's spontaneous speech. *Journal of Speech and Hearing Disorders, 36,* 315–340.

Lenneberg, E. (1967). *Biological foundations of language.* New York: Wiley.

Lerner, J. (1985). *Learning disabilities* (4th ed.). Boston: Houghton Mifflin.

Levine, E. (1974). Psychological tests and practices with the deaf: A survey of the state of the art. *Volta Review, 76,* 298–319.

Lindquist, E. F., & Feldt, L. S. (1980). *Iowa Tests of Educational Development.* Chicago: Science Research Associates.

Lindzey, G. (1959). On the classification of projective techniques. *Psychological Bulletin, 56,* 158–168.

Luria, A. (1966). *Higher cortical functions in man.* New York: Basic Books.

MacGinitie, W. (1978). *Gates-MacGinitie Reading Tests.* Chicago: The Riverside Publishing Company.

Madden, R., Gardner, E. F., & Collins, C. S. (1983). *Stanford Early School Achievement Test* (2nd ed.). Cleveland: The Psychological Corporation.

Mann, L. (1970a). Are we fractionating too much? *Academic Therapy, 5,* 85–91.

Mann, L. (1970b). Perceptual training: Misdirections and redirections. *American Journal of Orthopsychiatry, 40,* 30–38.

Mann, L. (1971a). Perceptual training revisited: The training of nothing at all. *Rehabilitation Literature, 32,* 322–335.

Mann, L. (1971b). Psychometric phrenology and the new faculty psychology: The case against ability assessment and training. *Journal of Special Education, 5,* 3–14.

Mardell-Czudnowski, C., & Goldenberg, D. (1983). *Developmental Indicators for the Assessment of Learning–Revised.* Edison, NJ: Childcraft Education Corp.

McCarthy, D. (1972). *Manual for the McCarthy Scales of Children's Abilities.* Cleveland: The Psychological Corporation.

Meeker, M. (1969). *The structure of intellect.* Columbus, OH: Merrill.

Mercer, J. (1973). The myth of 3% prevalence. In R. Eyman, C. E. Meyer, & G. Tarjan (Eds.), *Sociobehavioral studies in mental retardation.* AAMD Monograph.

Mercer, J. (1979). *System of Multicultural Pluralistic Assessment: Technical manual.* Cleveland: The Psychological Corporation.

Mercer, J., & Lewis, J. (1977). *SOMPA: Parent interview manual.* Cleveland: The Psychological Corporation.

Mercer, J., & Lewis, J. (1978). *SOMPA: Student assessment manual.* Cleveland: The Psychological Corporation.

Merriam, G., & Merriam, C. (1953). *Webster's new collegiate dictionary.* Cambridge, MA: Riverside Press.

Miller, L. C., Loewenfeld, R., Lindner, R., & Turner, J. (1963). Reliability of Koppitz' scoring system for the Bender Gestalt. *Journal of Clinical Psychology, 19,* 2111.

Mischel, W. (1970). Sex typing and socialization. In J. M. Tanner (Ed.), *Carmichael's manual of child psychology.* New York: Wiley.

Moss, M. (1979). *Tests of Basic Experiences: Norms and technical data book.* Monterey, CA: CTB/McGraw-Hill.

Mueller, M. (1965). *A comparison of the empirical validity of six tests of ability with young educable retardates* (IMRID Behavioral Science Monograph No. 1). Nashville: Institute on Mental Retardation and Intellectual Development.

Munday, L. A., & Rosenberg, G. L. (1979a). *How*

should the Stanford-Binet be used? Chicago: The Riverside Publishing Company.

Munday, L. A., & Rosenberg, G. L. (1979b). *How did the Stanford-Binet come about?* Chicago: The Riverside Publishing Company.

Munday, L. A., & Rosenberg, G. L. (1979c). *Social concerns and the Stanford-Binet.* Chicago: The Riverside Publishing Company.

Murray, H. (1943). *Thematic Apperception Test.* Cambridge, MA: Harvard University Press.

Naslund, R. A., Thorpe, L. P., & Lefever, D. W. (1978). *SRA Achievement Series.* Chicago, IL: Science Research Associates.

National Advisory Committee on Handicapped Children. (1968, January 31). *Special education for handicapped children.* First Annual Report. Washington, DC: U.S. Department of Health, Education and Welfare.

National Center for Education Statistics (1976). *The condition of education.* Washington, DC: NCES.

National Education Association. *Technical recommendations for achievement tests.* Washington, DC: National Education Association.

National Society for the Prevention of Blindness. (1961). *Vision screening in the schools.* New York: The Society.

National Society for the Prevention of Blindness. (1966). *Estimated statistics on blindness and vision problems.* New York: The Society.

Nelson, M., & French, J. (1974). *Henmon-Nelson Tests of Mental Ability: Primary Form 1.* Chicago: The Riverside Publishing Company.

Newland, T. E. (1969). *Blind Learning Aptitude Test.* Champaign, IL: T. Ernest Newland.

Newland, T. E. (1980). Psychological assessment of exceptional children and youth. In W. Cruickshank (Ed.), *Psychology of exceptional children and youth.* Englewood Cliffs, NJ: Prentice-Hall.

Nihira, K. (1969a). Factorial dimensions of adaptive behavior in adult retardates. *American Journal of Mental Deficiency, 73,* 868–878.

Nihira, K. (1969b). Factorial dimensions of adaptive behavior in mentally retarded children and adolescents. *American Journal of Mental Deficiency, 74,* 130–141.

Nihira, K., Foster, R., Shellhaas, M., & Leland, H. (1969). *Adaptive Behavior Scale.* Washington, DC: American Association on Mental Deficiency.

Nihira, K., Foster, R., Shellhaas, M., & Leland, H. (1974). *The AAMD Adaptive Behavior Scale manual.* Washington, DC: American Association on Mental Deficiency.

Nunnally, J. (1967). *Psychometric theory.* New York: McGraw-Hill.

Nunnally, J. (1978). *Psychometric theory.* New York: McGraw-Hill.

Nurss, J. R., & McGauvran, M. E. (1976a). *Metropolitan Readiness Tests, teacher's manual, Part II: Interpretation and use of test results (level I).* Cleveland: The Psychological Corporation.

Nurss, J. R., & McGauvran, M. E. (1976b). *Metropolitan Readiness Tests, teacher's manual, Part II: Interpretation and use of test results (level II).* Cleveland: The Psychological Corporation.

O'Neill, J., & Oyer, H. (1966). *Applied audiometry.* New York: Dodd, Mead.

Osgood, C. E. (1957a). Motivational dynamics of language behavior. In M. R. Jones (Ed.), *Nebraska symposium on motivation* (pp. 348–424). Lincoln, NB: University of Nebraska Press. Cited by Paraskevopoulos & Kirk, 1969.

Osgood, C. E. (1957b). A behavioristic analysis of perception and language as cognitive phenomena. In *Contemporary approaches to cognition* (pp. 75–118). Cambridge, MA: Harvard University Press. Cited by Paraskevopoulos & Kirk, 1969.

Otis, A., & Lennon, D. (1979). *Otis-Lennon Mental Ability Test.* Cleveland: The Psychological Corporation.

Paraskevopoulos, J. N., & Kirk, S. A. (1969). *The development and psychometric characteristics of the Revised Illinois Test of Psycholinguistic Abilities.* Champaign: University of Illinois Press.

Pennsylvania Association for Retarded Children v. *Commonwealth of Pennsylvania,* 334 F. Supp. 1257 (E.D. Pa. 1971).

Peterson, D. R. (1968). *The clinical study of social behavior.* New York: Appleton-Century-Crofts.

Piers, E., & Harris, D. (1969). *The Piers-Harris Children's Self Concept Scale.* Nashville: Counselor Recordings and Tests.

Piotrowski, Z. (1957). *Perceptanalysis.* New York: Macmillan.

Poland, S. F., Thurlow, M. L., Ysseldyke, J. E., & Mirkin, P. K. (1982). Current psychoeducational assessment and decision-making practices as reported by directors of special education. *Journal of School Psychology, 20,* 171–179.

Poole, I. (1934). Genetic development of articulation of consonant sounds in speech. *Elementary English Review, 11,* 159–161.

Prescott, G. A., Balow, I. H., Hogan, T. R., & Farr, R. C. (1978). *Metropolitan Achievement Tests: Survey Battery.* Cleveland: The Psychological Corporation.

Psychological Corporation. (1959). *Test Service Bulletin #54: On telling parents about test results.* Cleveland: The Psychological Corporation.

Quay, H. C., & Peterson, D. R., (1967). *Manual for the Behavior Problem Checklist.* Unpublished manuscript, University of Illinois.

Quick, A., Little, T., & Campbell, A. (1974). *Project MEMPHIS: Enhancing developmental progress in preschool exceptional children.* Belmont, CA: Fearon.

Rees, N. S. (1973). Auditory processing factors in language disorders: The view from Procrustes' bed. *Journal of Speech and Hearing Disorders, 38,* 304–315.

Reitan, R. (1966). A research program on the psychological effects of brain lesions in human beings. In N. Ellis (Ed.), *International review of research in mental retardation* (Vol. 1). New York: Academic Press.

Resnick, L. B., Wang, M. C., & Kaplan, J. (1973). Task analysis in curriculum design: A hierarchically sequenced introductory mathematics curriculum. *Journal of Applied Behavior Analysis, 6,* 679–710.

Reynolds, M. (1975). Trends in special education: Implications for measurement. In W. Hively & M. Reynolds (Eds.), *Domain-referenced testing in special education.* Minneapolis: Leadership Training Institute/Special Education, University of Minnesota.

Reynolds, M. C., & Balow, B. (1972). Categories and variables in special education. *Exceptional Children, 38,* 357–366.

Roach, E. F., & Kephart, N. C. (1966). *The Purdue Perceptual-Motor Survey.* Columbus, OH: Merrill.

Roberts, J. (1971). *Intellectual development of children by demographic and socioeconomic factors.* Washington, DC: DHEW No. (HSM) 72-1012.

Robinson, N., & Robinson, H. (1976). *The mentally retarded child.* New York: McGraw-Hill.

Rorschach, H. (1966). *Rorschach Ink Blot Test.* New York: Grune & Stratton.

Rubin, S. (1969). A re-evaluation of figure-ground pathology in brain-damaged children. *American Journal of Mental Deficiency, 74,* 111–115.

Salvia, J., & Good, R. (1982). Significant discrepancies in the classification of pupils: Differentiating the concept. In J. Neisworth (Ed.), *Assessment in Special Education.* Rockville, MD: Aspen Systems Corp.

Salvia, J., & Ysseldyke, J. E. (1972). Criterion validity of four tests for red-green color blindness. *American Journal of Mental Deficiency, 76,* 418–422.

Salvia, J., Ysseldyke, J., & Lee, M. (1975). 1972 revision of the Stanford-Binet: A farewell to the mental age. *Psychology in the Schools, 12,* 421–422.

Salvia, J., & Ysseldyke, J. (1978). *Assessment in special and remedial education.* Boston: Houghton Mifflin.

Sattler, J. M. (1965). Analysis of functions of the 1960 Stanford-Binet Intelligence Scale, Form L-M. *Journal of Clinical Psychology, 21,* 173–179.

Sattler, J. M. (1974). *Assessment of children's intelligence.* Boston: Allyn and Bacon.

Sattler, J. M. (1982). *Assessment of children's intelligence and special abilities* (2nd ed.). Boston: Allyn and Bacon.

Scannell, D. P. (1978). *Tests of Achievement and Proficiency.* Chicago: The Riverside Publishing Company.

Schaie, K. W., & Roberts, J. (1971). *School achievement of children by demographic and socioeconomic factors.* Washington, DC: DHEW No. (HSM) 72-1011.

Shub, A. N., Carlin, J. A., Friedman, R. L., Kaplan, J. M., & Katien, J. C. (1973). *Diagnosis: An Instructional Aid (Reading).* Chicago: Science Research Associates.

Sitlington, P. L. (1970). Validity of the Peabody Individual Achievement Test with educable mentally retarded adolescents. Unpublished master's thesis, University of Hawaii.

Skinner, B. (1957). *Verbal behavior.* New York: Appleton-Century-Crofts.

Slingerland, B. (1970). *Teacher's manual to accompany Slingerland Screening Tests for Identifying Children with Specific Language Disability.* Los Angeles: Western Psychological Services.

Slingerland, B. (1974). *Slingerland Screening Tests for Identifying Children with Specific Language Disability, form D for grade V and grade VI.* Cambridge, MA: Educators Publishing Service.

Slobin, D. I., & Welsh, C. A. (1973). Elicited imitation as a research tool in developmental psycholinguistics. In C. Ferguson & D. Slobin (Eds.), *Studies of child language development.* New York: Holt, Rinehart and Winston.

Slosson, R. L. (1971). *Slosson Intelligence Test.* East Aurora, NY: Slosson Educational Publications.

Solomon, I., & Starr, B. (1968). *School Apperception Method.* New York: Springer.

Sonnenschein, J. L. (1983). *Basic Achievement Skills Individual Screener.* Cleveland: The Psychological Corporation.

Spache, G. D. (1972). *Diagnostic Reading Scales.* Monterey, CA: CTB/McGraw-Hill.

Sparrow, S., Balla, D., & Cicchetti, D. (1984) *Vineland Adaptive Scales.* Circle Pines, MN: American Guidance Service.

Spivack, G., & Spotts, J. (1966). *Devereux Child Behavior Rating Scale.* Devon, PA: The Devereux Foundation Press.

Spivack, G., Spotts, J., & Haimes, P. (1967). *Devereux Adolescent Behavior Rating Scale.* Devon, PA: The Devereux Foundation Press.

Spivack, G., & Swift, M. (1967). *Devereux Elementary School Behavior Rating Scale.* Devon, PA: The Devereux Foundation Press.

Stake, R., & Wardrop, J. (1971). Gain score errors in performance contracting. *Research in the Teaching of English, 5,* 226–229.

Stevens, S. S. (1951). Mathematics, measurement, and psychophysics. In S. S. Stevens (Ed.), *Handbook of experimental psychology.* New York: Wiley.

Sullivan, E. T., Clark, W. W., & Tiegs, E. W. (1970). *Short Form Test of Academic Aptitude.* Monterey, CA: CTB/McGraw-Hill.

Sweney, A., Cattell, R. B., & Krug, S. (1970). *School Motivation Analysis Test.* Champaign, IL: Institute for Personality and Ability Testing.

Tanner, J. M. (1970). Biological bases of development. In J. M. Tanner (Ed.), *Carmichael's manual of child psychology.* New York: Wiley.

Taylor, O., & Swinney, D. (1972). The onset of language. In V. Irvin & M. Marge (Eds.), *Principles of childhood language disabilities.* Englewood Cliffs, NJ: Prentice-Hall.

Templin, M. C. (1957). Certain language skills in children. Institute of Child Welfare Monograph Series, No. 26. Minneapolis: University of Minnesota Press.

Terman, L., & Merrill, M. (1973). *Stanford-Binet Intelligence Scale.* Chicago: The Riverside Publishing Company.

Thorndike, R. (1963). *The concepts of over- and underachievement.* New York: Columbia University Press.

Thorndike, R., & Hagen, E. (1961, 1978b). *Measurement and evaluation in psychology and education.* New York: Wiley.

Thorndike, R., & Hagen, E. (1978a). *Cognitive Abilities Test.* Chicago: The Riverside Publishing Company.

Thorpe, L., Clark, W., & Tiegs, E. (1953). *California Test of Personality.* Monterey, CA: CTB/McGraw-Hill.

Thurstone, L. L. (1944). *A factorial study of perception.* Chicago: University of Chicago Press.

Thurstone, T. (1978). *Educational Ability Series.* Chicago: Science Research Associates.

Tiegs, E. W., & Clark, W. W. (1970). *California Achievement Test.* Monterey, CA: CTB/McGraw-Hill.

U.S.O.E. (1977, December 29). Assistance to states for education of handicapped children: Procedures for evaluating specific learning disabilities. *Federal Register, 42.*

U.S. Public Health Service. (1971). *Vision screening of children.* PHS Document #2042. Washington, DC: U.S. Public Health Service.

Urban, W. (1963). *Draw-a-Person.* Los Angeles: Western Psychological Services.

Valett, R. E. (1964). A clinical profile for the Stanford Binet. *Journal of School Psychology, 2,* 49–54.

Van Riper, C. (1963). *Speech correction: Principles and methods* (4th ed.). Englewood Cliffs, NJ: Prentice-Hall.

Vinter, R., Sarri, R., Vorwaller, D., & Schafer, E. (1966). *Pupil Behavior Inventory.* Ann Arbor: Campus Publishers.

Walker, D. K. (1973). *Socioemotional measures for preschool and kindergarten children.* San Francisco: Jossey-Bass.

Walker, H. (1970). *Walker Problem Identification Checklist.* Los Angeles: Western Psychological Services.

Walker, H. M., & Lev, J. (1953). *Statistical inference.* New York: Holt, Rinehart and Winston.

Wechsler, D. (1967). *Manual for the Wechsler Preschool and Primary Scale of Intelligence.* Cleveland: The Psychological Corporation.

Wechsler, D. (1974). *Manual for the Wechsler Intelligence Scale for Children–Revised.* Cleveland: The Psychological Corporation.

Wechsler, D. (1981). *Manual for the Wechsler Adult Intelligence Scale–Revised* New York: Psychological Corporation.

Weinberg, R., & Wood, R. (1975). *Observation of pupils and teachers in mainstream and special education settings: Alternative strategies.* Minneapolis: Leadership Training Institute/Special Education, University of Minnesota.

Weiner, F. (1979). *Phonological process analysis.* Baltimore: University Park Press.

Wellman, B. L., Case, I. M., Mengert, I. G., & Bradbury, D. E. (1931). Speech sounds of young children. University of Iowa Studies in Child Welfare. Iowa City: University of Iowa Press.

Wepman, J. M. (1973). *Auditory Discrimination Test* (rev. ed.). Chicago: Language Research Associates.

Werner, H., & Strauss, A. A. (1941). Pathology of figure-background relation in the child. *Journal of Abnormal and Social Psychology, 36,* 236–248.

Wiley, J. (1971). A psychology of auditory impairment. In W. Cruickshank (Ed.), *Psychology of exceptional children and youth.* Englewood Cliffs, NJ: Prentice-Hall.

Williams, G. C., & McReynolds, L. V. (1975). The relationship between discrimination and articulation training in children with misarticulations.

Journal of Speech and Hearing Research, 18, 401–412.

Winitz, H. (1975). *From syllable to conversation.* Baltimore: University Park Press.

Wittrock, M. C. (1970). The evaluation of instruction: Cause-and-effect relations in naturalistic data. In M. C. Wittrock & D. E. Wiley (Eds.), *The evaluation of instruction.* New York: Holt, Rinehart and Winston.

Wolfram, W. A. (1971). Social dialects from a linguistic perspective: Assumptions, current research and future directions. In R. Shuy (comp.), *Social dialects and interdisciplinary perspectives.* Washington, DC: Center for Applied Linguistics.

Woodcock, R. (1973). *Woodcock Reading Mastery Tests.* Circle Pines, MN: American Guidance Service.

Woodcock, R. (1978). *Woodcock-Johnson Psychoeducational Battery.* Hingham, MA: Teaching Resources Corporation.

Yates, A. J. (1954). The validity of some psychological tests of brain damage. *Psychological Bulletin, 51,* 359–379.

Ysseldyke, J. E. (1973). Diagnostic-prescriptive teaching: The search for aptitude-treatment interactions. In L. Mann & D. A. Sabatino (Eds.), *The first review of special education.* New York: Grune & Stratton.

Ysseldyke, J. E. (1975). Process remediation with secondary learning disabled children. In L. Goodman & L. Mann (Eds.), *Learning disabilities in the secondary school: Title III curricula development for secondary learning disabilities.* King of Prussia, PA: Montgomery County Intermediate Unit and the Pennsylvania Department of Education.

Ysseldyke, J. E. (1979). Issues in psychoeducational assessment. In G. Phye & D. Reschly (Eds.), *School psychology: Perspectives and issues.* New York: Academic Press.

Ysseldyke, J. E., & Algozzine, B. (1982). Where to begin in diagnosing reading problems. *Topics in Learning and Learning Disabilities, 2,* 60–69.

Ysseldyke, J. E., & Marston, D. (1982). Gathering decision-making information through the use of non-test-based methods. *Measurement and Evaluation in Guidance, 15,* 58–69.

Ysseldyke, J. E., & Salvia, J. (1974). Diagnostic-prescriptive teaching: Two models. *Exceptional Children, 41,* 181–186.

Zeaman, D., & House, B. J. (1963). The role of attention in retardate discrimination learning. In N. R. Ellis (Ed.), *Handbook of mental deficiency.* New York: McGraw-Hill.

Zweig, R. L. (1971). *Fountain Valley Teacher Support System in Reading.* Huntington Beach, CA: Richard L. Zweig Associates.

Cases and Statutory Materials

Brown v. Board of Education, 347 U.S. 483 (1954).

Covarrubias v. San Diego Unified School District, Civ. No. 70-394-S (S.D. Cal., filed Feb. 1971) (settled by consent decree, July 31, 1972).

Diana v. State Board of Education, C.A. No. C-70-37 R.F.P. (N.D. Cal., filed Feb. 3, 1970).

Frederick L. v. Thomas, 419 F. Supp. 960 (E.D. Pa. 1976), aff'd, 57 F. 2a 373 (3d Cir 1977).

Hansen v. Hobson, 269 F. Supp. 401 (D.D.C. 1967).

Larry P. v. Riles, 343 F. Supp. 1306 (N.D. Cal. 1972), aff'd, 502 F.2d 963 (9th Cir 1974).

Lora v. New York City Board of Education, 456 F. Supp. 1211, 1275 (E.D.N.Y. 1978).

PASE v. Hannon, 74C3586, (N.D. Ill. 1980).

Pennsylvania Association for Retarded Children v. Commonwealth of Pennsylvania, 334 F. Supp. 1257 (E.D. Pa. 1971); 343 F. Supp. 279 (E.D. Pa. 1972).

Pub. L. No. 94-142, 89 Stat. 773 (1975) (codified at 20 U.S.C. 1401–1461 (1978))

Rehabilitation Act of 1973, 29 U.S.C., 701–794 (1975).

Tinker v. Des Moines Ind. Community School Dist., 393 U.S. 503, 511 (1969).

TEST INDEX

AUTHOR/SOURCE INDEX

SUBJECT INDEX